D1201913

# NEW YORK FILM FESTIVAL GOLD

## *A 50th Anniversary Celebration*

EDITED BY LAURA KERN, JOANNE KOCH, AND RICHARD PEÑA · INTRODUCTION BY PEDRO ALMODÓVAR

# NEW YORK FILM FESTIVAL GOLD

## *A 50th Anniversary Celebration*

*Edited by*
LAURA KERN, JOANNE KOCH, AND RICHARD PEÑA

*introduction by*
PEDRO ALMODÓVAR

*historical overview by*
PHILLIP LOPATE
+
15 TALES FROM THE INSIDE

*film stills from*
THE KOBAL COLLECTION

film society lincoln center

*Published by*
THE FILM SOCIETY OF LINCOLN CENTER, INC.
70 LINCOLN CENTER PLAZA
NEW YORK, NY 10023-6595
WWW.FILMLINC.COM

*Designed by*
E.Y. LEE AND DANIEL CORNELL

*With funding generously provided by*
*William L. Bernhard*
*Roy Furman*
*Frederick R. Koch*
*Ira Resnick*
*John Roche*
*Bernard Schwartz*
*Martin E. Segal*

*Furthermore:* A PROGRAM OF THE J.M. KAPLAN FUND

COUNTRY OF FIRST PUBLICATION: UNITED STATES OF AMERICA
ISBN 978-0-615-66360-9

*Printed in Hong Kong SAR by*
ASIA PACIFIC OFFSET
Cover: *John Cassavetes'* Faces, *a selection of the 6th NYFF. Credit: Walter Reade Organization/The Kobal Collection/Sam Shaw.*
Endpapers: *Werner Herzog playing soccer in Alice Tully Hall in front of the NYFF's 20th Anniversary photo exhibition.*
© *Helaine Messer, 1982.* Back Cover: © *Susanne Faulkner Stevens.*

*This book is dedicated to the memory of Richard Roud, Amos Vogel, and Andrew Sarris, who were there at the beginning, to Martin E. Segal, whose generosity and guidance kept it going, and to William Schuman, who understood that film is a performing as well as a visual art, and who had the vision and audacity to bring the movies to Lincoln Center.*

# CONTENTS

# FOREWORD

*Rose Kuo*

For the past 50 years, the Opening Night of the New York Film Festival (dubbed "prom night" within the community), has ushered in the fall season of serious film-watching in New York City. For the Festival's two-week duration, the global film community gathers to consider the most significant works by the world's leading filmmakers.

My own NYFF rite of passage took place in the 1990s when I was still based in L.A. Each year, I would fly to New York and wait outside Alice Tully Hall hoping that an NYFF subscriber would offer me a ticket to a sold-out show. Down the road, I was invited to attend critics' and, later, public screenings. That was where I received my film education. The Festival has often been, as you will discover in reading the eyewitness testimonies gathered herein, a wild ride.

As Phillip Lopate's overview reminds us, the NYFF began at a time in American cultural life when film was not yet taken seriously as an art form. His account of the controversies and triumphs brought about by the pioneer programmers, Richard Roud and Amos Vogel, link the Festival's history to a golden age of European art cinema. It's somewhat awe-inspiring to think that a festival could introduce American audiences to Buñuel's *The Exterminating Angel* and then continue to tantalize them with new works by Rossellini, Godard, Pasolini, Resnais, Ozu, Bresson, and Polanski . . . all in its first year! To paraphrase Shakespeare: we will not live so long or see so much.

Two people have decisively led the Festival's selection process: the late Richard Roud, from 1963 to 1988, and my esteemed colleague Richard Peña, who, following his 25th festival, will retire at the end of 2012. They have each guided an astonishing group of critics, essayists, and scholars to pick the best of the best, year after year. The essays contributed by Roger

Greenspun, Richard Corliss, Molly Haskell, Jim Hoberman, David Thomson, David Ansen, Stuart Klawans, John Powers, Kent Jones, and Lisa Schwarzbaum—a veritable Dream Team of film criticism—relate five decades' worth of behind-the-scenes festival affairs. Their tales testify to the urgency and passion that accompany the best of critical debates.

The story of the NYFF, which includes the evolution of the Film Society of Lincoln Center itself, is told in these pages by staff and selection-committee members both past and present. Their insider histories deal with battles over censorship and distribution and offer a view of the future of our organization in a transformed visual culture, in which we find ourselves competing with thousands of festivals worldwide, as the role and value of cinema is being redefined on a daily basis.

This book has been made possible by the generosity of board members Martin E. Segal, Bernard Schwartz, Fred Koch, John Roche, Bill Bernhard, Roy Furman, and Ira Resnick, and the support of President Dan Stern and Chair Ann Tenenbaum, as well as the herculean labors of my dedicated colleagues Richard Peña, Laura Kern, and former Film Society Executive Director Joanne Koch.

I would also like to acknowledge both the enormous generosity and dedication of our Board of Directors, patrons, and members whose unwavering commitment has spanned five decades. Of equal importance is the dedicated staff of the Film Society of Lincoln Center, all of whom believe in inspiring and nurturing future generations through the art of the moving image.

The NYFF has, for half a century, discovered and rediscovered some of the finest films and filmmakers from around the world, and will continue to do so for the next 50 years—and beyond.

# INTRODUCTION

*Pedro Almodóvar*

My New York Film Festival debut was in 1988, in the last century, with *Women on the Verge of a Nervous Breakdown*. I wasn't the only one having a debut that year, so was Richard Peña. The city, the Festival, and its director have become an important personal reference, both emotionally and professionally. At that moment I began a conversation with New York City and its cinephiles that has only increased in intensity, fun, variety, and passion.

My films have been invited many times; besides being a huge honor, it has always been an opportunity to see the most recent world cinema and to return to New York, a city that always inspires me and that I need to soak up at least once a year.

Located on a privileged spot in the calendar, after the three big A-List festivals, and with an equally privileged sensibility on the part of its selection committee, the NYFF has always been the best showcase of what would be seen months and even years later on the world's screens. I think it has managed to maintain the difficult balance between low-budget cinema and big productions, paying attention to the quality and interest held by each individual film. I have always admired its eclectic nature and lack of prejudice—the films are what matter. That it's noncompetitive and has practically no glitz is a respite.

I remember every one of my presentations: how awkward, bold, and nervous I was; how the lively, uninhibited, and enormous audience reacted. I remember every one of the suits I wore, whom I embraced on stage, before going on, or at the after-party; the first encounter with a living film legend; the silence, stupor, or laughter of the audience. Each of the screenings gave me a sense of how the film would perform afterward in the American market. It was a baptism, a celebration, and an epiphany. I have discovered many auteurs in the Festival.

My first year, I was invited to visit the offices of the Festival and was impressed to see big black-and-white photos hanging from the walls, with dedications from auteurs who had participated in past Festivals. I remember Truffaut, Fassbinder, Bertolucci . . . and I thought that I didn't deserve to be a part of that club, even if I was European. I still believe this, and I thank the loyalty of the NYFF from the bottom of my heart. If it has survived 50 years, that means it is eternal. Happy Birthday!

# ESSAYS

*The Exterminating Angel* by Luis Buñuel

# THE NEW YORK FILM FESTIVAL

## ITS FIRST 50 YEARS

*Phillip Lopate*

THE NEW YORK FILM FESTIVAL, I WOULD argue, has had a profound effect on American film culture, helping to shape the discussion by setting high standards and calling attention to daring, demanding works of cinematic art year after year. To use Hollywood terms, it is a Success Story, and one key measure of that success is that it has survived for half a century. That it has managed to do so, in the face of skepticism, criticism, fiscal strains, and a vastly changing film culture, may be attributed to a combination of adapting to the ever-shifting global/ technological landscape while stubbornly refusing to budge on its principles or to alter its essential structure. That core identity may be summarized as follows: from the first it has been a relatively small festival (21-26 new features a year, as well as several retrospective gems), free of the hoopla of competitions and prizes; not a marketplace but a boutique-like selection, dedicated to the exigent art of cinema without yielding to commercial or censorship pressures; and rooted inside the high-culture campus of Lincoln Center.

Institutional history that aspires to be more than puff piece has much in common with biography, in that it must take into consideration the parentage, historical context, growing pains, identity crises, quarrels, treacheries, triumphs, stases, and challenges of aging. It makes sense to focus on strong, visionary leaders: and because of the peculiar circumstance that the film festival's first two program directors, Richard Roud and Richard Peña, each served exactly 25 years, one is tempted to frame the half-century chronicle in a Shakespearian manner, as the Reign of the Two Richards. But the story of many enduring nonprofit organizations also traces an arc from improvised utopian idealism to consolidation, bureaucratic organization, and self-perpetuation. The visionary founders wander off or die, leaving the organization to recast itself pragmatically, preserve its core identity, or both. In considering the history of the New York Film Festival

*Les vampires* by Louis Feuillade

(henceforth NYFF), there were so many kingmakers, supporting players, kibitzers, and unsung heroes that they too deserve to emerge from the shadows and have their contributions known.

Lincoln Center for the Performing Arts (LCPA), a suite of travertine-clad buildings on the West Side of Manhattan that would come to hold the Metropolitan Opera, the New York Philharmonic, the New York City Ballet, the Juilliard School, a repertory theater company, and other cultural institutions, opened its doors in 1962. The newly appointed president of Lincoln Center, William Schuman, got it into his head—or the idea was put there by Eugene Archer, then a second-string *New York Times* film critic—that the complex and New York needed a film festival, along the lines of the British Film Institute's London Film Festival. Schuman, a distinguished American composer with an appetite for administrating,

loved going to the movies—but his appreciation for the medium was not shared by some on the LCPA Board. John D. Rockefeller III, who had been so instrumental in getting Lincoln Center built, objected: "What next, baseball?" Others protested that the complex was supposed to be devoted to the lively arts. Schuman recalled: "I countered with the fact that it was livelier than lots of things that went on. The objection that was made to film was that 99 percent of it was junk. I absolutely agreed with that—and that 99 percent of music, theater, literature, and any other art is also junk; that you can't judge an art by the part that's not successful or not distinguished; and that this could be a great addition to the offerings of the Center. Eventually my view prevailed."

What's interesting to note is that, even as late as the 1960s, many cultivated highbrows and middlebrows still needed to be convinced that film was an art form. At that same moment, coincidentally, world cinema was

going through a renaissance, with the French New Wave, the Italian school (Antonioni, Visconti, Fellini, etc.), Satyajit Ray, Akira Kurosawa, Ingmar Bergman; the Poles and Czechs bestirring themselves, the American Independent and avant-garde filmmakers drawing attention, and the old Hollywood lions celebrated by the French as auteurs (Ford, Hawks, Hitchcock, Nicholas Ray, Welles, Minnelli, etc.) still around making good movies. It was as though all the stars were aligned; the classical elders like Renoir, Dreyer, and Lang, harking back to the silent era, and the cutting-edge iconoclasts like Godard and Oshima, sharing the stage. In response, a network of film magazines, art-house theaters, university clubs, and film-studies programs cropped up, which sought to integrate the excitement over the new movies, such as *L'avventura*, *Breathless*, *The 400 Blows*, *Wild Strawberries*, and *La Dolce Vita*, with an

Jean-Luc Godard, 1980

animation), Montreal, San Francisco (the only one in the U.S.)—and London. The London Film Festival was different from the others in that it did not insist on premiering a work, but chose the strongest films from other festivals, with an emphasis on those that might not otherwise have been shown in commercial British cinemas. That model of the small (15-20 titles), high-art, curated "Festival of Festivals" looked good to Schuman. He approached Richard Roud, then the 34-year-old program director of the London Film Festival, with the idea of bringing him over to New York to do the same, while continuing to run the London festival. It was understood that London and New York would be twins, or at least overlap in many of the selections.

Roud, an American born in Boston, had spent most of his adult life in Europe, dividing his time between Paris, where he then mostly resided, and London. Juggling many jobs and identities, he was a working journalist, the regular film critic for *The Guardian*, and an employee of the British Film Institute, programming multiple film series for the BFI throughout the year and selecting the London Film Festival's titles. Urbane, with a mustache and a rumpled-dapper appearance, a man of strong, confident, and (in retrospect) almost unerring good taste, Roud had a comprehensive take on the breakthroughs in European cinema. He was essentially an

appreciation of, even a reverence for, cinematic history. The phenomenon known as cinephilia had taken hold. In New York especially, there was a hunger to fill in gaps in the oeuvres of director-heroes that the vagaries of American distribution had denied us. European audiences may have been able to see in their proper order the intriguingly beautiful Antonioni movies that led up to *L'avventura* and *La Notte*, such as *Story of a Love Affair*, *Camille Without Camellias*, *Le amiche*, and *Il Grido*; but here,

those films were only rumors, phantoms whose glossy stills in film magazines tantalized our imaginations; the same with Visconti's early masterworks (*Ossessione*, *La terra trema*, *Senso*). New York cinephiles felt provincial, semi-isolated; we had a lot of catching up to do. It was the perfect moment to start a film festival here.

In the early 1960s, there were only a dozen or so film festivals scattered about the world: Cannes, Venice, Locarno, Berlin, Karlovy Vary, Edinburgh, Melbourne, Cork, Cartagena, Annecy (for

Richard Roud and Amos Vogel, 1965

Aaron and Irene Diamond, William Schuman, and Schuyler Chapin at the Opening Night of *Capricious Summer*, 1968

auteurist, sympathetic to the French/*Cahiers du cinéma* valuations of historical masters and contemporary innovators, and inclined to include in his festivals any picture by a director whose work he admired. What most excited him when he took on the NYFF post were the modernist, self-reflexive works of Jean-Luc Godard, Jean-Marie Straub, and Alain Resnais. He was a superb writer, as can be seen from his lucid, casually erudite, still-relevant books on Godard, Straub, and Henri Langlois, the larger-than-life collector-founder of the Cinémathèque Française. Though Roud worked for a rival film archive, the BFI, he and the touchy, suspicious Langlois got along well. Roud would use him as a consultant in the early years of the NYFF, and some of the Festival's most dazzling retrospective choices had all the earmarks of Langlois: Feuillade's *Les vampires*, Renoir's *Nana*, von Stroheim's *The Wedding March*, the tribute to Abel Gance, etc.

At the same time Schuman was courting Roud as Festival Organizer, he approached Amos Vogel (on the recommendation of the Museum of Modern Art's film curator, Richard Griffith) to serve as Festival Coordinator. Vogel, who had fled Nazi-occupied Austria as a teenager, was an esteemed, beloved figure in the New York movie scene, having since 1947 run Cinema 16, the high-minded film club that premiered many experimental and art films (including Bresson, Brakhage, Cassavetes, Oshima) over its 15-year history. Cinema 16 had run into financial trouble and been forced to shut down in 1962, so Vogel was looking for work. He was something of a luftmensch, an omnivorous reader, a man of irreproachable moral integrity, a self-declared Socialist, and a quintessential humanist, ill at ease in the corridors of power. The title of his survey book, *Film as a Subversive Art*, suggests his outsider outlook. More interested in politics and society than the formalist-inclined Roud, he was also determined that shorts, documentaries, and avant-garde films find a place in whatever this New York Film Festival might turn out to be. "That was what was so attractive about the offer that came from Lincoln Center, that I would go there and be able to continue on an expanded scale something that I had started at

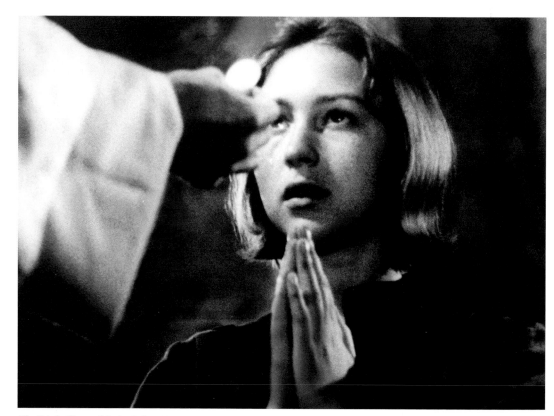

*The Trial of Joan of Arc* by Robert Bresson

Cinema 16," explains Vogel.

Schuman told both Roud and Vogel that they would be engaged on a year-to-year basis, with no contracts, no guarantees. Lincoln Center agreed to put up the money for the first year's festival, saying only, "If we like it we'll let you continue." The money would come from a discretionary fund set up at Lincoln Center

for new ventures, such as the Chamber Music Society. For the most part, Lincoln Center acted as a real-estate operation, providing an umbrella for its constituent institutions; but every so often it would initiate programming (such as the Mostly Mozart Festival, at the time still in the offing).

Roud and Vogel had less than six months

*Knife in the Water* by Roman Polanski

Roman Polanski at the 1st NYFF, 1963

to throw together the first NYFF, which was scheduled to debut in September 1963. They went to Cannes, scouted films there and at other festivals, screened hoped-for New York premieres, and agreed on a lineup of new releases. That first year they were able to offer an amazing program of 21 as-yet-unreleased films, which included Luis Buñuel's *The Exterminating Angel* (a natural for Opening Night, given its macabre trapped bourgeoisie plot), Roman Polanski's *Knife in the Water*, Robert Bresson's *The Trial of Joan of Arc*, Yasujiro Ozu's final work, *An Autumn Afternoon*, Ermanno Olmi's *The Fiancés*, Jean-Pierre Melville's *Magnet of Doom*, Joseph Losey's *The Servant*, Chris Marker's *Le joli mai*, Glauber Rocha's *Barravento*, and Alain Resnais's *Muriel*. Each film would be shown once, in the immense 2,300-seat Philharmonic Hall (later renamed Avery Fisher Hall).

At the same time these new art films were screening in Philharmonic Hall, the NYFF would also be showing, at the Museum of Modern Art, 10 programs of films from the recent past that had failed to find commercial distribution. That dreamy roster of retrospective gems included Kenji Mizoguchi's *Sansho the Bailiff*, Akira Kurosawa's *I Live in Fear*, Emile de Antonio's *Point of Order*, Kent Mackenzie's *The Exiles*, and Max Ophuls's *Lola Montès*—such were the rarities available for the picking. The retrospective series was partly an effort to placate MoMA, which had been nervous about this new upstart NYFF threatening to cut into its audience and patronage pie. Lincoln Center assured the museum it had no intentions of acquiring a film archive like MoMA's; it would strictly be screening films for two weeks a year.

I remember attending that first NYFF 50 years ago, covering it for the *Columbia Daily Spectator*. Ads had been placed in *The New York Times* and *The Village Voice* with promising stills and descriptions in tiny print (which I could then easily read). I had rushed down Sunday morning as soon as the ad appeared, and found myself about sixty-fifth in line. Word circulated that at the head of the line stood the senior actress Helen Hayes (or was it Lillian Gish?). I was able to secure tickets to everything I wanted to see (prices had been set intentionally low, so as to attract the enthusiastic public and countermand the black-tie reputation of Lincoln Center), and I spent the 10 days of the Festival rushing from Lincoln Center to MoMA, letting schoolwork fall by the wayside.

It had taken some doing, down to the wire, to retrofit the capacious Philharmonic Hall as a movie theater. The room had been bedeviled from the start with problematic acoustics, and renovations would be made periodically to get the sound right.[1] Then there was the seating pattern, with side-balconies containing boxes not ideal for film viewing. The projection looked excellent, in spite of the lengthy throw. But the hall had a red carpet pomp that ill-suited some of the smaller, more intimate

films. On the other hand, that very grandeur helped the reception of some films, lending them an extra air of importance. Many of the NYFF filmgoers were young; and, as one such at the time, I can attest to feeling privileged, even intimidated, by the swanky surroundings. You felt present at the start of something important. If there were still some doubts that film was a high art, what better way to assert its dignity than to screen movies in the Philharmonic?

The prestige that accrued to the NYFF for its placement in the fortress-like culture island that was Lincoln Center had complicated trade-offs. For one thing, it was perceived as stuffily Establishment by the downtown bohemian crowd who tended not to travel north of 14th Street. That crowd included a

large chunk of the avant-garde filmmakers. They were wary from the start (justifiably, as it turned out) that the NYFF would for the most part exclude their work, and contemptuous (less justifiably) of European art films as being only a smidgen less commercial and corrupt than the Hollywood product. Jonas Mekas, a *Village Voice* critic and champion of American experimental film, often castigated art-house films for their alleged appropriation of avant-garde techniques. Though the NYFF's initial lineup had made sure to include *Hallelujah the Hills*, a counter-cultural comedy by Adolfas Mekas, that sop was scarcely enough to quiet the rumblings. A rumor circulated that the avant-gardists were preparing a protest action at Lincoln Center during the running of the film

1   It was a barely kept secret over the years that it might be better to choose a foreign film with subtitles for Opening Night, which continued to be held at Avery Fisher Hall, than an American picture, where some of the dialogue might sound garbled.

*Alphaville* by Jean-Luc Godard

festival. Amos Vogel, who was sympathetic to avant-garde film and felt caught in the middle, sat through security meetings with the Lincoln Center brass as they speculated on possible scenarios, not excluding terrorist bombs. He was greatly relieved when the action turned out to be some pink dye added to the water at Lincoln Center's fountain!

Press coverage of the first NYFF was widespread and tended toward the very positive. Critics had been asked not to review individual films but to comment on the festival as a whole. The reason for that policy (which would change after the first two years) was concern that potential distributors might be scared off from acquiring a film by a negative or lukewarm review. The NYFF saw itself as a spur to film distribution. Richard Roud explained to a *Village Voice* reporter: "This is one way of changing the release pattern. We do the festival with a lot of publicity and create a lot of interest, and we get a lot of people who are really interested in films and will talk about them, and then there is a reason for distributors to bring out more films commercially." The regular *New York Times* critic, Bosley Crowther, then widely disdained by film buffs as a fuddy-duddy, quietly maneuvered behind the scenes to get distributors and production companies to give the NYFF their films. Down the road, Jack Valenti, President of the Motion

*Woman in the Dunes* by Hiroshi Teshigahara

Picture Association of America, and Michael F. Mayer, Executive Director of the IFIDA, would also be enlisted to secure the cooperation of studios and distributors. Mayer, speaking for the distributors in a festival program note, wrote pointedly: "There is no rule and there should not be, that each and every Festival film should go to the general market. Until we distributors go into the business of pure (rather than unintentional) philanthropy, there will be a certain number of pictures which should be

made available at Lincoln Center but which cannot be profitably distributed in this country."

Of course there were, from the start, grumblings from some members of the press about the obscurity or pretentiousness of various art films. Stanley Kauffmann, with his customary measured skepticism, asserted in his New Republic column, after praising the films of Olmi, Polanski, and Losey at the first NYFF: "The common denominator among most of the others—particularly the 'arty' ones—was tediousness. The persisting sin of serious film-makers, even some with talent, is reluctance to stop: a shot, a scene, a film. When the maker has no theatrical sense and his cinematic sense consists of lingering over very little, of trying to wring out meanings (usually symbolic) through insistence on trivia, the result is physically excruciating. I wriggled through many of these films. And I willingly risk a charge of philistinism in supposing that they have been declined by importers because they are too boring, not because they are too good."

This same Emperor's New Clothes charge would be made against the NYFF, more intemperately by John Simon and other critics, off and on during the years. There is no point in denying that a few stinkers managed to get on the festival roster each year (vide Patroni Griffi's 1963 *Il Mare*). The real question is: how

*Hallelujah the Hills* by Adolfas Mekas

*Hamlet* by Grigori Kozintsev

many films selected in any given year for the NYFF have proven worthy, and how many unworthy? Some viewers will always find tedious what others think sublime. But we may note, from a distance of 50 years and the consensus of film criticism since, that the common denominator for the first New York Film Festivals would seem to have been a phenomenally high level of quality. The 1964 NYFF followed with Godard's *Band of Outsiders* and *A Woman Is a Woman*, Kozintsev's *Hamlet*, Rossen's *Lilith*, Rosi's *Salvatore Giuliano* and *Hands Over the City*, Teshigahara's *Woman in the Dunes*, Mizoguchi's *The Taira Clan*, Munk's *Passenger*, Buñuel's *Diary of a Chambermaid* and *L'Age d'Or*, Bertolucci's *Before the Revolution*, and Satyajit Ray's *The Great City*. The 1965 NYFF brought Godard's *Alphaville* and *Le Petit Soldat*, Skolimowski's *Walkover* and *Identification Marks: None*, Ray's *Charulata*, Kadár & Klos's *The Shop on Main Street*, Penn's *Mickey One*, Antonioni's *Camille Without Camellias*, von Stroheim's *The Wedding March*, Feuillade's *Les vampires*, Bellocchio's *Fists in the Pocket*, Straub's *Unreconciled*, Dreyer's *Gertrud*, Marker's *The Koumiko Mystery*, and Kurosawa's *Red Beard*. By this point the Festival was no longer a one-shot experiment; it had proven itself, and was off and running.

Each year's program brochure, distributed at the public screenings, would contain brief essays by Roud and Vogel, and these exercises in tactful instruction, seduction, defensive self-justification, and combativeness make fascinating reading today. Roud, for instance, warned in his second essay that "a certain number of films will be found which can only be classified as difficult, films that demand more than passive enjoyment. Many of them are impressionistic in style, ambiguous, or open-ended—not from sheer perversity, but because what they are trying to express is too subtle to be handled otherwise," and he compared their technique to literary modernists such as Faulkner and Woolf. By the fourth essay Roud had grown testy, taking Kauffmann to task for his New Republic critique of Godard's *My Life to Live*, deploring the low status of film in New York and the tendency of local critics to judge films "more as illustrated

*Mickey One* by Arthur Penn

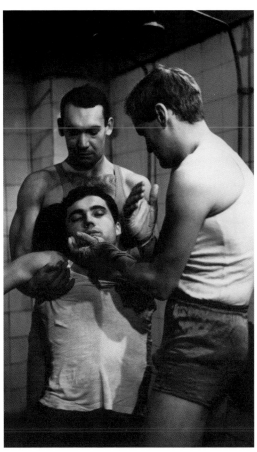

*Walkover* by Jerzy Skolimowski

literature than anything else" (which is curious, since he had defended difficult films the year before by comparing them to Faulkner and Woolf), while citing his friend Susan Sontag favorably as "a rare exception to the prevailing rule." In the fifth year, he began by quoting André Malraux, "The distinguishing feature of modern art is that it never tells a story," and ended by approving of Godard for his cinematic self-reflexiveness. Roud's 9th year's essay contained a defense against the complaint that he was too Eurocentric and that there were so few American films at the Festival. Listing all the ones included so far (not that many, to be frank), he went on to say that he would have liked to include "films like, say, *M\*A\*S\*H*, *Easy Rider*, *El Dorado* and *Point Blank*," but could not obtain them, either because "more films than ever before are now released in the summertime or the attitude toward festivals in general on the part of major film companies" (meaning, they did not want to harm the commercial potential of a movie by stigmatizing it as Art). In the 13th year he went back to sounding defiantly elitist, arguing that there was no reason why the NYFF should "select its repertory on the basis of a geographical spread. For the plain fact is that while all men may be created equal, all nations do not make equal achievements in the arts."

Vogel, in his essays, tended to draw attention to the way festival films reflected general social anxiety, changes in sexual mores or "existentialist complexities," as well as the surrealist and experimental crossovers from avant-garde film. Behind the scenes, he pushed for more variety. He chose many of the shorts, as Roud tended to be indifferent toward this form. Vogel, while respectful of his partner's cinematic knowledge, thought Roud was excessively Francophile, and was willing to let weak French films into the Festival while showing less interest in Eastern European or Japanese movies. Vogel himself had a passion for the emergent Czech cinema, and would soon curate an ambitious season featuring work from the Prague Spring directors, at MoMA. Eager to expand the intellectual content of the NYFF, he also began arranging special programs, sidebars featuring panel discussions,

Q&As with directors, a series on the Independent Cinema with programs devoted to Richard Leacock, Stan VanDerBeek, Peter Emmanuel Goldman, Tony Conrad, Shirley Clarke, Lionel Rogosin, Jonas Mekas, the Maysles Brothers, Harry Smith, Ed Emshwiller, Parker Tyler, and other artists and scholars.

Vogel's ultimate goal was to bring year-round film programming to Lincoln Center: he was now on full-time salary at Lincoln Center, and more to the point—he lived in New York City—was the local on the scene. Roud came to New York at most twice a year, for short periods—always by boat, since he hated flying and enjoyed the luxury of ocean liners. He was still running the London Film Festival (and would for several more years, until forced to choose one over the other), and he had little enthusiasm for more film programming at Lincoln Center beyond the annual two-week festival. Vogel, meanwhile, began drawing up plans for other activities during the year, which would eventually include Films in the Park, Movies for Kids, and cinemobiles in inner-city neighborhoods. It was the '60s, and bringing art to the people was very much in the air, championed by Mayor John Lindsay and Parks Commissioner Thomas Hoving. Vogel began urging Schuman to establish film as a regular constituent of Lincoln Center, alongside opera, ballet, music education, and theater. A feasibility study was made to see what that might entail; and at this point, as Vogel tells it, "there began to be noises at the highest level of Lincoln Center about whether we were in some way invading the Museum of Modern Art's turf." Nelson Rockefeller, who was on the MoMA Board, complained to his brother John D. Rockefeller III, who was Chairman of Lincoln Center's Board, that the Museum of Modern Art was already doing a fine job exhibiting films. Why did we need a new year-round film operation at Lincoln Center?

There being a limited number of very wealthy patrons interested in the arts even in a city the size of New York, it was inevitable that such tensions and divided institutional loyalties would arise. Schuman instructed Vogel to discuss the matter with Willard Van Dyke, at that point the head of MoMA's film department.

Willard Van Dyke, Vera Chytilová, Jiří Menzel, and Amos Vogel at MoMA for the Czech series, 1967

Since Van Dyke was an old friend who had collaborated with him on the Czech film series, Vogel expected no problems. He was surprised to find Van Dyke adamantly opposed to establishing a film society at Lincoln Center. Nevertheless, it came to pass. (Ultimately, these tensions would all be resolved when the two institutions began co-sponsoring its successful and still-running New Directors/New Films, the annual spring festival of emerging filmmakers.)

But other tensions now arose, inside the film festival itself. At the beginning, Roud and Vogel had gotten along beautifully, complementing each other's interests. Vogel's wife, Marcia, was particularly fond of Roud, a single man, and doted on him maternally. Vogel remembers him and Roud overseeing till four in the morning the erection of the screen for Philharmonic Hall that first year. "We were both sitting there, telling jokes, falling asleep, not knowing what to do because everything

3rd NYFF directors Elmar Klos, Miloš Forman, Ján Kadár, Jerzy Skolimowski, James Ivory, and Sidney Lumet, 1965

*Shadows of Forgotten Ancestors* by Sergei Parajanov

went wrong all the time!" The two festival co-directors spent hours discussing which films to include, often over late-night phone calls, and were enraptured when they stumbled together out of a darkened theater, having discovered an original work like Sergei Parajanov's *Shadows of Forgotten Ancestors*. In Vogel's mind, they were both programmers and administrators. By the third year, he began to be troubled by the difference in their titles: why was he the Festival Director and Roud the Program Director, when they'd been sitting together in screening rooms and thrashing over the same selections? Meanwhile, Vogel had been hearing from other festival directors that Roud was presenting himself as the one who decided programming, and characterizing Vogel as simply the administrator. (This should not have come as such a shock to Vogel: when a *Village Voice* reporter asked Roud in 1963, "But who actually chooses the films to be shown?"

Roud answered: "Me.") Vogel now proposed a change, that they be given the same co-director title, and Roud absolutely refused.

Perhaps as a way to make the process more democratic, Vogel advocated that there be a selection committee to assist Roud. The Lincoln Center administration liked the idea, and the suggestion became official policy. From then on, the NYFF would have rotating selection committees of ultimately five members—an advantageous arrangement that, besides bringing diverse points of view to the table, would also take the heat off the program director for unpopular selections. Roud, though concerned at first that the system might dilute his authority, came to work smoothly with the committees. For the most part they followed his lead, since he had a big say in picking the committee members (Arthur Knight, Susan Sontag, Andrew Sarris, Roger Greenspun, Molly Haskell, Richard Corliss,

and Charles Michener were among those who served under Roud) and he naturally gravitated toward friends or those whose tastes jibed with his own. Too, Roud was responsible for picking the majority of the movies that would be presented to the committee for their vote, and this preliminary screening was bound to govern much of the selection process. Even when it was decided that the selection members should all go to Cannes, Roud still attended many more film festivals and was in regular contact with filmmakers and responsible for gathering the bulk of examined materials.

Occasionally, a film might even be selected by Roud that the committee had not had a chance to see, because of print unavailability. Vogel began to suspect, rightly or wrongly, that Roud was manipulating the process so that he, Vogel, would not get a chance to see certain films that Roud was determined should go in—or be kept out. "It got so bad that we began to have very complicated voting formulas," said Vogel. "For example, he had the right to put two films in, then I had the right to put two films in that he didn't like. Then we each had the right to nix one or two films that the other had approved." Roud wryly compared them to a couple on the brink of divorce: "In marriages, the time comes when you say we no longer have the same bed or the same room, so I'm going to move to another office." Vogel realized that this wasn't working out; it was only a matter of time before one or the other man would have to resign.

At about the same time, Lincoln Center had become alarmed with the deficits that the NYFF was running—about $200,000 a year. Schuman and his Board came to the conclusion that a structure needed to be put into place that could fund-raise for the Festival and free Lincoln Center from footing the bill. As it happened, Schuman had been going to the movies every Friday night with his friend, the financier Martin E. Segal, and their wives.

Schuman asked Segal if he would agree to become president of a Film Society of Lincoln Center (FSLC). Martin Segal had been born in Russia, had come to this country when young and sold newspapers to help support his family; he went to work early, skipping college, and made a good deal of money. He had served in the municipal government under Mayors Wagner and Lindsay, and had a strong civic responsibility. Segal had also been interested in movies from the time he was a teenager, and agreed to take on the post. His friend, the corporate executive William F. May, would become chairman of the new organization, and together they would assemble a board of directors and solicit donors to close the budget deficit. It was urgent, they felt, that the NYFF be placed on a sound financial basis, with no time to spare.

Amos Vogel did not like having to answer to these corporate overseers. He was distressed that the Film Society and its Board had been put together without consulting him, the

Festival Director; he suddenly feared his input weighed no more than some businessmen who had scant knowledge of film. At the first FSLC Board meeting, in 1969, Vogel delivered an impassioned speech against the three proposals on the table: 1) that the budget be cut in half; 2) that ticket prices be raised; and 3) that all special events be eliminated, for the time being, as a way of saving money. According to Vogel, Segal approached him afterward: "'That was an interesting speech you made. I listened to it very attentively, and you seemed to indicate that no compromise was possible as far as you are concerned. But of course,' he said to me, with a big smile, 'you don't really mean that. Compromise is always possible.' So I said to him, 'No, I mean it.'" To Vogel, Segal's call for compromise was the final proof that in that corporate world, pragmatism always trumped principles. One of the Board members had approached Vogel with a suggestion that, since *The Shop on Main Street* had made money after it showed at the NYFF and gone on to win an

*The Shop on Main Street* by Ján Kadár and Elmar Klos

Oscar, maybe film producers should be charged a hefty fee to get their films into the Festival. It was a foolish suggestion that had no chance of being adopted, and Vogel could have dismissed it as such; but instead he became worried that the Board would begin to influence the festival-selection process. This was his primal nightmare, the corruption of art by commerce. As it turned out, nothing of the sort happened: the Board has never affected the selection process, and in fact, selection members almost never come into contact with Board members. But Vogel's fear of the new Mammon-tinged governing structure, his diminishing authority, and his tensions with Roud converged to make him decide to quit.

As Segal tells it, Vogel came to him and asked for a separate budget so that he could still work on various projects. Segal said no: you cannot have two chiefs, and Roud was their man in charge. "Vogel was useful but not central," Segal summarized. His resignation was accepted. The irony is that, with the newly formed FSLC, they had finally instituted a year-round film presence at Lincoln Center, as Vogel had consistently recommended; only he would no longer be around to participate in it.

No one knew exactly what the Film Society's mandate would be, beyond raising necessary funds, reining in the budget and monitoring the administration. The language of the FSLC's Certificate of Incorporation was intentionally vague: "the purposes for which the corporation is formed are to develop, stimulate and support the art of film and related media by (a) the presentation of a film festival or festivals at Lincoln Center or elsewhere, (b) the showing of selected programs of films, (c) the encouragement of the study of film through seminars, teaching programs, and otherwise at schools, colleges and other institutions, (d) the development of educational programs involving the use of film, (e) the use of film for training programs, employee services, and the improvement of social conditions and (f) participating in any and all matters in conjunction with or independent of others in sponsoring, promoting and improving the film media."

There was some talk among Board members that the NYFF should be assigned a "cut-off" date for the festival to break even, at which point its fate should be reconsidered, maybe even pulling the plug, if it failed to do so. Martin Segal cogently argued against a cut-off date. According to the minutes kept by the FSLC Board secretary, "He stated that the Board must have sufficient faith in its organization and its goals to be able to proceed in full knowledge of the anticipated deficit—as do all boards of performing arts institutions today. He noted that the Film Festival itself should be recast as the 'loss aspect' of the Society's operations, and the task was to re-cast it into more manageable form." Though many on the

Susan Rai and Martin Segal at the Opening Night of *One Sings, the Other Doesn't*, 1977

Board continued to insist that all the FSLC's programs should be self-supporting, Segal's position prevailed.

In 1969, the very same year that the Film Society of Lincoln Center was formed, Alice Tully Hall opened. Designed by the architect Pietro Belluschi for chamber music, favored with excellent acoustics and about a 1,000-seat capacity, it would serve from then on as the NYFF's home. It made a much more comfortable ad-hoc movie theater than the 2,300-seat Philharmonic (although the latter would continue to be used for Opening Night and

other festive functions). The NYFF had developed a reliable fan base, selling over 95 percent of its seats. You would even see scalpers holding up tickets in front of Alice Tully for last-minute purchases to "hot" screenings. With the move to Alice Tully came another change: each of the feature films would now be shown twice, except for the documentaries, which would still get only one screening.

The double-page ad placed in the Arts & Leisure section of *The New York Times* the first Sunday after Labor Day had become a New York tradition: film buffs waited impatiently for it to appear and ran down to stand in the box-office line, or else mailed in their choices immediately. The decision to hold the NYFF in late September–early October meant that the Festival became an annual autumn ritual, intersecting with the start of the academic year, the new blockbuster shows in the museums, the baseball playoffs, the Jewish High Holidays, and some of the most gorgeous weather available in the New York calendar. One might emerge from the darkened press screening of some miserabilist Eastern-European film to encounter the bluest of skies and pleasantest crisp-apple temperatures. Also the occasional squall, it being hurricane season as well.[2]

The establishment of the FSLC necessitated

---

2    I remember attending a press screening of Agnieszka Holland's *Angry Harvest* on a morning when we were warned by the Mayor to stay indoors: there, too, was Andrew Sarris, equally oblivious of Hurricane Gloria, or else scrupulously honoring his duties as a critic.

Wendy Keys and Richard Roud, 1983

Joanne Koch, 1989

a year-round administrative staff. The first Executive Director, Gerald Freund, had come from Yale University's front office and wanted to push the organization in a more educational, socially useful direction. He wrote a memorandum, according to Board minutes, which advocated less emphasis on the New York Film Festival and more on educational and socially significant activities, concluding with, "Proposed expanded educational programs and activities aimed as serving social ends, aiding artistic experiments, and creating relationships with other communications media, best lend themselves to foundation and other philanthropic support." He served from 1970-71 and was not a good fit, it was generally agreed, though he went on to a distinguished career in philanthropic and academic administration, at the Rockefeller Foundation, the MacArthur Foundation (where he initiated the "genius grants"), and Hunter College.

Sallie Wilensky, who had served capably as the Festival's coordinator since 1964, and then under Freund as administrative director, was especially devoted to Richard Roud. She resigned her post when she felt that the new administrative/board structure was trying to limit Roud's authority. Under her married name, Sallie Blumenthal, she assisted Henri Langlois in his efforts to establish a beachhead in New

York, and later joined the Board of the FSLC, where she served for many years.

The society's second administrative director was Joanne Koch, who had been programming Movies in the Park for the Film Society, and this time the appointment took. Koch would become one of the key figures in the organization's history during her 32 years of active involvement. Her background had included working for the Museum of Modern Art and Barney Rossett's Grove Press before coming to the Film Society. The mother of two girls, she established a familial atmosphere in the office, and was as loyal to her staff as she expected them to be to her. Her employees tended to stay for decades. She was especially strong at mentoring younger women for advancement and expanded responsibilities: everyone in the office got used to multitasking.

By now the Film Society had become engaged in a number of activities that went well beyond the NYFF. The gracious, tactful, Canadian-born Wendy Keys had joined the organization in its fourth year, at first as a part-time employee, then full-time, running an expanded education department under Freund. Outreach programs included Movies for Kids, paid for by the Helena Rubinstein Foundation, Movies in the Parks (sponsored by the Miller Brewing Company), and Films in Education, which would send filmmakers into schools,

hospitals, and church spaces. Often a filmmaker whose movie was being shown in the NYFF would arrive, accompanied by a 16mm projector and a projectionist, speak to a group, and take questions. The FSLC had also acquired from its previous owner a magazine, *Film Comment*, which it would publish bimonthly. One incentive for becoming an FSLC member would be a free subscription to *Film Comment*. It has never been a house organ, and continues to this day to cherish its independence. Richard Corliss, the magazine's first editor under the FSLC's ownership (and future *Time* critic) was determined to steer *Film Comment* away from academic jargon and to keep its articles lively, witty, and reader-friendly. In doing so, he helped build up its subscription base to 27,000, though the magazine still lost money, which the Board agreed to make up.

It was the Board and Koch's responsibility to find ways to close the organization's budget gap. One such fund-raising idea, which became a permanent feature of the Film Society, was to hold a gala tribute to some screen luminary, with tickets for the event and the dinner/party afterward priced according to the level of donor support. The first honoree was an inspired choice: Charlie Chaplin. There was enormous sympathy for the king of comedy, living in exile after the McCarthy era's attempts to brand him a Communist; and Chaplin's wife Oona

*Last Tango in Paris* by Bernardo Bertolucci

wanted to revisit her native land. The writer Brendan Gill, an FSLC board member, suggested the idea of honoring Chaplin to Martin Segal, the Board President of FSLC, who went to London and handled the negotiations with the star and his business partner, Mo Rothman. Subsequent galas paid tribute to such silver-screen legends as Fred Astaire, Alfred Hitchcock, George Cukor, Bob Hope (his fan Woody Allen helped prepare the clips), John Huston, Barbara Stanwyck, Sir Laurence Olivier, Claudette Colbert, Federico Fellini,

Elizabeth Taylor, and Audrey Hepburn, all of whom were conveniently still alive. It was helpful if the honorees were not only distinguished but well-known, so as to draw a large enough paying audience to fill Avery Fisher Hall.[3] From the sixth gala on, Wendy Keys took over the job of organizing each tribute, which entailed securing the screen lion's participation (not always easy: some viewed it superstitiously as a preliminary call from the Grim Reaper), managing the honoree's ego and those of the guests whom Keys had coaxed to

appear on stage to pay tribute, and gathering film clips into a reel that would make for an entertainingly varied career narrative. Some of the Galas were televised by WNET as "Live from Lincoln Center" specials.

The NYFF itself remained a relatively austere affair: a two-week revival-tent meeting consecrated to cinema as high art. Unlike Cannes, that rambling, market-place festival, there were no topless starlets or parties on yachts. Though Keys tried to make the Festival more "festive," with the occasional party at

---

3    William Schuman proposed the following criteria, which was adopted by the Board: 1) The individual should be living; 2) He or she should have drawing power for a benefit audience; 3) He or she should have a body of work of sufficient size and scope for an interesting evening; 4) The honored guest should be one with an aura—a special dimension of charisma; 5) The individual and the quality of his or her work in film should be suitable for sponsorship by the Film Society as an organization involved in the advancement of film as an art; 6) Not only the work of the individual, but also the availability of film material should be considered.

Alfred Stern, Rainer Werner Fassbinder, and Richard Koch at the Closing Night of *The Marriage of Maria Braun,* 1979

Studio 54 or the Rainbow Room, her efforts went against the overall no-nonsense tenor of the NYFF. There was very little coddling of the press, such as film journalists would become accustomed to at Toronto: a simple breakfast buffet would be laid out, followed by a diet of rigorous movies. There was no pressroom set aside for rendezvousing with colleagues, or for sending off faxes and, later, e-mails. Perhaps because the NYFF was held in New York, and not in a small tourist spot like Locarno or Telluride, it lacked central hangouts: critics and the public attended screenings and then dispersed, returning to their normal city lives.

What buzz the NYFF generated had more to do with the films themselves than celebrity-spotting. In 1972, the same year that the FLSC paid tribute to Chaplin, the NYFF's Closing Night was *Last Tango in Paris*. Keys remembers going into Elaine's, the fabled East Side eatery, and being importuned on all sides to describe the film before its showing. "In the early days," she noted, "to be part of the cultural conversation you had to go to the New York Film Festival." Pauline Kael wrote a famous review of *Last Tango* in which she compared its showing at the NYFF with the premiere of Stravinsky's *Rites of Spring*. (Kael, by the way, was invited to join the Festival's selection committee, but at an exploratory meeting she

and Roud argued so strenuously about movies that she declined the offer.)

By 1973, the FSLC was reporting that it was in sound financial shape. Subscriptions were up, as were donations and grants from sponsors and government agencies. Still, the NYFF continued to be a costly affair, in part because, now that it had its own organization and was no longer presented by Lincoln Center for the Performing Arts (LCPA), it was required to pay high, ever-escalating rentals for Alice Tully Hall and Avery Fisher Hall to the parent organization, Lincoln Center. (A chart that analyzed festival expenses from 1969 to 1984 indicated hall costs went from 30 percent of expenses to 58 percent.) Most festival patrons might naïvely assume the NYFF was getting these halls for free, but that was not the case. Labor costs were also steep, thanks to the stagehands' union contract. That contract had been designed for single three-hour events like chamber music concerts; but on weekends the NYFF might run four or five films from morning to midnight, and the stagehands would be paid considerable overtime. It bothered Joanne Koch, a fiscally prudent manager and a tigress in protecting the Film Society's interests, that 10 percent of the Festival's costs went to stage labor. Stagehands were in fact paid much more than projection-ists, although their duties were minimal in comparison. Koch haggled endlessly—some-times even successfully—with Lincoln Center's upper management, trying to come up with a more advantageous arrangement for the Film Society's use of the halls. Over the years, Koch would sometimes ponder whether it might not be better to take the film festival somewhere else, such as the Ziegfeld Theatre,[4] where rentals and labor costs would be half the amount, or the Loews Lincoln Square multi-plex. But in the end, it always seemed safer to keep it at Lincoln Center, partly because of the international prestige of that brand, and partly because the film festival's identity seemed bound up, for better or worse, with the cultural complex. (Another advantage was that the Film Society did receive a slice of

---

4    The Film Society did use Radio City Music Hall, for instance, for the showing of *Koyaanisqatsi* and *The New Babylon*, and it rented the Ziegfeld for a Gala showing of *That's Entertainment, Part 2* and several performances of *Vertigo* because Alice Tully was not equipped for 70mm projection.

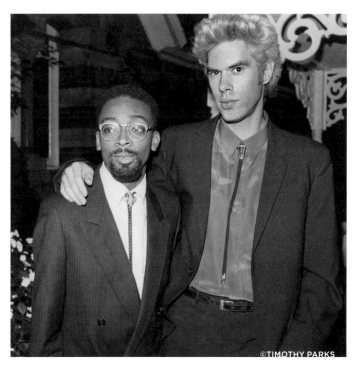

Jonathan Demme, Jason Robards, and Lois O'Connor at the Opening Night of *Melvin and Howard*, 1980

Spike Lee and Jim Jarmusch at the Opening Night of *Down by Law*, 1986

the Lincoln Center corporate fund drive, sometimes as much as $100,000, though they also had to pay into a general fund if Alice Tully Hall did not meet its annual budget.) Because of these disagreements over hall charges, the Film Society did not actually sign its official constituency agreement to become a resident member of Lincoln Center until 2004.

One of the most congenial traditions established from the very beginning of the

NYFF was to commission an artist to design a poster for each year's festival. These posters, initially paid for by the Vera List Foundation, resulted in some marvelous images by Larry Rivers, Saul Bass, Bruce Conner, Roy Lichtenstein, Andy Warhol, Marisol Escobar, James Rosenquist, Frank Stella, Josef Albers, Niki de Saint Phalle, Jean Tinguely, Jim Dine, Richard Avedon, Michelangelo Pistoletto, David Hockney, Robert Rauschenberg, Les Levine, Robert Breer, Tom Wesselmann, and

Diane Arbus, among others.

Richard Roud, as cultivated in the visual arts as in all things aesthetic, took an active interest in choosing the artists and securing their participation. But in other respects he tended to keep a distance from FSLC affairs— he never attended a Gala Tribute, for instance, as they did not occur when he made it his business to be in New York. No longer running the London Film Festival, he saw his job now as coming up with the best slate of films for the

Wim Wenders, 1984

Andy Warhol, James Ivory, and Felicity Kendal at a *Shakespeare Wallah* screening, 1965

*Dodsworth* by William Wyler

*Chariots of Fire* by Hugh Hudson

NYFF, along with the selection committee, and this function he continued to perform supremely well. He introduced to New York the exciting new German school of filmmakers, Rainer Werner Fassbinder, Wim Wenders, Volker Schlöndorff, Margarethe von Trotta, Werner Herzog, Rosa von Praunheim, Alexander Kluge, and Daniel Schmid; he continued to feature the French New Wave stalwarts like Truffaut, Godard, Chabrol, Rivette, Rohmer, Varda, Resnais, and Marker, while adding French newcomers such as Jean Eustache, André Téchiné, Maurice Pialat, Alain Tanner, and Bertrand Tavernier; he drew attention to Andrei Tarkovsky, Sergei Parajanov, Jerzy Skolimowski, Miklós Jancsó, Krzysztof Zanussi, Márta Mészáros, Andrzej Wajda, Agnieszka Holland, Krzysztof Kieślowski, István Szabó, Emir Kusturica, and others from the USSR and Eastern Europe; he was sympathetic to maverick American independents such as Terrence Malick, Jim Jarmusch, Robert Kramer, Jonathan Demme, Errol Morris, and the Coen Brothers; he remained a warm advocate of the Italians (Bertolucci, Olmi, Pier Paolo Pasolini, Gianni Amico, Marco Ferreri, Sergio Leone, the Taviani Brothers); he honored a very few British filmmakers, among them James Ivory, Joseph Losey, and Michael Apted; he continued to show audience-provoking films by Marguerite

Duras or Jean-Marie Straub and Danièle Huillet, and shrugged off the massive walkouts; and his retrospective programming of sublime, neglected gems by Ophuls, Renoir, Antonioni, Visconti, Feuillade, et al always demonstrated the highest taste.

Though he assured the Board that "there is not a single director who has had all of his films shown at the NYFF—we never automatically take films by a 'favorite' director, contrary to rumor," this was somewhat disingenuous: of course there were favorites. Roud was at heart a staunch auteurist—and what's so wrong with that, especially when the favorites were all clearly significant, innovative filmmakers? It only became an issue when a favorite was given the Opening Night slot, and the particular film turned out to be a disaster, as happened with Visconti's *Conversation Piece*. (That specific choice, a problematic but interesting picture, was further marred when a horrendously dubbed print arrived instead of the subtitled one the selection committee had expected to show.)

The selection for Opening Night (and to a lesser extent, Closing Night) became a touchy subject because tickets were priced higher and the Film Society counted on rewarding its donors with an entertaining night out and a party afterwards, as a fund-raising event. There was always a cultural divide between the more

moneyed audiences that went to Opening and Closing Nights and the cognoscenti who attended the regular NYFF screenings. A study of tickets purchased by major donors in 1995 indicated that 48 percent of these supporters were not interested in most of the NYFF showings and only cared about Opening and Closing Nights and the Gala Tributes. The cinephiles might look down on those swells in evening dress who cared more about fashion than Fassbinder, or might tut-tut when bunches of seats in a supposedly sold-out screening went empty because the subscription ticket holders could not be bothered to attend; but they ought to have appreciated that their own opportunity to see rarefied cinematic fare was being subsidized by these very donors.

Although Joanne Koch had set up a firewall between the Board and Roud's selection committees, ignoring those board members who suggested they should be given veto power over festival selections, she came to feel she had the right herself, as Executive Director, to register some input about Opening Night. Roud had originally agreed in 1969 to let the Board approve the choice of the Opening Night film. Later, this was changed to a promise on his part to consult with Koch about his selection. But in 1979 he committed the Opening Night slot to Bertolucci's *La Luna* before anyone else on the selection committee had seen the film, and it turned out to be a complete dud; many of the major donors walked out. Hard to get Opening Night exactly right: the 1981 selection, *Chariots of Fire*, proved a big success; everyone went off happy to the after-party at Tavern of the Green. The 1983 choice, *The Big Chill*, was another crowd-pleaser, but cineastes were entitled to wonder: what was the august NYFF doing showing such a crassly commercial Hollywood film? Was it a signal that one should expect the Opening Night film to be a little "soft" artistically from now on? In other years, Roud and the selection committee went back to their auteurist roots. Fassbinder's *Veronika Voss*, which opened the Festival in 1982 was visually elegant but drenched in druggy, thanatopsic sensibility, and went over like a lead balloon. (It did not help the mood that Fassbinder could not attend since he had died of a drug overdose the previous June.)

The *La Luna* fiasco started a serious disagreement between Roud and Koch. In the beginning of their working together they had been warmly collegial, sharing screenings and meals at Cannes, getting on famously. They had collaborated on "Saved," a wonderful sidebar at the NYFF of restored rarities, such as Murnau's *City Girl*; Walsh's *Regeneration*; *The Letter*, with Jeanne Eagels; *It's the Old Army Game*, with Louise

Brooks; King Vidor's *Wild Oranges*; Borzage's *Liliom*; and Wyler's *Dodsworth*. But over the years their relationship cooled. From Koch's perspective, it was Roud who became more distant, and seemed not to notice or, more to the point, appreciate that there was an organization, the Film Society, that toiled year-round to support his film festival. Roud thought she'd been the one who had changed, had become tenser, more difficult to deal with.

There were also problems because he would not fly (he had once been on a plane that had made an emergency landing and became permanently spooked), which meant he was restricted to festivals he could get to by train, thereby reinforcing the Festival's Eurocentric slant. He had wanted to visit New York annually in the spring, and Koch had partly set up the New Directors/New Films festival to accommodate him. (In fact, she took a grant Gerald Freund had secured to show films in prisons, and redirected it to provide crucial funding for the start-up of New Directors/New Films.) One spring, because the usual luxury liners were not sailing, Roud did not make it to New Directors/New Films.

The larger problem came down to respect, or lack of it. A charmer when he chose to be, Roud could also be brusquely dismissive toward anyone he decided was not in his league. There were ill feelings when Roud refused to

show Fellini's *Intervista*, a film key staffers had rooted for. Fellini had been the honoree at the previous Gala Tribute, but Roud, like many cinephile purists at the time, looked down on the Italian maestro. Technically, Roud was within his rights to exclude administration from program input, but it might have been more diplomatic at least to consider their views.

Eventually, things got so tense that Koch decided there should be some representation from the staff on the selection committee, and proposed Wendy Keys's appointment. At this point, Keys had been working for the NYFF and FSLC for over 20 years, had programmed Japanese film series, animation series, and films in the schools, had been on the New Directors/New Films selection committee, and had organized the Gala Tributes. She felt fully capable of serving on the committee. Moreover, she was—or considered herself—a close personal friend of Roud's, and even, as she put it, his protégé. But Roud refused to accept her on the committee, saying she had no credentials. (Looking back at what must have felt like a painful betrayal of their friendship, Keys says wistfully: "I blame myself, partly. I sometimes asked Richard questions I knew the answer to, the way women do, and played the eager student around him, and the result was that he didn't really respect me as a peer.")

Roud warned he would even circumvent the Board President and Chairman to prevent Keys from ever getting on the committee. Somehow the Rubicon had been crossed almost inadvertently. Roud was asked to resign. As with any unfortunate breakup, one cannot help wondering how easily it might have been avoided with a little less rigidity on both ends.

As soon as word leaked out that Roud had

*La Luna* by Bernardo Bertolucci

Bernardo Bertolucci and Jill Clayburgh at the Opening Night of *La Luna*, 1979

*Women on the Verge of a Nervous Breakdown* by Pedro Almodóvar

Pedro Almodóvar, *Talk to Her*, 2002

been fired, *The New York Times* and *The Village Voice* carried stories portraying him as the artist-martyr who had been unjustly dismissed by know-nothing bureaucrats wanting to censor or otherwise cheapen the integrity of the New York Film Festival. The press coverage was brutal; Koch was called "The Terminator" in one article. But what needs to be remembered is that by 1988, when all this brouhaha occurred, the NYFF had already become a beloved New York institution, and Roud was, in many people's minds, the Festival. It would be unthinkable to even imagine a New York Film Festival without him presiding.

We get some insight into Roud's own views about the structural tensions between programmer and administration in this passage from his 1983 book, *A Passion for Films: Henri Langlois and the Cinémathèque Française*: "But the biggest blow to Langlois came from the decision to split his job in two; in 1964 Langlois, who had officially been secretary-general, became artistic and technical director, and a certain Claude Fabrizio was 'parachuted' into the Cinémathèque as administrative and financial director. Officially and hierarchically, their posts were equal. Fabrizio was a pleasant young man with little experience of the cinema but with a solid grounding in administration. Whatever his qualities, however, it was an

impossible situation. The division between artistic and technical direction and administrative and financial direction was artificial, since almost any artistic or technical direction must affect finances and administration, and vice

Richard Peña in front of Alice Tully Hall, 1988

versa." It must be said that, since Roud had no desire to manage the administration of the Film Society, he brought upon himself that artificial division.

It must also be said that by the time Roud resigned, he had lost some of his enthusiasm for the current moment in cinema. As he wrote in his book on Langlois, "The great surge of talent that had started in the late fifties had, so it seemed, begun to lose momentum . . . By the mid-'70s, there seemed to be few new faces, few new talents. Is the cinema dying? Quite possibly: there is no guarantee of eternal life for any art form." If the New York Film Festival was to continue to play a vital role in discovering the best cinema had to offer, it would be necessary to find a more optimistic leadership, a new pulse. Roud had done a superb job, but he was tired, ill, and would in fact die the following year, in 1989, of heart failure, at the age of 59.

Richard Peña was 33 when he assumed the role as Director of the New York Film Festival, about the same age Roud had been when he started. A New Yorker of Puerto Rican and Spanish parentage, he had been a film buff from an early age, and had attended a NYFF screening of an Erich von Stroheim film at the age of 12. He went to Harvard, spent a year in Rio de Janeiro for his master's thesis on Brazilian and Argentine cinema, and took a master's degree in film at the Massachusetts Institute of Technology, during which he shot documentaries under the cinema vérité master

Ricky Leacock before concluding that he was not a filmmaker but a cinephile. He taught at several colleges before programming at the Harvard Film Archive and serving as director of the Film Center at the Art Institute of Chicago. There he ran series on Asian and Latin American filmmakers, including Raúl Ruiz. Unlike Roud, whose background had been that of a working journalist, Peña was more of a film scholar, who fit comfortably into academic settings. Like Roud, he was supremely confident of his taste and judgments, and took over the reins as Festival Director without missing a beat, assembling a new selection committee, composed of Peña himself, Wendy Keys, *The Christian Science Monitor* film critic David Sterritt, *The Philadelphia Inquirer* critic Carrie Rickey, who was the one holdover from the Roud committee, and—myself. (I had no particular allegiance to Roud, and was a warm acquaintance of Peña's, what did I have to lose? And I would get to go to Cannes.)

Several members of the old selection committee had resigned in solidarity with Roud. Critic Stephen Schiff was quoted as saying that anyone who joined the new committee would be equivalent to a Vichy government collaborator. I remember sitting at a large dinner the first week in Cannes next to Schiff and jokingly ordering Vichy water. Whatever lingering outrage the film community felt for the way Roud had been let go, on the surface things normalized quickly when it became apparent that Peña was capable of running the Festival without any diminution in quality. We had the luck that first year of being able to offer a knockout Opening Night film, Pedro Almodóvar's *Women on the Verge of a Nervous Breakdown*. Other standouts at the 1988 NYFF were Cassavetes' *Opening Night*, three English films (Mike Leigh's *High Hopes*, Terence Davies' *Distant Voices, Still Lives*, Derek Jarman's *The Last of England*), French newcomer Catherine Breillat's *36 fillette*, a brace of Asian films (Hou Hsiao-hsien's *Daughter of the Nile*, Lee Jang-ho's *The Man with Three Coffins*, Zhang Yimou's *Red Sorghum*), Bille August's *Pelle the Conqueror*, Marcel Ophuls's *Hotel Terminus: The Life and Times of Klaus Barbie*, the eccentric, dark

*Distant Voices, Still Lives* by Terence Davies

Canadian film *A Winter Tan* (now undeservedly forgotten), a bleak, powerful Romanian film, *Jacob*, and a newly initiated program, "Avant-Garde Voices."

The films were changing—no longer so Western Eurocentric, with Italian, German, and Scandinavian cinemas at a lull, and French cinema still active but not as prominent as it once had been. International film festivals were starting to give awards to polished, fascinating films from such places as Taiwan, Mainland China, Hong Kong, South Korea, Iran, Egypt, Israel, Palestine, the Philippines, Mali, Burkina Faso, Brazil, Mexico, Australia, Romania, Turkey… The NYFF had the satisfaction of knowing that it was showing some of the most exciting, critically acclaimed work on the planet. Sadly, these brilliant filmmakers from Asia, Africa, Latin America, and the Middle East would never generate the sort of name recognition or hero worship among American audiences that the European masters of a previous generation (Bergman, Antonioni, Godard, Truffaut) had garnered. Even auteurs recognized as giants abroad, such as Hou Hsiao-hsien or Abbas Kiarostami, would not get distributed in the U.S. on any but the most token level. It made the NYFF vulnerable to those who scoffed at all the seemingly obscure

filmmakers with funny names from remote places crowding the Festival's listings. The upside was it meant that the NYFF now had an even more valuable role to play, in making available to American audiences so many cinematic achievements they might otherwise have had no chance of seeing.

Richard Peña was clearly the right man to usher these globally broadened perspectives into the new NYFF. Multilingual, gregarious, with a lifelong interest in Latin American culture and a special sympathy for Asian and Middle Eastern cinemas, he would fly anywhere to check out a small festival or national archive. Though Peña was thoroughly grounded in film history and formalist theory, he had more of an ethnographic curiosity and a sociopolitical perspective than Roud. He might urge that a certain film be shown because it eloquently depicted the way of life of a little-known mountain people, or represented the maturation of a valiantly emerging national cinema. These were marginal cases, however: what tends to be overlooked is that Roud's and Peña's choices would have overlapped 80-85 percent of the time. "That was probably because my tastes were formed to a large extent by Roud," Peña explains, "all those years of my going to the New York Film Festival."

*Red Sorghum* by Zhang Yimou

Peña too had his pet auteurs. Though he was less inclined than Roud to stick loyally to everything by one of his favorites, especially if the new film seemed more a repetition than an advance, those who followed the NYFF would expect to find with regularity the work of Almodóvar, Manoel de Oliveira, Wong Kar Wai, Edward Yang, Mike Leigh, Raúl Ruiz, the Dardenne Brothers, Hou Hsiao-hsien, Jia Zhang-ke, Abbas Kiarostami, Jafar Panahi, Béla Tarr, Idrissa Ouedraogo, Abderrahmane Sissako, Frederick Wiseman, Youssef Chahine, Apichatpong Weerasethakul, Hong Sang-soo, Arnaud Desplechin, Guy Maddin, Lars von Trier, Lucrecia Martel, Nuri Bilge Ceylan, and Clint Eastwood. Peña's selection committees showed the early work of Jane Campion, Michael Moore, Aki Kaurismäki, Atom Egoyan, Leos Carax, Bruno Dumont, Agnès Jaoui, and continued to favor the older masters whom Roud had championed: Rohmer, Resnais, Godard, Rivette, the Taviani Brothers, Straub-Huillet.

Joanne Koch was less inclined, after the Roud Affair, to voice any opinions about programming, and gave Peña a free hand (if grumbling under her breath at times). There

Zhang Yimou, 1988

continued to be the occasional tensions over Opening Night, however. Roy Furman, who served as Chairman and/or President of the Film Society Board for 12 years during this period, took the position that "the board and staff should have no input on selections, but once the body of films for the Festival was chosen, the board should have a voice regarding the Opening Night selection, as it was so crucial to donors. I lobbied the selection committee, sometimes successfully, for certain films, and tried to educate them to the needs of our major contributors," he remembers.

Alfred Stern, who had succeeded Martin Segal as President, had made it known that he was determined that the Film Society should acquire its own year-round venue. The opportunity had arisen when Lincoln Center announced that it was erecting a tower, which would later be named the Rose Building, on the northwest corner of the complex. It would

Arsinée Khanjian and Atom Egoyan, *The Adjuster*, 1991

Roy Furman, George Clooney, and Frieda Furman at the Opening Night of *Good Night, and Good Luck.*, 2005

house a Juilliard dormitory, administrative offices, and whatever else its constituent organizations succeeded in lobbying to have included. The Film Society, which had long been considered (with some reason) a stepchild of Lincoln Center, managed to make the case this time that its needs should be addressed. The resulting Walter Reade Theater was named after an art-house chain owner and foreign-film distributor. Stern solicited the initial naming gift through negotiations with Sheldon Guns-berg, a Film Society Board member and officer in the Walter Reade Foundation. Subsequently, the bulk of the fund-raising fell to Roy Furman, who underwrote the adjacent Gallery with his wife Frieda, and was a pivotal figure in soliciting the film studios, and meeting often with the other board members, such as Dorothy Cullman and her husband Lewis, to map strategies. During these years, the Film Society enjoyed a very active board, spearheaded by Furman, Stern, Dorothy Cullman, and Julien Studley, who moved mountains to get the new facility financed. Meanwhile, Joanne Koch supervised every decision about its appointments, down to the angle of the incline and the upholstery fabric.

When it opened in 1999, the 268-seat house was immediately appreciated as one of the best places to see a movie in the city: every seat was comfortable, well-spaced, with perfect sight lines, and the acoustics functioned splendidly (so much so that the hall would occasionally rent out for chamber music concerts). The French director Louis Malle was so impressed with the facility that he rose to the stage after a screening of his motion picture *Damage* to declare that this theater was what a filmmaker dreams his movie will look and sound like when the picture is completed. The only problem was that it was hard to find, located on the second floor to the rear, virtually invisible from the sidewalk. Its tucked-away location reinforced the prejudices of those resistant to Lincoln Center as a refined, snooty enclave. You pretty much had to know before-hand what was playing at the Walter Reade and how to get there; but once you did, the rewards for film lovers were plentiful and continuous.

The Walter Reade Theater altered the way the NYFF and the FSLC did business. The selection committee could now view submitted movies there in the mornings, when the Walter Reade was not booked for public showings, instead of having to rent a midtown screening room for its two-week July sifting marathon, and it could then repair in the afternoons to the FSLC offices above for viewings on video-tape or, later, DVD. The Film Society, which had previously made do with crowded facilities in shabby basements, suddenly found itself housed in a bright, clean, corporate suite of offices.

The Walter Reade made it possible, during the two-week NYFF, to show ambitious sidebar series (such as memorable retrospectives of Sacha Guitry, Yasujiro Ozu, Youssef Chahine), as well as screening-worthy documentaries or avant-garde programs that could not have hoped to fill the Alice Tully. During the rest of the year, the Walter Reade would occasionally book a weeklong run of an intriguing film that had played in the NYFF but had not received distribution. Most of the theater's offerings, however, consisted of older movies or premieres that would be shown once or twice, as part of some curated series. Over the years, Peña and his associates developed a group of programs that would make annual appearances: Rendez-Vous with French Cinema, Spanish Cinema Now, Open Roads: New Italian Cinema, Latinbeat, the African Film Festival, Dance on Camera (curated by Joanna Ney), Film Com-ment Selects (an edgy *salon des refusés* put together by Gavin Smith, the magazine's editor). Kent Jones, film critic and filmmaker, was hired to assist Peña in programming the Walter Reade. He came up with a number of notable series, including Hou Hsiao-hsien, Jean Gabin, and Allan Dwan retrospectives, and he also traveled to Kazakhstan, Uzbekistan, and Kyrgyzstan to put together a groundbreaking show on the films of the Silk Road. Such adventurous programming was a special necessity for an art-film venue operating in New York City, where other local institutions such as the Museum of Modern Art, the American Museum of the Moving Image, the BAM Rose Cinemas, and the Film Forum had set the bar high. Following the demise of most art-houses and repertory theaters in the city, the legacy of film history seemed now to have passed largely into the hands of nonprofit cultural institutions. These half-dozen venues made it possible to still see movies projected full-size as they were intended, with bodies and faces larger than life, augmenting the dramatic spectacle, and with the crisp detail of film onscreen, though film prints were becoming scarcer and digital media rapidly replacing celluloid.

One side benefit of the proliferation of digital media was that the NYFF had many more pictures to choose from, it being easier and cheaper to mail in a DVD than a stack of film cans. A dozen features from Iran could now arrive in a single box. Entries to the NYFF have grown from 794 in 1988 (the year Peña began as Festival Director) to over 2,000. It has made for more global variety but has also required hundreds of additional hours of pre-screening. Fortunately, Peña had a robust constitution (growing from ectomorph to endomorph over the years) and a strong work ethic: he would come in on weekends and stay weeknights to plow through the piles. Each year he prefaced his remarks to the Opening Night audience with a special thanks to his wife and three children for their forbearance.

Under Joanne Koch's stable administration, the Film Society grew in sophistication and budget size, and tasks that had previously been farmed out to consultants were now done in-house. Since 1982 the FSLC had had its own director of public relations, Joanna Ney, and in 1993 it hired a director of development, Claudia Bonn, to oversee fund-raising. Bonn had come to the Film Society from the nonprofit cultural world, having worked at the Joffrey Ballet and the American Ballet Theater. After 10 years' service at the Film Society, however, Bonn was ready to take on more responsibility.

It was decided by the Board that Koch would step down and Bonn be named the new Executive Director. Koch was willing to give up the post, but after 32 years her life had become so inextricably tied to the Film Society that she found it difficult to walk away from it entirely. During Bonn's first year as Executive Director, Koch continued to work on projects involving expansion of the FSLC, which made for some awkwardness. Eventually they sorted it out. Bonn's style was less familial than Koch's, more businesslike. She recalls now: "I had to professionalize the office and make rules and regulations."

By all accounts, Bonn was seen as a calm, even-keeled, fair-minded administrator. "My job was to make Richard [Peña] a hero. To be a manager, to fund-raise, and stay away from curating. It helped that I knew nothing about films." Still, she had to rein in Peña from time

Claudia Bonn and Dan Stern at the Opening Night of *Look at Me*, 2004

to time, because he would go off on his own, making arrangements with the cultural ambassador of X county or Y national archive; and then bills for the series would start to come in. Eventually she had to confront him: "I won't tell you what to program and you won't do my budgets." Peña understood and made the necessary adjustments to include her more in the loop. "Tell me about that meeting you just had," she would inquire periodically. She admired his iconoclastic programming, though in her view "there was a lot of 'Sit down, shut up, and eat your spinach.'" He took seriously the mission to educate the public to what they might have been missing in world cinema.

Temperamentally, he was more of a teacher than a showman. (By this time, in fact, he had become an Associate Professor at Columbia University, specializing in film theory and international cinema, simultaneous with his duties at the FSLC.)

One of Bonn's biggest tasks was to raise tens of millions of dollars for a new addition to the Film Society: a complex of three theaters and a café that was to be built across the street from the Walter Reade. Lincoln Center had announced plans to redo West 65th Street, dismantling the overhead bridge, altering the design of Alice Tully Hall to make it more permeable to the city, and turning that corridor into a kind of colorful electronic marquee. The Film Society saw a chance that might never come again for a flexible screening center with expanded educational programs, and put in a bid to erect the complex where the old underground parking garage had been. They retained the architecture firm David Rockwell & Associates, who drew up plans for the project. It was now the Board's job to figure out a way to fund-raise for it in a difficult economic climate. Under the dynamic leadership of Daniel Stern and Ann Tenenbaum, the entire $40 million capital cost was raised before completion. Realtor and perennial Board member Julien Studley was crucial in brokering the property deal, and a long-time Board member, Elinor Bunin Munroe, generously pledged a substantial naming gift toward the cost of construction. Two other donors, Francesca Beale and Howard Gilman, stepped forward to provide naming gifts for the two screens. The new theater complex was well on its way to becoming a reality. But after five years of serving with skill and equanimity as Executive Director, Claudia Bonn decided she had had enough. She took a job running Wave Hill, a public garden and cultural center in the Bronx. "I moved from films to horticulture," she remarks cheerfully, "where I enjoy a peace and serenity I never had at the Film Society."

Over the years the press continued to cover the NYFF, with *The New York Times*, and for a while, the *New York Post* and other local papers printing daily reviews. The *Times* was the money review: it had acceded to the FSLC's

*Hotel Terminus: The Life and Times of Klaus Barbie* by Marcel Ophuls

request to run its assessment on the morning of the film's first showing (rather than the day after, as was usually done), so as to generate last-minute box-office purchases in the event of a positive notice. Of course, there was always the chance the reviewer would trash the picture, in which case not only would there be no last-minute box-office rush but the film's

chances of being picked up for U.S. distribution would likely be crushed. Still, it was worth the gamble to have each film reviewed separately, and it added to the prestige of being chosen by the NYFF. The selection committee certainly looked forward, whether optimistically or masochistically, to having its work graded each morning by the critics.

One of the rationales put forward for keeping the Festival relatively small was that if you expanded it beyond, say, 25 slots, the *Times* would stop reviewing each film. At a certain point, however, the *Times* critics decided to scrap its daily reviews anyway and substitute several wrap-ups punctuating the course of the Festival. As a result of these wrap-up articles, most films would get no more than a few sentences at best, preceded by some generalizing essayistic setup about the Festival's trends, grimness quotient, or level of quality. Such ruminations often veered toward discontent, as is perhaps inevitable when attempting to generalize about an uneven assortment of films. It would seem that from the mid-1990s on, the press in general began to express a sort of grouchy rather than grateful response to the NYFF, as if to say, "Yes, yes, the Festival is doing its thing, still showing masterpieces and challenging art films, but…" Part of that jaded response issued from the fact that these same reviewers had already caught up with most of the films on display, in Cannes, Toronto, Berlin, Sundance, or Telluride. The NYFF may very well have culled or curated (as it preferred to say) the best of the festivals, but there were no, or very few, premieres, hence no news to report; and film reviewers are journalists as well as critics.

Michael Barker, John C. Reilly, Ann Tenenbaum, and Jodie Foster at the Opening Night of *Carnage*, 2011

*Mystic River* by Clint Eastwood

There was criticism from both ends of the aesthetic spectrum: irritation on the part of cutting-edge film critics that the NYFF had turned down this or that radical piece of filmmaking, and annoyance on the part of the popular entertainment reviewers that the pictures selected seemed elitist, baffling, and drastically short on star power. The NYFF was slammed for occasionally showing films of wide appeal that it thought had artistic merit (such as *Beauty and the Beast, Mystic River, My Week with Marilyn,* or *The Descendants*), it was pilloried for showing too many pictures that had already secured distribution, and it was condemned for showing pictures so esoteric they had no chance of ever gaining distribution. Shrugging off such attacks, Peña and his selection committees wisely stuck to the rule of showing what they considered the 25 or so best movies of the year.

The organization had grown middle-aged, and hence vulnerable to attack for that very reason—it seemed predictable—regardless of whether the function it performed was still invaluable. It had come into existence at a time when there were only a handful of film festivals

worldwide, and New York desperately needed to catch up with world cinema. Several decades later, that was hardly the case. Indeed, the upstart, populist, celebrity-soaked Tribeca Film Festival was making a lot of noise, and surely the NYFF would have to respond to the challenge, it was said: make accommodations and offer something new and glitzy to confront the newcomer from downtown.

The Executive Director who replaced Claudia Bonn in 2008 was Mara Manus. She had come from The Public Theater; and she subscribed to the notion that major changes were in order. She thought it imperative that the FSLC attract a new, more demographically broad-based audience, and, as she told Peña: "Stop showing these movies that no one wants to see." She also fired half the old staff—in effect, the institutional memory of the Film Society—and put in people loyal to her. Along the way she dismantled the old subscription system for the NYFF, with less than desirable results. Perhaps some change was in order, but Manus had moved too quickly and unilaterally, and there was an outcry, and her tenure lasted just a little over a year.

Through it all, Peña has been a rock: steady,

imperturbable, reliable, and, in his way, unbudgeable. He has stubbornly refused to alter the basic concept he had inherited from Roud. Why give prizes? The NYFF doesn't need competitions and awards, he argues, because it's so small that just getting into it is a kind of award. Why expand the slate? As it is, each film gets focused attention, and the selection committee can't waffle or compromise its critical judgment. Why merge with other institutions, such as the Tribeca Film Festival (as was once proposed)? Tribeca might be advertised as "the people's festival," but after its initial splash, it has had a hard time securing films of the caliber the NYFF shows. Why move parts of the Festival away from Lincoln Center? The Festival's presence at Lincoln Center elevates film to the level of the opera and ballet, and Peña has never wanted it to lose that cachet. (Indeed, when the after-party at Tavern on the Green started to become too populous, well-wishers overwhelming the honorees, it was changed to a dinner-dance and moved to Lincoln Center, thanks to Bernard Schwartz, the Gala Tribute Chairman for three decades, who graciously covered the additional

*My Week with Marilyn* by Simon Curtis

With so many ways to watch moving pictures, from iPads to Netflix streaming to telephones, it may become necessary to entice people into theatrical settings by making the screening feel more like a special event. Repertory cinemas face a scarcity of prints, digital transfers are becoming increasingly expensive, many of the old art-film distributors have gone out of business, there is considerably more self-distribution, and the old financing model for independent filmmaking has collapsed and needs to be reinvented. Some predict that movies themselves will cease to exist. Through it all, ravishing, strange, exhilarating, tormenting films continue being made, enough to supply the NYFF with a full slate for the foreseeable future. Meanwhile, the riches of the cinematic past mount up, providing us with a priceless record of beauty, intelligence, behavioral complexity, vexation, anguish, and desire that must not be allowed to perish or slip away.

When the NYFF approached its 25th anniversary, there was a proposal in the works to publish a book commemorating that achievement, which came to naught. As it was about to turn 40, there was talk again of putting out a volume honoring the institution's history; and again the idea was tabled. Now we have arrived at the Festival's 50th anniversary, and you hold such a book in your hands. It is time to celebrate—and take stock.

expenditures himself.) Why contemplate inviting online video or other interactive media into the Festival? "I'm pretty old-fashioned, I really love the communal film experience, and that's what we do." He adds that he is stepping down now, after 25 years, because "like at any other cultural institution, change can be important. Someone new should take over, who will bring in fresh ideas."

The new Executive Director, Rose Kuo, represents the future of the Film Society. Her background is in film programming, and she is knowledgeable, energetic, and willing to experiment. How the old structural tensions between program director and administrator will be resolved after Peña has left remains to be seen.

As the New York Film Festival enters its second half-century, it encounters some remarkable opportunities and compelling challenges. The Film Society has never been more expansively replete. With the opening of the gorgeously

handsome, intimate, jewel-box screening halls at the Elinor Bunin Munroe Film Center, it now has a street-level presence and the chance to show a variety of first-run and retrospective programs that can complement the Walter Reade. It is still trying to figure out the best ways to program these new theaters, both to broaden the audience and cover the organization's resultant higher operating costs. The Film Society does not possess a theater of its own large enough to hold the NYFF, and is obliged to continue renting Alice Tully Hall; but that facility has been redesigned to make its entry a much more amiable public space, and its interior a welcoming gathering place open to the street. And *Film Comment* is still going strong.

As for the larger picture, the whole landscape of filmmaking and distribution is undergoing radical change. These forces cannot help but impact on the Film Society's future.

Michael Fassbender, Rose Kuo, and David Cronenberg, 2011

August 19, 1963: Larry Rivers painting a billboard of the poster he designed for the 1st NYFF. *Photograph by Bob Serating*

# OLD TIMES

*Roger Greenspun*

OF COURSE NEW YORK HAD A FILM CUL-
ture before it had a film festival. Not just at the
big Midtown theaters and the fancier of the
first-run little theaters. By the early 1960s there
were repertory houses, from the New Yorker
and the Thalia uptown to the Fifth Avenue and
Bleecker Street cinemas downtown, film series
at MoMA and Amos Vogel's Cinema 16,
second- or even third-run theaters like the East
Village's essential and long-lost Saint Marks.
Above all, there was 42nd Street between 7th
and 8th Avenues, after the time of legitimate
theater and before the time of utter degradation.
A 42nd Street double feature might cost 85
cents. The programming ranged from softcore
porn at the houses in the west, to a repertory of
American action cinema at the Times Square
midblock, to subtitled foreign films (some that
you would never find anyplace else) at the
Apollo, nearer 7th Avenue. Across 42nd Street
from the Apollo, the New Amsterdam played
horror and science fiction. I believe that's where
George Franju's *Eyes Without a Face* (*The Horror*

*Chamber of Dr. Faustus* on 42nd Street) and
Fritz Lang's final masterpiece *The 1,000 Eyes of
Dr. Mabuse* opened, both dubbed into English
and both to no reviews.

It was a haphazard film culture, serious and
somewhat arrogantly disreputable. It provided
the young and marginally employed with lots
of opportunity for feeding a passion, avoiding
the day's fresh air and sunshine, all without
spending much money.

Up-to-the-minute opinions and attitudes
took their cues from the pages of a very little
magazine, *The New York Film Bulletin*, but for
depth and perspective the authoritative text
would have been Andrew Sarris's 1963 "American Directors" issue of the journal *Film Culture*.
We were learning the history and quality of our
own movies by way of thinking that came from
Paris: you could buy the then-legendary *Cahiers
du cinéma* in a few stores here and absorb its
influence even if you couldn't actually read
French. It was a deeply rooted and still growing
history: John Ford's *The Man Who Shot Liberty*

*Le joli mai* by Chris Marker

*Valance* opened in 1962, Hitchcock's *The Birds* in 1963.

That year also saw the first New York Film Festival. It was a classy affair, with program cover art and poster by Larry Rivers, sidebar screenings at MoMA (Mizoguchi, Ophuls, Kurosawa, etc., free with museum admission), and a dazzling selection of films. Buñuel's *The Exterminating Angel*, Ozu's *An Autumn Afternoon*, Bresson's *The Trial of Joan of Arc*, Losey's *The Servant*, Chris Marker's *Le joli mai*, and Alain Resnais's *Muriel* are a few titles that remain current. It was an international list, and it resonated for those of us who, thanks in part to Andrew Sarris and to lessons from France, were becoming aware of our own legacy and were able to sense sublimity not just in imports but also in, say, Minnelli's 1962 *Two Weeks in Another Town*. For this audience the Festival arrived as a gift, an exceptionally generous one, with free talks, seminars, and screenings. Among the perks, I recall Andy Warhol loops—*Sleep*, *Empire*, etc.—running nonstop in the then–Philharmonic Hall's promenade during one of the early Festivals. The abundance owed a lot to good funding, to the enterprise and energy of the Festival Coordinator Amos Vogel, and to the taste, knowledge, and connections of the Festival Director Richard Roud, an American living in England, who in the early years brought the best of the

non-competitive London Film Festival to New York. The extent of Roud's influence I learned only years later, but from the start I assumed that he made the major decisions.

It helped that for all the city's access to current international film—think of the later 1950s and early 1960s for Bergman, Truffaut, Kurosawa, Antonioni, Fellini—much had not been released, and it was available. With the idea of a festival in play, exhibitor Dan Talbot began his own small one at the New Yorker,

now long gone from its corner at Broadway and 89th Street. And there was a dazzling series of French cinema at Rockefeller Center's Normandie Theater that included to my mind the greatest double bill ever to open in New York: Bresson's *Les dames du Bois de Boulogne* (1945) and Renoir's *The Crime of Monsieur Lange* (1935). You might look up the 1964 *New York Times* review of that show for a reminder of the utter fallibility of daily film criticism.

The daily reviewers weren't altogether fond of the Festival in its early years. From where I stood, on the outside, it had long seemed that the major movie critics were wrong about everything. At Festival press screenings you could gauge a film's worth, or at least its ambitions, by how much of the audience walked out on it. Jean-Marie Straub, Bresson, and Fassbinder were particular non-favorites. Later, when I actually began covering the Festival for the *Times* I could appreciate what it meant to have a load of new, usually difficult movies dumped on a reviewer just at the beginning of the busiest season of the year. Some of my colleagues felt that wanting to see a movie twice meant "not getting it" the first time. But at least twice is what the Festival typically demanded, and deserved, and I cannot count how often, the second time around, I was thankfully able to change my

*Muriel* by Alain Resnais

mind. Whatever else, for anyone given to thinking about movies, the New York Film Festival was an educational paradise.

Some years after the Festival opened I joined the film panel of the New York State Council on the Arts (NYSCA), a groundbreaking program and, I was told, a model for the National Endowment. NYSCA helped fund the Festival, but grudgingly so as far as the film panel was concerned. The Festival was too successful, too rich, too commercial, not sufficiently sensitive to the needs and efforts of local independent filmmakers. Mostly the panel consisted of independent filmmakers. In my time I was the only critic, and I believe I got there in part because the NYSCA staff felt the panel could use some non-independent-film balance. Previously all the gripes I had heard about the Festival came from the other side,

from over-challenged reviewers and the Philistine public. For me the Festival had been golden. And it was odd and uncomfortable to sit in a room full of people who thought it commercial dross. Having seen plenty of their movies, I of course had my own reservations about New York's independent filmmakers. And as for the question of art versus commerce, I recall one panelist bitterly resisting our giving money to a Long Island theater—no connection to the Festival—for a Howard Hawks series. Howard Hawks! He reminded us we were after all the New York State Council on the "Arts."

In 1975 I found myself on the selection committee, with Richard Corliss, Arthur Knight, Henri Langlois, Arthur Mayer, Charles Michener, Susan Sontag, and of course Richard Roud. I don't recall seeing Knight or Langlois

(who remained in France), but the rest of us did meet in the Fifth Avenue Screening Room, in a West 56th Street row house, to see and select movies—or what there was left to select. The selection-committee appointment had been an honor. It became a shock.

At least half the films had been pre-selected. We were to screen and choose the rest. I don't recall which selections fell into which category, but on the whole, 1975 was a good year. For a partial list: Visconti's *Conversation Piece*, Renoir's 1931 *La chienne*, Orson Welles's *F for Fake*, Werner Herzog's *Every Man for Himself and God Against All* (*The Mystery of Kaspar Hauser* in commercial release), Ousmane Sembene's *Xala*, the Straub-Huillet filming of Schönberg's *Moses und Aron*, Marguerite Duras's *India Song*, Michael Ritchie's wonderful *Smile*, Truffaut's *The Story of Adele H*. I

*F for Fake* by Orson Welles

*The Story of Adele H.* by François Truffaut

*Smile* by Michael Ritchie

*Xala* by Ousmane Sembene

couldn't have done better myself—or at least, not enough of it. Roud had done most of it, in Europe, before he arrived in New York with a screening list for the rest of us. Typically the reason given was that movies once offered had to be snapped up immediately, without time for consultation, if the Festival was to get them. This may have been true, though from this distance I'm not sure why. Certainly there were a few films, not on the list above, for which there wouldn't have been much competition.

Roud had remarkable taste and energy. His writing, in the Festival program notes, in books

Marguerite Duras, 1975

on Jean-Luc Godard and Henri Langlois, looks good to me today. And a Richard Roud film festival, which I believe we largely got, was in fact a pleasure. So far as I knew, in my time nobody else on the selection committee had his film sophistication or his access. That last remained important. He did all the tough work; the rest of us sat in a screening room and formed opinions. But Roud also decided what we did and didn't get to see. You could compile an interesting list of films and filmmakers that might have been but never were considered for the New York Film Festival.

I complained about the limited representation for the selection committee, and perhaps a bit for that reason it was decided we should all begin seeing movies at Cannes the following year. A better reason might have been that it cost the Festival less to help send us to France (of course we weren't paid, but we did get $1,000 for travel expenses, which even in the 1970s wouldn't take you far to, from, and in Cannes) than to ship cases of 35mm film back and forth for consideration.

Cannes was a great resource. Typically it meant half a dozen movies a day in whatever language with, if you were lucky, French subtitles. There was no accreditation for visiting selection committees, so we went as journalists and film critics, filing copy. Everyone who

has been there has written his or her first-experience-of-the-Cannes-Film-Festival piece, so I won't attempt another. In many ways the memory is better than the experience. Cannes, offering perhaps 70 movies a day (admittedly, many repeats) both in and out of competition and, I assume, all for sale, was famously the antithesis of New York. For me, without the crowds, the mass parties, the press hysteria, the actually not-so-great food, New York was decidedly more fun.

The selection committee had its battles at Cannes, and there were tense negotiations, both there and back home. Even if we decided on a film, distributors might balk at a Festival opening—too highbrow—or at risking a Festival newspaper review for a movie that might open much later to a condensed review or possibly no review at all. However, programs were put together, simply extraordinary programs, and they deserve more study. I find it worth writing this piece if only to bring to mind so many films from 30, 40, 50 years ago. Some are now repertory standards, some we are unlikely every to see again. But from them all there emerge moments that form a history of moods, styles, attitudes—memories that combine film and life in a heady mixture of nostalgia and delight. 🎥

*The Last Picture Show* by Peter Bogdanovich

# 17 SPRINGS AND SUMMERS

*Richard Corliss*

HERE'S A JOB FEW CRITICS WOULD TURN down: a two-week spring break at the Cannes Film Festival; then a two-week summer session watching movies in a Manhattan screening room; and (optional) 17 days in early autumn, seeing the fruits of our Solomonic labors shown to the public at the New York Film Festival. The immense power we wielded as members of the selection committee was balanced by a minor honorarium. But money was the least of it, since we got to see some excellent films and aim wry collegial derision at some bad ones. We helped choose works that set the fall cultural agenda for a generation of knowledgeable cinephiles who massed at Lincoln Center to prove that, yes, film was a high art. And all the while we spent quality time with the sharpest of American movie minds.

Sounds like fun, and, oh, it was. But at the beginning for me, in 1971, I was engorged with trepidation—or would have been, if I'd had any capacity for self-reflection. Serving on the

NYFF selection committee, after all, was an honor a movie person achieved in mid-life or later, like a seat on the Supreme Court. The members of the 1971 committee had surely earned their eminence. Richard Roud, in additional to running our festival, had programmed the National Film Theatre and the London Film Festival and authored monographs on Jean-Luc Godard and Max Ophuls. Arthur Knight, film critic for the *Saturday Review*, had written the seminal history *The Liveliest Art*—the first movie book I ever bought for the text, not the pictures. Arthur Mayer, who'd been in the movie business since the 1920s, had kick-started America's postwar interest in foreign films by importing Rossellini's *Open City*; he also taught at Dartmouth and USC. Susan Sontag, essayist, novelist, and filmmaker, possessed the most glamorous intellect of her time; when she troubled to smack down my review of Bergman's *Persona* in a footnote in her book *Styles of Radical Will*, a friend told me, "Kid, you've made it."

Peter Bogdanovich, 1980

Louis Malle, 1981

members, including Henri Langlois and Mary Meerson of the Cinémathèque Française and the *Times of London* film critic John Russell Taylor, but their function was to recommend movies, not to participate in the voting.) The year I joined the committee, Sarris and Roud were 42, Sontag was 38, Knight 55, Mayer a patrician 85; and it saddens me beyond words that, today, they are all dead.

I was 27 and, in their company, felt 12. My own meager résumé: a freelance reviewer of movies and pop music for *The New York Times*, *National Review*, and *Andy's Voice*, a contributor of essays to *Film Quarterly* and *Film Society Review*, and, for less than two years, the editor of *Film Comment* magazine. If I had any qualification for the NYFF job, it was probably my youth. In this year of retrenchment for the Festival, when only 18 feature programs were to play at Alice Tully Hall and sidebar programs had been cut, Richard had been encouraged to

The only one of the committee members I knew, except by their spectacular résumés, was Andy Sarris, my teacher and mentor at the New York University graduate film school. But he was also Andrew Sarris: *Village Voice* reviewer, Mr. Auteur Theory, and America's most adventurous and influential film historian. (Back then the Festival also had advisory

add a younger person to the selection committee. I later learned another finalist was the art critic Peter Schjeldahl. He would have been great (too), but I was younger by a couple of years. Joanne Koch, head of the Film Society of Lincoln Center, may have mentioned my name; she would play an important role in my Film Festival tenure, which lasted 17 years.

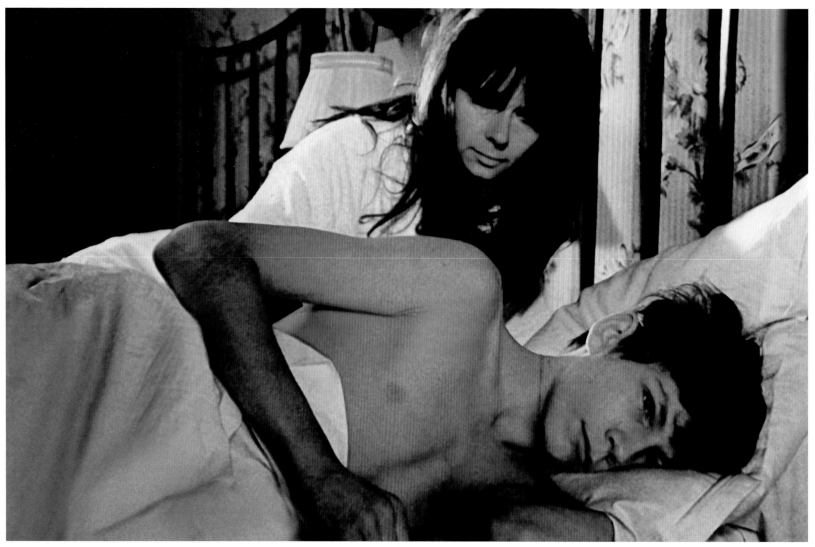

*Murmur of the Heart* by Louis Malle

*Fata Morgana* by Werner Herzog

As *Film Comment* editor I had accustomed myself to petitioning eminent film critics I didn't know to write pieces for a penny or two a word. So I suppose I was too confident or ignorant to be cowed by Richard's phone call, in the summer of 1971, offering me a place on the committee. And yet my first thought was the stupid one, which I even more stupidly voiced in that conversation, that I was not fluent in the foreign languages of most of the films we'd be seeing. "Don't worry," Richard assured me, "movies have subtitles now."

Thus it was that, in early August, I walked into the Preview 9 screening room at 1600 Broadway for my first day as a committee member. Richard, Susan, and Arthur Knight were already there. Two documentaries were on the afternoon schedule: Emile de Antonio's *Millhouse*, about Nixon, and Fred Wiseman's *Basic Training*. Assuming that the *Millhouse* screening would be followed by a high-minded debate, à la David Susskind's *Open End* talk show, I furiously took notes. But the film ended without comment, and we went directly

into the Wiseman. That was my first clue that the selection process would be informal: less like an oral exam for a doctorate, more like the upperclassmen's selection of pledges in a college fraternity.

Roud was of course the crafty face and booming voice of the NYFF, its prime mover and host. The selection committee, inaugurated in 1966, the fourth year of the Festival, was thought by outsiders to be window dressing, or insulation for Richard's more controversial film choices: "the Roudies," someone called us. Not so. The members—six when I joined, then five from 1976—met, saw movies, chatted, and voted; the films with the most positive votes got in. Simple as that. But in my first two years on the committee, only Richard had gone to Cannes and other European Festivals; some of the films he alone saw won spots in the final program. In 1973 I joined Richard at Cannes, and the following year all the members were invited—a policy that still applies.

That first year we showed a mix of old and young masters, including Akira Kurosawa (*Dodes'ka-den*), Robert Bresson (*Four Nights of a Dreamer*), Pier Paolo Pasolini (*The Decameron*), Louis Malle (*Murmur of the Heart*), Werner Herzog (*Fata Morgana*), Rainer Werner Fassbinder (*Recruits in Ingolstadt*—his first of nine consecutive years at the Festival), Marco Bellocchio (*In the Name of the Father*), Peter

*The Sorrow and the Pity* by Marcel Ophuls

Marcel Ophuls, 1988

Jean-Pierre Léaud, Suzanne Charity, Jacqueline Bisset, Mayor John Lindsay, Richard Roud, and Lillian Gish at the Opening Night of *Day for Night*, 1973

Watkins (*Punishment Park*) and Peter Bogdanovich (*The Last Picture Show*, plus the documentary *Directed by John Ford*). Two French films, each logging in at more than four hours, lent the Festival a solemn grandeur: Marcel Ophuls's *The Sorrow and the Pity* and Abel Gance's *Bonaparte and the Revolution*, the 82-year-old director's updated version of his 1927 epic *Napoleon*. I scan this list and think, Jeez, we were smart. But we had a rich crop to harvest; and perhaps half of these films had been chosen by Richard before the rest of the committee convened.

To me, though, 1971 was most memorable for two films: one discarded, one selected. We saw *The French Connection* at the Fox Screening Room one morning and had collectively forgotten it by lunchtime; the following spring it won Oscars for Best Picture, Director, Writer, and Actor. The other was *WR: Mysteries of the Organism*, a jaunty survey of the crackpot scientist Wilhelm Reich by Dušan Makavejev, the Yugoslav iconoclast whose *Love Affair, or the Case of the Missing Switchboard Operator* the Festival had shown four years earlier. Somehow

this grab bag of outrage, which contained Beat poetry, a severed talking head, and the "plaster-casting" of an erect penis, did not appeal to Richard. He said that as a member of the

Joanne Koch and Luis Buñuel, 1974

committee he loathed the film, and as the Director of the Festival he couldn't conscientiously defend it against charges of pornography. But it had the votes and got in—proof to me, in my first weeks on the committee, that the Great Dictator would take one for the team.

I think of 1972 as *l'année française*: 11 of the 21 features were in some way French, and reinforced the stereotype of the Festival boss, whom *Variety* had dubbed "Francophile Roud." But can you blame him, or us? The films included François Truffaut's *Two English Girls*, Jean-Luc Godard and Jean-Pierre Gorin's *Tout va bien* and Luis Buñuel's *The Discreet Charm of the Bourgeoisie*. The Opening Night selection was Eric Rohmer's *Chloe in the Afternoon*, the Closing Night, Bernardo Bertolucci's *Last Tango in Paris*. Pauline Kael compared that evening to the riotous 1913 debut of Stravinsky's *The Rite of Spring*, but I recall the after-party in the Tully Hall foyer as a decorous event; people were sipping wine, not tossing it in Bertolucci's face.

In 1973 I got to join Richard in Cannes. His hotel, the Martinez, was at one end of the Croisette; Mary Corliss and I, and Joanne and

Dick Koch were in the Splendid at the other end; and we met in the middle for screenings at the old Palais (now a Marriott hotel). In those dear, dead days Cannes was still a French festival; a familiarity with the language was necessary to order in the restaurants, haggle in the shops and, crucially, understand most of the movies: the French ones had English subtitles but all other "foreign-language" films were subtitled in French. (So my initial apprehension was correct: a good knowledge of French was virtually mandatory of selection-committee membership.) I recall a screening of an Algerian film with Mary and me perched on either side of Richard, who whispered the English translation to us (except that he was incapable of whispering); in the row behind, a man was translating into Italian for a friend of his. It was blissful Babel in the years before English became Cannes' lingua franca.

From Cannes we brought back Jean Eustache's *The Mother and the Whore*, that grand epic of bad behavior, and Truffaut's *Day for Night*—whose blithe, movie-wise charm so appealed to our Opening Night audience that we thought about opening every subsequent Festival with it. (We thought about it again two years later, when Luchino Visconti's *Conversation Piece*, in an ill-advised English-dubbed version, met with derisive howls on Opening Night 1975.) We showed Herzog's *Land of Silence and Darkness*, Fassbinder's near-great *The Bitter Tears of Petra von Kant* (which *New York Times* critic Nora Sayre invidiously compared to the Joan Crawford weepie *The Best of Everything*) and two prime melodramas from Claude Chabrol, *La Rupture* and *Just Before Nightfall*. Our oldie was Fritz Lang's *Dr. Mabuse the Gambler* from 1922.

But 1973 was the year of the Americans. Though James Frawley's sweet comic Western *Kid Blue* didn't leave a lasting imprint, two others did. Yet Martin Scorsese's *Mean Streets*, when it was screened for four members of the committee, received a split vote. That left the decision to the venerable Arthur Mayer. As a champion of the film, I saw it again with Arthur, hoping to coax him toward a positive vote. At the end, he said, "It meanders, it's obscene and it should be cut by a half-hour."

And, I asked, your vote? "Yes!" It got in.

The other American film was Terrence Malick's *Badlands*, a first feature with no pedigree, except that it might have been recommended by Arthur Penn; Jill Jakes, Terry's then-wife and a producer on the film, had once worked for Penn. I remember that a quiet young courier brought in the print from Los Angeles to the Preview screening facilities. We watched the movie, and afterward Richard said to the messenger, "Would you please tell Mr. Malick that we loved *Badlands* and want it as our Closing Night film?" The unassuming fellow replied, "I'm Mr. Malick." He was also friendly, shy-friendly, working with the Tully technicians on the proper sound mix for the press screening, possibly one of the last times this reclusive auteur was seen in public.

By this time, the Film Society had acquired *Film Comment* from its generous publisher, Austin Lamont. Now a full-time employee of the organization that produced the Film Festival, I joined Richard as one of the two permanent members of the selection committee. (Permanent: funny word.)

*Day for Night* by François Truffaut

*True Stories* by David Byrne

David Byrne, 1986

A few times each year I would introduce films at the public showings and moderate the Q&A sessions afterward. In the early '70s the Festival convened full-blown panels, of the Susskind sort, where learned minds discussed weighty issues such as The Documentary. But usually they were conversations with the film's director and actors. I was the designated specialist in movies featuring musicians. One after-film chat that filled me with dread was the *True Stories* panel with its director David Byrne; the leader of Talking Heads was supposedly unresponsive in his dealings with the press. Blessed relief: Byrne proved thoughtful and genial. The same year, 1986, Bertrand Tavernier came to the NYFF with the legendary tenor sax man Dexter Gordon for the jazzophonic *Round Midnight*; while Tavernier waxed authoritative on all subjects, Gordon wandered around the stage, as if performing a silent improv on an invisible axe. In 1987 we showed *Chuck Berry Hail! Hail! Rock 'n' Roll*, the Taylor Hackford doc about Berry's preparation for a 60th-birthday concert, with Keith Richards serving as musical director. Berry, who called himself not an artist but a businessman, was near mute that night, perhaps because he wasn't being paid for this gig; but Richards was an

Chuck Berry and Richard Corliss, 1987

Keith Richards and Chuck Berry, 1987

Sidney Lumet, Arthur Penn, and Bertrand Tavernier, 1996

*Tih Minh* by Louis Feuillade

elegant charmer. When he met Mary Corliss in the Tully green room before the panel, he leaned over and kissed her hand.

And since the prints of some foreign-language silent films chosen for retrospectives—Buñuel's *L'Age d'Or*, Fritz Lang's *Spies*, Louis Feuillade's *Tih Minh*—had no English intertitles, I took the job of reading translations into a microphone from a box in the rear of the auditorium. Tim Ward, the Tully Hall house manager who had a background in theater, schooled me in microphone diction. Before the screening I'd advise folks sitting in the back seats below me not to worry if they smelled cigarette smoke; it was just me, taking an occasional puff between readings. Ah, those wild outlaw days.

Richard and Joanne had more to worry about than visits from the Fire Marshall when, in the mid-'70s, the committee chose two films that contained some explicit sex. Jean-François Davy's *Exhibition* was a documentary whose subject was the hard life and hard-core career of French actress Claudine Beccarie. The committee members, finding the film a telling profile of an interesting woman with an unusual job, voted it in without any urgent debate that I recall. But there was *tsouris* aplenty when *Exhibition* was seized by the U.S. Customs Service and the Festival had to alert customers that they might not see the film. The U.S.

Attorney's office subsequently released the print and the show went on. (Other piquant films of '75: Herzog's *The Mystery of Kaspar Hauser*, Truffaut's *The Story of Adele H.*, the Maysles Brothers' *Grey Gardens*, Michael Ritchie's *Smile*, and Orson Welles's *F for Fake*.)

The *Exhibition* flap was the merest preliminary to the seizure and cancellation of another NYFF selection, Nagisa Oshima's *In the Realm of the Senses*, dealt with at length elsewhere in this volume. The point I want to

make is that the committee members—Sontag, Roger Greenspun, Charles Michener, and I that year—concerned ourselves only with the merits of films as we perceived them; our sole mission was to see films and vote on them. We worried neither about the response of the audience nor the jeopardy that the Festival and the Film Society might be placed in by showing "pornography." We left to Richard and Joanne, and to Joanne's invaluable associate Wendy Keys, the tasks of defending our choices and, if necessary, mounting a legal defense. Joanne was particularly suited to the latter task, having worked for Barney Rosset at Grove Press when it bought U.S. rights to the Swedish film *I Am Curious (Yellow)* and overcame myriad legal hassles to win the right to release it. Joanne enjoyed a good fight for a good cause.

As Richard Roud protected the high end of film culture, managing to find room for new films by Jean-Marie Straub, Marguerite Duras, and Gianni Amico, I aimed to infiltrate the Festival with popular fare that was every bit as worthy of being called art. Actually, both Richards were admirers of King Hu's kung-fu delight *A Touch of Zen* when we saw it at Cannes in 1975. That year the film was not voted in; so, for the only time I can remember, we waited a year, showed the same movie to other members and secured a spot for it. Eleven years later,

*Grey Gardens* by the Maysles Brothers, Ellen Hovde, and Muffie Mayer

Jackie Chan's *Police Story* (a Dave Kehr nomination) mined a similar appreciation of action balletics in the committee and the NYFF audience. In 1979 we had the thrill of seeing grand old cartoons invade Tully Hall. *The Bugs Bunny/Road Runner Movie*, a compilation of Warner Bros. shorts directed by Chuck Jones, helped bring this animation master some long-overdue academic respect.

Debates? We had a few. Andy was a fervent supporter of Fellini's *Amarcord*, which we'd seen at Cannes in 1974, but he couldn't muster enough votes to get it in the Festival; for years he used the film as an argument against the infallibility of the selection committee. And the voting system of 1 (disdain) to 5 (fervor), suggested by Molly Haskell in 1978, simplified the process but led to a few wrinkled brows, as when Richard and I went hog-wild 5 for Michelangelo Antonioni's video experiment *The Mystery of Oberwald* and the other three members registered apathy. Passion won that particular bout. David Thomson, in 1985, his final year on the committee, announced that he would be voting only 1s and 5s—all or nothing. I'm someone who believes that the great majority of movies reside in the gray middle area (I'd agonize over whether to give a film a 2.5 or a 3.5), but I respected David's argument that our role was to choose films, and that strong votes would speed the process.

Besides, as Hitchcock might have said, "It's only a movie, Richard."

Very rarely, conflicting views of a movie could seed clouds of ill feeling. In 1978 Richard Roud had a strong rooting interest in Peter Handke's *The Left-Handed Woman* and detested Bertrand Blier's *Get Out Your Handkerchiefs*; I was left cold by the first film and loved the second, which I'd discovered in the Cannes marketplace. In what was later known as the great Handke-Hankie affair, the disagreement escalated until it threatened to end a beautiful friendship. Eventually, both films were shown—catastrophe averted, amity restored. And at an intimate Festival dinner for Blier that I attended, Richard made a special point of showering his charm on the director. Which is what I call Acting!

Though I was in the Film Society offices because of my *Film Comment* job, I didn't take part in the discussions Richard and Joanne had about additions to the committee. (The three-year stint for three members meant a new recruit each year.) It happened that three of those who joined in the 1980s—Thomson, Jim Hoberman, and Dave Kehr—were frequent and valued contributors to the magazine, but they had plenty of crit cred on their own. My main value to Richard in those years, aside from good fellowship and the occasional film wrangle, was as his drug mule: Mary and I

would come home from Cannes with cartons of his favorite Gauloise cigarettes, which were much less expensive in Europe than in the U.S.

One potential Festival job that Joanne asked me to take on was hand-holder for Richard. He lived in London most of the year, coming to New York in the summer, leaving in November, and always by ship. Fear of flying had kept him from air travel for decades. When the Festival partnered with the Museum of Modern Art to produce the spring series New Directors/New Films (in whose selections I was not involved), Joanne wanted Richard to be there. The problem: no cruise ships. I was commissioned to fly over to London, get him on a plane and, on the flight back, occupy him with banter that would keep him so amused or sedated that he wouldn't jump out over the Atlantic. Well, the air-rescue mission never took place; I forget why. Either Joanne decided New Directors could proceed without Richard's presence, or he came over by Merchant Marine.

Like the fluttering pages of a calendar in an old Hollywood romance, the years of my Festival service flew by. The excitement of the early days became a routine that was always pleasant and challenging, never daunting. On this test of choosing films, there were no wrong answers. I can't recall any second-guessing. We somehow survived the entire Lina Wertmüller vogue of the mid-'70s without presenting any of the

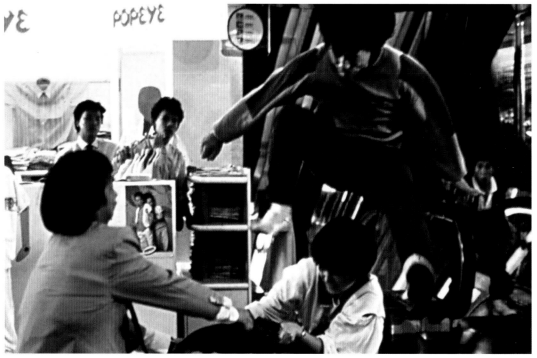

Jackie Chan, 1987

*Police Story* by Jackie Chan

Dave Kehr, Mary and Richard Corliss, and Wendy Keys, 1987

Italian director's films. We could have shown *Rocky* in 1976—at the summer screening we attended, Bertolucci acclaimed the movie to Richard—but didn't. I'm sorry that, a decade later, *Blue Velvet* wasn't in the Festival, though I think the distributor was demanding the Closing Night slot, which we'd already awarded to Francis Coppola's *Peggy Sue Got Married*. Anyway, all the films in our little *salon des refusés* did just fine without the NYFF bump.

If there's a surprise in the lineup of films from 1971 to 1987, it's how Eurocentric it was. Like programmers at virtually every other international festival of those years, we thought that scouring the world for movies meant scouring Europe. We were great on France and Germany, good on Hungary and Poland, selective or myopic on Italy: yes to Olmi, Amico, and the Taviani Brothers, no to Fellini, Scola, and Argento). We also did right by the Australian New Wave, which was like British cinema with its fly open. Once in a while we included a film from Africa—if the director had studied in France (Ousmane Sembene) or the U.S. (Youssef Chahine)—or Latin America.

But Asia—except for a few Japanese stalwarts like Kurosawa and Oshima, and Satyajit Ray and Mani Kaul from India, and for the prescient showing of *A Touch of Zen*—was for us a virtual no man's land (the title, by the way of a 1985 Festival film by Alain Tanner: Swiss). I grant that Chinese filmmakers of the Fifth Generation, including Chen Kaige and Zhang Yimou, were just beginning in the mid-'80s, and that the great spate of Hong Kong action epics by Tsui Hark, John Woo, and Ringo Lam was barely underway. But, like the swooning musical melodramas from Bollywood, those Hong Kong glories were

*The Left-Handed Woman* by Peter Handke

movies, not films; popular entertainments, not Mensa experiments. Their discovery would be left to the fanboys in video stores; we in the official culture were blinded by notions of good taste and high art. Our one '80s bow to Asian popular art: the selection of *Police Story* in 1987.

That was the year our founder foundered. After 25 years at the helm, Richard had a terminal dispute with Joanne and Wendy, and when that fall's Festival ended, so did his tenure. (Completing his biography of Langlois, Richard died in January, 1989, at 59; his demise can be attributed to his love of those unfiltered Gauloises, not to a lost job or a broken heart.) The story was in all the papers, though they didn't always get it right. *Variety* speculated that Richard was fired because he showed a Jackie Chan movie. I can testify that, in my 17 years, I never heard of flak from any executive or Board member about any NYFF selection. The contretemps between Richard and the Film Society was entirely an administrative matter.

Joanne asked me to replace Richard as the head of the selection committee. I said I would, on the condition that Richard be allowed to serve as a voting committee member. When

that proposal was turned down, I resigned, as did David Denby, then in his second year on the committee. So instead of Richard C. succeeding Richard R., the position went to Richard P.—Peña, then a rising star at the Art Institute of Chicago. He has kept the Festival floating for another 25 years, very much in the spirit Roud established: a few dozen provocative, accomplished films chosen by a panel of professional critics.

As the dust settled, Richard and I agreed that, for all the attendant controversy, no "Roudie" would boycott the New York Film Festival just because neither he nor I was involved. Thanks to his efforts, it had grown into an independent organism, its own Rite of Fall. And over the decades, with the fading of the crucial place foreign-language films had commanded in the 1960s, the NYFF necessarily became the prime missionary outpost for world cinema in the United States. The Festival, not its selection committee, is the thing, and I suspect it will remain so for the next 50 years. 🎥

*Au hasard Balthazar* by Robert Bresson

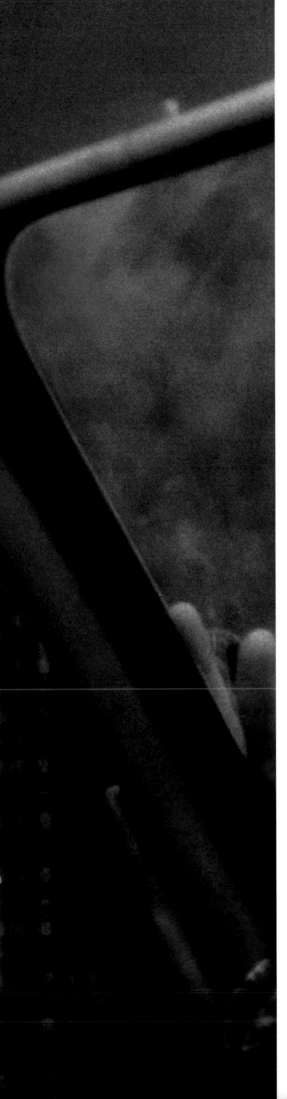

# MEMORIES OF
# THE NEW YORK FILM FESTIVAL

*Molly Haskell*

MY EARLIEST MEMORIES OF THE FESTIVAL and of the movie love it nourished are inseparably bound up with an existing passion, and another about to be born. The first was France and French films: I'd just begun working at the French Film Office, where I'd replaced Helen Scott (Truffaut's amanuensis and translator on *Fahrenheit 451*), and was writing a bulletin and newsletter for American journalists, as well as interpreting for directors when they came to New York. The second was my first sighting of the man who would become my husband. It was 1965. Andrew Sarris, whose writing I'd been following in *The Village Voice*, was on a panel with Pauline Kael and Jean-Luc Godard. (Is this possible? Was Godard's English good enough? Was there a translator? I'm pretty sure Richard Roud wasn't on the dais.) Maybe because it was the subject of Godard, but there Andrew and Pauline would have been in agreement (not "going at it," as one person remembers it), something that happened more often than people realize, and perhaps

more than either of them would have admitted. A caveat: recollections are unreliable. We know through daily bulletins from the ever-expanding field of brain science how complex and malleable those neural networks are, and how creatively and self-servingly we alter and adjust images of our past. I can't call on Andrew for confirmation: that once-phenomenal memory has sprung mighty leaks and mine was never that good to begin with.

This much is true: Andrew would become a member of the NYFF selection committee when it was formed in 1966 (he, Arthur Knight, and Susan Sontag joining Richard and Amos Vogel), but as a reviewer and champion of auteurs, he was very much a presence from the beginning. As was Godard, for whom the Festival might have been invented: two films in 1964 (*Band of Outsiders* and *A Woman Is a Woman*), two in 1965 (*Alphaville* and *Le Petit Soldat*), two in 1966 (*Masculin Féminin* and *Pierrot le fou*), and at least one for most years through the '60s. Andrew remembers (as do I)

*Get Out Your Handkerchiefs* by Bertrand Blier

*The Battle of Algiers* opening the 1967 Festival, and the black-tie audience cheering for the terrorists. Another occasion he remembers, possibly the same year, was being on stage (these events were at Alice Tully Hall) when I was in the audience. He was making a signal at me when a soon-to-be-former girlfriend of his from Toronto walked in and saw him. She immediately turned around, walked out, never to be heard from again. *A Woman Is a Woman* and *Girlfriends and Boyfriends*, circling and being encircled (and ensorceled) by cinema. Like characters in a Godard film, movie love was at the center of love itself. Whose dreams were we dreaming?

If Andrew were writing his recollections, he would mention the late Eugene Archer, friend and fellow auteurist, who was then reviewing for the *Times*, and with whom (along with Patrick Bauchau) he had spent long hours

discussing movies and making those lists that provoked in Pauline such sniggers of derision. Archer's favorable disposition toward the Festival would be crucial in a climate of resistance and suspicion on the part of "over-worked" reviewers (remember them?).

In 1966, Andrew alerted me to Bresson's *Au hasard Balthazar*, possibly the most transcendent experience in my moviegoing memory. In 1968, he reported the excitement among committee members over John Cassavetes' *Faces* and Maurice Pialat's *L'enfance nue*. Andrew wouldn't follow Cassavetes into his later you've-got-to-love-my-actors-whatever-they-do improvisations, but we both became and remain passionate fans of Pialat. Also that year, Rivette's beautiful *The Nun* (why is that never revived? Too classical?), and in 1969, *My Night at Maud's*, maybe the single most auspicious and exciting debut ever. I say debut,

but of course Rohmer had made other films, many of them, starting in the '50s, and we had seen some: *Le Signe du Lion* and *La Collectioneuse*, the latter using the aforementioned Archer and Bauchau playing dead-on replicas of themselves. That was the year Andrew and I married and went to the Berlin Film Festival (then in the summer) as part of our "wedding trip," and I vividly remember sitting in an outdoor café with Richard and Susan Sontag. I was meeting her for the first time and was apprehensive. Did I look too conventional? Would I say something stupid? She was of course utterly charming and disarming, and I already adored Richard, who could be intimidating as well. He had his "pets," Susan being one of them, Marguerite Duras another.

In the year of *L'enfance nue* and *Faces* was also *Lola Montès*, which Andrew had, with deliberate provocation, called the greatest film

*The Shout* by Jerzy Skolimowski

Molly Haskell and Andrew Sarris, early 1980s

of all time. In 1970, two more greats: Truffaut's *The Wild Child* and Chabrol's *Le Boucher*. Our first date, in 1966, had been to an afternoon screening of Chabrol's *Les Bonnes Femmes*. We were in rapturous accord over this film's bleakly beautiful pathos, and part of the rapture was in our own shared taste. Relationships have been founded on less.

What a lineup of directors, year after year, and how astonishingly our favorites produced consistently brilliant and engaging films. Rare was the Resnais, Truffaut, Bertolucci, Buñuel, Fassbinder, Bresson, Skolimowski, Herzog, Zanussi, Forman, Rohmer, Satyajit Ray, Jancsó one had to accept out of gratitude for past bounties—or excuse as the lesser work of a great director. As a replacement for the revival houses that were fast disappearing, the Festival

was my graduate school in the cinema of the past: Fritz Lang, Jean Renoir, Nicholas Ray, Mizoguchi, Melville, Stroheim, Feuillade. And then more discoveries. When I joined the committee in 1978, we introduced Phillip Noyce's *Newsfront* and Errol Morris's *Gates of Heaven*. There were the scandals: *Last Tango in Paris* during one of Andrew's years on the committee, *The Mother and the Whore* another. I remember seeing the Eustache film at Cannes at the Grand Palais, where the local petite bourgeoisie rose up as one in harrumphing horror. In my first year, Bertrand Blier's *Get Out Your Handkerchiefs*, with a crudely funny Gérard Depardieu (and Patrick Dewaere), was a Gallic buddy film with a nasty edge and the first of many unsettling, unpredictable comedies from Blier that would épater the

bourgeois and the cognoscenti alike. Also that year: Skolimowski's *The Shout*, Martin Scorsese's documentary about his family, *Italianamerican*, and Chabrol's chilling *Violette*.

Yes, we were definitely Eurocentric. The committees on which I served were basically in sync with our director who, according to critics, never met a French film he didn't like. Times would change, more non-European and American independent films would add their own kinds of edginess, but the French, Spanish, German, Italian, East European cinema that made its way into Alice Tully Hall during my years of tenure exhibited a festival that was far from insular or complacent. Rather, the records show selections to have been consistently ahead of their time. Women directors were increasing in numbers, if slowly (Agnès Varda would be represented regularly and Chantal Akerman and Mira Nair were to come). My second year on the committee saw Gillian Armstrong's *My Brilliant Career*. Also that year was the great Powell-Pressburger *Peeping Tom*, which today has lost none of its power to disturb. Fassbinder and Pialat were represented by two of their finest, Fassbinder with *The Marriage of Maria Braun* (along with the sad-crazy transsexual drama, *In a Year of 13 Moons*) and Pialat with a masterpiece, *Loulou*. In 1980, my last year until

Helen Scott and François Truffaut, 1981

Claude Chabrol, 1978

*The Marriage of Maria Braun* by Rainer Werner Fassbinder

1984, we had *The Life and Times of Rosie the Riveter* and Sergio Leone's incomparable *Once Upon a Time in the West*.

Andrew, who had rotated off in 1974, had told me about the arguments, the horse-trading. I was thus prepared for similar sly bargaining and weighted voting. But it was mostly fun and astonishingly harmonious. Whether in the 1960s, '70s, or '80s, we would often come up with a lineup fairly easily, then get bogged down on the Opening Night film. The Opening Night audience was by common

*Peeping Tom* by Michael Powell

consensus different from the film-buff attendees of the rest of the Festival, so something more massively pleasing and party-ready was required—but how to find one like that and still keep the Festival's rigorous (even "austere") art-house bona fides? In the early days, those overburdened reviewers out to get the Festival were on the offensive, looking for weaknesses that might bring it down, and an opener that was a little too pleasing, or conversely a later film that was too "difficult" was red meat for the weary. A bad review in the *Times* would kill the mood and maybe deplete the audience, as had Vincent Canby's slash-and-burn diatribe against *Bob & Carol & Ted & Alice* in 1969.

Back on the committee in 1984 I had no sooner started watching movies—a procedure once confined to several weeks of intense viewing that was now consuming the whole summer—when Andrew came down with a mysterious and life-threatening illness. He spent three months at New York Hospital, mostly in the ICU, and I would trudge back and forth from screening room to hospital, hardly knowing what I saw. Richard Corliss, David Thomson, and Jim Hoberman, my wonderful fellow committee members, were my comfort, consolation, stimulation. Their empathy was infinite. I could feel them cringe when anything conceivably related to my predicament appeared on screen: a disease, a loss, a death, someone named Andrew or Andrei or Andre or Andrusha, and especially hospital settings that seemed to come up with uncanny frequency. But it wasn't those scenes that bothered me (I was an illness-junkie and inveterate addict of hospital shows) but movies themselves—the idea of not seeing and talking about them with Andrew possibly ever again. The Festival was my escape nonetheless, and we came up with two dazzling first films, Jim Jarmusch's *Stranger Than Paradise*, and the Coen Brothers's *Blood Simple*, along with Tavernier's *A Sunday in the Country*, Márta Mészáros's *Diary for My Children*, and my favorite Pialat, *À nos amours*.

By the time of the Festival in October, Andrew was at Rusk Rehabilitation Institute, recovering and learning to walk again, while Truffaut, who'd fallen ill with a brain tumor at

*Peggy Sue Got Married* by Francis Ford Coppola

©CORI WELLS BRAUN

Akira Kurosawa in the green room, *Ran* Opening Night, 1985

the very same time, was getting worse and would die just after the Festival, on October 21.

I was on the committee for two more years. The 1985 edition saw films by Agnieszka Holland (*Angry Harvest*), Emir Kusturica (*When Father Was Away on Business*), Kurosawa (*Ran*), Alain Tanner (*No Man's Land*), Leos Carax (*Boy Meets Girl*), Michael Apted (*28 Up*, part of his extraordinary chronicle of British lives), and William Wellman (*Nothing Sacred*). Godard managed to stir things up with *Hail Mary*. My farewell year, 1986, seemed to cover wider ground, both geographically and aesthetically, with Tarkovsky, and Hou Hsiao-hsien at one end of the spectrum and *Peggy Sue Got Married* and *Sid and Nancy* at the other. Pialat's *Police* had a screenplay by Catherine Breillat, who would become an invigorating and sometimes controversial presence, along with Chantal Akerman and Claire Denis.

Meanwhile, as years passed, the losses added up, not of films, but of the people who made them and loved them. After Truffaut's early exit, the directorial roll call of death included Buñuel, Bergman, Fellini, and Rohmer, most in the ripeness of time. Closer to home, however, we lost Richard Roud at age 60 in 1989, and Vincent Canby (at a young 76) in 2000. I miss them as if it were yesterday. 🎥

*Je t'aime, Je t'aime* by Alain Resnais

# IN THE MARGIN OF HISTORY

RICHARD ROUD, THE NEW YORK FILM FESTIVAL, AND ME

*J. Hoberman*

IN THE FALL OF 1981, PERHAPS THE WEEK I reviewed *The Rocky Horror Picture Show*'s obscure sequel *Shock Treatment* for *The Village Voice*, I found one of those old-fashioned phone-message forms in my office mailbox: CALL RICHARD ROUD. I'd never met the man—although I had for years admired his taste and the brisk savoir faire with which he conducted the New York Film Festival's post-screening press conferences—and I had no idea why he would have telephoned. Perhaps, I thought (with little enthusiasm), the NYFF was planning some sort of avant-garde sidebar and he wanted to pick my brain. So when I returned his call, I was gobsmacked to hear the chatty voice on the line inviting me to join the New York Film Festival selection committee.

As though unsure of my response, the NYFF director further informed me that Susan Sontag was leaving the committee and had recommended me (the *Voice*'s third-string critic) as her replacement. I had never met Sontag either and was digesting this amazing information

when Mr. Roud, who, as I would discover, loved gossip, added that "Susan" stressed that she was recommending me despite the fact that I "hated" her own movies. (Published in the *Voice* some 18 months earlier, my positive review of Peter Handke's *The Left-Handed Woman* began with the observation that, "When serious writers turn to filmmaking, the results can be appalling. For every Jean Cocteau, the field is strewn with Norman Mailers, Susan Sontags, Alain Robbe-Grillets…")

Richard, as I could now call him, needn't have worried. This anointment, burnished by Sontagian approval, was the greatest honor of my professional life thus far—although to understand why, one has to know what the New York Film Festival meant to the teenage outer-borough cinephile that I had been. The two-page spread with which the NYFF would announce and annotate its lineup each September was the equivalent of a cloth laid out in a Baghdad marketplace, laden with exotic delights: *Shadows of Forgotten Ancestors*? Gotta see that!

*The Red and the White* by Miklós Jancsó

In 1968, I was enterprising enough to secure press credentials for a nonexistent college film magazine and thus attended the mind-blowing NYFF that included Bresson's *Mouchette*, Rivette's *The Nun*, Cassavetes' *Faces*, Forman's *The Firemen's Ball*, Ophuls' *Lola Montès*, Straub's *Chronicle of Anna Magdalena Bach*, Jancsó's *The Red and the White,* the baffling *Signs of Life*, the first feature by a German named Werner Herzog, and most vivid in my memory, the overhead coffee cup close-up from *2 or 3 Things I Know About Her.* I repeated the same brazen stunt in 1969 (which is where I saw Sontag's *Duet for Cannibals*) and even 1970 (*Je t'aime, je t'aime*). In 1971, however, publicist Sue Salter got wise to me. "Where are your clippings?" Clippings?

Eight years later, I returned to Lincoln Center with legitimate press credentials that, in addition to the movies afforded several memorable sightings: a cheery Pauline Kael and her retinue bustling through the Alice Tully lobby for the first, disastrous screening of *La Luna*, a smirking Fassbinder in full Hell's Angels drag and an even larger retinue striding in late for a

*In a Year of 13 Moons* press conference. I reviewed the 1980 NYFF for *Artforum*, was part of *The Village Voice*'s team coverage in 1981, and in May 1982 found myself on the committee in Cannes along with the two "permanent" members, the Richards Roud and Corliss, the latter whom I knew as *Film Comment* editor; the avuncular *Newsweek* culture critic Jack Kroll; and the Pacific Film Archives' inscrutable second director Tom Luddy.

Cannes was bewildering (white light off the Mediterranean, French everywhere) but the selection process was simple enough. Committee members attended movies, often on Richard R.'s suggestion, and then met to vote, assigning each possible selection a number from 1 to 5 (half points allowed). I don't know when this practice was instituted but, in explaining it, Richard would always invoke the formulation developed by Molly Haskell (who served on the committee from 1978-80). To rate a movie a 1 was to tell your colleagues that should this abomination be included in the Festival, you'd never speak to them again; bestowing a 5 carried the same threat if the movie was not in the Festival. Naturally

and under the influence of our supremely sociable leader Richard R., we all wanted to keep talking—or, at least, I did.

A dozen or so movies were chosen at Cannes; the rest selected after two weeks of marathon screenings in August. The NYFF's founding coordinator Amos Vogel advised me to keep a record of the voting "for history." With a skeptical sense of its ultimate significance but a nerd's appreciation for stats, I did and, nearly 30 years later, was actually able to find (at least some of) these scribblings buried in a box of old notebooks. Although some calculations were so arcane as to be no longer understandable, what's clear from the record is that consensus was often outvoted by (shared) passion. Although a movie generally needed at least a 3 average to gain admission, it really only required only a pair of enthusiasts or haters to determine a film's fate—two 5s or two 1s were always sufficient to get something in, or keep it out.

Some committee members were more generous than others. Jack had the highest average scores (3.5 and 3.4) in 1982 and 1983 and Richard R. was the most exacting (his were 2.6 and 2.5). But Richard's taste was far from absolute. In 1982, he gave 1s to the Cannes co-winner Şerif Gören's *Yol*, Miklós Jancsó's *The Tyrant's Heart*, and Paul Bartel's *Eating Raoul*, all of which ended up in the Festival; we also broke his heart that year, but also provided him cover, by giving Robert Altman's *Come Back to the Five and Dime, Jimmy Dean, Jimmy Dean* four 1s to his lone 5. Of course, Richard did manage to insert Joseph Losey's *The Trout* into, and ax Bertrand Tavernier's far more entertaining *Coup de Torchon* from the lineup at the last possible moment.

Richard was one of the most influential cine-tastemakers to ever give New York the benefit of his sensibility—an early, loyal champion of such once-outré geniuses as Bresson, Godard, Rivette, Varda, Parajanov, Makavejev, and Fassbinder, to name just a few. But other committee members had agendas as well. Tom Luddy was a strong advocate for American independent films; in 1982 he managed to fill the Festival with six documentary programs, not to mention the special world premiere of *Koyaanisqatsi* at Radio City. I remember that David Thomson, who, in 1983 took Tom's place on the committee, arrived

from San Francisco to, as he said, "instruct" us on what seemed to me the dubious merits of Francis Ford Coppola's *Rumble Fish*.

I too had a mission. On the one hand, I was eager to have the NYFF to reassert its relevance by showing the most challenging underappreciated European movies (Tarkovsky, Raúl Ruiz, and Chantal Akerman were my top three); on the other, I wanted it to include more Third World and avant-garde filmmakers. I was … a militant marginalist. In 1982, I was able to sell the committee on the "no wave" 16mm blockbuster *Vortex*, directed by Beth B and Scott B and starring Lydia Lunch, as well as the restored version of the long-lost Yiddish talkie *The Light Ahead*. (That year there were also shorts by Manuel De Landa, Ernie Gehr, and George Kuchar.) And I'd say that, were such a decoration given, I amply earned Hungary's *vörös csillag* for recruiting Kroll's help in packing the Festival with a record three Magyar productions—*The Tyrant's Heart*, Károly Makk's *Another Way*, and Péter Gothár's *Time Stands Still*—all chosen at Cannes yet! Festival coordinator Joanne Koch was incredulous. There were two more Hungarian films—Zsolt Kézdi-Kovács's *Forbidden Relations* and Gyula Gazdag's *Lost Illusions*—in the 1983 NYFF that, to my futile disapproval,

*Yol* by Şerif Gören

opened with *The Big Chill*. I had already learned that Opening Night was determined by Richard R. and Joanne with an eye to what Joanne jokingly called the Board's "bourgie" tastes, not to mention a distributor willing to foot the bill for the Opening Night party. In 1982, I naïvely argued that Antonioni's *Identification of a Woman*—a movie that topped the Cannes choices with a 4.1 average, including 5s from both Richards—would be an extremely glamorous opener. Richard R. listened to me for half a second before he dismissed the idea with a curt "pearls before swine." (As charming and solicitous as he could be, Richard didn't willingly suffer fools, a trait that had more than a little to do with his being ousted from Lincoln Center in 1987.)

The Opening Night movie might logically have been another Italian movie, the Taviani Brothers's crowd-pleasing *The Night of the Shooting Stars*, but that was a movie that Richard had given a 2. Then Fassbinder died that June and the opener turned out to be *Veronika Voss*—a fabulous downer that began the fête on an unmistakable feel-bad note. Still, Richard knew what he was doing. Vincent Canby concluded a rapturous review by noting that "the New York Film Festival honors itself by honoring Fassbinder." (One of Chairman Richard's maxims was that the then chief critics for *The New York Times* would pan or praise the Festival on alternate years.)

As an inveterate second-guesser, I was chastened to learn that a festival can only be as good as what's available. You can't always get what you want. There was no way, for example, that the suits at Paramount were going to let us look at Samuel Fuller's *White Dog*. (I think it

*Eating Raoul* by Paul Bartel

*Danton* by Andrzej Wajda

was Tom who explained to me that from the studio's point of view, it was a lose-lose proposition: if the film was badly reviewed it would hurt them but they would look even worse if it was well received.) In 1982, Jack and I teamed up to give our only 5s to Hans-Jürgen Syberberg's *Parsifal* only to have the ungrateful filmmaker pull the movie from the Festival in favor of a stand-alone screening some months later at Philharmonic Hall. Godard's *Passion* and Souleymane Cissé's *The Wind*, both voted into the 1982 festival at Cannes, had to wait for 1983—I don't remember exactly why but their presence added to what was without a doubt, the strongest NYFF lineup to which I ever contributed and one that I shamelessly used my *Village Voice* megaphone to promote.

Wajda's *Danton* and Bresson's *L'Argent* were the two big consensus choices, along with Diane Kurys's *Entre Nous*. There was nothing I could do for Oshima (*Merry Christmas, Mr. Lawrence*) or Imamura (*The Ballad of Nara-yama*) in 1983, but Richard Corliss and I did join forces to ensure Chantal Akerman's NYFF debut with a pair of 5s for *The Golden Eighties*. (With Akerman, Kurys, Ann Hui, Jackie Ochs, Patricia Gruben, Mira Nair, and Trinh T. Minh-ha—not to mention Ericka Beckman, whose *You the Better* nearly started a riot—the '83 NYFF had more women directors than any previous Festival.)

Making my one and only backroom deal, I privately offered to give Rohmer's generally unpopular *Pauline at the Beach* (a movie that even Jack accorded a mere 2.5) a 4 if Richard R. would give a 3 to *Nostalghia*—thus securing Tarkovsky's return to Lincoln Center. Done! He agreed without making a joke or missing a beat. (It turned out to be cost-free: *Pauline* dropped out anyway when its distributor decided to open it in the summer.) Back in the New York, I nudged the committee to see Mani Kaul's *Dhrupad*, which had been buried

in the market at Cannes, found the Howard Brookner documentary *Burroughs* on the VHS slush pile, successfully agitated for Jonathan Kaplan's "unreleasable" *Heart Like a Wheel*, promoted Rosa von Praunheim's *Red Love*, and persuaded Joanne that showing the 1929 Soviet silent *The New Babylon* at Radio City with the original Shostakovich score would be the event of the year. It was more like the debacle of the decade, but she never reproached me for it.

The day after we finished voting, one surprised Richard told the other Richard who then told me that "Jim did very well." That would not be so in 1984. Richard R.'s decision to return Molly Haskell to the selection committee meant that her husband, *Voice* lead critic Andrew Sarris, would also be in Cannes. And that meant that I wouldn't be able to cover the Festival for the *Voice*, which meant that I'd have an inferior pass, not to mention a film editor back in New York annoyed to have two-thirds of her section swanning around La Croisette. Thus marginalized, I went not to sunny Côte d'Azur but, for the first time, blustery Berlin.

My colleagues did find some terrific movies at Cannes, including Jim Jarmusch's *Stranger Than Paradise* and Márta Mészáros's *Diary for My Children*, which I was pleased to endorse—and Richard R. discovered the Coen Brothers's *Blood Simple* in the market. Still, as he admitted to

Joan Macintosh, Sooni Taraporevala, Susan Sontag, and Mira Nair, 1988

*The Night of the Shooting Stars* by Paolo and Vittorio Taviani

*Heart Like a Wheel* by Jonathan Kaplan

me, the lineup was a weak one. But because of that it was possible to get Straub-Huillet's *Class Relations*, which Richard and I had seen in Berlin, and *Three Crowns of the Sailor*, which had already been shown twice in March as part of the Metro Cinema's "Perspectives on French Cinema" (albeit under the title *Les trois couronnes du matelot*), into a festival that, as I ungraciously wrote in the *Voice*, was "overloaded with middle-brow bean-bags."

On that bittersweet note my career as a militant marginalist came to an end, at least at the NYFF. Some months later, one of the *Voice*'s star writers was so affronted by my playful reference to Bruce Springsteen as "the sweatless Stakhanovite of rock," casual use of the term "deconstruction," and off-handed name-dropping of Raúl Ruiz that he dashed off an irate letter and left it in my office mailbox. Had I saved that letter it could have been the basis for another memoir.

The Taviani Brothers, 1993

*Three Crowns of the Sailor* by Raúl Ruiz

*Kaos* by Paolo and Vittorio Taviani

# 2 OR 3 THINGS ABOUT
# THE NEW YORK FILM FESTIVAL

*David Thomson*

LOOKING BACK, I WONDER WHETHER "it" wasn't over before I began—still, I was excited to be asked to join the selection committee of the New York Film Festival in 1983. What do I mean by that "it"? Chiefly, the feeling that extraordinary things had been happening lately in film; perhaps even the most extraordinary; the sense that "everything was cinema"; and so it was not just legitimate but obligatory to spend most of one's time in the dark. As far as I was concerned, the panache of that dark was personified by Richard Roud.

For a moviegoer who was 20 in London in 1961, Richard was a key figure. He was film critic for "my" newspaper, *The Guardian*; he programmed the National Film Theatre; and he seemed to be the guiding light for the London Film Festival. That had begun in the '50s, but it became a central event after 1960, because of the French New Wave and the battle over the American moviemakers so admired by those French critics who were suddenly directors themselves. Richard was a whisk in that stir:

American by birth, based in London, but fluent in French and friends with most of the young Parisians.

He had a great influence on me, not just in his reviews (and his longer pieces in *Sight & Sound*), but at the NFT he was programming like a teacher: immense surveys of French cinema; thorough seasons on Renoir, Fritz Lang, and Hawks; and new attention to the American directors whose revised reputations were rattling *Sight & Sound*. But it was hard in those days to know every film that Anthony Mann, say, or Edgar Ulmer had made. There were no reference books or lists, though often *Cahiers du cinéma* took a shot at them. So a friend, Kieran Hickey, and I went to the BFI Library in an attempt to compile such lists. John Gillett helped us find the Hollywood trade papers—and in a couple of years we had lists on maybe 200 directors, from pantheon class to "lightly likeable." We went to Roud with these lists, like foundlings, and he recognized their value. He used some of them in NFT program notes. We were elated. Our Nicholas Ray filmography was published in *Movie*. Were we on our way? Of course, that way then was still to make films, not be their clerks.

Twenty years passed, and one day Roud telephoned me in San Francisco where I lived by then. I wasn't sure he remembered me as a London foundling, but he was asking if I'd join the selection committee for the New York Film Festival. It seemed like heaven. With Amos Vogel, Richard had founded the Festival, in 1963, based on the model of London in which a select group of films were shown—the cream. And those were creamy years: the first year's lineup included *The Exterminating Angel*, *Knife in the Water*, *Harakiri*, *An Autumn Afternoon*, *The Trial of Joan of Arc*, *RoGoPaG*, *The Servant*, *Magnet of Doom*, *Le joli mai*, *Muriel*, and as revivals of works not previously

shown theatrically in the U.S., *Lola Montès* and *Sansho the Bailiff*.

Jump forward 10 years to 1973, and the program offered *Day for Night*, *Illumination*, *Mean Streets*, *La Rupture*, *The Mother and the Whore*, *Land of Silence and Darkness*, *Andrei Rublev*, *Distant Thunder*, *The Bitter Tears of Petra von Kant*, *Badlands*, and the 1922 *Dr. Mabuse the Gambler* as a retrospective. You could make a top 10 from just those two years.

My debut was 1983, and . . . well, it's invidious to name too many films, and hard. The committee that year (Richards Roud and Corliss, Jack Kroll, Jim Hoberman, and I) could claim *L'Argent*, *Passion*, and *Nostalghia* (not that I exactly loved any of them) and *Rear Window* was part of the retrospectives (it had been unavailable). I liked *In the White City* that year. Next year we discovered *Blood Simple* and the fact that the Coen Brothers

*Dr. Mabuse the Gambler* by Fritz Lang

*Paris, Texas* by Wim Wenders

were discovering themselves, *Man of Flowers*, *A Sunday in the Country*, *À nos amours*, and *Paris, Texas*. The year after that was *Hail Mary*, *28 Up*, and *Kaos*.

I'm omitting a lot of films, and I'm not going to begin on the ones we rejected (or those that were never submitted). I just want to say that you could feel "it" was gone in the mid '80s, or resting. Instead, I found myself attending much more to the friendships in the system, and to a thought that had seemed impossible— that I might not actually like film festivals, not even at the very amiable Hotel Splendid in Cannes where New York festival people were gathered (for a good rate, I suppose) and to make sure we talked film at any moment when we were not seeing them.

For me, that meant deepening an existing friendship with Richard and Mary Corliss, discovering how much I liked Molly Haskell and Andrew Sarris, and getting to know Roud better. But that possibility of friendship led to an unexpected crisis, and maybe the thing I recall from the film festival above anything else. There was a year when at the end of Cannes I saw Andy and Molly leaving in a car, heading for Italy. It looked so much more fun than trying to see all or parts of six films in a day. That was a feeling I had every morning at the Splendid, of looking out at the Mediterranean

light and hurrying toward the dark and its duty.

But then that summer Andy fell ill. It was a mysterious malady, not easily pinned down, but by the time the committee gathered again in Manhattan in early August, to make the final selection (which meant sitting in a screening room, watching up to 10 films a day for two weeks), Andy was in the hospital, in a dangerous state, and Molly was in a kind of chaos, visiting the hospital and doing her best to keep up with the committee's load of films. (She wrote a very good memoir about that time, *Love and Other Infectious Diseases*.) Moreover, a further unkindness occurred. Molly would often arrive late, in the middle of a picture, and it did seem that some relentless auteur ensured that as she arrived someone on screen was dying, or very ill, or some especially hideous piece of violence was being put on display. (Violence, or cruelty, gained ground in the '80s.) I wouldn't name the films, if I could remember them. But the anguish we felt for a friend smothered the artistic horror that the directors were striving for on the screen.

So I came to like film festivals a little less, and I began to see *The Exterminating Angel* as their model. One year I managed to bring my wife along to Cannes, and every day as I trudged off to the Palais for screenings, she had her plans: there was a museum up in the hills;

*Sansho the Bailiff* by Kenji Mizoguchi

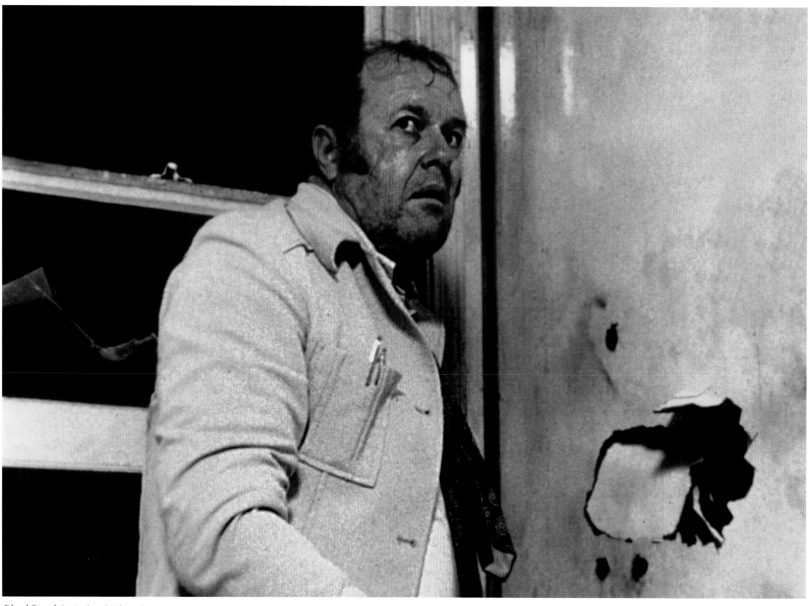

*Blood Simple* by Joel and Ethan Coen

something was happening in Nice; and she went on an overnight trip to Paris. It was an astonishing, casual, but revolutionary attitude, which said Cannes was a fine place to be because of all the other, un-movie things you could do from there. She came back from Nice with a straw hat she called "Char-lotte"—Charlotte and her jewels. I should add that when she heard there was to be a party on Clint Eastwood's yacht (he was in Cannes for *Pale Rider*, or to have a yacht for a fortnight) she managed to be available.

One purpose of these essays is to relate the New York Film Festival to film culture in general. Now, I don't think badly of the Festival or its organizers, but I did begin to develop a gentle antipathy to such gatherings

and the "community" they produced, and it seemed to me by the '80s that the festivity of any film festival was being let down by the quality or dismay of the films. Not everything, of course. But as I look back, I wonder that *The Big Chill* made the Festival but not *Blue Velvet*, and why not *The Singing Detective* (1986), or Mike Leigh's *Meantime*, or some of the films by Alan Clarke? Something we take for granted now was under way: films made for television were becoming more daring and more interest-ing than many film festival films. And it was plain that there were films made just for festivals, so that the makers—more or less—could travel around the world for a year.

Today of course, every crossroads and every ism has a film festival, and the insistence on a

The Coen Brothers, 1990

mood of festivity can become strained. No, I don't mean that there aren't still good or even great films. The '80s was not a rich period. But does anyone feel bound to claim that it's festivals that keep films alive, or is the stress sometimes a bitter struggle to fund the festival so that its wheel can keep turning?

I still like Telluride (it's brief, unexpected, and there's an impromptu air to it), and I enjoy the enthusiasm and the cold of Berlin. But the first time my wife and I went to Telluride even, driven there by Tom Luddy, we surprised some people by taking an afternoon off to visit the Anasazi cliff city of Mesa Verde (we had read Willa Cather's *The Professor's House*). The reason I liked *In the White City* so much, I think, was because it

was just a chance for Bruno Ganz to roam around the steep, narrow lanes of Lisbon. Not as a tourist, but as someone who wondered if he might live there—or come alive there.

This was a long time ago, but I still cherish the Corlisses and Andy and Molly. And the memory of Richard Roud. Not long after my term on the committee, the Festival cut him adrift. There's no need to refight that skirmish now. I'm sure he could be difficult, but he had grasped the moment of festivity in film when it meant everything, and he was happy to sit around after dinner and tell stories about . . . movies? . . . yes, but more than that, about life, about the possibility that everything was not cinema, and about a young woman and a hat named Charlotte. 🎥

*Rear Window* by Alfred Hitchcock

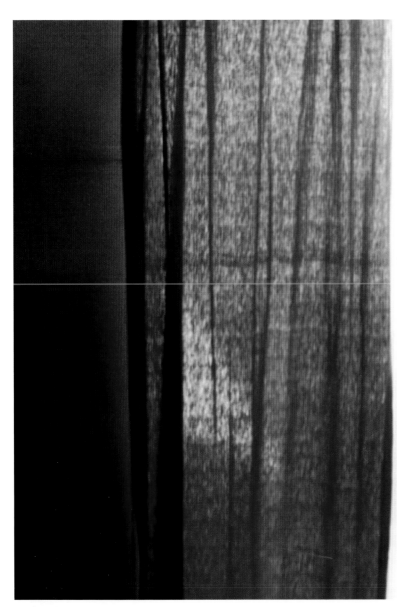

*In the White City* by Alain Tanner

*Shanghai Triad* by Zhang Yimou

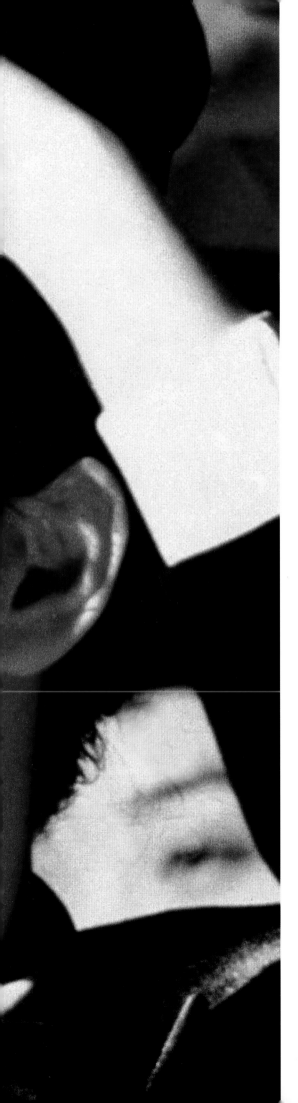

# CLOSE ENCOUNTERS
# OF THE FESTIVAL KIND

*David Ansen*

THE NEW YORK FILM FESTIVAL WILL always be, for me, the ur-festival. It was the first one I ever attended. The year was 1966—the 4th NYFF—and I was a college kid down from Boston with just a few days to cram in as many movies as possible. In that short, exalted time in Avery Fisher Hall I was blown away by two masterpieces—Bresson's *Au hasard Balthazar* and Godard's *Pierrot le fou*—caught Bertolucci's first feature *La commare secca*, Buñuel's sardonically unforgettable *Simon of the Desert*, Resnais's *La guerre est finie*, with Yves Montand, and a now forgotten film by the Argentine master Leopoldo Torre Nilsson called *The Eavesdropper*. I'd found my cinematic Mecca and I've been on my knees ever since.

So there was a lot of history roiling around in my excited head when Richard Peña asked me to serve on the Festival's selection committee in 1990. It was an offer to become an active part of that history, and how could I refuse? I felt like a kid being handed the keys to the candy store: little did I know how overstuffed

one could feel every August after two nonstop weeks of watching movies, starting in a screening room in the morning, moving on to the funky TV set in the Film Society's windowless room in the afternoon, and ending the day feeding tapes into a hotel-room VCR. It was an immersion in cinema so intense you could forget that reality came in three dimensions, as I discovered one day when I walked straight into a wall in the Film Society bathroom.

It was supposed to be a four-year stint, but it turned into eight: a glorious, grueling experience that broadened and altered my cinematic perspective, introduced me to the wonderland of Cannes (where we started our annual treasure hunt), and took me behind the curtains at Alice Tully Hall, where close encounters of the most improbable kind could occur.

Consider the unlikely sight of Don Johnson, Melanie Griffith, Jacques Derrida, and Peter Greenaway gathered together in the Tully green room one evening in 1991. Johnson and Griffith, married at the time, must have been guests of

*Simon of the Desert* by Luis Buñuel

Disney, whose *Beauty and the Beast* we were showing. (We'd rejected a Disney movie they'd starred in together, but they didn't seem to hold it against us.) Greenaway was there to introduce his screening of *Prospero's Books*. I can't remember why the French philosopher showed up, but he was heard telling Greenaway that he liked his movie very much, but didn't quite understand it. I introduced myself to the intimidatingly brainy Greenaway, telling him how much I admired *The Belly of an Architect*. The tall, imperious Englishman scanned me up and down. "Well, I can see why," he said, "you have quite an extraordinary belly yourself."

Nice to meet you, too.

The same year we showed Gus Van Sant's *My Own Private Idaho*. It was my job to conduct the Q&A after the screening. The *Idaho* gang—which included Van Sant, Keanu Reeves, Udo Kier, and River Phoenix—had been out partying during the screening, and they arrived in the green room in an advanced and blurry state of merriment, leaving cigarette butts in the carpet in their wake. I sensed the Q&A was going to be a challenge, and had to conduct a great part of it with Kier's hand distractingly gripping my thigh. The leather-jacketed Reeves was asked a question he barely seemed to hear, leaned back in his chair, made a deep rasping sound in his throat, and

expectorated mightily upon the Tully stage. (Years later, interviewing a sober and serious Keanu, I reminded him of the evening. He was astonished and didn't remember a thing.)

This, however, was a romp in the park compared to the Q&A following a Sunday afternoon screening of Kathryn Bigelow's wild futuristic action movie *Strange Days*. The first screening had been an enthusiastic success, the audience tamed by the presence of the film's stars, Ralph Fiennes and Angela Bassett. At the second screening only Bigelow and the screen-writer, Jay Cocks, came out to field questions, and the crowd was vociferously divided between lovers and haters. One accusatory woman, trembling with rage about a scene in which a woman is forced to watch her own rape, stood and asked the director if she'd ever known anyone who'd been raped. Bigelow, no shrinking violet, looked like a deer caught in the headlights. From the balcony came a booming, angry voice: "I've been coming to the New York Film Festival for 20 years and this is the worst piece of shit you've ever shown! And I want to know why you, David Ansen, programmed this garbage!" I tried to deflect his question by saying this was a Q&A for the filmmakers, not me, but he was having none of it. "Cop Out!" he shouted, whereupon I rattled off a defense of Bigelow's visionary, stylish, and challenging work, and

*My Own Private Idaho* by Gus Van Sant

Gus Van Sant and River Phoenix, 1991

was greeted with a mixed chorus of cheers and boos. We were all happy to get off the Tully stage that afternoon.

If our selections occasionally rubbed our patrons the wrong way (and New Yorkers are not shy about letting you know how they feel), they could also provoke international hissy fits. In 1995 our Opening Night film was Zhang Yimou's *Shanghai Triad*, and Zhang was expected to be there for the festivities. We were also showing, later in the Festival, the remarkable documentary *The Gate of Heavenly Peace*, about the occupation of Tiananmen Square, and the brutal crackdown on the protestors. The Chinese government (who hadn't seen it) demanded that we withdraw the film from our program, threatening to yank *Shanghai*. It was an empty threat, since Sony Pictures Classics controlled the U.S. rights, so when the Festival refused to back down, they instead punished Zhang, "advising" him not

to come to New York for the opening.

The '90s produced a great flowering of Chinese cinema, but the government pressure on these new filmmakers—the so-called Fifth Generation—was intense and unpredictable. You could fall in and out of favor overnight, as Tian Zhuangzhuang discovered. He was blacklisted after making *The Blue Kite* (NYFF 1993), a startling, frank depiction of the Cultural Revolution's tragic effect on a family, but a year later was overseeing production at the Beijing Film Studios. Zhang has bounced from banned outsider to Party pet. The year after the dust up over the Tiananmen documentary, Chen Kaige came to the Festival with *Temptress Moon*, a lavish period piece that many said contained a subversive subtext. We were wondering how the director would handle the inevitable political questions that would arise after the screening. It came time for the Q&A and there was no Chen in sight. We frantically

Peter Greenaway, 1991

*Prospero's Books* by Peter Greenaway

*Boogie Nights* by Paul Thomas Anderson

Paul Thomas Anderson, 1997

Quentin Tarantino, 1994

tried to reach him but he had found his own way to deal with the pressure: by passing out in his hotel room.

It was a breakthrough decade for Chinese filmmaking—and not just from the Mainland. Hong Kong's Wong Kar Wai and Taiwan's Hou Hsiao-hsien and Edward Yang became Festival staples, joining such august veterans as Manoel de Oliveira (*Valley of Abraham*), Jacques Rivette (*La belle noiseuse*), Eric Rohmer (*A Tale of Winter*), Ken Loach (*Land and Freedom*), and Agnès Varda (*Jacquot de Nantes*). There was a special excitement when you discovered a new filmmaking voice. I remember the thrill of seeing an early cut of Paul Thomas Anderson's *Boogie Nights* in Los Angeles, and vowing to premiere it at the Festival. At its 1997 centerpiece screening, Burt Reynolds, who was getting the best reviews of his career, presided over the Q&A like a proud papa, which was amusing to those of us who knew he'd threatened to fire his manager and agent for putting him in a dirty movie.

During those eight years, the Festival helped launch the singular career of Aki Kaurismäki, offering up such deadpan gems as *The Match Factory Girl* and *La vie de bohème*. We spotted Noah Baumbach's promise in *Kicking and Screaming* and Jacques Audiard's in *See How They Fall*, and marveled at the one-of-a-kind weirdness of Guy Maddin's *Careful*. Over the entire course of a sunny August afternoon we sat in front of a TV mired in the Hungarian muck and mud of Béla Tarr's astonishing, seven-and-a-half-hour *Sátántangó*. There was no doubt in our minds we had to show it.

It was the decade that saw Abbas Kiarostami (*Through the Olive Trees*), Jafar Panahi (*The White Balloon*), and Mohsen Makhmalbaf (*Gabbeh*) lead the new charge of Iranian cinema. *La Promesse* marked the dawn of the Dardenne Brothers's near-infallible careers. In Canada, Atom Egoyan (*The Adjuster*, *The Sweet Hereafter*) was doing his best work; in Italy, Nanni Moretti turned cinema into a comic personal essay (*Caro Diario*) and Gianni Amelio produced his majestic Albanian-set *Lamerica*. Arnaud Desplechin's fluid, tonally volatile sagas (*My Sex Life… or How I Got Into an Argument* and *La Sentinelle*) were a fresh remix of New Wave tropes; Jane Campion astonished us with *An Angel at My Table* and *The Piano*. These were the years of Mike Leigh's greatest works, *Naked* and *Secrets & Lies*, of Charles Burnett's *To Sleep with Anger*, André Téchiné's *Wild Reeds*, Arturo Ripstein's *Deep Crimson*,

*Pulp Fiction* by Quentin Tarantino

*Blue* by Derek Jarman

*Gabbeh* by Mohsen Makhmalbaf

Tim Burton's *Ed Wood*, great documentaries like *Hoop Dreams, Crumb, Theremin: An Electronic Odyssey*, and *Public Housing*, and Derek Jarman's radical farewell to life, *Blue*, whose visuals consisted entirely of a flickering blue screen. And I haven't even mentioned the notorious *Pulp Fiction* Opening Night, when an overwhelmed viewer slumped to the floor after fainting, the lights came on, the film was stopped, and Harvey Weinstein threw a tantrum.

Every title is a Festival memory, but they are sweeter because they were shared with my fellow selection-committee members. May I salute my brilliant partners in crime Phillip Lopate, David Sterritt, Stuart Klawans, Joan Juliet Buck, Jonathan Rosenbaum, and the late Robert Sklar, who allowed me to see what movies looked like through their discerning eyes, and in the process widen mine. And a special tip of the hat to our fearless, wise, and tireless leader Richard Peña, who whipped his ornery team of opinionated cineastes into shape, and to the evergreen Wendy Keys, whose boundless appetite for movies, friendship, and parties made those eight festival years a joy.

My last year on the committee was 1997, but I was asked, in 2001, to moderate a panel during the Festival called "Making Movies That Matter." It was originally conceived to be a broad discussion on social and political issues in film, but when the day came around there were other things on everyone's mind. This was just weeks after 9/11 and the city was in a state of shock. Tully was standing room only. Onstage were Oliver Stone, Christopher Hitchens, Bob Shaye, Tom Pollack, Raoul Peck, Christine Vachon, and bell hooks. I haven't the space to describe all the fireworks of that charged afternoon, which turned into a rancorous duel between Hitchens and Stone, who railed against the corporations that controlled the world and referred to the attack on the towers as "the revolt," prompting Hitchens to call him a "moral and intellectual idiot." The audience, electrified by the discussion, weighed in with applause, hisses, and impassioned questions. This was not a film-festival scene I, or anyone, could have imagined back in 1966, when cinephilia was young, and people were beginning to get the crazy notion that movies could change the world. It didn't quite work out that way, but the world certainly changed the movies. And the New York Film Festival, a kind of cultural first responder, listened and watched, ears to the ground, eyes on the screen, bringing us for 50 years the beautiful, awful, most exciting news. 🎥

*La belle noiseuse* by Jacques Rivette

Agnès Varda, 1991

*Topsy-Turvy* by Mike Leigh

# THE DECADE I DIDN'T YET KNOW
# HOW TO WATCH

DISCOVERING THE '90S WITH THE NEW YORK FILM FESTIVAL

*Stuart Klawans*

MOST MORNINGS A CHILL WOULD CREEP into me, despite the August blaze, because the Walter Reade Theater was cooled for an audience of 250, and there were just five of us sprawled inside. We tended to spread out, too, each claiming the same seat every day, so that half a row of cold air separated one member of the selection committee from the critical heat of the next. "Eyes on the screen," as Richard Peña liked to say, quoting his old Harvard mentor, Vlada Petric. And so we remained for hours, perfectly watchful but as still as hibernating reptiles, until my right hand would go numb from loss of circulation.

Talk about a cave of forgotten dreams. For five hours a day during the annual selection marathon for the New York Film Festival we warmed ourselves only by giving off catcalls, wisecracks, and sudden cries of amazement. In the urbane, laughing baritone of David Ansen, as the camera in *I Am Cuba* flew through a cigar factory and then right out the window: "I have no idea how they did that." In the

precise but excitable mid-Atlantic tones of Joan Juliet Buck, as the cool-burning color field of Derek Jarman's *Blue* seared into our retinas: "Masterpieces. Let's have nothing but masterpieces." The end credits rolled on the intricate satire of *A Confucian Confusion*, and from Jonathan Rosenbaum came one of those bursts of ardor he'd struggle to contain, this time about Edward Yang: "Nobody else is telling us as much about the way we live now." The sky dropped away in Ernie Gehr's *Side/Walk/ Shuttle* while the roof of an office building, upside-down, glided into the frame like a spaceship, and David Sterritt, usually a streetwise aphorist but now as wordless as the film, made no comment except to gasp.

Every year or two a year a visitor from outside might venture through the silent, darkened lobby and into our cave. Just before we watched *The Nightmare Before Christmas* a lanky, dark-stubbled man wearing sunglasses and jeans walked unannounced into the theater, said cheerfully that he hoped we liked the film,

*A Confucian Confusion* by Edward Yang

*The Nightmare Before Christmas* by Henry Selick

Krzysztof Kieślowski, 1994

and disappeared again with a wave: Tim Burton. Mostly, though, we were sealed off, the three rotating critics on the committee and its two standing members, Wendy Keys and Richard: Wendy, whose judgments of films were at once so sure and yet so gracefully voiced (as if the stinkers were unpleasant intruders at the party, whom she wished to usher away for our sake, while the good ones were guests of honor, whom the rest of us had of course known forever), and Richard, who never openly guided our decisions but made it seem as if he wanted only to make us laugh, or keep us on schedule. When the first scenes of a Scandinavian domestic drama seemed hopelessly derivative, he began supplying his own subtitles, but from the Japanese: "So, Noriko! You're going to get married!" When he'd decided the film on screen was not good enough even to be derivative, he would call out, with minutely calibrated impatience, "Shall we move on?"

We moved on. In the afternoon, when the

*Blue* by Krzysztof Kieślowski

*The Crying Game* by Neil Jordan

lights went on in the Walter Reade lobby, we went upstairs to the Film Society's office, to sink into the rump-sprung couches and chairs in the video room and watch tapes for another five or six hours. Here the quarters were close, the temperature a little too warm, and the image quality (in those VHS years) just irritating enough to induce eye fatigue. There was more chatter in the room, but also (at least for me) a greater danger of nodding off. On the Saturday when we came in specially to watch all seven and a half hours of *Sátántangó*, I stood for half the episodes, and not just out of respect.

This is what I remember best, and cherish most, about my time on the Festival: not the excitement of being one of those 5,000 very special journalists at Cannes, not the excellent dinners with directors, or the little Q&A performances we would put on from the stage of Alice Tully Hall, but the daily work of the

marathon, when we came to understand one another and also learned a little something about the world's filmmakers at that moment.

The titles I've mentioned tell part of the story. As the 1990s began, the repercussions of now-defunct Communism were reverberating through new films (not only *Sátántangó* but also *Underground*, *Lamerica*, *The Oak*, Kieślowski's Three Colors trilogy) and the occasional odd rediscovery, such as *I Am Cuba*. The devastation of AIDS, and the simultaneous outburst of the New Queer Cinema, were still keenly felt in films such as Jarman's *Blue*, *Totally F\*\*\*ed Up*, *Dottie Gets Spanked*, and even *The Crying Game*. It soon became common for the hip brigade of the early '90s to deny the impact of that latter film, saying about the big plot turn, "Of course I knew. It was obvious." I can testify that when the big moment came for the selection committee, five people with varied experience of life

Neil Jordan, 1992

*Underground* by Emir Kusturica

and not a little experience of movies all started shouting at one another, "Did you know?"

Another part of the story in the early '90s was the continuing decline in interest in experimental, non-narrative films, even among the hip brigade, while institutions devoted to such work struggled or sank. The inclusion of an annual, single-evening program titled "Avant-Garde Visions," into which *Side/Walk/Shuttle* might fit, testified both to the Festival's determination to keep these works before the public and to an uncertainty about what exactly to do with them. "Avant-Garde Visions" lasted eight years, from 1988 to 1995, after which the Festival came up with a different solution: a multi-program sidebar, "Views from the Avant-Garde."

Meanwhile, confronting another change in the culture of moving images, the Festival inaugurated a second sidebar, specifically for video. Here the uneasiness doubled. It was hard to tell why some of the videos shouldn't simply have been shown in "Views from the Avant-Garde" and equally hard to tell why others shouldn't have gone into the main program. The source of the difficulty—as demonstrated by the many hours the selection committee spent before a monitor—was that by the early 1990s video was already entrenched as a routine format for both distribution and production.

Capitulation was inevitable. The video sidebar migrated out of the Festival and withered away. By the end of the '90s the main program had become, in significant measure if quietly, a festival of videos transferred to celluloid.

As for Edward Yang and *A Confucian Confusion*: the one constant in this period, even amid change and uncertainty, was the elevation to authorial status of filmmakers who had recently emerged from all parts of the world,

bringing with them all sorts of news.

This wasn't exactly a novel process, but neither had it been entirely normal during the Festival's early years. I'm told that Richard Roud used to say, "There are no undiscovered masterpieces in Malaysia"—and that probably had been true, when Malaysians aspiring to make films might have despaired of acquiring the necessary cumbersome, expensive equipment and access to a lab. But by the early '90s, production

*Through the Olive Trees* by Abbas Kiarostami

Wes Anderson, 1998

*Rushmore* by Wes Anderson

*Happiness* by Todd Solondz

had become simpler, new waves had broken around the globe (in some countries, admittedly, for the second or third time) and New York had increased its appetite for fresh experiences—not necessarily of a lone genius and not simply of an exotic region but of a new filmmaker and subject matter together.

Which brings me to perhaps the most important event of the Festival in this decade, and my proudest moment with the committee: the afternoon in 1992 when Abbas Kiarostami stepped onto the stage of Alice Tully Hall for the first time, to discuss *Life and Nothing More...* with the press.

I wish I could say the journalists proved equal to the occasion. A little too aware that they had just seen the Festival's first selection from Iran, and a little too determined to make

of it an authentic encounter with the Other, they neglected the possibility that the calm, smooth-faced man with the tinted eyeglasses might be not only a sophisticated artist but also the most worldly person in the room. They repeatedly pressed Kiarostami about his use of a snatch of Vivaldi on the soundtrack, as if this might be the telltale sign of counterfeit. "I think of Vivaldi the way I think of the sun," he finally said through the interpreter, while letting only the slightest irritation disturb his aristocratic reserve. "He belongs to everyone." Fortunately, the audience soon caught on that Kiarostami, too, might belong to everyone. By the time the Festival showed *Through the Olive Trees* two years later, the mere mention of his name had begun to set off applause. By the time another two years passed, Festival audiences had also seen the work of Mohsen Makhmalbaf and Jafar Panahi and begun to grasp their very different personalities, and the rise of Iranian film had become one of the main stories of cinema in the '90s.

There were fallings-off, too. The Fifth Generation of Chinese cinema, which seemed so powerful at the start of the decade with Zhang Yimou and Chen Kaige, was noticeably flagging by the end; but then, in 2000, Jia Zhang-ke made his Festival debut with *Platform*, and the next phase began. Other noteworthy debuts during the '90s included Cheikh Oumar Sissoko, Djibril Diop Mambety, Abderrahamane Sissako, and Idrissa Ouedraogo, all part of a new wave from the Francophone countries of Africa; Wong Kar Wai from Hong Kong; Lars von Trier from Denmark; Michael Haneke from Austria; Aleksandr Sokurov from Russia; the Dardenne Brothers from Belgium;

and, from France, the dazzling quartet of Olivier Assayas, Jacques Audiard, Claire Denis, and Arnaud Desplechin.

First-time filmmakers from the United States—also a respectable group—included Wes Anderson with *Rushmore*, Paul Thomas Anderson with *Boogie Nights*, Todd Solondz with *Happiness*, and Steve James, Frederick Marx, and Peter Gilbert with one of the epochal films of any period of the Festival, *Hoop Dreams*.

For normal Saturday-night moviegoers, though, as distinguished from the art-house clique, one debut dominates the history of the Festival in these years: the presentation of Quentin Tarantino's *Pulp Fiction* on Opening Night 1994.

Whether the man who fainted during the overdose scene, halting the screening, really had

*Hoop Dreams* by Steve James, Frederick Marx, and Peter Gilbert

Todd Solondz, 1998

suffered a brief collapse or was (as rumored) performing a publicity stunt, I will never know. ("It was too exciting," the victim was reported to have explained upon recovering.) What I can say is that the premiere of *Pulp Fiction* decisively changed "independent film" from a description of the regional and handmade (such as Victor Nuñez's beautiful *Ruby in Paradise*) into a marketing category for mid-budget studio pictures. Whatever responsibility the Festival might have to accept for this development, both good and bad, I will stand by the decision to show *Pulp Fiction*. The talent was too extravagant to ignore, and the Festival had fulfilled one of its main purposes: to capture the moment.

That said, the shift from *Ruby in Paradise* to *Pulp Fiction*, from naturalistic observation to genre mash-up, tells another part of the story of the decade. For reasons that are less evident than the fall of Communism, the devastation of AIDS, or the triumph of video, but that may have had something to do with the shrinking

audience for the avant-garde, the '90s saw an overall movement away from narrative experiments and provocations (and from hybrids of fiction and documentary) toward a more settled mode of filmmaking.

Having directed the ferocious *Naked* earlier in the decade (and having alarmed Alice Tully Hall by giving the most violently contemptuous Q&A session in memory), Mike Leigh proceeded to make his splendid but far less challenging backstage musical, *Topsy-Turvy*. Atom Egoyan went from the puzzles of form and identity in *Calendar* to the dramatization of social problems in *The Sweet Hereafter*; Hou Hsiao-hsien from the ironies and real-life oddities of *The Puppetmaster* to the hyper-refinement of *Flowers of Shanghai*; Raúl Ruiz from the delirious games of *Three Lives and Only One Death* to the infinitely rich but well-established literary ground of *Time Regained*. The likelihood that *Time Regained* was Ruiz's supreme masterpiece suggests that this

movement toward (relatively) conventional narrative was neither good nor bad in itself. It's even arguable that another of the great stories of '90s cinema, the ripening of Pedro Almodóvar, was part of this trend.

I'm speaking in very broad terms, of course, and ignoring exceptional cases—the most important of which would be Jane Campion, who never conforms. She went from steeping the audience in a nice, hot genre bath in *The Piano* to flinging outrage in their faces in *Holy Smoke*. But in general, I think Richard Peña was right when he observed, toward the end of my time on the committee, "People just aren't looking anymore for a what-the-hell-was-that experience."

What was I looking for in those years? Joan Buck dared me to tell her, one afternoon in the video room, and the best I could say was, "A movie that I don't yet know how to watch." I found a few of those at the Festival. More than that, I found colleagues like Joan who pushed me to answer them and think more deeply, and

*Holy Smoke* by Jane Campion

*Naked* by Mike Leigh

challenged me by seizing on movies I hadn't been searching for at all.

When I rotated off the committee and Bob Sklar (may his memory be a blessing) came on, I dropped by the Walter Reade Theater on the first day of the marathon to present everyone with a gift bag containing snacks and a little bottle of Visine. I'd reverted to living outside the cave, but I wanted to feel, a little, the sting of the work, and especially the camaraderie.

Still, after that, I knew I couldn't hang around. Each year, when the selections were announced, I would wheedle news of favorite choices from committee members: John Anderson, Manohla Dargis, Dave Kehr, Kathleen Murphy, John Powers. But I now understood a little better the benevolent resignation of Joanne Koch, who watched over each successive committee with a gentle, attentive smile and let it get on with the job.

Did others feel the same way? When Manohla Dargis completed her first year on the committee and I asked how she'd enjoyed it, I got an earful of blistering satire about everything except the air conditioning. Then came the non-confession. Summing up her sufferings, she referred to the Stockholm syndrome.

And there she was: another willing hostage, happy to labor in the cave. 🎥

Raúl Ruiz, 1999

*Time Regained* by Raúl Ruiz

*Once Upon a Time in Anatolia* by Nuri Bilge Ceylan

# HOW THE WEST WAS LOST

*John Powers*

WHEN I WAS A BOY, MY FAMILY MOVED five blocks from the Indian Hills Theater in Omaha, which boasted the largest Cinerama screen in America. From the moment we first drove past this unlovely orange cylinder, I made my parents' lives miserable begging to see a movie there. And so, one Saturday afternoon in 1963—the same year the New York Film Festival began its half-century-and-counting run—my mother took my sister and me to see *How the West Was Won*. Almost sick with anticipation (I hadn't yet learned to dread the credit "Henry Hathaway"), I yelped with joy when I saw mom paying the cashier. But as she walked back toward us, I sensed something was wrong.

"I got us the tickets," she said, "but not for today."

"Why not?"

"The only seats were bad ones, way up front on the side."

"I don't care."

"Well, I do. It matters where you're sitting."

Then, as ever, my mom proved unable to resist using the occasion to reveal a Valuable Moral. "And remember," she said, "That's true of life, too."

Naturally, my sister and I rolled our eyes at her corn-fed wisdom, but when we went back the following weekend, I learned my lesson. Although the Hathaway parts were so lousy even a kid could tell, our seats were great, right in the center, where you seemed to be sucked into the Battle of Shiloh. Heading out to buy candy during a dull part, I noticed how, from the side aisle, the Cinerama image was so warped it was headache-inducing. My mother had been right.

Over the years, I realized that my mother was right in the larger sense, too: it really does matter where you're sitting. Although we like to think of ourselves as individuals who find and refine our own taste, our personal sense of cinema—of what movies are and how we should respond to them—is nearly always framed by the historical era in which we happened to be sitting as we grew up.

For my part, I long prided myself on discovering Godard when, if anything, it was he who'd discovered me.

Which is to say, I was privileged enough to pass from adolescence to young manhood during the 1960s and '70s when film was at the very center of culture. Le Grand Jean-Luc sent out bulletins from the front lines of consciousness; Michelangelo Antonioni revealed new possibilities in visual space; John Cassavetes played the extreme fringes of emotion as bebop once pushed the far reaches of melody; Francis Ford Coppola transformed the classic gangster movie into a rumination on the dark ironies of the American Dream—Michael Corleone had to destroy his family to save it. This was an era when, week after week, you went to the movies believing, foolishly or not, that you might see something that could change your life. And because so many millions shared this belief, the communal act of filmgoing endowed almost every trip to the cinema with a neon verve and brightness. The audience's excitement made the movies themselves more exciting.

Such idealistic giddiness had vanished by the time I moved to L.A. and became a professional film critic during the dark reign of "Morning in America." It wasn't that I found no movies to love—my review of *Blue Velvet* achieved a level of goo-goo-eyed kvelling that would embarrass the most doting of grandparents—but our culture no longer expected transcendent experiences from any film more demanding than *E.T.* Critics had begun thinking with their thumbs and the media paid vastly more attention to the weekend box-office grosses than any Cannes winner. By the time Richard Peña asked me to join the New York Film Festival selection committee—I would eventually do two stints, one in the late '90s, the other during the High Bush Years—even chefs were being taken more seriously than filmmakers. The buzz and prestige had begun migrating to TV, where today the chattering elite (including film critics) follow *Mad Men*, *The Wire*, *Breaking Bad*, and *Girls* with as much perfervid attention as they ever did the Nouvelle Vague; as before, such avidity only serves to make these shows feel richer, more resonant. Looked at from where most of American

*Flowers of Shanghai* by Hou Hsiao-hsien

culture is sitting—in front of the television or the iPad—the NYFF increasingly resembles a season of poetry readings by the likes of, oh, Les Murray, John Ashbery, and Wisława Szymborska—major talents no doubt, but aside from buffs, who the hell really cares?

I knew all of this when I first signed on to the committee, yet I was still delighted to be doing it, doubly so as I got to serve with my friend, the critical lodestar Dave Kehr. True, New York's weather during the annual August screening marathon prompted a certain nostalgia for the Bataan Death March. True, the job didn't exactly drench you in glamour: Harvey Weinstein once had his minions try to set up a special VIP area in the smallish green room at Alice Tully Hall so "the talent" wouldn't have to mingle with the rabble—viz., the members of the selection committee who'd invited them. And true, I would discover that, unlike such admirable committee members as Commissar Peña, Kent Jones, and the late Robert Sklar, I lack the patience (and splendidly callused backside) that enables a top-flight programmer to sift through unpromising movies deep into the night, hours after hothouse flowers like myself have wilted. "Having to see bad movies is hard on your soul," the great spiritual master Richard

Gere once told me in an interview, and having endured more than my share during those August sessions, I can only second his words with a hearty "Shanti."

On the other hand, discovering good movies is nirvana. As the NYFF's L.A. guy, I not only saw the very first screenings of *Rushmore* and *Election*—the terrific comedies that launched the still-soaring careers of Wes Anderson and Alexander Payne—but saw them in the same week. One night at Cannes, I stayed up insanely late to see *Flowers of Shanghai*, probably the greatest film by Hou Hsiao-hsien, the Taiwanese genius who has been, to my mind, the world's finest filmmaker over the last 30 years (a period, it's worth noting, that covers 60 percent of the New York Film Festival's entire existence). And then there was the day Lisa Schwarzbaum and I encountered Cristi Puiu's *The Death of Mr. Lazarescu* in the grotty upstairs screening room that (I'm told) Film Society employees use to house their kidnap victims. Lazy as ever, I wanted it to be rotten so we could turn it off, call it overrated, and get the heck out of there. After all, it was Friday afternoon and I knew the movie wasn't exactly *Trouble in Paradise*—it was two-and-a-half hours of an old guy in Bucharest dying. No matter. Within minutes we were

*Sympathy for Lady Vengeance* by Park Chan-wook

transfixed. Here was the kind of brilliant work that no longer has any commercial life in America (it eventually took in a mingy $79,934) but that the NYFF could properly treat as an artistic event.

Now, of course, it would've been a blast to have been on the committee in the '60s and '70s when film culture was booming—can you imagine the perverse Buñuelian pleasure of being in a position to turn down a film by Buñuel? Yet the important point is that *Flowers of Shanghai* and *The Death of Mr. Lazarescu* were not aberrations glittering like diamonds in a bucket of lard (to steal a line from Ben Hecht). If anything, they were evidence of a

massive sea change that still hasn't been fully acknowledged, let alone accepted, by many cultural gatekeepers or the traditional art-film audience. Just as the U.S. and Europe no longer dominate the world economy, they no longer dominate the world of international cinema. And they haven't for at least the last 25 years.

Don't get me wrong. I realize that, even as Hollywood moves move ever deeper into the theme-park business, America boasts astonishingly talented filmmakers like David Fincher, Paul Thomas Anderson, Kathryn Bigelow, and Quentin Tarantino. I'm equally well aware that Europe hasn't packed it in either. In fact, the NYFF annually hosts European auteurs known

by their first names—Pedro and Lars and Aki and Olivier (though I'm not sure even Frau Haneke thinks of her joyless husband as "Michael")—and it takes care to showcase slightly newer talents like Jacques Audiard and Matteo Garrone. Still, we're a long way from the time when the best and most exciting work came from places with which most of the American—indeed, most of the Western—audience feels comfortable. I keep meeting people who ask me why they don't make great movies like *Jules and Jim* anymore, and I always say, "They do, just not in France."

If you were looking to find the most exciting movies in recent decades you would do what

Bong Joon-ho, 2006

Tian Zhuangzhuang, 2006

Park Chan-wook, 2005

*The President's Last Bang* by Im Sang-soo

Corneliu Porumboiu, 2009

the NYFF has been doing ever since Richard Peña became director—look beyond Hollywood and Europe to what used to be considered the East. That's where the stories are. In the '80s, China began announcing its arrival with its Fifth Generation stars (Zhang Yimou, Chen Kaige, and Tian Zhuangzhuang); the afterthought island of Taiwan produced two world-class filmmakers in Hou and Edward

Yang, whose work possessed a cinematic intelligence and cultural richness that made most Western movies look simpleminded; meanwhile over in Hong Kong, there was an explosion of crowd-pleasing talent, from Jackie Chan and Tsui Hark, to Johnnie To and Wong Kar Wai, who by the late '90s would become the world's most imitated director. After this came the sunburst of Iranian cinema fired by

Mohsen Makhmalbaf, Jafar Panahi, and Abbas Kiarostami, whose apparently simple, deeply humane work may have been (come to think of it) even more emulated than Wong's.

By the time we reached the new millennium, we had entered the South Korean film boom, which would produce perhaps the deepest directorial bunch working anywhere. In my time on the committee, I was pleased to support (and write gaudy blurbs for) Bong Joon-ho's *The Host*, the best horror film of the '00s, Im Sang-soo's *The President's Last Bang*, a deeply subversive black comedy that's like a cross between *JFK* and *The Manchurian Candidate*, and Park Chan-wook's *Sympathy for Lady Vengeance*, which stands *Kill Bill* on its head—vengeance, however justified, soils you.

*4 Months, 3 Weeks and 2 Days* by Cristian Mungiu

Cristian Mungiu, 2007

Nuri Bilge Ceylan, 2011

I would have been equally happy to celebrate South Korea's two most literate filmmakers, Festival favorites Hong Sang-soo (whose Rohmer-esque work is, alas, becoming as formulaic as the Jason Statham oeuvre) and the far more expansive and original Lee Chang-dong, whose *Secret Sunshine* and *Poetry* are among the rare movies to deserve to be called novelistic.

Merely writing these names I recall other great ones: the wonderful Thai filmmaker Apichatpong Weerasethakul, mercifully known as "Joe," the Chinese master Jia Zhang-ke, involved in one of the new millenniums grand cinematic projects—chronicling the biggest modernization project in human history—and the startlingly good Turkish director Nuri Bilge Ceylan, whose masterful *Once Upon a Time in Anatolia* is that weirdest of hybrids, a Chekhovian epic. And I haven't even mentioned the treasures from we might call "the other East"—Eastern Europe—where, to everyone's astonishment, Romanian filmmakers like Puiu, Cristian Mungiu (*4 Months, 3 Weeks and 2 Days*), and Corneliu Porumboiu (*Police, Adjective*) emerged from the depressive shambles of post-Ceaușescu culture to create daring movies that, a few decades ago, would have won them articles in *Esquire* and *Newsweek*, and lengthy reviews in *The New Yorker* (okay, maybe I'm going too far). Meanwhile, in Israel, Joseph Cedar and Ari Folman…

But enough with the lists. Basta! Yet truly, it's hard to stop. Although nothing makes worse reading than a blizzard of names—Mexico's Gerardo Naranjo! Argentina's Lucrecia Martel! Chile's Pablo Larraín—it's worth reminding ourselves that, far from enduring some cinematic version of the End Times, we're living through a period when there are still more than enough good movies to occupy any critic's or any movie lover's attention, more than enough to keep the New York Film Festival stocked with films worth seeing. But you do need to look for them in places you didn't have to back when Fellini, Bergman, and Truffaut were part of the cultural air one breathed.

People love to quote that Orwell line about it being a constant struggle to see what's under one's nose. No doubt he's right, but it's an even greater struggle to see what isn't. To do that, you've got to get up from where you've been sitting, often all too comfortably, and go in search of something new.

*Police, Adjective* by Corneliu Porumboiu

*Che* by Steven Soderberg

# DAYS AND NIGHTS IN THE FOREST

*Kent Jones*

I SERVED ON THE NEW YORK FILM Festival selection committee for seven years, from 2002 to 2008. Every once in a while, around festival time, someone would interview either Richard Peña or me, sometimes both of us. The questions were specifically about that year's films and, inevitably, about the selection process itself. After a while, I found myself awaiting the inevitable: "What are the criteria for selecting movies?" Sometimes it would be differently shaded: "How exactly does the selection process work?" or "How did you arrive at these 25 films?" The hard-boiled approach became a particular favorite: "Okay—how does it really work with the selection committee?" As if we were Mormon elders, or machine politicians ca. 1942.

My answer was always the same: five people see as many movies as they can and then choose the 25-to-28 best, end of story. This always proved slightly disconcerting to whoever happened to be conducting the interview, and I was sincerely sorry to let the air out of the tire so quickly. In many cases, my interrogator remained undaunted.

"Were you pursuing a theme with this year's selections?" "What made you decide to choose so many films from Taiwan and fewer than usual from France?" "Why are there so many violent films this year?" Again, my answers were always the same: running themes or a preponderance of movies from a particular country were inevitable on a year-by-year basis, and they had everything to do with the year itself and zero to do with the selection process.

During my time, there were quite a few rotations among the three "guest" spots on the committee: Lisa Schwarzbaum, Dave Kehr, John Anderson, Geoffrey O'Brien, Phillip Lopate, John Powers, Manohla Dargis, Jim Hoberman, and Scott Foundas all served for varying terms, and with every shift in personnel there was a shift in the emotional and intellectual composition of the group. You could feel it in the geography of the screenings. With every new group of five, there would be a new set of vectors in the Walter Reade: each of us would invariably occupy the same position in the room day by day, and if one of us changed positions it would be remarked upon with mock grandiloquence.

A fairly coherent series of signals would always develop. We became quickly attuned to one another's individual expressions of disapproval or boredom during screenings—one of us would crack a joke, another would sigh, I myself would get up and pace. Of course, there were frequent disagreements, most of which played out tensely but quietly over the course of conversations that occasionally flared into arguments, all of which died out quickly. There were alliances, momentary deflations when one's favorites didn't make it in and spikes of elation when they did, and there was more than a little quiet indignation (as in: I can't believe that we're showing/not showing that!). I suppose many of us harbored an illusion that the process could be perfected. This was a fantasy, of course. Having achieved some distance, I think it worked very well. Group consensus between five passionate and stubbornly opinionated people doesn't drop from the sky.

It was Richard who kept everything functioning and on track. At times he was like a pre-K teacher getting everyone settled down after recess, at other times like an activities director on a cruise, but he always behaved as a good and interested colleague. I realize now that he worked hard to keep things from devolving into either chaos or groupthink. He

chose many people whose opinions diverged from his own, and while he was as disappointed as any of us when one of the films he loved was shot down, I think that maintenance of the integrity of the process itself was much more important to him than the inclusion of this or that movie. This was no small task since it was carried out in the midst of not one but two immersive situations (10 days in Cannes and two weeks in a screening room in New York in August) during which a measure of social deprivation sets in: no matter how much you love movies, I can tell you right now that you aren't quite prepared to do nothing but see movies, and talk about movies, while (in the case of Cannes) you're standing on line to see more movies. "It must be great to go to the Riviera once a year," people often tell me with a smile. It is. But vast swaths of the Cannes Film Festival could just as well be taking place in Dubuque or Tampa.

Richard's job also involved telling people—in some cases great artists, in other cases powerful studio heads—that absolutely everything was done by the book, that nothing was accepted unilaterally and every film had to be seen and voted on by the committee, that if something had been rejected there was no reversing it. One indignant young filmmaker whose film didn't make the cut haughtily reminded Richard that he had been referred to

in the press as "the white Spike Lee." For not asking me to make that call, and so much more, I will always be indebted to Richard. We all owe him a lot, and by "we," I mean committee members and film culture at large.

During most of my tenure on the committee, Joanne Koch was the Executive Director of the Film Society. If Richard was the taskmaster, Joanne was the parental figure, nervously hovering behind the scenes, trying her best to remain silent and let the kids work things out on their own. During the Festival itself, we would go like compliant children to the office she shared with her successor, the lovely Claudia Bonn, to ask for our tickets, which she would patiently dole out from the stash in her top drawer. Joanne assumed the role of mother to us all, and she gave me precious moral support during a tough moment in my life. A few years later, she and Claudia found it in their hearts to look the other way from some careless behavior on my part, something I will never forget.

The Festival plays out in my mind as a series of encounters and onstage discussions with filmmakers and their collaborators, and urgent journeys from the office to the green room to the stage to some neighboring restaurant and back again. From one angle, I remember all the Q&As as variations on a remarkably uniform set of questions—"What was your budget?" "What was your shooting

Steven Soderbergh, 2008

Bill Murray, Anjelica Huston, Gwyneth Paltrow, and Wes Anderson at the 10th anniversary screening of *The Royal Tenenbaums*, 2011

ratio?" "What was your process with the actors?" "What do you think happened to the characters at the end of the film?" "Who are your influences?" and so on. If this sounds rudely dismissive, I don't mean it to. I often sensed that many audience members had something more delicate in mind, but would shyly resort to one of these standbys just so they could engage with the filmmaker; similarly, I often found myself resorting to an old chestnut (such as "What was your starting point?") without embarrassment: the point was simply to start a conversation. Most of the filmmakers who appeared were extremely gracious, understanding that awkward questions were simply manifestations of one's desire to acknowledge an investment in the film. Not all of them, though, and some became positively venomous, especially during press conferences. One filmmaker greeted a clueless but benign comment from a NY critic with the most withering sarcasm I've ever seen displayed in public: "That's one of the most idiotic comments I've ever heard and I shall be repeating it at dinner parties for years to come." Fortunately, few filmmakers are so contemptuous. And few critics are as venomous as the grey eminence who introduced himself to a young first-time filmmaker and calmly explained that he thought her film was "a piece of shit." Welcome to New York.

I have many fond memories—Bill Murray getting up and wandering off the stage in the

*The Royal Tenenbaums* by Wes Anderson

*Sideways* by Alexander Payne

The Dardennes Brothers, 1996

Alexander Payne, 2004

Don Rickles and John Landis, 2007

middle of the *Royal Tenenbaums* Q&A; Jia Zhang-ke breaking into gales of laughter when he looked at the screen from the booth and realized that the subtitles of *Che* had somehow infiltrated his own *24 City*; my father meeting Jean-Pierre and Luc Dardenne after a screening of *L'Enfant*, which was the last movie he would ever see in a theater; Laura Dern asking David Lynch how many characters she actually wound up playing in *Inland Empire*. But the high point came when I shared the stage with Don Rickles. During the 2007 selection process, as we considered films by Béla Tarr, Carlos Reygadas, and Catherine Breillat, good

old Lisa Schwarzbaum brought in a DVD of John Landis's *Mr. Warmth: The Don Rickles Project*. Not since *Sideways* had the entire committee been reduced so consistently to helpless laughter—we were literally spilling out of our chairs. Old pro that he was—81 at that point—Rickles showed up for the intro and Q&A despite the fact that he had cracked a rib on the stationary bicycle at his hotel that afternoon. Nothing that a series of vodka and tonics couldn't take care of. "Have you read my book?" he asked me backstage. I had not. "You should go buy it now—it's terrific." During the Q&A, I was compared to a potted plant, told

that I was "even worse than Regis" (who was in the back of the house), and I got this when I took too long with my next question: "Come on, it's like NASA over here . . . 10, 9, 8, 7 . . ." I'm proud to say that I actually made Rickles laugh. It was a spit-take.

When I was a teenager, I used to wait for the autumn Sunday *Times* two-page NYFF ad with anticipation, and I would pore over it for hours. The Festival is now one of New York's most venerable institutions and, when all is said and done, a beacon of American film culture. It was an honor to have taken part in its shaping and presentation for a few years. 🎥

*L'Enfant* by Jean-Pierre and Luc Dardenne

*24 City* by Jia Zhang-ke

*Pan's Labyrinth* by Guillermo del Toro

# NEW MILLENNIUM, NEW "WORLD"

*Lisa Schwarzbaum*

SOME ASPECTS OF SERVING ON THE selection committee of the New York Film Festival are, I like to imagine, unchanged since the beginning of recorded selection-committee time. I'm sure that everyone who has ever sat in the Walter Reade Theater before me has also known the exquisite feeling of anticipation that precedes the unspooling of the first frame of a completely unknown film. I'm sure that every predecessor has also experienced the group exhilaration that follows the discovery of new movie greatness (*Pan's Labyrinth*! *Wendy and Lucy*! *Secret Sunshine*!), and the group disappointment that precedes the acknowledgment that it's time to phone the projection booth and move on to the next entry (names redacted!). We've all endured the velvet-coffin disorientation that comes from spending hours on end huddled with colleagues in rooms without sunlight, absorbing all or part of six or seven or eight films in a day. And we've all—at least all those of us fortunate to have served during Richard Peña's 25-year tenure as Program

Director—marveled at Richard's extraordinary breakfast buffets of nuts, red pepper slices, raisins, almonds, cheese cubes, chocolate bits, twigs, and, hmmm Tinker Toys?, brought from home and laid out for vegetarian morning grazing before the hard, privileged work of screening entries for the NYFF began each day.

Well, I don't want to talk about those universal experiences. Nor about how splendid it is to be part of the process, even though it is. (It's splendid even when, deep into the summer season of marathon screenings, one wants to throttle one's esteemed colleagues simply because one or another will not stop boasting about being buddies with Olivier Assayas, or telling cute stories about Manny Farber, or chewing funny.) Instead, I'd like to linger over a handful of situations, observations, and moments that, to me, not only defined my five years on the committee, from 2004-2008, but also defined the times, as well as the movies that arose out of them. In inviting me into this swanky literary salon, Richard has encouraged

Lee Chang-dong, 2007

*Secret Sunshine* by Lee Chang-dong

Jim Hoberman and Cristi Puiu, 2010

me to write about my experience in the "new millennium." So let's begin with this: before the New Millennium, I doubt I would have ever been invited to the NYFF-selection-committee table to begin with.

This isn't aw-shucksism on my part. I know I bring a lot to the party, not least of which is a talent for herding rambling audience "questions" at after-screening Q&As, an ability to keep press conferences with taciturn Coen Brothers from deteriorating into grunts and mumbles, and a highly developed appreciation for foreign-language films involving camels, incest, and deadpan fatalism. (Finnish accents are a plus.) But the fact is, I write for a mass-market consumer entertainment magazine pitched to readers more familiar with the oeuvre of hunky actor Channing Tatum than that of Thai auteur Apichatpong Weerasethakul. The truth is, I have not seen every film Manoel de Oliveira has ever made. (Only Scott Foundas has.) The reality is, I was invited to work with my erudite NYFF colleagues because I am a woman. And although some forceful, brilliant women have contributed to the selection committee over the years—Susan Sontag, Molly Haskell, Joan Buck, Carrie Rickey, and Manohla Dargis among them—only in the New Millennium has gender sensitivity been elevated to a committee staffing goal. Which is, to be sure, a not inconsiderable challenge, since, historically, film criticism and scholarship have been predominantly male pursuits. (That situation is changing. Good times!) So, to be clear, I'm aware of my assets and my circumstances. And I've got no problem with being an affirmative-action hire. With great respect, I call my place

in the screening room, among my very sharp, very erudite male colleagues the Vagina Seat. I salute that saddle as a force for good.

And oh, the wonders I saw occupying that metaphorical chair, wherever our furniture was assembled! In the mornings we gathered in the Walter Reade Theater (brrrr, cold as a meat locker, but with space to spread out, each of us an individual island of aesthetic vigilance and

*The World* by Jia Zhang-ke

extra sweaters in a small sea of empty theater cushions). In the afternoons, we repaired upstairs to the shabby FSLC back-office rumpus room that J. Hoberman dubbed the House of Peña; there we squinted at a crap-quality screen while FSLC staffers regularly wandered by to log DVD inventory or, I don't know, eat hummus sandwiches. Sometimes,

we traveled as a group to various screening rooms around the city. Each was the site of peak viewing experiences, including:

1) *The World*, by Jia Zhang-ke, 2004, Walter Reade. The English subtitling was missing on the last reel of Jia's great distillation of Chinese globalization and its discontents, set in an Epcot-like theme park. It didn't matter. We watched, rapt, and brought *The World* to New York, the third NYFF selection from the masterful Jia following *Platform* (2000) and *Unknown Pleasures* (2002). Long may he lead the way for Sixth Generation Chinese filmmakers.

2) *The Death of Mr. Lazarescu*, Cristi Puiu, 2005, House of Peña. Three of our selection committee comrades had already seen Puiu's

Laura Dern and David Lynch, 2006

*Inland Empire* by David Lynch

gem at Cannes, heralding an exciting New Wave of Romanian filmmaking creativity just beginning to roll in. But John Powers and I needed to catch up. So we shoehorned into the House of Peña late one day after the rest of the team had been dismissed and the hummus wrappers had been discarded. The video quality was punk. The movie was a treasure.

3) *Sideways*, Alexander Payne, 2004, Dolby 24 Screening Room. The viewing conditions were ideal: small room in Midtown Manhattan, comfy chairs, good sound, perfect sightlines. But the movie, we immediately knew, was ideal quite apart from our cushy surroundings. We sat, enchanted, through the complete closing credits, then all five of us levitated and floated out of the room, dazzled to be among the very first to see so lovely a goblet-sized work of art from one of America's finest contemporary filmmakers.

4) *Inland Empire*, David Lynch, 2006, Walter Reade. Peak viewing experience? For me, that's debatable; three viewings later, I'm still confounded. Peak thriller experience? Definitely, since the screening event itself was the satisfying conclusion to a tense episode of Festival brinksmanship. Could Lynch finish a version in time to make the NYFF submission deadline? Would he? Could Peña grant the

exacting filmmaker any deadline leeway? Would he? At the last minute of the last hour of the last day, an honor guard (well, at least an intern) flew red-eye from L.A. to NY, clutching a still-wet print. (I speak poetically: the picture was shot digitally, a first for him.) We all felt very . . . Top Secret. Not to mention, we felt excited about being confused by primo cinematic weirdness. Anyone claiming to make sense of the work after one viewing is a big, fat liar. The whole thing is so . . . Lynchian! And we were so proud to feature *Inland Empire* in the 2006 New York Film Festival.

Lynch's embrace of digital video is one notable aspect of the New Millennium as reflected in NYFF programming. My years on the committee coincided with a burst of liberating narrative experimentation made possible by the flexibility and economy of digital technology in offerings as varied as Steven Soderbergh's 2005 hi-def video experiment *Bubble* (2005), and Jonathan Caouette's 2004 autobiographical assemblage *Tarnation*, originally made using iMac software. Vital American filmmakers played with new story shapes—among them Todd Solondz with *Palindromes* (2004), Lodge Kerrigan with *Keane* (2004), and Todd Haynes with his tour-de-force Bob Dylan reverie *I'm Not There* (2007).

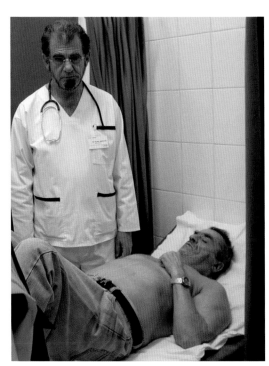

*The Death of Mr. Lazarescu* by Cristi Puiu

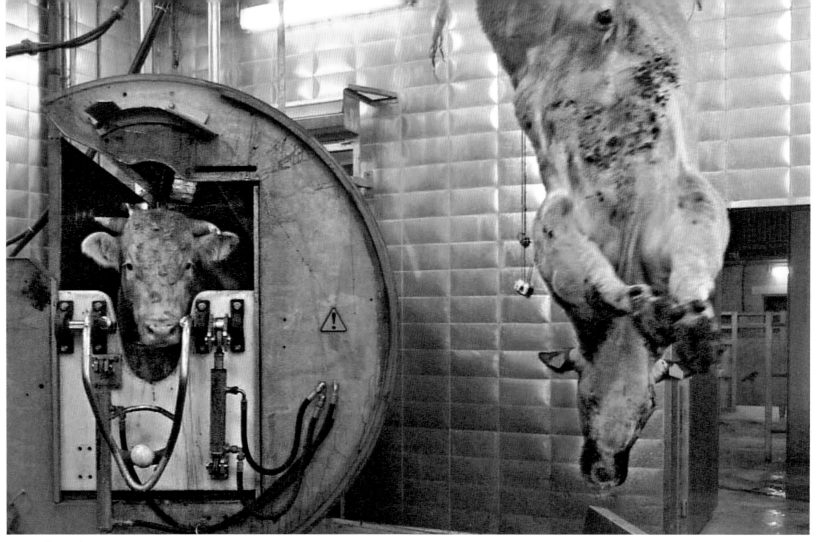

*Our Daily Bread* by Nikolaus Geyrhalter

But, true to my pop-culture bona fides, I was even more excited by the creative leaps taken by the animation arts. And I'm especially proud that during my NYFF term we brought two spectacular animated features to the NYFF, great cinematic works that took advantage of the accessibility, beauty, and friendliness of the animated line to tell powerful political stories: the autobiographical Iranian saga *Persepolis* (2007) by Marjane Satrapi and Vincent Paronnaud (based on Satrapi's own gorgeous graphic novels) and the autobiographical Israeli saga *Waltz with Bashir* (2008) by Ari Folman. In my ideal NYFF of the future, there would be room for even more animation in the lineup. And monster movies, like Bong Joon-ho's pointed tale *The Host*. And for more documentaries, too! (If calling the category "nonfiction filmmaking" increases its sex appeal, I'm all for a change of nomenclature.) A television-lover among Criterion Collection–collecting colleagues (I lay claim to a past life spent working at public television

WGBH in Boston, the home of the standard-setting series *Frontline*), I was frustrated, at times, by the hit-or-miss quality of the nonfiction movies available for our consideration. Under the circumstances, John Landis's

*I'm Not There* by Todd Haynes

expertly steered *Mr. Warmth: The Don Rickles Project* (2007) was a sight for sore laugh muscles. Then again, I also loved *Our Daily Bread* (2006), Nikolaus Geyrhalter's cool-toned, wordless look at industrial-level

food production. We should have included more; documentaries are hot.

Finally, the ladies, yes. My experience on the NYFF selection committee in the New Millennium included the opportunity to program new work by old masters—Eric Rohmer, Ousmane Sembene, Sidney Lumet, Claude Chabrol, Ingmar Bergman; the chance to program youthful work by mature masters—Pedro Almodóvar, Zhang Yimou, Mike Leigh, Hou Hsiao-hsien, Stephen Frears; and the luck to program arresting work by new masters—Apichatpong Weerasethakul, Arnaud Desplechin, Hong Sang-soo, Nuri Bilge Ceylan. But nothing gave me more pleasure than to acknowledge the work of female masters working in top form. My very first NYFF "hosting" activity was conducting the inaugural HBO Films Directors Dialogues with the witty, spirited, astute Agnès Jaoui, whose *Look at Me* (2005) sparkles with a bright understanding of feminine insecurity. My love of Argentinian director Lucrecia

Martel deepened (after her striking 2001 debut, *La Ciénaga*) with *The Holy Girl* (2004), about awakening female sexual feelings and religious impulses; I was aroused by the erotic fire in Catherine Breillat's *The Last Mistress* (2007); and I was head-over-heels dazzled, as any NYFF committee member throughout all history would be, by Kelly Reichardt's spare and cut-to-the-core meditation on American rootlessness and economic struggle, *Wendy and Lucy* (2008).

I'm pretty sure that all these great movies would have made it into the NYFF with or without my position in the Vagina Seat. But I'm glad and grateful, nonetheless, that I was the one who was able to be in that place, in those years, in that group of ardent cinephiles. I loved every debate, every breakfast soybean, and, most of all, that moment, every time, as the lights went down and we were filled with hope, all of us together, faces tilted toward the screen. 🎥

*Wendy and Lucy* by Kelly Reichardt

*The Last Mistress* by Catherine Breillat

The newly renovated exterior of Alice Tully Hall. *Photograph by Mark Bussell*

# THE FUTURE

*Scott Foundas*

WHERE DO WE GO NOW? SURELY, AS THE movie universe simultaneously expands (in terms of the number of available offerings) and contracts (in terms of an ever more fragmented public), this is the question foremost on the minds of decision makers in every corner of the industry. And make no mistake: the world of film festivals is hardly immune. As has been noted elsewhere in this book, when the New York Film Festival began a half-century ago, there were but a handful of such events in the world. Now, in cities major and minor, there are practically a handful each week—festivals devoted to the films of specific countries or cultural backgrounds, festivals of children's films, of gay and lesbian films, of movies about the environment, of movies on dance. Even at Lincoln Center, the NYFF is now but one of a dozen or so annual film festivals of one sort or another produced by the Film Society in concert with other leading local and international cultural organizations.

This is, I am inclined to think, mostly a good thing. The proliferation of regional and specialty festivals across the country and around the world is allowing interested audiences access to films they might otherwise never see, and which, in some cases, might not even be made. That there are dedicated audiences for these programs, however specific they might be, is a sign that film culture is thriving. Of course, many films still fall silently in the celluloid (or, nowadays, digital) forest, and— unfashionable as it may be to say in this culture of endless positive reinforcement—a lot of them deserve to. Just because inexpensive digital technology now makes it possible for anyone to make a movie doesn't mean that just anyone should, much as *American Idol* has reminded us that not everyone with a voice has any business around a microphone. All of which is to say that the role played by film festivals today—as curators, as educators—seems more important than ever. How else to navigate one's way through this surfeit of "content"?

At the same time, the growth of festivals

has led to an often unpleasant jockeying for position that calls to mind the rioting moviegoers at the end of Nathanael West's *The Day of the Locust*. "Today, if you're a young filmmaker with a good short film, there are already three satellites focused on you," Thierry Frémaux, director of the Cannes Film Festival, told me in a 2007 interview, referring to the fervent desire of the world's leading festivals—specifically Cannes, Berlin, and Venice—to get in on the ground floor with the next generation of important filmmakers, and to somehow brand them as their discoveries. Whereas it was still possible, in the not too distant past, for a film like the Mexican director Carlos Reygadas's *Japón* to premiere at a modest festival like Rotterdam and still go on to an official screening in Cannes, world premieres are now insisted on by the majors as a matter of course. And many festivals, big and small, have instituted screenplay labs and production and post-production grants designed to link themselves to films that have not even yet been made.

All of which is well and good so long as the guiding principle remains talent cultivation, and not flattering the egos of festival organizers, corporate sponsors, and important donors. For at the risk of alienating a few friends and colleagues, I will propose that there is only one festival in the world, Sundance, that has truly entered the pop-culture lexicon as something more than a mere arts organization, its name invoking not just an annual gathering in the mountains of Utah but a particular strain of independent film—and independent filmmaker—that the festival and its associated Institute have played a major role in cultivating. It is, in short, the film festival as lifestyle brand—and whether or not this has ultimately been for the betterment of movies remains, I think, very much an open question.

Whither NYFF in all this? As it so happens, more or less right where it began. My dear colleague and mentor Richard Peña is fond of saying that when he assumed leadership of the Festival from Richard Roud in 1988, his personal mandate, being a longtime NYFF devotee, was to avoid fixing what wasn't broken. Now, as Richard II himself prepares to abdicate the throne, the identity of the Festival remains something of an

*Paradise Lost 3: Purgatory* by Joe Berlinger and Bruce Sinofsky

unassailable constant. True, we screen many more films—and types of films—than ever before, thanks to the addition of the Walter Reade Theater (in 1991) and, just last year, the Elinor Bunin Munroe Film Center. The retrospectives are more comprehensive, the adventurous "Views From the Avant-Garde" program more encyclopedic. There is even, new this year, a "convergence" of leading thinkers from the realm of "immersive media," who are seeking ways we can experience moving pictures beyond the realm of conventional cinemas. (In 2062, as you prepare to download the 100th edition of NYFF directly into your brain, you'll have them to thank.)

But the core of NYFF remains the nightly screenings in the gloriously renovated Alice Tully Hall, where many of the most lauded and anticipated films from the previous 10 months make their New York (and, in many cases, U.S., North American, or world) premieres, before crowds of up to 1,100 people, and in the presence of their makers. The screen is large, the seating is reserved, and the air is suitably reverential—the feeling one associates with performances at the other Lincoln Center constituents, but all too infrequently (in the multiplex and home-viewing era) with going to the movies. Indeed, for all the debates over digital methods of production and exhibition versus traditional analog ones, the real battle at the movies today is one that the very pioneers of the moving image first fought more than a century ago: namely, whether cinema is effectively a solitary art form, to be experienced

Inside Alice Tully Hall, Opening Night 2011

in small viewing boxes of the kind invented by Thomas Edison and perfected by Steve Jobs, or if movies should be a collective experience, as Edison's transatlantic rivals, the brothers Auguste and Louis Lumière, believed. Night after night at NYFF, I like to think that we score points for the French team.

When I first came to NYFF in the early years of the last decade—initially as a spectator, and later as a journalist—I was quickly seduced by this concert-hall atmosphere, rivaled only by the grand "palais" of Cannes, Venice, and Berlin. I can remember loitering about the outside of Alice Tully, hoping to score a spare ticket to a sold-out screening, or craning my neck from the balcony as the lights went down, in search of an unclaimed orchestra seat. Not in my wildest imagination did I think that one day that would be me in the spotlight, introducing this or that world-renowned auteur or auspicious newcomer to the New York audience. And even now, six years into my tenure on the selection committee and three as a full-time Film Society staffer, I still feel an electric charge as I wait in the Alice Tully wings, watching the crowd file in, hoping to see a really good show. To be sure, there are festivals that make more noise than us, that seem intent on having you remember their names above and beyond the titles of any of the films that played there. Yet it is only at the NYFF where, just in the last few years, you could attend the world premieres of *The Social Network* and Martin Scorsese's glorious *Hugo* (the latter as a secret, work-in-progress screening); where the extraordinary documentary *Paradise Lost 3: Purgatory* screened for the first time in the presence of its own subjects—three wrongfully accused young men newly released from prison; and where, in

*Hugo* by Martin Scorsese

a rare U.S. appearance, the legendary French filmmaker Alain Resnais—an alumnus of the very first NYFF—took to the stage for the premiere of his new *Wild Grass* and received a thunderous standing ovation. Somewhere, I dare say, the Lumière Brothers are smiling.

In an unpublished editorial submitted to *The New York Times* on the occasion of NYFF's 20th edition in 1982, the Festival's esteemed co-founder, Amos Vogel, had some choice words for what he deemed "the unfulfilled promise of film at Lincoln Center." At the time, the plans for the year-round cinema that would eventually become the Walter Reade Theater had been put on hold due to budgetary problems, while the Festival itself had become, in Amos's opinion, a victim of "the American marriage of culture and corporation," beholden to deep-pocketed sponsors and an ossified selection process. Twenty-nine years later, in what would prove to be his last public appearance, Amos took his first steps inside the new

Film Center for a special screening of Luis Buñuel's *The Exterminating Angel*—the Opening Night film of the 1st NYFF—to kick off our yearlong countdown to this historic 50th edition. It was the only time I had the pleasure of meeting this storied figure, and in the course of helping Amos's son Steve escort him into the building, something rather wonderful happened. As we passed the Film Center's enormous plasma-screen monitor, emblazoned with an animated version of the bright orange Film Society logo, Amos stopped in his tracks, grabbed my arm tightly, and with the twinkle in his eye that so many have spoken of, he said proudly, "The Film Society of Lincoln Center? I started that!"

At the half-century mark, has the promise of film at Lincoln Center finally been fulfilled? I won't hazard to say, except that a dream fulfilled leaves nothing to work toward. Where do we go now? How about we go to the movies. 🎥

*Wild Grass* by Alain Renais

The Elinor Bunin Munroe Film Center Amphitheater

The Walter Reade Theater

*Zorns Lemma* by Hollis Frampton

# IN THE REALM OF THE SENSES,

## OR HOW THE NYFF LEARNED TO STOP WORRYING AND LOVE AVANT-GARDE FILM

*Gavin Smith*

FROM ITS INCEPTION, THE NYFF DEMON-strated a commitment to showing films that subverted, disrupted, or overthrew conventional cinema and narrative. Its first decade saw the cultural ferment of the 1960s give rise to the emergence of a generation of modernist filmmakers who tore up the rule book. Most of them turned up in the Festival: Chris Marker, Alain Resnais, Jean-Marie Straub, Alexander Kluge, Sergei Parajanov, Marguerite Duras, Miklós Jancsó, Pier Paolo Pasolini, Nagisa Oshima, Jean-Luc Godard, and so on. Even after the experimentation of the '60s had waned on many fronts, the Festival still found room for challenging and even radical work that pushed the envelope formally, conceptually, or both—Jacques Rivette's *Out 1: Spectre*, Raúl Ruiz's *Three Crowns of the Sailor*, Derek Jarman's *The Last of England*, Béla Tarr's *Sátántangó*, Aleksei Guerman's *Khrustalyov, My Car!*, to name just a few.

The '60s was also a watershed decade for avant-garde filmmaking in the U.S. The so-called American Independent Film movement that emerged in the '50s came into its own in the '60s with an explosion of cinematic experimentation from coast to coast. Appointed alongside Richard Roud to program the NYFF in 1962, the late Amos Vogel was himself a pioneer of this movement. He was the man behind Cinema 16, the weekly film club that from the late '40s to the early '60s had introduced New York audiences to an eclectic range of new and exciting discoveries in experimental and documentary cinema from all over the world, including work by many of the founding figures of the American avant-garde—among them Maya Deren, Stan Brakhage, Kenneth Anger, Bruce Conner, and Gregory Markopoulos. Vogel hoped to bring the Cinema 16 ethos to Lincoln Center and align it with Roud's art-film tastemaking. The first two editions of the NYFF suggested the possibilities: alongside a who's who of contemporary world cinema (Buñuel, Polanski, Godard, Rocha, Bresson, Satyajit Ray, Bertolucci, Resnais) there were such Cinema 16–worthy offerings as Adolfas Mekas's

*Hallelujah the Hills*, Jonas and Adolfas Mekas's *The Brig*, and future Italian softcore-porn director Tinto Brass's found-footage study of 20th-century revolutionary movements, *Ça ira*—not to mention short-form works like Robert Frank's *O.K. End Here*, Joris Ivens's *Valparaiso*, and Alfred Leslie's *The Last Clean Shirt*. There was also a selection of experimental animation pieces by Walerian Borowczyk, Robert Breer, Norman McLaren, and Stan VanDerBeek, all of whom would become NYFF regulars.

In subsequent editions of the Festival, however, Vogel's input was mainly kept at the margins in expansive and ambitious supplementary free-admission programs, most notably the 27-event "Independent Cinema" sidebar that was held at the Library Museum of Performing Arts in 1966. This featured, among other things, in-person presentations of Harry Smith's early abstract shorts and his *Heaven and Earth Magic* feature, Tony Conrad's *The Flicker*, Peter Goldman's *Echoes of Silence*, and Ed Emshwiller's *Relativity*, while among the participants in the numerous panel discussions and lectures were Rudolf Arnheim, Shirley Clarke (whose *Portrait of Jason* would debut in the Festival the following year), Parker Tyler, P. Adams Sitney, and Henry Geldzahler, while Annette Michelson's lecture, "Radicalism in Film," went on to become the basis for her famous essay "Film and Radical Aspiration." Though Jonas Mekas was an old rival of Vogel's, he was announced as a participant in three separate events—but in the end boycotted the whole thing.

Vogel's interests were catholic, and not confined to experimental film—for instance in 1967 he mounted a nine-film tribute to Abel Gance and organized the 20-event "Social Cinema in America" sidebar—during which, in a lecture entitled "Social Reality and the Avant-Garde," he discussed, per the Festival program's telling description "how non-realist films (intentionally or not) frequently render a more complex view of reality, as illustrated in the films of Brakhage, Conner, Emshwiller, VanDerBeek, and Warhol." But where *were* the films of Brakhage, and indeed Conner and Warhol, who had both designed exceptional posters for the Festival in 1965 and 1967

respectively? Conner didn't make the cut until 1978 with *Valse Triste*. As for Warhol, while 20-minute loops from four of his silents—*Kiss*, *Eat*, *Haircut*, and *Sleep*—were presented in a partitioned-off booth-like structure in the lobby of Philharmonic Hall in 1964 on four Fairchild 400 projection systems (a portable device that projected 8mm reduction prints onto a built-in screen) accompanied by a La Monte Young score, it wasn't until 2005 that this avant-garde film giant made his big-screen debut in the Festival with a restoration of his 1968 feature *Blue Movie*—18 years after his death. It would seem that Vogel's ideal fusion of Cinema 16 avant-gardism and Eurocentric art-film connoisseurship was a pipe dream, with just a handful of experimental films finding their way into the Festival as opening shorts, including works by James Whitney, Scott Bartlett, and James Broughton, as well as Robert Nelson's famous, and for some scandalizing, 1966 lampoon of racist stereotypes, *Oh Dem Watermelons*.

Ironically, the NYFF's failure to include the latest breakthroughs by experimental filmmakers in the main slate (partly because Avery Fisher Hall didn't acquire xenon 16mm projection capability until 1966) left it open to attack by Mekas—and this despite his inclusion in the Festival's second edition! Mekas was

not only one of the avant-garde's prime movers and a major filmmaker in his own right, but also wrote about film for *The Village Voice*. Columns protested against the Festival's rejection of Brakhage's *The Art of Vision* and Markopoulos's *Galaxie*. Much was made of the Festival's balking at paying a rental charge for Brakhage's *Songs* ("the festival saved $75 and lost probably its greatest film"), although how it would have been technically possible to project this 22-film Super-8 cycle in Alice Tully Hall is unclear. Mekas's attacks culminated in his August 1968 column, "Ten Reasons Why The New York Film Festival Should Be Closed." Curiously, he never lists those 10 reasons, but he does quote from a radical group's manifesto denouncing the Festival as "reactionary" and declaring that "its function is coping with rebellion . . . Lincoln Center's presentation of radical art, by plucking it out of the social context which could give it life and meaning, effectively nullifies whatever explosive content it might have had." Needless to say, this would hardly be the last time that the avant-garde film community would launch a polemical assault on the NYFF.

Vogel resigned after the Festival's 1968 edition, partly over the way he'd been sidelined by Roud, partly because he anticipated that the incorporation of the Festival as a not-for-profit

Jonas Mekas, Allen Ginsberg, and Richard Roud, 1966

*Flaming Creatures* by Jack Smith

under the auspices of the newly formed Film Society of Lincoln Center would open the door to board interference with its programming, and partly because his demand that a commitment to year-round film programming at Lincoln Center was rebuffed. As if to confirm Vogel's worst fears about compromise, the 1969 edition's Opening Night film was *Bob & Carol & Ted & Alice*, a Hollywood "zeitgeist" comedy starring Natalie Wood and Elliott Gould about two couples experimenting with swinging. Was it to head off accusations of "selling out" that Roud and his team saw fit not only to select films by Breer and Broughton, but also Jerome Hill, George Landow (aka Owen Land), Kenneth Anger, and Jordan Belson? Maybe— but that year also saw the presentation of an unprecedented nine-program survey of Californian experimental film, "Avant-Garde West," organized by Bob Sitton and featuring work by Bruce Baillie, Pat O'Neill, Chick Strand, Will Hindle, Larry Jordan, and soon-to-be-Festival-regulars Nelson and Belson—five of whom went on to become part of Anthology Film Archives' "Essential Cinema" canon. And in 1970 Roud made a rare endorsement of contemporary avant-garde film with the (as the Festival program would have it) world premiere of Hollis Frampton's *Zorns Lemma*, which was paired with British filmmaker Dick Fontaine's

experimental autobiographical documentary *Double Pisces*, *Scorpio Rising*, featuring Amanda Lear, Eduardo Paolozzi, Jean Shrimpton, Norman Mailer, and music by Pete Townshend. Frampton's film provoked a small riot in the theater, but the filmmaker was invited back the following year to show *Nostalgia* and the Festival's engagement with the avant-garde would culminate in 1972 when none other than Jonas Mekas would return to Lincoln Center with his feature-length *Reminiscences of a Journey to Lithuania*, which was programmed with his brother Adolfas's companion piece film, *Going Home*. That year also saw the notorious screening of Philippe Garrel's decidedly avant *The Inner Scar*, starring Pierre Clémenti and Nico, which seems to have been the straw that broke the camel's back—according to one eyewitness, the audience loudly ridiculed the film and sought to disrupt the screening, with one viewer, taking his cue from Garrel's endless circular tracking shots, leading a chorus of "I've been working on the railroad."

It wouldn't be until the appointment of J. Hoberman to the Festival selection committee in 1982 that avant-garde film would make a brief comeback. Probably no other committee member since Vogel had demonstrated as deep a commitment to and knowledgeability about underground and avant-garde cinema past and

present, as a viewer, maker, and sometime programmer and writer. (Indeed, the *Village Voice* film critic's own experimental collage film, *Mission to Mongo*, had screened the previous year in the "Movies for Cynics" sidebar in "Short Cuts," a program devoted to satirical shorts that also included pieces by Conner and Nelson.) Hoberman's influence was immediately apparent with the inclusion of Beth B and Scott B's feature *Vortex* in the 1982 lineup—nothing probably seemed less likely than that these quintessential denizens of the No Wave cinema scene (a short-lived Downtown New York post-punk movement) would wind up in Alice Tully Hall. That said, Godfrey Reggio's ersatz-avant *Koyaanisqatsi* also made the cut, screening at Radio City no less.

In retrospect it could be argued that Hoberman's activism came at a pivotal moment—an indisputably establishment festival had become almost completely disengaged from and indifferent to an avant-garde movement that many both inside and outside the experimental scene were beginning to regard as moribund and irrelevant. In fact, the American avant-garde, far from stagnating, had already moved on and was in the process of another renaissance—but the landscape had shifted. In broad strokes, if the '60s represented an era of dramatic sociocultural upheaval and possibility, the '70s was America's dark night of the soul, and a sense of malaise and doubt seemed to permeate the cultural landscape—and just around the corner were the culture wars and backlash of Reagan's '80s. These sea changes manifested themselves in all the arts, but whereas avant-garde cinema had once seemed almost fashionable, at least within the context of '60s counterculture, many of its prime movers had spent the '70s entrenching themselves in academia and to the casual observer must have seemed off the radar—if they had ever been on it, that is. The influence of the first generation of the American avant-garde on mainstream filmmakers is now an accepted fact. NYFF discovery Martin Scorsese, for one, has cited the impact on him of films like Anger's *Scorpio Rising*, while Jack Smith's *Flaming Creatures*, a relatively widely seen and notoriously transgressive film certainly had an effect on and intersected with the work of filmmakers as diverse as Fellini, Waters, and Fassbinder, even if the effect on them was unquantifiable and there were a number of degrees of separation between them. (The NYFF's presentation of a restoration of Smith's landmark in 1991 might be taken as confirmation of this.) By the end of the '60s, the ranks of the first generation were swelled by artists such as Michael Snow, Hollis Frampton, Morgan Fisher, Paul Sharits, and George Landow, exponents of what P. Adams Sitney dubbed "structural cinema."

By the late 1970s, a second generation of artists born in the '40s and '50s was beginning to emerge. Hoberman demonstrated that the avant-garde had continued to advance and evolve, successfully lobbying on behalf of more established second-generation filmmakers like Ernie Gehr and George Kuchar but also emerging figures like Manuel De Landa, Trinh T. Minh-ha, and Ericka Beckman, whose *You the Better* was paired with Godard's *Passion*. (Her film received the requisite hostile reception from the audience, but then Godard took to the stage and declared himself glad to have had his film shown with Beckman's.)

Predictably, with the departure of Hoberman, the Festival reverted to the tokenist approach that had prevailed since 1972—every now and then an experimental film of real stature would somehow sneak in, as Fisher's *Standard Gauge* did in 1985, while multimedia artist Anita Thacher's films were included a number of times—and Thacher was also responsible for the Festival's first bona fide installation, *Light*house, which was presented in Alice Tully Hall's lobby in 1981 and paid tribute to a recently deceased photographer by the name of Francesca Woodman.

Roud's successor, Richard Peña, broke with the past in a number of ways. Among other things, he launched an annual dedicated experimental film slot, initially dubbed "Avant-Garde Voices," and renamed "Avant-Garde Visions" in 1989. Far more knowledgeable and appreciative of experimental film than Roud, Peña paid equal homage to figures from the older generation who continued to endure (Strand, Brakhage, Ken Jacobs, Pat O'Neill,

*Side/Walk/Shuttle* by Ernie Gehr

and most notably Ernie Gehr's *Side/Walk/Shuttle*) and to younger artists, who came of age in the late '70s (important films such as Su Friedrich's *Sink or Swim* as well as work by Warren Sonbert, Abigail Child, Vivienne Dick, Isaac Julien). The audience walkout rate was often high, and schizophrenically, filmmakers regarded "Visions" as both tokenist and prestigious, if only because it enjoyed equal status with the Festival's other offerings. Peña and his team, myself among them from the mid-90s onward, also programmed the opening short films with additional experimental work by new-to-the-Festival artists such as Lewis Klahr, Robert Beavers, and Janie Geiser, as well as Germany's Matthias Müller and Austria's Martin Arnold, at long last internationalizing the scope of the avant-garde selections. It was also on Peña's watch that Yvonne Rainer finally made her NYFF debut— with 1990's *Privilege*, her fifth feature. Despite claims to the contrary, there continued to be a tremendous outpouring of avant-garde work in the '80s and '90s, but the increasingly moribund state of avant-garde exhibition had rendered much of the new generation invisible. Moreover, while the culture wars of the '80s

saw unprecedented attacks on the avant-garde community by forces hostile to its activities, factionalization also undermined the movement from within. "Visions" was only the tip of the iceberg of experimental filmmaking during this period—but at least the Festival acknowledged the iceberg's existence and significance.

Peña also began to redress the Festival's previous obliviousness to new media forms that began to emerge in the art world and elsewhere in the '70s, including commercial derivations of avant-garde aesthetics, such as music videos (another thing that Hoberman had managed to program in the 1984 edition). In 1992, "Videorama," the first edition of an annual sidebar in the Walter Reade dedicated exclusively to work made on video was launched with 11 programs curated by Peña and Marian Masone. (The following year it was rebranded as "Video Visions," and from the third edition onward became the New York Video Festival.) An incredibly wide spectrum of work was presented here, much of it with an avant-garde emphasis. Suddenly the playing field was level: experimental filmmakers like Kuchar, Ken Kobland, Peggy Ahwesh, Mark Rappaport, and Joe Gibbons, early adopters of video all, mingled freely with both avant-leaning art-cinema renegades like Ruiz, Godard, Greenaway, and Marker, and contemporary video artists like Bill Viola, Cheryl Donnegan, and Matthew Barney—and now there was a space for fascinating feature-length experiments like the Wooster Group's *White Homeland Commando* and Sophie Calle's collaboration with Gregory Shephard, *Double Blind (No Sex Last Night)*. While a new wing of the avant-garde was already materializing in the still-evolving realm of video, with its own distinct aesthetic possibilities in terms of hybridity and non-filmic expressive values, only the Walter Reade was equipped with video projection, and so a de facto segregation of film and video came into effect. It was only with the advent of the digital revolution that these aesthetic restrictions no longer held.

Rigid categories were also breaking down in other ways. By the early '90s, it was clear that there were now other players in the game who didn't necessarily identify themselves as avant-garde filmmakers. Whether from the art world or from independent film, people like the Quay Brothers, Guy Maddin, Tracey Moffat, Luc Moullet, and John Greyson began to appear in the Festival with work that exhibited more or less experimental qualities. This development was encouraging in the sense that it represented an escape from narrow definitions of avant-garde film that had held in the Festival even into the '90s—hence the inclusion of films like Todd Haynes's *Dottie Gets Spanked* in "Visions" in 1993. On the face of it the 1994 program, consisting of Mani Kaul's *The Cloud Door*, Aleksandr Sokurov's *Whispering Pages*, and Teresa De Pelegri's short *Roig*, appeared to further this broadening of definitions. In reality, the selection committee was drawing a blank when it came to experimental work that year, and it was presumably expedient to shuffle the Kaul and Sokurov films, which had been selected but needed to be placed, into the section. It was less a matter of the committee being unable to find interesting experimental work per se and more that no one knew how to program them together and make them work as a coherent whole. The avant-garde leanings and affinities of the Kaul and Sokurov films were undeniable (*Roig* not so much) but the resulting program was odd in light of earlier editions. Finally, although there was an abundance of new avant-garde work out there to be had, in 1996 the selection committee were unable to come up with a program for "Visions" at all—despite the fact that experimental films by Janie Geiser, Robert Beavers, Lewis Klahr, and David Sherman, not to mention a music video by Robert Frank, were chosen as opening shorts.

Although the non-appearance of "Visions" in 1996 wasn't necessarily a shot heard round the world, it presented an opening. I proposed that the Festival invite programmer Mark McElhatten to take charge of the section, with me as co-pilot. As a 20-year veteran experimental-film curator, McElhatten was

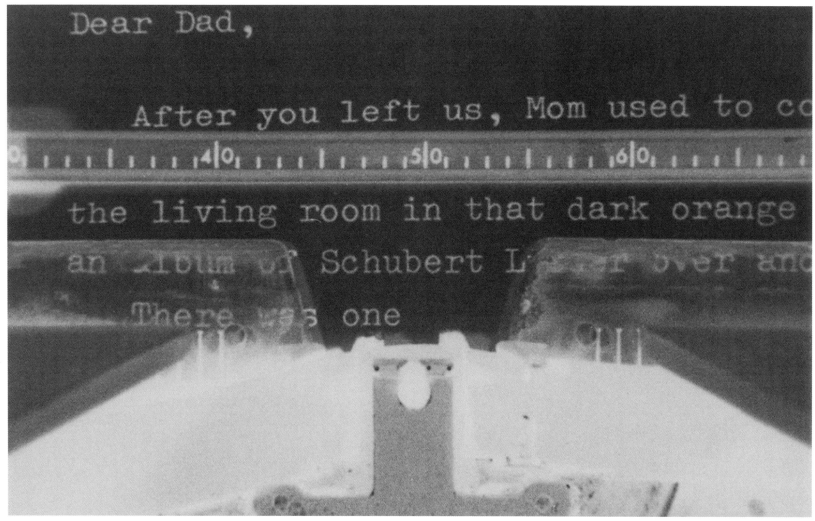

*Sink or Swim* by Su Friedrich

*Twilight Psalm II: Walking Distance* by Phil Solomon

uniquely qualified to bring a combination of expertise, experience, and in-depth knowledge of the field—not to mention the strong relationships with many artists both near and far—to reinvent the Festival's avant-garde programs. At the same time, his distinctive sensibility and discerning point of view would take things to a new level. Peña generously agreed to delegate responsibility for the selection of experimental film to the two of us. In 1997, an expanded, four-program section was launched, relocated from Alice Tully Hall to the Walter Reade Theater, which though a much smaller house, was vastly superior in terms of projection and sound, more flexible, and conducive to growth. The first edition of the section, renamed "Views from the Avant-Garde," attracted large audiences who were ready to make the necessary commitment to watch sometimes demanding work with attentiveness—in contrast to the Alice Tully Hall ticket holders of former years, many of whom voted with their feet. The gradual expansion every year thereafter (there were 24 programs in 2011) was only slightly a result of the backlog of important work that had never previously screened in New York. For the most part, it was a testament to the sheer volume of work

that was being produced every year in America and, to a lesser extent, overseas. Moreover, in the fifth year of "Views," with increasing numbers of avant-garde artists migrating from 16mm to digital or working in both media, the artificial segregation of video from film (resulting, ironically, from jurisdictional competition with the New York Video Festival, which was decoupled from the NYFF in 1996) finally came to an end, greatly increasing the size of the pool of work eligible for selection.

This expanded showcase for the avant-garde wasn't intended to address the diminishing of experimental work at the NYFF or to pretend to revive what the Festival had attempted in the Vogel era so much as create a new context and opportunity that was very modest at first.

Although some regarded the move to the Walter Reade as a downgrading of experimental film, "Views" had tremendous impact and a lot of critical pressure came to bear on it because it arrived at a moment of need in New York and had a high profile. Before its advent, exhibition of experimental film in New York was polarized between high (the Museum of Modern Art) and low (peripatetic, intermittent microcinemas in makeshift settings) with little activity happening week to week in any stable

midrange alternative space. Within a few years of "Views"'s launch, an ongoing revival in the exhibition of avant-garde work in New York gained momentum, while "Views"'s success also inspired other major film festivals—most notably Toronto, London, and Hong Kong, to create programs of a similar character. "Views" also represented the strong reassertion of the tradition of formalist experimentation that many felt was in danger of being disenfranchised.

To caricature the situation, after the splintering of the avant-garde film community in the '80s and '90s, things had become polarized between those championing issue-oriented work and those favoring aesthetic experimentation—as if the two things need be mutually exclusive. Those who attended those early editions of "Views" stood ready to be counted and heard according to whether they upheld or disavowed its unmistakable affirmation of formalist explorations—within a framework that welcomed and embraced avant-garde tendencies of every stripe.

Many key second-generation filmmakers made their NYFF debuts in the first years of "Views"—Mark LaPore (*Five Bad Elements*), Phil Solomon (*Twilight Psalm II: Walking Distance*), Julie Murray, Leslie Thornton, Peter Hutton, Peggy Ahwesh, Luther Price, Jim Jennings, Scott Stark, Fred Worden, Vincent Grenier—and all became mainstays. Filmmakers reaching the top of their game and attaining international acclaim such as James Benning (*RR*) would also become part of the mix. Nathaniel Dorsky returned to New York to show new work for the first time in years, kicking off in the flagship edition of "Views" with *Triste* and going on to became one of its defining figures.

Meanwhile, the emergence of a new, third generation of filmmakers was well underway, and "Views" became an important place for them to show their work: among those it would be impossible not to mention are David Gatten, Kerry Laitala, Jennifer Reeves, Stephanie Barber, Bobby Abate, Michael Robinson, Ben Rivers, Laida Lertxundi, Jonathan Schwartz, Deborah Stratman, and Tomonari Nishikawa—and there are dozens more.

In terms of international work, Austrian and

*RR* by James Benning

*Triste* by Nathaniel Dorsky

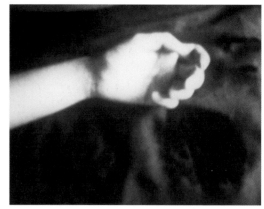

*Five Bad Elements* by Mark LaPore

German artists in particular had demonstrated a long-standing affinity with the American avant-garde dating back to the films of Peter Kubelka and Kurt Kren in the '60s. "Views," like "Avant-Garde Visions" before it, championed the work of Peter Tscherkassky (particularly his stunning *Outer Space*), Martin Arnold, Dietmar Brehm, Matthias Müller, and Heinz Emigholz.

The reach of "Views'"s programming has also extended in several other ways. Firstly, it has regularly presented restorations of vintage work, ranging from major first generation filmmakers—Markopoulos, Anger, Warhol, Conner, Mekas, Jacobs, Strand, Kuchar, Larry Gottheim, Saul Levine—to lesser known or overlooked figures such as Canada's Arthur Lipsett, England's Jeff Keen, and Italy's Paolo Gioli. Secondly, it has been able to mount a

handful of projection performances, including Ken Jacobs's Nervous System presentation in 1998 and Nervous Magic Lantern show in 2002, and 16mm and Super-8 performances by Bruce McClure and Paul Clipson respectively.

To bring things full circle, to Vogel's idea of what the NYFF could aspire to, in a modest way "Views" has also managed to some degree to create a wider space in which the definition of avant-garde film is able to encompass filmmakers who have been fixtures of mainstream art cinema and the NYFF itself for in some cases many years—work by Godard, Pasolini, Oliveira, Costa, Apichatpong, Maddin, Straub-Huillet, and Norman Mailer has all appeared in "Views."

If the experimental programming at the NYFF during the Vogel era was exciting, partially representative, but not crucial, and during the

early Peña era became a small but important gesture, with the advent and robust growth of "Views," it has moved to the forefront, functioning as a vital and valuable program even as the definitions and contours of the avant-garde remain in flux. In this sense "Views" makes a significant contribution to the enterprise of the NYFF. New York remains one of the world's cultural capitals and, as one of the city's leading cultural events, the NYFF's prestige remains undimmed. However, in an era where film festivals have proliferated across the U.S., the NYFF now has competition when it comes to agenda-setting—while "Views," as the country's only event of its kind in terms of scale and visibility, can lay claim to having a significant national and international impact. 🎥

*Outer Space* by Peter Tscherkassky

*Napoleon* by Abel Gance

# FRINGE BENEFITS

SIDEBARS, SYMPOSIA, AND OTHER SPECIAL EVENTS

*Wendy Keys*

THE NEW YORK FILM FESTIVAL IS MORE than the sum of its films. While adhering to the idea of being a small, strongly curated affair, four years in it cautiously branched out to create sidebar events that reflected its ever-evolving tastes, desire for experimentation, and the zeitgeist of the times. These events—which stirred up controversy and excitement and helped to widen the Festival's scope—took a variety of forms: film series (both contemporary and revival), thematic panels, art installations, and summer retrospectives.

## FILM SERIES

In 1966, I began my career at the New York Film Festival, which was then entering its 4th year. Among my duties were the side programs, some of which reflected the rebellious nature of the era. Others were documentary and experimental-film surveys with titles like "Direct Cinema," "Radical Cinema," "Personal Cinema," and "Expanded Cinema." We introduced the independent filmmakers Jim McBride, the Maysles Brothers, Tony Conrad, Stan VanDerBeek, and in 1967 we premiered Frederick Wiseman's *Titicut Follies* to a rioting turn-away crowd. All sidebar events were offered free of charge in the auditorium of the Library Museum of Lincoln Center and, to our great delight, often attracted large, unruly audiences. During the early years we also presented the award winners from the National Student Film Festival, auto-documentaries by street gangs (*Let's Get Nice* by the Potheads comes to mind), beautifully animated films by kindergarten children from the Yellow Ball Workshop, public-television documentaries, and war and propaganda films.

During our 1967 series "Social Cinema in America," I vividly recall a screening of Santiago Álvarez's *Now*, a Cuban film about the American civil-rights movement that featured scenes of police assaulting peaceful demonstrators with high-pressure water hoses set to the rousing music of "Hava Nagila." Halfway through the film the police entered the theater, stopped the

*Blood and Sand* by Rouben Mamoulian

projection, and told everyone to look under their seats; apparently someone had lost some valuable jewelry. The crowd went wild, the police were quickly routed, and the screening resumed. I later learned that there had been a bomb scare, and the police, furious with the reception of their disruption, seemed inclined to let the bomb go off.

Over the years the NYFF organized retrospectives of Abel Gance (in 1967 at Avery Fisher Hall we screened the first of many iterations of *Napoleon* to come), Jean Renoir, and Luis Buñuel. William K. Everson curated a marvelous retrospective of the early Western, which included *Tumbleweeds*, the film that features William S. Hart's touching farewell speech, in which, astride his horse, he bids adieu to his fans. And in 1969 we began our commitment to experimental cinema with a program called "Avant-Garde West," which introduced young filmmakers who were among the stalwarts of the avant-garde movement—Bruce Baillie, the Whitney Brothers, Larry Jordan, James Broughton, and Jordan Belson, to name a few.

In 1970 we presented a series called "Cinema and Color." The program notes emphatically announced that the majority of films in the Festival were now in color, and because black

and white was the exception rather than the rule it was time to survey the different color processes. We displayed examples of hand-painted films, tinted and toned, Fujicolor and Technicolor. The gorgeous saturated colors of *Blood and Sand* left the biggest impression on me. Henri Langlois, the curator of this event, met Martin Scorsese, whose *Street Scenes 1970* was showing in the main slate, and alerted him to the difficulties with the preservation of color negatives and prints. Scorsese's advocacy in this

area is now widely known.

There are four series that I remember with particular fondness because they provided me with the opportunity to do some creative programming. In 1976 we presented an ambitious survey of animation, featuring a total of five programs and 76 films that ranged from Walt Disney and Tex Avery to the contemporary works of Robert Breer and George Griffin, whose charming short *The Club* featured penises frequenting a traditional men's club. I submitted a still from Griffin's film to *The New York Times* as part of our promotion, and for some reason I took it as a personal triumph when they printed it. This program of animation for adults was accompanied by a splendid exhibit of storyboards, clay figures, and sandboxes—all works of participating filmmakers. It was also well attended and enthusiastically reviewed—the *Times* cited it as "an innovative festival; both a constructive service for the artists involved and for discriminating moviegoers . . . proof that the film animation genre has come a long way."

The NYFF collaborated with the American Film Institute on a few retrospectives of salvaged and restored films, and in 1977 we presented a series called "Saved!" made up of 11 films culled from a variety of American archives. An example of the interaction between the different sections of the Festival occurred in the midst of this series when Bernardo Bertolucci, after seeing

*The Club* by George Griffin

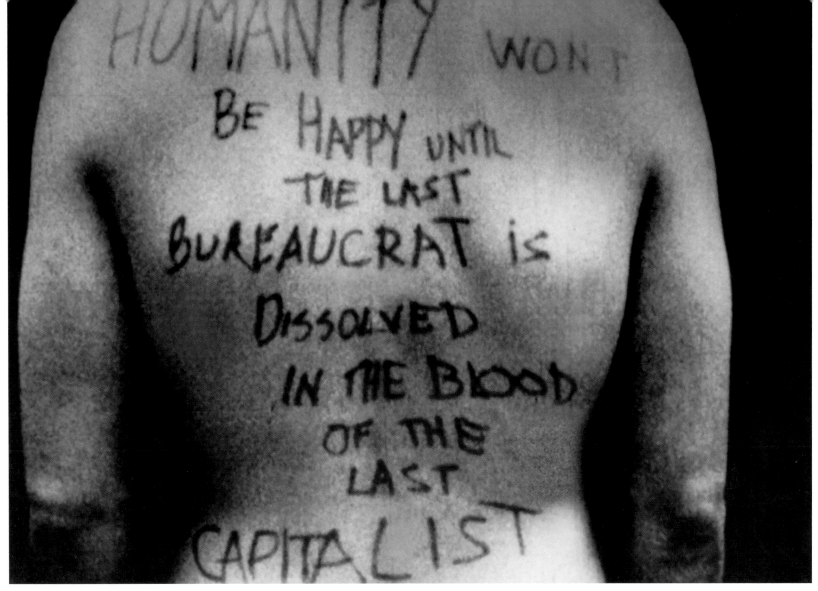

*Ice* by Robert Kramer

Murnau's *City Girl*, decided then and there to make some changes to his *1900* because Murnau's film provided him with an idea for a scene transition that he hadn't thought of previously.

The next year brought "New Currents in Japanese Cinema," which included an extraordinary light show employing stepladders and stagehands being directed by Shuji Terayama (in Japanese) on the stage of Alice Tully Hall.

Another highlight of this series was a reconstructed version of Shohei Imamura's *The Pornographers*, which Alan Poul from the Japan Society and I helped to assemble from pieces of film found all over the world, including a cave in Southern France.

In response to the criticism that the Festival was too Eurocentric, we featured a significant series of American Independent film in 1979.

It included Shirley Clarke's *The Cool World*, Paul Morrissey's *Trash*, Robert Kramer's *Ice*, Terrence Malick's *Badlands*, as well as films by Mark Rappaport, the Mekas Brothers, Melvin Van Peebles, Robert M. Young, and Richard Pearce. Subsequently some of these filmmakers entered the mainstream—Pearce, whose *Country* opened the NYFF in 1984, and Malick, perhaps most notably.

The following year, in conjunction with the

Martin Sheen and Terrence Malick on the set of *Badlands*

Nicolas Roeg, 1980

Jessica Lange and Richard Pearce, 1984

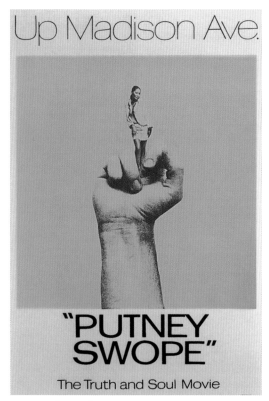

## Up Madison Ave.

"PUTNEY SWOPE"

The Truth and Soul Movie

Poster for *Putney Swope* by Robert Downey Sr.

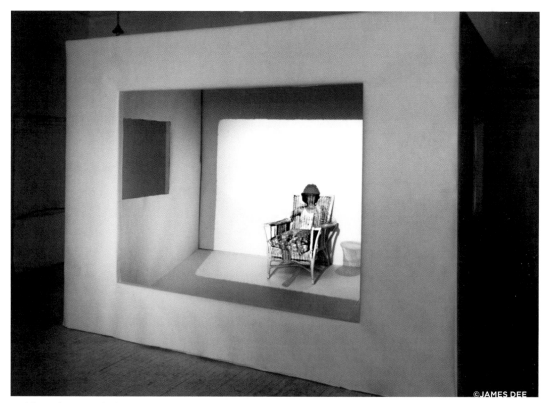

*Light*house by Anita Thacher, 1981

British Film Institute, we presented "British Film Now," which featured works by Nicolas Roeg, Derek Jarman, and Ken Loach and introduced new British talents Mike Leigh and Stephen Frears to American audiences. Princess Michael of Kent gave an Opening Night speech in which she quoted Prince Charles saying that he hoped that after several days of film-watching we all wouldn't end up with square eyes. All the cinephiles groaned.

Amidst the new cinema on display, our popular homages to the past remained popular, and they were twice offset by surveys illustrating the future of film technology. In 1980 more than 50 organizations exhibited new devices for us, and the following year we had an all-day event titled "Channeling the Future: Cable and New TV." Alan Hirschfield, Chairman of 20th Century Fox, gave the keynote address and we had a series of town-hall meetings and panels, one of which was called "The New TV – Will It Be Gutenberg or Glut," with Gloria Steinem, Lincoln Center's John Goberman, and others weighing in. The day generated a great deal of interest from the industry.

In 1981, supplementing the 19th NYFF, came one of my favorite series from my long tenure at the Film Society. "Movies for Cynics"

was devoted to social and political satire and commentary. Among those who participated in lively discussions following their films were Robert Downey Sr., Bill Richert, John Guare, and Buck Henry. Colorful and iconoclastic, they all contributed greatly to the renegade spirit of the series. I remember chatting happily on stage with Downey following the screening of *Putney Swope* when his cinematographer, who was in the audience, pointed out that reels 4 and 5 had been reversed. Bob took it well—he said he hadn't even noticed and everyone laughed. This was the first of only two projection glitches I can remember over 49 years. Not bad!

### THEMATIC PANELS

NYFF panels and lectures started out being closely associated to the themes of our special events and post-screening Q&As, but in 1971 I coordinated stand-alone panels not specifically tied to anything appearing at the Festival. Three stick out in my memory—not for their erudition but for their lack of decorum. The first was "Screenwriters and Novelists," which was moderated by Brendan Gill and included James Dickey, Terry Southern, Kurt Vonnegut Jr., David Newman, and Buck Henry. The bad

behavior began at an elegant dinner hosted by Martin Segal at Le Poullaillier, where Dickey became very drunk and argumentative and Southern was stoned. To make matters worse, Dickey threw up backstage just before they all went on. The other panelists, considered to be a voluble bunch, were muted with terror onstage and Gill ended up doing all the talking, for which he was chastised in *Variety* the next day.

The second unfortunate event sabotaged by bad behavior started at a dinner preceding the panel called "Women in Film" that was moderated by Molly Haskell and included Barbara Loden, Eleanor Perry, and Nadine Trintignant. The Board member hosting the dinner made insulting remarks about the abilities of women, which rattled this highly accomplished group. During the panel John Simon pointed out how it was "interesting that supposedly behind every great man there was a women and that each of the women on stage had a great man behind them." This was greeted by a stunned silence until Eleanor Perry looked out into the audience and said with contempt, "Oh, is that you, John?" and everyone laughed, diffusing the tension. Ah, 1971!

A week later David Steinberg moderated

a panel on Hollywood, "The Establishment and the Challengers," whose participants included Henry Jaglom, Jack Nicholson, Dennis Hopper, and Otto Preminger. Hopper stole the spotlight that night with a drug-fueled stream-of-consciousness monologue, leaving the usually voluble Preminger speechless. We presented additional panels that were of interest—and more civilized. But in 1972 we returned to our earlier format of filmmakers discussing their work post-screening.

In addition to poster and photo exhibits displayed each year in the lobby of Alice Tully Hall we presented three art installations of which we were proud. The first, in 1977, was developed at MIT by Stan VanDerBeek and Joan Brigham. Evocative and charmingly mysterious, it consisted of an animated film projected onto a screen of steam vapor.

In 1981 we featured Anita Thacher's

*Light*house, in which the spectator would enter a small house with a wicker chair to view projected life-sized images of a young woman. Dedicated to photographer Francesca Woodman, who had just committed suicide at the age of 22, the installation invited viewers to become part of the space, in which the film offers the haunting effect of Woodman being brought back to life.

The third installation was *Chain Reaction* by Lynn Hershman. It consisted of film projected onto the six south-facing windows of the old Tully Hall, offering the passersby on 65th Street a narrative told by six characters who give the illusion that they are really inside the building. The grand finale made it look as though Tully Hall was on fire!

Also drawing in the art crowd (as well as the film crowd and the in-crowd in general) were our two must-see Radio City Music Hall screenings in 1982-83: *Koyaanisqatsi*, with a live score by Philip Glass, and the 1929 silent classic, *The New Babylon*, with a live orchestra performing a newly discovered score by Dmitry Shostakovich. *The New Babylon* screening was immortalized by Don DeLillo in his master-piece *Underworld*.

### SUMMER RETROSPECTIVES

In the first 25 years we presented three summer retrospectives as offshoots of the NYFF. The first, in 1983, included an outstanding array of 52 of the most cherished films from our first decade. The following year we presented 46 films from our second decade. It was a terrific way to demonstrate the impact and influence the Festival had had on American film culture during those years. In the summer of 1985, six months after François Truffaut's death, we presented "Truffaut Plus," a full retrospective of his work, matched with the films he most loved. Standing on the stage to welcome audiences on Opening Night, I said: "For many years François Truffaut stood on this stage…"—and then burst into uncontrollable sobbing. After what seemed like an eternity, I got a grip on myself and continued. Mortified, I considered leaving the country forever, until people assured me they had cried along with me.

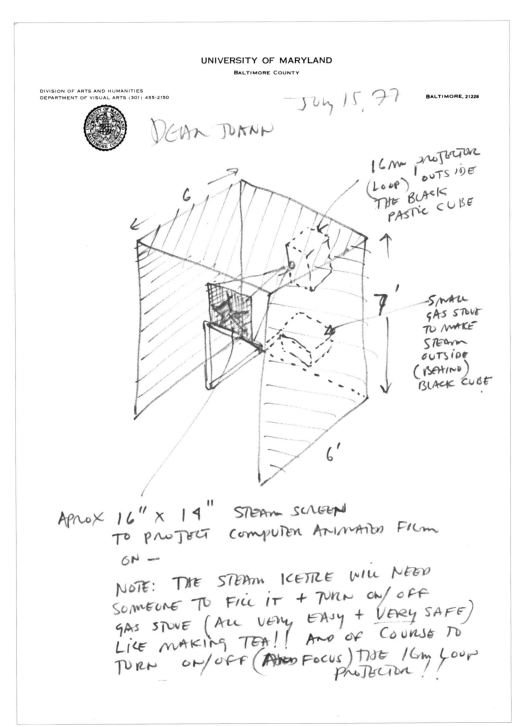

The specifications that Stan VanDerBeek sent to the NYFF for his steam projection machine, 1977

*The New Babylon* by Grigori Kozintsev and Leonid Trauberg

*Koyaanisqatsi* by Godfrey Reggio

At the 26th New York Film Festival, Richard Peña succeeded Richard Roud as director, and he went on to oversee the retrospectives and special events that complemented the main slate. I joined the Festival's selection committee and assumed other Film Society responsibilities, but I will always think fondly of those rough-and-tumble years when the NYFF was forging its identity and film viewing in America was coming of age. 🎥

Gérard Depardieu and François Truffaut, 1981

Radio City Music Hall showing *Koyaanisqatsi*, 1982

*In the Realm of the Senses* by Nagisa Oshima

# HOT PEPPERS & HOT TICKETS

## COPING WITH CENSORSHIP

*Joanne Koch*

*HAIL MARY, TITICUT FOLLIES*, AND *IN THE Realm of the Senses* are just a few of the films that faced obstacles before they were able to fill New York Film Festival screens. The concerns they raised included censorship (mostly due to sexual content), rights of privacy, political and religious conflicts, and the boundaries of copyright law.

The assumed responsibility of the Festival's administration has from the beginning been to assure the exhibition of any and all films chosen by its programmers. This applied to the Film Society as well as to Lincoln Center, the presenter of the event for its first six years, before the Film Society became an independent constituent. Fortunately, the Boards of both institutions firmly supported this mandate.

The most immediate challenge international film programmers faced in the early years was U.S. Customs, which would ordinarily screen all films entering the country to look for content that did not meet its stringent guidelines. The New York State Board of Regents and the City Department of Licenses were also potential hurdles.

Fortunately for the Festival, Amos Vogel, who had been hired to run it, called upon John Mazzola, Lincoln Center's legal counsel, to deal with film-import regulations. Mazzola had a history with U.S. Customs—earlier in his career he had established a friendship with a customs agent when expediting a large shipment of capsicum peppers from Africa. That friendship was later instrumental in arranging a waiver of censorship requirements for any film bound for the Festival. Each film was personally addressed to Mazzola, who was then responsible for overseeing the number of screenings and the return of the films to their source or distributor. After U.S. Customs issued the waiver, both the Regents and the City Department of Licenses followed along. So in its formative years, the Festival owes it freedom from government censorship in large measure to a shipment of chili peppers!

This arrangement prevailed from 1963-67.

*Exhibiton* by Jean-François Davy

Subsequently, we were permitted to import films for selection purposes without prior examination. Once slated for public exhibition, though, they had to be offered to Customs for screening. Over the next 10 years, just two films were challenged: *Exhibition*, in 1975, a minor snafu, and *In the Realm of the Senses*, in 1976, which provoked a major contretemps.

### EXHIBITION, 1975

When *Exhibition*, Jean-François Davy's documentary about the public and private life of France's premiere sex-film star, Claudine Beccarie, screened at the Cannes Film Festival, the French cultural Ministry Chief, Hubert Astier, issued a statement recognizing that although the film "goes quite far in its sex sequences, to a graphicness and permissiveness

of vision never before achieved, it could not propose a total prohibition because of its exceptional human testimony." It was suggested that the screening be prefaced with the words: "Very provocative film in its expression and images. Not recommended for a delicate public."

*Exhibition* was allowed into the U.S. on bond, but once selected by the Festival committee it was delivered to Customs for the required screening. In early September we were notified that the film had been seized under U.S. Code, Title 19 (a Federal law prohibiting the importation of obscene materials) and that Customs had requested the U.S. Attorney for the Eastern District of New York to begin forfeiture proceedings.

Tickets for the Festival had already gone

on sale so we quickly informed ticket buyers of the situation, and assured them that we would contest the seizure and offer refunds or a substitute film if necessary. After being screened by Department of Justice attorneys in New York and Washington, the film was released. But for the first time, the Festival refused admittance to anyone under 18. Needless to say, *Exhibition* was an especially hot ticket.

### IN THE REALM OF THE SENSES, 1976

A sensation at Cannes, Nagisa Oshima's film follows an obsessive love affair in the '30s—between a middle-aged man, who's married to a geisha house owner, and a newly arrived geisha—that ends in a graphic castration. It was described in our program guide as

*Titicut Follies* by Frederick Wiseman

"marking a genuine breakthrough for the serious artistic treatment of explicit sex." Although the selection committee was divided on the film (Richard Roud was not a fan), it was enthusiastically supported by those who voted for its inclusion.

In the January-February 1977 issue of *Film Comment*, Film Society attorney and Board member James Bouras, who has worked tirelessly, pro bono, for more than three decades to clear up all legal matters concerning potential programming interference, detailed what happened next.

In summary, the print of *In the Realm of the Senses* arrived in Los Angeles and was released by Customs without being screened. New York Customs officials questioned the propriety of the film's entry into L.A. and insisted that Government representatives attend our press screening. Following that, Customs advised the Film Society and Anatole Dauman, *Realm*'s producer, that had the film entered through New York it would have been detained and turned over to the U.S. Attorney. We were then told that the print would be seized if we attempted to show it, and it was ominously implied that other legal proceedings might ensue. As a result, for the first time in the history of the NYFF, the public screenings were canceled. An earlier Oshima film, *The*

*Ceremony*, was substituted, and audiences were offered the option of a refund or to hold on to their tickets for a later performance in the event the original film could be shown. Just 565 refunds were issued, leaving 1,570 people willing to hold out for possible later screenings.

The Film Society's Board President, Martin E. Segal, read a statement to the audience describing Customs' actions as an "unwarranted interference with artistic freedom and artistic judgment" that threatens a "dangerous precedent."

An additional brouhaha occurred following the press conference in which Dauman asked a question regarding Customs' still-pending action that Roud refrained from answering, in adherence to Bouras's instruction. Roud had previously panned the film in *The Guardian*, so when he refused to respond to the question, Dauman accused Roud of attempting to sabotage the entry of the film.

Dauman refused to surrender the print and filed suit against the Commissioner of Customs for the New York area and the United States. On November 9, after further legal back-and-forth, Federal District Judge Marvin E. Frankel characterized the Customs actions against *In the Realm of the Senses* as an "outrage" and announced that he would forbid Customs from pursuing its recall demand or "from otherwise proceeding against the film in question or

prints thereof" under the Federal law against the importation of obscene material. This had nothing to do with whether the film was obscene—but it was a firm condemnation of New York Customs procedures.

Alice Tully Hall wasn't available to the Film Society at this time, so the Museum of Modern Art offered their theater, where I introduced *In the Realm of the Senses* at four separate screenings shortly after the film's release from Customs. Thus, we did not damage our record. Over the life of the Festival, every film scheduled has eventually reached the screen.

This was our final run-in with Customs. Some 20 years ago, the laws were changed to prohibit only what is considered obscene in terms of community values. Because New York City, as one would expect, has a broad definition of redeeming artistic value, the New York Import Compliance Division was disbanded, although the Festival is still required to sign an affidavit stating that an incoming film "contains no obscene or immoral matter."

### TITICUT FOLLIES, 1967

The Festival's first censorship challenge outside of Customs came with Frederick Wiseman's debut documentary, described by Vincent Canby in *The New York Times* as "a calm, cool and ultimately horrifying look at conditions at

*Last Tango in Paris* by Bernardo Bertolucci

the state prison for the criminally insane at Bridge-water, Mass. … An extraordinarily candid picture of a modern Bedlam, where the horrors are composed of indifference and patronizing concern." Titicut is the Indian name for Bridgewater, and the film's title comes from a talent show presented by the hospital's inmates. The film was scheduled to screen as part of the Festival's special program called "Social Cinema in America." Embarrassed by the film, the Massachusetts government tried to secure an injunction prohibiting its release, claiming it violated the patients' privacy and dignity. Wiseman had obtained the patients' permission, but the state claimed they needed formal releases. The issue went to trial in the Supreme Court of the State of New York. John Mazzola argued for Lincoln Center, on behalf of the Festival, and the film was shown in the courtroom to the presiding judge, Timothy Murphy. The day before the scheduled Festival screening, Judge Murphy ruled there was no cause to prohibit the film. Consequently, *Titicut Follies* was presented at Lincoln Center's Bruno Walter Auditorium and several hundred people stood in the rain clamoring for tickets. Soon after, it opened at the Cinema Rendezvous in Manhattan. The distributor of *Titicut Follies* was Grove Press, where, coincidentally, I was working at that time as the personal assistant to Grove's publisher, Barney Rosset. A month after the film's Festival screening,

I received a subpoena issued on behalf of the correctional officers featured in the film, who claimed defamation and invasion of privacy. A Federal Court decision ruled that the First Amendment overrides traditional laws of libel where subjects of public interest are involved, even though the plaintiffs are government employees of subordinate status and not at all known to the public.

Then, in 1968, a Massachusetts judge ordered that the film be yanked from distribution and all copies be destroyed, claiming that Wiseman still hadn't obtained valid releases from the inmates who appear in the film, some of them naked and others in the throes of mental illness. Wiseman appealed this decision and in 1969 the Massachu-setts Supreme Judicial Court allowed it to be screened for mental-health and legal professionals. Wiseman then appealed to the U.S. Supreme Court, which refused to review the case. This was the first time in American history that a film was banned for reasons other than obscen-ity, immorality, or national security. In 1992, the ban was lifted because all the inmates who had appeared in the film were dead, and that September *Titicut Follies* aired on PBS. This saga might have played quite differently had Lincoln Center, on behalf of the NYFF, successfully resisted Massachusetts' attempt to prevent the Festival's screening in 1967.

Dušan Makavejev, 1971

Makavejev's birthday cake, 1971

## WR: MYSTERIES OF THE ORGANISM, 1971

The Festival described Yugoslavian director Dušan Makavejev's film as an attempt to "discover the failure of the Communist revolution in the sexual repression of its leaders and to chart a new, liberated course based on the teachings of Wilhelm Reich." In *The New York Times*, Vincent Canby called it a "Third World cinematic hallucination . . . An occasionally comic and brilliant collage movie." Although the film was a respectful probing of the teachings of Reich, the creator of the orgone box, it included some satirical elements, and his followers were not amused. Doctors at the International Institute of Bioenergetic Analysis tried to prohibit the film and threatened to sue Makavejev for $1 million, and both Lincoln Center for the Performing Arts and Cinema 5, the distributor, for $600,000. They claimed the film was pornographic and that Makavejev had told them he was shooting an educational film about Reich, to be shown on German television. They denied signing releases, which in fact they had. Cinema 5 owner Don Rugoff was an irascible but impassioned exhibitor who welcomed controversy, especially when it meant publicity. Lawyers for the Film Society and Cinema 5 contested the injunction and shortly before the scheduled Festival showing, the film was screened for a New York Supreme Court judge. Rugoff enlisted Wendy Keys and Brooks Riley, two highly attractive members of the Festival staff, to attend the screening dressed as prim schoolgirls. The injunction was denied and the premiere of *WR* took place on Makavejev's birthday. Rugoff paid for a cake large enough to feed the entire audience of the 1,100-seat Vivian Beaumont Theater, the Festival's home that year. He insisted on trying a sample of the cake before it was served and asked us to place a hammer and sickle on top. We compromised with a large phallic candle. The audience thoroughly enjoyed the cake.

## LAST TANGO IN PARIS, 1972

When we requested that Bernardo Bertolucci's wildly anticipated film close the 10th NYFF, David Picker at United Artists insisted that we forego the usual mandatory press screening. We reluctantly agreed, and the result was a

*W.R.: Mysteries of the Organism* by Dušan Makavejev

*The Bitter Tears of Petra Von Kant* by Rainer Werner Fassbinder

hysterical demand for tickets that surpassed anything we had ever experienced, or ever would. Pauline Kael wrote in *The New Yorker* that the date of the public screening should become a landmark in movie history comparable to the first performance of *The Rite of Spring* in 1913. But in this instance, the protests occurred not before, but during the screening, when dozens fled Alice Tully Hall as the notorious "butter scene" unspooled. In the lobby, one Film Society Board member shouted that Richard Roud had "destroyed the New York Film Festival." Far from it.

## THE BITTER TEARS OF PETRA VON KANT, 1973

The following year, a group of lesbians picketed the presentation of Rainer Werner Fassbinder's depiction of virtual slavery in the workplace. The Festival promoted the film as portraying "power relationships with universal application, not merely tortured lesbian relationships." But on the flipside, Nora Sayre's hysterically funny colossal pan in *The New York Times* asserted that Fassbinder wanted the audience to remember how unnatural these relationships are and has filmed the women "under lighting that makes them look pastier and stranger than anyone encountered by flashlight in a sewer." Undoubtedly, those women on the picket line had good reason for their indignation.

## HAIL MARY, 1985

The programming of Jean-Luc Godard's modernization of the Annunciation and Nativity stories provoked the most prolonged and dramatic protests the NYFF has ever experienced.

The Catholic Church's objections to *Hail Mary* resounded throughout the world and, in 1993, a scholarly book of essays about the film and its controversy, edited by Maryel Locke

and Charles Warren, was published by the Southern Illinois University Press.

In Godard's film, Mary is a basketball player who refuses to make love to her boyfriend, Joseph. After finding out from her family doctor that she is pregnant while still a virgin, she is seen naked in her bedroom, wondering what has happened and why. She gives birth to a child named Jesus and the final scene is a close-up of Mary smoking and putting on lipstick. Our Festival program described *Hail Mary* as "a disturbing meditation on the divine enigma of womanhood."

Early on we received a message from the Vatican condemning the film, accusing Godard of understanding nothing, and arguing that the real Mary was cultured and certainly aware of her destiny.

We were besieged with phone calls immediately after the film's inclusion was announced, nearly two months before it was scheduled to screen. At the time, Lincoln Center had a central switchboard, which was jammed by hundreds of calls. We were also barraged by letters, most of them identical. Because we were presenting the U.S. premiere of *Hail Mary* it was highly unlikely that any of the callers or writers had even seen the film.

I was personally threatened with predictions of perdition. As my cardiologist will attest, it was a disturbing time.

We issued a statement, written by Richard

*Hail Mary* protesters, 1985

*Hail Mary* by Jean-Luc Godard

Corliss, a member of the selection committee, and a Catholic, contending that "*Hail Mary* is a serious work by one of the world's most important and innovative film artists—that the film is an audacious work in which Godard's attitude is both critical and sympathetic—ironic, perhaps even irreverent, but not disrespectful."

The pressure continued. I ended up on network television for a brief debate with John Cardinal O'Connor, during which I insisted that it was not our intention to offend, but that art must also be respected. Then, after notifying the press, a purported emissary from the Vatican presented a document of protest to Richard Roud and me, at a strange ceremony outside Alice Tully Hall. The Festival was vilified from pulpits throughout the city, and

the day before the public screening the Cardinal denounced the film at St. Patrick's Cathedral. Neither he nor the Pope had seen it.

Godard was present for the press screening of *Hail Mary*, but I was told he'd be leaving New York before the public screenings. I remember it was pouring and I dashed across the street to the Gaumont offices to ask him to stay. We had, after all, endured months of harassment defending the film. His response: "It's only a movie." Later, I learned that his decision might have had something to do with fear for his personal safety, partly caused by the memory of John Lennon's assassination.

On the night of the first public screening, close to 3,000 protesters were bussed in from the suburbs and 65th Street was closed to traffic.

Holy water was sprinkled and rosaries were recited, but fortunately no violence occurred. There were some 1,000 protesters at the second screening and a full audience for both shows.

The New York press had decidedly mixed views on *Hail Mary*. Vincent Canby, in *The New York Times*, said that "it may be a serious film, but it was not especially provocative or entertaining." David Denby, in *New York* magazine, called it "a celebration of the blessedness of life on earth, one of the most tenderly religious movies ever made," and, perhaps most interesting of all, Andrew Sarris, in *The Village Voice*, called the situation "a debate in a vacuum, a confrontation between people who never go to church and people who never patronize French films, and ultimately, a dialogue of the deaf."

### THÉRÈSE, 1986, AND DOGMA, 1989

Catholics took issue with two other films presented by our Festival. In 1986 Alain Cavalier's film, starring Catherine Mouchet as St. Thérèse of Lisieux, drew letters of protest due to its depiction of the neurotic side of saintliness. And in 1989, Kevin Smith's comedy about two renegade angels, long ago tossed out of heaven, who discover what they perceive as a loophole in church dogma that will allow them to return, inspired several hundred protesters. *Dogma* was produced by Miramax but distributed by Lion's Gate, so as not to embarrass Miramax's parent company at that time, Disney.

### LOOKING FOR LANGSTON, 1989

Isaac Julien's meditation on the Harlem Renaissance and the life and art of the poet Langston Hughes takes the position that Hughes should have come out of the closet. Presumably displeased with the film's stance, the Hughes estate claimed copyright infringement. In order to avoid legal action, the Festival blocked out the sound in two short clips from a 1959 television show in which Hughes read from his poetry.

### ROGER & ME, 1989

Michael Moore's blackly comic first documentary takes on Roger Smith, the Chairman of General Motors, who eliminated 40,000 jobs when he closed the factories in Flint, Michigan. General Motors was a substantial donor to Lincoln Center's Corporate Fund Drive, and George Weissman, the Center's Chairman, visited me to find out if we had indeed programmed Moore's film. When I told him we had, he smiled with resignation and said he would deal with it. Weissman cared about the Film Society *and* about cinema—and deal with it he did. Interestingly, the following year the General Motors Foundation continued to donate to the Fund at the same level.

### THE GATE OF HEAVENLY PEACE, 1995

Richard Gordon and Carma Hinton's documentary about the 1989 occupation of Beijing's Tiananmen Square by students and

*Thérèse* by Alain Cavalier

*The Gate of Heavenly Peace* by Richard Gordon and Carma Hinton

workers reveals the complexity of the event that led, tragically, to deepening political repression in China. Also in 1995, Zhang Yimou's *Shanghai Triad* had been invited to open the Festival. In an effort to force us to cancel the screenings of the documentary, the Chinese government attempted to withdraw the opening film. Having failed—*Shanghai Triad* had an American distributor (Sony Pictures Classics)—they "asked" Zhang not to attend. Sadly, he had to comply, but the incident provoked a letter of protest to *The New York Times* signed by such luminaries as Jonathan Demme, Louis Malle, Alan Pakula, and Oliver Stone. We can speculate that if Zhang had defied the Chinese government in this

instance, he may not have been selected to direct the opening and closing ceremonies for the 2008 Summer Olympics in Beijing.

It is gratifying that more than a decade has passed without any substantive challenges to the Festival's selections. Attitudes and procedures have changed—imagine how U.S. Customs would have reacted to Lars von Trier's *Antichrist* in the '70s. Undoubtedly new issues will arise, especially if there is a shift in our government's perception of morality. However, I am confident that the Film Society's present and future leadership will continue to respect and support the aesthetic expertise of its programmers. 🎥

*Roger & Me* by Michael Moore

*The Social Network* by David Fincher

# THE PROCESS

*Richard Peña*

NEXT TO "DO YOU EVER GET TIRED OF watching movies?" the question I've been asked most frequently over my years at the New York Film Festival has been "How in fact do you choose the films?" In the Festival's very first years, they were selected by its two directors, Richard Roud and Amos Vogel, according to a complex formula Amos once described to me as having a certain number of "solo picks" in addition to a number of films both had to agree on. By 1966, it was decided that this arrangement was too unwieldy, and a selection committee, made up of both permanent Film Society staff members and outside, rotating critics was established, a system that continues to this day.

When I came on board in 1988, a few festival-world colleagues asked me if I was going to try to abolish the selection committee, deeming it an unnecessary encumbrance to my programming. The answer was, of course, no. First of all, I was in no position to request anything of the kind, and second, I was

looking forward to working with a team that, for my first year, included friends such as Wendy Keys, Phillip Lopate, and Carrie Rickey (David Sterritt would also soon become a friend). Collaborating with the ever-changing committees of the NYFF over the past 24 years has been a source of great joy, some real education, and a lot of laughs, and it's one of the things I will miss most about the job when I leave in December 2012.

Each year the actual NYFF selection process begins after the lineup has been finalized for New Directors/New Films (a festival on which I've also worked), and I would head off, most years, to Berlin. I try as much as possible to separate ND/NF from the NYFF so as to avoid favoritism a title for the NYFF. Just about every filmmaker accepted to ND/NF asks me if they should hold out for the Festival; my response is always that being invited to screen at New Directors in no way guarantees inclusion in the NYFF, as they're programmed with vastly different criteria.

A NYFF selection committee reunion, 2006. TOP ROW: David Ansen, Robert Sklar, Stuart Klawans, Geoffrey O'Brien, Phillip Lopate, Kent Jones, Dave Kehr. BOTTOM ROW: Lisa Schwarzbaum, Wendy Keys, Carrie Rickey

Amos Vogel and Richard Peña, 1996

In Berlin I see as many films as I can, but perhaps even more valuable are the many meetings I have with producers, sales agents, critics, and national film agency representatives. Collectively, they help provide some sense of that year's lay of the land—which films would be ready for Cannes in May, and which others might be available for us to see before our August deadline. Whatever information I glean is added to the notebooks where I keep track of the films I should be on the lookout for. Back in New York I then do all the necessary follow-up, reminding producers or sales agents of our deadlines. In the months between Berlin and Cannes we are also often asked to look at potential films, especially those that might be assigned an earlier release date if the Festival didn't want them. This always includes a number of Opening Night contenders, but more on that dreaded subject in a moment.

The entire NYFF selection committee attends Cannes, which most years proves to be our principal hunting ground. Under consideration are the offerings in the various sections of that festival, as well as the films I liked in Berlin, which could often now be seen in the Cannes Market or in a special screening. There were also new films to be discovered in the Market, which offers hundreds of films from all over the world beyond the festival's curated sections. At first I tried to assign committee members to specific sections—"You cover the Directors' Fortnight, I'll take Un Certain Regard"—but that never seemed to work, so instead we began to fan out as best we could, sending notes (and later, text messages) about what should be seen—or avoided.

Near the end of Cannes, the five of us get together to go over the entire festival; at this point we decide to put forward anywhere from five to eight invitations, which might also include works we had seen before arriving in France. After returning from Cannes a few additional screenings are set up for the committee between early June and when we come together for our final selection sessions in late July and early August. When we enter our final phase we have 10-12 films, a bit less than half the program, already in place.

Now to the issue of Opening Night. For nearly a quarter of a century selecting a film for that slot has been the bane of my existence. The chosen title not only must be worthy of the Festival's high standards but also accessible enough for a broad, non-cinephile audience. And it must have a distributor attached who can help pay for the Opening Night party, which is, to many, the single greatest annual event within the New York film community.

*Secrets & Lies* by Mike Leigh

Mike Leigh, 1996

A few times in my tenure the perfect Opening Night film has come our way: *Secrets & Lies, All About My Mother, The Social Network*, among a few others. Most years, though, we pretty much just held our breath until it was over—even when we knew we had a terrific film.

During those final selection weeks, our days are long, often 10-12 hours, with some viewing still to be done at home. By this time, the many hundreds of films submitted have been whittled down (mainly by me) to about 80-100 from which we choose the remaining 15 or so titles. About half of those drop out pretty quickly, but picking the final films from the 40 or 50 still in the running can be really difficult. Nearly every one of them are worthy, yet less than a third will wind with an invitation.

How do we actually make those final selections? Because I believe that each edition of the NYFF is essentially a program, as opposed to a collection of individual films, I've always tried to avoid voting on individual films.

Rather, during each stage in our decision-making process—at Cannes, in the weeks following our return, and in our final sessions—I've preferred to have long discussions about all of the films under consideration, during which each committee member will speak his or her mind about all of them. Based on the comments I hear—and my own prejudices—I propose a slate of five to eight films that we as a committee can vote for or against. Ideally, in each of these slots there are films each member is passionate about, though of course in many cases there will be one or two that he or she likes less than his or her colleagues. I'm greatly swayed by passion, and hearing someone expound enthusiastically on a film has often led me to think that, even if it's not my cup of tea, there should still be a place for it. In the end, we read through the list of everything we've invited, express our assent, then go home and sleep it off.

The selection process is often an intense, hothouse experience, and on a few occasions tempers have flared and feelings have been hurt. But overall I have been truly blessed with the committees with which I've worked—men and women who have given extraordinarily of themselves and put together the best Festival that we, together, are able to create. I could never repay them. 🎥

*All About My Mother* by Pedro Almodóvar

# *Behind the* SCENES AT THE NYFF

TOP LEFT

**SALLIE WILENSKY BLUMENTHAL AND RICHARD ROUD:** 1966. *By ©Elliott Moss Landy*

LEFT

**ADOLPH GREEN, JASON ROBARDS, AND LAUREN BACALL:** 1966. *By ©Elliott Moss Landy*

BOTTOM LEFT

**CATHERINE BREILLAT:** *36 fillette.* 1988. *By ©GODLIS*

ABOVE

**GÉRARD DEPARDIEU, CAROLE BOUQUET, AND BERTRAND BLIER:** Opening Night, *Too Beautiful for You.* 1989. *By ©Jonathan Levine*

TOP RIGHT

**VITTORIO GASSMAN AND LAUREN HUTTON:** *A Wedding.* 1977. *©By Sonia Moskowitz*

RIGHT

**RENÉ ALLIO, AGNÈS VARDA, AND FRIEND:** 1966. *By ©Elliott Moss Landy*

BOTTOM RIGHT

**JULIEN STUDLEY, FRIEND, AND WILLIAM MAY:** Opening Night, *Capricious Summer.* 1968. *By ©Bob Serating*

ABOVE
**FRANK STELLA:** In front of his NYFF poster. 1971.

TOP RIGHT
**SARA DRIVER, JIM JARMUSCH, AND NICOLETTA BRASCHI:** *Down by Law.* 1986. *By ©Timothy Parks*

UPPER RIGHT
**THEO ANGELOPOLOUS:** *The Suspended Step of the Stork.* 1991. *By ©Stephanie Berger*

LOWER RIGHT
**HENRI LANGLOIS:** 1966.

BOTTOM RIGHT
**LILLIAN GISH AND JAMES FRASHER:** Opening Night, *A Wedding.* 1978. *By ©Sonia Moskowitz*

LEFT
**FAYE DUNAWAY AND BARBET SCHROEDER:** *Barfly.* 1987.
*By ©Timothy Parks*

TOP LEFT
**CLINT EASTWOOD, DIANE VENORA, AND FOREST
WHITAKER:** *Bird.* 1988. *By ©Star Black*

MIDDLE LEFT
**DIANA MICHENER, CHINA MACHADO, CHARLES
MICHENER, BULLE OGIER, AND GATO AND MICHELLE
BARBIERI:** *Last Tango in Paris.* 1972. *By ©Helaine Messer*

TOP RIGHT
**MALCOLM MCDOWELL AND MARY STEENBURGEN:**
Opening Night, *Melvin and Howard.* 1980. *By ©Helaine Messer*

MIDDLE RIGHT
**ROBERT ALTMAN AND PHYLLIS GEORGE BROWN:**
Opening Night, *A Wedding.* 1980. *By ©Helaine Messer*

BOTTOM RIGHT
**JOHN BOORMAN AND SARAH MILES:**
*Hope and Glory.* 1987. *By ©Timothy Parks*

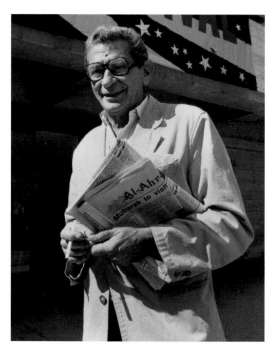

TOP LEFT

**ISMAIL MERCHANT AND INDRANI RAHMAN:**
*Roseland.* 1977. *By ©Tony De Nonno*

ABOVE

**WENDY KEYS, RICHARD KOCH, MARIAN MASONE, AND DAVID MAMET:** *House of Games.* Ticket crisis. 1987.
*By ©Timothy Parks*

TOP RIGHT

**LINDSAY CROUSE AND DAVID MAMET:** *House of Games.*
1987. *By ©Timothy Parks*

MIDDLE RIGHT

**RICHARD ROUD, ROBERTO BENIGNI, TERRY KANE, SUSAN JACOBS, NICOLETTA BRASCHI, AND JIM JARMUSCH:** *Opening Night, Down by Law.* 1986.
*By ©Timothy Parks*

BOTTOM RIGHT

**WENDY KEYS AND TIM BURTON:** *Ed Wood.* 1994.
*By ©Stephanie Berger*

LEFT
**MARTIN SCORSESE AND MICHELANGELO ANTONIONI:** *1991. By ©Stephanie Berger*

MIDDLE LEFT
**CATHERINE CAHILL, ELLIE CULLMAN, AND WILLIAM BERNHARD:** *1991. By ©Stephanie Berger*

BOTTOM LEFT
**JOHN HURT:** *Love and Death on Long Island. 1997. By ©Stephanie Berger*

BELOW
**JESSICA LANGE AND ROBERT DE NIRO:** *Night and the City. 1992. By ©Stephanie Berger*

BOTTOM RIGHT
**OUSMANE SEMBENE:** *1991. By ©Stephanie Berger*

TOP LEFT
**AGNIESZKA HOLLAND:** Opening Night, *Olivier Olivier.*
*By ©GODLIS*

TOP RIGHT
**RICHARD LINKLATER AND ERIC BOGOSIAN:** *SubUrbia.*
1996. *By ©GODLIS*

MIDDLE LEFT
**RICHARD PEÑA AND MARK RAPPAPORT:** *From the Journals of Jean Seberg.* 1996. *By ©Stephanie Berger*

ABOVE
**MARK WAHLBERG AND BURT REYNOLDS:** *Boogie Nights.*
1997. *By ©Stephanie Berger*

BOTTOM RIGHT
**KEN LOACH:** 1993. *By ©Robin Holland*

TOP LEFT
**HAYAO MIYAZAKI:** *Princess Mononoke.* 1999.
*By ©Stephanie Berger*

ABOVE
**WOODY HARRELSON, COURTNEY LOVE, MILOŠ FORMAN, DONNA HANOVER, AND EDWARD NORTON:** *The People vs. Larry Flynt.* 1996. *By ©GODLIS*

BOTTOM LEFT
**BILLY BOB THORNTON:** *Sling Blade.* 1996. *By ©GODLIS*

TOP RIGHT
**CHEN KAIGE:** *Farewell My Concubine.* 1980. *By ©GODLIS*

MIDDLE RIGHT
**TODD FIELD, VICTOR NUÑEZ, AND ASHLEY JUDD:** *Ruby in Paradise.* 1993. *By ©GODLIS*

RIGHT
**KEVIN SMITH:** *Dogma.* 1999. *By ©Stephanie Berger*

TOP LEFT
**CAMERON DIAZ, CATHERINE KEENER, JOHN MALKOVICH, SPIKE JONZE, AND JOHN CUSACK:** *Being John Malkovich.* 1999. *By ©Stephanie Berger*

ABOVE
**CHARLES BURNETT:** *To Sleep with Anger.* 1990. *By ©GODLIS*

TOP RIGHT
**THELMA SCHOONMAKER:** 1999. *By ©GODLIS*

MIDDLE RIGHT
**KENNETH ANGER AND ALBERT MAYSLES:** 2006. *By ©GODLIS*

BOTTOM RIGHT
**WILLEM DAFOE, JIM JARMUSCH, ABEL FERRARA, AND AMOS POE:** *You Are Not I.* 2011. *By ©GODLIS*

TOP LEFT
**LEOS CARAX:** *Bad Blood.* 1987. *By ©GODLIS*

ABOVE
**TODD FIELD AND KATE WINSLET:** *Little Children.* 2006.
*By ©Stephanie Berger*

TOP RIGHT
**DERMOT MULRONEY, JACK NICHOLSON, AND HOPE
DAVIS:** Opening Night, *About Schmidt.* 2002. *By ©GODLIS*

CENTER
**AGNÈS JAOUI:** Opening Night, *Look at Me.* 2004.
*By ©Stephanie Berger*

CENTER RIGHT
**APICHATPONG WEERASETHAKUL:** *Uncle Boonmee Who
Can Recall His Past Lives.* 2010. *By ©GODLIS*

RIGHT
**ROSSY DE PALMA AND MARISA PAREDES:** *The Flower of
My Secret.* 1995. *By ©Stephanie Berger*

ABOVE LEFT
**TODD HAYNES:** *I'm Not There.* 2007. *By ©Stephanie Berger*

MIDDLE LEFT
**MANOEL DE OLIVEIRA AND RICHARD PEÑA:**
*The Convent.* 1995. *By ©GODLIS*

BOTTOM LEFT
**JAVIER BARDEM:** *No Country for Old Men.* 2007.

ABOVE
**OLIVIER ASSAYAS AND NATHALIE RICHARD:** *Irma Vep.*
1996. *By ©GODLIS*

TOP RIGHT
**TERENCE DAVIES:** *The House of Mirth.* 2000. *By ©Stephanie Berger*

RIGHT
**REGINALD HUDLIN AND WESLEY SNIPES:** *King of New
York.* 1990. *By ©GODLIS*

BELOW
**HILARY SWANK, KIMBERLY PEIRCE, AND CHLOË
SEVIGNY:** *Boys Don't Cry.* 1999. *By ©GODLIS*

OPPOSITE PAGE
**PENÉLOPE CRUZ:** *Volver.* 2006. *By ©GODLIS*

TOP LEFT
**DAVID STRATHAIRN, FRANK LANGELLA, PATRICIA CLARKSON, AND GEORGE CLOONEY:** *Opening Night, Good Night, and Good Luck.* 2005. *By ©Dave Allocca/Starpix*

MIDDLE LEFT
**ALEJANDRO GONZÁLEZ IÑÁRRITU AND BENICIO DEL TORO:** *21 Grams.* 2003. *By ©Stephanie Berger*

BOTTOM LEFT
**AKIRA KUROSAWA AND RICHARD GERE:** *Opening Night, Ran.* 1985. *By ©Fernando Diaz*

TOP RIGHT
**BRIAN DE PALMA:** *Redacted.* 2007. *By ©GODLIS*

MIDDLE RIGHT
**WARREN BEATTY AND ANNETTE BENING:** *Reds* 25th Anniversary. 2006. *By ©GODLIS*

BOTTOM RIGHT
**ED HARRIS AND MARCIA GAY HARDEN:** *Pollock.* 2000. *By ©GODLIS*

TOP LEFT
**JACQUES RIVETTE:** Opening Night, *Va Savoir*. 2001.
*By ©GODLIS*

MIDDLE LEFT
**BONO AND JULIAN SCHNABEL:** *The Diving Bell and the Butterfly*. 2007. *By ©GODLIS*

BOTTOM LEFT
**LUCRECIA MARTEL:** *La Ciénaga*. 2001. *By ©Stephanie Berger*

TOP RIGHT
**TILDA SWINTON AND EWAN MCGREGOR:** *Young Adam*. 2003. *By ©GODLIS*

ABOVE MIDDLE
**DIANE KEATON, GUS VAN SANT, AND MICHAEL LYNNE:** *Elephant*. 2003. *By ©GODLIS*

LOWER MIDDLE
**LIV ULLMANN:** *Faithless*. 2000. *By ©Stephanie Berger*

LEFT
**SIDNEY LUMET AND JOHN LANDIS:** *Before the Devil Knows You're Dead*. 2007. *By ©GODLIS*

ABOVE
**LEONARDO DICAPRIO:** Opening Night, *Celebrity*. 1998.
*By ©Stephanie Berger*

TOP LEFT
**GABOUREY SIDIBE AND LEE DANIELS:** *Precious: Based on the Novel "Push" by Sapphire.* 2009. *By ©GODLIS*

ABOVE
**ISAACH DE BANKOLÉ AND CLAIRE DENIS:** *White Material.* 2009. *By ©GODLIS*

TOP RIGHT
**KEN BURNS:** 2004. *By ©GODLIS*

CENTER
**HENRY MCGEE, IRA RESNICK, AND ARTHUR SULZBERGER JR.:** 2003. *By ©Stephanie Berger*

MIDDLE RIGHT
**MICKEY ROURKE AND SYLVIA MILES:** *The Wrestler.* 2008. *By ©Stephanie Berger*

RIGHT
**TODD SOLONDZ, JENNIFER JASON LEIGH, AND ELLEN BARKIN:** *Palindromes.* 2004. *By ©GODLIS*

TOP LEFT

**ARNAUD DESPLECHIN:** *A Christmas Tale*, 2004.
*By ©GODLIS*

ABOVE

**JASON SCHWARTZMAN AND WES ANDERSON:**
Autographing *Film Comment*. Opening Night, *The Darjeeling Limited*. 2007. *By ©GODLIS*

TOP RIGHT

**HELEN MIRREN AND STEPHEN FREARS:** Opening Night,
*The Queen*. 2006. *By ©GODLIS*

CENTER

**JOANNA NEY AND MICHAEL HANEKE:** *Caché*. 2005.
*By ©GODLIS*

MIDDLE RIGHT

**PETER MULLAN:** *The Magdalene Sisters*. 2002.
*By ©Stephanie Berger*

RIGHT

**CATHERINE KEENER AND PHILIP SEYMOUR HOFFMAN:**
*Capote*. 2004. *By ©GODLIS*

*Complete* FILM LISTINGS

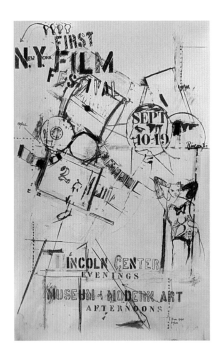

# 1963

PROGRAMMED BY RICHARD ROUD (FROM LONDON) AND AMOS VOGEL (NEW YORK). RICHARD GRIFFITH, CURATOR OF FILM AT MOMA, PRESENTED A PROGRAM OF RETROSPECTIVES.

THE 1ST NYFF POSTER ARTWORK WAS CREATED BY LARRY RIVERS. ©LIST ARTS POSTERS FOR LINCOLN CENTER.

**THE EXTERMINATING ANGEL**
*Mexico, 1962. Written and Directed by Luis Buñuel, based on a story by Luis Alcoriza and Buñuel.*
With Silvia Pinal, Jacqueline Andere, Augusto Benedico, Luis Beristain. (Opening Night.)

**SWEET AND SOUR (DRAGÉES AU POIVRE)**
*France/Italy, 1963. Directed by Jacques Baratier.*
Written by Baratier and Guy Bedos. With Bedos, Jean-Paul Belmondo, Anna Karina, Simone Signoret, Alexandra Stewart, Roger Vadim, Monica Vitti, Marina Vlady. (Closing Night.)

**ALL THE WAY HOME**
*USA, 1963. Directed by Alex Segal.*
Written by Phillip Reisman Jr., based on Tad Mosel's play and James Agee's novel *A Death in the Family*. With Jean Simmons, Robert Preston, Pat Hingle, Aline MacMahon.

◀ **AN AUTUMN AFTERNOON**
*Japan, 1962-3. Directed by Yasujiro Ozu.*
Written by Kogo Noda and Ozu. With Chishu Ryu, Shinichiro Mikami, Keiji Sada, Mariko Okada, Shima Iwashita.

**BARRAVENTO**
*Brazil, 1962. Directed by Glauber Rocha.*
Written by Luiz Paulino dos Santos, Rocha, and José Telles de Magalhaes. With Antonio Sampaio, Luiza Maranhão, Aldo Teixeira, Lucy Carvalho.

**ELEKTRA (ELEKTRA AT EPIDAURUS)**
*Greece, 1962. Directed by Ted Zarpas.*
Sophocles' play staged by Takis Mouzenidis. With Anna Synodinou, Thanos Cotsopoulos, Kakia Panayotou, Theodoros Moridis.

**THE FIANCÉS**
*Italy, 1963. Written and Directed by Ermanno Olmi.*
With Carlo Cabrini, Anna Canzi.

**+ THE CHAIR**
*USA, 1963. Directed by Richard Leacock, Jim Lipscombe, D.A. Pennebaker, and Hope Ryden.*
Executive Produced by Robert Drew. A documentary about the last days of Paul Crump, before he is was electrocuted.

## HALLELUJAH THE HILLS
*USA, 1963. Written and Directed by Adolfas Mekas.*
With Peter H. Beard, Martin Greenbaum, Sheila Finn, Peggy Steffans.

## HARAKIRI
*Japan, 1963. Directed by Masaki Kobayashi.*
Written by Shinobu Hashimoto, based on Yasuhiko Takiguchi's novel. With Tatsuya Nakadai, Shima Iwashita, Akira Ishihama, Yoshio Inaba.

## IN THE MIDST OF LIFE (AU COEUR DE LE VIE)
*France, 1962-3. Written and Directed by Robert Enrico, based on stories by Ambrose Bierce.*
With François Frankiel, Eric Frankiel, Edwin Moatti, Roger Jacquet, Anne Cornaly.

## LE JOLI MAI
*France, 1963. Directed by Chris Marker.*
Written by Catherine Varlin; commentary spoken by Simone Signoret written by Chris Marker. With the people of Paris.

## KNIFE IN THE WATER
*Poland, 1962. Directed by Roman Polanski.*
Written by Jakub Goldberg, Polanski, and Jerzy Skolimowski. With Leon Niemczyk, Jolanta Umecka, Zygmunt Malanowicz.

## LOVE IN THE SUBURBS
*Hungary, 1963. Directed by Tamás Fejér.*
Written by István Csurka. With Miklos Gábor, György Palos, Margit Bara.

## MAGNET OF DOOM
*France/Italy, 1963. Written and Directed by Jean-Pierre Melville, based on Georges Simenon's novel.*
With Jean-Paul Belmondo, Charles Vanel, Michèle Mercier, Malvina Silberberg, Stefania Sandrelli.

## IL MARE (THE SEA)
*Italy, 1962. Written and Directed by Giuseppe Patroni Griffi.*
With Umberto Orsini, Françoise Prévost, Dino Mele.

## MURIEL
*France/Italy, 1963. Directed by Alain Resnais.*
Written by Jean Cayrol. With Delphine Seyrig, Jean-Pierre Kérien, Jean-Baptiste Thierrée, Nita Klein, Claude Sainval.

## ROGOPAG
*Italy/France, 1962. Segments include:*

- **Virginity (Illibatezza).** Written and Directed by Roberto Rossellini. With Rosanna Schiaffino, Bruce Balaban, Maria Pia Schiaffino, Carlo Zappavigna.

- **The New World (Il Nuovo Mondo).** Written and Directed by Jean-Luc Godard. With Jean-Marc Bory, Alexandra Stewart.

- **Cream Cheese (La Ricotta).** Written and Directed by Pier Paolo Pasolini. With Orson Welles, Mario Cipriani, Laura Betti, Edmonda Aldini, Ettore Garofolo.

- **The Range-Grown Chicken (Il Pollo Ruspante).** Written and Directed by Ugo Gregoretti. With Ugo Tognazzi, Lisa Gastoni, Ricky Tognazzi, Antonella Taito.

◄ ## THE SERVANT
*UK, 1963. Directed by Joseph Losey.*
Written by Harold Pinter, based on Robin Maugham's novel. With Dirk Bogarde, James Fox, Sarah Miles, Wendy Craig.

## THE SKY aka GLORY SKY (OURANOS)
*Greece, 1962-63. Directed by Takis Kanellopoulos.*
Written by Kanellopoulos and Georges Kitsopoulos. With Emilie Pitta, Phedon Georgitsis, Takis Emmanouil, Nikos Tsahiridis.

## THE TERRACE (LA TERRAZA)
*Argentina, 1963. Directed by Leopoldo Torre Nilsson.*
Written by Beatriz Guido. With Graciela Borges, Leonardo Favio, Marcela López Rey, Héctor Pellegrini.

## THE TRIAL OF JOAN OF ARC
*France, 1962. Written and Directed by Robert Bresson.*
With Florence Carrez, Jean-Claude Fourneau, Roger Honorat, Marc Jacquier.

## + THE CRISIS
*USA, 1963. Directed by Richard Leacock, Jim Lipscombe, D.A. Pennebaker, and Hope Ryden.*
Executive Produced by Robert Drew. Behind the scenes with President Kennedy's struggle to get two black students into the University of Alabama.

SELECTIONS SHOWN AT MoMA were described as "distinguished films of the recent past never before shown theatrically in the U.S." They included: *The Bread of Our Former Years*, by Herbert Vesely, West Germany, 1962; *The End of the Fiesta*, by Leopoldo Torre Nilsson, Argentina, 1959; *The Exiles*, by Kent Mackenzie, USA, 1958-61; *I Live in Fear*, by Akira Kurosawa, Japan, 1955; *Lola Montès*, by Max Ophuls, France/West Germany, 1955; *The New Angels*, by Ugo Gregoretti, Italy, 1962; *The Olive Trees of Justice*, by James Blue, France, 1961; *Point of Order*, by Emile de Antonio, USA, 1963; *Sansho the Bailiff*, by Kenji Mizoguchi, Japan, 1954. Short films shown: *Assembly Line*, USA, by Morton Heilig (at MoMA); *Boiled Egg*, France, by Marc Andrieux and Bernard Brévent; *The Ceiling*, Czechoslovakia, by Vera Chytilová; *Clap Vocalism*, Japan, by Yoji Kuri; *Concert*, Hungary, by István Szabó; *Cybernetic Grandmother*, Czechoslovakia, by Jiří Trnka; *The Flying Man*, UK, by George Dunning; *Gallina Vogelbirdae*, Czechoslovakia, by Jiří Brdečka; *The Game*, Yugoslavia, by Dušan Vukotić; *Girl on the Road*, France, by Louis Terme; *Grandmother's Encyclopedia*, France, by Walerian Borowczyk; *Labyrinth*, Poland, by Jan Lenica; *O.K. End Here*, USA, by Robert Frank; *Pianissimo*, USA, by Carmen D'Avino; *The Pistol*, West Germany, by Wolfgang Urchs; *The Plain Man's Guide to Advertising*, UK, by Bob Godfrey; *Skullduggery*, USA, by Stan VanDerBeek; *They Have All Gone Away*, USA, by Mark Weiss (at MoMA); *The Two Castles*, Italy, by Bruno Bozzetto; *We Are Hanging by a Thread*, Denmark, by Jorgen Roos; *The Winner*, USA, by Bert Brown (at MoMA).

# 1964

PROGRAMMED BY RICHARD ROUD, PROGRAM DIRECTOR, AND AMOS VOGEL, FESTIVAL DIRECTOR.

THE 2ND NYFF POSTER ARTWORK WAS CREATED BY SAUL BASS. LIST ART POSTERS, ©LCPA.

2nd NEW YORK FILM FESTIVAL
Sept. 14-26 1964 · Philharmonic Hall
Lincoln Center.

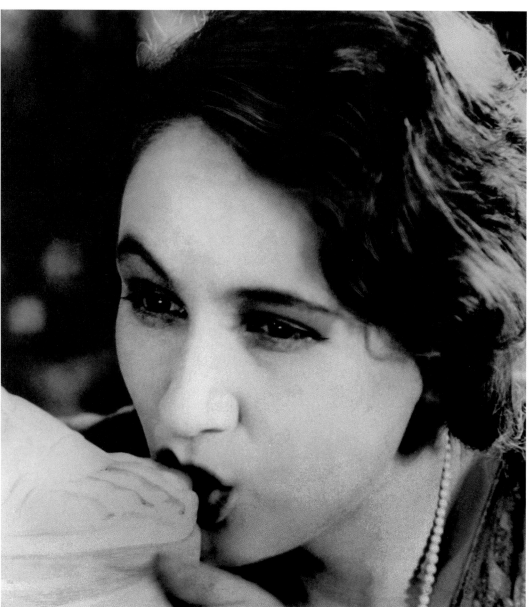

### HAMLET
*USSR, 1964. Written and Directed by Grigori Kozintsev, based on Shakespeare's play.*

With Innokenti Smoktunovski, Michal Nazwanov, Elza Radzin-Szolkonis, Y. Tolubeev. (Opening Night.)

### THE GREAT CITY aka THE BIG CITY (MAHANAGAR)
*India, 1963. Written and Directed by Satyajit Ray, based on a story by Narenda Nath Mitra.*

With Madhabi Mukherjee, Anil Chatterjee, Haradhan Banerjee, Haren Chatterjee. Shown with *Fotel*, Poland. Directed by Daniel Szczechura. (Closing Night.)

### ◀ L'AGE D'OR
*France, 1930. Directed by Luis Buñuel.*

Written by Buñuel and Salvador Dalí. With Gaston Modot, Lya Lys, Max Ernst, Germaine Noizet, Lionel Salem, Pierre Prévert. (Retrospective.)

### ALONE ON THE PACIFIC aka MY ENEMY, THE SEA
*Japan, 1963. Directed by Kon Ichikawa.*

Written by Natto Wada, based on a logbook by Kenichi Horie. With Yujiro Ishihara, Masayuki Mori, Kinuyo Tanaka, Ruriko Asaoka. Shown with *Breathing*, USA. Directed by Robert Breer.

### BAND OF OUTSIDERS (BANDE À PART)
*France, 1964. Written and Directed by Jean-Luc Godard, based on D. and B. Hitchens's novel* Fool's Gold.

With Anna Karina, Sami Frey, Claude Brasseur, Louisa Colpeyn. Shown with *Renaissance*, France. Directed by Walerian Borowczyk.

### BEFORE THE REVOLUTION
*Italy, 1964. Written and Directed by Bernardo Bertolucci.*

With Adriana Asti, Francesco Barilli, Allen Midgette, Morando Morandini. Shown with *Francis Bacon*, UK. Directed by David Thompson.

### THE BRIG
*USA, 1964. Directed by Adolfas and Jonas Mekas.*

Written by Kenneth H. Brown. Photographed on the stage of the Living Theatre. With James Tiroff, Steven Ben Israel, Gene Lipton. Rufus Collins. Shown with *The Last Clean Shirt*, USA. Directed by Alfred Leslie.

*Band of Outsiders* by Jean-Luc Godard

### ÇA IRA
*Italy, 1964. Written and Directed by Tinto Brass.*

Documentary made up of never-before-seen newsreel footage. Shown with *Allo, Allo*, Romania. Directed by Ion Popescu-Gopo.

### CONFLAGRATION
*Japan, 1959. Directed by Kon Ichikawa.*

Written by Keiji Hasebe and Natto Wada, based on Yukio Mishima's novel *Kinkakuji*. With Raizo Ichikawa, Tatsuya Nakadai, Ganjiro Nakamura, Yoko Uraji. Shown with *Corps Profond*, France. Directed by Igor Barrère and Étienne Lalou.

### CYRANO ET D'ARTAGNAN
*France/Italy/Spain, 1963-64. Directed by Abel Gance.*

Written by Gance and Nelly Kaplan. With José Ferrer, Jean-Pierre Cassel, Sylva Koscina, Dahlia Lavi, Michel Simon. Shown with *Love*, Japan. Directed by Yoji Kuri.

### DIARY OF A CHAMBERMAID
*France, 1964. Directed by Luis Buñuel.*

Written by Buñuel and Jean-Claude Carrière. With Jeanne Moreau, Michel Piccoli, Georges Géret, Françoise Lugagne. Shown with *Canon*, Canada. Directed by Norman McLaren.

### FAIL-SAFE
*USA, 1964. Directed by Sidney Lumet.*

Written by Walter Bernstein, based on the book by Eugene Burdick and Harvey Wheeler. With Henry Fonda, Dan O'Herlihy, Walter Matthau, Frank Overton. Shown with *Cow at the Border*, Yugoslavia. Directed by Dragutin Vunak.

### HANDS OVER THE CITY
*Italy, 1963. Directed by Francesco Rosi.*

Written by Enzo Forcella, Raffaele La Capria, Enzo Provenzale, and Rosi. With Salvo Randone, Rod Steiger, Guido Alberti, Marcello Cannavale. Shown with *One, Two, Three*, Hungary. Directed by Gyula Macskássy.

### THE INHERITANCE (LA HERENCIA)
*Argentina, 1963. Written and Directed by Ricardo Alventosa, based on a story by Guy de Maupassant.*

With Juan Verdaguer, Nathán Pinzón, Marisa Grieben, Alba Mujica. Shown with *Joseph Killian*, Czechoslovakia. Directed by Pavel Jurácek and Jan Schmidt.

### KING & COUNTRY
*UK, 1964. Directed by Joseph Losey.*

Written by Evan Jones, based on John Wilson's play, adapted from a story by James Lansdale Hodson. With Dirk Bogarde, Tom Courtenay, Leo McKern, Barry Foster. Shown with *Alf, Bill and Fred*, UK. Directed by Bob Godfrey.

### LIFE UPSIDE DOWN aka INSIDE OUT
*France, 1964. Written and Directed by Alain Jessua.*

With Charles Denner, Anna Gaylor, Guy Saint-Jean, Jean Yanne. Shown with *Mammals*, Poland. Directed by Roman Polanski.

### LILITH
*USA, 1964. Written and Directed by Robert Rossen, based on J.R. Salamanca's novel.*

With Warren Beatty, Jean Seberg, Peter Fonda, Kim Hunter, Gene Hackman. Shown with *Bahing*, France. Directed by Jean-Charles Meunier.

### NOBODY WAVED GOODBYE
*Canada, 1964. Written and Directed by Don Owen.*

With Peter Kastner, Julie Biggs, Claude Rae, Toby Tarnow. Shown with *Interview with Bruce Gordon*, USA. Directed by Harold Becker.

### NOTHING BUT A MAN
*USA, 1964. Directed by Michael Roemer.*

Written by Roemer and Robert M. Young. With Ivan Dixon, Abbey Lincoln, Gloria Foster, Julius Harris, Yaphet Kotto. Shown with *Snow*, UK. Directed by Geoffrey Jones.

### PASSENGER
*Poland, 1961-63. Directed by Andrzej Munk, completed by Witold Lesiewicz.*

Written by Munk and Zofia Posmysz-Piasecka. With Aleksandra Slaska, Jan Kreczmar, Anna Ciepielewska, Franciszek Pieczka. Shown with *Valparaiso*, France/Chile. Directed by Joris Ivens.

### SALVATORE GIULIANO
*Italy, 1961. Directed by Francesco Rosi.*

Written by Suso Cecchi D'Amico, Enzo Provenzale, Rosi, and Franco Solinas. With Frank Wolff, Salvo Randone, Federico Zardi, Pietro Cammarata. Shown with *Red Type*, UK. Directed by Albert Noble.

### SHE AND HE
*Japan, 1963. Written and Directed by Susumu Hani.*

With Sachiko Hidari, Kikuji Yamashita, Eiji Okada, Akio Hasegawa, Mariko Igarashi. Shown with *Trope*, USA. Directed by Barry H. Prince.

### TALES OF THE TAIRA CLAN aka THE TAIRA CLAN
*Japan, 1955. Directed by Kenji Mizoguchi.*

Written by Masashige Narusawa and Yoshikata Yoda, based on a story by Eiji Yoshikawa. With Yoshiko Kuga, Michiyo Kogure, Ichijiro Oya, Mitsusaburo Ramon. Shown with *L'Adage*, France. Directed by Dominique Delouche.

### TO LOVE
*Sweden, 1964. Written and Directed by Jörn Donner.*

With Harriet Andersson, Zbigniew Cybulski, Isa Quensel, Tomas Svanfeldt, Jane Friedmann. Shown with *The Peaches*, UK. Directed by Michael Gill.

### WOMAN IN THE DUNES
*Japan, 1964. Directed by Hiroshi Teshigahara.*

Written by Kobo Abe, based on his novel. With Eiji Okada, Kyoko Kishida, Hiroko Ito. Shown with *Insects*, UK. Directed by Teru Murakami.

### A WOMAN IS A WOMAN
*France/Italy, 1961. Written and Directed by Jean-Luc Godard.*

With Anna Karina, Jean-Claude Brialy, Jean-Paul Belmondo, Nicole Paquin. Shown with *Le Poulet*, France. Directed by Claude Berri.

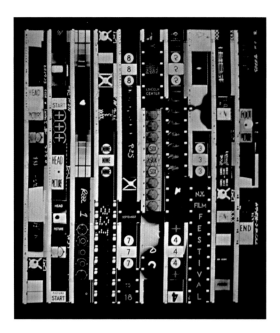

# 1965

PROGRAMMED BY RICHARD ROUD AND AMOS VOGEL.

THE 3RD NYFF POSTER ARTWORK WAS CREATED BY BRUCE CONNER. LIST ART POSTERS, ©LCPA.

### ALPHAVILLE
*France, 1965. Written and Directed by Jean-Luc Godard.*

With Eddie Constantine, Anna Karina, Akim Tamiroff, Howard Vernon. Shown with *Overture*, Hungary. Directed by János Vadász. (Opening Night.)

◀ **RED BEARD**
*Japan, 1965. Directed by Akira Kurosawa.*

Written by Masato Ide, Ryuzo Kikushima, Kurosawa, and Hideo Oguni. With Toshiro Mifune, Yuzo Kayama, Yoshio Tsuchiya, Reiko Dan. (Closing Night.)

### BLACK PETER
*Czechoslovakia, 1964. Directed by Milos Forman.*

Written by Forman and Jaroslav Papoušek. With Ladislav Jakim, Pavla Martínková, Pavel Sedlacek, Jan Ostroil. Shown with *Insomnie*, France. Directed by Pierre Etaix.

### "BUSTER AND BECKETT" – three short films:
- **Film**, USA, 1965. Directed by Alan Schneider. Written by Samuel Beckett. With Buster Keaton, Nell Harrison, James Karen, Susan Reed.

- **The Railrodder**, Canada, 1965. Written and Directed by Gerald Potterton. With Buster Keaton.

- **Seven Chances**, USA, 1925. Directed by Buster Keaton. Written by Clyde Bruckman, Jean C. Havez, and Joseph A. Mitchell, based on Roi Cooper Megrue's play. With Keaton, Frankie Raymond, T. Roy Barnes, Snitz Edwards. Piano accompaniment by Arthur Kleiner.

### CAMILLE WITHOUT CAMELLIAS
*Italy, 1952-3. Directed by Michelangelo Antonioni.*

Written by Antonioni, Suso Cecchi D'Amico, Francesco Maselli, P.M. Pasinetti, based on a story by Antonioni. With Lucia Bosé, Andrea Checchi, Gino Cervi, Ivan Desny, Alain Cuny. (Retrospective.) Shown with *The Top*, USA. Directed by Teru Murakami.

### CARESSED aka SWEET SUBSTITUTE
*Canada, 1965. Written and Directed by Larry Kent.*

With Robert Howay, Angela Gann, Lanny Beckman, Carol Pastinsky, Bob Silverman. Shown with *People*, USA. Directed by Max Katz. Also, *Hollywood in Yugoslavia*, West Germany. Directed by Ulrich Schamoni.

**CHARULATA** ▲
*India, 1964. Written and Directed by Satyajit Ray.*
With Soumitra Chatterjee, Madhabi Mukherjee, Sailen Mukherjee, Shyamal Ghoshal. Shown with *Portraits*, Poland. Directed by Mirowslaw Kijowicz.

**FISTS IN THE POCKET**
*Italy, 1965. Written and Directed by Marco Bellocchio.*
With Lou Castel, Paola Pitagora, Marino Masé, Liliana Gerace. Shown with *The Beach*, Poland. Directed by Edward Sturlis.

**GERTRUD** ▲
*Denmark, 1964. Written and Directed by Carl Theodor Dreyer, based on Hjalmar Söderberg's play.*
With Nina Pens Rode, Bendt Rothe, Ebbe Rode, Baard Owe, Axel Strøbye. Shown with *The Fifth*, Yugoslavia. Directed by Zlatko Grgić and Pavao Stalter.

**IDENTIFICATION MARKS: NONE**
*Poland, 1964. Written and Directed by Jerzy Skolimowski.*
With Elżbieta Czyżewska, Skolimowski, Tadeusz Mins, Andrzej Zarnecki, Jacek Szczęk. Shown with *Araby*, Poland. Directed by Zbigniew Raplewski. Also, *One Man Band*, UK. Directed by Bob Godfrey.

**KNAVE OF HEARTS** aka **MONSIEUR RIPOIS**
*UK, 1954. Directed by René Clément.*
Written by Clément and Hugh Mills. With Gérard Philipe, Natasha Parry, Valerie Hobson, Joan Greenwood, Margaret Johnson. (Retrospective.) Shown with *Dermis probe*, UK. Directed by Richard Williams.

**THE KOUMIKO MYSTERY**
*France, 1965. Written and Directed by Chris Marker.*
With Koumiko Muraoka. Shown with *Twilight of Empire*, UK, 1965. Directed by Kevin Billington. The return of Malcolm Muggeridge to India, with commentary by Muggeridge.

**MICKEY ONE**
*USA, 1965. Directed by Arthur Penn.*
Written by Alan Surgal. With Warren Beatty, Hurd Hatfield, Alexandra Stewart, Teddy Hart, Jeff Corey, Kamatari Fujiwara, Franchot Tone. Shown with *Mosaic*, Canada. Directed by Norman McLaren.

**OF HUMAN BONDAGE**
*USA, 1934. Directed by John Cromwell.*
Written by Lester Cohen, based on W. Somerset Maugham's novel. With Bette Davis, Leslie Howard, Frances Dee, Kay Johnson, Reginald Denny, Alan Hale. (Retrospective.)

**PARIS VU PAR… (SIX IN PARIS)**
*France, 1965. Six short films (produced by Barbet Schroeder) in which different Paris neighborhoods are seen by six New Wave directors:*

- **La Muette**. Written and Directed by Claude Chabrol. With Chabrol, Stéphane Audran.
- **Saint-Germain-des-Prés**. Written and Directed by Jean Douchet. With Barbara Wilkin, Jean-François Chappey, Jean-Pierre Andréani.
- **Montparnasse et Levallois**. Written and Directed by Jean-Luc Godard. With Johanna Shimkus, Philippe Hiquily, Serge Davri.
- **Rue Saint-Denis**. Written and Directed by Jean-Daniel Pollet. With Micheline Dax, Claude Melki.
- **Place de l'Etoile**. Written and Directed by Eric Rohmer. With Jean-Michel Rouzière, Marcel Gallon.
- **Gare du Nord**. Written and Directed by Jean Rouch. With Nadine Ballot, Barbet Schroeder, Gilles Quéant.

Shown with *La Cloche*, France. Directed by Jean L'Hôte.

**LE PETIT SOLDAT**
*France, 1960. Written and Directed by Jean-Luc Godard.*
With Michel Subor, Anna Karina, Henri-Jacques Huet, Paul Beauvais. Shown with *Screening Room*, USA. Directed by Lincoln Diamant. Also, *The Longest Bridge*, USA. Directed by Richard Longo.

**RAVEN'S END**
*Sweden, 1964. Written and Directed by Bo Widerberg.*
With Thommy Berggren, Keve Hjelm, Emy Storm, Ingvar Hirdwall. Shown with *The Hoffnung Symphony*, UK. Directed by Harold Whitaker.

**SANDRA**
*Italy, 1965. Directed by Luchino Visconti.*
Written by Suso Cecchi D'Amico, Enrico Medioli, and Visconti. With Claudia Cardinale, Jean Sorel, Michael Craig, Renzo Ricci. Shown with *Study in Wet*, USA. Directed by Homer Groening.

**SHAKESPEARE WALLAH**
*India, 1965. Directed by James Ivory.*
Written by Ivory and Ruth Prawer Jhabvala. With Shashi Kapoor, Geoffrey Kendal, Laura Liddell, Felicity Kendal, Madhur Jaffrey. Shown with *Enter Hamlet*, USA. Directed by Fred Mogubgub.

**THE SHOP ON MAIN STREET** aka **THE SHOP ON HIGH STREET**
*Czechoslovakia, 1964. Directed by Ján Kadár and Elmar Klos.*
Written by L. Grosman, Kadár, and Klos. With Josef Kroner, Ida Kaminská, Hana Slivková, František Zvarík.

◀ **THOMAS THE IMPOSTER**
*France, 1965. Directed by Georges Franju.*
Written by Raphael Cluzel, Jean Cocteau, Franju, and Michael Worms, based on Cocteau's novel. Narrated by Jean Marais, with Emmanuelle Riva, Jean Servais, Fabrice Rouleau, Sophie Darès. Shown with *Yeats Country*, Ireland. Directed by Patrick Carey.

**UNRECONCILED (NICHT VERSÖHNT)** ▼
*West Germany, 1965. Directed by Jean-Marie Straub.*
Written by Straub and Danièle Huillet, based on Henrich Böll's novel *Billiards at Half Past Nine*. With Henning Harmssen, Ulrich Hopmann, Heiner Braun, Heinrich Hargesheimer, Joachim Weiler. Shown with *A*, West Germany. Directed by Jan Lenica. Also, *Les jeux des anges*, France. Directed by Wladimir Borowczyk. Also, *Fist Fight*, USA. Directed by Robert Breer.

**LES VAMPIRES**
*France, 1915. Written and Directed by Louis Feuillade.*
With Edouard Mathé, Delphine Renot, Louise Lagrange, Jeanne Marie-Laurent, Marcel Lévesque, Musidora. Piano accompaniment by Arthur Kleiner. (Retrospective.)

**WALKOVER**
*Poland, 1965. Written and Directed by Jerzy Skolimowski.*
With Skolimowski, Alexandra Zawieruszanka. This is in a sense a continuation of *Identification Marks: None*. Shown with *We Insist*, Italy. Directed by Gianni Amico.

**THE WEDDING MARCH**
*USA, 1925-7. Written and Directed by Erich von Stroheim.*
With von Stroheim, George Fawcett, Maude George, Fay Wray, ZaSu Pitts. (Retrospective.)

# 1966

SELECTION COMMITTEE INITIATED. IT INCLUDED RICHARD ROUD, AMOS VOGEL, ARTHUR KNIGHT, AND ANDREW SARRIS.

THE 4TH NYFF POSTER ARTWORK WAS CREATED BY ROY LICHTENSTEIN. LIST ART POSTERS. ©LCPA.

SEPTEMBER 12-22 1966
4TH NEW YORK · FILM · FESTIVAL
PHILHARMONIC · HALL

### LOVES OF A BLONDE ▲
*Czechoslovakia, 1965. Directed by Milos Forman.*

Written by Forman, Jaroslav Papoušek, and Ivan Passer. With Hana Brejchová, Vladimir Pucholt, Vladimír Menšík, Milada Jezková. Shown with *The Last Mohican*, USA. Directed by Paul E. Leaf. (Opening Night.)

### LA GUERRE EST FINIE (THE WAR IS OVER)
*France/Sweden, 1966. Directed by Alain Resnais.*

Written by Jorge Semprún. With Yves Montand, Ingrid Thulin, Geneviève Bujold, Michel Piccoli. Shown with *Joachim's Dictionary*, France. Directed by Walerian Borowczyk. (Closing Night.)

### ACCATONE
*Italy, 1961. Written and Directed by Pier Paolo Pasolini.*

With Franco Citti, Franca Pasut, Roberto Scaringella, Adele Cambria. Shown with *Tarantella*, USA. Directed by Carmen D'Avino.

### ALMOST A MAN
*Italy, 1966. Directed by Vittorio De Seta.*

Written by Fabio Carpi, De Seta, and Vera Gherarducci. With Jacques Perrin, Lea Padovani, Gianni Garko, Rosemary Dexter. Shown with *Diagram*, Poland. Directed by Daniel Szczechura.

### AU HASARD BALTHAZAR
*France/Sweden, 1966. Written and Directed by Robert Bresson.*

With Anne Wiazemsky, François Lafarge, Philippe Asselin, Nathalie Joyaut. Shown with *Adolescence*, France. Directed by Vladimir Forgency.

### THE BURMESE HARP
*Japan, 1956. Directed by Kon Ichikawa.*

Written by Natto Wada. With Rentaro Mikuni, Shoji Yasui, Tatsuya Mihashi, Taniye Kitabayashi. (Retrospective.)

### LA CHIENNE
*France, 1931. Written and Directed by Jean Renoir, based on Georges de la Fouchardière's novel.*

With Michel Simon, Janie Mareze, Georges Flament, Madeleine Bérubet. (Retrospective.)

### LA COMMARE SECCA (THE GRIM REAPER)
*Italy, 1962. Directed by Bernardo Bertolucci.*

Written by Bertolucci, Sergio Citti, and Pier Paolo Pasolini. With Francesco Ruiu, Giancarlo De Rosa, Vincenzo Ciccora, Alvaro d'Ercole. Shown with *Pestilent City*, USA. Directed by Peter Goldman.

### THE CREATURES (LES CRÉATURES)
*France/Sweden, 1966. Written and Directed by Agnès Varda.*

With Catherine Deneuve, Michel Piccoli, Eva Dahlbeck, Britta Pettersson. Shown with *Aquarelle*, France. Directed by Dominique Delouche.

### DO YOU KEEP A LION AT HOME?
*Czechoslovakia, 1963. Directed by Pavel Hobl.*

Written by Sheila Ochová and Bohumil Sobotka, based on a story by Ochová. With Ladislav Očenášek, Josef Filip, Olga Machoninova, Jan Brychta. Shown with *Le Poisson prof*, France. Directed by Philippe de Poix.

### THE EAVESDROPPER (EL OJO DE LA CERRADURA)
*Argentina/USA, 1964. Directed by Leopoldo Torre Nilsson.*

Written by Edmundo Eichelbaum, Joe Goldberg, Beatriz Guido, Mabel Itzocovich, and Torre Nilsson, based on an original story by Guido and Torre Nilsson. With Janet Margolin, Stathis Giallelis, Lautaro Murúa, Leonardo Favio. Shown with *Oh Dem Watermelons*, USA. Directed by Robert Nelson. Also, *Chamber Piece*, Denmark. Directed by Ole Gammeltoft.

**THE HAWKS AND THE SPARROWS** ▲
*Italy, 1966. Written and Directed by Pier Paolo Pasolini.*
With Toto, Ninetto Davoli, Femi Benussi, Umberto Bevilacqua. Shown with *Piano Lesson*, Sweden. Directed by Vera Nordin.

**HUNGER (SULT)**
*Denmark/Norway/Sweden, 1966. Directed by Henning Carlsen.*
Written by Carlsen and Peter Seeberg, based on Knut Hamsun's novel. With Per Oscarsson, Gunnel Lindblom, Oswald Helmuth, Birgitte Federspiel. Shown with *Contrepied*, France. Directed by Manuel Otero.

**THE HUNT (LA CAZA)**
*Spain, 1966. Directed by Carlos Saura.*
Written by Angelino Fons and Saura. With Ismael Merlo, Alfredo Mayo, José María Prada, Emilio Gutiérrez Caba. (Discovered by Bosley Crowther in Madrid!) Shown with *The Pop Show*, USA. Directed by Fred Mogubgub. Also, *Les escargots*, France. Directed by R. Laloux and R. Topor.

◀ **INTIMATE LIGHTING**
*Czechoslovakia, 1965. Directed by Ivan Passer.*
Written by Jaroslav Papoušek, Passer, and Václav Sasek. With Vera Kresadlová, Zdenek Bezusek, Jan Vostrcil, Vlastimila Viková.

**THE MAN WITH THE SHAVEN HEAD** aka **THE MAN WHO HAD HIS HAIR CUT SHORT**
*Belgium, 1966. Directed by André Delvaux.*
Written by Delvaux and Anna De Pagter, based on Johan Daisne's novel. With Senne Rouffaer, Beata Tyszkiewicz, Hector Camerlynck.

+ **SIMON OF THE DESERT**
*Mexico, 1965. Written and Directed by Luis Buñuel, dialogue by Julio Alejandro and Buñuel.*
With Claudio Brook, Silvia Pinal.

**MASCULIN FÉMININ**
*France/Sweden, 1965. Written and Directed by Jean-Luc Godard, very loosely based on two stories by Guy de Maupassant.*
With Jean-Pierre Léaud, Chantal Goya, Marlène Jobert, Michel Debord. Shown with *A la source, la femme aimée*, France. Directed by Nelly Kaplan. Also, *How Do You Like Dem Bananas*, USA. Directed by Lionel Rogosin.

**PEARLS OF THE DEEP** aka **PEARLS ON THE GROUND**
*Czechoslovakia, 1965. Five separate segments, all written by Bohumil Hrabal, based on his own short stories:*
  • **Mr. Baltazar's Death**. Directed by Jiří Menzel. With Pavla Maršálková, Ferdinand Kruta, Jan Pech.

- **The Imposters**. Directed by Jan Němec. With Milos Ctrnacty, František Havel, Josef Heji.
- **The House of Happiness**. Directed by Ewald Schorm. With Václav Žák, Josefa Pechlatová, Ivan Vyskočil.
- **The Snackbar World**. Directed by Vera Chytilová. With Vladimír Boudník, Vera Mrázková, Alzbeta Lastovková.
- **Romance**. Directed by Jaromil Jireš. With Karel Jerábek, Dana Valtová.

Shown with *9 Variations on a Dance Theme*, USA. Directed by Hilary Harris.

◀ **PIERROT LE FOU**
*France/Italy, 1965. Written and Directed by Jean-Luc Godard, based on Lionel White's novel* Obsession.

With Jean-Paul Belmondo, Anna Karina, Dirk Sanders, Raymond Devos. Shown with *Son of Dada*, USA. Directed by Robert Preston. Also, *Ceremonie pour une Victoire*, France. Directed by Jacques Kébadian.

**THE ROUND-UP**
*Hungary, 1966. Directed by Miklós Jancsó.*

Written by Gyula Hernádi. With János Görbe, Tibor Molnár, Andras Kozak, Gabor Agardy. Shown with *La brûlure de mille soleils*, France. Directed by Pierre Kast.

**"THE SCENE"** – three cinéma-vérité films:
- **Meet Marlon Brando**, USA, 1966. Directed by the Maysles Brothers.
- **Troublemakers**, USA, 1966. Directed by Norman Fruchter and Robert Machover.
- **Notes for a Film on Jazz**, Italy, 1966. Directed by Gianni Amico. With Steve Lacy, Annie Ross, Roni Pondexter, Mal Waldron.

**SHADOWS OF FORGOTTEN ANCESTORS**
*USSR, 1964. Directed by Sergei Parajanov.*

Written by Ivan Chendey and Parajanov, based on M. Kotsiubinsky's novel. With Ivan Nikolaichuk, Larisa Kadochnikova, Tatiana Bestaeva, Spartak Bagashvili. Shown with *The Hand*, Czechoslovakia. Directed by Jiří Trnka.

**THE SHAMELESS OLD LADY**
*France, 1964. Written and Directed by René Allio, based on a story by Bertolt Brecht.*

With Sylvie, Etienne Bierry, Malka Ribovska, Victor Lanoux. Shown with *The Woman*, Hungary. Directed by Ivan Lakatos.

**THREE**
*Yugoslavia, 1965. Directed by Aleksandar Petrovič.*

Written by Antonije Isakovič and Petrovič, based on Isakovič's novel *The Fern and the Fire*. With Velimir Bata Živojinović, Ali Raner, Senka Veletanlić-Petrović, Voja Mirić.

**THE WAR GAME**
*UK, 1966. Written and Directed by Peter Watkins.*

With "some of the people of Kent."

**+ WHOLLY COMMUNION**
*UK, 1966. Directed by Peter Whitehead.*

With Allen Ginsberg, Lawrence Ferlinghetti, Gregory Corso, Harry Fainlight. Shown with *St. Matthew Passion*, Hungary. Directed by Tamás Czigány.

**A WOMAN OF AFFAIRS**
*USA, 1929. Directed by Clarence Brown.*

Written by Bess Meredyth, based on Michael Arlen's novel *The Green Hat*. With Greta Garbo, John Gilbert, Lewis Stone, John Mack Brown, Douglas Fairbanks Jr.

**+ THE CHEAT**
*USA, 1915. Directed by Cecil B. DeMille.*

Written by Hector Turnbull. With Fannie Ward, Jack Dean, Sessue Hayakawa, James Neill. Piano accompaniment by Arthur Kleiner. (Retrospective.)

*The Shameless Old Lady* by René Allio

NYFF SPECIAL EVENTS began this year with **"The Independent Cinema"** – a program of 27 events covering various aspects of current independent filmmaking in the U.S. that was presented, free of charge, at the Library Museum of Performing Arts. Amos Vogel was the Program Director, John Brockman the Coordinator. Wendy Keys also worked on the program. The lineup: Discussions – Amos Vogel on the present state of indie cinema; directors from abroad on indie filmmaking; Bert Stern and Harold Becker, plus screenings of TV commercials; Harry Smith, plus screenings of early abstract films and *Magic Feature*; Hilary Harris, plus portions of his film about New York City; new concepts of film, moderated by Henry Geldzahler; independent-film distribution, with Shirley Clarke, Lionel Rogosin, Jonas Mekas, and Louis Brigante; the problems with indie-film distribution, moderated by Michael Mayer; the Maysles Brothers, plus excerpts from their films; Stan VanDerBeek and Robert Breer, plus screenings of their films; Open interviews – Miloš Forman; Richard Roud and visiting foreign film directors; Presentation of Robert Whitman's new film-oriented "theater piece"; Lectures – Andrew Sarris on cinematic style; Annette Michelson on radicalism in film; George Amberg on the psychology of vision; Parker Tyler – "What Are the New Critics Saying?"; Richard Kostelanetz on how mixed media relates to film; Screenings – *Echoes of Silence*, plus discussion with Peter Goldman; *The Flicker and Archangel*, plus discussion with Tony Conrad and Victor Grauer; *Relativity*, plus discussion with Ed Emshwiller; selections from the UCLA's National Student Film Festival; *Stravinsky*, plus discussion with Richard Leacock; *Vali*, plus discussion with Sheldon Rochlin.

# 1967

SELECTION COMMITTEE: RICHARD ROUD, AMOS VOGEL, ARTHUR KNIGHT, ANDREW SARRIS, AND SUSAN SONTAG.

THE 5TH NYFF POSTER ARTWORK WAS CREATED BY ANDY WARHOL. ©LCPA AND THE ANDY WARHOL FOUNDATION FOR THE VISUAL ARTS, INC./ARTISTS RIGHTS SOCIETY (ARS), NEW YORK.

## THE BATTLE OF ALGIERS ▶

*Italy/Algeria, 1965. Directed by Gillo Pontecorvo.*

Written by Franco Solinas. With Jean Martin, Yacef Saadi, Brahim Haggiag, Tommaso Neri. Note: the black-tie audience cheered on the Algerian terrorist liberationists. Shown with *What on Earth*, Canada. Directed by Les Drew and Kaj Pindal. (Opening Night.)

## FAR FROM VIETNAM

*France, 1967. Directed by Jean-Luc Godard, Joris Ivens, William Klein, Claude Lelouch, Alain Resnais, and Agnès Varda.*

Six important directors in Paris express their views on the Vietnam War. Shown with *12-12-42*, USA. Directed by Dick Gerendasy, Tom McDonough, and Bernard Stone. (Closing Night.)

## APPLAUSE

*USA, 1929. Directed by Rouben Mamoulian.*

Written by Garrett Fort, based on Beth Brown's novel. With Helen Morgan, Joan Peers, Fuller Mellish Jr., Jack Cameron.

## + SHOW PEOPLE

*USA, 1929. Directed by King Vidor.*

Written by Agnes Christine Johnson and Laurence Stalling. With Marion Davies, William Haines, Dell Henderson, Paul Ralli, and a large roster of celebrity walk-ons. Piano accompaniment by Arthur Kleiner. (Retrospective.)

## BARRIER

*Poland, 1966. Written and Directed by Jerzy Skolimowski.*

With Jan Nowicki, Joanna Szczerbic, Tadeusz Lomnicki, Zdzisław Maklakiewicz. Shown with *Le Voyage*, France. Directed by Jacques Simonet. Also, *See Saw Seems*, USA. Directed by Stan VanDerBeek.

## LES CARABINIERS

*France/Italy, 1962. Directed by Jean-Luc Godard.*

Written by Godard, Jean Gruault, and Roberto Rossellini, based on Benjamin Joppolo's play. With Geneviève Galéa, Catherine Ribero, Marino Masé, Albert Juross. Shown with *Minute Waltz*, Poland. Directed by Andrzej Kaminski and Marian Marzynski. Also, *The Secret Cinema*, USA. Directed by Paul Bartel.

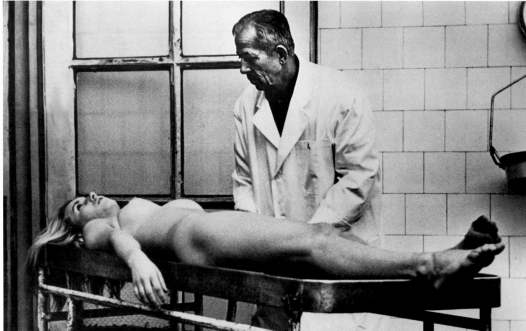

Both photos above from *Love Affair, or the Case of the Missing Switch Board Operator* by Dušan Makavejev

### THE LION HUNTERS (LA CHASSE AU LION À L'ARC)
*France, 1965. Written and Directed by Jean Rouch.*

### + MEMORANDUM
*Canada, 1966. Directed by Donald Brittain and John Spotton.*

### "THE LONDON SCENE" – two 1967 films directed by Peter Whitehead:
- **Tonite Let's All Make Love in London.** With Michael Caine, Vanessa Redgrave, Julie Christie, David Hockney, Lee Marvin. Music by Pink Floyd, the Rolling Stones.
- **The Benefit of the Doubt.** Excerpts from the Royal Shakespeare Company's presentation of *US*, directed by Peter Brook, interspersed with interviews with the actors. With Eric Allan, Mary Allen, Jeremy Anthony, Hugh Armstrong.

### LOVE AFFAIR, OR THE CASE OF THE MISSING SWITCHBOARD OPERATOR aka AN AFFAIR OF THE HEART
*Yugoslavia, 1967. Written and Directed by Dušan Makavejev.*

With Eva Ras, Slobodan Aligrudić, Ružica Sokić, Miodrag Andrić. Shown with *The Fly*, Yugoslavia. Directed by Aleksandar Marks. Also, *Calanda*, France. Directed by Juan Luis Buñuel.

### MADE IN U.S.A.
*France, 1966. Written and Directed by Jean-Luc Godard, based on Richard Stark's novel* The Jugger.

With Anna Karina, Lászlo Szabó, Jean-Pierre Léaud, Yves Afonso. Shown with *Crazy Murder*, Japan. Directed by Yoji Kuri. Also, *Cages*, Poland. Directed by Mirosław Kijowicz.

### NAPOLEON
*France, 1923-27. Written and Directed by Abel Gance.*

Music by Arthur Honegger. With Albert Dieudonné, Vladimir Roudenko, Antonin Artaud. Piano accompaniment by Arthur Kleiner. (Retrospective.)

### THE OTHER ONE (L'UNE ET L'AUTRE)
*France, 1967. Written and Directed by René Allio.*

With Malka Ribovska, Philippe Noiret, Marc Cassot, Christian Alers. Shown with *Ares Contra Atlas*, France. Directed by Manuel Otéro. Also, *Lighthouse*, France. Directed by Lucien Clergue.

### PORTRAIT OF JASON
*USA, 1967. Written and Directed by Shirley Clarke.*

With Jason Holliday. Shown with *Lapis*, USA. Directed by James Whitney.

### REBELLION aka SAMURAI REBELLION
*Japan, 1967. Directed by Masaki Kobayashi.*

Written by Shinobu Hashimoto, based on a story by Yasuhiko Takiguchi. With Toshiro Mifune, Takeshi Kato, Yoko Tsukasa, Tatsuyoshi Ebara.

### SONS AND MOTHERS (SERDTSE MATERI)
*USSR, 1966. Directed by Mark Donskoi.*

Written by I. Donskoia and Z. Voskrensenskaia. With Elena Fadeyeva, Danili Sagal, Nina Menichkova, Guennady Tchertov. Shown with *Nadar*, France. Directed by Michel Boschet and André Martin.

### THE TAKING OF POWER BY LOUIS XIV
*France, 1966. Directed by Roberto Rossellini.*

Written by Philippe Erlanger and Jean Gruault. With Jean-Marie Patte, Raymond Jourdan, Silvagni, Katharina Renn, Dominique Vincent. Shown with *Lumberjacks*, USSR. Directed by Igor Grabovsky.

### LE DÉPART
*Belgium, 1967. Directed by Jerzy Skolimowski.*

Written by Andrzej Kostenko and Skolimowski. With Jean-Pierre Léaud, Catherine Duport, Jacqueline Bir, Paul Roland. Shown with *Five-Minute Thriller*, Hungary. Directed by József Nepp.

### ELVIRA MADIGAN
*Sweden, 1967. Written and Directed by Bo Widerberg.*

With Pia Degermark, Thommy Berggren, Lennart Malmen, Nina Widerberg. Shown with *Calypso*, USA. Directed by Paul Glickman. Also, *Minestrone with Music*, USA. Directed by Carmen D'Avino.

### FATHER (APA)
*Hungary, 1966. Written and Directed by István Szabó.*

With Miklós Gábor, Klári Tolnay, András Bálint, Dani Erdelyi. Shown with *Screen Test*, Hungary. Directed by György Kárpáti.

### THE FEVERISH YEARS
*Yugoslavia, 1966. Directed by Dragoslav Lazić. Written by Ljubiša Kozomara and Gordan Mihić.*

With Bekim Fehmiu, Ana Matic, Dušica Žegarac, Milan Jelić. Shown with *Dancing Songs*, Yugoslavia. Directed by Zlatko Bourek. Also, *Lourdes*, France. Directed by Christian Gion.

### FUNNYMAN
*USA, 1967. Directed by John Korty.*

Written by Peter Bonerz and Korty. With Bonerz, Sandra Archer, Carol Androsky, Larry Hankin. Shown with *Bach to Bach*, USA. Directed by Paul Leaf.

### HUGS AND KISSES
*Sweden, 1967. Written and Directed by Jonas Cornell.*

With Agneta Ekmanner, Håkan Serner, Lena Granhagen, Sven-Bertil Taube. Shown with *Balade d'Emile*, France. Directed by Manuel Otéro. Also, *God Is Dog Spelled Backwards*, USA. Directed by Dan McLaughlin.

**YESTERDAY GIRL (ABSCHIED VON GESTERN)**
*West Germany, 1966. Written and Directed by
Alexander Kluge, based on a story from his book*
Attendance List for a Funeral.

With Alexandra Kluge, Günther Mack, Eva Maria Meineke,
Hans Korte. Shown with *Numbers*, Poland. Directed by
Stefan Schabenbeck. Also, *Shadow of the Apple*, France.
Directed by Robert Lapoujade.

**YOUNG TÖRLESS**
*Germany, 1966. Written and Directed by Volker
Schlöndorff, based on Robert Musil's novel.*

With Mathieu Carrière, Marian Seidowsky, Bernd Tischer,
Fred Dietz. Shown with *People from the Neretva River*,
Yugoslavia. Directed by Obrad Gluscevic.

## Special Events

PRESENTED AT LINCOLN CENTER'S LIBRARY & MUSEUM OF
PERFORMING ARTS

**"A Tribute to Abel Gance"** – presented in conjunction
with the Cinémathèque Française and George Eastman
House. Films shown: *La dixième symphonie*, 1918; *La fin du
monde*, 1929; *Un grand amour de Beethoven*, 1935; *J'accuse*
(silent version), 1919; *J'accuse*, 1937; *Marie Tudor*, 1965;
*Napoleon*, 1927 (presented at Philharmonic Hall as part of
the main slate); *Paradis perdu*, 1939; *La roue*, 1922.

**"The Social Cinema in America"** – selected by Gordon
Hitchens, Arthur Knight, Perry Miller, Andrew Sarris,
Amos Vogel, and Edith Zornow. Included: Amos Vogel –
"Social Reality and the Avant-Garde"; Discussion with
Richard Roud and visiting foreign directors; *Every 7th
Child*, by Jack Willis; Four Vietnam War films: *While
Brave Men Die*, by Fulton Lewis III, *The Unique
War*, by the U.S. Army, *Victory Will Be Ours*, by the
National Liberation Front of South Vietnam, and
*Napalm by Don Lerner*; *Home for Life*, by Gordon
Quinn and Gerald Temaner; George Amberg – "The
Ambiguity of Reality"; *The Holy Ghost People*, by
Peter Adair; *Lay My Burden Down*, by Jack Willis;
*Malcolm X: Struggle for Freedom*; *Now*, by Santiago
Álvarez, Cuba; and *Black Natchez*, by David

Neuman; *Mills of the Gods*, by Beryl Fox; Open inter-
view with visiting directors; Panels: "The Ethics of the
Documentary"; "Reality Cinema: Whose Truth?"; and
"The Television Documentary and the Establishment";
*Sons and Daughters*, plus discussion with Jerry Stoll;
*This Time the World*; *Titicut Follies*, by Frederick
Wiseman, plus discussion with anti-censorship
lawyer Ephraim London; *Warrendale*, by Alan King;
Workshop – "New Materials Available in Film."

*J'accuse* (1919) by Abel Gance

# 1968

SELECTION COMMITTEE: RICHARD ROUD, CHAIRMAN, AMOS VOGEL, ANDREW SARRIS, AND SUSAN SONTAG.

THE 6TH NYFF POSTER ARTWORK WAS CREATED BY HENRY PEARSON. STUDY #2 – LIST ART POSTERS, ©LCPA.

LINCOLN CENTER'S
SIXTH NEW YORK FILM FESTIVAL
PHILHARMONIC HALL
September 17-28

### CAPRICIOUS SUMMER
*Czechoslovakia, 1968. Written and Directed by Jiří Menzel, based on Vladislav Vančura's novel.*

With Rudolf Hrušínský, Mila Myslíková, František Rehák. Shown with *Koncertissimo*, Hungary. Directed by József Gémes. Also, *The Dove*, USA. Directed by George Coe and Anthony Lover. (Opening Night.)

### THE FIREMEN'S BALL
*Czechoslovakia, 1967. Directed by Miloš Forman.*

Written by Forman, Ivan Passer, and Jaroslav Papoušek. With Vaclav Stockel, Josef Svet, Jan Vostrcil, Josef Kolb. Shown with *The Big Shave*, USA. Directed by Martin Scorsese. Also, *French Lunch*, USA. Directed by Nell Cox. (Closing Night.)

### ARTISTS UNDER THE BIG TOP: PERPLEXED
*West Germany, 1968. Written and Directed by Alexander Kluge.*

Shown with *Off On*, USA. Directed by Scott Bartlett.

### BEYOND THE LAW
*USA, 1968. Written and Directed by Norman Mailer.*

With Rip Torn, George Plimpton, Mailer, Mickey Knox, Marcia Mason. Shown with *Permutations*, USA. Directed by John Whitney.

### ◀ LES BICHES (THE DOES)
*France/ Italy, 1967. Directed by Claude Chabrol.*

Written by Chabrol and Paul Gégauff. With Jean-Louis Trintignant, Jacqueline Sassard, Stéphane Audran, Nane Germon. Shown with *T.G.I.F.*, USA. Directed by Alan Arkin.

### THE BOY WITH GREEN HAIR
*USA, 1949. Directed by Joseph Losey.*

Written by Ben Barzman and Alfred Lewis Levitt, based on a story by Betsy Beaton. With Pat O'Brien, Robert Ryan, Barbara Hale, Dean Stockwell.

### + THEY LIVE BY NIGHT
*USA, 1949. Directed by Nicholas Ray.*

Written by Charles Schnee, adaptation by Ray, based on Edward Anderson's novel *Thieves Like Us*. With Farley Granger, Cathy O'Donnell, Howard Da Silva. (Retrospectives—presented in cooperation with the AFI.)

### CHRONICLE OF ANNA MAGDALENA BACH
*Italy/West Germany, 1968. Directed by Jean-Marie Straub.*

Written by Straub and Danièle Huillet. With Gustav Leonhardt, Christiane Lang. Shown with *Poem Field No. 1*, USA. Directed by Stan VanDerBeek.

### L'ENFANCE NUE (NAKED CHILDHOOD)
*France, 1968. Written and Directed by Maurice Pialat.*

With Michel Terrazon, Marie-Louise Thierry, René Thierry, Linda Gutemberg, Raoul Billerey, Pierrette Deplanque. Shown with *Concerto for an Exile*, France/Ivory Coast. Directed by Désiré Ecaré.

### FACES
*USA, 1968. Written and Directed by John Cassavetes.*

With John Marley, Gena Rowlands, Lynn Carlin, Fred Draper, Seymour Cassel.

### HUGO AND JOSEFIN
*Sweden, 1968. Directed by Kjell Grede.*

Written by Grede and Maria Gripe, based on Gripe's novel. With Marie Öhman, Fredrik Becklen, Beppe Wolgers. Shown with *A Day with Timmy Page*, USA. Directed by David Hoffman.

### THE IMMORTAL STORY
*France, 1968. Written and Directed by Orson Welles, based on a story by Karen Blixen (Isak Dinesen).*

With Orson Welles, Jeanne Moreau, Roger Coggio, Norman Eshley. Shown with *Historia Naturae*, Czechoslovakia. Directed by Jan Svankmajer. Also, *When Angels Fall*, Poland. Directed by Roman Polanski.

### KAYA, I'LL KILL YOU
*Yugoslavia/France, 1967. Directed by Vatroslav Mimica.*

Written by Mimica and Kruno Quien. With Zaim Muzaferija, Uglješa Kojadinović, Antun Nalis, Jolanda Dacic. Shown with *Rope Trick*, UK. Directed by Bob Godfrey. Also, *Hop-Jan*, Yugoslavia. Directed by Vlatko Filipović.

### LOLA MONTÈS ▼
*France/Germany, 1955. Directed by Max Ophuls.*

Written by Franz Geiger, Ophuls, and Annette Wademant, based on Cécil Saint-Laurent's novel *La Vie Extraordinaire de Lola Montès*. With Martine Carol, Peter Ustinov, Anton Walbrook, Oskar Werner. (Retrospective.)

### MONEY (L'ARGENT)
*France/Germany, 1927. Written and Directed by Marcel L'Herbier, based on Emile Zola's novel.*

With Brigitte Helm, Pierre Alcover, Mary Glory, Raymond Rouleau, Yvette Guilbert. Piano accompaniment by Arthur Kleiner. (Retrospective.)

### MOUCHETTE
*France, 1967. Written and Directed by Robert Bresson, based on Georges Bernanos's novel* Nouvelle Histoire de Mouchette.

With Nadine Nortier, Jean-Claude Guilbert, Marie Cardinal, Paul Hébert, Jean Vimenet. Shown with *The Apple*, USA. Directed by Norman Gollin. Also, *Uncle Yanco*, France. Directed by Agnès Varda.

### THE NUN (LA RELIGIEUSE)
*France, 1965. Directed by Jacques Rivette.*

Written by Jean Gruault and Rivette, based on Denis Diderot's novel. With Anna Karina, Liselotte Pulver, Micheline Presle, Christiane Lénier.

### ONE PLUS ONE aka SYMPATHY FOR THE DEVIL
*UK, 1968. Directed by Jean-Luc Godard.*

With the Rolling Stones and Anne Wiazemsky. Godard's first English-language film.

### PARTNER
*Italy, 1968. Directed by Bernardo Bertolucci.*

Written by Gianni Amico and Bertolucci, freely based on Fyodor Dostoevsky's *The Double*. With Pierre Clémenti, Stefania Sandrelli, Tina Aumont, Sergio Tofano.

### THE RED AND THE WHITE
*Hungary/USSR, 1967. Directed by Miklós Jancsó.*

Written by Gyula Hernádi, Jancsó, and Giorgi Mdivani. With Tatyana Konyukhova, Krystyna Mikolaiewska, Mikhail Kozakov, Viktor Avdiushko. Shown with *The Other Side*, Belgium. Directed by Herman Wuyts.

### A REPORT ON THE PARTY AND THE GUESTS aka THE PARTY AND THE GUESTS
*Czechoslovakia, 1966. Directed by Jan Němec.*

Written by Ester Krumbachová and Němec. With Jan Klusák, Ivan Vyskočil, Jiří Němec, Zdena Skvorecka, Pavel Bosek, Karel Mares. Shown with *Quodlibet*, UK. Directed by Nancy Hanna and Vera Linnecar. Also, *The Bed*, USA. Directed by James Broughton.

### SIGNS OF LIFE
*West Germany, 1968. Written and Directed by Werner Herzog.*

With Peter Brogle, Wolfgang Reichmann, Athina Zacharopoulou, Wolfgang von Ungern-Sternberg. Shown with *Hobby*, Poland. Directed by Daniel Szczchura.

### TONI
*France, 1934. Directed by Jean Renoir.*

Written by Carl Einstein and Renoir, based on the material gathered by J. Levert for his novel. With Charles Blavette, Jenny Hélia, Celia Montalvan, Delmont. (Retrospective.) Shown with *Fairy Story*, UK. Directed by Tony Cattaneo.

### TROPICS (TROPICI)
*Italy, 1968. Directed by Gianni Amico.*

Written by Amico and Francesco Tullio Altan. With Joel Barcelos, Janira Santiago, Graciele Campos, Batista Campos. Shown with *Whatever Happened to Uncle Fred?*, UK. Directed by Bob Godfrey.

### TWENTY-FOUR HOURS IN THE LIFE OF A WOMAN
*France/West Germany, 1967. Directed by Dominique Delouche.*

Written by Delouche, Marie-France Rivière, and Albert Valentin, based on Stefan Zweig's novel. With Danielle Darrieux, Robert Hoffmann, Romina Power, Léna Skerla, Marthe Alycia. Shown with *You Can*, USA. Directed by Rose Neiditch. Also, *Pax de deux*, Canada. Directed by Norman McLaren.

### 2 OR 3 THINGS I KNOW ABOUT HER
*France, 1967. Written and Directed by Jean-Luc Godard.*

With Marina Vlady, Anny Duperey, Roger Montsoret, Raoul Lévy, narrated by Godard. Shown with *Ciné Tracts I*, France. Directors: Anonymous.

### WEEKEND
*France/Italy, 1967. Written and Directed by Jean-Luc Godard.*

With Mireille Darc, Jean Yanne, Jean-Pierre Kalfon, Valérie Lagrange, Jean-Pierre Léaud. Shown with *Ciné Tracts II*, France. Directors: Anonymous.

# Special Events

PRESENTED AT LINCOLN CENTER'S LIBRARY & MUSEUM OF THE PERFORMING ARTS

**"Personal Cinema"** – personal-story films, portraits, and auto-documentaries programmed by Henry English, Wendy Keys, Bob Sitton, and Amos Vogel. Films shown: *The Amazing Colossal Man, Cinder City Plus Six*, and *Yellow Ball Cache*, by children of the Yellow Ball Workshop; *Anti-1*, by Michel Maquesee; *Arabesque*, by Nancy Linde; *The Attempt*, by Ivan Quilles; *Black Spring*, by LeRoi Jones; *Bridge*, by Ted Benzer; *The Children of Cardoza*, by William Gaddis and William Hansard; *Child's Eye View*, by Bank Street College students; *Clarence*, by Jud Yalkut; *David Holzman's Diary*, by Jim McBride; *Douglas, James and Joe*, by Grover Dale; *The End* and *The Pot Heads in 'Let's Get Nice,'* by Alfonso Sanchez; *Fat Fred*, by students in the North of England; *The Fight Against the Borrowers*, by Orson Montez; *Film Club*, by James Barrios, plus discussion moderated by Bob Sitton; *The First Step*, by Greer Morton Jr. and Bill Peltz; *From the Inside Out*, by residents of a California ghetto; *Georg*, by Stanton Kaye; *Ghetto*, by Richard Mason; *The Grandfather*, by Peter Hoving; *I Love You, I Think*, by Woodard Archie; *I'm Here Now*, by NY ghetto residents, Bud Wirschafter, project director; *Intrepid Shadows*, by Al Clah; *The Journey*, by Marvin Silbersher; *The Jungle*, by the Oxford Street Gang of Philadelphia; *Laughing Bear*, by Mark Sadan; *Male and Female*, by Miguel Sanchez; *Memory of John Earl*, by Earl McFadden; *Menagerie*, by students at the Lexington School of Modern Dance; *Nyala*, by Glen Denny; *The Picnic*, by British students; *Profiles Cast Long Shadows*, by Bob Sperry; *Prospera*, by Linda Yellin; *The Revenge*, by Miguel Sanchez; *Song of Innocence*, by Mark Sadan; *Spirit of the Navajo*, by Maxinne and Maryjane Tsossie; *Tell It Like It Is*, by Harry Dolan and other Watts writers; *That's Where I'm At*, by Alvin Fiering and Lois Ginandes; *The Thief*, by Raymond Esquelin; *Trio at 19*, by Judith Kurtz; *Yesterday*, by Paul Tepper; *You Dig It?*, by members of Mobilization for Youth; *You See What I'm Trying To Say?*, by Henry English.

**"The Western"** – prepared with the assistance of William K. Everson. Films shown: *Broken Arrow*, 1950, by Delmer Daves, plus excerpts from *The Red Raiders*, 1927, by Ken Maynard; *The Covered Wagon*, 1923, by James Cruze; *Cowboy Ambrose*; Discussion titled "The Western: Art or Entertainment?," with Andrew Sarris, Henry Fonda, and William K. Everson; Excerpts from "B" Westerns – *The Phantom Empire, Deadwood Dick, The Red Rider*, and *Zorro's Fighting Legion*; *The Heart of an Indian*, 1913, by Thomas Ince; *From Hell to Texas*, 1958, by Henry Hathaway; *The Gunfighter*, 1950, and *Jesse James*, 1939, by Henry King; *Hell's Hinges*, 1916, plus excerpts from *Wild Bill Hickok* and *Tumbleweeds*, by William S. Hart; *High Noon*, 1952, by Fred Zinnemann; *The Iron Horse*, 1924, and *My Darling Clementine*, 1946, by John Ford; *The Last Drop of Water*, 1911, by D.W. Griffith; *Massacre*, 1934, by Alan Crosland; *The Plainsman*, 1937, by Cecil B. DeMille; *The Real West*, an NBC documentary with Gary Cooper, plus panel discussion moderated by Bob Sitton; *Red River*, 1947, by Howard Hawks; *Shane*, 1953, by George Stevens; *Sky High*, 1922, by Lynn Reynolds; *The Texas Rangers*, 1936, by King Vidor; *Thundering Hoofs*, 1924, by Albert S. Rogell; *When Outlaws Meet*, 1919, by Al Jennings; *Wild and Woolly*, 1919, by John Emerson.

**"Film-makers on New Life-Styles"** – movies dealing with the new generation's attempts to create alternative styles of living. Films shown: *God Respects Us When We Work, But Loves Us When We Dance*, by Les Blank and Skip Gerson, plus *The Alternative*, by Fred Thorne; *Last Summer Won't Happen*, by Peter Gessner and Tom Hurwitz; *No Vietnamese Ever Called Me Nigger*, by David Loeb Weiss; *One Step Away*, by David Neuman and Ed Pincus; *Sally's Hounds*, by Robert Edelstein; *Sometimes I Like Even Me*, by Peter Levin, plus *Summerhill*, by Dennis Miller.

*The Covered Wagon* by James Cruze

*Jesse James* by Henry King

*My Darling Clementine* by John Ford

# 1969

SELECTION COMMITTEE: RICHARD ROUD, CHAIRMAN, PENELOPE HUSTON, ARTHUR KNIGHT, ANDREW SARRIS, SUSAN SONTAG.
CONSULTANT: HENRI LANGLOIS (RETROSPECTIVES).

THE 7TH NYFF POSTER ARTWORK WAS CREATED BY MARISOL ESCOBAR. LIST ART POSTERS, ©LCPA.

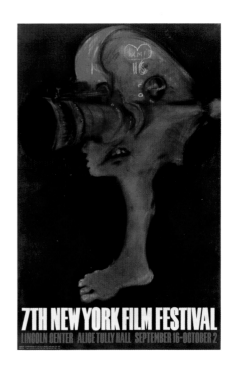

7TH NEW YORK FILM FESTIVAL
LINCOLN CENTER · ALICE TULLY HALL · SEPTEMBER 16–OCTOBER 2

**BOB & CAROL & TED & ALICE**
*USA, 1969. Directed by Paul Mazursky.*

Written by Mazursky and Larry Tucker. With Natalie Wood, Robert Culp, Elliott Gould, Dyan Cannon. (Opening Night.) Note: This was the first ON film from the U.S.; it was introduced by Mayor John Lindsay.

◀ **OH! WHAT A LOVELY WAR**
*UK, 1969. Directed by Richard Attenborough.*

Written by Len Deighton, based on Charles Chilton's play and Joan Littlewood's musical. With Ralph Richardson, Ian Holm, John Gielgud, Jack Hawkins, John Mills, Jean-Pierre Cassel, Maggie Smith, Michael Redgrave, Laurence Olivier, Susannah York, Dirk Bogarde, Vanessa Redgrave. (Closing Night.)

**ÅDALEN '31**
*Sweden, 1968. Written and Directed by Bo Widerberg.*

With Peter Schildt, Kerstin Tidelius, Roland Hedlund, Stefan Feierbach.

**BOY (SHONEN)**
*Japan, 1969. Directed by Nagisa Oshima.*

Written by Tsutomu Tamura. With Fumio Watanabe, Tetsuo Abe, Akiko Koyama, Tsuyoshi Kimoshita. Shown with *Passing Days*, Yugoslavia. Directed by Nedeljko Dragić.

**THE DESERTER AND THE NOMADS**
*Czechoslovakia/Italy, 1968. Directed by Juraj Jakubisko.*

Written by Jakubisko, Karol Sidon, and Ladislav Ťažký, based on Ťažký's novel. With Ferencz Gejza, Helena Gorovova, Mikulás Ladizinsky, Alexandra Sekulova. Shown with *The Serendipity Bomb,* France. Directed by Jean-Françoise Laguionie.

**DESTROY, SHE SAID**
*France, 1969. Written and Directed by Marguerite Duras.*

With Catherine Sellers, Nicole Hiss, Henri Garcin, Michael Lonsdale, Daniel Gélin. Shown with *Momentum*, USA. Directed by Jordan Belson.

**DUET FOR CANNIBALS**
*Sweden, 1969. Written and Directed by Susan Sontag.*

With Adriana Asti, Lars Ekborg, Gösta Ekman, Agneta Ekmanner.

## THE EPIC THAT NEVER WAS (I, CLAUDIUS)

*UK, 1965.* A BBC anatomy of a film that was never finished provides a posthumous confrontation between its dictatorial director, Josef von Sternberg, and an anarchic actor, Charles Laughton, with comments by those who saw it, including von Sternberg. Narrated by Dirk Bogarde. *I, Claudius* was directed by von Sternberg, based on the novel by Robert Graves. With Charles Laughton, Emlyn Williams, Merle Oberon, Flora Robson, Robert Newton.

## UNE FEMME DOUCE (A GENTLE WOMAN)

*France, 1969. Written and Directed by Robert Bresson, based on a story by Fyodor Dostoevsky.*

With Dominique Sanda, Guy Frangin, Jane Lobre. Shown with *Cambridge Steam Engine*, UK. Directed by Charlie Jenkins. Also, *The Noose*, Hungary. Directed by Sandor Albert.

## LE GAI SAVOIR

*France/West Germany, 1968. Written and Directed by Jean-Luc Godard, loosely based on Jean-Jacques Rousseau's Emile.*

With Jean-Pierre Léaud, Juliet Berto. Shown with *69*, USA. Directed by Robert Breer. Also, *Institutional Quality*, USA. Directed by George Landow.

## GOTO, ISLAND OF LOVE

*France, 1968. Written and Directed by Walerian Borowczyk.*

With Pierre Brasseur, Ligia Branice, Ginette Leclerc, René Dary. Shown with *Invocation of My Demon Brother*, USA. Directed by Kenneth Anger.

## HE WHO GETS SLAPPED ▼

*USA, 1924. Directed by Victor Sjöström.*

Written by Sjöström and Carey Wilson, based on Leonid Andreyev's play. With Lon Chaney, Norma Shearer, John Gilbert, Ruth King, Tully Marshall. Piano accompaniment by Arthur Kleiner. (Retrospective—presented in association with the AFI.)

## THE JOKE

*Czechoslovakia, 1968. Written and Directed by Jaromil Jireš, based on Milan Kundera's novel.*

With Josef Somr, Jana Dítětová, Luděk Munzar, Jaromír Hanzlík. Shown with *Cosmic Zoom*, Canada. Directed by Joe Koenig and Robert Verrall. Also, *To See or Not to See*, Canada. Directed by Bretislav Pojar.

## THE LADY FROM CONSTANTINOPLE

*Hungary, 1969. Directed by Judit Elek.*

Written by Ivan Mandy, based on an original idea by Elek. With Manyi Kiss. Shown with *The World of Man*, USA. Directed by Michael Collyer and Albert Fischer. Also, *At Home*, Canada. Directed by Martin Lavut.

## LIONS LOVE

*USA, 1969. Written and Directed by Agnès Varda.*

With Viva, Jerry Ragni, James Rado, Shirley Clarke, Carlos Clarens, Eddie Constantine. Shown with *Mean to Me*, USA. Directed by Daniel Rosenwein.

## THE MERRY WIDOW

*USA, 1925. Directed by Erich von Stroheim.*

Written by Benjamin Glazer and von Stroheim, based on Franz Lehar, Victor Leon, and Leo Stein's operetta. With Mae Murray, John Gilbert, Roy D'Arcy, Josephine Crowell. Piano accompaniment by Arthur Kleiner. (Retrospective—presented in association with the AFI.)

## THE MONEY ORDER (MANDABI)

*Senegal/France, 1968. Written and Directed by Ousmane Sembene, based on L.S. Senghor's short story.*

With Mamadou Guye, Ynousse N'Diaye, Issa Niang, Serigne N'Diayes. Shown with *How Do You Seduce a Man?*, USA. Directed by Jeremy Paul Kagan.

## ◀ MY NIGHT AT MAUD'S

*France, 1969. Written and Directed by Eric Rohmer.*

With Jean-Louis Trintignant, Françoise Fabian, Marie-Christine Barrault, Antoine Vitez. Shown with *The Canaries*, USA. Directed by Jerome Hill.

## ONE FINE DAY

*Italy, 1969. Written and Directed by Ermanno Olmi.*

With Brunetto Del Vita, Lidia Fuortes, Vitaliano Damioli, Giovanna Ceresa.

## PIERRE & PAUL

*France, 1969. Written and Directed by René Allio.*

With Pierre Mondy, Bulle Ogier, Madeleine Barbulée, Pierre Santini. Shown with *The Emperor's New Armor*, USA. Directed by R.O. Blechman. Also, *Harvesting*, Canada. Directed by Arthur Lamothe.

## PORCILE (PIGPEN)

*Italy/France, 1969. Written and Directed by Pier Paolo Pasolini.*

With Jean-Pierre Léaud, Anne Wiazemsky, Alberto Lionello, Margherita Lozano, Pierre Clémenti, Ugo Tognazzi.

## THE RITE aka THE RITUAL

*Sweden, 1969. Written and Directed by Ingmar Bergman.*

With Ingrid Thulin, Anders Ek, Gunnar Björnstrand, Erik Hell. Shown with *Dr. Murke's Collected Silences*, Sweden. Directed by Per Berglund.

## LA RONDE ▶

*France, 1950. Directed by Max Ophuls.*

Written by Jacques Natanson and Ophuls, based on Arthur Schnitzler's play Reigen. With Anton Walbrook, Simone Signoret, Serge Reggiani, Simone Simon, Daniel Gélin, Danielle Darrieux, Fernand Gravey, Odette Joyeux, Jean-Louis Barrault, Isa Miranda, Gérard Philipe. (Retrospective.) Shown with *A Paris Never Seen*, France. Directed by Albert Lamorisse.

# Special Events

PRESENTED AT LINCOLN CENTER'S LIBRARY & MUSEUM OF THE PERFORMING ARTS

**"Jean Renoir: A One-Man Show"** – presented by the Film Society and the Cinémathèque Française. Films shown: *Le bled,* 1929; *Boudu Saved from Drowning,* 1932; *La chienne,* 1931; *Chotard and Company,* 1933; *The Crime of Monsieur Lange,* 1936; *Le déjeuner sur l'herbe,* 1959; *Diary of a Chambermaid,* 1946; *Elena and Her Men,* 1956; *The Elusive Corporal,* 1962; *Experiment in Evil (Le testament du Dr. Cordelier),* 1959; *French Cancan,* 1954; *The Golden Coach,* 1951; *Grand Illusion,* 1937; *The Little Match Girl,* 1928; *The Lower Depths,* 1936; *Madame Bovary,* 1933; *La Marseillaise,* 1938; *Nana,* 1926; *Night at the Crossroads,* 1932; *On purge bébé,* 1931; *Partie de Campagne,* 1936; *The River,* 1951; *The Rules of the Game,* 1939; *The Sad Sack,* 1928; *The Southerner,* 1945; *Swamp Water,* 1941; *Toni,* 1935; *Whirlpool of Fate,* 1925.

**"The National Film Collection"** – American films from the Library of Congress, presented by the Film Society in association with the AFI. Included: *Broadway,* 1919, by Paul Fejos; *The Cameraman,* 1928, by Edward Sedgwick; *The Canadian,* 1926, by William Beaudine; Clips from *Elvira Madigan* and *Adalen '31,* plus a discussion with Bo Widerberg; *The Conquering Power,* 1921, by Rex Ingram; *The Criminal Code,* 1931, by Howard Hawks; *Dirigible,* 1931, by Frank Capra; Discussion about film preservation, with John Kuiper from the Library of Congress and Sam Kula from the AFI, moderated by Bob Sitton; *Exit Smiling,* 1926, by Sam Tayor; *The Goose Woman,* 1925, by Clarence Brown; *The Kiss Before the Mirror,* 1933, by James Whale; *Little Man, What Now?,* 1934, by Frank Borzage; *The Man Who Laughs,* 1928, by Paul Leni; *Men Without Women,* 1930, by John Ford; *The Mysterious Island,* 1929, by Lucien Hubbard; *The Old Dark House,* 1932, by James Whale; *The Patsy,* 1928, by King Vidor; *The Power and the Glory,* 1933, by William K. Howard; *Pride of the Clan,* 1916, by Maurice Tourneur; *The Scarlet Letter,* 1926, by Victor Sjöström; *So's Your Old Man,* 1926, by Gregory La Cava; *Stark Love,* 1927, by Karl Brown; *The Third Degree,* 1926, by Michael Curtiz; *The Vanishing American,* 1926, by George B. Seitz.

**"Avant-Garde West"** – works by West Coast filmmakers:

**Program 1:** *7362,* by Pat O'Neill, *Still Life,* by Bruce Baillie; *Anselmo,* by Chick Strand; *Orange,* by Karen Johnson; *Castro Street,* by Bruce Baillie, *The Empire of Things,* by Philip Makanna, *3-Screen Film,* by John and James Whitney.

**Program 2:** *Yantra,* by James Whitney; *Oiley Peloso, the Pump Man,* by Robert Nelson, *Gymnopedies,* by Larry Jordan; *Free Form,* by Michael Stewart; *Music with Balls,* by John Coney.

**Program 3:** *Untitled,* by John Whitney; *Project #1,* by David Lourie; *Ephesus,* by Fred Padula; *The Last Days of Spring,* by Lawrence and Sheila Booth.

**Program 4:** *I Change, I Am the Same,* by Shelby Kennedy; *Vicious Cycles,* by Len Janson and Charles Manville; *Momentum,* by Jordan Belson; *Mainstream,* by Jerry Abrams, *Hard Core,* by Walter De Maria; *3-Screen Film,* by John and James Whitney.

**Program 5:** *The Ineluctible Modality of the Visible* and *Happy Birthday, Lenny,* by Lenny Lipton; *Watersmith,* by Will Hindle; *3-Screen Film,* by John and James Whitney.

**Program 6:** *Cria,* by John and Michael Whitney, *2x2,* by Al Razutis; *Nuptiae,* by James Broughton; *Tung,* by Bruce Baillie; *Flesh Tones,* by Walter Chappell; *War Is Hell,* by Robert Nelson.

**Program 7:** *Cybernetik 5.3,* by John Stenhura; *Billabong,* by Will Hindle; *Epiphanies,* by Dan McLaughlin; *Invocation of My Demon Brother,* by Kenneth Anger; *Our Lady of the Sphere,* by Larry Jordan.

**Program 8:** *Binary Bit Patterns,* by Michael Whitney, *E Pluribus Unum,* by Alan S. Jacobson; *Duo Concertantes,* by Larry Jordan; *Lady Reddog Returns,* by Don Symanski; *Chinese Firedrill,* by Will Hindle; *3-Screen Film,* by John and James Whitney.

**Program 9:** *Feast of Friends,* by Paul Ferrara; *Charles Lloyd – Journey Within,* by Eric Sherman; *Cycles,* by Bill Tannen.

**"Open Programs"** – designed to ensure that no worthwhile film is excluded from the NYFF due to failure to fit a category. Included: *Apollon: An Occupied Factory,* Italy, by Ugo Gregoretti; *Dr. Chicago,* USA, by George Manupelli, with *Naughty Nurse,* by Paul Bartel; *Herostratus,* UK, by Don Levy; *High School,* USA, by Frederick Wiseman, with *Eddie,* by Peter Barton; *My Girlfriend's Wedding,* USA, by Jim McBride, with *Breakfast,* by William Sachs; *No Man's Land,* 1931, Germany, by Victor Trivas, with *Cockfight,* by Bill Fertik; A selection of animated films by Walerian Borowczyk; *This Is What Biafra Is,* USA, by Harry Lapham; *Some Won't Go,* USA, by Gil Toff, with *War Is Hell,* by Robert Nelson.

*The Crime of Monsieur Lange* by Jean Renoir

*The Man Who Laughs* by Paul Leni

*High School* by Frederick Wiseman

8th New York Film Festival
September 10-20, 1970
Philharmonic Hall, Lincoln Center

# 1970

SELECTION COMMITTEE: RICHARD ROUD, CHAIRMAN, ARTHUR KNIGHT, ANDREW SARRIS, AND SUSAN SONTAG. CONSULTANT: HENRI LANGLOIS (RETROSPECTIVES).

THE 8TH NYFF POSTER ARTWORK WAS CREATED BY JAMES ROSENQUIST. LIST ART POSTERS, ©LCPA.

### THE WILD CHILD (L'ENFANT SAUVAGE)
*France, 1969. Directed by François Truffaut.*

Written by Jean Gruault and Truffaut, based on Jean Itard's *Mémoire et rapport sur Victor de l'Aveyron*. With Jean-Pierre Cargol, Truffaut, Françoise Seigner, Paul Ville. Shown with *The "What Did You Think of the Movie?" Movie*, USA. Directed by Jeremy Paul Kagan. (Opening Night.)

### TRISTANA
*Italy/France/Spain, 1970. Directed by Luis Buñuel.*

Written by Julio Alejandro and Buñuel, based on Benito Pérez Galdós's novel. With Catherine Deneuve, Fernando Rey, Franco Nero, Lola Gaos. Shown with *Visages de femmes*, France. Directed by Peter Foldes. (Closing Night.)

### LE BOUCHER (THE BUTCHER)
*France/Italy, 1969. Written and Directed by Claude Chabrol.*

With Stéphane Audran, Jean Yanne, Antonio Passalia, Roger Rudel. Shown with *Henry 9 'til 5*, UK. Directed by Bob Godfrey and Bev Roberts.

### THE CANNIBALS
*Italy, 1970. Directed by Liliana Cavani.*

Written by Cavani and Italo Moscati, based on Sophocles' *Antigone*. With Britt Ekland, Pierre Clémenti, Delia Boccardo, Marino Masé. Shown with *Bleu Shut*, USA. Directed by Robert Nelson.

### CHIKAMATSU MONOGATARI
*Japan, 1954. Directed by Kenji Mizoguchi.*

Written by Matsutaro Kawaguchi and Yoshikata Yoda, based on Monzaemon Chikamatsu's classic Kabuki drama *The Legend of the Grand Scroll-Makers*. With Kazuo Hasegawa, Kyoko Kagawa, Yoko Minamida, Eitaro Shindo. (Retrospective.) Shown with *The Magic Machines*, USA, Directed by Bob Curtis.

### COMRADES
*France, 1970. Directed by Marin Karmitz.*

Written by Jean-Paul Giquel, Karmitz, and Lia Wajntal. With Giquel, Juliet Berto, Dominique Labourier, Jean-Pierre Melec, André Julien. Shown with *Making "Love,"* USA. Directed by Finbar Harvey.

### THE CONFORMIST
*Italy/France/West Germany, 1970. Written and Directed by Bernardo Bertolucci, based on Alberto Moravia's novel.*

With Jean-Louis Trintignant, Stefania Sandrelli, Dominique Sanda, Pierre Clémenti.

### DAYS AND NIGHTS IN THE FOREST
*India, 1969. Written and Directed by Satyajit Ray, based on a story by Sunil Ganguly.*

With Soumitra Chatterjee, Subhendu Chatterjee, Samit Bhanja, Robi Ghose.

### EVEN DWARFS STARTED SMALL
*West Germany, 1970. Written and Directed by Werner Herzog.*

With Helmut Döring, Gerd Gickel, Paul Glauer, Erna Gschwendtner. Shown with *The Want-Ad*, Germany. Directed by Bernd Upnmoor.

### FIVE EASY PIECES
*USA, 1970. Directed by Bob Rafelson.*

Written by Adrien Joyce, based on a story by Joyce and Rafelson. With Jack Nicholson, Karen Black, Sally Struthers, Lois Smith, Susan Anspach. Shown with *Arena*, USA. Directed by István Ventilla.

### "FROM LUMIÈRE TO LANGLOIS: THE FRENCH SILENT CINEMA" – excerpts from silent french films:

With piano accompaniment by Arthur Kleiner. Shown with *Langlois*, USA. Directed by Roberta Guerra and Eila Hershon. With Jeanne Moreau, Ingrid Bergman, Simone Signoret, Lillian Gish, Catherine Deneuve, François Truffaut.

### THE GARDEN OF DELIGHTS
*Spain, 1970. Directed by Carlos Saura.*

Written by Rafael Azcona and Saura. With José Luis López Vázquez, Luchy Soto, Francisco Pierrá. Shown with *Even the Sun Cries*, France. Directed by François Bel.

### HARRY MUNTER
*Sweden, 1969. Written and Directed by Kjell Grede.*

With Jan Nielsen, Carl-Gustaf Lindstedt, Gun Jönsson, George Adelly, Alan Simon. Shown with *Three Days*, USA. Directed by Phillip Frey.

### THE INHERITORS
*Brazil, 1969. Written and Directed by Carlos Diegues.*

With Sérgio Cardoso, Odette Lara, Mario Lago, Jean-Pierre Léaud.

### JE T'AIME, JE T'AIME
*France, 1968. Directed by Alain Resnais.*

Written by Resnais and Jacques Sternberg. With Olga Georges-Picot, Claude Rich, Anouk Ferjac, Marie-Blanche Vergne. Shown with *Invasion*, Poland. Directed by Stefan Schabenbeck.

### KES
*UK, 1969. Directed by Ken Loach.*

Written by Barry Hines and Loach, based on Hines's novel *A Kestrel for a Knave*. With David Bradley, Freddie Fletcher, Lynne Perrie, Colin Welland. Shown with *Hands, Knees and Bumps-a-Daisy*, UK. Directed by George Dunning.

### MISTREATMENT
*Sweden, 1970. Written and Directed by Lasse Forsberg.*

With Knut Pettersen, Björn Granath, Berit Persson. Shown with *The-End-of-One*, USA. Directed by Paul Kocela.

### LA MUSICA
*France, 1966. Directed by Marguerite Duras and Paul Seban.*

Written by Duras, based on her play. With Delphine Seyrig, Robert Hossein, Julie Dassin. Shown with *Subterraneans*, France. Directed by Roberto E. Castro.

### OTHON (LES YEUX NE VEULENT PAS EN TOUT TEMPS SE FERMER OU PEUT-ÊTRE QU'UN JOUR ROME SE PERMETTRA DE CHOISIR À SON TOUR)
*West Germany, 1970. Written and Directed by Jean-Marie Straub and Danièle Huillet, based on Pierre Corneille's play.*

With Adriano Aprà, Anne Brumagne, Ennio Lauricella, Olimpia Carlisi. Shown with *Reunion*, USA. Directed by Gerry Matthews and Ton Scheuer.

### PRAISE MARX AND PASS THE AMMUNITION
*UK, 1968. Written and Directed by Maurice Hatton, based on an original idea by Hatton and Michael Wood.*

With John Thaw, Edina Ronay, Louis Mahoney. Shown with *Richard Hamilton*, UK. Directed by James M. Scott.

*The Conformist* by Bernardo Bertolucci

### THE SCAVENGERS (I RECUPERANTI)
*Italy, 1970. Directed by Ermanno Olmi.*

Written by Tullio Kezich, Olmi, and Mario Rigoni Stern. With Antonio Lunardi, Andreino Carli, Alessandra Micheletto. *Shown with P.B.L. #2*, USA. Directed by Robert Breer.

### UNE SIMPLE HISTOIRE
*France, 1958. Written and Directed by Marcel Hanoun, based on a true incident.*

With Micheline Bezançon. Considered to be one of the great "lost" films. Shown with *Kyoto*, Japan. Directed by Kon Ichikawa.

### THE SPIDER'S STRATAGEM
*Italy, 1969-70. Directed by Bernardo Bertolucci.*

Written by Bertolucci, Eduardo de Gregorio, and Marilù Parolini, based on a story by Jorge Luis Borges. With Giulio Brogi, Alida Valli, Tino Scotti, Pippo Campanini. Shown with *The Battle*, UK. Directed by Derek Phillips.

### STREET SCENES 1970
*USA, 1970. A Project of New York Cinetracts Collective. Production Supervisor and Post Production Director: Martin Scorsese.*

A film about the demonstrations on Wall Street and Washington in the spring of 1970. Note: Among others, Harvey Keitel and Ira Resnick are credited with the still photography. Also features Jay Cocks, Verna Bloom, and camerawork by Oliver Stone. Shown with *The Golden Positions*, USA. Directed by James Broughton.

### WIND FROM THE EAST (LE VENT D'EST)
*Italy/France/West Germany, 1969. Directed by Jean-Luc Godard.*

Written by Daniel Cohn-Bendit and Godard. With Gian Maria Volonté, Anne Wiazemsky, Cristiana Tullio-Altan, Glauber Rocha. Shown with *The Giants*, Czechoslovakia. Directed by Gene Deitch.

### ZORNS LEMMA
*USA, 1970. Directed by Hollis Frampton.*

With the voices of Rosemarie Castoro, Ginger Michels, Marcia Steinbrecher, Twyla Tharp.

### + DOUBLE PISCES, SCORPIO RISING
*UK, 1970. Directed by Dick Fontaine.*

Written by Fontaine and Mike Myers. With Robert Brownjohn, Amanda Lear, Jean Shrimpton, Norman Mailer.

## Special Events
PRESENTED AT LINCOLN CENTER'S LIBRARY & MUSEUM OF THE PERFORMING ARTS

**"1927-1933: Medium Rare"** – presented in association with the Film Society and the AFI. Films shown: *Back Street*, 1932, by John M. Stahl; *The Front Page*, 1931, by Lewis Milestone; *Kid Brother*, 1927, by Ted Wilde; *The Emperor Jones*, 1933, by Dudley Murphy; *King of Jazz*, 1930, by John Murray Anderson; *The Last Flight*, 1931, by William Dieterle; *Laughter*, 1930, by Henri d'Abbadie d'Arrast; *The Miracle Woman*, 1932, by Frank Capra; *Mystery of the Wax Museum*, 1933, by Michael Curtiz; *Once in a Lifetime*, 1932, by Russell Mack.

**"American Voices"** – a survey of films by and about minority groups in America today, presented by the Department of Film of the Museum of Modern Art in association with the Film Society. Selected by Edith Zornow. Films shown: *America Is in Real Trouble*, by Tom Palazzo; *Before the Mountain Was Moved*, by Robert Sharpe; *Bessie Smith*, by Charles Levine; *Black Roots*, by Lionel Rogosin; *El Teatro Campesino*, by Victoria Hochberg, Janet Sternberg, and Jac Venza; *How Can I Not Be Among You?*, by Thomas Reichman; *I Am Also You*, by Bruce Kerner; *I Am Somebody*, by Madelyne Anderson; *I'm a Man*, by Peter Rosen; *Ira, You'll Get Into Trouble*, by Stephen Sbarge; *The Land*, 1942, by Robert Flaherty; *Lenny Bruce*, by John Magnuson; *Lord Thing*, by Dewitt Beall; *March of Time*, produced by Time Life, Inc. and Louis de Rochemont; *Mississippi Summer*, by William Bayer; *Miss Nude America*, by Tony Silver; *Nothing But a Man*, by Michael Roemer; *The Other America*, by Krainin/Savage Productions; *The Plow That Broke the Plains*, 1936, and *The River*, 1937, by Pare Lorentz; *Susan After the Sugar Harvest*, by Peter Robinson; *This Is the Home of Mrs. Levant Graham*, by Eliot Noyes Jr. and Claudia Weill; *Trail of Tears*, by Lane Slate; *Uptown: A Portrait of the South Bronx*, by Herb Danska; *Woo Who? May Wilson*, by Amalie R. Rothschild; *You Are on Indian Land, Encounter with Saul Alinsky, Part II (Rama Indian Reserve)*, and *Ballad of Crowfoot*, courtesy of the National Film Board of Canada.

**"Cinema and Color"** – presented by the Cinémathèque Française in association with the Film Society. Selected by Henri Langlois. Included: *All These Women*, 1963, by Ingmar Bergman; *Banjo on My Knee*, 1936, by John Cromwell; *Blood and Sand*, 1941, by Rouben Mamoulian; *The Bowery*, 1933, by Raoul Walsh; "Color in Animation," with examples of works by Max Fleischer, Norman McLaren, and others; *A Double Tour (Web of Passion)*, 1960, by Claude Chabrol; *Folies Bergere*, 1935, by Roy Del Ruth; "Hand-Painted Films," with examples of works by Georges Méliès and others; *King of Jazz* (two-color Technicolor), 1930, by John Murray Anderson; *Othello*, 1955, by Sergei Yutkevich; *The Princess Yang Kwei-Fei*, 1955, by Kenji Mizoguchi; *Rapsodia Satanica*, Italy, by Carmine Gallone; *The Return of Frank James*, 1940, and *Western Union*, 1941, by Fritz Lang; "Three Early Films Produced by Darryl F. Zanuck"; "Tinted and Toned Films," including the French-tinted *Cabinet of Dr. Caligari*.

### COMPANY
*USA, 1970. Directed by D.A. Pennebaker.*

A documentary about the original cast recording of the musical, followed by a Q&A with the filmmakers.

*The Front Page* by Lewis Milestone

*Mystery of the Wax Museum* by Michael Curtiz

*Western Union* by Fritz Lang

9TH NEW YORK FILM FESTIVAL

OCT. 1-16 1971

VIVIAN BEAUMONT THEATER

THE FILM SOCIETY OF LINCOLN CENTER

# 1971

SELECTION COMMITTEE: RICHARD ROUD, CHAIRMAN, RICHARD CORLISS, ARTHUR KNIGHT, ARTHUR L. MAYER, ANDREW SARRIS, AND SUSAN SONTAG. CONSULTANT: HENRI LANGLOIS (RETROSPECTIVES).

THE 9TH NYFF POSTER ARTWORK WAS CREATED BY FRANK STELLA. LIST ART POSTERS, ©LCPA.

### THE DEBUT
*USSR, 1971. Directed Gleb Panfilov.*

Written by E. Gavrilovich and Panfilov. With Inna Churikova, V. Telichkina, T. Stepanova, L. Kuravlyov. Shown with *Replay*, USA. Directed by Robert Deubel. (Opening Night.)

### MURMUR OF THE HEART
*France/Italy/West Germany, 1971. Written and Directed by Louis Malle.*

With Lea Massari, Benoît Ferreux, Daniel Gélin, Michel Lonsdale. (Closing Night.)

### BONAPARTE AND THE REVOLUTION
*France, 1971. Written and Directed by Abel Gance.*

With Albert Dieudonné, Vladimir Roudenko, Antonin Artaud, Abel Gance, Annabella.

### BORN TO WIN
*USA, 1971. Directed by Ivan Passer.*

Written by David Scott Milton and Passer. With George Segal, Jay Fletcher, Paula Prentiss, Karen Black, Hector Elizondo. Shown with *I Never Promised You a Long Run*, USA. Directed by Paul Leaf.

### ◀ THE DECAMERON (IL DECAMERON)
*Italy, 1971. Written and Directed by Pier Paolo Pasolini, based on stories by Boccaccio.*

With Franco Citti, Ninetto Davoli, Angela Luce, Patrizia Capparelli. Shown with *The Further Adventures of Uncle Sam*, USA. Directed by Dale Case and Robert Mitchell.

### DIRECTED BY JOHN FORD
*USA, 1971. Written and Directed by Peter Bogdanovich.*

Produced by George Stevens Jr. and James R. Silke for the AFI. With Henry Fonda, James Stewart, John Wayne, Orson Welles, John Ford. Presented in association with the AFI. Shown with *What Fixed Me*, USA. Directed by Thomas Rickman.

### DODES'KA-DEN
*Japan, 1971. Directed by Akira Kurosawa.*

Written by Shinobu Hashimoto, Kurosawa, and Hideo Oguni, based on a story by Shugoro Yamamoto. With Yoshitaka Zushi, Junzaburo Ban, Kiyoko Tange, Hisashi Igawa, Kunie Tanaka.

*The Last Picture Show* by Peter Bogdanovich

### FAMILY LIFE
*Poland, 1971. Written and Directed by Krzysztof Zanussi.*

With Daniel Olbrychski, Jan Kreczmar, Maja Komorowska, Jan Nowicki. Shown with *Passing Quietly Through*, USA. Directed by Dinitia Smith McCarthy.

### FATA MORGANA
*West Germany, 1971. Written and Directed by Werner Herzog.*

Shown with *'70*, USA. Directed by Robert Breer. Also, *Nostalgia*, USA. Directed by Hollis Frampton.

### FOUR NIGHTS OF A DREAMER
*France, 1971. Written and Directed by Robert Bresson, based on Fyodor Dostoevsky's story "White Nights."*

With Guillaume des Forêts, Isabelle Weingarten, Jean-Maurice Monnoyer. Shown with *New Arts*, USA. Directed by Howard Chesley and Eric Saarinen.

### IN THE NAME OF THE FATHER
*Italy, 1971. Written and Directed by Marco Bellocchio.*

With Yves Beneyton, Renato Scarpa, Aldo Sassi, Laura Betti. Shown with *Mummy, Mummy*, UK. Directed by John Beech.

### IN THE SUMMERTIME (DURANTE L'ESTATE)
*Italy, 1971. Directed by Ermanno Olmi.*

Written by Olmi and Fortunato Pasqualino. With Renato Paracchi, Rosanna Callegari, Gabriele Fontanesi, Mario Cazzaniga. Shown with *Little Man, Big City*, Yugoslavia. Directed by Gyula Macskássy and György Várnai.

### THE LAST PICTURE SHOW
*USA, 1971. Directed by Peter Bogdanovich.*

Written by Bogdanovich and Larry McMurtry, based on McMurtry's novel. With Timothy Bottoms, Jeff Bridges, Cybill Shepherd, Ben Johnson, Cloris Leachman, Ellen Burstyn, Eileen Brennan, Randy Quaid. Shown with *Abraham and Isaac*, USA. Directed by R.O. Blechman.

### PIONEERS IN INGOLSTADT aka RECRUITS IN INGOLSTADT
*West Germany, 1971. Written and Directed by Rainer Werner Fassbinder, based on Marieluise Fleisser's play.*

With Irm Hermann, Hanna Schygulla, Harry Baer, Rudolf Waldemar Brem. Shown with *The Caterpillar and the Wild Animals*, USA. Directed by Gerard H. Baldwin. Also, *The Last Winters*, France. Directed by Jean-Charles Tacchella.

### PUNISHMENT PARK
*USA, 1971. Written and Directed by Peter Watkins.*

With Carmen Argenziano, Stan Armsted, Jim Bohan, Fredrick Franklyn. Shown with *Fable Safe*, USA. Directed by Erik Barnouw.

### A SAFE PLACE ▼
*USA, 1971. Written and Directed by Henry Jaglom.*

With Tuesday Weld, Orson Welles, Jack Nicholson, Philip Proctor, Gwen Welles. Shown with *Synchromy*, USA. Directed by Norman McLaren.

### THE SORROW AND THE PITY
*Switzerland, 1970. Directed by Marcel Ophuls.*

Written by André Harris and Ophuls. An epic documentary about the occupation of France.

### WR: MYSTERIES OF THE ORGANISM
*Yugoslavia, 1971. Written and Directed by Dušan Makavejev.*

With Milena Dravić, Jagoda Kaloper, Ivica Vidović, Zoran Radmilović. *WR* provoked protests from the local followers of Wilhelm Reich. Shown with *A Child's Alphabet with Casual References to DNA Replication in the Garden of Eden*, USA. Directed by Thomas Spence. Also, *Work*, USA. Directed by Fred Wardenburg.

THERE WERE NO special events in connection with this year's Festival (due to economizing after serious losses in 1970), but there were panel discussions organized by Wendy Keys following several of the films. They included: "Writers and Directors: Who Tells the Story?" Moderated by David Frost, with Brian De Palma, Bill Gunn, Frank Perry, and Krzysztof Zanussi; "Women in Film." Moderated by Molly Haskell, with Barbara Loden, Susan Martin, Eleanor Perry, Nadine Trintignant, and Kitty Winn; "The Film Business." Moderated by Leonard Harris, with Paul Bartel, Chris Dewey, Cliff Frazier, Werner Herzog, David Picker, and Donald Rugoff; "Screenwriters and Novelists." Moderated by Brendan Gill, with James Dickey, Buck Henry, David Newman, Terry Southern, and Kurt Vonnegut Jr.; "The Political Power of Film." Moderated by Richard Corliss, with Pete Hamill, Marcel Ophuls, and Peter Watkins; "Socialism and Capitalism: A Filmmaker's Point of View." Moderated by Antonin Liehm, with Jan Kadar, Tuli Kufperberg, Dušan Makavejev, and Dr. Myron Schrage; "Hollywood: The Establishment and the Challengers." Moderated by David Steinberg, with Kit Carson, Dennis Hopper; Henry Jaglom, Jack Nicholson, and Otto Preminger.

Note: The NYFF presented these panel discussions for just one year. Aside from the enormous amount of work that went into organizing them, it was found that audiences really preferred to talk about a film just screened, rather than discuss an unrelated topic.

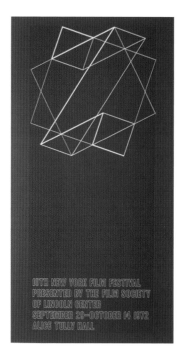

# 1972

SELECTION COMMITTEE: RICHARD ROUD, CHAIRMAN, RICHARD CORLISS, ARTHUR KNIGHT, ARTHUR L. MAYER, ANDREW SARRIS, SUSAN SONTAG, AND JOHN RUSSELL TAYLOR. CONSULTANT: HENRI LANGLOIS (RETROSPECTIVES).

THE 10TH NYFF POSTER ARTWORK WAS CREATED BY JOSEF ALBERS. LIST ART POSTERS, ©LCPA.

### CHLOE IN THE AFTERNOON
*France, 1972. Written and Directed by Eric Rohmer.*

With Bernard Verley, Zouzou, Françoise Verley, Daniel Ceccaldi. Shown with *American Pie*, USA. Directed Fred Mogubgub and Al Brodax. (Opening Night.)

### LAST TANGO IN PARIS
*Italy/France, 1972. Directed by Bernardo Bertolucci.*

Written by Franco Arcalli and Bertolucci. With Marlon Brando, Maria Schneider, Darling Légitimus, Jean-Pierre Léaud. Note: During the projection, Bertolucci was in the booth continuing to edit the film. (Closing Night.)

### THE ADVERSARY
*India, 1971. Written and Directed by Satyajit Ray.*

With Dhritiman Chatterjee, Krishna Bose, Jayshree Roy, Kalyan Chatterjee. Shown with *Silences*, Yugoslavia. Directed by Predrag Golubovic.

### L'AMOUR FOU
*France, 1968. Directed by Jacques Rivette.*

Written by Marilù Parolini and Rivette. With Bulle Ogier, Jean-Pierre Kalfon, Josée Destoop, Michèle Moretti. (Retrospective.)

### THE ASSASSINATION OF TROTSKY
*Italy/France, 1972. Directed by Joseph Losey.*

Written by Nicholas Mosley. With Richard Burton, Alain Delon, Romy Schneider, Valentina Cortese. Shown with *100*, East Germany. Directed by Peter Voigt.

### BAD COMPANY ▶
*USA, 1972. Directed by Robert Benton.*

Written by Benton and David Newman. With Jeff Bridges, Barry Brown, Jim Davis, David Huddleston. Note: This film was a Paramount release and Stanley Jaffee had a tantrum in our pressroom because Abe Weiler, a second-string *New York Times* critic had reviewed it rather than Vincent Canby. Jaffee thought the NYFF should be able to dictate reviewing policy to the *Times*. One of the Paramount publicists was so freaked out by Jaffee's ranting that he virtually inhaled an entire box of Ritz crackers. Shown with *Joshua & the Blob*, USA. Directed by John C. Lange. Also, *White Grease*, USA. Directed by Barry Bialik.

*The King of Marvin Gardens* by Bob Rafelson

## THE DISCREET CHARM OF THE BOURGEOISIE
*France, 1972. Directed by Luis Buñuel.*

Written by Buñuel and Jean-Claude Carrière. With Fernando Rey, Jean-Pierre Cassel, Stéphane Audran, Paul Frankeur, Delphine Seyrig, Bulle Ogier, Julien Bertheau, Claude Piéplu, Michel Piccoli. Shown with *Two Marches*, Yugoslavia. Directed by Dušan Povh.

## FAMILY LIFE
*UK, 1972. Directed by Ken Loach.*
Written by David Mercer. With Sandy Ratcliff, Bill Dean, Grace Cave, Malcolm Tierney. Shown with *The Black Beach*, UK. Directed by John Bulmer.

## HEAT
*USA, 1972. Written and Directed by Paul Morrissey, based on an idea by John Hollowell.*

Produced by Andy Warhol. With Joe Dallesandro, Sylvia Miles, Pat Ast, Andrea Feldman. Shown with *The Prayer*, Yugoslavia. Directed by Radivoj Gvozdanović. Also, *Make Love, Not War*, Yugoslavia. Directed by Zlatko Grgić.

## IMAGES
*Ireland, 1972. Written and Directed by Robert Altman.*

With Susannah York, René Auberjonois, Marcel Bozzuffi, Hugh Millais. Shown with *The Collector*, Yugoslavia. Directed by Milan Blažeković.

## THE INNER SCAR (LA CICATRICE INÉRIEURE)
*France, 1971. Written and Directed by Philippe Garrel.*

With Pierre Clémenti, Nico, Garrel. Shown with *Dangling Participle*, USA. Directed by Standish D. Lawder. Also, *Judas*, Yugoslavia. Directed by Vlatko Gilić.

## THE KING OF MARVIN GARDENS
*USA, 1972. Directed by Bob Rafelson.*

Written by Jacob Brockman, based on a story by Brockman and Rafelson. With Jack Nicholson, Bruce Dern, Ellen Burstyn, Julia Anne Robinson. Shown with *Meatloaf*, USA. Directed by Don Cirillo.

## LOVE
*Hungary, 1971. Directed by Károly Makk.*
Written by Tibor Déry. With Lili Darvas, Mari Törőcsik, Iván Darvas. Shown with *Façades*, Yugoslavia. Directed by Suad Mrkonjic.

## THE MERCHANT OF FOUR SEASONS
*West Germany, 1971. Written and Directed by Rainer Werner Fassbinder.*

With Irm Hermann, Hanna Schygulla, Hans Hirschmüller. Shown with *Sheila*, UK. Directed by Jeff Schwartz.

## NATHALIE GRANGER
*France, 1972. Written and Directed by Marguerite Duras.*

With Lucia Bosé, Jeanne Moreau, Gérard Depardieu, Dionys Mascolo. Note: The audience response to the lack of action in this film was to kick their chairs in unison. Depardieu saved the day with his brief appearance as a refrigerator repairman. Shown with *Sunday Breakfast*, USA. Directed by Peter Virsis.

## RED PSALM
*Hungary, 1972. Directed by Miklós Jancsó.*
Written by Gyula Hernádi. With Andrea Drahota, Lajos Balázsovits, András Bálint.

## + BEHIND THE WALL
*Poland, 1971. Directed by Krzysztof Zanussi.*
Written by Zanussi and Edward Zebrowski. With Maja Komorowska, Zbigniew Zapasiewicz.

## REMINISCENCES OF A JOURNEY TO LITHUANIA
*USA, 1972. Directed by Jonas Mekas.*

## + GOING HOME
*USA, 1972. Directed by Adolfas Mekas.*
After 25 years, the Mekas Brothers return to their hometown.

## A SENSE OF LOSS
*USA/Switzerland, 1972. Directed by Marcel Ophuls.*

A documentary addressing the problems of Northern Ireland and the conflict between the occupying army of Great Britain and the IRA.

## SUMMER SOLDIERS
*Japan, 1971. Directed by Hiroshi Teshigahara.*
Written by John Nathan. With Keith Sykes, Reisen Lee, Kazuo Kitamura, Toshiko Kobayashi.

## TOUT VA BIEN
*France/Italy, 1972. Written and Directed by Jean-Luc Godard and Jean-Pierre Gorin.*

With Yves Montand, Jane Fonda, Vittorio Caprioli, Elizabeth Chauvin, Éric Chartier, Jean Pignol. Shown with *A Letter to Jane*, France. Directed by Jean-Luc Godard and Jean-Pierre Gorin.

## TWO ENGLISH GIRLS (LES DEUX ANGLAISES ET LE CONTINENT)
*France, 1971. Directed by François Truffaut.*

Written by Jean Gruault and Truffaut, based on Henri-Pierre Roché's novel. With Jean-Pierre Léaud, Kika Markham, Stacey Tendeter, Sylvia Marriott. Shown with *Fantoro & the Last Enforcer*, France. Directed by Jan Lenica.

## WE WON'T GROW OLD TOGETHER
*France/Italy, 1972. Written and Directed by Maurice Pialat.*

With Marlène Jobert, Jean Yanne, Macha Méril, Christine Fabréga. Shown with *An American Liaison*, USA. Directed by Robert Brennan.

# 1973

SELECTION COMMITTEE: RICHARD ROUD, CHAIRMAN, RICHARD CORLISS, ARTHUR KNIGHT, ARTHUR L. MAYER, ANDREW SARRIS, AND SUSAN SONTAG. CONSULTANT: HENRI LANGLOIS (RETROSPECTIVES).

THE 11TH NYFF POSTER ARTWORK WAS CREATED BY NIKI DE SAINT PHALLE. LIST ARTS POSTERS, ©LCPA.

### DAY FOR NIGHT (LA NUIT AMÉRICAINE)
*France/Italy, 1973. Directed by François Truffaut.*

Written by Jean-Louis Richard, Suzanne Schiffman, and Truffaut. With Jacqueline Bisset, Valentina Cortese, Alexandra Stewart, Jean-Pierre Aumont, Jean-Pierre Léaud, Truffaut, Jean Champion, Nathalie Baye. Shown with *Pierre*, France. Directed by Dominique Cheminal. (Opening Night.)

### BADLANDS ▲
*USA, 1973 Written and Directed by Terrence Malick.*

With Martin Sheen, Sissy Spacek, Warren Oates. Note: Arthur Penn recommended this film to the selection committee. Because it had a double track, Malick was in the projection booth while it screened. The committee was stunned, knowing they had just discovered a major talent. Malick humbly asked if they liked the film—they could hardly respond, they were so overwhelmed. Shown with *Frank Film*, USA. Directed by Frank Mouris. (Closing Night.)

### ANDREI RUBLEV
*USSR, 1966-69. Directed by Andrei Tarkovsky.*

Written by Andrei Mikhalkov-Kontchalovsky and Tarkovsky. With Anatoli Solonitzine, Ivan Lapikov, Nikolai Grinko, Nikolai Sergeyev.

### THE BITTER TEARS OF PETRA VON KANT ▶
*West Germany, 1972. Written and Directed by Rainer Werner Fassbinder.*

With Margit Carstensen, Hanna Schygulla, Irm Hermann, Eva Mattes. Shown with *The Artichoke*, Belgium. Directed by Michel Clarence. Note: Both the feature and the short film provoked protests by the Lesbian Feminist Liberation.

### DISTANT THUNDER
*India, 1973. Written and Directed by Satyajit Ray.*

With Soumitra Chatterjee, Babita, Sandhya Roy, Gobinda Chakravarty. Shown with *Alphon in Wonderland*, France. Directed by Maxim Ferrier and Gerald Poussin. Also, *Mediana*, USA. Directed by Scott Bartlett.

### A DOLL'S HOUSE
*UK, 1973. Directed by Joseph Losey.*

Written by David Mercer, based on Henrik Ibsen's play. With Jane Fonda, David Warner, Trevor Howard, Delphine Seyrig, Edward Fox, Anna Wing. Shown with *Sandman*, USA. Directed by Eliot Noyes Jr. Also, *When Roobarb Made a Spike*, UK. Directed by Bob Godfrey.

### DR. MABUSE: THE GAMBLER
*Germany, 1922. Directed by Fritz Lang.*

Written by Thea von Harbou, based on Norbert Jacques's novel. Piano accompaniment by Arthur Kleiner. (Retrospective.)

### HISTORY LESSONS
*West Germany/Italy, 1972. Directed by Jean-Marie Straub.*

Written by Straub and Danièle Huillet. With Gottfried Bold, Benedikt Zulauf, Johann Unterpertinger, Henri Ludwigg. Shown with *Introduction to Schönberg's Accompanying Music for a Film Scene*, West Germany/Italy. Directed by Jean-Marie Straub.

### ILLUMINATION
*Poland, 1973. Written and Directed by Krzyzstof Zanussi.*

With Stanislaw Latallo, Maigorzata Pritulak, Monika

Dzienisiewicz-Olbrychska, Edward Zebrowski. Shown with *Pulcinella*, Italy. Directed by Giulio Gianini and Emanuele Luzzati. Also, *For a Few Performances Only*, Greece. Directed by Theodor Kalomirakis.

### ISRAEL, WHY (POURQUOI ISRAËL)
*France, 1973. Written and Directed by Claude Lanzmann.*

A documentary that probes deeply into Israeli reality.

### JUST BEFORE NIGHTFALL
*France/Italy, 1971. Written and Directed by Claude Chabrol, based on Edward Atiyah's novel* The Thin Line.

With Stéphane Audran, Michel Bouquet, François Périer, Jean Carmet. Shown with *Butterfly † 1975*, The Netherlands. Directed by Peter Brouwer. Also, *Colter's Hell*, UK. Directed by Robin Lehman.

### KID BLUE ▲
*USA, 1973. Directed by James Frawley.*

Written by Edwin Shrake. With Dennis Hopper, Warren Oates, Peter Boyle, Ben Johnson, Lee Purcell, Janice Rule. Shown with *Pin Ball Wizard*, USA. Directed by Rod McCall.

### LAND OF SILENCE AND DARKNESS
*West Germany, 1971. Directed by Werner Herzog.*

With Fini Straubinger. Narrated by Rolf Illig. Shown with *The Train That Never Stopped*, France. Directed by Chris Marker/SLON.

### MEAN STREETS ▲
*USA, 1973. Directed by Martin Scorsese.*

Written by Mardik Martin and Scorsese. With Harvey Keitel, Robert De Niro, David Proval, Amy Robinson, Richard Romanus. Shown with *Background*, USA. Directed by Carmen D'Avino.

### THE MOTHER AND THE WHORE ▲
*France, 1973. Written and Directed by Jean Eustache.*

With Bernadette Lafont, Jean-Pierre Léaud, Françoise Lebrun, Isabelle Weingarten.

### RÉJEANNE PADOVANI
*Canada, 1973. Directed by Denys Arcand.*

Written by Arcand and Jacques Benoit. With Jean Lajeunesse, Luce Gullbeault, Roger Lebel, Pierre Thériault. Shown with *Australian History*, Australia. Directed by Bruce Petty.

### RETURN (RITORNO)
*Italy, 1972. Directed by Gianni Amico.*

Written by Amico and Enzo Ungari, with the collaboration of Domenico Rafele. With Ilaria Occhini, Luigi Diberti, Laura Betti, Carla Calò. Shown with *Opera*, Italy. Directed by Bruno Bozzetto. Also, *Coming On*, USA. Directed by Doe Mayer.

### LA RUPTURE (THE BREAK UP)
*France/Italy/Belgium, 1970. Written and Directed by Claude Chabrol.*

With Stéphane Audran, Jean-Pierre Cassel, Michel Bouquet, Marguerite Cassan. Shown with *Dans la vie*, Canada. Directed by Pierre Veilleux.

*Andrei Rublev* by Andrei Tarkovsky

# 1974

SELECTION COMMITTEE: RICHARD ROUD, CHAIRMAN, RICHARD CORLISS, ARTHUR KNIGHT, ARTHUR L. MAYER, ANDREW SARRIS, AND SUSAN SONTAG. CONSULTANT: HENRI LANGLOIS (RETROSPECTIVES).

THE 12TH NYFF POSTER ARTWORK WAS CREATED BY JEAN TINGUELY. LIST ART POSTERS, ©LCPA.

## DON'T CRY WITH YOUR MOUTH FULL (PLEURE PAS LA BOUCHE PLEINE)
*France, 1973. Directed by Pascal Thomas.*

Written by Roland Duval, Suzanne Schiffman, and Thomas. With Annie Colé, Jean Carmet, Christiane Chamaret, Hélène Dieudonné. Shown with *A Bird's Life*, Czechoslovakia. Directed by H. Born, J. Doubrava, and Miloš Macourek. (Opening Night.)

## THE PHANTOM OF LIBERTY
*France, 1974. Directed by Luis Buñuel.*

Written by Buñuel and Jean-Claude Carrière, based on a story by Gustavo A. Bécquer. With Jean-Claude Brialy, Monica Vitti, Milena Vukotic, Michael Lonsdale, Claude Piéplu, Michel Piccoli, Julien Bertheau, Adriana Asti. (Closing Night.) Note: This was a harrowing end for the NYFF. The print of the film was brought over at the last minute by the producer, Serge Silberman, who kept it in his hotel room. He refused to give it to the Festival because he was unhappy with his seats in the director's box, which were in the first tier and less expensive than orchestra seats. Subsequently director's box seats were printed at top price!

## ALICE IN THE CITIES ▶
*West Germany, 1974. Directed by Wim Wenders.*

Written by Veith der Furstenberg and Wenders. With Rüdiger Vogeler, Yella Rottländer, Elisabeth Kreuzer. Edda Köchl. Shown with *Punishment*, The Netherlands. Directed by Olga Madsen.

## ALI: FEAR EATS THE SOUL
*West Germany, 1974. Written and Directed by Rainer Werner Fassbinder.*

With Brigitte Mira, El Hedi ben Salem, Marquard Bohm, Walter Sedlmayr, Doris Mattes. Shown with *Jabberwocky*, Czechoslovakia. Directed by Jan Svankmajer.

## A BIGGER SPLASH
*UK, 1974. Directed by Jack Hazan.*

Written by Hazan and David Mingay. With (as themselves) David Hockney, Peter Schlesinger, Ossie Clark, Celia Birtwell, Mo McDermott, Henry Geldzahler. Shown with *Braverman's Condensed Cream of Beatles*, USA. Directed by Charles Braverman.

## CELINE AND JULIE GO BOATING
*France, 1973. Directed by Jacques Rivette.*

Written by Juliet Berto, Eduardo de Gregorio, Dominique Labourier, Bulle Ogier, Marie-France Pisier, and Rivette. With Berto, Labourier, Ogier, Pisier, Barbet Schroeder.

## THE CIRCUMSTANCE
*Italy, 1974. Written and Directed by Ermanno Olmi.*

With Ada Savelli, Gaetano Porro, Raffaella Bianchi, Mario Sireci. Shown with *Diary Found with the Ants*, France. Directed by George Sénéchal.

## LES ENFANTS TERRIBLES
*France, 1950. Directed by Jean-Pierre Melville.*

Written by Jean Cocteau, based on his novel. With Nicole Stéphane, Edouard Dermithe, Renée Cosima, Jacques Bernard. (Retrospective.)

## "HOMAGE TO BUÑUEL" – four of Buñuel's most important works:

- **L'Age d'Or**, France, 1930. Written by Buñuel and Salvador Dalí. With Gaston Modot, Lya Lys.

- **The Discreet Charm of the Bourgeoise**, France, 1972. Written by Buñuel and Jean-Claude Carrière. With Fernando Rey, Jean-Pierre Cassel, Stéphane Audran, Paul Frankeur, Delphine Seyrig, Bulle Ogier.

- **The Exterminating Angel**, Mexico, 1962. Written by Buñuel. With Silvia Pinal, Jacquelin Andere, Augusto Benedico, Luis Beristáin.

- **The Milky Way**, France, 1969. Written by Buñuel and Jean-Claude Carrière. With Paul Frankeur, Laurent Terzieff, Alan Cuny, Edith Scob. (Retrospective.)

**LACOMBE, LUCIEN**
*France/Italy/West Germany, 1974. Directed by Louis Malle.*
Written by Malle and Patrick Modiano. With Pierre Blaise, Aurore Clément, Holger Löwenadler, Therese Giehse.

**LANCELOT DU LAC**
*France/Italy, 1974. Written and Directed by Robert Bresson.*
With Luc Simon, Laura Duke Condominas, Humbert Balsan, Vladimir Antolek-Oresek. Shown with *Sea Creatures*, UK. Directed by Robin Lehman.

**LIEBELEI**
*Germany, 1932. Directed by Max Ophuls.*
Written by Curt Alexander and Hans Wilhelm, based on Arthur Schnitzler's play. With Wolfgang Liebeneiner, Magda Schneider, Luise Ulllrich, Willy Eichenberger. (Retrospective.)

**THE MIDDLE OF THE WORLD**
*Switzerland, 1974. Directed by Alain Tanner.*
Written by John Berger and Tanner. With Olimpia Carlisi, Philippe Léotard, Juliet Berto, Jacques Denis. Shown with *Optimist and Pessimist*, Yugoslavia. Directed by Zlatko Grgic.

**THE NIGHT OF THE SCARECROW**
*Brazil, 1974. Directed by Sérgio Ricardo.*
Written by Nilson Barbosa, Jean-Claude Bernardet, Maurice Capovila, Plíneo Pacheco, and Ricardo. With Rejane Medeiros,
José Pimentel, Gilson Moura, Alceu Valença. Shown with *Along These Lines*, Canada. Directed by Peter Pearson.

**OUT 1: SPECTRE**
*France, 1972-74. Directed by Jacques Rivette.*
With Bernadette Lafont, Jean-Pierre Léaud, Michael Lonsdale, Bulle Ogier, Eric Rohmer, Juliet Berto, Michèle Moretti, François Fabian, Sylvain Corthay, Michel Delahaye. A four-plus-hour journey into an underground world of anxiety and terror. Each member of its cast was invited by Rivette to invent his or her own character and dialogue, based loosely on Balzac's *Story of the 13*.

**LA PALOMA**
*Switzerland/France, 1974. Written and Directed by Daniel Schmid.*
With Ingrid Caven, Peter Kern, Peter Chatel, Jérôme Nicolin, Béatrice Stoll, Bulle Ogier. Shown with *Superior Force*, Yugoslavia. Directed by Zlatko Pavlinic. Also, *Oh! Oh!*, Poland. Directed by Bronislaw Zeman.

**PART-TIME WORK OF A DOMESTIC SLAVE**
*West Germany, 1974. Directed by Alexander Kluge.*
Written by Hans Drawe and H.D. Müller. With Alexandra Kluge, Franz Bronski, Sylvia Gartmann, Traugott Buhre, Ursula Birichs, Bion Steinborn. Shown with *The Bench of Desolation*, France. Directed by Claude Chabrol.

**ROME WANTS ANOTHER CAESAR**
*Italy, 1973. Directed by Miklós Jancsó.*
Written by Giovanna Gagliardo and Janscó. With Daniel Olbrychsky, Hiram Keller, Lino Troisi, Gino Lavagetto. Shown with *Light*, USA. Directed by Jordan Belson.

**"ROOTS"** – a program of four featurettes celebrating the contribution of many ethnic strands to the fabric of American life:
- **From These Roots**, USA, 1974. Directed by William Greaves.
- **Italianamerican**, USA, 1974. Directed by Martin Scorsese, treatment by Larry Cohen and Mardik Martin.
- **Old Fashioned Woman**, USA, 1974. Written and Directed by Martha Coolidge.
- **Yudie**, USA, 1974. Written and Directed by Mirra Bank.

**STAVISKY**
*France/Italy, 1974. Directed by Alain Resnais.*
Written by Jorge Semprún. With Jean-Paul Belmondo, Anny Duperey, Charles Boyer, François Périer, Roberto Bisacco, Michael Lonsdale, Gérard Depardieu.

**A WOMAN UNDER THE INFLUENCE ▼**
*USA, 1974. Written and Directed by John Cassavetes.*
With Peter Falk, Gena Rowlands, Matthew Cassel, Matthew Laborteaux, Christina Grisanti, Katherine Cassavetes, Lady Rowlands, Fred Draper.

# 1975

SELECTION COMMITTEE: RICHARD ROUD, CHAIRMAN, RICHARD CORLISS, ROGER GREENSPUN, ARTHUR L. MAYER, AND CHARLES MICHENER. CONSULTANT: HENRI LANGLOIS (RETROSPECTIVES).

THE 13TH NYFF POSTER ARTWORK WAS CREATED BY CAROL SUMMERS. LIST ART POSTERS, ©LCPA.

## CONVERSATION PIECE ▶

*Italy/France, 1975. Directed by Luchino Visconti.*

Written by Suso Cecchi D'Amico, Enrico Medioli, and Visconti, based on a story by Medioli. With Burt Lancaster, Silvano Mangano, Helmut Berger, Claudia Marsani, Stefano Patrizi, Elvira Cortese, Dominique Sanda, Claudia Cardinale. Shown with *Coney*, USA. Directed by Frank Mouris and Caroline Ahlfors Mouris. (Opening Night.) Note: This was one of the most disastrous openings of the NYFF. The print the selection committee had initially screened was the subtitled version, not the dubbed one that was shown to the public.

## THE STORY OF ADELE H.

*France, 1975. Directed by François Truffaut.*

Written by Jean Gruault, Suzanne Schiffman, and Truffaut, based on *The Diary of Adèle Hugo*, edited by Frances V. Guille. With Isabelle Adjani, Bruce Robinson, Sylvia Marriott, Reubin Dorey. Shown with *The Imprint*, France. Directed by Jacques Cardon. (Closing Night.)

## AUTOBIOGRAPHY OF A PRINCESS

*UK, 1975. Directed by James Ivory.*

Written by Ruth Prawer Jhabvala. With James Mason, Madhur Jaffrey, Keith Varnier.

## + COMPAÑERO

*Chile/UK, 1975. Directed by Martin Smith.*

A filmed interview with Joan Turner, the English widow of Chilean political folk singer Victor Jara, about the last days of Jara's life.

## BLACK MOON

*France/West Germany, 1975. Directed by Louis Malle.*

Written by Joyce Buñuel, Malle, and Ghislain Uhry. With Cathryn Harrison, Therese Giehse, Alexandra Stewart, Joe Dallesandro. Shown with *Thanksgiving*, Canada. Directed by Ken Wallace. Also, *Cycles*, USA. Directed by Stephen Beck and Jordan Belson.

## LA CHIENNE (THE BITCH)

*France, 1931. Directed by Jean Renoir.*

Written by André Girard and Renoir, based on Georges de La Fouchardière's novel. With Michel Simon, Janie Marèze, Georges Flamant, Magdeleine Bérubet. (Retrospective.)

## ELECTRA, MY LOVE

*Hungary, 1975. Directed by Miklós Jancsó.*

Written by László Gyurkó and Gyula Hernádi. With Mari Töröcsik, József Madaras, György Cserhalmi. Shown with *Fuji*, USA. Directed by Robert Breer. Also, *Screentest*, USA. Directed by Frank Mouris and Caroline Ahlfors Mouris.

## EXHIBITION

*France, 1975. Directed by Jean-François Davy.*

With Claudine Beccarie, Benoît Archenoul, Frédéric Barral, Béatrice Harnois. Documentary on the public and private life of France's premiere sex-film actress. Note: This film caused NYFF's first serious confrontation with censorship. Shown with *Café Bar*, UK. Directed by Alison de Vere.

## F FOR FAKE

*France, 1973. Written and Directed by Orson Welles.*

With (as themselves) Welles, Oja Kodar, Elmyr de Hory, Clifford Irving. Edith Irving, François Reichenbach, Joseph Cotten. Shown with *Arthur and Lillie*, USA. Directed by Kris Samuelson. A documentary about Arthur and Lillie Mayer. Arthur was a former member of the NYFF selection committee.

## FOX AND HIS FRIENDS

*West Germany, 1975. Directed by Rainer Werner Fassbinder.*

Written by Fassbinder and Christian Hohoff. With Fassbinder, Peter Chatel, Karl-Heinz Böhm, Harry Baer. Shown with *Way Out*, UK. Directed by Ted Rockley.

*Electra, My Love* by Miklós Jancsó

**GREY GARDENS**
*USA, 1975. Directed by Ellen Hovde, Albert and David Maysles, and Muffie Meyer.*

With (as themselves) Edith Beale (mother), Edith Beale (daughter), Jerry Torre, Lois Wright, Jack Helmuth, Brooks Hires. Shown with *Longing for Darkness*, USA. Directed by Peter Beard.

**HEARTS OF THE WEST**
*USA, 1975. Directed by Howard Zieff.*

Written by Rob Thompson. With Jeff Bridges, Andy Griffith, Donald Pleasence, Blythe Danner, Alan Arkin. Shown with *The Unanimous Declaration of the 13 United States of America*, USA. Directed by A.P. Ferullo and R.A. Mayes.

**INDIA SONG**
*France, 1974. Written and Directed by Marguerite Duras.*

With Delphine Seyrig, Michel Lonsdale, Mathieu Carrière, Claude Mann.

**THE LOST HONOR OF KATHARINA BLUM ▶**
*West Germany, 1975. Written and Directed by Volker Schlöndorff and Margarethe von Trotta, based on Heinrich Böll's novel.*

With Angela Winkler, Mario Adorf, Dieter Laser, Heinz Bennent. Shown with *Don't*, USA. Directed by Robin Lehman.

**MILESTONES**
*USA, 1975. Written and Directed by John Douglas and Robert Kramer.*

With Amber, Bobby Buechler, Mary Chapelle, Pola Chapelle, Grace Paley.

**MOSES AND AARON**
*West Germany/France/Italy, 1974. Written and Directed by Jean-Marie Straub and Danièle Huillet, based on Arnold Schönberg's opera.*

With Günter Reich, Louis Devos, Roger Lucas, Eva Csapò.

**THE MYSTERY OF KASPAR HAUSER** aka **EVERY MAN FOR HIMSELF AND GOD AGAINST ALL**

*West Germany, 1974. Written and Directed by Werner Herzog.*

With Bruno S., Walter Ladengast, Brigitte Mira. Shown with *Homage to Magritte*, USA. Directed by Anita Thacher.

**SMILE**
*USA, 1975. Directed by Michael Ritchie. Written by Jerry Belson.*

With Bruce Dern, Barbara Feldon, Michael Kidd, Geoffrey Lewis, Nicholas Pryor, Melanie Griffith.

**SOUVENIRS D'EN FRANCE (FRENCH PROVINCIAL)**
*France, 1975. Directed by André Téchiné.*

Written by Marilyn Goldin and Téchiné. With Jeanne Moreau, Michel Auclair, Marie-France Pisier, Claude Mann. Shown with *Classical Cartoon*, UK. Directed by Bill Mather.

**THE WONDERFUL CROOK**
*Switzerland/France, 1975. Directed by Claude Goretta.*

Written by Charlotte Dubreuil and Goretta. With Marlène Jobert, Gérard Depardieu, Dominique Labourier, Philippe Léotard. Shown with *This Is Not a Museum*, USA. Directed by John Haugse.

**XALA**
*Senegal, 1974. Written and Directed by Ousmane Sembene.*

With Thierno Leye, Seun Samb, Younouss Seye, Myriam Niang.

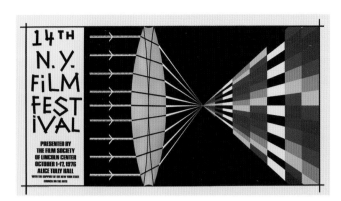

# 1976

SELECTION COMMITTEE: RICHARD ROUD, CHAIRMAN, RICHARD CORLISS, ROGER GREENSPUN, CHARLES MICHENER, AND SUSAN SONTAG. CONSULTANTS: ARTHUR KNIGHT, (WEST COAST) AND HENRI LANGLOIS.

THE 14TH NYFF POSTER ARTWORK WAS CREATED BY ALLAN D'ARCANGELO. LIST ART POSTERS, ©LCPA.

### SMALL CHANGE ▲

*France, 1976. Directed by François Truffaut written by Suzanne Schiffman and Truffaut.*

With Richard Golfier, Laurent Devlaeminck, Bruno Staab, Sébastien Marc. Shown with *Doubletalk*, USA. Directed by Alan W. Beattie. (Opening Night.)

### ◄ THE MARQUISE OF O (DIE MARQUISE VON O)

*West Germany/France, 1975. Written and Directed by Eric Rohmer, based on a story by Heinrich von Kleist.*

With Edith Clever, Bruno Ganz, Peter Lühr, Edda Seippel. Shown with *Sweet Sounds*, USA. Directed by James Ivory, Ismail Merchant, and Richard Robbins. (Closing Night.)

### CADAVERI ECCELLENTI (ILLUSTRIOUS CORPSES)

*Italy, 1976. Directed by Francesco Rosi.*

Written by Tonino Guerra, Lino Januzzi, and Rosi, based on Leonardo Sciascia's novel *The Context*. With Lino Ventura, Charles Vanel, Fernando Rey, Max von Sydow.

### DERSU UZALA

*USSR/Japan, 1975. Directed by Akira Kurosawa.*

Written by Kurosawa and Yuri Nagibin, based on a book by Vladimir Arseniev. With Maxim Munzuk. Note: This film was screened off the Lincoln Center campus, at the Ziegfeld Theatre, because at that time Alice Tully Hall did not have an adequate surround-sound system.

### DUELLE

*France, 1976. Directed by Jacques Rivette.*

Written by Eduardo de Gregorio and Marilù Parolini. With Bulle Ogier, Juliet Berto, Jean Babilée, Hermine Karagheuz, Nicole Garcia, Claire Nadeau. Shown with *Nightlife*, USA. Directed by Robin Lehman.

### FEAR OF FEAR

*West Germany, 1975. Written and Directed by Rainer Werner Fassbinder.*

With Margit Cartensen, Ulrich Faulhaber, Brigitte Mira, Irm Hermann, Armin Meier. Shown with *Organism*, USA. Directed by Hilary Harris.

### HARLAN COUNTY, U.S.A.

*USA, 1976. Directed by Barbara Kopple.*

A documentary about a miners' strike in Kentucky. With (as themselves) Bessie Lou Parker, Jerry Wynn, Bob Davis, Lois Scott. Shown with *Steelworkers from Village Borovica Gornja*, Yugoslavia. Directed by Mirjana Zizkovic.

### IN THE REALM OF THE SENSES ▼

*France/Japan, 1976. Written and Directed by Nagisa Oshima.*

With Eiko Matsuda, Tatsuya Fuji, Taiji Tonoyama. Note: Due to a run-in with U.S. Customs, this is the only time in NYFF history that we were unable to show a scheduled film.

It was later screened at MoMA. Shown with *In a Rehearsal Room*, USA. Directed by David Hahn.

### JONAH WHO WILL BE 25 IN THE YEAR 2000

*Switzerland, 1976. Directed by Alain Tanner.*

Written by John Berger and Tanner. With Jean-Luc Bideau, Myriam Boyer, Jacques Denis, Roger Jendly, Dominique Labourier. Shown with *No Noise*, USA. Directed by Carmen D'Avino.

### KINGS OF THE ROAD

*West Germany, 1976. Written and Directed by Wim Wenders.*

With Rüdiger Vogler, Hanns Zischler, Lisa Kreuzer, Rudolf Schündler.

### THE MEMORY OF JUSTICE

*USA, 1976. Written and Directed by Marcel Ophuls.*

With (as themselves) Daniel Ellsberg, Telford Taylor, Albert Speer, Admiral Karl Dönitz, Marie-Claude Vaillant-Couturier, Edgar Faure. The investigation of national and individual responsibility in the wake of Auschwitz, Katyn, Dresden, Hiroshima, Algeria, and Vietnam.

### THE MIDDLEMAN

*India, 1975. Written and Directed by Satyajit Ray, based on Sankar's novel.*

With Pradip Mukherjee, Satya Banerjee, Dipankar Dey, Lily Chakravorty.

### NANA

*France, 1926. Directed by Jean Renoir.*

Written by Pierre Lestringuez, based on Emile Zola's novel, adapted by Renoir. With Catherine Hessling, Jean Angelo, Werner Krauss, Raymond Guérin-Catelain. Piano accompaniment by Arthur Kleiner. (Retrospective.)

### OSSESSIONE

*Italy, 1942. Directed by Luchino Visconti.*

Written by Mario Alicata, Giuseppe De Santis, Antonio Pietrangeli, Gianni Puccini, and Visconti. With Clara Calamai, Massimo Girotti, Juan de Landa, Elio Marcuzzo. Visconti's first film. (Retrospective.)

*A Touch of Zen* by King Hu

**"RITES OF PASSAGE" – three featurettes:**
- **Bernice Bobs Her Hair**, USA, 1976. Written and Directed by Joan Micklin Silver, based on a story by F. Scott Fitzgerald. With Shelley Duvall, Veronica Cartwright, Bud Cort, Patrick Reynolds.
- **In the Region of Ice**, USA, 1976. Written and Directed by Peter Werner, based on a story by Joyce Carol Oates. With Fionnula Flanagan, Peter Lempert, Malachi Throne, Shirley Slater.
- **Sunday Funnies**, USA, 1976. Written and Directed by Ray Karp, based on a story by Douglas Kenney. With Bette Anderson, Buddy Anderson, Frank Morrow.

**SÉRAIL**
*France, 1976. Directed by Eduardo de Gregorio.*
Written by de Gregorio and Michael Graham. With Leslie Caron, Bulle Ogier, Marie-France Pisier, Corin Redgrave. Shown with *Women's Answers*, France. Directed by Agnès Varda.

**THE STORY OF SIN**
*Poland, 1975. Written and Directed by Walerian Borowczyk, based on Stefan Żeromski's novel.*
With Grażyna Długołęcka, Jerzy Zelnik, Olgierd Łukaszewicz, Marek Walczewski.

**STRONGMAN FERDINAND**
*West Germany, 1975. Written and Directed by Alexander Kluge, based on his story "A Capitalist Bolshevik."*
With Heinz Schubert, Vérénice Rudolph, Joachim Hackethal, Heinz Schimmelpfennig. Shown with *Two Cops*, USA. Directed by Charles Braverman.

**A TOUCH OF ZEN**
*Hong Kong, 1975. Written and Directed by King Hu.*
With Hsu Feng, Pai Ying, Roy Chiao Hung, Shih Chun.

# 1977

SELECTION COMMITTEE: RICHARD ROUD, CHAIRMAN, RICHARD CORLISS, ROGER GREENSPUN, CHARLES MICHENER, AND SUSAN SONTAG. CONSULTANT: ARTHUR KNIGHT (WEST COAST).

THE 15TH NYFF POSTER ARTWORK WAS CREATED BY ©JIM DINE.

## ONE SINGS, THE OTHER DOESN'T
*France, 1977. Written and Directed by Agnès Varda.*

With Valérie Mairesse, Thérèse Liotard, Robert Dadiès, Ali Raffi. Shown with *Music of the Spheres*, USA. Directed by Jordan Belson. (Opening Night)

## THAT OBSCURE OBJECT OF DESIRE ▶
*France/Spain, 1977. Directed by Luis Buñuel.*

Written by Buñuel and Jean-Claude Carrière, based on Pierre Louÿs's novel *La Femme et le Pantin*. With Fernando Rey, Carole Bouquet, Angela Molina, Julien Bertheau. Shown with *Kudzu*, USA. Directed by Marjie Short. (Closing Night.)

## THE AMERICAN FRIEND ▼
*West Germany/France, 1977. Written and Directed by Wim Wenders, based on Patricia Highsmith's novel* Ripley's Game.

With Bruno Ganz, Dennis Hopper, Lisa Kreuzer, Gérard Blain, Nicholas Ray, Samuel Fuller, Daniel Schmid, Jean Eustache, Lou Castel.

## LE CAMION (THE TRUCK)
*France, 1977. Written and Directed by Marguerite Duras.*

With Duras, Gérard Depardieu. Shown with *Grandpa*, USA. Directed by Paul Desaulniers and Stephen L. Forman.

## THE DEVIL, PROBABLY
*France, 1977. Written and Directed by Robert Bresson.*

With Antoine Monnier, Tina Irissari, Henri de Maublanc, Laetitia Carcano. Shown with *Glove Story*, USA. Directed by Eli Noyes.

## L'ENFANT DE PARIS
*France, 1913. Written and Directed by Léonce Perret, based on Adolphe d'Ennery's play* Les Deux Orphelines.

With Perret, Suzanne Le Bret, Maurice Lagrenée, Louis Leubas. Piano accompaniment by William Perry. (Retrospective.)

## HANDLE WITH CARE aka CITIZENS BAND
*USA, 1977. Directed by Jonathan Demme.*

Written by Paul Brickman. With Paul Le Mat, Candy Clark, Bruce McGill, Roberts Blossom. Shown with *Froggie Went A-Courtin'*, USA. Directed by Frank Gladstone.

## HEART OF GLASS
*West Germany, 1976. Directed by Werner Herzog.*

Written by Herbert Achternbusch and Herzog. With Josef Bierbichler, Stefan Güttler, Clemens Scheitz, Volker Prechtel. Shown with *La Soufrière*, West Germany. Directed by Werner Herzog.

## HOT TOMORROWS
*USA, 1977. Written and Directed by Martin Brest.*

With Ken Lerner, Ray Sharkey, Hervé Villechaize, Victor Argo.

## + MOYA BABUSHKA (MY GRANDMOTHER)
*USSR, 1929. Directed by Kote Mikaberidze.*

Written by S. Dolidze, G. Mdivani, and Mikaberidze. With A. Takaishvili, B. Chernova. A satire of Russian bureaucrats that was suppressed for half a century.

## THE LACEMAKER ▼
*France/Switzerland/West Germany, 1977. Directed by Claude Goretta.*

Written by Goretta and Pascal Lainé, based on Lainé's novel. With Isabelle Huppert, Yves Beneyton, Florence Giorgetti, Annemarie Düringer.

## THE MAN WHO LOVED WOMEN
*France, 1977. Directed by François Truffaut.*

Written by Michel Fermaud, Suzanne Schiffman, and Truffaut. With Charles Denner, Brigitte Fossey, Nelly Borgeaud, Geneviève Fontanel, Nathalie Baye, Leslie Caron, Valérie Bonnier, Jean Dasté, Sabine Glaser.

### MEN OF BRONZE
*USA, 1977 Directed by William Miles.*

A documentary about WWI's 15th Army Brigade, an outfit of black volunteers who fought in the trenches with the French.

### + CHILDREN OF LABOR
*USA, 1977. Directed by Richard Broadman, Noel Buckner, Mary Dore, and Al Gedicks.*

A documentary about Finnish immigrants to the American North who organized to demand decent working conditions.

### 1900
*Italy, 1976. Directed by Bernardo Bertolucci.*

Written by Franco Arcalli and Bernardo and Giuseppe Bertolucci. With Burt Lancaster, Romolo Valli, Anna-Maria Gherardi, Laura Betti, Robert De Niro, Paolo Pavesi, Dominique Sanda, Sterling Hayden, Gérard Depardieu, Stefania Sandrelli. Note: Alberto Grimaldi, the producer, would or could not commit this film to the NYFF until after our annual *New York Times* ad had gone to press. Rather than lose the film we filled the spot with a question mark, but word got out and it was the first film to sell out.

### OMAR GATLATO
*Algeria, 1977. Written and Directed by Merzak Allouache.*

With Boualem Benani, Farida Guenaneche, Aziz Degga, Abdelkader Chaou. Shown with *Striptease*, Italy. Directed by Bruno Bozzetto and Guido Manuli.

### PADRE PADRONE
*Italy, 1977. Written and Directed by Paolo and Vittorio Taviani, based on a book by Gavino Ledda.*

With Omero Antonutti, Saverio Marconi, Marcella Michelangeli, Nanni Moretti.

### PAFNUCIO SANTO
*Mexico, 1976. Written and Directed by Rafael Corkidi.*

With Pablo Corkidi, María de la Luz Zendejas, Jorge Humberto Robles, Gina Morett. Shown with *Nightmare*, Yugoslavia. Directed by Aleksandar Marks.

### ROSELAND
*USA, 1977. Directed by James Ivory.*

Written by Ruth Prawer Jhabvala. With Teresa Wright, Lou Jacobi, Geraldine Chaplin, Helen Gallagher, Joan Copeland, Christopher Walken, Lilia Skala, David Thomas. Shown with *Part of Your Loving*, USA. Directed by Tony De Nonno.

### ◀ SALÒ
*Italy/ France, 1975. Directed by Pier Paolo Pasolini.*

Written by Sergio Citti and Pasolini, based on the Marquis de Sade's novel *120 Days of Sodom*. With Paolo Bonacelli, Giorgio Cataldi, Umberto P. Quintavalle, Aldo Valletti.

### SHORT EYES
*USA, 1977. Directed by Robert M. Young.*

Written by Miguel Piñero, based on his play. With Bruce Davison, José Pérez, Nathan George, Don Blakely.

### TENT OF MIRACLES
*Brazil, 1977. Directed by Nelson Pereira dos Santos.*

Written by Jorge Amado and dos Santos, based on Amado's novel. With Hugo Carvana, Sonia Dias, Anecy Rocha.

### WOMEN
*Hungary, 1977. Directed by Márta Mészáros.*

Written by József Balázs, Géza Bereményi, and Ildikó Korody. With Marina Vlady, Lili Monori, Miklós Tolnay, Jan Nowicki. Shown with *What I Did Not Tell the Prince*, Czechoslovakia. Directed by Jiří Brdečka. Also, *Single Fathering*, USA. Directed by Ron Taylor.

## Special Events

**"Animation Festival"** – an adult program selected by Wendy Keys. Shown in Alice Tully Hall in the afternoons.

**Program 1:** *Flamingo Boogy*, by Richard Protovin; *Marguerite*, by Betty Chen; *Mindscape*, by Jacques Drouin; *Thru the Mirror*, by Walt Disney; *Arabesque*, by John Whitney; *Tête en Fleurs*, by Bernard Longpre; *Sonoma*, by Dennis Pies; *Duo Concertantes*, by Larry Jordan; *Snow Sound*, by Robert Dvorak; *Opening and Closing*, by Kathleen Laughlin; *The 40's*, by John Canemaker; *The Nose*, by Alexander Alexeiff and Claire Parker; *Feasting*, by Louis Grenier; *Dreamstealer*, by Eric Durst; *Music of the Spheres*, by Jordan Belson.

**Program 2:** *Chow Fun*, by Sally Cruikshank; *Fantabiblical*, by Bruno Bozzetto; *Teatime*, by Mary Szilagyi, *Manga*, by Yoji Kuri; *Lady Fishbourne's Complete Guide to Better Table Manners*, by Janet Perlman; *Der Fuehrer's Face*, by Walt Disney; *The Family That Dwelt Apart*, by Yvon Mallette; *Made for Each Other*, by Barbara Bottner; *The Killing of an Egg*, by Paul Driessen; *Miss Glory*, by Tex Avery; *Exercise*, by R.O. Blechman; *When Roobarb Made a Spike*, by Bob Godfrey; *The Club*, by George Griffin; *Duck Amuck*, by Chuck Jones; *Ransom*, by Ron Skinner; *Ten Short Films*, by Karen Fredericks; *Freud Explains*, by A. Valma.

**Program 3:** *Autosong*, by Al Jarnow; *Olympiad*, by Lillian Schwarz; *UFO Noah*, by Jean Luc de Reymaecker; *In Plain Sight*, by Jane Aaron; *Fuji*, by Robert Breer; *Rapid Eye Movements*, by Jeff Carpenter; *Fantasy*, by Vincent Collins; *Pasadena Freeway Stills*, by Gary Beydler; *Phoenix*, by Petar Gligorovski; *Coney*, by Frank Mouris; *Neuron*, by Robert Russett; *Pin Ball Wizard*, by Rod McCall; *The Revenge of the Objects*, by Pierre Veilleux; *Roll 'Em Lola*, by Fred Burns.

**Program 4:** *Sandman*, by Eli Noyes; *Notes on a Triangle*, by Rene Jodoin; *The Band Concert*, by Walt Disney; *The Bead Game*, by Ishu Patel; *What's Opera, Doc?*, by Chuck Jones; *Two Stars*, by Lisze Bechtold; *Googleplex*, by Lillian Schwartz; *Improvisation*, by Doris Chase; *Musical Pig*, by Zlatko Grgić and Turido Paus; *Composition in Blue*, by Oskar Fischinger; *Pianissimo*, by Carmen D'Avino; *Morning, Noon and Nightclub*, by Max Fleischer; *Afternoon of a Nose*, by Robert Stuhmer; *Hallelujah*, by Mark Henrikson.

**Program 5:** *Whirling Ecstasy*, by Dennis Pohl; *Snow Show*, by Stan VanDerBeek; *The Doodlers*, by Kathy Rose; *Thumbnail Sketches*, by George Griffin; *The Sandcastle*, by Coe Hoedeman; *The Dream of Inca Yupanqui*, by Jose Gelabert; *Jabberwocky*, by Jan Svankmajer; *Honeymation*, by Ferenc Varsanyi; *Seed Reel*, by Mary Beams; *A Recent Animation*, by Lowell Bodger; *Leaves in Space*, by Kenneth Hoffman; *Album*, by Linda Heller; *The Intruder*, by Scott Morris; *I Change, I Am the Same*, by Shelby Kennedy and Ann Severson; *Evolution of the Red Star*, by Adam Beckett; *High Tide*, by David Bruce.

**"Saved!"** – a retrospective of 12 American films from the preservation vaults of the AFI, George Eastman House, MoMA, and UCLA, also shown during afternoons at Alice Tully Hall. This program was organized by Richard Roud and Joanne Koch. Films shown: *City Girl*, 1930, by F.W. Murnau; *Dodsworth*, 1936, by William Wyler; *Downstairs*, 1932, *The Letter*, 1929, and *The Torrent*, 1926, by Monta Bell; *It*, 1927, by Clarence Badger and (uncredited) Josef von Sternberg; *It's the Old Army Game*, 1926, by Edward Sutherland; *Liliom*, 1930, by Frank Borzage; *Paid*, 1930, by Sam Wood; *Regeneration*, 1915, by Raoul Walsh; *Transatlantic*, by William K. Howard; and *Wild Oranges*, 1924, by King Vidor.

*The Torrent* by Monta Bell

# PRESENTED BY THE FILM SOCIETY OF LINCOLN CENTER

The 16th New York Film Festival made possible with the support of the New York State Council on the Arts

**SEPTEMBER 22 - OCTOBER 8, 1978 · ALICE TULLY HALL**

# 1978

SELECTION COMMITTEE: RICHARD ROUD, CHAIRMAN, RICHARD CORLISS, ROGER GREENSPUN, AND MOLLY HASKELL. CONSULTANTS: TOM LUDDY (WEST COAST) AND MARY MEERSON (RETROSPECTIVES).

THE 16TH NYFF POSTER ARTWORK WAS CREATED BY ©RICHARD AVEDON. DESIGN: ELIZABETH PAUL.

## A WEDDING
*USA, 1978. Directed by Robert Altman.*

Written by Altman, John Considine, Allan Nicholls, and Patricia Resnick, based on a story by Altman and Considine. With Lillian Gish, Desi Arnaz Jr., Vittorio Gassman, Dina Merrill, Carol Burnett, Paul Dooley, Amy Stryker, Mia Farrow, Peggy Ann Garner, Geraldine Chaplin, Viveca Lindfors, Lauren Hutton. (Opening Night.)

## VIOLETTE (VIOLETTE NOZIÈRE) ▶
*France/Canada, 1978 Directed by Claude Chabrol.*

Written by Odile Barski, Hervé Bromberger, and Frédéric Grendel, based on a book by Jean-Marie Fitère. With Isabelle Huppert, Stéphane Audran, Jean Carmet, Lisa Langlois. (Closing Night.)

## AMERICAN BOY: A PROFILE OF STEVEN PRINCE
*USA, 1978. Directed by Martin Scorsese.*

Written (treatment) by Julia Cameron and Mardik Martin. People in the room: Prince, Scorsese, George Memmoli, Martin, Cameron, Kathy McGinnis.

## + MOVIES ARE MY LIFE
*UK, 1978. Directed by Peter Hayden.*

A profile of Martin Scorsese with John Cassavetes, Jay Cocks, Robert De Niro, Brian De Palma, Jodie Foster, Mardik Martin, Liza Minnelli, Steven Prince, Robbie Robertson, Scorsese.

## THE APPLE GAME
*Czechoslovakia, 1976. Directed by Věra Chytilová.*

Written by Chytilová and Kristina Vlachová. With Dagmar Bláhová, Jiří Menzel, Evelyna Steimarová, Jiří Kodet. Shown with *Eggs*, USA. Directed by Ruth C. Hayes.

## BLOODBROTHERS
*USA, 1978. Directed by Robert Mulligan.*

Written by Walter Newman, based on Richard Price's novel. With Paul Sorvino, Tony Lo Bianco, Richard Gere, Lelia Goldoni.

## CAMOUFLAGE
*Poland, 1977. Written and Directed by Krzysztof Zanussi.*

With Piotr Garlicki, Zbigniew Zapasiewicz, Christine Paul, Mariusz Dmochowski. Shown with *The Discipline of D.E.*, USA. Directed by Gus Van Sant.

## DESPAIR
*West Germany/France, 1978. Directed by Rainer Werner Fassbinder.*

Written by Tom Stoppard, based on Vladimir Nabokov's novel. With Dirk Bogarde, Andréa Ferréol, Volker Spengler, Klaus Löwitsch.

## DOSSIER 51
*France/West Germany, 1978. Directed by Michel Deville.*

Written by Deville and Gilles Perrault, based on Perrault's novel. With François Marthouret, Claude Mercault, Philippe Rouleau. Shown with *Duane Michals (1939-1997)*, USA. Directed by Theodore Haimes and Ed Howard.

## ELECTIVE AFFINITIES
*Italy, 1978. Directed by Gianni Amico.*

Written by Amico, I. Alighiero Chiusano, and Marco Melani, based on Johann Wolfgang von Goethe's novel. With Francesca Archibugi, Paolo Graziosi, Nino Castelnuovo, Veronica Lazar.

## GATES OF HEAVEN
*USA, 1978. Directed by Errol Morris.*

An analytical study of contemporary America as portrayed by California pet cemeteries.

## + MANIMALS
*USA, 1978. Directed by Robin Lehman.*

Shown with *The Dogs*, USA. Directed by Aviva Slesin.

## GET OUT YOUR HANDKERCHIEFS
*France/Belgium, 1978. Written and Directed by Bertrand Blier.*

With Gérard Depardieu, Patrick Dewaere, Carol Laure, Riton.

## THE GREEN ROOM (LA CHAMBRE VERTE) ▲
*France, 1968. Directed by François Truffaut.*

Written by Jean Gruault and Truffaut, based on themes from Henry James's life and work. With François Truffaut, Nathalie Baye, Jean Dasté, Jean-Pierre Moulin. Shown with *Going Out of Business*, USA. Directed by Christopher Gamboni.

## THE LEFT-HANDED WOMAN
*West Germany, 1978. Written and Directed by Peter Handke.*

With Edith Clever, Markus Mühleisen, Bruno Ganz, Michael Lonsdale, Angela Winkler, Gérard Depardieu.

## LIKE A TURTLE ON ITS BACK
*France, 1978. Directed by Luc Béraud and Hubert Niogret.*

Written by Béraud and Claude Miller. With Jean-François Stévenin, Bernadette Lafont, Virginie Thévenet, Véronique Silver, Miller, Sandy Whitelaw.

## THE MIRACLE OF THE WOLVES
*France, 1924. Directed by Raymond Bernard.*

Written by A. Paul Antoine, based on Henry Dupuy-Mazuel's novel. With Charles Dullin, Vanni-Marcoux, Romuald Joube, Yvonne Sergyl. A love story set in the time of Louis XI. Piano accompaniment by Bill Perry. (Retrospective.)

## NEWSFRONT
*Australia, 1978. Directed by Phillip Noyce.*

Written by Bob Ellis and Noyce, based on an idea by David Elfick. With Bill Hunter, Wendy Hughes, Gerard Kennedy, Chris Haywood.

## PERCEVAL (PERCEVAL LE GALLOIS)
*France, 1978. Written and Directed by Eric Rohmer, based on the poem by Chrétien de Troyes.*

With Fabrice Luchini, André Dussolier.

## THE SHOUT
*UK, 1978. Directed by Jerzy Skolimowski.*

Written by Michael Austin and Skolimowski, based on a story by Robert Graves. With Alan Bates, Susannah York, John Hurt, Robert Stephens, Tim Curry. Shown with *Valse Triste*, USA. Directed by Bruce Conner. Also, *Sea Travels*, USA. Directed by Anita Thacher.

## SPIES
*Germany, 1928. Directed by Fritz Lang.*

Written by Lang and Thea von Harbou, based on her novel. With Rudolf Klein-Rogge, Gerda Maurus, Lien Deyers, Louis Ralph. Piano accompaniment by Curtis Salke. (Retrospective.)

## SKIP TRACER
*Canada, 1977. Written and Directed by Zale R. Dalen.*

With David Petersen, John Lazarus, Rudy Szabo, Mike Grigg. Shown with *Bruce & His Things*, USA. Directed by Mike Haller.

**"STYLES OF RADICAL WILL"** – with a title borrowed from Susan Sontag, these three films investigate various aspects of contemporary politics:

• **CIA: Case Officer**, USA, 1978. Directed by Saul Landau. Cinematography by Haskell Wexler. A portrait of John Stockwell, a CIA officer in Angola who had to choose between his career and his conscience.

• **They Are Their Own Gifts**, USA, 1978. Directed by Margaret Murphy and Lucille Rhodes. A portrait of Muriel Rukeyser, a politically committed and brilliant poet.

• **With Babies and Banners: Story of the Women's Emergency Brigade**, USA, 1978. Directed by Lorraine Gray. A mixture of footage from the General Motors sit-down strike in 1937 and interviews with the survivors at their 40th-anniversary reunion.

# Special Event

**"New Currents in Japanese Cinema"** – a collaboration between the Film Society and the Japan Society. The series was programmed by the Film Society's Wendy Keys and the Japan Society's Alan Poul, in association with Peter Grilli, Joanne Koch, and Donald Richie. Five independent Japanese films were shown in the afternoons in Alice Tully Hall: *Pastoral Hide-and-Seek*, 1974, by Shuji Terayama; *The Pornographers*, 1966, by Shohei Imamura; *Preparation for the Festival*, 1975, by Kazuo Kuroki; *Sanrizuka: The Skies of May*, 1977, by Shinsuke Ogawa, shown with *Nito-jo*, by Shuji Terayama; and *Third Base*, 1978, by Yoichi Higashi.

*Pastoral Hide-and-Seek* by Shuji Terayama

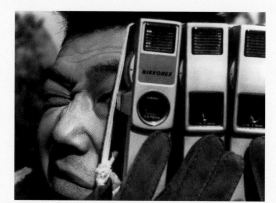

*The Pornographers* by Shohei Imamura

*Preparation for the Festival* by Kazuo Kuroki

# 1979

SELECTION COMMITTEE: RICHARD ROUD, CHAIRMAN, RICHARD CORLISS, MOLLY HASKELL, TOM LUDDY, AND CHARLES MICHENER.
CONSULTANT: MARY MEERSON (RETROSPECTIVES).

THE 17TH NYFF POSTER ARTWORK WAS CREATED BY ©MICHELANGELO PISTOLETTO.

**LA LUNA**
*Italy/USA, 1979. Directed by Bernardo Bertolucci.*

Written by Bernardo and Giuseppe Bertolucci and Clare Peploe, based on a story by Franco Arcalli and Bernardo and Giuseppe Bertolucci. With Jill Clayburgh, Matthew Barry, Veronica Lazar, Renato Salvatori, Fred Gwynne, Tomas Milian, Alida Valli, Roberto Benigni. (Opening Night.)

**THE MARRIAGE OF MARIA BRAUN ▲**
*West Germany, 1978. Directed by Rainer Werner Fassbinder.*

Written by Pea Fröhlich and Peter Märthesheimer. With Hanna Schygulla, Klaus Löwitsch, Ivan Desny, Gottfried John, Gisela Uhlen, Elsiabeth Trissenaar, Hark Bohm, Fassbinder. (Closing Night.)

**ALEXANDRIA... WHY?**
*Egypt/Algeria, 1978. Directed by Youssef Chahine.*

Written by Chahine and Mohsen Zayed. With Naglaa Fathi, Farid Shawki, Ezzat El Alayli, Gerry Sundquist.

**ANGI VERA**
*Hungary, 1979. Directed by Pál Gábor.*

*Nosferatu the Vampyre* by Werner Herzog

Written by Gábor, based on Endre Vészi's novel. With Veronika Papp, Erzsi Pásztor, Tamás Dunai, Éva Szabó. Shown with *Since '45*, USA. Directed by Michael Korolenko.

### BEST BOY
*USA, 1979. Directed by Ira Wohl.*

A documentary about the filmmaker's 52-year-old cousin, who has the emotional and intellectual capacity of an 8-year-old. It won an Oscar for best documentary feature. Shown with *LMNO*, USA. Directed by Robert Breer.

### BLACK JACK
*UK, 1979. Written and Directed by Ken Loach, based on Leon Garfield's novel.*

With Jean Franval, Andrew Bennett, Stephen Hirst, Pat Wallis. Shown with *Every Child*, Canada. Directed by Eugene Fedorenko.

### THE BLACK STALLION
*USA, 1979. Directed by Carroll Ballard.*

Written by Melissa Mathison, Jeanne Rosenberg, and William D. Wittliff, based on Walter Farley's novel. Executive produced by Francis Ford Coppola. With Mickey Rooney, Kelly Reno, Teri Garr, Clarence Muse.

### THE BUGS BUNNY/ROAD RUNNER MOVIE
*USA, 1979. Directed by Chuck Jones.*

Written by Jones and Mike Maltese. Voice Characterizations by Mel Blanc. With Bugs Bunny, Road Runner, Wile E. Coyote, Elmer Fudd, Pepé Le Pew, Daffy Duck. "Bugs Bunny At Home" sequence co-directed by Phil Monroe.

### THE EUROPEANS
*UK, 1979. Directed by James Ivory.*

Written by Ruth Prawer Jhabvala, based on Henry James's novel. With Lee Remick, Robin Ellis, Wesley Addy, Lisa Eichhorn, Nancy New. Shown with *Impasse*, USA. Directed by Frank and Caroline Mouris.

### THE GOLDEN COACH
*Italy/ France, 1953. Directed by Jean Renoir.*

Written by Renzo Avanzo, Ginette Doynel, Jack Kirkland, Giulio Macchi, and Renoir, based on Prosper Mérimée's play *La Carosse du Saint-Sacrement*. With Anna Magnani, Duncan Lamont, Odoardo Spadaro, Riccardo Rioli. (Retrospective.) Shown with *Jean Renoir's Direction of Actors*, France. Directed by Gisèle Braunberger.

### IN A YEAR OF 13 MOONS
*West Germany, 1976. Written and Directed by Rainer Werner Fassbinder.*

With Volker Spengler, Ingrid Caven, Gottfried John, Elisabeth Trissenaar.

### MAD WEDNESDAY aka THE SIN OF HAROLD DIDDLEBOCK
*USA, 1950. Written and Directed by Preston Sturges.*

With Harold Lloyd, Frances Ramsden, Jimmy Conlin, Raymond Walburn, Edgar Kennedy, Arline Judge, Franklin Pangborn, Lionel Stander. (Retrospective.)

### MOLIÈRE
*France, 1978. Written and Directed by Ariane Mnouchkine.*

With Philippe Caubère, Joséphine Derenne, Brigitte Catillon, Claude Merlin. A four-and-a-half-hour biography of the great French playwright, as well as a spectacular portrait of 17th-century France.

### MY BRILLIANT CAREER ▼
*Australia, 1979. Directed by Gillian Armstrong.*

Written by Eleanor Witcombe, based on Miles Franklin's novel. With Judy Davis, Sam Neill, Wendy Hughes, Robert Grubb. Shown with *The Bronswik Affair*, Canada. Directed by Robert Awad and André Leduc.

### NOSFERATU THE VAMPYRE
*West Germany/USA, 1978. Written and Directed by Werner Herzog.*

With Klaus Kinski, Isabelle Adjani, Bruno Ganz, Roland Topor. Shown with *Euclidean Illusions*, USA. Directed by Stan VanDerBeek.

### OTHER PEOPLE'S MONEY (L'ARGENT DES AUTRES)
*France, 1978. Directed by Christian de Chalonge.*

Written by de Chalonge and Pierre Dumayet, based on Nancy Markham's novel. With Jean-Louis Trintignant, Claude Brasseur, Michel Serrault, Catherine Deneuve, François Perrot, Juliet Berto, Umberto Orsini. Shown with *Special Delivery*, Canada. Directed by Eunice Macaulay and John Weldon.

### PEEPING TOM ▶
*UK, 1959. Directed by Michael Powell.*

Written by Leo Marks. With Carl Boehm, Moira Shearer, Anna Massey, Maxine Audley. (Retrospective.)

### PRIMAL FEAR
*Canada, 1978. Directed by Anne Claire Poirier.*

Written by Marthe Blackburn and Poirier, based on a story by Andrée Major. With Julie Vincent, Germain Houde, Paul Savoie, Monique Miller. Shown with *Pretend You're Wearing a Barrel*, Canada. Directed by Jan-Marie Martell.

### SCARFACE
*USA, 1932. Directed by Howard Hawks.*

Written by W.R. Burnett, John Lee Mahin, and Seton I. Miller, adaptation by Ben Hecht, based on Armitage Trail's novel. With Paul Muni, Ann Dvorak, Karen Morley, Osgood Perkins, Boris Karloff, C. Henry Gordon, George Raft. (Retrospective.)

### SHORT MEMORY (LA MÉMOIRE COURTE)
*France/Belgium, 1979. Directed by Eduardo de Gregorio.*

Written by Edgardo Cozarinsky and de Gregorio. With Nathalie Baye, Philippe Léotard, Bulle Ogier, Xavier Saint-Macary.

### WISE BLOOD
*USA, 1979. Directed by John Huston.*

Written by Benedict Fitzgerald, based on Flannery O'Connor's novel. With Brad Dourif, Ned Beatty, Harry Dean Stanton, Dan Shor, Amy Wright, Mary Nell Santacroce, John Huston. Shown with *Why Me?*, Canada. Directed by Derek Lamb and Janet Perlman.

### WITHOUT ANESTHESIA
*Poland, 1978. Directed by Andrzej Wajda.*

Written by Agnieszka Holland and Wajda. With Zbigniew Zapasiewicz, Ewa Dalkowska, Andrzej Seweryn, Krystyna Janda.

### THE WOBBLIES
*USA, 1979. Directed by Stewart Bird and Deborah Shaffer.*

A history of the Industrial Workers of the World, the radical American labor union founded in 1905. Shown with *Modeling the Universe*, USA. Directed by Jaime Snyder.

### YOUNG GIRLS OF WILKO
*Poland/France, 1979. Directed by Andrzej Wajda.*

Written by Zbigniew Kaminski, based on Jarosław Iwaszkiewicz's novella. With Daniel Olbrychski, Krystyna Zachwatowicz, Anna Seniuk, Maja Komorowska.

## Special Event

"American Independents" – presented by the Film Society and the Film Fund at the Paramount Theater, 61st Street and Broadway, prior to the NYFF. Films shown: *Alambrista!* aka *The Illegal*, by Robert M. Young; *Badlands*, by Terrence Malick; *Bush Mama*, by Haile Gerima; *The Cool World*, by Shirley Clarke; *Crazy Quilt*, by John Korty; *Gal Young 'Un*, by Victor Nuñez; *Glen and Randa*, by Jim McBride; *Heartland*, by Richard Pearce; *Ice*, by Robert Kramer; *Killer's Kiss*, by Stanley Kubrick, with *The Brig*, by Jonas Mekas; *Northern Lights*, by Jon Hanson and Rob Nilsson; *The Scenic Route*, by Mark Rappaport; *Sweet Sweetback's Baadasssss Song*, by Melvin Van Peebles; and *Trash*, by Paul Morrissey.

# 1980

SELECTION COMMITTEE: RICHARD ROUD, CHAIRMAN, RICHARD CORLISS, MOLLY HASKELL, TOM LUDDY, AND SUSAN SONTAG.
CONSULTANT: MARY MEERSON (RETROSPECTIVES).

THE 18TH NYFF POSTER ARTWORK WAS CREATED BY ©LES LEVINE.

*Melvin and Howard* by Jonathan Demme

## MELVIN AND HOWARD
*USA, 1980. Directed by Jonathan Demme.*

Written by Bo Goldman. With Jason Robards, Paul Le Mat, Mary Steenburgen, Michael J. Pollard, Pamela Reed, Gloria Grahame, Charles Napier, Jack Kehoe, Dabney Coleman. Shown with *Dance Space*, USA. Directed by John G. Avildsen. (Opening Night.)

## THE LAST METRO
*France, 1980. Directed by François Truffaut.*

Written by Suzanne Schiffman and Truffaut, with additional dialogue by Jean-Claude Grumberg. With Catherine Deneuve, Gérard Depardieu, Heinz Bennent, Jean Poiret, Andréa Ferréol. (Closing Night.)

## "AMERICANA" – a program of three featurettes:
- *New York Story*, USA, 1980. Written and Directed by Jackie Raynal. With Sid Geffen, Raynal, Gary Indiana, Jim Dradfield.
- *Night at O'Rear's*, USA, 1980. Directed by Robert Mandel. Written by Maurice Noel, based on a story by Patricia Griffith. With Craig Wasson, Linda Gillin, Louise Hoven, Sally Julian.
- *Rush*, USA. Directed by Evelyn Purcell. A documentary about sorority pledge week at the University of Mississippi.

## BYE BYE BRAZIL
*Brazil, 1980. Written and Directed by Carlos Diegues.*

With Betty Faria, José Wilker, Fébio Júnior, Zaira Zambelli. Shown with *The Solar Film*, USA. Directed by Saul and Elaine Bass.

## CAMERA BUFF ▲
*Poland, 1979. Written and Directed by Krzysztof Kieślowski, with additional dialogue by Jerzy Stuhr.*

With Stuhr, Małgorzata Ząbkowska, Ewa Pokas, Stefan Czyzewski, Jerzy Nowak.

## THE COLOR OF POMEGRANATES
*Armenia, 1969-72. Directed by Sergei Parajanov.*

An evocation of the poetry of Sayat Nova, the great 18th-century Armenian poet. With Sophico Tchiaourelli, M. Alekyan, V. Galestian, G. Gueguetchkori. Shown with *T.Z.*, USA. Directed by Robert Breer. Also, *Dog's Dialogue*, France. Directed by Raúl Ruiz.

## CONFIDENCE
*Hungary, 1979. Directed by István Szabó.*

Written by Szabó, based on an idea by Szabó and Erika Szántó. With Ildikó Bánsági, Péter Andorai.

## THE CONSTANT FACTOR
*Poland, 1980. Written and Directed by Krzysztof Zanussi.*

With Tadeusz Bradecki, Zofia Mrozowska, Małgorzata Zajączkowska, Cezary Morawski. Shown with *Backdrop*, France. Directed by Arthur Joffe.

## EUROPA '51 ▲
*Italy, 1952. Directed by Roberto Rossellini.*

Written by Sandro De Feo, Diego Fabbri, Mario Pannunzio, Ivo Perilli, Antonio Petrangeli, Brunello Rondi, and Rossellini, based on a story by Rossellini. With Ingrid Bergman, Alexander Knox, Sandro Franchina, Ettore Giannini, Giulietta Masina. (Retrospective.)

## EVERY MAN FOR HIMSELF (SAUVE QUI PEUT (LA VIE))
*France/Switzerland, 1980. Directed by Jean-Luc Godard.*

Written by Jean-Claude Carrière and Anne-Marie Miéville. With Isabelle Huppert, Jacques Dutronc, Nathalie Baye.

## HANDICAPPED LOVE
*Switzerland, 1979. Directed by Marlies Graf.*

Written by Brigitt Baumeler, Graf, Ursula Eggli, Matthias Loretan, Wolfgang Suttner, Theres Scherer, and Therese Zemp. With Zemp, Jules Burgener, Christoph and Ursula Eggli.

## + HERE'S LOOKING AT YOU KID
*USA, 1979. Directed by William E. Cohen.*

These two films are unflinching looks at the struggles of amputees, paraplegics, and burn victims. The first is the record of a Swiss therapy program encouraging human, loving contact. The second is a documentary about Rob Cole, a burn victim who was able, through love and self-respect, to return to a "normal" life.

## THE HANDYMAN (L'HOMME À TOUT FAIRE)
*Canada, 1980. Written and Directed by Micheline Lanctôt.*

With Jocelyn Bérubé, Andrée Pelletier, Janette Bertrand, Paul Dion, Madeleine Guérin.

## KAGEMUSHA ▼
*Japan, 1980. Directed by Akira Kurosawa.*

Written by Masato Ide and Kurosawa. With Tatsuya Nakadai, Tsutomu Yamazaki, Kenichi Hagiwara, Kota Yui.

## THE LIFE AND TIMES OF ROSIE THE RIVETER ▶
*USA, 1980. Directed by Connie Field.*

A documentary about four women who worked in the factories during WWII, only to be told to get the hell out when the war ended.

## + QUILTS IN WOMEN'S LIVES
*USA, 1980. Directed by Pat Ferrero.*

Demolishes any notion that "little old ladies" make quilts because they have nothing better to do.

## LOULOU
*France, 1980. Directed by Maurice Pialat.*

Written by Arlette Langmann and Pialat. With Isabelle Huppert, Gérard Depardieu, Guy Marchand, Humbert Balsan.

## MASOCH – THE CONFESSIONS OF WANDA VON SACHER-MASOCH
*Italy, 1980. Written and Directed by Franco Brogi Taviani.*

With Paolo Malco, Francesca de Sapio, Fabrizio Bentivoglio, Inga Alexandrova.

## ONCE UPON A TIME IN THE WEST (presented as The Martin Scorsese Color Show)
*Italy, 1969. Directed by Sergio Leone.*

Written by Sergio Donati and Leone, based on a story by Dario Argento, Bernardo Bertolucci, and Leone. With Henry Fonda, Claudia Cardinale, Jason Robards, Charles Bronson, Frank Wolff, Gabriele Ferzetti, Keenan Wynn, Paolo Stoppa, Lionel Stander, Jack Elam, Woody Strode. This first-time screening of the complete version of Leone's masterpiece—in a beautiful three-color imbibition print, was presented as part of Scorsese's campaign for preservation of color films.

## ONE DAY LIKE ANOTHER
*India, 1980. Written and Directed by Mrinal Sen, based on a story by Amalendu Chakraborty.*

With Satya Banerjee, Gita Sen, Mamata Shankar, Sreela Majumdar. Shown with *Marathon Woman*, Miki Gorman, USA. Directed by Ellen Freyer.

## THE ORCHESTRA CONDUCTOR aka THE CONDUCTOR
*Poland, 1980. Directed by Andrzej Wajda.*

Written by Andrzej Kijowski, based on conversations with conductor Andrzej Markowski. With John Gielgud, Krystyna Janda, Andrzej Seweryn.

## SPECIAL TREATMENT
*Yugoslavia/USA. Directed by Goran Paskaljević.*

Written by Filip David, Dušan Kovačević, and Paskaljević. With Ljuba Tadić, Dušica Žegarac, Danilo Stojković, Milena Dravić, Petar Kralj. Shown with *Worm Dance*, USA. Directed by Eliot Noyes Jr.

## SUNDAY DAUGHTERS
*Hungary, 1980. Written and Directed by János Rózsa.*

With Julianna Nyakó, Melinda Szakács, Julianna Balogh, Andrea Blizik.

## TIH MINH
*France, 1918. Directed by Louis Feuillade.*

With May Harald, René Cresté, Georges Biscot, Édouard Mathé. Piano accompaniment by Curtis Salke. In a sense, a continuation of *Les vampires*. (Retrospective.)

# 1981

SELECTION COMMITTEE: RICHARD ROUD, CHAIRMAN, RICHARD CORLISS, JACK KROLL, TOM LUDDY, AND SUSAN SONTAG. CONSULTANTS: MARY MEERSON (RETROSPECTIVES) AND MARK N. WEISS (AMERICAN INDEPENDENT FILM).

THE 19TH NYFF POSTER ARTWORK WAS CREATED BY ©DAVID HOCKNEY, 1970, COURTESY OF PETERSBURG PRESS.

## CHARIOTS OF FIRE
*UK, 1981. Directed by Hugh Hudson.*

Written by Colin Welland. With Ben Cross, Ian Charleson, Nigel Havers, Nicholas Farrell. (Opening Night.)

## MAN OF IRON ▶
*Poland, 1981. Directed by Andrzej Wajda.*

Written by Aleksander Ścibor-Rylski. With Jerzy Radziwiłowicz, Krystyna Janda, Marian Opania, Irena Byrska. (Closing Night.)

## THE AVIATOR'S WIFE
*France, 1981. Written and Directed by Eric Rohmer.*

With Philippe Marlaud, Marie Rivière, Anne-Laure Meury, Mathieu Carrière. Shown with *The Ballad of Lucy Jordan*, USA. Directed by Ian Moo Young. Also, *Couples and Robbers*, UK. Directed by Clare Peploe.

## THE BEADS OF ONE ROSARY
*Poland, 1981. Written and Directed by Kazimierz Kutz, based on A Siekerski's short story "This House Is No Longer Here."*

With Marta Straszna, Augustyn Halotta, Franciszek Pieczka, Jan Bógdol. Shown with *Coming Soon*, USA. Directed by Eugene Ferraro.

## BEAU PÈRE
*France, 1981. Written and Directed by Bertrand Blier, based on his novel.*

With Patrick Dewaere, Ariel Besse, Maurice Ronet, Nicole Garcia, Nathalie Baye.

◀ ## BOB LE FLAMBEUR
*France, 1956. Written and Directed by Jean-Pierre Melville.*

With Isabelle Corey, Roger Duchesne, Daniel Cauchy, Guy Decomble. (Retrospective.)

## CONTRACT
*Poland, 1980. Written and Directed by Krzysztof Zanussi.*

With Tadeusz Łomnicki, Zofia Mrozowska, Krzysztof Kolberger, Magda Jaroszowna. Shown with *America Is Waiting*, USA. Directed by Bruce Conner.

## FIT TO BE UNTIED
*Italy, 1975. Directed by Silvano Agosti, Marco Bellocchio, Sandro Petraglia, and Stefano Rulli.*

A study of a radical approach to mental illness, letting former inmates work in factories and live with families.

## GRADUATE FIRST (PASSE TON BAC D'ABORD)
*France, 1980. Written and Directed by Maurice Pialat.*

With Sabine Haudepin, Philippe Marlaud, Annik Alane, Michel Caron. Shown with *Flying Fur*, USA. Directed by George Griffin.

**HOPPER'S SILENCE**

*USA, 1980. Written and Directed by Brian O'Doherty.*

With Helen Hayes, Alan Novak, and (as themselves) Edward and Jo Hopper, John Clancy, Lloyd Goodrich, Barbara Novak. About the marriage of the painters Edward and Jo Hopper, with demonstrations of how Edward Hopper's landscapes were achieved.

**THE LAST TO KNOW**

*USA, 1981. Directed by Bonnie Friedman.*

With (as themselves) Lori Schmidt, Sandy Feil, Loretta Jaye, Sharon Bell. An examination of women's dependency on alcohol and tranquilizers.

**LIGHTNING OVER WATER**

*West Germany/Sweden, 1980. Directed by Nicholas Ray and Wim Wenders.*

With Ed Lachman, Martin Mueller, Craig Nelson, Wenders, Nicholas, Susan, and Timothy Ray. A documentation of Ray's decline from cancer and an examination of the motives of friendship and generosity that kept this project going. Shown with *Act of God*, UK. Directed by Peter Greenaway.

**LOOKS AND SMILES**

*UK, 1981. Directed by Ken Loach.*

Written by Barry Hines. With Graham Green, Carolyn Nicholson, Tony Pitts, Roy Haywood. Shown with *Mirrored Reason*, USA. Directed by Stan VanDerBeek.

**MEPHISTO**

*Hungary/West Germany, 1981. Directed by István Szabó.*

Written by Péter Dobai and Szabó, based on Klaus Mann's novel. With Klaus Maria Brandauer, Krystyna Janda, Ildikó Bánsági, Karin Boyd.

**MURS MURS**

*USA, 1980. Written and Directed by Agnès Varda.*

A documentary about the murals of Los Angeles with Juliet Berto as "*The Visitor.*"

**+ DOCUMENTEUR: AN EMOTION PICTURE**

*USA, 1981. Written and Directed by Agnès Varda.*

With Sabine Mamou, Mathieu Demy, Tina Odom, Lisa Blok.

**MY DINNER WITH ANDRE ▲**

*USA, 1981. Directed by Louis Malle.*

Written by Andre Gregory and Wallace Shawn. With Shawn, Gregory, Jean Lenauer, Roy Butler. Shown with *Cecilia*, USA. Directed by Diana Michener.

**THE MYSTERY OF OBERWALD ▶**

*Italy, 1980. Directed by Michelangelo Antonioni.*

Written by Antonioni, and Tonino Guerra, based on Jean Cocteau's play *The Eagle Has Two Heads*. With Monica Vitti, Paolo Bonacelli, Franco Branciaroli, Luigi Diberti.

**ONLY A MOTHER**

*Sweden, 1949. Directed by Alf Sjöberg.*

Written by Ivar Lo-Johansson and Sjöberg, based on Lo-Johansson's novel. With Eva Dahlbeck, Ragnar Falck, Ulf Palme, Hugo Björne.

**+ KARIN MÅNSDOTTER**

*Sweden, 1954. Written and Directed by Alf Sjöberg, based on August Strindberg's play* Erick XIV.

With Ulla Jacobsson, Jarl Kulle, Ulf Palme, Per Oscarsson. (Retrospective.)

**PASSION OF LOVE**

*Italy/France, 1981. Directed by Ettore Scola.*

Written by Ruggero Maccari and Scola, based on Iginio Ugo Tarchetti's story "Fosca." With Bernard Giraudeau, Valeria D'Obici, Laura Antonelli, Jean-Louis Trintignant.

**LE PONT DU NORD**

*France, 1981. Directed by Jacques Rivette.*

Written by Rivette and Suzanne Schiffman. With Bulle Ogier, Pascale Ogier, Jean-François Stévenin, Pierre Clémenti.

**RESURGENCE: THE MOVEMENT FOR EQUALITY VS. THE KU KLUX KLAN**

*USA, 1981. Directed by Pamela Yates and Newton Thomas Sigel.*

The resurgence of the KKK, shot in Greensboro, North Carolina, after the murder of five anti-Klan demonstrators in 1979.

**SOLDIER GIRLS**

*USA, 1981. Directed by Nick Broomfield and Joan Churchill.*

A hard look at a platoon of young army volunteers during training at Fort Benning, Georgia.

**STATIONS OF THE ELEVATED**

*USA, 1980. Directed by Manfred Kirchheimer.*

With music by Charles Mingus. Graffiti-covered trains hurtling through a strange urban landscape filled with the debris of a decaying civilization. Shown with *The Climate of New York*, USA. Directed by Edgar B. Howard.

**+ VERNON, FLORIDA**

*USA, 1981. Directed by Errol Morris.*

Documentary about private obsessions in a small northwest Florida town.

**TAXI ZUM KLO ▲**

*West Germany, 1980. Written and Directed by Frank Ripploh.*

With (as themselves) Ripploh, Bernd Broaderup, Gitte Lederer, Hans-Gerd Mertens. Shown with *Friday and Clyde*, USA. Directed by Kerry L.B. Feltham.

*Mephisto* by István Szabó

### TIGHTEN YOUR BELTS, BITE THE BULLET
*USA, 1980. Directed by James Gaffney, Martin Lucas, and Jonathan Miller.*

An analysis of the municipal crises in New York City and Cleveland that contrasts the different approaches of their respective mayors.

### TRANCES
*France/Morocco, 1981. Written and Directed by Ahmed El Maanouni.*

With (as themselves) Nass El Ghiwane, Boujemaa Hgour, Omar Sayed, Allal Yaala, Aberrahman Paco, Larbi Batma. A depiction of the group musical group Nass El Ghiwane. Shown with *Overseas*, France. Directed by Jacques Fieschi.

### WE WERE GERMAN JEWS
*USA/West Germany, 1981. Directed by Michael Blackwood.*

With (as themselves) Herbert and Lotte Strauss. A portrait of a couple who escaped Nazi Germany together in 1943 and their return to Germany after 35 years.

### THE WITNESS
*Hungary, 1968. Written and Directed by Péter Bascó.*

With Ferenc Kállai, Lili Monori, Zoltán Fábri, Lajos Öze. Shown with *Egg City*, USA. Directed by David Kellogg.

### ◀ THE WOMAN NEXT DOOR
*France, 1981. Directed by François Truffaut.*

Written by and Jean Aurel, Suzanne Schiffman, and Truffaut. With Gérard Depardieu, Fanny Ardant, Henri Garcin, Michèle Baumgartner.

## Special Events

**"Movies for Cynics"** – a program of American political satire and commentary presented at the Paramount Theater. Films shown: *An Acquired Taste*, 1981, by Ralph Arlyck; *The Americanization of Emily*, 1964, by Arthur Hiller; *El Salvador: Another Vietnam*, 1981, by Glenn Silber and Tete Vasconcellas; *First Family*, 1980, by Buck Henry; *The Great Dictator*, 1940, by Charlie Chaplin; *The Great McGinty*, 1940, by Preston Sturges; *The Hungry I Reunion*, 1981, by Thomas Cohen; *Nixon: From Checkers to Watergate*, 1980, by Charles Braverman; *The Private Files of J. Edgar Hoover*, 1977, by Larry Cohen; *Putney Swope*, 1969, by Robert Downey; "SHORT CUTS," satirical shorts by R.O. Blechman, Jeff Carpenter, Bruce Conner, George Griffin, J. Hoberman, Andrew Lack, James McPhearson, Daniel Nauke, Robert Nelson, Janet Perlman, and Jimmy Picker; *Smile*, 1975, by Michael Ritchie; *Taking Off*, 1971, by Miloš Forman; and *Winter Kills*, 1979, by William Richert.

**"Channeling the Future: Cable and the New TV"** – a daylong event exploring the promise of new technologies for independent producers and directors. Presented by New Medium in cooperation with the Film Society of Lincoln Center. Topic headings were: "The Expanding Universe"; "The New TV… Toward Gutenberg or Glut?"; "What's Coming Next?"; and "What's on Cable Now?". (This event was chaired by Alan Hirschfield, then Chairman of Columbia Pictures.)

**Installation in the lobby of Alice Tully Hall** – *Light*house, by Anita Thacher. Dedicated to Francesca Woodman, a young photographer who died in 1981, this installation explored the relationship between two- and three-dimensionality by creating a "real" space—a room with a wicker chair—into which life-size images of a young woman are projected. The viewer who enters *Light*house becomes part of the space in which a film is being created.

*The Americanization of Emily* by Arthur Hiller

*The Great Dictator* by Charlie Chaplin

*The Great McGinty* by Preston Sturges

# 1982

SELECTION COMMITTEE: RICHARD ROUD, CHAIRMAN, RICHARD CORLISS, J. HOBERMAN, JACK KROLL, AND TOM LUDDY.
CONSULTANTS: MARY MEERSON (RETROSPECTIVES) AND MARC N. WEISS (AMERICAN INDEPENDENT FILM).

THE 20TH NYFF POSTER ARTWORK WAS CREATED BY ROBERT RAUCHENBERG. ©UNTITLED PRESS, 1982.

*Fitzcarraldo* by Werner Herzog

### VERONIKA VOSS
*West Germany, 1982. Directed by Rainer Werner Fassbinder.*

Written by Fassbinder, Pea Fröhlich, and Peter Märthesheimer. With Rosel Zech, Hilmar Thate, Cornelia Froboess, Annemarie Düringer. Shown with *Pianissimo*, USA. Directed by Carmen D'Avino. (Opening Night.)

### FITZCARRALDO
*West Germany, 1982. Written and Directed by Werner Herzog.*

With Klaus Kinski, Claudia Cardinale, José Lewgoy, Miguel Ángel Fuentes, the Ashininka-Campa Indians of the Gran Pajonal, the Campas of the Rio Tambo, the Machinguengas of the Rio Camisea. (Closing Night.)

### ANOTHER WAY
*Hungary, 1982. Directed by Károly Makk.*

Written by Erzsébet Galgóczi and Makk, based on Galgóczi's novel. With Jadwiga Jankowska-Cieślak, Grażyna Szapolowska, Jozef Kroner, Gábor Reviczky.

### ARSHILE GORKY
*USA, 1982. Written and Directed by Charlotte Zwerin.*

With (as themselves), Peter Blume, Elaine and Willem de Kooning, Agnes Fielding, Sidney Janis. Shown with *Letter to Freddy Buache*, Switzerland. Directed by Jean-Luc Godard.

### + BEFORE THE NICKELODEON: THE EARLY CINEMA OF EDWIN PORTER

*USA, 1982. Directed by Charles Musser.*

Written by Warren D. Leight and Musser. Narrated by Blanche Sweet, with the voices of Jay Leyda, Robert Sklar, Robert Rosen, D.A. Pennebaker, Milos Forman, Louis Malle, Robert Altman.

### THE BURNING BRAZIER
*France, 1923. Written and Directed by Ivan Mozhukhin.*

With Mozhukhin, Nathalie Lissenko, Nicolai Koline. Piano accompaniment by Curtis Salke. (Retrospective.)

### CITY LOVERS
*South Africa, 1982. Written and Directed by Barney Simon, based on a story by Nadine Gordimer.*

With Joe Stewardson, Denise Newman.

### + COMING OF AGE
*USA, 1982. Directed by Josh Hanig.*

With (as themselves) Neil and Bernice VanSteenbergen, Bernieh Cuthbertson, Glen Poling. A diverse group of inner-city teenagers meet for an "encounter" week to reveal their "unspoken thought."

### DARK CIRCLE
*USA, 1982. Directed by Chris Beaver, Judy Irving, and Ruth Landy.*

Written by Beaver and Irving. With (as themselves), Don Gabel, Marlene Batley, Raye Fleming, Rex Haag. Near Denver, a nuclear weapons facility may have contaminated the water supply in a suburban community. Shown with *For the Next Sixty Seconds*, USA. Directed by John Penhall. Also, *Science Fiction*, USA. Directed by J.J. Murphy.

### THE DRAUGHTSMAN'S CONTRACT
*UK, 1982. Written and Directed by Peter Greenaway.*

With Anthony Higgins, Janet Suzman, Anne-Louise Lambert, Hugh Fraser. Shown with *Shift*, USA. Directed by Ernie Gehr.

### EATING RAOUL
*USA, 1982. Directed by Paul Bartel.*

Written by Bartel and Richard Blackburn. With Mary Woronov, Bartel, Robert Beltran, Ed Begley Jr., Buck Henry. Shown with *Louise Smells a Rat*, USA. Directed by Anne Flournoy.

### IDENTIFICATION OF A WOMAN
*Italy, 1982. Directed by Michelangelo Antonioni.*

Written by Antonioni and Gerard Brach, with the collaboration of Tonino Guerra. With Tomas Milian, Christine Boisson, Daniela Silverio, Marcel Bozzuffi.

### KOYAANISQATSI
*USA, 1982. Directed by Godfrey Reggio.*

Music by Philip Glass. Taking its title from the Hopi word for "world out of balance," *Koyaanisqatsi* presents a mind-boggling view of natural and man-made environments. A special event sponsored by the Film Society and Radio City Music Hall, where it was presented.

**LETTER FROM SIBERIA**
*France, 1957. Directed by Chris Marker.*
Featuring Marker's parodies of both capitalist and communist propaganda.
**+ DESCRIPTION OF A STRUGGLE**
*Israel/France, 1959. Directed by Chris Marker.*

**THE LIGHT AHEAD**
*USA, 1939. Directed by Edgar G. Ulmer.*
Written by Chaver Pahver, based on a story by Mendele Mocher Sforim. With Isidore Cashier, Helen Beverly, David Opatoshu, Rosetta Bialis. (Retrospective.) Shown with *Ted Baryluk's Grocery*, Canada. Directed by Mike Mirus and John Paskievich.

**LITTLE PEOPLE**
*USA, 1982. Directed by Jan Krawitz and Thomas Ott.*
With (as themselves) Tina and George Baehn, Karla Eastburg, Martha Holland. Shown with *Up*, USA. Directed by Robert Kukes.

**LITTLE WARS**
*Lebanon, 1982. Written and Directed by Maroun Baghdadi.*
With Soraya Khoury, Nabil Ismail, Roger Hawa, Reda Khoury. A thriller set against the conflicts between Christians and Muslims in Beirut.

**MADAM SATAN**
*USA, 1930. Directed by Cecil B. DeMille.*
Written by Jeanie Macpherson. With Kay Johnson, Reginald Denny, Lillian Roth, Roland Young, Elsa Peterson, Jack King, Tyler Brooke. (Retrospective.)

**MOONLIGHTING**
*UK, 1982. Written and Directed by Jerzy Skolimowski.*
With Jeremy Irons, Eugene Lipinski, Jiří Stanislav, Eugeniusz Hackiewicz. Shown with *Swiss Army Knife with Rats and Pigeons*, USA. Directed by Robert Breer.

**THE NIGHT OF THE SHOOTING STARS**
*Italy, 1982. Directed by Paolo and Vittorio Taviani.*
Written by Giuliani G. De Negri and the Tavianis, with the collaboration of Tonino Guerra. With Omero Antonutti, Margarita Lozano, Claudio Bigagli, Massimo Bonetti.

**ONE MAN'S WAR**
*France, 1981. Written and Directed by Edgardo Cozarinsky, based on Ernst Jünger's* Parisian Diaries.
Newsreels of Nazi-occupied France against the journals of Ernst Jünger, German poet, novelist, and career army officer. Shown with *Three Postcards from Saigon*, France. Directed by Edgardo Cozarinsky.

**SAY AMEN, SOMEBODY**
*USA, 1982. Directed by George T. Nierenberg.*
With (as themselves), Willie Mae Ford Smith, Thomas A. Dorsey, Sallie Martin, Delois Barrett Campbell. A profile of the pioneers of gospel music. Shown with *Remembering Thelma*, USA. Directed by Kathe Sandler.

**THE STATIONMASTER'S WIFE ▼**
*West Germany, 1977. Written and Directed by Rainer Werner Fassbinder, based on Oskar Maria Graf's novel.*
With Kurt Raab, Elisabeth Trissenaar, Gustl Bayrhammer, Bernhard Helfrich.

**TEX**
*USA, 1982. Directed by Tim Hunter.*
Written by Charlie Haas and Hunter, based on S.E. Hinton's novel. With Matt Dillon, Jim Metzler, Meg Tilly, Bill McKinney. Shown with *Zea*, Canada. Directed by André and Jean-Jacques Leduc.

**TIME STANDS STILL**
*Hungary, 1981. Directed by Péter Gothár.*
Written by Géza Bereményi and Gothár. With István Znamenák, Henrik Pauer, Sándor Söth, Péter Gálfy. Shown with *Miami Is OK*, USA. Directed by Steven S. Weiss.

**THE TROUT (LA TRUITE) ▲**
*France, 1982. Directed by Joseph Losey.*
Written by Monique Lange and Losey, based on Roger Vailland's novel. With Isabelle Huppert, Jacques Spiesser, Jeanne Moreau, Jean-Pierre Cassel. Shown with *Delivery Man*, USA. Directed by Emily Hubley.

**THE TYRANT'S HEART** aka **BOCCACCIO IN HUNGARY**
*Hungary, 1981. Directed by Miklós Jancsó.*
Written by Giovanna Gagliardo, Gyula Hernádi, and Jancsó. With Ninetto Davoli, László Galffy, Teresa Ann Savoy, József Madaras.

**VORTEX**
*USA, 1982. Written and Directed by Beth B and Scott B.*
With James Russo, Lydia Lunch, Bill Rice, Ann Magnuson. Shown with *Wild Night in El Reno*, USA. Directed by George Kuchar. Also, *Harmful or Fatal if Swallowed*, USA. Directed by Manuel De Landa.

**YOL (THE WAY)**
*Turkey/Switzerland/France, 1982. Directed by Şerif Gören.*
Written by Yilmaz Güney. With Tarik Akan, Şerif Sezer, Halil Ergün, Necmettin Çobanoğlu, Meral Orhonsoy.

# 1983

SELECTION COMMITTEE: RICHARD ROUD, CHAIRMAN, RICHARD CORLISS, J. HOBERMAN, JACK KROLL, AND DAVID THOMSON.
CONSULTANTS: TOM LUDDY (WEST COAST), MARY MEERSON (RETROSPECTIVES), AND MARC N. WEISS (AMERICAN INDEPENDENT FILM).

THE 21ST NYFF POSTER ARTWORK WAS CREATED BY ©JACK YOUNGERMAN.

*Life Is a Bed of Roses* by Alain Resnais

*Nostalghia* by Andrei Tarkovsky

## THE BIG CHILL
*USA, 1983. Directed by Lawrence Kasdan.*

Written by Barbara Benedek and Kasdan. With Tom Berenger, Glenn Close, Jeff Goldblum, William Hurt, Kevin Kline, Mary Kay Place, Meg Tilly, JoBeth Williams. (Opening Night.)

## STREAMERS
*USA, 1983. Directed by Robert Altman.*

Written by David Rabe, based on his play. With Matthew Modine, Michael Wright, Mitchell Lichtenstein, David Alan Grier, Paul Lazar. (Closing Night.)

## L'ARGENT
*France/Switzerland, 1983. Written and Directed by Robert Bresson.*

With Christian Patey, Sylvie Van den Eisen, Michel Briguet, Caroline Lang. Shown with *Trial Balloons*, USA. Directed by Robert Breer. Also, *En rachâchant*. Directed by Jean-Marie Straub and Danièle Huillet.

## BOAT PEOPLE
*Hong Kong, 1982. Directed by Ann Hui.*

Written by K.C. Chiu, based on a story by Tien Kor. With George Lam, Cora Miao, Season Ma, Andy Lau.

## DANTON
*France/Poland, 1983. Directed by Andrzej Wajda.*

Written by Jean-Claude Carrière, based on Stanislawa Przybyszewska's *The Danton Affair*, with the collaboration of Jacek Gasiorowski, Agnieszka Holland, Boleslaw Michalek, and Wajda. With Gérard Depardieu, Wojciech Pszoniak, Patrice Chéreau, Angela Winkler.

## ENTRE NOUS
*France, 1983. Written and Directed by Diane Kurys.*

With Miou-Miou, Isabelle Huppert, Guy Marchand, Jean-Pierre Bacri.

## ERENDIRA
*Mexico/France/West Germany, 1983. Directed by Ruy Guerra.*

Written by Gabriel Garcia Márquez, based on his story. With Irene Papas, Claudia Ohana, Michael Lonsdale, Oliver Wehe.

## FORBIDDEN RELATIONS
*Hungary, 1982. Written and Directed by Zsolt Kézdi-Kovács.*

With Lili Monori, Miklós B. Székely, Mari Töröcsik, József Tóth. Shown with *Lady Tree*, USA. Directed by Howard Danelowitz.

## THE GOLDEN EIGHTIES (LES ANNÉES 80)
*Belgium, 1983. Directed by Chantal Akerman.*

Written by Akerman and Jean Gruault. A flurry of videotape rehearsals, culled from 40 hours of material that blossoms into a series of Arthur Freed–type production numbers. Shown with *Camilla Horn Watching Herself Play Gretchen in Murnau's Silent Film "Faust,"* West Germany. Directed by Hedda Rinneberg and Hans Sachs.

## HEART LIKE A WHEEL
*USA, 1983. Directed by Jonathan Kaplan.*

Written by Ken Friedman. With Bonnie Bedelia, Beau Bridges, Leo Rossi, Bill McKinney.

## IN THE WHITE CITY
*Portugal/Switzerland, 1982. Written and Directed by Alain Tanner.*

With Bruno Ganz, Teresa Madruga, Julia Vonderlinn, José Carvalho.

## LAST NIGHT AT THE ALAMO
*USA, 1983. Directed by Eagle Pennell.*

Written by Kim Henkel. With Sonny Carl Davis, Lou Perry, Steve Mattila, Tina Bess Hubbard. Shown with *Sifted Evidence*, Canada. Directed by Patricia Gruben.

**LIFE IS A BED OF ROSES**
*France, 1983. Directed by Alain Resnais.*

Written by Jean Gruault. With Vittorio Gassman, Ruggero Raimondi, Geraldine Chaplin, Fanny Ardant, Pierre Arditi, Sabine Azéma.

**LOST ILLUSIONS**
*Hungary, 1982. Directed by Gyula Gazdag.*

Written by Gazdag, Miklós Györffy, and György Spiró, based on the second part of Balzac's novel. With Gábor Máté, Dorottya Udvaros, Robert East, Boguslaw Linda. Shown with *Sundae in New York*, USA. Directed by James Picker.

**THE NEW BABYLON**
*USSR, 1929. Written and Directed by Grigori Kozintsev and Leonid Trauberg, based on an idea by P. Bliakin.*

With Elena Kuzmina, Piotr Sobolevskii, David Gutman, Sophie Magarill. (Special Event—sponsored by the Film Society and Radio City Music Hall.) Accompanied by the Radio City Music Hall Chamber Orchestra, Omri Hadari, conductor, performing the newly recovered original score by Shostakovich provided by the British Film Institute.

**NOSTALGHIA**
*Italy/USSR, 1983. Directed by Andrei Tarkovsky.*

Written by Tonino Guerra and Tarkovsky. With Oleg Yankovsky, Domiziana Giordano, Erland Josephson, Patrizia Terreno.

**PASSION**
*France/Switzerland, 1982. Written and Directed by Jean-Luc Godard.*

With Isabelle Huppert, Hanna Schygulla, Michel Piccoli, Jerzy Radziwilowicz. Shown with *You the Better*, USA. Directed by Ericka Beckman.

**REAR WINDOW**
*USA, 1954. Directed by Alfred Hitchcock.*

Written by John Michael Hayes, based on a story by Cornell Woolrich. With James Stewart, Grace Kelly, Wendell Corey, Thelma Ritter, Raymond Burr. (Retrospective.)

**RED LOVE (ROTE LIEBE)**
*West Germany, 1981. Written and Directed by Rosa von Praunheim.*

With Sascha Hammer, Mark Eins, Helga Goetze, Olga Demetriescu. Shown with *The Woman and the Dress*, USA. Directed by George Kuchar.

**RUMBLE FISH ▲**
*USA, 1983. Directed by Francis Ford Coppola.*

Written by Coppola and S.E. Hinton, based on Hinton's novel. With Matt Dillon, Mickey Rourke, Diane Lane, Dennis Hopper, Diana Scarwid, Vincent Spano, Nicolas Cage.

**SEEING RED**
*USA, 1983. Directed by James Klein and Julia Reichert.*

With (as themselves) Bill Bailey, Dorothy Healey, Howard "Stretch" Johnson, Pete Seeger, Stanley Postak, Rose Krysak, as well as Ronald Reagan, Richard Nixon, Hubert Humphrey, J. Edgar Hoover. A documentary subtitled "Stories of American Communists."

**LA SIGNORA DI TUTTI**
*Italy, 1934. Directed by Max Ophuls.*

Written by Curt Alexander, Ophuls, and Hans Wilhelm, based on Salvator Gotta's novel. With Isa Miranda, Memo Benassi, Tatiana Pavlova, Federico Benfer. (Retrospective.)

**SO FAR FROM INDIA**
*India/USA, 1982. Directed by Mira Nair.*

A documentary about an Indian town where a new bride waits for the call to join her husband, and the subway station in New York where he sells newspapers.

**+ DHRUPAD**
*India, 1982. Directed by Mani Kaul.*

The titular form of Indian classical music dating from the 15th century is the pretext for this documentary.

◄ **THE STORY OF PIERA (STORIA DI PIERA)**
*Italy/France/West Germany, 1983. Directed by Marco Ferreri.*

Written by Piera Degli Esposti, Ferreri, and Dacia Maraini, based on a story by Degli Esposti and Maraini. With Isabelle Huppert, Hanna Schygulla, Bettina Gruhn, Marcello Mastroianni.

**VIETNAM: THE SECRET AGENT**
*USA, 1983. Directed by Jacki Ochs.*

An account of Agent Orange.

**+ BURROUGHS**
*USA, 1983. Directed by Howard Brookner.*

With (as themselves) Lauren Hutton, William S. Burroughs, Patti Smith, Terry Southern, Allen Ginsberg.

**THE WIND (FINYE)**
*Mali, 1982. Written and Directed by Souleymane Cissé.*

With Balla Moussa Keita, Ismaila Sarr, Fousseyni Sissoko, Goundo Guissé. Shown with *Reassemblage*, USA. Directed by Trinh T. Minh-ha.

22nd NEW YORK FILM FESTIVAL
presented by
THE FILM SOCIETY OF LINCOLN CENTER
SEPTEMBER 28 – OCTOBER 14    1984
ALICE TULLY HALL

*THE 22nd NEW YORK FILM FESTIVAL IS MADE POSSIBLE, IN PART, WITH PUBLIC FUNDS FROM THE NEW YORK STATE COUNCIL ON THE ARTS AND THE NATIONAL ENDOWMENT FOR THE ARTS*

# 1984

SELECTION COMMITTEE: RICHARD ROUD, CHAIRMAN, RICHARD CORLISS, MOLLY HASKELL, J. HOBERMAN, AND DAVID THOMSON. CONSULTANTS: TOM LUDDY (WEST COAST), MARY MEERSON (RETROSPECTIVES), AND LAWRENCE SAPADIN (AMERICAN INDEPENDENT FILM).

THE 22ND NYFF POSTER ARTWORK WAS CREATED BY ©ROBERT BREER.

*Blood Simple* by Joel Coen

## COUNTRY
*USA, 1984. Directed by Richard Pearce.*
Written by William D. Wittliff. With Jessica Lange, Sam Shepard, Wilford Brimley, Matt Clark. (Opening Night.)

## PARIS, TEXAS
*West Germany/France, 1984. Directed by Wim Wenders.*
Written by Sam Shepard, adaptation by L.M. Kit Carson. With Harry Dean Stanton, Nastassja Kinski, Dean Stockwell, Aurore Clément, John Lurie. (Closing Night.)

## AMERICA AND LEWIS HINE
*USA, 1984. Directed by Nina Rosenblum.*
Written by Daniel V. Allentuck, with L.S. Block and John Crowley. With the voices of Jason Robards, Maureen Stapleton, and Crowley (narrator). A documentary about America's pioneer social photographer.

## À NOS AMOURS ▼
*France, 1983. Directed by Maurice Pialat.*
Written by Arlette Langmann and Pialat. With Sandrine Bonnaire, Pialat, Evelyne Kerr, Dominique Besnehard.

## BECKY SHARP
*USA, 1935. Directed by Rouben Mamoulian.*
Written by Francis Edward Faragoh, based on Langdon Mitchell's play, adapted from W.M. Thackeray's novel *Vanity Fair*. With Miriam Hopkins, Sir Cedric Hardwicke, Nigel Bruce, Frances Dee. (Retrospective.)

## BLOOD SIMPLE
*USA, 1983. Directed by Joel Coen.*
Written by Joel and Ethan Coen. With John Getz, Frances McDormand, Dan Hedaya, M. Emmet Walsh, Samm-Art Williams.

## CAMMINA CAMMINA (KEEP WALKING)
*Italy, 1983. Written and Directed by Ermanno Olmi.*
With Alberto Fumagalli, Antonio Cucciarrè, Eligio Martellacci, Renzo Samminiatesi.

## CLASS RELATIONS
*West Germany/France, 1983. Written and Directed by Jean-Marie Straub and Danièle Huillet, based on Franz Kafka's unfinished novel* Amerika.
With Christian Heinisch, Reinald Schnell, Klaus Traube, Hermann Hartmann.

## ◀ DIARY FOR MY CHILDREN
*Hungary, 1983. Written and Directed by Márta Mészáros.*
With Zsuzsa Czinkóczi, Anna Polony, Jan Nowicki, Tamás Tóth.

## A FLASH OF GREEN
*USA, 1984. Written and Directed by Victor Nuñez, based on John D. MacDonald's novel.*
With Ed Harris, Blair Brown, Richard Jordan, George Coe.

*À nos amours* by Maurice Pialat

## A HILL ON THE DARK SIDE OF THE MOON
*Sweden, 1983. Directed by Lennart Hjulström.*

Written by Agneta Pleijel. With Gunilla Nyroos, Thommy Berggren, Lina Pleijel, Bibi Andersson.

## THE HOLY INNOCENTS
*Spain, 1984. Directed by Mario Camus.*

Written by Camus, Antonio Larreta, and Manuel Matji, based on Miguel Delibes's novel. With Alfredo Landa, Francisco Rabal, Terele Pávez, Belén Ballesteros. Shown with *The Bewitching*, Venezuela. Directed by John Petrizzelli.

## LOS SURES
*USA, 1984. Directed by Diego Echeverria.*

A documentary exploring the community in one of New York's poorest Puerto Rican neighborhoods.

## A LOVE IN GERMANY
*West Germany/France, 1983. Directed by Andrzej Wajda.*

Written by Agnieszka Holland, Boleslaw Michalek, and Wajda, based on Rolf Hochhuth's novel. With Hanna Schygulla, Marie-Christine Barrault, Armin Mueller-Stahl, Elisabeth Trissenaar. Shown with *Pies*, Canada. Directed by Sheldon Cohen.

## LOVE ON THE GROUND (L'AMOUR PAR TERRE)
*France, 1984. Directed by Jacques Rivette.*

Written by Pascal Bonitzer, Marilù Parolini, Rivette, and Suzanne Schiffman. With Geraldine Chaplin, Jane Birkin, André Dussolier, Jean-Pierre Kalfon.

## MAN OF FLOWERS
*Australia, 1983. Directed by Paul Cox.*

Written by Cox and Bob Ellis. With Norman Kaye, Alyson Best, Chris Haywood, Sarah Walker. Shown with *Boxing Booth*, UK. Directed by Adrin Neatrour.

## MEMOIRS OF PRISON
*Brazil, 1984. Written and Directed by Nelson Pereira dos Santos, based on Graciliano Ramos's autobiographical novel.*

With Carlos Vereza, Glória Pires, Paulo Porto, David Pinheiro.

## ONCE UPON A TIME IN AMERICA ▲
*USA/Italy, 1984. Directed by Sergio Leone.*

Written by Franco Arcalli, Leonardo Benvenuti, Piero De Bernardi, Franco Ferrini, Enrico Medioli, and Leone, based on Harry Grey's novel *The Hoods*. With Robert De Niro, James Woods, Elizabeth McGovern, Treat Williams, Tuesday Weld, Burt Young, Joe Pesci, Danny Aiello, William Forsythe, Jennifer Connelly, James Russo, Richard Bright.

## SHIVERS
*Poland, 1981. Written and Directed by Wojciech Marczewski.*

With Tomasz Hudziec, Teresa Marczewska, Marek Kondrat, Zdzislaw Wardejn. Shown with *Urban Update*, USA. Directed by Edward Hoch.

## STRANGER THAN PARADISE
*USA/West Germany, 1984. Written and Directed by Jim Jarmusch.*

With John Lurie, Eszter Balint, Richard Edson, Cecillia Stark. Shown with *New Frontier*, UK. Directed by Annabel Jankel and Rocky Morton.

## STRIKEBOUND
*Australia, 1983. Written and Directed by Richard Lowenstein.*

With Chris Haywood, Carol Burns, Hugh Keays-Byrne, Rob Steele, Nik Forster, David Kendall. Shown with *How Far Home: Veterans After Vietnam*, USA. Directed by Bestor Cram.

## A SUNDAY IN THE COUNTRY
*France, 1984. Directed by Bertrand Tavernier.*

Written by Bertrand and Colo Tavernier, based on Pierre Bost's novel *Monsieur Ladmiral va bientôt mourir*. With Louis Ducreux, Sabine Azéma, Michel Aumont, Geneviève Mnich. Shown with *Pleasure of Love*, UK. Directed by Annabel Jankel and Rocky Morton.

## THREE CROWNS OF THE SAILOR
*France, 1982. Directed by Raúl Ruiz.*

Written by Ruiz, with Emilio de Solar and François Ede. With Jean-Bernard Guillard, Philippe Deplanche, Jean Badin, Nadège Clair.

## THE TIMES OF HARVEY MILK
*USA, 1984. Directed by Robert Epstein.*

Narrated by Harvey Fierstein.

## TOKYO OLYMPIAD
*Japan, 1965. Directed by Kon Ichikawa.*

Narration written by Ichikawa, Yoshio Shirasaka, Shuntaro Tanikawa, and Natto Wada. (Retrospective.)

## TWO ENGLISH GIRLS
*France, 1971. Directed by François Truffaut.*

Written by Jean Gruault and Truffaut, based on Henri-Pierre Roché's novel. With Jean-Pierre Léaud, Kika Markham, Stacy Tendeter, Sylvia Marriott, Marie Mansart, Philippe Léotard.

*The Times of Harvey Milk* by Robert Epstein

23rd NEW YORK FILM FESTIVAL
PRESENTED BY THE FILM SOCIETY OF LINCOLN CENTER

SEPTEMBER 27 - OCTOBER 13  ALICE TULLY HALL
The 23rd New York Film Festival is made possible, in part, with public funds from the New York State Council on the Arts and the National Endowment for the Arts.

# 1985

SELECTION COMMITTEE: RICHARD ROUD, CHAIRMAN, RICHARD CORLISS, MOLLY HASKELL, DAVE KEHR, AND DAVID THOMSON.
CONSULTANTS: MARY MEERSON (RETROSPECTIVES) AND LAWRENCE SAPADIN (AMERICAN INDEPENDENT FILM).

THE 23RD NYFF POSTER ARTWORK WAS CREATED BY ©TOM WESSELMANN.

*Black Narcissus* by Michael Powell and Emeric Pressburger

### RAN ▲
*France/Japan, 1985. Directed by Akira Kurosawa.*

Written by Masato Ide, Kurosawa, and Hideo Oguni. With Tatsuya Nakadai, Akira Terao, Jinpachi Nezu, Daisuke Ryu. (Opening Night.) Note: Hurricane Gloria struck on this day—we had dozens of cancellations and our bus service refused to provide transportation for audiences to get from the theater to the Tavern on the Green. About an hour before the first screening the skies parted and the sun came out. Lincoln Center security stopped traffic on 65th Street so that Kurosawa could be walked from Alice Tully to Avery Fisher Hall on a beautiful evening.

### KAOS
*Italy, 1984. Directed by Paolo and Vittorio Taviani.*

Written by Tonino Guerra and the Tavianis, based on Luigi Pirandello short stories. With Margarita Lozano, Claudio Bigagli, Massimo Bonetti, Franco Franchi, Ciccio Ingrassia, Biagio Barone, Salvatore Rossi, Omero Antonutti, Regina Bianchi. (Closing Night.) Note: Both ON and CN film titles mean chaos!

### ANGRY HARVEST
*West Germany, 1985. Directed by Agnieszka Holland.*

Written by Paul Hengge and Holland, based on Hermann H. Field and Stanislaw Mierzenski's novel. With Armin Mueller-Stahl, Elisabeth Trissenaar, Käthe Jaenicke, Hans Beerhenke.

### BLACK NARCISSUS
*UK, 1947. Written and Directed by Michael Powell and Emeric Pressburger, based on Rumer Godden's novel.*

With Deborah Kerr, Flora Robson, Jenny Laird, Judith Furse. (Retrospective—a tribute to the 50th Anniversary of the National Film Archive of the British Film Institute.)

### BLISS
*Australia, 1985. Directed by Ray Lawrence.*

Written by Peter Carey and Lawrence, based on Carey's novel. With Barry Otto, Lynette Curran, Helen Jones, Miles Buchanan.

### BOY MEETS GIRL
*France, 1984. Written and Directed by Leos Carax.*

With Denis Lavant, Mireille Perrier, Carroll Brooks, Elie Poicard.

### CHAIN LETTERS
*USA, 1985. Written and Directed by Mark Rappaport.*

With Mark Arnott, Reed Birney, David Brisbin, Randy Danson. Shown with *Standard Gauge*, USA. Directed by Morgan Fisher.

### CITY OF PIRATES
*Portugal/France, 1983. Written and Directed by Raúl Ruiz.*

With Hugues Quester, Anne Alvaro, Melvil Poupaud, André Engel.

### COLONEL REDL
*Hungary/West Germany/Austria, 1985. Directed by István Szabó.*

Written by Szabó and Péter Dobai. With Klaus Maria Brandauer, Armin Mueller-Stahl, Gudrun Landgrebe, Jan Niklas.

### DESTROYED TIME (LE TEMPS DÉTRUIT)
*France, 1985. Directed by Pierre Beuchot.*

Narrated by Jean-Marc Bory, Frédéric Leidgens, Philippe Nahoun, Anne Terrier. A documentary about three men killed in 1940 during the early stages of WWII.

*Colonel Redl* by István Szabó

### FIRE FESTIVAL (HIMATSURI)
*Japan, 1984. Directed by Mitsuo Yanigimachi.*

Written by Kenji Nakagami. With Kinya Kitaoji, Kiwako Taichi, Ryota Nakamoto, Norihei Miki.

### HAIL MARY
*Switzerland/France, 1984. Written and Directed by Jean-Luc Godard.*

With Myriem Roussel, Thierry Rode, Philippe Lacoste, Manon Anderson, Malachi Jara Kohan. Shown with *The Book of Mary*, Switzerland/France. Directed by Anne-Marie Miéville.

### HARVEST OF DESPAIR
*Canada, 1984. Directed by Slavko Nowytski.*

Narrated by Jon Granik, Joan Karasevych, Eric Peterson. A documentary about the 1932-33 famine in Ukraine.

### HUEY LONG
*USA, 1985. Directed by Ken Burns.*

Written by Geoffrey C. Ward. Narrated by David McCullough. A documentary that captures the thrills and menace of one of the greatest natural politicians America has ever known.

### NO MAN'S LAND
*Switzerland/France, 1985. Written and Directed by Alain Tanner.*

With Hugues Quester, Myriam Mézières, Jean-Philippe Écoffey, Betty Berr, Marie-Luce Felber.

### ◀ NOTHING SACRED
*USA, 1937. Directed by William Wellman.*

Written by Ben Hecht, Ring Lardner Jr., Dorothy Parker, and Budd Schulberg, based on James H. Street's short story "Letter to the Editor." With Carole Lombard, Fredric March, Charles Winninger, Walter Connolly. (Retrospective—a tribute to the 50th Anniversary of the Department of Film of the Museum of Modern Art.) Shown with *Manhole Covers*, USA. Directed by Ruth Cade.

### ORIANA
*Venezuela/France, 1985. Directed by Fina Torres.*

Written by Antoine Lacomblez and Torres, based on a short story by Marvel Moreno. With Doris Wells, Daniela Silverio, Maya Oloe, Claudia Venturini. Shown with *Shapes, Forms and Robots*, USA, 1985. Directed by Cathy Karol.

### PRIVATE CONVERSATIONS
*USA, 1985. Directed by Christian Blackwood.*

With Arthur Miller, Dustin Hoffman, John Malkovich, Volker Schlöndorff. A documentary about the making of Schlöndorff's film *Death of a Salesman*. Shown with *Destrux: Bring the Horror Home*, USA. Directed by Conrad Fink.

### RENOIR, THE BOSS (RENOIR, LE PATRON)
*France, 1967. Directed by André S. Labarthe and Jacques Rivette.*

With Jean Renoir and Marcel Dalio. Concentrates on excerpts from *The Rules of the Game*, discussed in interviews with Renoir and the surviving actors.

### + JEAN COCTEAU – SELF-PORTRAIT OF A MAN UNKNOWN
*France, 1983. Written and Directed by Edgardo Cozarinsky, based on an idea by Carole Weiswiller.*

Footage from Cocteau's 16mm movies, television interviews, and other archival sources.

### THE SATIN SLIPPER aka UNDER THE WINDS OF THE BALEARIC ISLANDS
*France/Portugal, 1984. Written and Directed by Manoel de Oliveira, based on Paul Claudel's play.*

With Luis Miguel Cintra, Patricia Barzyk, Anne Consigny, Frank Oger.

### STEAMING ▼
*UK, 1984. Directed by Joseph Losey.*

Written by Patricia Losey, based on Nell Dunn's play. With Vanessa Redgrave, Sarah Miles, Diana Dors, Patti Love. Shown with *Traveling Light*, USA, 1985. Directed by Jane Aaron.

### SUGARBABY (ZUCKERBABY)
*West Germany, 1984. Written and Directed by Percy Adlon.*

With Marianne Sägebrecht, Eisi Gulp, Toni Berger, Manuela Denz, Will Spindler, Hans Stadlbauer. Shown with *Boomtown*, USA. Directed by Connie D'Antuon, Bill Plympton, and Valeria Vasilevski.

### 28 UP
*UK, 1985. Directed by Michael Apted.*

With (as themselves) Nicholas Hitchon, Paul Kligerman, Charles Furneaux, Andrew Brackfield, Jacqueline Bassett, Susan Sullivan, Symon Basterfield. Twenty-one years later, a study of the children featured in Apted's *7 Up*. Shown with *7 Up*, UK, 1963. Prepared by Paul Almond with Michael Apted.

### WHEN FATHER WAS AWAY ON BUSINESS
*Yugoslavia, 1985. Directed by Emir Kusturica.*

Written by Abdulah Sidran. With Moreno D'E Bartolli, Miki Manojlović, Mustafa Nadarević, Mira Furlan, Predrag Laković, Pavle Vujisić.

### A YEAR OF THE QUIET SUN ▼
*Poland/USA/West Germany, 1984. Written and Directed by Krzysztof Zanussi.*

With Scott Wilson, Maja Komorowska, Hanna Skarzanka, Ewa Dalkowska, Vadim Glowna, Danny Webb, Zbigniew Zapasiewicz, Tadeusz Bradecki.

# 1986

SELECTION COMMITTEE: RICHARD ROUD, CHAIRMAN, RICHARD CORLISS, DAVID DENBY, MOLLY HASKELL, AND DAVE KEHR.
CONSULTANTS: MARY MEERSON (RETROSPECTIVES) AND LAWRENCE SAPADIN (AMERICAN INDEPENDENT FILM).

THE 24TH NYFF POSTER ARTWORK WAS CREATED BY ©ELINOR BUNIN.

### DOWN BY LAW ▲
*USA, 1986. Written and Directed by Jim Jarmusch.*
With Tom Waits, John Lurie, Roberto Benigni, Nicoletta Braschi, Ellen Barkin. Shown with *Loose Corner*, USA. Directed by Anita Thacher. (Opening Night.)

### PEGGY SUE GOT MARRIED
*USA, 1986. Directed by Francis Ford Coppola.*
Written by Jerry Leichtling and Arlene Sarner. With Kathleen Turner, Nicolas Cage, Barry Miller, Catherine Hicks, Joan Allen, Kevin J. O'Connor, Jim Carrey, Sofia Coppola. (Closing Night.)

### THE BLIND DIRECTOR aka THE ASSAULT OF THE PRESENT ON THE REST OF TIME
*West Germany, 1985. Written and Directed by Alexander Kluge.*
With Jutta Hoffmann, Armin Mueller-Stahl, Hans-Michael Rehberg, Peter Roggisch.

## CACTUS
*Australia, 1986. Directed by Paul Cox.*

Written by Cox, Bob Ellis, and Norman Kaye. With Isabelle Huppert, Robert Menzies, Kaye, Monica Maughan. Shown with *Passionless Moments,* Australia. Directed by Jane Campion and Gerard Lee.

## CHARLOTTE AND LULU (L'EFFRONTÉE)
*France, 1985. Directed by Claude Miller.*

Written by Luc Béraud, Annie and Claude Miller, and Bernard Stora. With Charlotte Gainsbourg, Bernadette Lafont, Jean-Claude Brialy, Raoul Billerey, Julie Glenn, Jean-Philippe Écoffey, Clothilde Baudon.

## DANCING IN THE DARK
*Canada, 1986. Written and Directed by Leon Marr, based on Joan Barfoot's novel.*

With Martha Henry, Neil Munro, Rosemary Dunsmore, Richard Monette. Shown with *My Socks*, West Germany. Directed by Martin Gressman.

## THE DECLINE OF THE AMERICAN EMPIRE
*Canada, 1986. Written and Directed by Denys Arcand.*

With Dominique Michel, Dorothée Berryman, Louise Portal, Geneviève Rioux.

## DIRECTED BY WILLIAM WYLER
*USA, 1986. Directed by Aviva Slesin.*

Narrated by Harry S. Murphy, with (as themselves) Bette Davis, Samantha Eggar, Greer Garson, Lillian Hellman, Audrey Hepburn, William Wyler. A portrait of the director featuring interviews with admirers and excerpts from his films.

## + DODSWORTH
*USA, 1936. Directed by William Wyler.*

Written by Sidney Howard, based on his play and Sinclair Lewis's novel. With Walter Huston, Ruth Chatterton, Paul Lukas, Mary Astor, David Niven. (Retrospective.)

## ISAAC IN AMERICA: A JOURNEY WITH ISAAC BASHEVIS SINGER
*USA, 1986. Directed by Amran Nowak.*

Readings from Singer's work by Judd Hirsh.

## + THE INTERNATIONAL SWEETHEARTS OF RHYTHM: AMERICA'S HOTTEST ALL-GIRL BAND
*USA/UK, 1986. Directed by Greta Schiller and Andrea Weiss.*

With (the band) Anna Mae Winburn, Tiny Davis, Rosaline Cron, Helen Jones, Helen Saine, Evelyn McGee, Jesse Stone. Shown with *Set in Motion*, USA. Directed by Jane Aaron.

## MALANDRO (ÓPERA DO MALANDRO)
*Brazil/France, 1986. Directed by Ruy Guerra.*

Written by Chico Buarque, Guerra, Orlando Senna, based on Buarque's opera. With Edson Celulari, Claudia Ohana, Elba Ramalho, Ney Latorraca. Shown with *Honky Tonk Bud*, USA. Directed by Scott Laster.

## MARLENE
*West Germany, 1983. Directed by Maximilian Schell.*

Written by Meir Dohnal and Schell. A portrait of Marlene Dietrich as an old woman that turns into a funny struggle between two kinds of German sensibility—Dietrich's cynicism versus Schell's earnest humanism. Shown with *A Girl's Own Story*, Australia. Directed by Jane Campion.

## MÉNAGE
*France, 1986. Written and Directed by Bertrand Blier.*

With Gérard Depardieu, Michel Blanc, Miou-Miou, Bruno Cremer. Shown with *Girls in Suits at Lunch*, USA. Directed by Ruth Charny.

## NO END
*Poland, 1984. Directed by Krzysztof Kieślowski.*

Written by Kieślowski and Krzysztof Piesiewicz. With Grazyna Szapolowska, Maria Pakulnis, Aleksander Bardini, Jerzy Radziwilowicz, Artur Barcis.

## POLICE
*France, 1985. Directed by Maurice Pialat.*

Written by Catherine Breillat, Sylvie Danton, Jacques Fieschi, and Pialat, based on an idea by Breillat. With Gérard Depardieu, Sophie Marceau, Richard Anconina, Pascale Rocard, Sandrine Bonnaire.

## ROUND MIDNIGHT ▶
*USA, 1986. Directed by Bertrand Tavernier.*

Written by David Rayfiel and Tavernier. With Dexter Gordon, François Cluzet, Gabrielle Haker, Sandra Reaves-Phillips, Herbie Hancock, Martin Scorsese, Philippe Noiret.

## THE SACRIFICE
*Sweden/France, 1986. Written and Directed by Andrei Tarkovsky.*

With Erland Josephson, Susan Fleetwood, Valérie Mairesse, Allan Edwall, Sven Wollter.

*Scene of the Crime* by André Téchiné

### THE WEDDING MARCH
*USA, 1928. Written and Directed by Erich von Stroheim.*

With von Stroheim, George Fawcett, Maude George, Fay Wray, ZaSu Pitts, Matthew Betz, Maude George. With the original music score transferred to the film by the Cinémathèque Française. (Retrospective—a celebration of the 50th anniversary of the Cinémathèque.)

### A ZED & TWO NOUGHTS
*UK, 1985. Written and Directed by Peter Greenaway.*

With Andréa Ferréol, Brian Deacon, Eric Deacon, Frances Barber, Joss Ackland, Jim Davidson, Agnès Brulet, Guusje van Tilborgh, Gerard Thoolen.

### SCENE OF THE CRIME
*France, 1986. Directed by André Téchiné.*

Written by Olivier Assayas, Pascal Bonitzer, and Téchiné. With Catherine Deneuve, Victor Lanoux, Danielle Darrieux, Wadeck Stanczak.

### SID AND NANCY ▶
*UK, 1986. Directed by Alex Cox.*

Written by Cox and Abbe Wool. With Gary Oldman, Chloe Webb, Drew Schofield, David Hayman.

### THÉRÈSE
*France, 1986. Directed by Alain Cavalier.*

Written by Cavalier and Camille de Casabianca. With Catherine Mouchet, Aurore Prieto, Sylvie Habault, Ghislaine Mona, Hélenè Alexandridis.

### A TIME TO LIVE AND A TIME TO DIE
*Taiwan, 1985. Directed by Hou Hsiao-hsien.*

Written by Chu Tien-wen and Hou Hsiao-hsien. With Yu An-shun, Hsin Shu-fen, Tien Feng, Mei Fang, Tang Ru-yun.

### TO SLEEP SO AS TO DREAM
*Japan, 1986. Written and Directed by Kaizo Hayashi.*

With Moe Kamura, Shiro Sano, Koji Otake. Shown with *Attack on a Bakery*, Japan. Directed by Yamakawa Naoto.

### TRUE STORIES
*USA, 1986. Directed by David Byrne.*

Written by Byrne, Beth Henley, and Stephen Tobolowsky. With Byrne, John Goodman, Swoosie Kurtz, Spalding Gray, Annie McEnroe. Shown with *0*, USA. Directed by Michael Sciulli and Melissa White.

## Special Event

**"Celluloid Cathedrals"** – a photo exhibit of color photographs of American movie theaters by John Margolies was installed in Alice Tully Hall.

25TH NEW YORK FILM FESTIVAL
presented by the Film Society of Lincoln Center

ALICE TULLY HALL
SEPTEMBER 25 - OCTOBER 11, 1987

# 1987

SELECTION COMMITTEE: RICHARD ROUD, CHAIRMAN, RICHARD CORLISS, DAVID DENBY, DAVE KEHR, AND CARRIE RICKEY.
CONSULTANTS: MARY MEERSON (RETROSPECTIVES) AND LILLIAN JIMENEZ (AMERICAN INDEPENDENT FILM).

THE 25TH NYFF POSTER ARTWORK WAS CREATED BY ©SOL LEWITT.

*Babette's Feast* by Gabriel Axel

*Bad Blood* by Leos Carax

**DARK EYES**
*Italy, 1987. Directed by Nikita Mikhalkov.*

Written by Alexander Adabachian and Mikhalkov, with the collaboration of Suso Cecchi D'Amico, based on short stories by Anton Chekhov. With Marcello Mastroianni, Silvana Mangano, Marthe Keller, Elena Sofonova. Shown with *The First 25 Years,* USA. A NYFF-anniversary short. Directed by Wendy Keys and Doug Wyles. (Opening Night.)

**HOUSE OF GAMES**
*USA, 1987. Written and Directed by David Mamet, based on a story by Jonathan Katz and Mamet.*

With Lindsay Crouse, Joe Mantegna, Mike Nussbaum, Lilia Skala. (Closing Night.)

**ANITA - DANCES OF VICE**
*West Germany, 1987. Directed by Rosa von Praunheim.*

Written by H. Limpach and von Praunheim. With Lotti Huber, Ina Blum, Mikael Honesseau. Shown with *Imagine,* USA. Directed by Zbigniew Rybcyzński. Also, *Academy Leader Variations,* USA/Switzerland/Poland/China. Film "snippits" by A Da, Jane Aaron, Skip Battaglia, Chang Guang Xi, Piotr Dumala, David Ehrlich, Paul Glabicki, George Griffin, Al Jarnow, He Yu Men, Hu Jing Quing, Krzysztof Kiwerski, Jerzy Kucia, Stanisław Lenartowicz, Lin Wen Xiao, Claude Luyet, Georges Schwizgebel, Daniel Suter, Martial Wannaz, Yan Ding Xian.

**ANNA**
*USA, 1986. Directed by Yurek Bogayevicz.*

Written by Agnieszka Holland, based on a story by Bogayevicz and Holland. With Sally Kirkland, Robert Fields, Paulina Porizkova. Shown with *When I Grow Too Old to Dream,* USA. Directed by Priscilla Olson.

**BABETTE'S FEAST**
*Denmark, 1987. Written and Directed by Gabriel Axel, based on the novella by Isak Dinesen.*

With Stéphane Audran, Bodil Kjer, Birgitte Federspiel. Shown with *Fiddle-de-dee,* Canada, 1947. Directed by Norman McLaren. (Part of a tribute to McLaren.)

**BAD BLOOD (MAUVAIS SANG)**
*France, 1987. Written and Directed by Leos Carax.*

With Denis Lavant, Juliette Binoche, Michel Piccoli, Hans Meyer, Julie Delpy.

**BARFLY**
*USA, 1987. Directed by Barbet Schroeder.*

Written by Charles Bukowski. With Mickey Rourke, Faye Dunaway, Alice Krige, Jack Nance. Shown with *Arena Brains,* USA. Directed by Robert Longo.

**THE BELLY OF AN ARCHITECT**
*UK/Italy, 1987. Written and Directed by Peter Greenaway.*

With Brian Dennehy, Chloe Webb, Lambert Wilson, Sergio Fantoni. Shown with *Blinkity Blank,* Canada, 1955. Directed by Norman McLaren. Also, *Finger Wave,* Hungary. Directed by Gyula Nagy.

**BOYFRIENDS AND GIRLFRIENDS** aka **MY GIRLFRIEND'S BOYFRIEND**
*France, 1987. Written and Directed by Eric Rohmer.*

With Emmanuelle Chaulet, Sophie Renoir, Anne-Laure Meury, Eric Viellard. Shown with *This Is Just to Say,* USA. Directed by Maureen Selwood.

**BRIGHTNESS (YEELEN)**
*Mali, 1987. Written and Directed by Souleymane Cissé.*

With Issiaka Kane, Aoua Sangare, Niamanto Sanogo, Balla Moussa Keita.

**CHUCK BERRY HAIL! HAIL! ROCK 'N' ROLL**
*USA, 1987. Directed by Taylor Hackford.*

With (as themselves) Chuck Berry, Keith Richards, Linda Ronstadt, Julian Lennon, Robert Cray, Eric Clapton, Etta James, Little Richard, Bruce Springsteen, Jerry Lee Lewis. Chuck Berry reenacts his early years, then leads a welcome-home concert at the Fox Theatre in St. Louis. The interaction of Berry and Keith Richards at the NYFF made this a night to remember!

**DIARY FOR MY LOVED ONES**
*Hungary, 1987. Directed by Márta Mészáros.*

Written by Mészáros and Éva Pataki. With Zsuzsa Czinkóczi, Anna Polony, Jan Nowicki, Pál Zolnay.

**FIRE FROM THE MOUNTAIN**
*USA, 1987. Directed by Deborah Shaffer.*

A documentary chronicling the Sandinistas' triumph over the Somoza regime in Nicaragua. Shown with *The Centerfielder*, Nicaragua. Directed by Ramiro Lacayo Deshon.

**HOPE AND GLORY ▲**
*UK, 1987. Written and Directed by John Boorman.*

With Sebastien Rice-Edwards, Sarah Miles, David Hayman, Derrick O'Connor, Susan Woolridge, Ian Bannen.

**HOROWITZ PLAYS MOZART**
*USA, 1987. Directed by Susan Froemke, Albert Maysles, and Charlotte Zwerin.*

Horowitz rehearses and performs Mozart's Concerto No. 23 in A major. Shown with *One Art*, USA. Directed by Anita Thacher. Also, *Young at Heart*, USA. Directed by Pat Conn and Sue Marx.

**JACKIE CHAN'S POLICE STORY**
*Hong Kong, 1985. Directed by Jackie Chan.*

Written by Edward Tang. With Chan, Brigitte Lin, Maggie Cheung, Chor Yuen. Shown with *Pas de deux*, Canada, 1967. Directed by Norman McLaren.

**JOAN OF ARC AT THE STAKE ▼**
*Italy, 1954. Directed by Roberto Rossellini.*

Oratorio written by Paul Claudel. With Ingrid Bergman, Tullio Carminati, Augusto Romani, Agnese Dobbini.

*The Manchurian Candidate* by John Frankenheimer

**+ THE HUMAN VOICE**
*Italy, 1948. Written and Directed by Roberto Rossellini, based on Jean Cocteau's one-act play* La Voix Humaine.

With Anna Magnani. A telephone monologue of a woman about to be deserted by her lover. (Retrospective program commemorating the 10th anniversary of Rossellini's death.)

**THE MANCHURIAN CANDIDATE**
*USA, 1962. Directed by John Frankenheimer.*

Written by George Axelrod, based on Richard Condon's novel. With Frank Sinatra, Laurence Harvey, Janet Leigh, Angela Lansbury. (Retrospective.) Note: The NYFF had wanted to show this for years. Finally, through the efforts of our Board member Bob Towbin, who knew Mickey Rudin, Frank Sinatra's lawyer, Sinatra agreed to release the film to us. Sinatra had bought the rights to this film, along with *Suddenly* (also about presidential assassinations), and shelved them after JFK was killed. After the NYFF screening the film was rereleased theatrically.

**MÉLO**
*France, 1986. Written and Directed by Alain Resnais, based on Henry Bernstein's play.*

With Sabine Azéma, Fanny Ardant, Pierre Arditi, André Dussollier. Shown with *Conrapunctus*, USA. Directed by Laura Companeitz.

**A MONTH IN THE COUNTRY**
*UK, 1987. Directed by Pat O'Connor.*

Written by Simon Gray, based on J.L. Carr's novel. With Colin Firth, Kenneth Branagh, Natasha Richardson, Patrick Malahide, Jim Carter. Shown with *Begone Dull Care*, Canada, 1949. Directed by Norman McLaren.

**RADIUM CITY**
*USA, 1987. Directed by Carole Langer.*

The story of women in Ottawa, Illinois, employed by an alarm-clock company that produced glow-in-the-dark dials.

**A TAXING WOMAN ▲**
*Japan, 1987. Written and directed by Juzo Itami.*

With Nobuko Miyamoto, Tsutomu Yamazaki, Masahiko Tsugawa, Hideo Murota.

**THEME (TEMA)**
*USSR, 1979/86. Directed by Gleb Panfilov.*

Written by Alexander Chernivsky and Panfilov. With Inna Churikova, Mikhail Ulyanov, Stanislav Lyubshin, Yevgeny Vesnik, Yevgeniya Nechayeva.

**UNDER THE SUN OF SATAN**
aka **UNDER SATAN'S SUN**
*France, 1987. Directed by Maurice Pialat.*

Written by Sylvie Danton and Pialat, based on Georges Bernanos's novel. With Gérard Depardieu, Sandrine Bonnaire, Pialat, Alain Artur. Shown with *Stars and Stripes*, Canada, 1949. Directed by Norman McLaren.

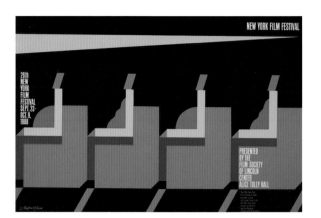

SELECTION COMMITTEE: RICHARD PEÑA, CHAIRMAN, WENDY KEYS, PHILLIP LOPATE, CARRIE RICKEY, AND DAVID STERRITT.
CONSULTANTS: LILLIAN JIMENEZ (AMERICAN INDEPENDENT FILM), MARY MEERSON (RETROSPECTIVES), AND RICHARD ROUD
(EUROPEAN CONSULTANT AND NEW YORK FILM FESTIVAL DIRECTOR EMERITUS).

THE 26TH NYFF POSTER ARTWORK WAS CREATED BY ©MILTON GLASER.

*Hard Times* by João Botelho

## WOMEN ON THE VERGE OF A NERVOUS BREAKDOWN

*Spain, 1988. Written and Directed by Pedro Almodóvar.*

With Carmen Maura, Antonio Banderas, Julieta Serrano, María Barranco, Rossy de Palma. Shown with *Night of the Living Duck*, USA. Directed by Greg Ford and Terry Lennon. (Opening Night.)

## RED SORGHUM

*People's Republic of China, 1987. Directed by Zhang Yimou.*

Written by Chen Jianyu, Zhu Wei, and Mo Yan, based on a story by Mo Yan. With Gong Li, Jiang Wen, Liu Ji, Teng Ru-Jun, Ji Cun Hua. Shown with *Words*, USA. Directed by Chuck Workman. (Closing Night.)

## ASHIK KERIB

*USSR, 1988. Directed by Sergei Parajanov.*

Written by Georgy Badridze, based on themes from Mikhail Lermontov's short story. With Yuri Goyan, Veronika Metonidze, Levan Natroshvili, Sofiko Chiaureli.

## ASYA'S HAPPINESS

*USSR, 1967. Directed by Andrei Konchalovsky.*

Written by Yury Klepikov. With Iya Savina, Alexander Surin, Ljubov Sokolova, Geniadij Egorytschev.

## "AVANT-GARDE VOICES"

- **Fake Fruit Factory**, USA, 1986, Directed by Chick Strand.

- **Honor and Obey**, USA, 1988. Directed by Warren Sonbert.

- **I... Dreaming** and **Marilyn's Window**, USA, 1988. Directed by Stan Brakhage.

- **Lived in Quotes**, USA, 1987. Directed by Laurie Dunphy.

## BIRD ▲

*USA, 1988. Directed by Clint Eastwood.*

Written by Joel Oliansky. With Forest Whitaker, Diane Venora, Michael Zelniker, Samuel E. Wright. Shown with *Koko*, USA. Directed by George Griffin.

## DAUGHTER OF THE NILE

*Taiwan, 1987. Directed by Hou Hsiao-hsien.*

Written by Chu Tien-wen, based on a story by Chen Hwai-en, Huang Jian-he, Jiang Bao-de, and Wang Cen-ru. With Yang Lin, Kao Jai, Yang Fan, Li Tien-lu. Shown with *Astronomy*, USA. Directed by Susan Rogers.

## DISTANT VOICES, STILL LIVES

*UK, 1988. Written and Directed by Terence Davies.*

With Freda Dowie, Pete Postlethwaite, Angela Walsh, Dean Williams. Shown with *The Short and Curlies*, UK. Directed by Mike Leigh.

## FELIX

*West Germany, 1987. Four episodes directed by Christel Buschmann, Helke Sander, Helma Sanders-Brahms, and Margarethe von Trotta.*

Written by Buschmann, Silvo Lahtela, Sander, Sanders-Brahms, and von Trotta. With Ulrich Tukur, Danuta Lato, Gabriela Herz, Eva Mattes. Shown with *Chet's Romance*, France. Directed by Bertrand Fèvre.

## GOLUB

*USA, 1988. Directed by Jerry Blumenthal and Gordon Quinn.*

A portrait of the expressionist painter Leon Golub.

USSR, 1967. Part l: *Angel*. Directed by Andrei Smirnov. Written by Ilya Suslov, Mikhail Suslov, and Boris Yermolaev, based on a story by Yury Olesha. Part 2: *Homeland of Electricity* (*Rodina elektrichestva*). Written and Directed by Larisa Shepitko, based on short stories by Andrei Platonov. An omnibus film made to commemorate the 50th anniversary of the October Revolution. (Retrospective.)

### OPENING NIGHT

*USA, 1978. Written and Directed by John Cassavetes.*

With Gena Rowlands, Cassavetes, Ben Gazzara, Joan Blondell. Shown with *Central Park in the Dark*, USA. Directed by Rudy Burckhardt and Christopher Sweet.

### ◀ PELLE THE CONQUEROR

*Denmark, 1987. Directed by Bille August.*

Written by August, Per Olov Enquist, and Bjarne Reuter, based on Martin Andersen Nexø's novel. With Max von Sydow, Pelle Hvenegaard, Erik Paaske, Kristina Törnqvists. Shown with *Junior*, USA. Directed by Gus Van Sant.

### SALAAM BOMBAY!

*India, 1987. Directed by Mira Nair.*

Written by Sooni Taraporevala, based on a story by Nair and Taraporevala. With Shafiq Syed, Sarfuddin Quarassi, Raju Barnad, Raghubir Yadav.

### 36 FILLETTE

*France, 1988. Directed by Catherine Breillat.*

Written by Breillat and Roger Salloch. With Delphine Zentout, Etienne Chicot, Olivier Parnière, Jean-Pierre Léaud, Jean-Françoise Stévenin. Shown with *Elle et lui*, France. Directed by François Margolin.

### A WINTER TAN

*Canada, 1987. Directed by Jackie Burroughs, Louise Clark, John Frizzell, John Walker, and Aerlyn Weissman.*

Written by Burroughs, based on the book *Give Sorrow Words, Maryse Holder's Letters from Mexico*. With Burroughs, Erando Gonzalez, Anita Olanick. Shown with *Ray's Male Heterosexual Dance Hall*, USA. Directed by Bryan Gordon.

### + FALKENAU, THE IMPOSSIBLE (SAMUEL FULLER BEARS WITNESS)

*France, 1988. Directed by Emil Weiss.*

Written by Samuel Fuller and Weiss. Includes Fuller's "home movie" footage shot when he was a U.S. soldier liberating a concentration camp.

### HARD TIMES

*Portugal, 1988. Written and Directed by João Botelho, based on Charles Dickens's novel.*

With Henrique Viana, Eunice Muñoz, Júlia Britton, Ruy Furtado. Shown with *April 16th, 1989*, USA. Directed by David Byrne.

### HIGH HOPES

*UK, 1988. Written and Directed by Mike Leigh.*

With Philip Davis, Ruth Sheen, Edna Doré, Philip Jackson. Shown with *Treacle*, UK. Directed by Peter Chelsom.

### HOTEL TERMINUS: THE LIFE AND TIMES OF KLAUS BARBIE

*USA, 1988. Directed by Marcel Ophuls.*

A four-and-a-half-hour account of the infamous Nazi war criminal.

### JACOB

*Romania, 1988. Written and Directed by Mircea Daneliuc, based on the works of Geo Bogza.*

With Dorel Visan, Cecilia Birbora, Ion Fiscuteanu, Maria Seles. Shown with *The Zip*, UK. Directed by Jo Ann Kaplan.

### ◀ THE LAST OF ENGLAND

*UK, 1987. Written and Directed by Derek Jarman.*

With Tilda Swinton, Nigel Terry, Spencer Leigh, Spring, Gay Gaynor. A glimpse of Western civilization on the brink of apocalypse. Shown with *Cause and Effect*, USA. Directed by Mary Perillo and John Sanborn.

### THE MAN WITH THREE COFFINS

*South Korea, 1987. Directed by Lee Jang-ho.*

Written by Jue-ha and Lee, based on Jue-ha's novel *A Wanderer Never Sleeps Even on the Road*. With Kim Myung-kon, Lee Bo-hee, Woo Ok-joo. Shown with *Souvenir*, USA. Directed by Adele Friedman.

### MAPANTSULA

*South Africa, 1988. Directed by Oliver Schmitz.*

Written by Thomas Mogotlane and Schmitz. With Mogotlane, Thembi Mtshali, Marcel Van Heerden, Dolly Rathebe. Shown with *Utter*, South Africa. Directed by Henion Han.

### LA MASCHERA

*Italy, 1988. Directed by Fiorella Infascelli.*

Written by Adriano Apra and Infascelli, with the collaboration of Ennio De Concini and Enzo Ungari. With Helena Bonham Carter, Michael Maloney, Feodor Chaliapin, Roberto Herlitzka. Shown with *Sarah*, France. Directed by Edgardo Cozarinsky. A meditation on the career of Sarah Bernhardt, narrated by Susan Sontag.

*Salaam Bombay!* by Mira Nair

27th New York Film Festival
September 22–October 9, 1989 · Alice Tully Hall

Presented by
The Film Society
of Lincoln Center

# 1989

SELECTION COMMITTEE: RICHARD PEÑA, CHAIRMAN, WENDY KEYS, PHILLIP LOPATE, CARRIE RICKEY, AND DAVID STERRITT.

THE 27TH NYFF POSTER ARTWORK WAS CREATED BY ©JENNIFER BARTLETT.

*Intolerance* by D.W. Griffith

**TOO BEAUTIFUL FOR YOU**
*France, 1989. Written and Directed by Bertrand Blier.*
With Gérard Depardieu, Josiane Balasko, Carole Bouquet, Roland Blanche. Shown with *No More Disguises*, USA, 1989. Directed by Tom Sigel and Boryana Varbanov. (Opening Night.)

**BREAKING IN**
*USA, 1989. Directed by Bill Forsyth.*
Written by John Sayles. With Burt Reynolds, Casey Siemaszko, Sheila Kelley, Lorraine Toussaint. Shown with *Animated Self Portraits* by Sally Cruikshank, David Ehrlich, Candy Kugel, Bill Plympton, Maureen Selwood (USA); Mati Kutt, Priit Pärn, Riho Unt, Hardi Volmer (Estonia); Borivoj Dovniković, Nikola Majdak, Joško Marušić, Dušan Vukotić (Yugoslavia); Jiří Barta, Pavel Koutsky, Jan Švankmajer (Czechoslovakia); Kihachiro Kawamoto, Renzo Kinoshita, Osamu Tezuka (Japan). Nineteen animators join for a series of animated impressions of themselves. (Closing Night.)

**ARIEL**
*Finland, 1988. Written and Directed by Aki Kaurismäki.*
With Turo Pajala, Susanna Haavisto, Matti Pellonpää. Eetu Hilkamo. Shown with *London Suite*, UK. Directed by Vivienne Dick (one the Super-8 superstars of the 1970s).

**"AVANT-GARDE VISIONS"**
- **Friendly Witness**, USA, 1989. Directed by Warren Sonbert.
- **Mercy**, USA, 1989. Directed by Abigail Child.
- **Water and Power**, USA, 1989. Directed by Pat O'Neill.

**BLACK RAIN ▶**
*Japan, 1989. Directed by Shohei Imamura.*
Written by Imamura and Toshiro Ishido, based on Masuji Ibuse's novel. With Yoshiko Tanaka, Kazuo Kitamura, Etsuko Ichihara, Shoichi Ozawa.

**A CITY OF SADNESS**
*Taiwan, 1989. Directed by Hou Hsiao-hsien.*
Written by Chu Tien-wen and Wu Nien-jen. With Tony Leung, Hsin Shu-fen, Chen Sown-yung, Kao Jai. Shown with *Super Soap*, People's Republic of China. Directed by Ah Da and Ma Kexuan.

**CONFESSION: A CHRONICLE OF ALIENATION**
*USSR, 1988. Directed by Georgi Gavrilov.*
Written by Gavrilov and Yu Kotliar. Portrait of a Moscow drug addict and the drug subculture among alienated Soviet youth. Shown with *The Inspector*, Brazil. Directed by Artur Omar.

**CURRENT EVENTS**
*USA, 1989. Directed by Ralph Arlyck.*
An examination of the news media and social and political activism. Shown with *Dreams from China*, USA. Directed by Fred Marx. A lyrical observation of today's China.

**DANCING FOR MR. B: SIX BALANCHINE BALLERINAS**
*USA, 1989. Directed by Anne Belle and Deborah Dickson.*
With Maria Tallchief, Mary Ellen Moylan, Melissa Hayden, Allegra Kent, Merrill Ashley, Darci Kistler. Shown with *This Time Around*, USA. Directed by Jane Aaron.

**THE DOCUMENTATOR (DER DOKUMENTATOR)**
*Hungary, 1988. Written and Directed by István Dárday and Györgyi Szalai.*
With Mihály Dés, Lilla Pászti, János Ágoston.

**INTOLERANCE**
*USA, 1916. Directed by D.W. Griffith.*
With Mae Marsh, Fred Turner, Howard Gaye, Lillian Langdon, Margery Wilson, Eugene Pallette, Constance Talmadge, Elmer Clifton. Presented in Avery Fisher Hall accompanied by the Brooklyn Philharmonic Orchestra and Chorus under the baton of Gillian B. Anderson. Print courtesy of the Museum of Modern Art. (Retrospective.)

**◀ LIFE AND NOTHING BUT**
*France, 1989. Directed by Bertrand Tavernier.*
Written by Jean Cosmos and Tavernier. With Philippe Noiret, Sabine Azéma, Pascale Vignal, Maurice Barrier. Shown with *Please Don't Stop*, USA. Directed by Stephanie Maxwell.

**LOOKING FOR LANGSTON**
*UK, 1988. Directed by Isaac Julien.*
With Ben Ellison, Matthew Baidoo, John Wilson, Akim Mogaji. A meditation of the Harlem Renaissance and Langston Hughes.

**+ BOOK OF DAYS**
*USA, 1986. Directed by Meredith Monk.*
Written by Tone Blevins and Monk. With Robert Een, Andrea Goodman, Lanny Harrison, Wayne Hankin. Shown with *Black-Eyed Susan (Portrait of an Actress)*, USA. Directed by Stuart Sherman.

**THE MAHABHARATA**
*France/UK/USA, 1989. Directed by Peter Brook.*
With Robert Langdon Lloyd, Antonin Stahly-Viswanadhan, Bruce Myers, Vittorio Mezzogiorno. Brook reconceived his theatrical staging of this great Sanskrit epic for the screen.

**MONSIEUR HIRE**
*France, 1989. Directed by Patrice Leconte.*

Written by Patrick Dewolf and Leconte, based on Georges Simenon's novel *Les Fiançailles de M. Hire*. With Michel Blanc, Sandrine Bonnaire, Luc Thullier, André Wilms. Shown with *C'mon Babe (Danke Schoen)*, USA. Directed by Sharon Sandusky.

**MY LEFT FOOT ▲**
*Ireland, 1989. Directed by Jim Sheridan.*

Written by Sheridan and Shane Connaughton, based on the book by Christy Brown. With Daniel Day-Lewis, Brenda Fricker, Alison Whelan, Kirsten Sheridan. Shown with *J.P. Somersaulter's Dot to Dot Cartoon Cartoon*, USA. Directed by J.P. Somersaulter.

**MYSTERY TRAIN**
*USA, 1989. Written and Directed by Jim Jarmusch.*

With Masatoshi Nagase, Youki Kudoh, Screamin' Jay Hawkins, Nicoletta Braschi, Elizabeth Bracco, Joe Strummer, Rick Aviles, Steve Buscemi. Shown with *The Black Tower*, UK. Directed by John Smith.

**NEAR DEATH**
*USA, 1989. Directed by Frederick Wiseman.*

A monumental work shot in the intensive-care unit of a Boston hospital.

**THE PLOT AGAINST HARRY ▲**
*USA, 1969-89. Written and Directed by Michael Roemer.*

With Martin Priest, Ben Lang, Maxine Woods, Henry Nemo. It took 20 years to raise post-production funds. (Retrospective.) Shown with *Pas è deux*, The Netherlands. Directed by Monique Renault and Gerrit van Dijk.

**ROGER & ME**
*USA, 1989. Written, Directed, and Narrated by Michael Moore.*

Subtitled "A Humorous Look at How General Motors Destroyed Flint, Michigan," this was Moore's debut film. Shown with *A Western*, USA. Directed by Laurie Dunphy.

**A SHORT FILM ABOUT KILLING**
*Poland, 1987. Directed by Krzysztof Kieślowski.*

Written by Kieślowski and Krzysztof Piesiewicz. With Mirosław Baka, Krzysztof Globisz, Jan Tesarz. Shown with *The Mourner*, Poland. Directed by Helene Dabrowski-Torres.

**SPEAKING PARTS**
*Canada, 1989. Written and Directed by Atom Egoyan.*

With Michael McManus, Arsinée Khanjian, Gabrielle Rose, Tony Nardi. Shown with *Under the Sea*, USA. Directed by Paul Glabicki.

**STRAPLESS**
*UK, 1988. Written and Directed by David Hare.*

With Blair Brown, Bruno Ganz, Bridget Fonda, Alan Howard, Hugh Laurie. Shown with *The Soulful Shack*, UK. Directed by John Roberts.

**SWEETIE**
*Australia, 1989. Directed by Jane Campion.*

Written by Campion and Gerard Lee. With Geneviève Lemon, Karen Colston, Tom Lycos, Jon Darling. Shown with *Kitchen Sink*, New Zealand. Directed by Alison Maclean.

**A TALE OF THE WIND**
*France, 1988. Directed by Joris Ivens and Marceline Loridan.*

Written by Ivens and Loridan, with Elizabeth D. With Ivens, Liu Guilian, Liu Zhuang, Han Zhenxiang. Shown with *Rain*, The Netherlands, 1929. Directed by Joris Ivens.

**THELONIOUS MONK: STRAIGHT, NO CHASER ▲**
*USA, 1988. Directed by Charlotte Zwerin.*

Narrated by Samuel E. Wright. With the music of Monk, Charlie Rouse, Larry Gales, Ben Riley, Phil Woods, Johnny Griffin, Ray Copeland and Jimmy Cleveland, Tommy Flanagan, Barry Harris, Dick Hyman. Shown with *Ostensibly*, USA. Directed by Rudy Burckhardt.

**◄ YAABA**
*Burkina Faso, 1988. Written and Directed by Idrissa Ouedraogo.*

With Fatimata Sanga, Noufou Ouedraogo, Roukietou Barry, Adama Ouedraogo. Shown with *Kakania*, USA. Directed by Karen Aqua.

# 1990

SELECTION COMMITTEE: RICHARD PEÑA, CHAIRMAN, DAVID ANSEN, WENDY KEYS, PHILLIP LOPATE, AND DAVID STERRITT.

THE 28TH NYFF POSTER ARTWORK WAS CREATED BY ©ERIC FISCHL.

*Miller's Crossing* by Joel Coen

**L'ATALANTE**
*France, 1934. Directed by Jean Vigo.*

Written by Albert Riéra and Vigo, based on an original scenario by Jean Guinée. With Dita Parlo, Jean Dasté, Michel Simon, Louis Lefebvre (Retrospective.) Shown with *To the Top*, USA. Directed by Anita Thacher.

**"AVANT-GARDE VISIONS"**
• **Pièce touchée**, Austria, 1989. Directed by Martin Arnold.
• **Scenes from the Life of Andy Warhol**, USA, 1990. Directed by Jonas Mekas.
• **Sink or Swim**, USA, 1990. Directed by Su Friedrich.

**DR. PETIOT**
*France, 1990. Directed by Christian de Chalonge.*

Written by de Chalonge and Dominique Garner. With Michel Serrault, Pierre Romans, Zbigniew Horoks, Bérangère Bonvoisin. Shown with *Hang Up* and *The Space Between the Door and the Floor*, Australia. Both directed by Pauline Chan.

**FREEZE-DIE-COME TO LIFE**
*USSR, 1989. Written and Directed by Vitaly Kanevsky.*

With Dinara Drukarova, Pavel Nazarov, Yelena Popova, Vyacheslav Bambushek.

**THE GOLDEN BOAT**
*USA, 1990. Written and Directed by Raúl Ruiz.*

With Michael Kirby, Kate Valk, Federico Muchnik, Michael Stumm, Mary Hestand, Jim Jarmusch, Brett Alexander, Barbet Schroeder. Shown with *Inside the Circle of Love*, USA. Directed by J.P. Somersaulter.

**GOLDEN BRAID**
*Australia, 1990. Directed by Paul Cox.*

Written by Cox and Barry Dickins, inspired by a short story by Guy de Maupassant. With Chris Haywood, Gosia Dobrowolska, Paul Chubb, Norman Kaye. Shown with *Touch My Lips*, Canada. Directed by Jim Garrard.

**I HIRED A CONTRACT KILLER**
*Finland/Sweden, 1990. Written and Directed by Aki Kaurismäki.*

With Jean-Pierre Léaud, Margi Clarke, Kenneth Colley, Trevor Bowen, Joe Strummer, Serge Reggiani.

◀ **JU DOU**
*China/Japan, 1990. Directed by Zhang Yimou.*

Written by Lui Heng. With Gong Li, Li Baotian, Li Wei, Zhang Yi, Zhen Jian. Shown with *Macha's Curse*, USA. Directed by Rose Bond.

**KING OF NEW YORK** ▶
*USA/Italy, 1989. Directed by Abel Ferrara.*

Written by Nicholas St. John. With Christopher Walken, David Caruso, Laurence Fishburne, Victor Argo, Wesley Snipes. Shown with *Nowon*, USA. Directed by Peter Judson.

**LISTEN UP: THE LIVES OF QUINCY JONES**
*USA, 1990. Directed by Ellen Weissbrod.*

With (as themselves) Quincy Jones, Miles Davis, Frank Sinatra, Ray Charles, Ella Fitzgerald, Lionel Hampton, Barbra Streisand. A documentary on the life and music of Jones.

**THE MATCH FACTORY GIRL**
*Finland, 1990. Written and Directed by Aki Kaurismäki.*

With Kati Outinen, Elina Salo, Esko Nikkari, Vesa Vierikko, Silu Seppälä. Shown with *That Burning Question*, USA. Directed by Alan Taylor.

**MILLER'S CROSSING**
*USA, 1990. Directed by Joel Coen.*

Written by Joel and Ethan Coen. With Gabriel Byrne, Marcia Gay Harden, John Turturro, Jon Polito, J.E. Freeman, Albert Finney. Shown with *Eternity*, Canada. Directed by Sheryl Sardina. (Opening Night.)

**THE NASTY GIRL**
*West Germany, 1990. Written and Directed by Michael Verhoeven.*

With Lena Stolze, Monika Baumgartner, Michael Gahr, Fred Stillkrauth. Shown with *The Lunch Date*, USA. Directed by Adam Davidson. (Closing Night.)

**AMERICAN DREAM**
*USA, 1990. Directed by Barbara Kopple.*

A documentary about a strike against a Hormel meatpacking plant in Minnesota. Shown with *Siberian Summer*, Hungary. Directed by Andras Der.

**AN ANGEL AT MY TABLE**
*New Zealand, 1990. Directed by Jane Campion.*

Written by Laura Jones, based on Janet Frame's autobiographies. With Kerry Fox, Alexia Keogh, Karen Fergusson, Iris Churn.

**NIGHT SUN**

*Italy/France/West Germany, 1990. Directed by Paolo and Vittorio Taviani.*

Written by the Tavianis, with the collaboration of Tonino Guerra, loosely based on Leo Tolstoy's story "Father Sergius." With Julian Sands, Charlotte Gainsbourg, Nastassja Kinski, Massino Bonetti. Shown with *Mr. Tao*, Italy. Directed by Bruno Bozzetto.

**NO, OR THE VAIN GLORY OF COMMAND**

*Portugal, 1990. Written and Directed by Manoel de Oliveira.*

With Luís Miguel Cintra, Diogo Dória, Miguel Guilherme, Luis Lucas. Shown with *The Magical Stories*, USA. Directed by Ondrej Rudavsky.

**NOUVELLE VAGUE**

*Switzerland/France, 1990. Written and Directed by Jean-Luc Godard.*

With Alain Delon, Domiziani Giordano, Roland Amstutz, Laurence Côte. Shown with *Save the Last Dance for Me*, France/Canada. Directed by Lewis Furey.

**OPEN DOORS**

*Italy, 1990. Directed by Gianni Amelio.*

Written by Amelio and Vincenzo Cerami, with the collaboration of Alessandro Sermoneta, based on Leonardo Sciascia's novel. With Gian Maria Volonté, Ennio Fantastichini, Renzo Giovampietro, Renato Carpentieri. Shown with *Hiding Out from Heaven*, USA. Directed by Fred Marx.

**PRIVILEGE**

*USA, 1990. Written and Directed by Yvonne Rainer.*

With Alice Spivak, Novella Nelson, Blaire Baron, Rico Elias, Yvonne Rainer. Shown with *Night Cries: A Rural Tragedy*, Australia. Directed by Tracey Moffatt.

**SIDDHESHWARI**

*India, 1988. Written and Directed by Mani Kaul.*

With Mita Vasisht, Ranjana Srivastava, Pandit Narayan Misra, Shravani Mukherjee. A fantasia based on the life of Siddheshwari Devi, great singer of Thumri music. Shown with *A Nice Arrangement*, UK. Directed by Gurinder Chadha.

**THE STING OF DEATH**

*Japan, 1990. Written and Directed by Kohei Oguri, based on Toshio Shimao's novel.*

With Keiko Matsuzaka, Ittoku Kishibe, Takenori Matsumura, Yuri Chikamori, Midori Kiuchi. Shown with *Another Damaging Day*, USA. Directed by Stacy Cochran.

**A TALE OF SPRINGTIME**

*France, 1990. Written and Directed by Eric Rohmer.*

With Anne Teyssèdre, Hugues Quester, Florence Darrel, Eloise Bennett, Sophie Robin.

**TAXI BLUES**

*USSR/France, 1990. Written and Directed by Pavel Lounguine.*

With Pyotr Mamonov, Piotr Zaitchenko, Vladimir Kachpur, Natalia Kolyakanova. Shown with *Wonderland*, USA. Directed by Zoe Beloff.

**TILAI**

*Burkina Faso, 1990. Written and Directed by Idrissa Ouedraogo.*

With Rasmane Ouedraogo, Ina Cisse, Roukietou Barry, Assane Ouedraogo. Shown with *All My Relations*, USA. Directed by Joanna Priestley.

**TO SLEEP WITH ANGER**

*USA, 1990. Written and Directed by Charles Burnett.*

With Danny Glover, Paul Butler, Mary Alice, Carl Lumbly. Shown with *Fat Monroe*, USA. Directed by Andrew Garrison.

**A WOMAN'S REVENGE**

*France, 1989. Directed by Jacques Doillon.*

Written by Doillon and Jean-François Goyet, loosely based on Dostoevsky's story "The Eternal Husband." With Isabelle Huppert, Béatrice Dalle, Jean-Louis Murat, Laurence Côte, Sebastian Roché.

29th NEW YORK FILM FESTIVAL

# 1991

SELECTION COMMITTEE: RICHARD PEÑA, CHAIRMAN, DAVID ANSEN, WENDY KEYS, PHILLIP LOPATE, AND DAVID STERRITT.

THE 29TH NYFF POSTER ARTWORK WAS CREATED BY ©PHILIP PEARLSTEIN.

### AMELIA LÓPES O'NEILL
*Chile/France/Spain, 1990. Directed by Valeria Sarmiento.*

Written by Raúl Ruiz and Sarmiento. With Laura del Sol, Franco Nero, Laura Benson, Valérie Mairesse. Shown with *Cairo As Told by Youssef Chahine*, Egypt/France. Directed by Chahine.

### "AVANT-GARDE VISIONS"
- **Flaming Creatures**, USA, 1962. Directed by Jack Smith.
- **The Making of "Monsters,"** Canada, 1991. Directed by John Greyson.
- **Opening the Nineteenth Century: 1896**, USA, 1990. Directed by Ken Jacobs.

### BEAUTY AND THE BEAST
*USA, 1991. Directed by Gary Trousdale and Kirk Wise.*

Written by Linda Woolverton. With the voices of Robby Benson, Jessi Conti, Rex Everhart, Angela Lansbury. Screened as a work-in-progress illustrating various stages of the animation process.

### THE DOUBLE LIFE OF VÉRONIQUE ▲
*France/Poland, 1991. Directed by Krzysztof Kieślowski.*

Written by Kieślowski and Krzysztof Piesiewicz. With Irène Jacob, Philippe Volter, Claude Duneton, Wladyslaw Kowalski. Shown with *Home Stories*, Germany, 1991. Directed by Matthias Müller. (Opening Night.)

### HOMICIDE
*USA, 1991. Written and Directed by David Mamet.*

With Joe Mantegna, William H. Macy, Natalija Nogulich, Ving Rhames, Rebecca Pidgeon, Ricky Jay. Shown with *Fast Food Matador*, USA. Directed by Vincent Cafarelli and Candy Kugel. (Closing Night.)

### ADAM'S RIB
*USSR, 1990. Directed by Vyacheslav Krishtofovich.*

Written by Vladimir Kunin, based on Anatoly Kurchatkin's novel *House of Young Women*. With Inna Chirikova, Svetlana Ryabova, Masha Golubkina, Yelena Bogdanova. Shown with *The Tennis Ball*, Australia. Directed by John Dobson.

### THE ADJUSTER
*Canada, 1991. Written and Directed by Atom Egoyan.*

With Elias Koteas, Arsinée Khanjian, Maury Chaykin, Gabrielle Rose. Shown with *The Visible Compendium*, USA. Directed by Larry Jordan.

*Delicatessen* by Marc Caro and Jean-Pierre Jeunet

**LA BELLE NOISEUSE**
*France, 1990. Directed by Jacques Rivette.*

Written by Pascal Bonitzer, Christine Laurent, and Rivette, based on Balzac's novella. With Michel Piccoli, Jane Birkin, Emmanuelle Béart, Marianne Denicourt.

**DELICATESSEN**
*France, 1991. Directed by Marc Caro and Jean-Pierre Jeunet.*

Written by Gilles Adrien, Caro, and Jeunet. With Dominique Pinon, Marie-Laure Dougnac, Jean-Claude Dreyfus, Karin Viard. Shown with *New Fangled*, USA. Directed by George Griffin.

◀ **ENTRANCED EARTH (TERRA EM TRANSE)**
*Brazil, 1966. Written and Directed by Glauber Rocha.*

With Jardel Filho, José Lewgoy, Glauce Rocha, Paulo Autran. Shown with *Suburban Route*, Brazil. Directed by Francisco Cesar Filho.

**INTIMATE STRANGER**
*USA, 1991. Directed by Alan Berliner.*

A witty portrait of Berliner's grandfather, a Palestinian Jew raised in Egypt who worked in Japan while his family lived in Brooklyn.

+ **THE BODY BEAUTIFUL**
*UK, 1991. Written and Directed by Ngozi Onwurah.*

With (as themselves) Madge Onwurah, Sian Martin, Maureen Douglass, Brian Bovell. A lyrical, tough/gentle look at the white, cancer-stricken mother of the filmmaker, a black model.

**INVENTORY**
*Poland/Germany, 1989. Written and Directed by Krzysztof Zanussi.*

With Krystyna Janda, Maja Komorowska, Artur Żmijewski. Shown with *With Raised Hands*, Poland. Directed by Mitko Panov.

**JACQUOT DE NANTES**
*France, 1991. Written and Directed by Agnès Varda.*

With Philippe Maron, Edouard Joubeaud, Laurent Monnier, Jacques Demy. A biography of and tribute to Jacques Demy, Varda's husband.

**LIFE ON A STRING**
*China/UK/Germany, 1991. Written and Directed by Chen Kaige, based on a short story by Shi Tiesheng.*

With Liu Zhongyuan, Huang Lei, Xu Qing, Ma Ling. Shown with *A Year Along the Abandoned Road*, Norway. Directed by Morten Skallerud.

**LOCKED UP TIME**
*Germany, 1990. Directed by Sibylle Schönemann.*

An autobiographical film about East German filmmaker Schönemann's imprisonment in 1984 for requesting an exit visa. Shown with *Great Regular Flavor*, USA. Directed by Rudy Burckhardt.

**MY OWN PRIVATE IDAHO**
*USA, 1991. Written and Directed by Gus Van Sant.*

With River Phoenix, Keanu Reeves, James Russo, William Richert, Chiara Caselli, Udo Kier, Grace Zabriskie. Shown with *Backyard Movie*, USA, 1991. Directed by Bruce Weber.

**NIGHT ON EARTH**
*USA, 1991. Written and Directed by Jim Jarmusch.*

With Winona Ryder, Gena Rowlands, Giancarlo Esposito, Armin Mueller-Stahl, Rosie Perez, Roberto Benigni, Isaach De Bankolé, Béatrice Dalle, Matti Pellonpää.

**NO LIFE KING**
*Japan, 1989. Directed by Jun Ichikawa.*

Written by Hiroaki Jinno, based on Seikou Ito's novel. With Ryo Takayama, Saeko Suzuki, Neko Saito, Ogata Ittsusei, Kyusaku Shimada. Shown with *Shirt*, USA. Directed by Kenji Larsen.

*The Suspended Step of the Stork* by Theo Angelopoulos

### THE OTHER EYE
*Austria/USA, 1991. Written and Directed by Johanna Heer and Werner Schmiedel.*

With Rudolph S. Joseph, Anne Friedberg, Harold Nebenzal, Francis Lederer. A documentary about G.W. Pabst, the liberal, cosmopolitan filmmaker who returned to Austria in 1939 to direct movies for the Third Reich. Shown with *Shönberg, Austria*. Directed by Gerhard Ertl and Sabine Hiebler.

### PICTURES FROM A REVOLUTION
*USA, 1991. Directed by Alfred Guzzetti, Susan Meiselas, and Richard P. Rogers.*

A provocative study of the revolution in Nicaragua and its aftermath. Shown with *Post No Bills*, USA. Directed by Clay Walker.

### PROSPERO'S BOOKS
*The Netherlands/UK, 1991. Written and Directed by Peter Greenaway, based on Shakespeare's* The Tempest.

With John Gielgud, Michael Clark, Michel Blanc, Erland Josephson, Isabelle Pasco.

### THE RAPTURE
*USA, 1990. Written and Directed by Michael Tolkin.*

With Mimi Rogers, David Duchovny, Patrick Bauchau, Kimberly Cullum, Will Patton. Shown with *Resonance, Australia*. Directed by Stephen Cummins and Simon Hunt.

### ROCCO AND HIS BROTHERS ▶
*France/Italy, 1960. Directed by Luchino Visconti.*

Written by Suso Cecchi D'Amico, Vasco Pratolini, and Visconti, based on Giovanni Testori's novel *The Bridge of Ghisolfa*. With Alain Delon, Renato Salvatori, Annie Girardot, Katina Paxinou. (Retrospective—a restored three-hour version never before seen in the U.S.)

### A ROOM IN TOWN (UNE CHAMBRE EN VILLE)
*France, 1982. Written and Directed by Jacques Demy.*

With Dominique Sanda, Danielle Darrieux, Richard Berry, Michel Piccoli. (Retrospective—an homage to Demy.) Shown with *La Plage*, France. Directed by François Goize.

### THE SUSPENDED STEP OF THE STORK
*Greece/France, 1991. Directed by Theo Angelopoulos.*

Written by Angelopoulos, Tonino Guerra, and Petros Markaris. With Marcello Mastroianni, Jeanne Moreau, Gregory Karr, Dora Chrysikou, Ilias Logothetis.

### TOTO THE HERO
*Belgium/France/Germany, 1991. Written and Directed by Jaco van Dormael.*

With Michel Bouquet, Mireille Perrier, Jo De Backer, Gisela Uhlen. Shown with *Puppenhead*, Australia. Directed by David Cox.

### WOMAN OF THE PORT
*Mexico/USA, 1991. Directed by Arturo Ripstein.*

Written by Paz Alicia Garciadiego, based on a story by Guy de Maupassant. With Patricia Reyes Spindola, Alejandro Parodi, Evangelina Sosa, Damián Alcázar. Shown with *After the Fall*, USA. Directed by Joanna Priestly.

### ZOMBIE AND THE GHOST TRAIN
*Finland, 1991. Written and Directed by Mika Kaurismäki, based on a story by Sakke Järvenpää, Kaurismäki, and Pauli Pentti.*

With Silu Seppälä, Marjo Leinonon, Matti Pellonpää, Vieno Saaristo, Juhani Niemelä. Shown with *Tender, Slender and Tall*, USA. Directed by Lesley Ellen. An intimate look at the musician Shorty Jackson.

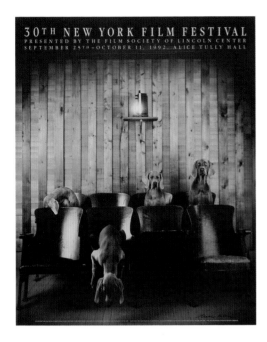

30TH **NEW YORK FILM FESTIVAL**
PRESENTED BY THE FILM SOCIETY OF LINCOLN CENTER
SEPTEMBER 25TH–OCTOBER 11, 1992. ALICE TULLY HALL

# 1992

SELECTION COMMITTEE: RICHARD PEÑA, CHAIRMAN, DAVID ANSEN, WENDY KEYS, STUART KLAWANS, AND DAVID STERRITT.

THE 30TH NYFF POSTER ARTWORK WAS CREATED BY ©WILLIAM WEGMAN.

### OLIVIER OLIVIER ▲
*France, 1992. Written and Directed by Agnieszka Holland.*
With François Cluzet, Brigitte Roüan, Grégoire Colin, Marina Golovine, Jean-François Stévenin, Alexis Derlon, Mathias Jung. Shown with *Omnibus*, France. Directed by Sam Karmann. (Opening Night.)

### NIGHT AND THE CITY
*USA, 1992. Directed by Irwin Winkler.*
Written by Richard Price, based on Gerald Kersh's novel. With Robert De Niro, Jessica Lange, Cliff Gorman, Jack Warden, Alan King. Shown with *Revolver*, UK. Directed by Chester Dent. (Closing Night.)

### ALLAH TANTOU
*Guinea/France, 1991. Directed by David Achkar.*
A documentary about Achkar's father, a Guinean diplomat who became a political prisoner.

*Dream of Light* by Victor Erice

**+ LUMUMBA: DEATH OF A PROPHET**
*Germany/Switzerland, 1991. Directed by Raoul Peck.*
The rise and fall of a seminal figure.

**AUTUMN MOON**
*Hong Kong/Japan, 1992. Directed by Clara Law.*
Written by Fong Ling Ching. With Masatoshi Nagase, Li Pui Wai, Choi Siu Wan, Maki Kiuchi, Suen Ching Hung. Shown with *Are We Still Married?*, UK, 1992. Directed by the Brothers Quay.

**"AVANT-GARDE VISIONS"**
- **John Five**, USA, 1992. Directed by James Herbert.
- **Short Fuse**, USA, 1991. Directed by Warren Sonbert.
- **Side/Walk/Shuttle**, USA, 1992. Directed by Ernie Gehr.

**BENNY'S VIDEO**
*Austria, 1992. Written and Directed by Michael Haneke.*
With Arno Frisch, Angela Winkler, Ulrich Mühe, Ingrid Stassner. Shown with *Deeper Still*, UK. Directed by Anthony Nielson.

**CAREFUL**
*Canada, 1992. Directed by Guy Maddin.*
Written by Maddin and George Toles, based on a story by Toles. With Kyle McCulloch, Gosia Dobrawolska, Sarah Neville, Brent Neale. Shown with *Amelia Rose Towers*, Australia. Directed by Jackie Karkas.

**THE CRYING GAME**
*Ireland/UK, 1992. Written and Directed by Neil Jordan.*
With Forest Whitaker, Miranda Richardson, Stephan Rea, Adrian Dunbar, Jaye Davidson, Jim Broadbent.

**DELIVERED VACANT**
*USA, 1992. Directed by Nora Jacobson.*
A documentation of Hoboken, New Jersey's battles over gentrification. Shown with *Southwest*, USA. Directed by Richard R. Hall.

**DREAM OF LIGHT** aka **QUINCE TREE OF THE SUN**
*Spain, 1992. Directed by Victor Erice.*
Written by Erice and Antonio López. With (as themselves) López, Maria Moreno, Enrique Gran, José Carretero. A meditation on art, technique, and expression following the creation of a painting by López of a quince tree in his backyard.

**HYENAS**
*Senegal/Switzerland/France, 1992. Directed by Djibril Diop Mambety.*
With Mansour Diouf, Ami Diakhate, Mahouredia Gueye, Issa Ramagelissa Samb. Shown with *Perpetual Motion*, USA. Directed by Karen Aqua.

**IDIOT**
*India, 1992. Directed by Mani Kaul.*
Written by Anup Singh, based on Fyodor Dostoyevsky's novel *The Idiot*. With Ayub Khan-Din, Shah Rukh Khan, Mita Vashisth, Navjot Hansra.

**IN THE SOUP**
*USA, 1992. Directed by Alexandre Rockwell.*
Written by Tim Kissell and Rockwell. With Steve Buscemi, Seymour Cassel, Jennifer Beals, Pat Moya, Jim Jarmusch, Carol Kane, Stanley Tucci. Shown with *Milk of Amnesia*, USA. Directed by Jeffrey Noyes Scher.

**LÉOLO**
*Canada, 1992. Written and Directed by Jean-Claude Lauzon.*
With Gilbert Sicotte, Maxime Collin, Ginette Reno, Julien Guiomar. Shown with *One Thousand Dollars*, USA. Directed by Sergio Castilla.

**LIFE AND NOTHING MORE... aka AND LIFE GOES ON**
*Iran, 1992. Written and Directed by Abbas Kiarostami.*
With Farhad Kheradmand, Pooya Pievar, and the people of Quokar and Poshteh. Shown with *My Little Eye*, UK. Directed by Benjamin Ross.

**THE LOVERS ON THE BRIDGE (LES AMANTS DU PONT-NEUF)**
*France, 1991. Written and Directed by Leos Carax.*
With Juliette Binoche, Denis Lavant, Klaus-Michael Grüber.

**MAN BITES DOG**
*Belgium, 1992. Directed by Rémy Belvaux, André Bonzel, and Benoît Poelvoorde.*
Written by Belvaux, Bonzel, Poelvoorde, and Vincent Tavier, based on an idea by Belvaux. With Poelvoorde, Jacqueline Poelvoorde-Pappaert, Nelly Pappaert, Hector Pappaert. Shown with *Rapture*, USA. Directed by Sara Whitely.

**THE OAK**
*Romania/France, 1992. Written and Directed by Lucian Pintilie, based on Ion Baiesu's novel* Balanta.
With Maia Morgenstern, Razvan Vasilescu, Victor Rebengiuc, Dorel Visan.

**LA SENTINELLE**
*France, 1992. Directed by Arnaud Desplechin.*
Written by Desplechin, Pascale Ferran, Noémie Lvovsky, and Emmanuel Salinger. With Salinger, Thibault de Montalembert, Jean-Louis Richard, Valérie Dréville.

**STONE**
*Russia, 1992. Directed by Aleksandr Sokurov.*
Written by Yuri Arabov. With Leonid Mozgovoy, Peter Alexandrov. Shown with *Definitely Sanctus*, Austria. Directed by Gerhard Ertl and Sabine Hiebler.

**THE STORY OF QUI JU**
*China, 1992. Directed by Zhang Yimou.*
Written by Liu Heng, based on Chen Yuan Bin's novel *The Wan Family's Lawsuit*. With Gong Li, Lei Lao Sheng, Liu Pei Qi, Ge Zhi Jun. Shown with *Square of Heroes, March 12, 1988*, Austria. Directed by Johannes Rosenberger.

**STRICTLY BALLROOM**
*Australia, 1992. Directed by Baz Luhrmann.*
Written by Andrew Bovell and Luhrmann, based on the play by Luhrmann and Craig Pearce. With Paul Mercurio, Tara Morice, Bill Hunter, Pat Thomson. Shown with *Mon Desir*, New Zealand. Directed by Nicky Marshall.

**"TAKING THE PULSE"** – three short works by master cinematic satirists:
- **Pets or Meat: The Return to Flint**, USA, 1992. Directed by Michael Moore. A chronicle of Moore's return to Flint, where he catches up with Deputy Fred, Bob Eubanks, and the Bunny Lady.
- **Seen from Elsewhere** (a sketch from *Montréal vu par...*), Canada, 1992. Directed by Denys Arcand. Written by Paule Baillargeon. With Domini Blythe, Rémy Girard, Baillargeon, Raoul Trujillo.
- **A Sense of History**, UK, 1992. Directed by Mike Leigh. Written by Jim Broadbent. With Broadbent.

**A TALE OF WINTER**
*France, 1992. Written and Directed by Eric Rohmer.*
With Charlotte Véry, Frédéric van den Driessche, Michel Voletti, Hervé Furic.

**LA VIE DE BOHÈME**
*Finland, 1992. Written and Directed by Aki Kaurismäki, based on Henri Murger's novel* Scènes de la Vie de Bohème.
With Matti Pellonpää, Evelyn Didi, André Wilms, Kari Väänänen. Shown with *The Addict*, USA. Directed by Matt Thomas Draper.

**ZEBRAHEAD**
*USA, 1992. Written and Directed by Anthony Drazan.*
With Michael Rapaport, N'Bushe Wright, DeShonn Castle, Ron Johnson. Shown with *Light Years Through the Heart: The Story of Fei & Miguel*, USA. Directed by Catherine Tse.

*Two Mules for Sister Sara* by Don Siegel

## Special Events
PRESENTED AT THE WALTER READE THEATER

**"Masters of Shadows: A Tribute to Gabriel Figueroa"** – selected films shot by the great cinematographer, organized by the Film Society in collaboration with the Mexican Film Institute and the UCLA Film Archive. Included: *Enamorada* (*Woman in Love*), Mexico, 1946, by Emilio Fernández; *The Fugitive*, USA, 1947, by John Ford; *Macario*, Mexico, 1959, by Roberto Gavaldón; *The Night of the Iguana*, USA, 1964, by John Huston; *The Pearl*, Mexico, 1945, by Fernández; "A Tribute to Don Gabriel Figueroa," with excerpts introduced by Mexican film specialist Michael Donnelly; *Two Mules for Sister Sara*, USA, 1970, by Don Siegel; *The White Rose*, Mexico, 1961, by Roberto Gavaldón; *The Young One*, Mexico, 1960, by Luis Buñuel.

**"Videorama: A Celebration of International Video Art"** – films from the USA unless otherwise noted.

**Program 1:** *Splash*, by Thomas Harris; *Juggling Gender*, by Tami Gold; *Rock Hudson's Home Movies*, by Mark Rappaport.

**Program 2:** *Damaged Visions*, 1991, by Shalom Gorewitz; *Neighbours*, Israel, by Dannah Nayblat; *'66 Was a Good Year for Tourism*, Israel, by Amit Goren.

**Program 3:** *Dog Baseball*, 1986, by William Wegman; *Dangerous Ideas: Todd Alcott*, by Skip Blumberg; *White Homeland Commando*, by Elizabeth LeCompte.

**Program 4:** *Tonbe/Leve*, by Patricia Benoit; *Haiti: Killing the Dream*, by Babeth, Katherine Kean, Hart Perry, and Rudi Stern.

**Program 5:** *Identity Crisis*, 1990, by Mindy Faber; *Black and White in Color*, UK, 1991, by Isaac Julien.

**Program 6:** *The Creeping Crimson*, 1987, by George Kuchar; *New York Conversations*, UK, 1990, by Vivienne Dick; *Les oeufs à la coque*, France, by Valerie Lalonde and Richard Leacock.

**Program 7:** *Teddy Dibble's Video Shorts*, 1991, by Teddy Dibble; *Long Distance Love*, Spain, by Franc Planas Guillot; *The Passing*, 1991, by Bill Viola.

**Program 8:** *Glass Jaw*, 1991, by Michael O'Reilly; *It Wasn't Love*, by Sadie Benning; *Doin' Time in Times Square*, 1991, by Charles Ahearn.

**Program 9:** *History and Memory*, 1991, by Rea Tajiri; *Palestinian Diaries*, 1991, by Tamouz Media.

**Program 10:** *Majorca-Fantasia*, 1991, by Nam June Paik, with Paul Garrin and Amy Greenfield; *The Nervous Thing*, Brazil, 1991, by Éder Santos; *TV Dante-Cantos 9-14*, UK, by Raúl Ruiz.

**Program 11:** *Visions of Light: The Art of Cinematography*. Directed by Arnold Glassman, Todd McCarthy, and Stuart Samuels. This documentary, shown in HDTV, was presented in association with the AFI and the Sony Corporation.

# 1993

SELECTION COMMITTEE: RICHARD PEÑA, CHAIRMAN, DAVID ANSEN, JOAN JULIET BUCK, WENDY KEYS, AND STUART KLAWANS.

THE 31ST NYFF POSTER ARTWORK WAS CREATED BY ©SHEILA METZNER.

### SHORT CUTS
*USA, 1993. Directed by Robert Altman.*

Written by Altman and Frank Barhydt, based on the writings of Raymond Carver. With Andie MacDowell, Bruce Davison, Jack Lemmon, Julianne Moore, Matthew Modine, Robert Downey Jr., Tim Robbins, Lily Tomlin, Frances McDormand, Lyle Lovett, Buck Henry. (Opening Night.) Note: It was quite a challenge to move this all-star cast from Alice Tully Hall to Avery Fisher Hall on Opening Night especially since Lyle Lovett was then married to Julia Roberts, who was the focus of the crowd and the paparazzi.

### THE PIANO
*France/Australia, 1992. Written and Directed by Jane Campion.*

With Holly Hunter, Harvey Keitel, Sam Neill, Anna Paquin. Shown with *The Perfect Woman*, USA. Directed by Illeana Douglas. (Closing Night.)

### AILEEN WUORNOS: THE SELLING OF A SERIAL KILLER ▶
*USA, 1993. Directed by Nick Broomfield.*

A documentary that explores the media circus surrounding the prostitute convicted of murdering seven men, and raises serious questions about the legality of Wuornos's trial. Shown with *Small Change*, UK. Directed by David Farr.

### "AVANT-GARDE VISIONS"
- **Dottie Gets Spanked**, USA, 1993. Directed by Todd Haynes.
- **Passage à l'acte**, Austria. Directed by Martin Arnold.
- **Poverties**, USA. Directed by Laurie Dunphy.

### BIRTHPLACE
*Poland, 1992. Directed by Paweł Łoziński.*

A documentary about the last days of a Polish-born American Jew's father during the Holocaust. Shown with *Libertas*, Yugoslavia. Directed by Zoran Jovanović. Also, *The Unproductives*, France. Directed by Pierre Isoard.

### BLUE
*UK, 1993. Written and Directed by Derek Jarman.*

With the voices John Quentin, Nigel Terry, Jarman, Tilda Swinton. Dying from AIDS, Jarman lays bare his personal state in a narration over a blue screen whose only images are those produced by your own retina: orange squares, flashes,

shadows. Shown with *Sleepy Haven*, Germany. Directed by Matthias Müller.

### BLUE (TROIS COULEURS: BLEU)
*France/Switzerland/Poland, 1993. Directed by Krzysztof Kieślowski.*

Written by Kieślowski and Krzysztof Piesiewicz, with Agnieszka Holland, Sławomir Idziak, and Edward Zebrowski. With Juliette Binoche, Benoît Régent, Florence Pernel, Charlotte Véry, Emmanuelle Riva. Shown with *Deraillement*, France/Norway. Directed by Unni Straume.

### THE BLUE KITE
*Hong Kong/China, 1993. Directed by Tian Zhuangzhuang.*

Written by Xiao Mao. With Yi Tian, Zhang Wenyao, Chen Xiaoman, Lu Liping.

### CALENDAR
*Canada/Germany/Armenia, 1993. Written and Directed by Atom Egoyan.*

With Arsinée Khanjian, Ashot Adamian, Egoyan.

### + MOVING IN (LE DÉMÉNAGEMENT)
*France, 1993. Written and Directed by Chantal Akerman.*

A Sami Frey monologue. Shown with *Just Desserts*, Australia, 1993. Directed by Monica Pellizzari.

### FAREWELL MY CONCUBINE
*Hong Kong/China, 1993. Directed by Chen Kaige.*

Written by Lilian Lee and Lu Wei, based on Lee's novel. With Leslie Cheung, Zhang Fengyi, Gong Li, Lu Qi.

### FIORILE
*Italy/France/Germany, 1992. Directed by Paolo and Vittorio Taviani.*

*Farewell My Concubine* by Chen Kaige

Written by Sandro Petraglia and the Tavianis. With Claudio Bigagli, Galatea Ranzi, Michael Vartan, Lino Capolicchio. Shown with *Pitchmaster 2000*, USA. Directed by Bill Allard.

## IT'S ALL TRUE: BASED ON AN UNFINISHED FILM BY ORSON WELLES
*Brazil/France/USA, 1993. Directed by Bill Krohn, Myron Meisel, and Richard Wilson. Original producer and director: Orson Welles.*

About the discovery of 314 cans of film in California, which turned out to be the remains of Welles's 1942 Brazilian project *It's All True*, one of the most legendary and controversial film ventures of all time. Shown with *Humboldt Street Family*, Brazil. Directed by Luciano Moura.

## NAKED ▲
*UK, 1993. Written and Directed by Mike Leigh.*

With David Thewlis, Lesley Sharp, Katrin Cartlidge, Greg Cruttwell, Claire Skinner, Peter Wight. Shown with *These Boots*, Finland. Directed by Aki Kaurismäki.

## THE NIGHT
*Syria/Lebanon/France, 1992. Directed by Mohamad Malas.*

Written by Malas and Oussma Mohamad. With Sabah Jazairi, Fares Al Helou, Omar Malas, Maher Sleibi.

## THE PUPPETMASTER
*Taiwan, 1993. Directed by Hou Hsiao-hsien.*

Written by Wu Nien-jen and Chu Tien-wen. With Cho Ju-wei, Cheng Kuei-chung, Lin Chung, Hung Liu.

## RAINING STONES
*UK, 1993. Directed by Ken Loach.*

Written by Jim Allen. With Bruce Jones, Julie Brown, Gemma Phoenix, Ricky Tomlinson. Shown with *The Darra Dogs,* Australia. Directed by Dennis Tupicoff.

## RUBY IN PARADISE
*USA, 1993. Written and Directed by Victor Nuñez.*

With Ashley Judd, Todd Field, Bentley Mitchum, Allison Dean. Shown with *Excursions to the Bridge of Friendship*, Australia. Directed by Christina Andreef.

## THE SCENT OF GREEN PAPAYA ▶
*Vietnam/France, 1993. Directed by Tran Anh Hung.*

Written by Tran Anh Hung with Patricia Petit. With Tran Nu Yen-Khe, Lu Man San, Truong Thi Loc, Nguyen Anh Hoa. Shown with *First Train*, Indonesia. Directed by Dicky Irawan.

## SHADES OF DOUBT (L'OMBRE DU DOUTE)
*France, 1993. Directed by Aline Issermann.*

Written by Issermann, with Martine Fadier-Nisse and Frédérique Gruyer. With Sandrine Blancke, Alain Bashung, Mireille Perrier, Josiane Balasko. Shown with *Grown Up*, USA. Directed by Joanna Priestly.

## THE SNAPPER
*UK, 1993. Directed by Stephen Frears.*

Written by Roddy Doyle, based on his novel. With Tina Kellegher, Colm Meaney, Ruth McCabe, Colm O'Byrne. Shown with *Dinner with Malibu*, France. Directed by Jon Carnoy.

## THE STORY OF A CHEAT
*France, 1936. Written and Directed by Sacha Guitry, based on his novel* Mémoires d'un tricheur.

With Guitry, Jacqueline Delubac, Marguerite Moreno, Rosine Deréan. (Retrospective.) Shown with *The Taste of Iron*, France. Directed by Rémi Bernard.

## TIM BURTON'S THE NIGHTMARE BEFORE CHRISTMAS
*USA, 1993. Directed by Henry Selick.*

With the voices of Chris Sarandon, Danny Elfman, Catherine O'Hara, Glenn Shadix. Shown with *Vincent*, USA, 1982. Directed by Tim Burton.

## TOTALLY F***ED UP
*USA, 1993. Written and Directed by Gregg Araki.*

With James Duval, Roko Belic, Susan Behshid, Jenee Gill. Shown with *Coffee and Cigarettes*, USA. Directed by Jim Jarmusch.

## VALLEY OF ABRAHAM aka ABRAHAM'S VALLEY
*Portugal/France/Switzerland, 1993. Written and Directed by Manoel de Oliveira, based on Agustina Bessa-Luís's novel* Vale Abraão.

With Leonor Silveira, Cecile Sanz de Alba, Luís Lima Barreto.

## THE WAR ROOM
*USA, 1993. Directed by Chris Hegedus and D.A. Pennebaker.*

A political documentary about Bill Clinton's presidential campaign. Shown with *Hoping for Better Times*, Switzerland. Directed by Jonas Raeber.

## WENDEMI (WENDEMI, L'ENFANT DU BON DIEU)
*Burkina Faso/France/Switzerland, 1993. Directed by S. Pierre Yameogo.*

Written by René Sintzel and Yameogo. With Sylvain Minoungou, Abdoulaye Komboudri, Sylvie Yameogo, Moussognouma Kouyate. Shown with *Untrue Stories*, Venezuela. Directed by Cezary Jaworski and John Petrizelli.

## THE WONDERFUL, HORRIBLE LIFE OF LENI RIEFENSTAHL
*Germany/Belgium/UK, 1993. Directed by Ray Müller.*

An exhaustive documentary in which the director grills Riefenstahl on her politics and gets responses that form a counterpoint to the film's extraordinary revelations.

*The Piano* by Jane Campion

## Special Events

**"L'Auteur complet: Sacha Guitry in Retrospect"** – selected films from 1915-1957, organized by the Film Society with the French Ministry for Foreign Affairs (Paris) and Interama Films (New York). Films shown: *Champs-Élysées*, 1938; *The Fabulous Destiny of Desiree Clary*, 1942; *Good Luck!*, 1935; *The Lame Devil*, 1948; *Let Us Dream*, 1936; *Pasteur*, 1935; *The Pearls of the Crown*, 1937; *Royal Affairs in Versailles*, 1954.

**"From the Dawn of Sound to Virtual Reality"** – an exhibit produced by AT&T for the International Video Arts Festival.

**"Video Visions"** – the Film Society's International Video Arts Festival:

**Program 1:** *Double Blind* (*No Sex Last Night*), France/USA, by Sophie Calle and Gregory Shephard; *Ex Memoriam*, France, by Bériou.

**Program 2:** *The Last Bolshevik*, France, by Chris Marker.

**Program 3:** *The Spirit of TV*, Brazil, by Vincent Carelli; *Saputi*, Canada, by Norm Cohn, Zacharias Kunuk, and Paulossie Qulitalik; *The Couple in the Cage: A Guatinaui Odyssey*, USA, by Coco Fusco and Paula Heredia.

**Program 4:** *Work in Progress*, USA, by Luis Valdovino; *No Rubber, No Way*, Brazil, by Sergio Goldenberg; *The Scavengers*, Brazil, by Eduardo Coutinho.

**Program 5:** "SA – Life I," Bosnia/Herzegovina. The faces behind the headlines of the war.

**Program 6:** "SA – Life II," Bosnia/Herzegovina. The living that goes on despite the war.

**Program 7:** "Change the Style: Pop Videos Reinvent 'Black Film,'" USA. Armond White presents a selection of music videos.

**Program 8:** *Ernst Will's Picture Book*, Australia, by Peter Callas; *The Magnum Eye*, USA, 18 portraits by Magnum agency photographers; *The Color Line: Racism in America*, USA, by Steve Zehentner.

**Program 9:** *Voices of the Morning*, USA, by Meena Nanji; *Escape from China*, China, by Iris Kung.

**Program 10:** "Meeting Points: A Tribute to Juan Downey" – a program of Downey's videotapes, including *The Laughing Alligator*, 1979, *Information Withheld*, 1983, and *Hard Times and Culture: Part One, Vienna 'fin-de-sièclé*, 1990.

**Program 11:** *Shiver*, USA, by Abigail Child; *Greetings from Out Here*, USA, by Ellen Spiro; *Finally Destroy Us*, *Darling Child*, and *Nomads*, USA, by Tom Kalin.

**Program 12:** "Who, What, When, How? Writing About Video" – a panel discussion.

**Program 13:** *Delirium*, USA, by Mindy Faber; *Joan Sees Stars*, USA, by Joan Braderman.

**Program 14:** *Bleeding Heart*, Mexico, by Ximena Cuevas; *Inversion of Solitude: A Fictional Documentary*, USA, by Terri Hanlon; *Heaven, Earth and Hell*, USA/Canada, by Thomas Allen Harris.

# 1994

SELECTION COMMITTEE: RICHARD PEÑA, CHAIRMAN, DAVID ANSEN, WENDY KEYS, STUART KLAWANS, AND JONATHAN ROSENBAUM.

THE 32ND NYFF POSTER ARTWORK WAS CREATED BY ©WILLIAM COPLEY.

## PULP FICTION

*USA, 1994. Directed by Quentin Tarantino.*

Written by Tarantino, based on stories by Roger Avary and Tarantino. With John Travolta, Samuel L. Jackson, Uma Thurman, Harvey Keitel, Tim Roth, Amanda Plummer, Maria de Medeiros, Ving Rhames, Eric Stoltz, Rosanna Arquette, Christopher Walken, Bruce Willis, Tarantino. (Opening Night.) Note: The ON performance of this film was interrupted when a member of the audience fainted during the hypodermic scene. Shown with *Michelle's Third Novel*, Australia. Directed by Karryn de Cinque.

## BULLETS OVER BROADWAY ▶

*USA, 1994. Directed by Woody Allen.*

Written by Allen and Douglas McGrath. With Jim Broadbent, John Cusack, Harvey Fierstein, Chazz Palminteri, Mary-Louise Parker, Rob Reiner, Jennifer Tilly, Dianne Wiest. (Centerpiece.)

## HOOP DREAMS

*USA, 1994. Directed by Peter Gilbert, Steve James, and Frederick Marx.*

A documentary made over five years about two children of the Chicago ghetto who dream of becoming professional basketball players. (Closing Night.) Note: The audiences' standing ovation for this film surpassed just about anything that had come before it.

## AMATEUR

*USA/France, 1994. Written and Directed by Hal Hartley.*

With Isabelle Huppert, Martin Donovan, Elina Löwensohn, Damian Young. Shown with *Suspicious*, USA. Directed by David Koepp.

## "AVANT-GARDE VISIONS"

• **The Cloud Door**, Germany/India, 1994. Directed by Mani Kaul.

• **Whispering Pages**, Russia/Germany, 1993. Directed by Aleksandr Sokurov.

Shown with *Roig*, Spain. Directed by Teresa de Pelegri.

## CARO DIARIO

*Italy/France, 1994. Written and Directed by Nanni Moretti.*

With (as themselves) Moretti, Jennifer Beals, Alexandre Rockwell. A personal visual diary in three parts. Shown with *Attempt at an Opening*, France, 1988. Directed by Luc Moullet.

**CHUNGKING EXPRESS ▶**
*Hong Kong, 1994. Written and Directed by Wong Kar Wai.*

With Brigitte Lin, Takeshi Kaneshiro, Tony Leung Chiu-wai, Faye Wong. Shown with *Eating Out*, Norway. Directed by Pål Sletaune.

**COLD WATER (L'EAU FROIDE)**
*France, 1994. Written and Directed by Olivier Assayas.*

With Virginie Ledoyen, Cyprien Fouquet, László Szabó, Jean-Pierre Darroussin. Shown with *Jump*, USA. Directed by Melissa Painter.

**A CONFUCIAN CONFUSION**
*Taiwan, 1994. Written and Directed by Edward Yang.*

With Chen Xiangqi, Ni Shu-chun, Wang Weiming, Wang Zongzheng.

**CRUMB ▼**
*USA, 1994. Directed by Terry Zwigoff.*

With Robert Crumb and his family. An in-depth look at underground comic-book artist R. Crumb. Shown with *Shut Up Jerk!*, USA. Directed by Craig McGillivray. Also, *Spot-Check*, Austria. Directed by Gerhard Ertl and Sabine Hiebler.

**ED WOOD**
*USA, 1994. Directed by Tim Burton.*

Written by Scott Alexander and Larry Karaszewski, based on Rudolph Grey's book *Nightmare of Ecstasy: The Life and Art of Edward D. Wood, Jr.* With Johnny Depp, Martin Landau, Bill Murray, Sarah Jessica Parker, Patricia Arquette.

**EXOTICA ▶**
*Canada, 1994. Written and Directed by Atom Egoyan.*

With Bruce Greenwood, Mia Kirshner, Don McKellar, Arsinée Khanjian, Elias Koteas. Shown with *All the Kind People*, UK. Directed by Erlend Eriksson.

**LADYBIRD LADYBIRD**
*UK, 1994. Directed by Ken Loach.*

Written by Rona Munro. With Crissy Rock, Vladimir Vega, Sandie Lavelle, Mauricio Venegas. Shown with *Cross Examination*, USA. Directed by Lori Hiris.

**MARTHA**
*West Germany, 1973. Written and Directed by Rainer Werner Fassbinder, based on Cornell Woolrich's novel.*

With Margit Carstensen, Karlheinz Böhm, Gisela Fackeldey, Adrian Hoven, Ingrid Caven. (Retrospective.) Shown with *Mrs. Matisse*, USA. Directed by Debra Solomon.

**POSTCARDS FROM AMERICA**
*USA, 1994. Written and Directed by Steve McLean, based on the writings of David Wojnarowicz.*

With Jim Lyons, Michael Tighe, Olmo Tighe, Michael Imperioli. Shown with *The Salesman and Other Adventures*, USA. Directed by Hannah Weyer.

**RED (TROIS COULEURS: ROUGE)**
*Switzerland/France/Poland, 1994. Directed by Krzysztof Kieślowski.*

Written by Kieślowski and Krzysztof Piesiewicz. With Irène Jacob, Jean-Louis Trintignant, Frédérique Feder, Jean-Pierre Lorit. Shown with *Bête de Scène*, France. Directed by Bernard Nissille.

**THE RED LOTUS SOCIETY**
*Taiwan, 1994. Written and Directed by Stan Lai.*

With Ying Zhaode, Chen Wenming, Na Weixun, Li Tongcun.

**SÁTÁNTANGÓ**
*Hungary/Germany/Switzerland, 1993. Directed by Béla Tarr.*

Written by Lázló Krasznahorkai and Tarr, with Agnes Hranitzky, based on Krasznahorkai's novel. With Mihály Vig, Dr. Putyi Horváth, Erika Bók, Peter Berling.

**SEE HOW THEY FALL**
*France, 1994. Directed by Jacques Audiard.*

Written by Audiard and Alain Le Henry, based on Teri White's novel *Triangle*. With Jean-Louis Trintignant, Jean Yanne, Mathieu Kassovitz, Bulle Ogier. Shown with *A Pair of Boots*, USA. Directed by John Cassavetes. A Civil War tale, made for *The Lloyd Bridges Show*, with John Marley, Royal Dano, Seymour Cassel, Beau Bridges.

### THE SILENCES OF THE PALACE
*Tunisia/France, 1994. Directed by Moufida Tlatli.*

Written by Tlatli, adaptation and dialogue by Nouri Bouzid. With Amel Hedhili, Hend Sabri, Najia Ouerghi, Ghalia Lacroix.

### STRAWBERRY AND CHOCOLATE
*Cuba/Mexico/Spain, 1993. Directed by Tomás Gutiérrez Alea and Juan Carlos Tabío.*

Written by Senel Paz. With Jorge Perugorría, Vladimir Cruz, Mirta Ibarra, Francisco Gattorno. Shown with *Catalina*, USA. Directed by Tommy O'Haver.

### THEREMIN: AN ELECTRONIC ODYSSEY
*USA, 1993. Directed by Steven M. Martin.*

With (as themselves) Leon Theremin, Clara Rockmore, Robert Moog, Brian Wilson. A documentary tracing the strange career of the world's first electronic musical instrument, and the even stranger career of its inventor. Shown with *Carnival*, USA. Directed by Ondrej Rudavsky.

### THROUGH THE OLIVE TREES
*Iran, 1994. Written and Directed by Abbas Kiarostami.*

With Hossein Rezai, Mohamad Ali Keshavarz, Farhad Kheradmand, Zarifeh Shiva.

### TO LIVE
*China 1994. Directed by Zhang Yimou.*

Written by Yu Hua and Lu Wei, based on Yu Hua's novel. With Ge You, Gong Li, Niu Ben, Guo Tao.

### TO THE STARRY ISLAND
*South Korea, 1994. Directed by Park Kwang-su.*

Written by Im Chul-woo, Lee Chang-dong, and Park Kwang-su, based on Im Chul-woo's novel. With Ahn Sung-ki, Moon Sung-kuen, Shm Hae-jin, Ahn So-young. Shown with *Home*, Israel. Directed by David Ofek.

### THE TROUBLES WE'VE SEEN (VEILLÉES D'ARMES)
*France, 1994. Written and Directed by Marcel Ophuls.*

With (as themselves) Philippe Noiret, Jon Duncanson, Sergio Appollonio, Colonel Hans Heckner. Focusing on the war in Bosnia, an examination of how the style, methods, and attitudes of war correspondents affect the information received by the public.

### WILD REEDS
*France, 1994. Directed by André Téchiné.*

Written by Olivier Massart, Gilles Taurand, and Téchiné. With Élodie Bouchez, Gaël Morel, Stéphane Rideau, Frédéric Gorny. Shown with *Crawl*, USA. Directed by Lara Shapiro.

## Special Events

PRESENTED AT THE WALTER READE THEATER

**"The Heady Comedy of Jacques Tati"** – films shown: *Jour de féte*, 1948; *Mon oncle*, 1958; *Mr. Hulot's Holiday*, 1953; *Parade*, 1973; *Playtime*, 1968; *Traffic*, 1971.

**"The Third New York Video Festival"** – included: *The Children Play Russian*, France/Switzerland/Russia, by Jean-Luc Godard, shown with *NYC 3/94*, USA, by Hal Hartley and *Cyclic*, Holland, by Pieter Thoenes; "Exploring the Digital Frontier: Bob Stein, High-Tech Explorer" – a presentation; *Former East/Former West*, USA, by Shelly Silver, preceded by *The Castle?*, Germany, by Calvez Bilbo and Vivien Laurent; *Free Fall*, USA/Germany, by Douglas Ferguson and Gea Kalthegener, followed by *End Credits*, USA, by Ken Kobland; *The Hair Opera*, Japan, by Obitani Yuri, preceded by *Pretty Boy*, USA, by Joe Gibbons, *No Sex*, France, by Eric Coignoux, and *Hair*, USA, by Maria Elena Venuto; *I Have Graduated*, China, by Structure, Wave, Youth and Cinema Experimental Group, preceded by *Knee Play 1*, Germany, 1988, by Claus Blume and *In Memory of L. Brezhnev*, Poland, by Jozef Robakowski; *Interrotron Stories*, USA, by Errol Morris; *In the Land of the Oranges*, France, directed by German Bobe; *Humpty Dumpty*, Germany, by Veit-Lup, and *The Tower of the Astro-Cyclops*, USA, by George Kuchar; *Moscow X*, USA, by Ken Kobland, preceded by *Blind Grace*, USA, by Adam Cohen; "New Voices, New Visions" – three works on CD-ROM: *The Dream of Time*, by Hsin-Chien Huang, *An Anecdoted Archive of the Cold War*, by George Legrady, and *Sound Toy*, by Todd Robbins; "The Philosophical Toy: Pixelvision Triumphant": *His Master's Voice*, USA, by Joe Gibbons, *Strange Weather*, USA, by Peggy Ahwesh and Margie Strosser, and *Orion Climbs*, USA, by Michael O'Reilly; "TurboVideo: High Definition Television": *Graffiti War*, USA, by Marc Levin, *Painted Memories, Spider's Garden*, USA/Japan, by Kit Fitzgerald, *On the Far Side of Twilight*, Japan, by Kohei Ando, and *Exterior Night*, USA, by Mark Rappaport; *Uh-Oh!*, USA, by Julie Zando, preceded by *Head, Kiss My Royal Irish Ass, GracefulPhatSheba*, and *Practisse*, USA, by Cheryl Donegan; *Girlpower*, USA, by Sadie Benning, *Tomboyshik*, USA, by Sandi Dobowski, and *Mad About the*

*Mon Oncle* by Jacques Tati

*Boy*, USA, by Lisel Banker and Alix Umen; *United States of Guns*, Sweden, by Folke Rydén, preceded by *Top Gun*, Latvia, by Artis Dzerye, *Wings for Fan*, Italy, by Alberto Noti, *Armed Man*, USA, by Stuart Bender and Angelo Funicelli, and *State of Emergency: Inside the Los Angeles Police Department*, USA, by Elizabeth Canner and Julia Meltzer; "West of MTV: Armond White on Music Video" – a presentation; *X 1/2: The Legacy of Malcolm*, USA, by Not Channel Zero, preceded by *I Know You Know*, USA, by Jerome Thomas, *All in the Family*, USA, by Thomas Allen Harris, and *Drive-by Shoot!*, USA, by Portia Cobb.

THE 33RD NEW YORK FILM FESTIVAL
PRESENTED BY THE FILM SOCIETY OF LINCOLN CENTER

SEPTEMBER 29 – OCTOBER 15, 1995  ALICE TULLY HALL

# 1995

SELECTION COMMITTEE: RICHARD PEÑA, CHAIRMAN, DAVID ANSEN, WENDY KEYS, STUART KLAWANS, AND JONATHAN ROSENBAUM. SHORT FILM ADVISORS: GAVIN SMITH AND GENEVIEVE VILLAFLOR.

THE 33RD NYFF POSTER ARTWORK WAS CREATED BY DIANE ARBUS. ©THE ESTATE OF DIANE ARBUS, LLC.

### SHANGHAI TRIAD
*China/France, 1995. Directed by Zhang Yimou.*

Written by Bi Feiyu, based on Li Xiao's novel. With Gong Li, Li Baotian, Li Xuejian, Sun Chun. Shown with *The First Screening*, France, 1895. Directed by the Lumière Brothers. A celebration of the birth of cinema. (Opening Night.)

### STRANGE DAYS ▶
*USA, 1995. Directed by Kathryn Bigelow.*

Written by James Cameron and Jay Cocks, based on a story by Cameron. With Ralph Fiennes, Angela Bassett, Juliette Lewis, Tom Sizemore. (Centerpiece.)

### CARRINGTON
*UK, 1995. Written and Directed by Christopher Hampton, based on Michael Holroyd's book* Lytton Strachey.

With Emma Thompson, Jonathan Pryce, Steven Waddington, Samuel West. Shown with *Surprise!*, Germany. Directed by Veit Helmer. (Closing Night.)

### "AVANT-GARDE VISIONS"
• **Alpsee**, Germany, 1994. Directed by Matthias Müller.

• **River Colors**, Germany, 1994. Directed by Christoph Janetzko.

• **Zone**, Japan, 1995. Directed by Takashi Ito.

Shown with *Warren*, USA. Directed by Jeffrey Noyes Scher.

### THE CELLULOID CLOSET
*USA, 1995. Directed by Rob Epstein and Jeffrey Friedman.*

Story by Epstein, Friedman, and Sharon Wood, narration written by Armistead Maupin. Narrated by Lily Tomlin. A documentary inspired by Vito Russo's study of Hollywood's portrayal of homosexuality in the movies. Shown with *Alkali, Iowa*, USA. Directed by Mark Christopher.

### CINEMA OF UNEASE
*New Zealand/UK, 1995. Written and Directed by Sam Neill and Judy Rymer.*

Neill's autobiographical tour through New Zealand cinema.

### + CITIZEN LANGLOIS
*France, 1995. Directed by Edgardo Cozarinsky.*

A portrait of Langlois, the founder of the Cinémathèque Française. Shown with *Evidence*, Italy. Directed by Angela Melitopulos and Godfrey Reggio.

*The Flower of My Secret* by Pedro Almodóvar

### THE CONVENT
*Portugal/France, 1995. Written and Directed by Manoel de Oliveira, based on an original idea by Agustina Bessa-Luís.*
With Catherine Deneuve, John Malkovich, Luís Miguel Cintra, Leonor Silveira. Shown with *Odilon Redon*, Canada. Directed by Guy Maddin.

### CYCLO
*France/Vietnam, 1995. Directed by Tran Anh Hung.*
Written by Tran, with dialogue by Tran and Nguyen Trung Bing. With Le Van Loc, Tony Leung Chiu-Wai, Tran Nu Yen-Khe. Shown with *Supermarket*, USA. Directed by David Byrne.

### DEAD PRESIDENTS
*USA, 1995. Directed by Albert and Allen Hughes.*
Written by Michael Henry Brown. With Larenz Tate, Keith David, Chris Tucker, Freddy Rodriguez.

### "DISCOVERING MAX LINDER" – a selection of seven short films
*France, 1912-16. Directed by, written by, and starring Max Linder.*
*Arranged Marriage*, 1916; *A Disturbing Night*, 1912; *The Little Novel*, 1912; *Max Afraid of the Water*, 1912; *Max and His Mother-in-Law*, 1915; *Max and the Bag*, 1916; *Max Creates a Fashion*, 1912. Presented by Linder's daughter, Maud, with piano accompaniment by Jean-Marie Sénia. (Retrospective.)

### FLAMENCO
*Spain, 1995. Directed by Carlos Saura.*
With Paco de Lucía, Manolo Sanlúcar, Lole y Manuel, Joaquín Cortés.

### FLIRT
*USA/Germany/Japan, 1995. Written and Directed by Hal Hartley.*
With Bill Sage, Parker Posey, Martin Donovan, Dwight Ewell, Geno Lechner, Peter Fitz, Miho Nikaido, Toshizo Fujiwara, Chikako Hara, Michael Imperioli. Shown with *The Beast*, USA. Directed by Ric Montgomery.

### THE FLOWER OF MY SECRET
*Spain, 1995. Written and Directed by Pedro Almodóvar.*
With Marisa Paredes, Juan Echanove, Imanol Arias, Carmen Elias, Rossy de Palma. Shown with *Altair*, USA. Directed by Lewis Klahr.

### "FORTUNE SMILES" – two comedies about remarkable reversals of fortune:
• **Le Franc**, Senegal/Switzerland, 1994. Written and Directed by Djibril Diop Mambety. With Dieye Ma Dieye, Aminata Fall, Demba Bâ.

• **Augustin**, France, 1995. Written and Directed by Anne Fontaine. With Jean-Chrétien Sibertin-Blanc, Stéphanie Zhang, Guy Casabonne, Nora Habib. Shown with *When It Rains*, USA. Directed by Charles Burnett.

### FROM THE JOURNALS OF JEAN SEBERG
*USA, 1995. Written and Directed by Mark Rappaport.*
With Mary Beth Hurt. Shown with *Joy Street*, USA. Directed by Suzan Pitt. Also, *A Thousand Years of Cinema*, Austria. Directed by Kurt Kren.

### THE GATE OF HEAVENLY PEACE
*USA, 1995. Directed by Richard Gordon and Carma Hinton.*
Written by Geremie Barmé and John Crowley. With Wuer Kaixi, Wang Dan, Chai Ling, Hou Dejian. A documentary about the 1989 occupation of Beijing's Tiananmen Square by students and workers.

### GEORGIA
*France/USA, 1995. Directed by Ulu Grosbard.*
Written by Barbara Turner.
With Jennifer Jason Leigh, Mare Winningham, Ted Levine, Max Perlich. Shown with *Depth Solitude*, Norway. Directed by Thomas Lien and Joachim Solum.

### GOOD MEN, GOOD WOMEN
*Taiwan/Japan, 1995. Directed by Hou Hsiao-hsien.*
Written by Chu Tien-wen, based on a play by Chiang Bi-yu and Lan Bo-chow. With Annie Shizuka Inoh, Lim Giong, Jack Kao, Vicky Wei. Shown with *Revolver*, Sweden. Directed by Stig Bergquist, Martti Ekstrand, Jonas Odell, and Lars Ohlson.

**GUIMBA**
*Mali/Burkina Faso/France, 1995. Written and Directed by Cheikh Oumar Sissoko.*

With Falaba Issa Traoré, Balla Moussa Keita, Habib Dembélé, Lamine Diallo. Shown with *Coloured*, UK. Directed by Barrie White.

**LA HAINE ▲**
*France, 1995. Written and Directed by Mathieu Kassovitz.*

With Vincent Cassel, Hubert Koundé, Saïd Taghmaoui, Karim Belkhadra. Shown with *Flying Geraldo*, Brazil. Directed by Bruno Vianna.

**KICKING AND SCREAMING**
*USA, 1995. Written and Directed by Noah Baumbach, based on a story by Baumbach and Oliver Berkman.*

With Josh Hamilton, Eric Stoltz, Elliot Gould, Olivia d'Abo, Cara Buono, Chris Eigeman, Parker Posey. Shown with *White Autumn Chrysanthemum*, USA. Directed by Patrick Ruane. Also, *Swinger*, Australia. Directed by Gregor Jordan.

**LAMERICA**
*Italy/France, 1994. Directed by Gianni Amelio.*

Written by Amelio, Andrea Porporati, and Alessandro Sermoneta. With Enrico Lo Verso, Michele Placido, Carmelo Di Mazzarelli, Piro Milkani. Shown with *Bathing Boxes*, Australia. Directed by Ann Turner.

**◄ LAND AND FREEDOM**
*UK, 1995. Directed by Ken Loach.*

Written by Jim Allen. With Ian Hart, Rosana Pastor, Icíar Bollaín, Tom Gilroy. Shown with *Mausoleum*, Russia. Directed by Alexei Khanyutin.

**THE NEON BIBLE**
*UK, 1995. Written and Directed by Terence Davies, based on John Kennedy Toole's novel.*

With Gena Rowlands, Diana Scarwid, Denis Leary, Jacob Tierney. Shown with *Polio Water*, USA. Directed by Caroline Kava.

**"THE ROSSELLINI WAR TRILOGY"**
- **Open City (Roma, città aperta)**, Italy, 1945. Written by Sergio Amidei and Alberto Consiglio, based on an adaptation by Amidei, Federico Fellini, and Rossellini, with dialogue by Fellini and S. Midi. With Anna Magnani, Aldo Fabrizi, Marcello Pagliero, Harry Feist, Nando Bruno.

- **Paisan (Paisà)**, Italy, 1946. Written by Federico Fellini and Rossellini, based on ideas by Sergio Amidei, Fellini, Alfred Hayes, Klauss Mann, Marcello Pagliero, Rossellini. With Carmela Sazio, Robert Van Loon, Dots M. Johnson, Alfonsino.

- **Germany Year Zero**, Italy, 1949. Written by Rossellini, Max Kolpet, and Carlo Lizzani, based on a story by Rossellini. With Edmund Moeshke, Franz Krüger, Barbara Hintz. (Retrospective Tribute.)

**SIXTEEN-OH-SIXTY (16060)**
*Brazil, 1995. Directed by Vinicius Mainardi.*

Written by Diogo and Mainardi. With Antônio Calloni, Maitê Proença, Marcélia Cartaxo, Carlos Meceni. Shown with *Red Card*, Brazil. Directed by Lais Bodanzky.

*Germany Year Zero* by Roberto Rossellini

**THE SON OF GASCOGNE**
*France, 1995. Directed by Pascal Aubier.*
Written by Aubier and Patrick Modiano. With Jean-Claude Dreyfus, Grégoire Colin, Dinara Droukarova, Nino Lapiachvili. Shown with *Sheller Shares Her Secret*, UK. Directed by Sarah Turner.

**THE WHITE BALLOON**
*Iran, 1995. Directed by Jafar Panahi.*
Written by Abbas Kiarostami, based on an original idea by Panahi and Parviz Shahbazi. With Aida Mohammadkhani, Mohsen Kafili, Fereshteh Sadr Orfani, Anna Bourkowska. Shown with *The Silence Between*, USA. Directed by Jacqueline Turnure.

# Special Events
PRESENTED AT THE WALTER READE THEATER

**"Celebrating Grigori Kozintsev"** – a presentation of rare works by the great Soviet director. Films shown: *Alone*, 1931. With a score by Dmitri Shostakovich; *The Devil's Wheel*, 1926 (silent fragment), with *The Overcoat*, 1926 (with piano accompaniment); *Don Quixote*, 1957; *Hamlet*, 1965; *King Lear*, 1970. With a score by Shostakovich; *The New Babylon*, 1929; *The Youth of Maxim*, 1935, with *Young Fritz*, 1942 (fragment).

**"The Fourth New York Video Festival"** – curated by Graham Leggat, Marian Masone, Richard Peña, and Gavin Smith, and presented with the support of the Association of Independent Video and Filmmakers. Included: Meta Media – two evenings devoted to the creative aspects of digital interactive media, presented in collaboration with the American Museum of the Moving Image and curated by Carl Goodman of AMMI (from USA unless otherwise noted):

1. "Liquid Libraries" – works on CD-ROM: *Our Secret Century*, by Richard Prelinger; *Public Shelter*, by Jayne Loader; *Visionary of Theater: Robert Wilson*, by Paul Kaiser.

2. "Digital Fictions" – *Psychic Detective*, by John Sanborn; *ScruTiny in the Great Round*, by Tennessee Rice Dixon and Jim Gasperini; *Bad Day on the Midway*, by Michael Nash.

3. *At Sundance*, by Michael Almereyda and Amy Hobby.

4. "Hidden Histories" – *Jane: An Abortion Service*, by Kate Kirtz and Nell Lundy; *Can't Help Lovin' Dat Man*, by Alix Umen; *Obsessive Becoming*, by Daniel Reeves.

5. *Stairs 1 Geneva*, Switzerland, by Peter Greenaway; *Iris*, by Tracy Leipold and Stephen Vitiello.

6. "Matthew Barney – After and Before" – *Cremaster 4* and *Cremaster 1*.

7. "Culture Shear" – *Raza*, by Adolfo Dávila; *Some Questions for 28 Kisses, Asian Studs Nightmare*, and *Game of Death*, by Kip Fulbeck; *A.K.A. Don Bonus*, by Spencer Nakasako and Sokly "Don Bonus" Nye.

8. "Signal to Noise: TV Inside Out" – *Watching TV Watching Us* and *Remote Control*, made up of segments by various independent videomakers.

9. "Journeys to the Interior" – *Buried in Light*, by Jem Cohen, preceded by *The Imagined, the Longed-for, the Conquered, and the Sublime*, by Roddy Bogawa; *Deserts*, by Bill Viola; *Lovely Desert*, by G.M. Auletta.

10. "Romanek Fiction" – music videos by Mark Romanek presented by Armond White.

11. "Live on Tape: Performance Video" – *Rehearsal*, by Cheryl Donegan; *No Accident*, USA/Germany, by Michel Negroponte; *German Song*, by Sadie Benning; *Salt Transfer Cycle*, by Michael Joo; *Barbie's Audition*, by Joe Gibbons; *Topless Cellist*, by Nam June Paik and Howard Weinberg.

12. "Fractured Selves" – *Next Life*, by Florence Bonneville; *My Failure to Assimilate*, by Cecilia Dougherty; *Kore, Operculum*, and *Aletheia*, by Tran T. Kim-Trang.

13. "Pranks, Subversions, and Interventions" – *Neglectosphere* and *Touch Tone*, by Eric Saks; *Dance of Death*, by Ron Rochleau; *Spiraling and Spoiling*, by G.M Auletta; *Mudflaps, Husband*, and *The Quick and the Dead Open*, by Deke Weaver; *How I Spent My Summer Vacation*, by Kate Wrobel.

14. "Reality: It's What's for Dinner" – *The Free Space of the Commodity*, by Les Leveque; *Signal to Noise Part II: TV Reality?*, by Cara Mertes; *Spin*, by Brian Springer.

# 1996

SELECTION COMMITTEE: RICHARD PEÑA, CHAIRMAN, DAVID ANSEN, WENDY KEYS, JONATHAN ROSENBAUM, AND ROBERT SKLAR.
SHORT FILM ADVISORS: GAVIN SMITH AND GENEVIEVE VILLAFLOR.

THE 34TH NYFF POSTER ARTWORK WAS CREATED BY ©JUAN GATTI.

### SECRETS & LIES
*France/UK, 1996. Written and Directed by Mike Leigh.*

With Brenda Blethyn, Timothy Spall, Phyllis Logan, Marianne Jean-Baptiste, Elizabeth Berrington. Shown with *Pieces of the Moon*, UK. Directed by Kirkham Jackson. (Opening Night.)

### THIEVES (LES VOLEURS)
*France, 1996. Directed by André Téchiné.*

Written by Gilles Taurand and Téchiné, in collaboration with Michel Alexandre and Pascal Bonitzer. With Catherine Deneuve, Daniel Auteuil, Laurence Côte, Benoît Magimel. (Centerpiece.)

### THE PEOPLE VS. LARRY FLYNT
*USA, 1996. Directed by Miloš Forman.*

Written by Scott Alexander and Larry Karaszewski. With Woody Harrelson, Courtney Love, Edward Norton, Donna Hanover (then Mrs. Rudy Giuliani), Brett Harrelson. Shown with *Tracks (Binari)*, Italy. Directed by Carlotta Cerquetti. (Closing Night.) Note: After the event at the NYFF, Larry Flynt flew Forman and some of the actors to Prague on his private jet to show the film to Václav Havel.

### BEYOND THE CLOUDS ▶
*France/Italy/Germany, 1996. Directed by Michelangelo Antonioni.*

Written by Antonioni, Tonino Guerra, and Wim Wenders, based on Antonioni's book *That Bowling Alley on the Tiber: Tales of a Director*. With Inés Sastre, Kim Rossi-Stuart, Sophie Marceau, John Malkovich, Fanny Ardant, Jeanne Moreau, Marcello Mastroianni. Antonioni's first film since 1982. Shown with *The Grateful Dead,* UK. Directed by Paul McCartney. A reworking of Linda Eastman McCartney's photographs.

### BREAKING THE WAVES
*Denmark, 1996. Written and Directed by Lars von Trier.*

With Emily Watson, Stellan Skarsgård, Katrin Cartlidge, Jean-Marc Barr.

### "CULTURE SHOCK" – two films about nationalism, culture, and their discontents:
- •Frantz Fanon: Black Skin, White Mask, UK, 1996. Directed by Isaac Julien. Written by Julien and Mark Nash. A meditation of the Afro-Caribbean psychiatrist and political activist.

- •Umm Kulthum: A Voice Like Egypt, USA, 1996. Written and Directed by Michal Goldman, based on Virginia Danielson's book *The Voice of Egypt*. Narrated by Omar Sharif. A portrait of the Egyptian singer.

### EMIGRATION, N.Y. (DIE GESCHICHTE EINER VERTREIBUNG)
*Austria, 1995. Written and Directed by Egon Humer.*

With Rosa Ully Axelrod, Ann Branden, Susanne Edelman, Frank Eisinger, Amos Vogel. Twelve Viennese Jews recount their lives as children in Austria, as emigrants, as New Yorkers.

### FIRE
*Canada/India, 1996. Written and Directed by Deepa Mehta.*

With Shabana Azmi, Nandita Das, Kulbhushan Kharbanda, Jaaved Jaaferi. Shown with *The Secret Story*, USA. Directed by Janie Geiser.

### GABBEH
*Iran/France, 1996. Written and Directed by Mohsen Makhmalbaf.*

With Shaghayegh Djodat, Hossein Moharami, Roghieh Moharami, Abbas Sayahi. Shown with *The Mail*, Latvia. Directed by Laila Pakalnina.

### LE GARÇU
*France, 1995. Directed by Maurice Pialat.*

Written by Sylvie Danton and Pialat. With Gérard Depardieu, Géraldine Pailhas, Antoine Pialat, Dominque Rocheteau. Shown with *So Many Things to Consider*, USA. Directed by Sandye Wilson.

### GOODBYE SOUTH, GOODBYE
*Japan/Taiwan, 1996. Directed by Hou Hsiao-hsien.*

Written by Chu Tien-wen, based on a story by Jack Kao and King Jieh-wen. With Kao, Hsu Kuie-ying, Lim Giong, Annie

Shizuka Inoh. Shown with *Summer Cannibals*, USA. Directed by Robert Frank. A portrait of Patti Smith and her band.

### ILLTOWN
*USA, 1996. Written and Directed by Nick Gomez.*

With Michael Rapaport, Lili Taylor, Adam Trese, Kevin Corrigan. Shown with *15th February*, UK. Directed by Tim Webb.

### IRMA VEP ▶
*France, 1996. Written and Directed by Olivier Assayas.*

With Maggie Cheung, Jean-Pierre Léaud, Nathalie Richard, Antoine Basler, Natalie Boutefeu, Bulle Ogier. Shown with *Tuning the Sleeping Machine*, USA. Directed by David Sherman.

### LILIES
*Canada, 1996. Directed by John Greyson.*

Written by Michel Marc Bouchard, based on his play *Le Feluettes ou La Répétition d'un drame romantique.* With Brent Carver, Marcel Sabourin, Aubert Pallascio, Jason Cadieux. Shown with *Amor*, Italy. Directed by Robert Beavers.

### MAHJONG
*Taiwan, 1996. Written and Directed by Edward Yang.*

With Virginie Ledoyen, Congsheng Tang, Yulun Ke, Zhen Zhang.

### MANDELA
*USA, 1996. Directed by Angus Gibson and Jo Menell.*

Produced by Jonathan Demme. A portrait of the South African leader.

### MY SEX LIFE… OR HOW I GOT INTO AN ARGUMENT
*France, 1996. Directed by Arnaud Desplechin.*

Written by Emmanuel Bourdieu and Desplechin. With Mathieu Amalric, Emmanuelle Devos, Emmanuel Salinger, Marianne Denicourt, Chiara Mastroianni, Jeanne Balibar, Denis Podalydès.

### NOBODY'S BUSINESS
*USA, 1996. Directed by Alan Berliner.*

A study of Berliner's family history, focusing on his reclusive father.

### + TROFIM
*Russia, 1995. Directed by Alexei Balabanov.*

A fantasy that leaps from the dawn of cinema to today.

### LA PROMESSE
*Belgium/France/Tunisia/Luxembourg, 1996. Written and Directed by Jean-Pierre and Luc Dardenne.*

With Jérémie Renier, Olivier Gourmet, Assita Ouedraogo, Rasmané Ouedraogo. Shown with *Lulu*, USA. Directed by Lewis Klahr.

### SALUT COUSIN!
*France/Algeria, 1996. Directed by Merzak Allouache.*

Written by Allouache and Caroline Thivel. With Gad Elmaleh, Mess Hattou, Magaly Berdy, Ann-Gisel Glass. Shown with *The Day "Close Up" Premiered*, Italy. Directed by Nanni Moretti.

### A SELF-MADE HERO
*France, 1996. Directed by Jacques Audiard.*

Written by Audiard and Alain Le Henry, based on Jean-François Deniau's novel. Shown with *Bad Animal*, USA. Directed by Doug Aitkin.

### SLING BLADE
*USA, 1996. Written and Directed by Billy Bob Thornton.*

With Thornton, Dwight Yoakam, J.T. Walsh, John Ritter, Robert Duvall.

### SUBURBIA
*USA, 1996. Directed by Richard Linklater.*

Written by Eric Bogosian, based on his play. With Jayce Bartok, Amie Carey, Nicky Katt, Steve Zahn, Parker Posey.

### SUZANNE FARRELL: ELUSIVE MUSE
*USA, 1996. Directed by Anne Belle and Deborah Dickson.*

With (as themselves) Suzanne Farrell, Jacques d'Amboise, Maria Calegari, Arthur Mitchell. An intimate portrait of the ballerina.

### ◀ TEMPTRESS MOON
*China, 1996. Directed by Chen Kaige.*

Written by Shu Kei, based on a story by Chen Kaige and Wang Anyi. With Leslie Cheung, Gong Li, Kevin Lin, He Saifei.

### THREE LIVES AND ONLY ONE DEATH
*France/Portugal, 1995. Directed by Raúl Ruiz.*

Written by Pascal Bonitzer and Ruiz. With Marcello Mastroianni, Anna Galiena, Marisa Paredes, Melvil Poupaud, Chiara Mastroianni.

### UNDERGROUND
*France/Germany, 1995. Directed by Emir Kusturica.*

Written by Dušan Kovačević and Kusturica, based on Kovačević's play. With Miki Manojlović, Lazar Ristovski, Mirjana Joković, Slavko Štimac.

*Lilies* by John Greyson

## Special Events

**"Ritwik Ghatak's Unknown Masterworks"** – India, 1925-1976. Films shown: *The Citizen*, 1953; *The Cloud-Capped Star* aka *Hidden Star*, 1960; *E-Flat*, 1961; *Pathetic Fallacy*, 1958; *Reason, Debate and a Story*, 1974; *A River Called Titash*, 1972; *The Runaway*, 1959; *Subarnarekha*, 1965.

**VERTIGO** ▶
*USA, 1958. Directed by Alfred Hitchcock.*
Written by Alec Coppel and Maxwell Anderson (uncredited), based on Pierre Boileau and Thomas Narcejac's novel *D'entre les morts*. With James Stewart, Kim Novak, Barbara Bel Geddes, Tom Helmore. Shown at the Ziegfeld Theatre; a benefit for the Walter Reade programming fund.

**THE ROLLING STONES ROCK AND ROLL CIRCUS**
*UK, 1968-96. Directed by Michael Lindsay-Hogg.*
The world premiere of this film, which had never been released. It was shot over two days and featured performances by Jethro Tull, the Who, Marianne Faithfull, the Dirty Mac Band, Yoko Ono, the Rolling Stones. There were nine sold-out screenings at the Walter Reade and all audience members received a poncho.

# 1997

SELECTION COMMITTEE: RICHARD PEÑA, CHAIRMAN, DAVID ANSEN, WENDY KEYS, JONATHAN ROSENBAUM, AND ROBERT SKLAR. SHORT FILM ADVISORS: GAVIN SMITH AND GENEVIEVE VILLAFLOR.

THE 35TH NYFF POSTER ARTWORK WAS CREATED BY ©LARRY RIVERS.

### THE ICE STORM ▲
*USA, 1997. Directed by Ang Lee.*

Written by James Schamus, based on Rick Moody's novel. With Kevin Kline, Sigourney Weaver, Joan Allen, Jamey Sheridan, Christina Ricci, Elijah Wood, Adam Hann-Byrd, Tobey Maguire. Shown with *Knitwits*, USA. Directed by Vincent Cafarelli and Candy Kugel. With the voice of Joan Rivers. (Opening Night.)

### THE SWEET HEREAFTER ▶
*Canada, 1997. Written and Directed by Atom Egoyan, based on Russell Banks's novel.*

With Ian Holm, Sarah Polley, Bruce Greenwood, Tom McCamus. Shown with *Today*, Finland. Directed by Eija-Liisa Ahtila. (Centerpiece.)

### LIVE FLESH
*Spain, 1997. Written and Directed by Pedro Almodóvar, based on Ruth Rendell's novel.*

With Liberto Rabal, Javier Bardem, Francesca Neri, Angela Molina. Shown with *The Bloody Olive*, Belgium. Directed by Vincent Bal. (Closing Night.)

### THE APOSTLE
*USA, 1997. Written and Directed by Robert Duvall.*

With Duvall, Farrah Fawcett, Miranda Richardson, Todd Allen, Billy Bob Thornton, June Carter Cash.

### BOOGIE NIGHTS
*USA, 1997. Written and Directed by Paul Thomas Anderson.*

With Mark Wahlberg, Julianne Moore, Burt Reynolds, Don Cheadle, John C. Reilly, William H. Macy.

### DEEP CRIMSON
*Mexico/France, 1996. Directed by Arturo Ripstein.*

Written by Paz Alicia Garciadiego. With Regina Orozco, Daniel Giménez Cacho, Marisa Paredes, Patricia Reyes Spíndola.

### DESTINY
*Egypt/France, 1997. Directed by Youssef Chahine.*

Written by Chahine and Khaled Youssef. With Nour El Cherif, Laila Eloui, Mahmoud Hemeida, Safia El Emary.

### FALLEN ANGELS
*Hong Kong, 1995. Written and Directed by Wong Kar Wai.*

With Leon Lai Ming, Takashi Kaneshiro, Charlie Yeung, Michelle Reis, Karen Mok. Shown with *The Rocking Horse Winner*, USA. Directed by Michael Almereyda.

### FAST, CHEAP & OUT OF CONTROL
*USA, 1997. Directed by Errol Morris.*

Interviews with a wild animal trainer, a topiary gardener, a mole-rat specialist, and a robot scientist. Shown with *Whiplash, USA*. Directed by Warren Sonbert.

### FIREWORKS (HANA-BI)
*Japan, 1997. Written and Directed by Takeshi Kitano.*

With Beat Takeshi, Kayoko Kishimoto, Ren Osugi, Susumu Terajima. Shown with *Balloons, Streamers*, USA. Directed by Josh Sternfeld.

### FROM TODAY UNTIL TOMORROW (DU JOUR AU LENDEMAIN)
*France/Germany, 1996. Directed by Jean-Marie Straub and Danièle Huillet.*

With Christine Whittlesey, Richard Salter, Claudia Barainsky, Ryszard Karczykowski. Arnold Schönberg's 1929 comic opera about married life. Shown with *The Man Who Couldn't Open Doors*, UK. Directed by Paul Arden.

### HAPPY TOGETHER
*Hong Kong, 1997. Written and Directed by Wong Kar Wai.*

With Tony Leung Chiu-wai, Leslie Cheung, Chang Chen. Shown with *The Hidden*, Sweden. Directed by Carina Reich and Bogdan Szyber.

### KISS OR KILL
*Australia, 1997. Written and Directed by Bill Bennett.*

With Frances O'Connor, Matt Day, Chris Haywood, Barry Otto. Shown with *Where's the Money, Ronnie?*, UK. Directed by Shane Meadows.

### KITCHEN
*Hong Kong, 1977. Written and Directed by Yim Ho, based on Banana Yoshimoto's novel.*

With Jordan Chan, Yasuko Tomita, Law Kar Ying, Karen Mok.

### LOVE AND DEATH ON LONG ISLAND
*UK/Canada, 1997. Written and Directed by Richard Kwietniowski, based on Gilbert Adair's novel.*

With John Hurt, Jason Priestley, Fiona Loewi, Sheila Hancock, Harvey Atkin.

### MARCELLO MASTROIANNI: I REMEMBER
*Italy, 1997. Directed by Anna Maria Tatò.*

Mastroianni's cinematic memoir. Shown in Avery Fisher Hall.

*Taste of Cherry* by Abbas Kiarostami

**MARTIN (HACHE)**
*Argentina/Spain, 1997. Directed by Adolfo Aristarain.*
Written by Aristarain and Kathy Saavedra. With Federico Luppi, Juan Diego Botto, Eusebio Poncela, Cecilia Roth.

**MA VIE EN ROSE (MY LIFE IN PINK)**
*Belgium/France/UK, 1997. Directed by Alain Berliner.*
Written by Berliner and Chris Vander Stappen. With Michèle Laroque, Jean-Philippe Écoffey, Hélène Vincent, Georges Du Fresne, Daniel Hanssens. Shown with *Breeze*, USA. Directed by Barbara Sanon.

**MOTHER AND SON**
*Germany/Russia, 1997. Directed by Aleksandr Sokurov.*
Written by Yuri Arabov. With Gudrun Geyer, Alexei Ananishnov. Shown with *Insight*, UK. Directed by Georg Misch.

**POST COITUM, ANIMAL TRISTE**
*France, 1997. Directed by Brigitte Roüan.*
Written by Santiago Amigorena, Philippe Le Guay, Jean-Louis Richard, Roüan, and Guy Zilberstein. With Roüan, Patrick Chesnais, Boris Terral, Nils Tavernier. Shown with *Majorettes in Space*, France. Directed by David Fourier.

**PUBLIC HOUSING**
*USA, 1997. Directed by Frederick Wiseman.*
An examination of life in Chicago's Ida B. Wells public-housing development.

**THE SARAGOSSA MANUSCRIPT**
*Poland, 1965. Directed by Wojciech Has.*
Written by Tadeusz Kwiatkowski, based on Jan Potocki's novel. With Iga Cembrzyńska, Zbigniew Cybulski, Aleksander Fogiel, Joanna Jędryka. (Retrospective—restored with the help of Martin Scorsese.)

**TASTE OF CHERRY**
*Iran, 1997. Written and Directed by Abbas Kiarostami.*
With Homayoun Ershadi, Abdolrahman Bagheri, Afshin Khorshid Bakhtiari, Safar Ali Moradi. Shown with *The House Is Black*, Iran, 1962. Directed by Forough Farrokhzad. A documentary about a leper colony by the great Persian poet.

**TELLING LIES IN AMERICA**
*USA, 1997. Directed by Guy Ferland.*
Written by Joe Eszterhas. With Kevin Bacon, Brad Renfro, Maximilian Schell, Calista Flockhart, Paul Dooley.

**LA VIE DE JÉSUS**
*France, 1997. Written and Directed by Bruno Dumont.*
With David Douche, Marjorie Cottreel, Geneviève Cottreel, Kader Chaatouf. Shown with *Sans Titre*, France. Directed by Leos Carax.

**VOYAGE TO THE BEGINNING OF THE WORLD**
*Portugal/France, 1997. Written and Directed by Manoel de Oliveira.*
With Marcello Mastroianni, Jean-Yves Gautier, Leonor Silveira, Diogo Dória. Shown with *Sea Space*, USA. Directed by William Farley.

**WASHINGTON SQUARE**
*USA, 1997. Directed by Agnieszka Holland.*
Written by Carol Doyle, based on Henry James's novel. With Jennifer Jason Leigh, Albert Finney, Maggie Smith, Ben Chaplin, Judith Ivey.

*Fireworks* by Takeshi Kitano

## Special Events

PRESENTED AT THE WALTER READE THEATER

**THE KINGDOM, PART 2**
*Denmark, 1997. Directed by Morten Arnfred and Lars von Trier.*
Written by von Trier and Niels Vørsel. With Ernst-Hugo Järegård, Kirsten Rolffes, Holger Juul Hansen, Søren Pilmark, Ghita Nørby, Jens Okking, Udo Kier.

**"Logic of Dream, Logic of Labyrinth: The Fantastic Journeys of Wojciech Jerzy Has"** – a retrospective of one of the great Polish directors. Films shown: *Codes,* 1966; *The Doll,* 1969; *Farewells,* 1958; *The Hourglass Sanatorium* aka *The Sandglass,* 1973; *How to Be Loved,* 1963; *The Memoirs of a Sinner,* 1986; *The Noose,* 1958; *The Tribulations of Balthazar Kober,* 1988; *An Uneventful Story,* 1982; *Write and Fight,* 1985.

**ORPHANS OF THE STORM**
*USA, 1921. Directed by D.W. Griffith.*
Written by Marquis de Trolignac, based on Eugene Cormon and Adolphe Philippe Dennery's play *The Two Orphans*. With Lillian Gish, Dorothy Gish, Joseph Schildkraut, Catherine Emmett, Morgan Wallace. Shown in Avery Fisher Hall, with live accompaniment by the Brooklyn Philharmonic Orchestra.

**"Views from the Avant-Garde"** – films from the USA unless otherwise noted.

**Program 1:** "Stirrings, Still" – *Commingled Containers,* by Stan Brakhage; *Triste,* by Nathaniel Dorsky; *The Five Bad Elements,* by Mark LaPore; *Retrospectroscope,* by Kerry Laitala; *Pensao Globo,* Germany, by Matthias Müller; *Secure the Shadow,* by Kerry Laitala; *The Idea of North,* by Rebecca Baron; *The Present,* by Robert Frank; *Flight,* by Greta Snider.

**Program 2:** "The World Happens Twice" – *Gladly Given,* by Jerome Hiler; *Pony Glass,* by Lewis Klahr; *Happy End,* Austria, by Peter Tscherkassky; *If You Stand With Your Back to the Slowing Speed of Light in Water,* by Julie Murray; *Yggdrasil Whose Roots Are Stars in the Human Mind,* by Stan Brakhage; *...or lost,* by Leslie Thornton; *Prost,* Austria, by Gerhard Ertl and Sabine Hiebler; *Life Wastes Andy Hardy,* Austria, by Martin Arnold; *Shulie,* by Elisabeth Subrin.

**Program 3:** Robert Beavers: *Efpsychi, Windseed,* and *The Stoas,* all Greece/USA.

**Program 4:** Gregory Markopoulos: *Eniaios* cycle 1, Greece/USA.

**YEAR OF THE HORSE**
*USA, 1997. Directed by Jim Jarmusch.*
A concert movie featuring Neil Young and his band Crazy Horse on their 1996 tour.

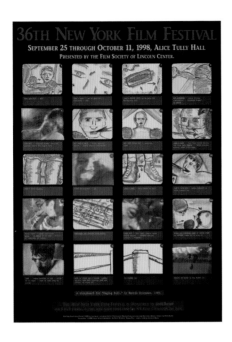

# 1998

SELECTION COMMITTEE: RICHARD PEÑA, CHAIRMAN, DAVE KEHR, WENDY KEYS, JOHN POWERS, AND ROBERT SKLAR. SHORT FILM ADVISORS: GAVIN SMITH AND GENEVIEVE VILLAFLOR.

THE 36TH NYFF POSTER ARTWORK WAS CREATED BY MARTIN SCORSESE. DESIGNED BY DEBORAH LYONS, ©THE FILM SOCIETY OF LINCOLN CENTER; *RAGING BULL*: ©1980, UNITED ARTISTS CORP.

## CELEBRITY
*USA, 1998. Written and Directed by Woody Allen.*

With Hank Azaria, Kenneth Branagh, Judy Davis, Leonardo DiCaprio, Melanie Griffith, Famke Janssen, Michael Lerner, Joe Mantegna, Bebe Neuwirth, Winona Ryder, Charlize Theron. Shown with *Yours*, USA. Directed by Jeff Scher. (Opening Night.)

## BLACK CAT, WHITE CAT
*Yugoslavia/Germany/France, 1998. Directed by Emir Kusturica.*

Written by Kusturica and Gordan Mihić. With Bajram Severdzan, Florijan Ajdini, Jasar Destani, Adnan Bekir. (Centerpiece.)

## THE DREAMLIFE OF ANGELS ▶
*France, 1998. Directed by Erick Zonca.*

Written by Roger Bohbot and Zonca, with the collaboration of Virginie Wagon. With Elodie Bouchez, Natacha Régnier, Grégoire Colin, Jo Prestia, Patrick Mercado. Shown with *Fetch*, Australia. Directed by Lynn-Maree Danzey. (Closing Night.)

## THE APPLE
*Iran/France, 1998. Directed by Samira Makhmalbaf.*

Written by Mohsen Makhmalbaf. With Massoumeh Naderi, Zahra Naderi, Ghorbanali Naderi, Azizeh Mohamadi, Zahra Saghrisaz. Shown with *Gasman*, UK. Directed by Lynn Ramsay.

## AUTUMN TALE
*France, 1998. Written and Directed by Eric Rohmer.*

With Marie Rivière, Béatrice Romand, Alain Libolt, Didier Sandre. Shown with *Theo, Are You There?*, France, 1998. Directed by Julie Lipinski.

## THE CELEBRATION (FESTEN)
*Denmark, 1998. Directed by Thomas Vinterberg.*

Written by Vinterberg and Mogens Rukov, based on an idea by Vinterberg. With Ulrich Thomsen, Henning Moritzen, Thomas Bo Larsen, Paprika Steen. Shown with *Let's Be Friends!*, France. Directed by Thomas Bardinet.

## DR. AKAGI
*Japan, 1998. Directed by Shohei Imamura.*

Written by Imamura and Daisuke Tengan, based on Ango Sakaguchi's novel *Dr. Liver*. With Akira Emoto, Kumiko Aso, Jyuro Kara, Masnori Sera.

## FLOWERS OF SHANGHAI
*Taiwan, 1998. Directed by Hou Hsiao-hsien.*

Written by Chu Tien-wen, based on Han Ziyun's novel *Hai Shang Hua*. With Tony Leung Chiu-wai, Michiko Hada, Lee Yu-ming, Carina Lau Ka-ling.

## THE GENERAL
*Ireland, 1998. Written and Directed by John Boorman.*

With Brendan Gleeson, Adrian Dunbar, Sean McGinley, Maria Doyle Kennedy.

## GODS AND MONSTERS
*USA, 1998. Written and Directed by Bill Condon, based on Christopher Bram's novel* Father of Frankenstein.

With Ian McKellen, Brendan Fraser, Lynn Redgrave, Lolita Davidovich. Shown with *My Ex*, USA. Directed by Steve Salinaro.

## HAPPINESS
*USA, 1998. Written and Directed by Todd Solondz.*

With Jane Adams, Elizabeth Ashley, Dylan Baker, Lara Flynn Boyle, Ben Gazzara, Jared Harris, Philip Seymour Hoffman, Louise Lasser, Jon Lovitz, Camryn Manheim.

## THE INHERITORS
*Austria, 1998. Written and Directed by Stefan Ruzowitzky.*

With Simon Schwarz, Sophie Rois, Lars Rudolph, Julia Gschnitzer.

## I STAND ALONE (SEUL CONTRE TOUS)
*France, 1998. Written and Directed by Gaspar Noé.*

With Philippe Nahon, Blandine Lenoir, Frankye Pain, Martine Audrain. Shown with *Horseshoe*, UK. Directed by David Lodge.

**THE JOYLESS STREET**
*Germany, 1925. Directed by G.W. Pabst.*

Written by Willy Haas, based on Hugo Bettauer's novel. With Greta Garbo, Valeska Gert, Einar Hanson, Werner Krauss, Asta Nielsen, Marlene Dietrich (an extra). Presented with German intertitles and simultaneous English translation. Piano accompaniment by pianist/composer Aljosha Zimmermann. (Retrospective.)

**KHRUSTALYOV, MY CAR!**
*Russia/France, 1998. Directed by Aleksei Guerman.*

Written by Svetlana Karmalita and Guerman. With Yuri Tsourilo, Nina Rouslanova, Yuri Yarvet, Michael Dementiev, A.Bachirov.

**LATE AUGUST, EARLY SEPTEMBER**
*France, 1998. Written and Directed by Olivier Assayas.*

With Mathieu Amalric, Virginie Ledoyen, François Cluzet, Jeanne Balibar. Shown with *Day to Day*, Brazil. Directed by Flavio Frederico, Alex Descas, Nathalie Richard.

**MY NAME IS JOE**
*UK, 1998. Directed by Ken Loach.*

Written by Paul Laverty. With Peter Mullan, Louise Goodall, David McKay, Gary Lewis. Shown with *Keep in a Dry Place and Away from Children*, UK. Directed by the Bolex Brothers.

◀ **POINT BLANK**
*USA, 1967. Directed by John Boorman.*

Written by Alexander Jacobs and David and Rafe Newhouse, based on Richard Stark's novel *The Hunter*. With Lee Marvin, Angie Dickinson, John Vernon, Keenan Wynn, Carroll O'Connor. (Retrospective.) Shown with *The Sickroom*, Canada. Directed by Serge Marcotte.

**RIVER OF GOLD**
*Portugal, 1998. Directed by Paulo Rocha.*

Written by Rocha and Cláudia Tomaz, based on an idea by Rocha. With Isabel Ruth, Lima Duarte, Joana Bárcia, António Capelo, Filipe Cochofel. Shown with *Shaman*, USA. Directed by Ondrej Rudavsky.

**RUSHMORE**
*USA, 1998. Directed by Wes Anderson.*

Written by Anderson and Owen Wilson. With Jason Schwartzman, Olivia Williams, Brian Cox, Seymour Cassel, Connie Nielsen, Bill Murray. Shown with *Interview*, France. Directed by Xavier Giannoli.

**SAME OLD SONG (ON CONNAÎT LA CHANSON)**
*France, 1998. Directed by Alain Resnais.*

Written by Jean-Pierre Bacri and Agnès Jaoui. With Pierre Arditi, Sabine Azéma, André Dussollier, Jaoui, Bacri.

**SLAM**
*USA, 1998. Directed by Marc Levin.*

Written by Levin, Bonz Malone, Sonja Sohn, Richard Stratton, and Saul Williams, based on a story by Levin and Stratton. With Williams, Sohn, Malone, Lawrence Wilson.

**"2000 SEEN BY..." – two of the 10 films commissioned by French television set on December 31, 1999:**

- **Life on Earth**, France/Mauritania/Mali, 1998. Written and Directed by Abderrahmane Sissako. With Abderrahmane Sissako, Nana Baby, Mohamed Sissako, Bourama Coulibaly.

- **The Book of Life**, USA/France, 1998. Written and Directed by Hal Hartley. With Martin Donovan, P.J. Harvey, Thomas Jay Ryan, Dave Simonds.

*Black Cat, White Cat* by Emir Kusturica

**VELVET GOLDMINE**
*USA/UK, 1998. Written and Directed by Todd Haynes, based on a story by Haynes and James Lyons.*

With Ewan McGregor, Jonathan Rhys Meyers, Toni Collette, Christian Bale, Eddie Izzard, Emily Woof. Shown with *Tangerine Dream*, Australia. Directed by Keri Light.

**YOU LAUGH (TU RIDI)**
*Italy, 1998. Written and Directed by Paolo and Vittorio Taviani, loosely based on stories by Luigi Pirandello.*

With Antonio Albanese, Sabrina Ferilli, Turi Ferro, Lello Arena, Steve Spedicato, Orio Scaduto, Ludovico Calderera. Shown with *I'm on Fire*, USA. Directed by Ryan Rowe.

# Special Events

PRESENTED AT THE WALTER READE THEATER

## IN THE PRESENCE OF A CLOWN
*Sweden, 1997. Written and Directed by Ingmar Bergman.*
With Börje Ahlstedt, Marie Richardson, Erland Josephson, Pernilla August.

## STRIKE
*USSR, 1924. Directed by Sergei M. Eisenstein.*
Written by Eisenstein and Grigory Alexandrov. With Alexandrov, Aleksandr Antonov, Yduif Glizer, Mikhail Gomorov. With live accompaniment by the Alloy Orchestra. (Retrospective.)

**"Views from the Avant-Garde"** – curated by Mark McElhatten and Gavin Smith.

**Program 1:** *Julio en Chapala*, by Bruce Baillie; *Glass: Memories of Water #25*, by Leighton Pierce; *Variations*, by Nathaniel Dorsky; *Arrival (1997A)*, by Steve Polta; *Korridor*, Austria, by Dietmar Brehm; *Alone: Life Wastes Andy Hardy*, by Martin Arnold.

**Program 2:** *Immur Zu*, by Janie Geiser; *Intrigue*, by Jim Jennings; *Nocturne*, by Peggy Ahwesh; *An W + B*, Austria, by Kurt Kren; *Noema*, by Scott Stark; *Wandelt*, The Netherlands, by R.G.A. Gerlach; *Emily Died*, by Anne Robertson; *19 Scenes Relating to a Trip to Japan*, by Konrad Steiner.

**Program 3:** *Ontic Antics Starring Laurel and Hardy*, by Ken Jacobs; *One*, by Fred Worden.

**Program 4:** "Arthur Lipsett Retrospective" – *21-87*, 1964; *Free Fall*, 1964; *A Trip Down Memory Lane*, 1965; *Fluxes*, 1968; *N-Zone*, 1968; *Very Nice, Very Nice*, 1961.

**"Youssef Chahine: Egyptian Auteur"** – films shown: *Alexandria Again and Forever*, 1989; *Alexandria…Why?*, 1978; *Cairo Station*, 1958, shown with *Cairo As Seen by Youssef Chahine*, 1991; *The Choice*, 1970; *Destiny*, 1997 (a film that *Variety* called "the most courageous frontal attack on Islamic fundamentalism to come out of the Arab cinema to date." There were 22 screenings of this film at the NYFF); *An Egyptian Story*, 1982; *It's You My Love*, 1957; *The Land*, 1969; *Once Upon a Time the Nile*, 1968-70; *The Return of the Prodigal Son*, 1978; *Saladin*, 1963; *Sky of Hell*, 1954; *The Sparrow*, 1973.

*Strike* by Sergei M. Eisenstein

# 1999

SELECTION COMMITTEE: RICHARD PEÑA, CHAIRMAN, DAVE KEHR, WENDY KEYS, JOHN POWERS, AND ROBERT SKLAR. SHORT FILM ADVISORS: GAVIN SMITH AND GENEVIEVE VILLAFLOR. SILENT FILM ADVISOR: SAYRE MAXFIELD.

THE 37TH NYFF POSTER ARTWORK WAS CREATED BY ©IVAN CHERMAYEFF.

## ALL ABOUT MY MOTHER
*Spain, 1999. Written and Directed by Pedro Almodóvar.*

With Cecilia Roth, Marisa Paredes, Penélope Cruz, Antonia San Juan, Candela Peña, Rosa María Sardá. (Opening Night.)

## TOPSY-TURVY
*UK, 1999. Written and Directed by Mike Leigh.*

With Jim Broadbent, Allan Corduner, Timothy Spall, Lesley Manville. (Centerpiece.)

## FELICIA'S JOURNEY
*UK/Canada, 1999. Written and Directed by Atom Egoyan, based on William Trevor's novel.*

With Bob Hoskins, Arsinée Khanjian, Elaine Cassidy, Sheila Reid. Shown with *Hero*, UK. Directed by John Mustafa. (Closing Night.)

## BEAU TRAVAIL
*France, 1999. Directed by Claire Denis.*

Written by Denis and Jean-Pol Fargeau, inspired by Herman Melville's *Billy Budd*. With Denis Lavant, Michel Subor, Grégoire Colin. Shown with *Cousin*, Australia. Directed by Adam Benjamin Elliot.

## BEING JOHN MALKOVICH
*USA, 1999. Directed by Spike Jonze.*

Written by Charlie Kaufman. With John Cusack, Cameron Diaz, Catherine Keener, John Malkovich, Orson Bean, Mary Kay Place. Shown with *Little Echo Lost*, Australia. Directed by Armagan Ballantyne.

## BOYS DON'T CRY ▲
*USA, 1999. Directed by Kimberly Peirce.*

Written by Andy Bienen and Peirce. With Hilary Swank, Chloë Sevigny, Peter Sarsgaard, Brendan Sexton III.

## ◀ THE CARRIERS ARE WAITING (LE CONVOYEURS ATTENDENT)
*Belgium/France, 1999. Directed by Benoît Mariage.*

Written by Mariage, with the collaboration of Emmanuelle Bada and Jean-Luc Seigle. With Benoît Poelvoorde, Morgane Simon, Bouli Lanners, Dominique Baeyens.

## THE COLOR OF PARADISE
*Iran, 1999. Written and Directed by Majid Majidi.*

With Hossein Mahjub, Salime Feizi, Mohsen Ramezani, Elham Sharifi, Farahnaz Safari. Shown with *Even the Wind*, France/Senegal. Directed by Laurence Attali.

## DOGMA
*USA, 1999. Written and Directed by Kevin Smith.*

With Ben Affleck, Matt Damon, Linda Fiorentino, Salma Hayek, Jason Lee, Alan Rickman, Chris Rock, Janeane Garofalo, George Carlin, Jason Mewes, Smith.

## THE EDGE OF THE WORLD
*UK, 1937. Written and Directed by Michael Powell.*

With John Laurie, Belle Chrystall, Eric Berry, Kitty Kirwan, Finlay Currie. (Retrospective.) Shown with *Closing Time*, Hungary. Directed by Bálint Kenyeres.

## HOLY SMOKE
*Australia, 1999. Directed by Jane Campion.*

Written by Anna and Jane Campion. With Kate Winslet, Harvey Keitel, Julie Hamilton, Tim Robertson.

**JUHA**

*Finland, 1999. Written and Directed by Aki Kaurismäki, based on Juhani Ano's novel.*

With Sakari Kuosmanen, Kati Outinen, André Wilms, Elina Salo. Shown with *La comtesse de Castiglione*, UK. Directed by David Lodge.

**JULIEN DONKEY-BOY**

*USA, 1999. Written and Directed by Harmony Korine.*

With Ewen Bremner, Chloë Sevigny, Werner Herzog, Evan Neumann.

**THE LETTER (LA LETTRE)**

*France/Portugal, 1999. Written and Directed by Manoel de Oliveira, inspired by Madame de La Fayette's* La Princesse de Clèves.

With Chiara Mastroianni, Pedro Abrunhosa, Antoine Chappey, Leonor Silveira. Shown with *September 5:10PM*, USA. Directed by Mitch McCabe.

**LICENSE TO LIVE**

*Japan, 1999. Written and Directed by Kiyoshi Kurosawa.*

With Hidetoshi Nishijima, Shun Sugata, Lily, Kumiko Asou, Koji Yakusho.

**MOBUTU, KING OF ZAÏRE**

*Belgium, 1999. Directed by Thierry Michel.*

Narrated by Simon Shrimpton Smith. A portrait of Mobutu's rise and fall.

**THE OTHER**

*Egypt/France, 1999. Directed by Youssef Chahine.*

Written by Chahine and Khaled Youssef. With Nabila Ebeid, Mahmoud Hemeida, Hanane Tork, Hani Salama. Shown with *Darwin's Evolutionary Stakes*, Australia. Directed by Andrew Horne.

**POLA X**

*France, 1999. Directed by Leos Carax.*

Written by Carax, Jean-Pol Fargeau, and Lauren Sedofsky, based on Herman Melville's *Pierre or the Ambiguities*. With Guillaume Depardieu, Katerina Golubeva, Catherine Deneuve, Delphine Chuillot, Sharunas Bartas, Laurent Lucas.

**PRINCESS MONONOKE**

*Japan, 1997. Directed by Hayao Miyazaki.*

Written by Miyazaki, with English adaptation by Neil Gaiman. With the voices of Billy Crudup, Claire Danes, Minnie Driver, Billy Bob Thornton, Gillian Anderson, Keith David. Shown in Avery Fisher Hall.

**PRIPYAT**

*Austria, 1999. Directed by Nikolaus Geyrhalter.*

Written by Geyrhalter and Wolfgang Widerhofer. Interviews with "returnees" to Chernobyl, 10 years after the nuclear accident. Shown with *Andares in the Time of War*, UK/Colombia. Directed by Alejandra Jiménez López.

**RIEN SUR ROBERT**

*France, 1999. Written and Directed by Pascal Bonitzer.*

With Fabrice Luchini, Sandrine Kiberlain, Valentina Cervi, Michel Piccoli, Bernadette Lafont. Shown with *Time Flies*, USA. Directed by Robert Breer.

**ROSETTA**

*Belgium, 1999. Written and Directed by Jean-Pierre and Luc Dardenne.*

With Émilie Dequenne, Fabrizio Rongione, Anne Yernaux, Olivier Gourmet. Shown with *End of the Century*, Germany/Argentina. Directed by Maike Höhne.

**SET ME FREE (EMPORTE-MOI)**

*Canada/Switzerland, 1999. Directed by Léa Pool.*

Written by Pool, with the collaboration of Nancy Huston and Monique H. Messier. With Karine Vanasse, Alexandre Mérineau, Pascale Bussières, Miki Manojlović. Shown with *2 ÷ 3*, USA. Directed by Richard Press.

**SICILY (SICILIA!)**

*France/Italy, 1999. Written and Directed by Jean-Marie Straub and Danièle Huillet, loosely based on Elio Vittorini's novel* Conversazione in Sicilia.

With Gianni Buscarino, Vittorio Vigneri, Angela Nugara. Shown with *Machorka-Muff*, West Germany, 1963. Directed by Jean-Marie Straub.

**TIME REGAINED**

*France, 1999. Directed by Raúl Ruiz.*

Written by Ruiz and Gilles Taurand, based on Marcel Proust's novel. With Catherine Deneuve, Emmanuelle Béart, Vincent Perez, John Malkovich, Marie-France Pisier, Pascal Greggory, Chiara Mastroianni, Marcello Mazzarella, Arielle Dombasie, Elsa Zylberstein, Melvil Poupaud.

**THE WOMAN CHASER**

*USA, 1999. Written and Directed by Robinson Devor, based on Charles Willeford's novel.*

With Patrick Warburton, Eugene Roche, Ron Morgan, Emily Newman. Shown with *hITCH*, USA. Directed by Bradley Rust Gray.

*Princess Mononoke* by Hayao Miyazaki

*The Color of Paradise* by Majid Majidi

# Special Events
PRESENTED AT THE WALTER READE THEATER

**"Pietro Germi: The Latin Loner"** – a retrospective of one of the greatest and most underrated Italian directors. Included: *Alfredo, Alfredo*, 1976; *The Birds, the Bees and the Italians*, 1965; *The Brigand of Tacca del Lupo*, 1952; Conference: Pietro Germi and the Italian Cinema, moderated by Richard Peña; *Divorce Italian Style*, 1961; *The Facts of Murder*, 1959; *Four Ways Out (La città si difende)*, 1951; *In the Name of the Law*, 1948; *My Friends*, 1975; *The Railroad Man*, 1956; *Seduced and Abandoned*, 1963; *The Straw Man*, 1958; *The Way of Hope*, 1950.

## UNDERGROUND
*France/Germany, 1995. Directed by Emir Kusturica.* Written by Dušan Kovačević and Kusturica, based on Kovačević's play. With Miki Manojlović, Lazar Ristovski, Mirjana Joković, Slavko Štimac. The original, full-length television version (312 minutes).

## A VISITOR FROM THE LIVING
*France, 1997. Directed by Claude Lanzmann.* A 1979 interview with Maurice Rossel, during the filming of *Shoah*.

## THE MAN WHO LAUGHS
*USA, 1928. Directed by Paul Leni.* Written by J. Grubb Alexander, based on Victor Hugo's novel. With Conrad Veidt, Mary Philbin, Julius Molnar Jr., Olga Baclanova. Accompanied by a new score composed by Gabriel Thibaudeau and performed by the ensemble Octuor de France.

**"Views from the Avant-Garde"** – curated by Mark McElhatten and Gavin Smith. Films from the USA unless otherwise noted.

**Program 1**: "The Demon of Analogy (Serpentine Dance)" – *Chimp for Normal Short*, by Leslie Thornton; *Quarry Movie*, by Greta Snider; *Filter Beds*, UK, by Guy Sherwin; *Zillertal*, Germany, by Jürgen Reble; *Moebius Strip*, by Luis Recoder; *Angus Mustang*, by Stephanie Barber; *Another Worldy*, by Leslie Thornton; *Removed*, by Naomi Uman; *Outer Space*, Austria, by Peter Tscherkassky.

**Program 2**: "in residue..." – *Fool's Spring (Two Personal Gifts)*, by Jerome Hiler and Nathaniel Dorsky; *Painting the Town*, by Jim Jennings; *Muktikara*, by Jeanne Liotta; *Moxon's Mechanick Exercises*, by David Gatten; *Silver Rush*, France, by Cécile Fontaine; *Hospital Fragment*, Canada, by Guy Maddin; *Twilight Psalm I: The Lateness of the Hour*, by Phil Solomon; *Home*, by Luther Price; *Twilight Psalm II: Walking Distance*, by Phil Solomon.

**Program 3**: "Winged Distance/Sightless Measure" – three films by Robert Beavers: *From the Notebook of...*, *Work Done*, and *The Painting*.

**Program 4**: *Spectres of the Spectrum*, by Craig Baldwin.

# 2000

SELECTION COMMITTEE: RICHARD PEÑA, JOHN ANDERSON, MANOHLA DARGIS, DAVE KEHR, AND KATHLEEN MURPHY. SHORT FILM ADVISORS: GAVIN SMITH AND GENEVIEVE VILLAFLOR. SILENT FILM ADVISOR: SAYRE MAXFIELD.

THE 38TH NYFF POSTER ARTWORK WAS CREATED BY ©TAMAR HIRSCHL.

### DANCER IN THE DARK
*Denmark/Sweden/France, 2000. Written and Directed by Lars von Trier.*

With Björk, Catherine Deneuve, Peter Stormare, David Morse. (Opening Night.)

### POLLOCK
*USA, 2000. Directed by Ed Harris.*

Written by Susan J. Emshwiller and Barbara Turner, based on Steven Naifeh and Gregory White Smith's book *Jackson Pollock: An American Saga*. With Harris, Marcia Gay Harden, Amy Madigan, Jennifer Connelly, Jeffrey Tambor, Bud Cort, John Heard, Val Kilmer. (Centerpiece.)

### CROUCHING TIGER, HIDDEN DRAGON
*Taiwan, 2000. Directed by Ang Lee.*

Written by James Schamus, Wang Hui Ling and Tsai Kuo Jung, based on Wang Du Lu's novel. With Chow Yun Fat, Michelle Yeoh, Zhang Ziyi, Chang Chen. (Closing Night.)

### AMORES PERROS ▶
*Mexico, 2000. Directed by Alejandro González Iñárritu.*

Written by Guillermo Arriaga. With Emilo Echevarría, Gael García Bernal, Goya Toledo, Álvaro Guerrero.

### BEFORE NIGHT FALLS ▼
*USA, 2000. Directed by Julian Schnabel.*

Written by Cunningham O'Keefe, Lázaro Gómez Carriles, and Schnabel. With Javier Bardem, Olivier Martinez, Andrea Di Stefano, Johnny Depp, Sean Penn.

### BOESMAN AND LENA
*France/South Africa, 2000. Written and Directed by John Berry, based on Athol Fugard's play.*

With Danny Glover, Angela Bassett, Willie Jonah. Shown with *Purse*, Russia. Directed by Valentina Elina.

### BROTHER
*USA, 2000. Written and Directed by Takeshi Kitano.*

With Kitano, Omar Epps, Claude Maki, Masaya Kato, Susumu Terajima.

### CHRONICALLY UNFEASIBLE
*Brazil, 2000. Directed by Sérgio Bianchi.*

Written by Bianchi and Gustavo Steinberg. With Cecil Thiré, Betty Gofman, Umberto Magnani. Shown with *You Are What You Are Born For*, Brazil. Directed by Roberto Berliner.

### CHUNHYANG
*South Korea, 2000. Directed by Im Kwon-taek.*

Written by Kim Myong-kon, based on the pansori song by Cho Sang-hyun. With Lee Hyo-jung, Cho Seung-woo, Kim Sung-nyu, Lee Jung-hun.

### THE CIRCLE
*Iran/Italy, 2000. Directed by Jafar Panahi.*

Written by Kambozia Partovi, based on a story by Panahi. With Fereshteh Sadr Orafai, Fatemah Naghavi, Nargess Mamizadeh, Maryam Parvin Almani. Shown with *Anino*, Philippines. Directed by Raymond Red.

*In the Mood for Love* by Wong Kar Wai

*The House of Mirth by Terence Davies*

## COMEDY OF INNOCENCE
*France, 2000. Directed by Raúl Ruiz.*

Written by Françoise Dumas and Ruiz, based on Massimo Bontempelli's novel. With Isabelle Huppert, Jeanne Balibar, Charles Berling, Nils Hugon. Shown with *Donuts for Breakfast*, New Zealand. Directed by Felicity Morgan-Rhind.

## EUREKA
*Japan, 2000. Written and Directed by Shinji Aoyama.*

With Koji Yakusho, Aoi Miyazaki, Masaru Miyazaki, Yohichiroh Saitoh.

## FAITHLESS
*Sweden, 2000. Directed by Liv Ullmann.*

Written by Ingmar Bergman. With Lena Endre, Erland Josephson, Krister Henriksson, Thomas Hanzon.

## GEORGE WASHINGTON
*USA, 2000. Written and Directed by David Gordon Green.*

With Candace Evanofski, Donald Holden, Curtis Cotton III, Eddie Rouse, Paul Schneider.

## THE GLEANERS AND I
*France, 2000. Directed by Agnès Varda.*

An intimate inquiry into French life and those who sift through our detritus, including Varda herself. Shown with *Later* (*Plus tard*), France. Directed by Eric Oriot.

## GOHATTO (TABOO)
*Japan, 1999. Written and Directed by Nagisa Oshima, based on novellas by Ryotaro Shiba.*

With Takeshi Kitano, Ryuhei Matsuda, Shinji Takeda, Tadanobu Asano. Shown with *Every Day Here*, USA. Directed by Frazer Bradshaw.

## THE HOUSE OF MIRTH
*UK/USA, 2000. Written and Directed by Terence Davies, based on Edith Wharton's novel.*

With Gillian Anderson, Dan Aykroyd, Eleanor Bron, Terry Kinney, Anthony LaPaglia, Laura Linney, Eric Stoltz, Elizabeth McGovern, Jodhi May.

## IN THE MOOD FOR LOVE
*Hong Kong, 2000. Written and Directed by Wong Kar Wai.*

With Tony Leung Chiu-wai, Maggie Cheung, Rebecca Pan, Lai Chen. Shown with *Walking Home*, UK. Directed by Oliver Krimpas.

## KIPPUR
*Israel/France, 2000. Directed by Amos Gitai.*

Written by Gitai and Marie-José Sanselme. With Liron Levo, Tomer Russo, Uri Ran Klauzner, Yoram Hattab.

## KRAPP'S LAST TAPE
*Canada/Ireland, 2000. Directed by Atom Egoyan.*

Written by Samuel Beckett. With John Hurt.

### + NOT I
*Ireland, 2000. Directed by Neil Jordan.*

Written by Samuel Beckett. With Julianne Moore's mouth in extreme close-up.

## PLATFORM
*China/Japan, 2000. Written and Directed by Jia Zhang-ke.*

With Wang Hong-wei, Zhao Tao, Liang Jing-dong, Yang Tian-yi.

## SMELL OF CAMPHOR, FRAGRANCE OF JASMINE
*Iran, 2000. Written and Directed by Bahman Farmanara.*

With Farmanara, Roya Nonahali, Reza Kianan, Valiyollah Shirandami. Shown with *Motorcycle*, Thailand. Directed by Aditya Assarat.

## SEVEN MEN FROM NOW
*USA, 1956. Directed by Budd Boetticher.*

Written by Burt Kennedy. With Randolph Scott, Gail Russell Lee Marvin, Walter Reed. (Retrospective.) Shown with *Forgotten Pilots*, UK. Directed by Cairo Cannon.

## THE TASTE OF OTHERS
*France, 2000. Directed by Agnès Jaoui.*

Written by Jean-Pierre Bacri and Jaoui. With Jaoui, Bacri, Anne Alvaro, Brigitte Catillon, Alain Chabat Shown with *Move It, Girl*, France. Directed by Caroline Vignal.

## YI YI (A ONE AND A TWO...)
*Taiwan/Japan, 2000. Written and Directed by Edward Yang.*

With Nianzhen Wu, Issey Ogata, Elaine Jin, Kelly Lee. Shown with *Brother*, Australia. Directed by Adam Elliot.

# Special Events
PRESENTED AT THE WALTER READE THEATER

## BODY AND SOUL
*USA, 1925. Directed by Oscar Micheaux.*

With Paul Robeson, Mercedes Gilbert, Julia Theresa Russell, Lawrence Chenault. Presented in Avery Fisher Hall and produced in collaboration with Jazz at Lincoln Center. The Lincoln Center Jazz Orchestra with Wynton Marsalis and guest pianist Eric Reed premiered a commissioned score by trombonist and composer Wycliffe Gordon.

**"Passion and Defiance: Silent Divas of the Italian Cinema"** – films shown: *Assunta Spina*, 1915, by Gustavo Serena, with *Vedi Napoli e Poi muori*, 1924, by Eugenio Perego; *Der Bastard*, 1926, by Gennaro Righelli; *Blue Blood*, 1914, by Nino Oxilia, with *The Lover*, 1920, by Righelli; *Flower of Evil*, 1915, by Carmine Gallone; *Malombra*, 1917,

by Gallone, with *Cenere*, 1917, by Febo Mari; *Mother Doll*, 1919, by Gallone; *Nobody's Child Part 1 & 2*, 1921, by Ubaldo Maria Del Colle; *The Painting of Osvaldo Mars*, 1921, by Guido Brignone; *Royal Tiger*, 1916, by Piero Fosco; *Satanic Rhapsody*, 1917, by Nino Oxilia, 1917; *Scampolo*, 1928, by Augusto Genina; *Story of a Woman*, 1920, by Perego. The films in this program were accompanied by Guido Sodo and François Laurent, artists of the Neapolitan tradition, providing guitar, mandolin, and voice; pianists Marco Dal Pane, Curtis Salke, and Donald Sosin; and singer Joanna Seaton.

**"Views from the Avant-Garde"** – curated by Mark McElhattan and Gavin Smith. Films from the USA unless otherwise noted.

**Program 1:** "Light Spill" – *The Heart of the World*, Canada, by Guy Maddin; *The Fourth Watch*, by Janie Geiser; *The Glass System*, by Mark LaPore; *Surface Noise*, by Abigail

Child; *Moon Streams*, by Mary Beth Reed; *Like a Dream That Vanishes*, Canada, by Barbara Sternberg; *Origin of the 21st Century*, France, by Jean-Luc Godard.

**Program 2:** Peter Hutton & Nathaniel Dorsky – *Time and Tide*, by Peter Hutton; *Arbor Vitae*, by Nathaniel Dorsky.

**Program 3:** "Beneath the Second Hand" – *Prelude*, Canada, by Michael Snow; *Dellamorte Dellamorte Dellamore*, France, by David Matarasso; *Spiral Vessel*, by Janie Geiser; *The Adventure Parade*, by Kerry Laitala; *The Zero Order*, by Bobby Abate; *Lost Motion*, by Janie Geiser; *Not Resting*, UK, by Nicky Hamlin; *Blitze*, Austria, by Dietmar Brehm; *Slow Death*, USA/Japan, by Stom Sogo; *Twig*, by Michael Mideke; *In Absentia*, UK, by the Quay Brothers, in collaboration with Karlheinz Stockhausen.

**Program 4:** *Teatro Amazonas*, by Sharon Lockhart.

39th New York Film Festival

Presented by The Film Society of Lincoln Center
September 28th - October 14th 2001, Alice Tully Hall

# 2001

SELECTION COMMITTEE: RICHARD PEÑA, CHAIRMAN, JOHN ANDERSON, MANOHLA DARGIS, DAVE KEHR, AND KATHLEEN MURPHY.
SHORT FILM ADVISORS: GAVIN SMITH AND GENEVIEVE VILLAFLOR. SILENT FILM ADVISOR: SAYRE MAXFIELD.

THE 39TH NYFF POSTER ARTWORK WAS CREATED BY ©MANNY FARBER.

## VA SAVOIR (WHO KNOWS?)
*France, 2001. Directed by Jacques Rivette.*

Written by Pascal Bonitzer, Christine Laurent, and Rivette, based on Luigi Pirandello's play *As You Desire Me*. With Jeanne Balibar, Sergio Castellitto, Marianne Basler, Jacques Bonnaffé. (Opening Night.) Note: Jacques Rivette attended the NYFF for the first time. He said he came to show his support for a post-9/11 New York.

## MULHOLLAND DRIVE ▶
*France/USA, 2001. Written and Directed by David Lynch.*

With Naomi Watts, Laura Elena Haring, Justin Theroux, Ann Miller. Shown with *Music for One Apartment and Six Drummers*, Sweden. Directed by Johannes Stjärne Nilsson and Ola Simonsson. (Centerpiece.)

## IN PRAISE OF LOVE (ÉLOGE DE L'AMOUR)
*Switzerland/France, 2001. Written and Directed by Jean-Luc Godard.*

With Bruno Putzulu, Cécile Camp, Jean Davy, Françoise Verney. Shown with *V.O.*, Spain. Directed by Antonia San Juan. (Closing Night.)

## ALL ABOUT LILY CHOU-CHOU
*Japan, 2001. Written and Directed by Shunji Iwai.*

With Hayato Ichihara, Shugo Oshinari, Ayumi Ito, Yu Aoi.

## BARAN ▲
*Iran, 2001. Written and Directed by Majid Majidi.*

With Hossein Abedini, Zahra Bahrami, Mohammad Amir Naji, Hossein Mahjoub, Abbas Rahimi. Shown with *Inja* (*Dog*), Australia/South Africa. Directed by Steve Pasvolsky.

## LA CIÉNAGA
*Argentina/Spain, 2001. Written and Directed by Lucrecia Martel.*

With Martín Adjemián, Diego Baenas, Leonora Balcarce, Silvia Baylé. Shown with *Measure*, USA. Directed by Dayna and Gaelen Hanson.

## FAT GIRL (À MA SOEURI)
*France/Italy, 2001. Written and Directed by Catherine Breillat.*

With Anaïs Reboux, Roxane Mesquida, Libero de Rienzo, Arsinée Khanjian, Romain Goupil, Laura Betti. Shown with *Asylums*, USA. Directed by Jason Bolling.

## I'M GOING HOME
*Portugal/France, 2001. Written and Directed by Manoel de Oliveira.*

With Michel Piccoli, Antoine Chappey, Catherine Deneuve, John Malkovich. Shown with *Could Have Been Utah*, USA. Directed by Frazer Bradshaw.

## INTIMACY
*France, 2001. Directed by Patrice Chéreau.*

Written by Chéreau and Anne-Louise Trividic, based on Hanif Kureishi's stories "Intimacy" and "Night Light." With Kerry Fox, Mark Rylance, Timothy Spall. Shown with *Contemporary Case Studies*, Australia. Directed by Janet Merewether.

## ITALIAN FOR BEGINNERS
*Denmark, 2001. Written and Directed by Lone Scherfig.*

With Anders W. Berthelsen, Ann Eleonora Jørgensen, Anette Støvelbæk, Peter Gantzler. Shown with *Swimming Out to Holly*, USA. Directed by Jesse Peyronel.

### THE LADY AND THE DUKE ▲
*France, 2001. Written and Directed by Eric Rohmer, inspired by Grace Elliott's* Journey of My Life During the French Revolution.

With Lucy Russell, Jean-Claude Dreyfus, François Marthouret, Léonard Cobiant.

### "MEN AT WORK"
• **La libertad**, Argentina, 2001. Written and Directed by Lisandro Alonso. With Misael Saavedra, Humberto Estrada, Rafael Estrada, Omar Didino, Javier Didino.

• **That Old Dream That Moves (Ce vieux rêve qui bouge)**, France, 2001. Written and Directed by Alain Guiraudie. With Pierre Louis-Calixte, Jean-Marie Combelles, Jean Ségani, Yves Dinse.

### "MAKING MOVIES THAT MATTER: THE ROLE OF FILM IN THE NATIONAL DEBATE"
An HBO Films Public Forum moderated by *Newsweek* Senior Critic David Ansen. Participants included Christopher Hitchens; filmmaker Raoul Peck; former head of Universal Tom Pollock; Chairman of New Line Cinema Robert Shaye; filmmaker Oliver Stone; and producer Christine Vachon.

### ◄ THE NIGHT OF THE HUNTER
*USA, 1955. Directed by Charles Laughton.*

Written by James Agee, based on David Grubb's novel. With Robert Mitchum, Shelley Winters, Lillian Gish, James Gleason. (Retrospective—at this screening the first FIAF Preservation Award was presented to Martin Scorsese.)

### THE ROYAL TENENBAUMS
*USA, 2001. Directed by Wes Anderson.*

Written by Anderson and Owen Wilson. With Gene Hackman, Anjelica Huston, Ben Stiller, Gwyneth Paltrow, Luke Wilson, Danny Glover, Owen Wilson, Bill Murray. Shown with *InBetweening America*, USA. Directed by Candy Kugel.

### SILENCE...WE'RE ROLLING
*Egypt/France, 2001. Written and Directed by Youssef Chahine.*

With Latifa, Ahmed Wafik, Ahmed Bedeir, Magda El Khatib. Shown with *Tuesday*, UK. Directed by Geoff Dunbar.

### SOBIBOR, OCTOBER 14, 1943, 4 P.M.
*France, 2001. Written and Directed by Claude Lanzmann.*

With Yehuda Lerner. The heart of this documentary is a 1979 interview with a Holocaust survivor about the uprising at the Polish extermination camp Sobibor.

### THE SON'S ROOM
*Italy, 2001. Directed by Nanni Moretti.*

Written by Linda Ferri, Moretti, and Heidrun Schleef. With Moretti, Laura Morante, Jasmine Trinca, Giuseppe Sanfelice. Shown with *Just Little Birds*, France. Directed by Fred Louf.

### LE SOUFFLE (DEEP BREATH)
*France, 2001. Written and Directed by Damien Odoul.*

With Pierre-Louis Bonnetblanc, Dominique Chevallier, Maxime Dalbrut, Jean-Claude Lecante. Shown with *Golden Gate (Palace II)*, Brazil. Directed by Katia Lund and Fernando Meirelles.

### STORYTELLING
*USA, 2001. Written and Directed by Todd Solondz.*

With Selma Blair, Robert Wisdom, Leo Fitzpatrick, Paul Giamatti, Mark Webber, Noah Fleiss, John Goodman, Julie Hagerty, Jonathan Osser. Shown with *Superhero*, France. Directed by Eric Guirado.

### TIME OUT (L'EMPLOI DU TEMPS)
*France, 2001. Directed by Laurent Cantet.*

Written by Robert Campillo and Cantet. With Aurélien Recoing, Karin Viard, Serge Livrozet, Jean-Pierre Mangeot, Monique Mangeot, Nicolas Kalsch.

## Special Events
PRESENTED AT THE WALTER READE THEATER

### BLUE WILD ANGEL: JIMI HENDRIX LIVE AT THE ISLE OF WIGHT
*USA, 2001. Directed by Murray Lerner.*
With Hendrix and his sidemen, Mitch Mitchell (drums) and Billy Cox (bass), during the 1970 concert.

### MY VOYAGE TO ITALY (IL MIO VIAGGIO IN ITALIA)
*USA, 200l. Directed by Martin Scorsese.*
Written by Suso Cecchi D'Amico, Raffaele Donato, Kent Jones, and Scorsese. A four-plus-hour spiritual autobiography of Scorsese focused on his love for Italian cinema.

### "The Outsider Looking In: The Films of Leonardo Favio" – a retrospective of the Argentinean actor-writer-director. Films directed by Favio, unless otherwise noted.
Films shown: *The Boss*, 1958, by Fernando Ayala; *Chronicle of a Lonely Child*, 1965; *Dream, Dream*, 1976; *The Employee* aka *The Clerk*, 1968; *Gatica*, 1993; *Hand in the Trap*, 1961, Leopoldo Torre Nilsson; *Juan Moreira*, 1973; *The Kidnapper*, 1958, by Torre Nilsson; *Nazareno Cruz and the Wolf*, 1974; *Perón, A Symphony of Feeling*, 1999; *The Romance of Aniceto and Francisca*, 1967.

### "Views from the Avant-Garde" – curated by Mark McElhattan and Gavin Smith. Films from the USA unless otherwise noted.

**Program 1:** "Dorsky, Brakhage & Beavers" – *Love's Refrain*, by Nathaniel Dorsky; *Micro-Garden*, by Stan Brakhage; *The Ground*, by Robert Beavers.

**Program 2:** "Circumference—Factual Telepathy" – *The Or Cloud*, by Fred Worden; *Light Licks 5*, by Saul Levine; *Patina*, by Peter Herwitz; *Impossible Love*, by Jim Jennings; *Fear of Blushing*, by Jennifer Reeves; *Nebel (Mist)*, Germany, by Matthius Müller; *The Enjoyment of Reading (Lost and Found)*, by David Gatten; *Interior*, by Jim Jennings; *Looking at the Sea*, by Peter Hutton.

**Program 3:** *Time Being*, by Andrew Noren.

**Program 4:** "Carnal Ghosts" – *The Dark Room*, USA/Korea, by Minyong Jang; *Her Glacial Speed*, by Eve Heller; *Dream Work (For Man Ray)*, Austria, by Peter Tscherkassky; *The Last Long Shot*, France, by Cécile Fontaine; *Montessori Sword Fight*, by Mary Beth Reed; *Dark Dark*, by Abigail Child; *The Aperture's Ghostings*, by Lewis Klahr; *Hallowed*, by Kerry Laitala; *Angel Beach*, by Scott Stark.

**Program 5:** "The Moon Stood Still" – *Meditations on Revolution III: Soledad*, by Robert Fenz; *Notes Before the Revolution*, Hong Kong, by Ip Yuk-Yiu; *Introduction to Living in a Closed System*, by Brittany Gravely; *Have a Nice Day Alone*, by Leslie Thornton; *Conquered*, by Kerry Laitala; *Their Idols Disintegrate*, by Jennifer Fieber; *Going to the Ocean*, by Matt McCormick.

### WAKING LIFE
*USA, 2001. Written and Directed by Richard Linklater.*
With an animated Julie Delpy, Adam Goldberg, Timothy "Speed" Levitch, Wiley Wiggins, Ethan Hawke, Caveh Zahedi, Linklater. Shown with *Saturday Morning*, Spain. Directed by Santi Trullenque.

### WARM WATER UNDER A RED BRIDGE
*Japan, 2001. Directed by Shohei Imamura.*
Written by Imamura, Daisuke Tengan, and Motofumi Tomikawa, based on Henmi Yo's novel. With Koji Yakusho, Misa Shimizu, Mitsuko Baisho, Mansuku Fuwa.

### WHAT TIME IS IT THERE?
*Taiwan/France, 200l. Directed by Tsai Ming-liang.*
Written by Tsai Ming-liang, in collaboration with Yang Pi-ying. With Lee Kang-sheng, Chen Shiang-chyi, Lu Yi-Ching, Miao Tien. Shown with *Gourmet Baby*, Singapore/USA. Directed by Sandi Tan.

### ◀ Y TU MAMÁ TAMBIÉN
*Mexico, 2001. Directed by Alfonso Cuarón.*
Written by Alfonso and Carlos Cuarón. With Maribel Verdú, Diego Luna, Gael García Bernal. Shown with *Beautiful*, New Zealand. Directed by Adam Stevens.

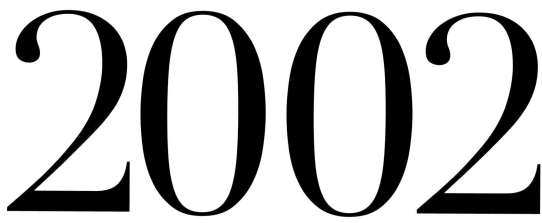

SELECTION COMMITTEE: RICHARD PEÑA, CHAIRMAN, JOHN ANDERSON, MANOHLA DARGIS, KENT JONES, AND DAVE KEHR. SHORT FILM SELECTION COMMITTEE: RICHARD PEÑA, GAVIN SMITH, AND GENEVIEVE VILLAFLOR. SILENT FILM ADVISOR: SAYRE MAXFIELD.

THE 40TH NYFF POSTER ARTWORK WAS CREATED BY ©JULIAN SCHNABEL.

### ABOUT SCHMIDT

*USA, 2002. Directed by Alexander Payne.*

Written by Payne and Jim Taylor. With Jack Nicholson, Kathy Bates, Hope Davis, Dermot Mulroney, Howard Hesseman, Len Cariou, June Squibb. Shown with *Tick*, New Zealand. Directed by Rebecca Hobbs. (Opening Night.)

### PUNCH-DRUNK LOVE

*USA, 2002. Written and Directed by Paul Thomas Anderson.*

With Adam Sandler, Emily Watson, Philip Seymour Hoffman, Luis Guzmán. Shown with *Hyper*, USA. Directed by Michael Canzoniero and Marco Ricci. (Centerpiece.)

### TALK TO HER

*Spain, 2002. Written and Directed by Pedro Almodóvar.*

With Javier Cámara, Darío Grandinetti, Leonor Watling, Rosario Flores, Geraldine Chaplin. Shown with *Play with Me*, The Netherlands. Directed by Esther Rots. (Closing Night.)

### AUTO FOCUS

*USA, 2002. Directed by Paul Schrader.*

Written by Michael Gerbosi. With Greg Kinnear, Willem Dafoe, Rita Wilson, Maria Bello.

### BLIND SPOT: HITLER'S SECRETARY

*Austria, 2002 Directed by André Heller and Othmar Shmiderer.*

Interviews with Traudi Junge, Hitler's secretary. Shown with *The ErlKing*, USA. Directed by Ben Zelkowicz.

### BLOODY SUNDAY

*UK/Ireland, 2002. Written and Directed by Paul Greengrass.*

With James Nesbitt, Tim Pigott-Smith, Nicholas Farrell, Gerard McSorley. A retelling of the massacre that took place in Londonderry, Northern Ireland, on January 20, 1972. Shown with *Burn*, USA. Directed by Patrick Jolley and Reynold Reynolds.

### CHIHWASEON

*South Korea, 2002. Directed by Im Kwon-taek.*

Written by Im Kwon-taek and Kim Yong-ok. With Choi Min-sik, Ahn Sung-ki, Yu Ho-Jeong, Kim Yeo-jin.

### DIVINE INTERVENTION

*France/Palestine, 2002. Written and Directed by Elia Suleiman.*

With Suleiman, Manal Khader, Nayef Fahoum Daher. A provocative expression of Palestinian outrage. Shown with *We Wuz Robbed*, USA. Directed by Spike Lee. About the 2000 election.

### FRIDAY NIGHT (VENDREDI SOIR)

*France, 2002. Directed by Claire Denis.*

Written by Emmanuèle Berheim and Denis. With Valérie Lemercier, Vincent Lindon, Hélène de Saint-Père, Hélène Fillières. Shown with *Tango de Olvido*, France/Argentina. Directed by Alexis Mital Toledo.

### LOVE AND DIANE

*USA/France, 2002. Directed by Jennifer Dworkin.*

With (as themselves) Diane, Donyaeh, and Love Hazzard. An epic documentary that follows many years of a recovering crack addict and a penitent parent.

### THE MAGDALENE SISTERS

*Scotland/Ireland, 2002. Written and Directed by Peter Mullan.*

With Geraldine McEwan, Anne-Marie Duff, Dorothy Duffy, Nora-Jane Noone, Eileen Walsh. Shown with *A Social Call*, UK. Directed by Jonathan Romney.

### ◀ THE MAN WITHOUT A PAST

*Finland, 2002. Written and Directed by Aki Kaurismäki.*

With Markku Peltola, Kati Outinen, Juhani Niemelä, Kaija Pakarinen. Shown with *Don't Have, Don't Give*, Poland/USA. Directed by David Turner.

### MONDAY MORNING

*France/Italy, 2002. Written and Directed by Otar Iosseliani.*

With Jacques Bidou, Anne Kravz-Tarnavsky, Narda Blanchet, Radslav Kinski.

## Special Events
PRESENTED AT THE WALTER READE THEATER

**"The Actor as Activist: Celebrating Shabana Azmi"** – films shown: *Congregation*, India, 1986, by Muzaffar Ali; *The Crossing*, India, 1984, by Goutam Ghose; *Death Sentence*, India, 1997, by Prakash Jha; *Fire*, Canada/India, 1996, by Deepa Mehta; *Godmother*, India, 1999, by Vinay Shukla; *Immaculate Conception*, UK, 1992, by Jamil Dehlavi; *In Custody*, UK/India, 1993, by Ismail Merchant; *Kamla*, India, 1985, by Jagmohan Mundhra; *The Marketplace*, India, 1983, by Shyam Benegal; *The Ruins*, India, 1983, by Mrinal Sen; *Sati*, India, 1989, by Aparna Sen; *The Seedling*, India, 1973, Shyam Benegal; *Shabana! Actor, Activist, Woman*, India, 2002, by Dev Benegal.

*Faust* by F.W. Murnau

### COME DRINK WITH ME
*Hong Kong, 1965. Directed by King Hu.*
Written by King Hu and Yang Erh. With Cheng Pei-pei, Yueh Hua.

### FAUST (FAUST – EINE DEUTSCHE VOLKSSAGE)
*Germany, 1926. Directed by F.W. Murnau.*
With Emil Jannings, Gösta Ekman, Camila Horn. Score by Phillip Johnston, lyrics by Hilary Bell, performed live by Johnston's quartet.

**"Views from the Avant-Garde"** – curated by Mark McElhatten and Gavin Smith. Films from the USA unless otherwise noted.

**Program 1:** *Song of the Firefly*, Canada, by Izabella Pruska-Oldenhof; *Yes? Oui? Ja?*, Germany, by Thomas Drashchan and Ulrich Wiesner; *Switch Center*, by Ericka Beckman; *Excerpts from a Work in Progress (Undesirables)*, by Owen Land; *Night Mulch* and *Very*, by Stan Brakhage; *Where the Girls Are*, by Abigail Child; *Guiding Fictions*, by Mark Street; *Snowdrift* aka *Snowstorm*, Sweden, by Gunvor Grundel Nelson; *Osmosis*, by Bradley Eros; *Film Number 15 Untitled Seminole Patchwork Film*, c. 1965-66, by Harry Smith, *Toccata*, Switzerland, by Hannes Schüpbach.

**Program 2:** Heinz Emigholz – Germany: *Sullivan's Banks*, 1993-2000; *Maillart's Bridges*, 1995-2000; *The Basis of Makeup Part II*, 1996-2000.

**Program 3:** *The Decay of Fiction*, by Pat O'Neill.

**Program 4:** *The Man We Want to Hang*, by Kenneth Anger; *Metropolis of Recklessness*, Germany, by Thomas Draschan and Ulrich Wiesner; *Homesick, Vagaries of Madness, Untitled, Theresa, Eulogies,* and *Silence of the Bride*, by José Rodriguez; *Mother (Revised)*, by Luther Price; *Mullroy*, by Tracey MacCullion.

**Program 5:** Ken Jacobs – *A Place Where There Is No Trouble*, A Ken Jacobs Nervous Magic Lantern Performance.

**Program 6:** *Regarding Penelope's Wake*, by Michele Smith.

**Program 7:** Ernie Gehr – *Glider, Crystal Palace,* and *City*.

**Program 8:** *The Visitation*, by Nathaniel Dorsky; *Cleft*, by Peter Bianco and Madison Brookshire; *Untitled*, by Julie Murray; *Across the Rappahannock*, by Brian Frye; *Daylight Moon*, by Lewis Klahr; *1305*, France, by Augustin Gimel; *Mekong*, by Mark LaPore; *Ultima Thule*, by Janie Geiser; *Psalm III: Night of the Meek*, by Phil Solomon.

---

### MY MOTHER'S SMILE
*Italy, 2002. Written and Directed by Marco Bellocchio.*
With Sergio Castellitto, Jacqueline Lustig, Chiara Conti, Gigio Alberti. Shown with *Lifeline*, Spain. Directed by Victor Erice.

### RUSSIAN ARK
*Russia/Germany, 2002. Directed by Aleksandr Sokurov.*
Written by Anatoly Nikiforov and Sokurov. With Sergei Dreiden, Maria Kuznetsova, Leonid Mozgovoy, Mikhail Piotrovsky. Shown with *The Projectionist*, Australia. Directed by Michael Bates.

### SAFE CONDUCT (LAISSEZ-PASSER)
*France, 2002. Directed by Bertrand Tavernier.*
Written by John Cosmos and Tavernier. With Jacques Gamblin, Denis Podalydès, Marie Gillain, Charlotte Kady.

### THE SON (LE FILS)
*Belgium/France, 2002. Written and Directed by Jean-Pierre and Luc Dardenne.*
With Olivier Gourmet, Morgan Marinne, Isabella Soupart, Rémy Renaud. Shown with *Lamb*, Australia, 2002. Directed by Emma Freeman.

### SPRINGTIME IN A SMALL TOWN
*China, 2002. Directed by Tian Zhuangzhuang. Written by Zhung Ah Cheng.*
With Hu Jingfan, Wu Jun, Xin Bajqing, Ye Xiaokeng, Lu Sisi. Shown with *Jealousy*, Spain. Directed by Dania Saragovia.

### TEN
*Iran/France, 2002. Written and Directed by Abbas Kiarostami.*
With Mania Akbari, Amin Maher, Roya Arabshahi, Katayoun Taleidzadeh, Mandana Sharbaf, Amene Moradi.

### TO BE AND TO HAVE
*France, 2002. Directed by Nicolas Philibert.*
With Georges Lopez and the pupils (and their families) of the one-room schoolhouse in Northern France's Saint-Étienne-sur-Usson. Shown with *Two Hundred Dirhams*, Morocco/France. Directed by Laïla Marrakchi.

### "TRUE LIVING COLOR: RACE IN FILM AND TELEVISION IN AMERICA TODAY AND TOMORROW" – an HBO Films Public Forum:
Participants included: John Leguizamo, casting director Reuben Cannon, independent distributor Jeff Lipsky, and *Yellow* author Frank H. Wu.

### TURNING GATE
*South Korea, 2002. Written and Directed by Hong Sang-soo.*
With Kim Sang-kyung, Yeh Ji-won, Chu Sang-mi. Shown with *Hammerbrook*, Germany. Directed by Elmar Freels.

### THE UNCERTAINTY PRINCIPLE
*Portugal/France, 2002. Written and Directed by Manoel de Oliveira.*
With Leonor Baldaque, Leonor Silveira, Isabel Ruth, Ricardo Trepa.

### UNKNOWN PLEASURES
*China/Japan, 2002. Written and Directed by Jia Zhang-ke.*
With Zhao Tao, Zhao Wei Wei. Wu Qiong. Shown with *Exceed*, USA. Directed by Julien M. Kheel.

### WAITING FOR HAPPINESS (HEREMAKONO)
*Mauritania/France, 2002. Written and Directed by Abderrahmane Sissako.*
With Khatra Ould Abder Kader, Maata Ould Mohamed Abeid, Mohamed Mahmoud Ould Mohamedou, Nana Diakité. Shown with *Candidate*, Iran. Directed by Mohammad Shirvani.

DECADE 4 LISTINGS | 287

*Russian Ark* by Aleksandr Sokurov

# 2003

41st New York Film Festival
presented by The Film Society of Lincoln Center
October 3rd -19th, 2003  Avery Fisher Hall, Alice Tully Hall, Walter Reade Theater

SELECTION COMMITTEE: RICHARD PEÑA, CHAIRMAN, JOHN ANDERSON, KENT JONES, DAVE KEHR, AND GEOFFREY O'BRIEN. SHORT FILM SELECTION COMMITTEE: RICHARD PEÑA, GAVIN SMITH, AND GENEVIEVE VILLAFLOR. SILENT FILM ADVISOR: SAYRE MAXFIELD.

THE 41ST NYFF POSTER ARTWORK WAS CREATED BY ©JUNICHI TAKI.

### MYSTIC RIVER
*USA, 2003. Directed by Clint Eastwood.*

Written by Brian Helgeland. With Sean Penn, Tim Robbins, Kevin Bacon, Laurence Fishburne, Marcia Gay Harden, Laura Linney. (Opening Night.)

### THE FOG OF WAR
*USA, 2003. Directed by Errol Morris.*

A dialogue with the conscience of Robert S. McNamara, who was Secretary of Defense during the escalation of the Vietnam War. (Centerpiece.)

### 21 GRAMS
*USA, 2003. Directed by Alejandro González Iñárritu.*

Written by Guillermo Arriaga. With Sean Penn, Benicio Del Toro, Naomi Watts, Charlotte Gainsbourg, Melissa Leo. (Closing Night.)

### THE BARBARIAN INVASIONS
*Canada, 2003. Written and Directed by Denys Arcand.*

With Rémy Girard, Stéphane Rousseau, Marie-Josée Croze, Marina Hands. Shown with *Destino*, USA/France. Directed by Dominique Monfery.

### BRIGHT LEAVES
*USA, 2003. Directed and Narrated by Ross McElwee.*

McElwee returns to his North Carolina birthplace to root out the story of his father's agricultural downfall. Shown with *The Rest of the World*, USA. Directed by Frazer Bradshaw.

### CRIMSON GOLD
*Iran, 2003. Directed by Jafar Panahi.*

Written by Abbas Kiarostami. With Hossain Emadeddin, Kamyar Sheissi, Azita Rayeji, Shahram Vaziri. Shown with *Bus 44*, China. Directed by Dayyan Eng.

*Distant* by Nuri Bilge Ceylan

# 2004

SELECTION COMMITTEE: RICHARD PEÑA, CHAIRMAN, KENT JONES, PHILLIP LOPATE, JOHN POWERS, AND LISA SCHWARZBAUM. SHORT FILM SELECTION COMMITTEE: RICHARD PEÑA, GAVIN SMITH, AND GENEVIEVE VILLAFLOR. SILENT FILM ADVISOR: SAYRE MAXFIELD.

THE 42ND NYFF POSTER ARTWORK WAS CREATED BY ©JEFF BRIDGES.

*Bad Education* by Pedro Almodóvar

**LOOK AT ME**
*France, 2004. Directed by Agnès Jaoui.*
Written by Jean-Pierre Bacri and Jaoui. With Marilou Berry, Jaoui, Bacri, Laurent Grévill. (Opening Night.)

**BAD EDUCATION**
*Spain, 2004. Written and Directed by Pedro Almodóvar.*
With Gael García Bernal, Fele Martínez, Javier Cámara, Daniel Giménez-Cacho. (Centerpiece.)

**SIDEWAYS**
*USA, 2004. Directed by Alexander Payne.*
Written by Payne and Jim Taylor, based on Rex Pickett's novel. With Paul Giamatti, Thomas Haden Church, Sandra Oh, Virginia Madsen. Shown with *Never Even*, Germany. Directed by Jan Schomburg. (Closing Night.)

**THE BIG RED ONE: THE RECONSTRUCTION**
*USA, 1980 (restored 2004). Written and Directed by Samuel Fuller.*
Print reconstruction by Richard Schickel and Brian Jamieson. With Lee Marvin, Mark Hamill, Robert Carradine, Bobby Di Cicco, Stéphane Audran, Kelly Ward.

**CAFÉ LUMIÈRE**
*Japan/Taiwan, 2004. Directed by Hou Hsiao-hsien.*
Written by Chu Tien-wen and Hou Hsiao-hsien. With Yo Hitoto, Tadanobu Asano, Masato Hagiwara, Kimiko Yo, Nenji Kobayashi.

**THE GATE OF THE SUN**
*Egypt/France, 2004. Directed by Yousry Nasrallah.*
Written by Nasrallah and Mohamed Soueid, based on Elias Khoury's novel. With Rim Turki, Orwa Nyrabeya, Hiam Abbass, Bassel Khayyat.

**THE HOLY GIRL (LA NIÑA SANTA)**
*Argentina/Spain, 2004. Written and Directed by Lucrecia Martel.*
With Mercedes Morán, Carlos Belloso, Alejandro Urdapilleta, María Alcé. Shown with *Flowers for Diana*, France. Directed by Reynald Bertrand.

**HOUSE OF FLYING DAGGERS**
*China, 2004. Directed by Zhang Yimou.*
Written by Li Feng, Wang Bin, and Zhang Yimou. With Takeshi Kaneshiro, Andy Lau, Ziyi Zhang, Song Dandan.

**IN THE BATTLEFIELDS**
*Lebanon/France/Belgium, 2004. Written and Directed by Danielle Arbid.*
With Marianne Feghali, Rawia Elchab, Laudi Arbid, Aouni Kawass, Carmen Lebbos. Shown with *The Patio*, Switzerland/Argentina. Directed by Milagros Mumenthaler.

**KEANE**
*USA, 2004. Written and Directed by Lodge Kerrigan.*
With Damian Lewis, Abigail Breslin, Amy Ryan, Tina Holmes, Christopher Evan Welch. Shown with *Nits*, UK. Directed by Harry Wootliff.

**KINGS AND QUEEN (ROIS ET REINE)**
*France, 2004. Directed by Arnaud Desplechin.*
Written by Roger Bohbot and Desplechin. With Mathieu Amalric, Emmanuelle Devos, Valentin Lelong, Jean-Paul Roussillon, Catherine Deneuve, Geoffrey Carey, Thierry Bosc, Maurice Garrel.

**MOOLAADÉ**
*Senegal/France, 2004. Written and Directed by Ousmane Sembene.*
With Fatoumata Coulibaly, Maïmouna Hélène Diarra, Salimata Traoré.

**NOTRE MUSIQUE ▼**
*France/Switzerland, 2004. Written and Directed by Jean-Luc Godard.*
With Sarah Adler, Nade Dieu, Rony Kramer, Georges Aguilar.

**OR (MY TREASURE)**
*Israel, 2004. Directed by Keren Yedaya.*
Written by Sari Ezouz and Yedaya. With Dana Ivgy, Ronit Elkabetz, Meshar Cohen, Katia Zimbris, Shmuel Edelman. Shown with *Frozen River*, USA. Directed by Courtney Hunt.

**PALINDROMES**
*USA, 2004. Written and Directed by Todd Solondz.*
With Ellen Barkin, Stephen Adly Guirgis, Jennifer Jason Leigh, Richard Masur, Debra Monk.

**ROLLING FAMILY (FAMILIA RODANTE)**
*Argentina/Spain, 2004. Written and Directed by Pablo Trapero.*
With Graciana Chironi, Liliana Capuro, Ruth Dobel, Federico Esquerro. Shown with *Supermarket*, USA. Directed by Illeana Douglas.

**SARABAND**
*Sweden, 2004. Written and Directed by Ingmar Bergman.*
With Liv Ullmann, Erland Josephson, Börge Ahlstedt, Julia Dufvenius, Gunnel Fred.

**TARNATION**
*USA, 2004. Written and Directed by Jonathan Caouette.*
A documentary portrait of family life, focusing on the director's relationship with his mother, a diagnosed schizophrenic. Shown with *Boy*, New Zealand. Directed by Welby Ings.

**THE 10TH DISTRICT COURT: MOMENTS OF TRIAL**
*France, 2004. Directed by Raymond Depardon.*
With (as herself) Michèle Bernard-Requin. The inner workings of a Parisian courtroom.

**TRIPLE AGENT**
*France, 2004. Written and Directed by Eric Rohmer.*
With Katerina Didaskalou, Serge Renko, Amanda Langlet, Emmanuel Salinger. Shown with *Highway 403, Mile 39*, USA. Directed by Mitch McCabe.

**TROPICAL MALADY**
*Thailand/France, 2004. Written and Directed by Apichatpong Weerasethakul.*
With Banlop Lomnoi, Sakda Kaewbuadee.

**UNDERTOW**
*USA, 2004. Directed by David Gordon Green.*
Written by Joe Conway and Green. With Dermot Mulroney, Jamie Bell, Devon Alan, Josh Lucas, Kristen Stewart.

**VERA DRAKE**
*UK, 2004. Written and Directed by Mike Leigh.*
With Imelda Staunton, Phil Davis, Peter Wight, Daniel Mays, Eddie Marsan, Lesley Manville, Sally Hawkins.

**WOMAN IS THE FUTURE OF MAN**
*South Korea/France, 2004. Written and Directed by Hong Sang-soo.*
With Yoo Ji-tae, Kim Tae-woo, Sung Hyun-ah. Shown with *Little Apocrypha No.2*, Hungary. Directed by Kornél Mundruczó.

**THE WORLD**
*China/Japan/France, 2004. Written and Directed by Jia Zhang-ke.*
With Zhao Tao, Chen Taisheng, Jing Jue, Jiang Zhong-wei.

*Palindromes* by Todd Solondz

*Infernal Affairs* by Andrew Lau and Alan Mak

# Special Events
PRESENTED AT THE WALTER READE THEATER

**"Elegance, Passion, and Cold Hard Steel: A Tribute to Shaw Brothers Studios"** – films shown (from Hong Kong): *Blood Brothers*, 1973 by Zhang Che; *Clans of Intrigue* aka *Killer Clans*, 1976, by Chor Yuen; *The Empress Dowager*, 1975, by Li Han-hsiang; *Heroes Two*, 1973, by Zhang Che; *Hong Kong Nocturne*, 1966, by Inoue Umetsugu; *The House of 72 Tenants*, 1973, by Chor Yuen; *Intimate Confessions of a Chinese Courtesan*, 1972, by Chor Yuen; *The Kingdom and the Beauty*, 1958, by Li Han-hsiang; *The Last Tempest*, 1975, by Li Han-hsiang; *The Love Eterne*, 1962, by Li Han-hsiang; *Love Without End*, 1961, by Doe Chin; *Vermillion Door*, 1964, by Lo Chen.

**"HBO Films Directors Dialogues"** – Agnès Jaoui in conversation with Lisa Schwarzbaum and Mike Leigh in conversation with Phillip Lopate.

**THE INFERNAL AFFAIRS TRILOGY**
*Hong Kong. Directed by Andrew Lau and Alan Mak.* Written by Felix Chong and Mak. With Andy Lau, Tony Leung, Edison Chen, Shawn Yue. Three crime thrillers, the first made in 2002, the next two in 2003.

**MACUNAÍMA**
*Brazil, 1969. Written and Directed by Joaquim Pedro de Andrade, based on Mário de Andrade's novel.* With Grande Otelo, Paulo José, Jardel Filho, Dina Sfat.

**MILES ELECTRIC: A DIFFERENT KIND OF BLUE**
*USA, 2004. Directed by Murray Lerner.* With (as themselves) Miles Davis, Carlos Santana, Joni Mitchell, Stanley Crouch, Bob Belden. Miles Davis's performance at the 1970 Isle of Wight Festival, plus reminiscences by other musicians who were by his side or influenced by him.

**"Selling Democracy: Films of the Marshall Plan 1947-1953"** – five programs of films made under the auspices of the Marshall Plan Film Unit. Selected from more than 250 films from 18 countries by Richard Peña and Sandra Schulberg.

**UNFORGIVABLE BLACKNESS: THE RISE AND FALL OF JACK JOHNSON**
*USA, 2004. Directed by Ken Burns.* Written by Geoffrey C. Ward. Narrated by Keith David, with Samuel L. Jackson as the voice of Jack Johnson. A study of a gifted athlete, with a score by Wynton Marsalis. Co-presented with Jazz at Lincoln Center.

**"Viva Pedro!"** – an evening with Pedro Almodóvar, including highlights from his career.

**"Views from the Avant-Garde"** – curated by Mark McElhatten and Gavin Smith. Films from the USA unless otherwise noted.

**Program 1:** *The Orientalist Chapters 1-5*, by Michele Smith.

**Program 2:** "Informed by Fire" – *Terrace 49*, by Janie Geiser; *Orchard*, USA/Ireland, by Julie Murray; *Let Me Count the Ways: Minus 10, 9, 8, 7…*, by Leslie Thornton; *Anaconda Targets*, by Dominic Angerame; *The Future Is Behind You*, by Abigail Child; *Isahn*, South Korea/USA, by Soon-mi Yoo; *Paradise Crushed* and *End in New World*, by Leslie Thornton.

**Program 3:** Lewis Klahr – *The Two Minutes to Zero Trilogy* and *Daylight Moon (A Quartet)*.

**Program 4:** "The Mind Moves Upon Silence" – *Redshift*, UK, by Emily Richardson; *Behind This Soft Eclipse*, by Eve Heller; *Deliquium*, by Julie Murray; *Luke*, by Bruce Conner (1967/2004); *Tabula Rasa*, USA/Canada, by Vincent Grenier; *#6: Okkyung*, by Andrew Lampert; *Mirror*, Germany, by Christoph Girardet and Matthias Müller; *Michelangelo Eye to Eye*, Italy, by Michelangelo Antonioni.

**Program 5:** "Mike and George Kuchar Preserved," with host John Waters – *Sylvia's Promise*, 1962, *Born of the Wind*, 1962, *The Thief and the Stripper*, 1959, and *A Town Called Tempest*, 1963.

**Program 6:** *The Orientalist Chapters 6-8*, by Michele Smith.

**Program 7:** Nina Fonoroff – *The Eye in the Mask* and *The Accursed Mazurka*, 1994.

**Program 8:** Ernie Gehr – *Precarious Garden*, *The Astronomer's Dream*, *The Collector*, and *Passage*.

**Program 9:** Peter Kubelka – *Truth and Poetry*, Austria, 2003, and *Mosaic im Vertauen*, Austria, 1954/55.

**Program 10:** "Pang Epoch" – *Play*, Germany, by Christoph Girardet and Matthias Müller; *Chasmic Dance*, Canada, by Daichi Saito; *Aspect*, UK, by Emily Richardson; *Life on Mars*, Belgium, by Isabelle Nouzha aka Ahzuon Ellebasi; *Phantom*, Germany, by Matthias Müller; *Axe*, Germany, by Christoph Janetzko; *Stable*, by Robert Todd; *Echo, Echo*, Austria, by Dietmar Brehm; *Palermo – "History" Standing Still*, Australia, by Janet Merewether; *Come to See 'Ya and Dirt*, by Eric Saks.

# 2005

SELECTION COMMITTEE: RICHARD PEÑA, CHAIRMAN, KENT JONES, PHILLIP LOPATE, JOHN POWERS, AND LISA SCHWARZBAUM. SHORT FILM SELECTION COMMITTEE: RICHARD PEÑA, GAVIN SMITH, AND GENEVIEVE VILLAFLOR. SILENT FILM ADVISOR: SAYRE MAXFIELD.

THE 43RD NYFF POSTER ARTWORK WAS CREATED BY ©MAURICE PIALAT.

**GOOD NIGHT, AND GOOD LUCK.**
*USA, 2005. Directed by George Clooney.*
Written by Clooney and Grant Heslov. With David Strathairn, Clooney, Patricia Clarkson, Jeff Daniels, Robert Downey Jr. Shown with *Stop!*, The Netherlands. Directed by Mathijs Geijskes. (Opening Night.)

**BREAKFAST ON PLUTO**
*Ireland/UK, 2005. Written and Directed by Neil Jordan.*
With Cillian Murphy, Liam Neeson, Ruth Negga, Laurence Kinlan, Stephen Rea. (Centerpiece.)

**CACHÉ ▼**
*France, 2005. Written and Directed by Michael Haneke.*
With Daniel Auteuil, Juliette Binoche, Maurice Bénichou, Annie Girardot. (Closing Night.)

**AVENGE BUT ONE OF MY TWO EYES**
*Israel/France, 2005. Written and Directed by Avi Mograbi.*
A documentary that ponders the relationship between stories of Jewish struggles for freedom and the Palestinian resistance. Shown with *Your Dark Hair Ihsan*, Morocco/USA. Directed by Tala Hadid.

**BUBBLE**
*USA, 2005. Directed by Steven Soderbergh.*

Written by Coleman Hough. With Debbie Doebereiner, Dustin James Ashley, Misty Dawn Wilkins, Omar Cowan. Shown with *Heydar, An Afghan in Tehran*, Iran/UK. Directed by Babak Jalali.

**CAPOTE**
*USA, 2005. Directed by Bennett Miller.*

Written by Dan Futterman. With Philip Seymour Hoffman, Catherine Keener, Clifton Collins Jr., Chris Cooper, Bruce Greenwood, Bob Balaban, Amy Ryan.

**THE DEATH OF MR. LAZARESCU**
*Romania, 2005. Directed by Cristi Puiu.*

Written by Puiu and Razvan Radulescu. With Ioan Fiscuteanu, Luminta Gheorghiu, Gabriel Spahiu, Doru Ana.

**L'ENFANT (THE CHILD)**
*Belgium/France, 2005. Written and Directed by Jean-Pierre and Luc Dardenne.*

With Jérémie Renier, Déborah François, Jérémie Segard, Fabrizio Rongione, Olivier Gourmet. Shown with *Blue Tongue*, Australia. Directed by Justin Kurzel.

**GABRIELLE**
*France, 2005. Directed by Patrice Chéreau.*

Written by Chéreau and Anne-Louise Trividic. With Isabelle Huppert, Pascal Greggory, Thierry Hancisse.

**I AM**
*Poland, 2005. Written and Directed by Dorota Kędzierzawska.*

With Piotr Jagielski, Agnieszka Nagórzycka, Edyta Jungowska. Shown with *Lâl*, Germany. Directed by Dirk Schaefer.

**MANDERLAY**
*Denmark/Sweden/France, 2005. Written and Directed by Lars von Trier.*

With Bryce Dallas Howard, Isaach De Bankolé, Danny Glover, Willem Dafoe, Michaël Abiteboul, Lauren Bacall, John Hurt, Jean-Marc Barr.

**METHADONIA**
*USA, 2006. Directed by Michel Negroponte.*

A tour of the borderland of recovering heroin addicts on methadone maintenance. Shown with *Victoria para Chino*, USA/Mexico. Directed by Cary Fukunaga.

**PARADISE NOW ▶**
*The Netherlands/Germany/France, 2005. Directed by Hany Abu-Assad.*

Written by Abu-Assad and Bero Beyer. With Ali Suliman, Kais Nashef.

**THE PASSENGER**
*Italy/USA/France, 1975. Directed by Michelangelo Antonioni.*

Written by Antonioni, Mark Peploe, and Peter Wollen. With Jack Nicholson, Maria Schneider, Jenny Runacre, Ian Hendry Steven Berkoff, Ambroise Bia. (Retrospective—Antonioni's preferred cut.)

**THE PRESIDENT'S LAST BANG**
*South Korea, 2005. Written and Directed by Im Sang-soo.*

With Han Suk-kyu, Baik Yoon-sik, Song Jae-ho, Kim Eung-soo. Shown with *Machulenco*, Spain. Directed by David Blanco.

**REGULAR LOVERS**
*France, 2005. Directed by Philippe Garrel.*

Written by Marc Cholodenko, Garrel, and Arlette Langmann. With Louis Garrel, Clotilde Hesme, Julien Lucas, Eric Rulliat.

**SOMETHING LIKE HAPPINESS ▼**
*Czech Republic, 2005. Written and Directed by Bohdan Sláma.*

With Tatiana Vilhelmová, Pavel Liska, Ana Geislerová, Marek Daniel. Shown with *Truant*, New Zealand. Directed by Michael Duignan.

*Breakfast on Pluto* by Neil Jordan

**THE SQUID AND THE WHALE ▼**

*USA, 2005. Written and Directed by Noah Baumbach.*
With Jeff Daniels, Laura Linney, Jesse Eisenberg, Owen Kline, Halley Feiffer, Anna Paquin, William Baldwin. Shown with *Be Quiet*, France. Directed by Sameh Zoabi.

**THE SUN**

*Russia/Italy/France/Switzerland, 2005. Directed by Aleksandr Sokurov.*
Written by Yuri Arabov. With Issey Ogata, Robert Dawson, Kaori Momoi, Shiri Sano. Shown with *Cigarette Break*, Germany. Directed by Ralf Stadler.

**SYMPATHY FOR LADY VENGEANCE**

*South Korea, 2005. Directed by Park Chan-wook.*
Written by Jeong Seo-kyung and Park Chan-wook. With Lee Young-ae, Choi Min-sik, Oh Dal-su, Kim Si-hu.

**TALE OF CINEMA**

*South Korea/France, 2005. Written and Directed by Hong Sang-soo.*
With Uhm Ji-won, Lee Ki-woo, Kim Sang-kyung. Shown with *Snow*, UK. Directed by Emily Greenwood.

**THREE TIMES**

*Taiwan, 2005. Directed by Hou Hsiao-hsien.*
Written by Chu Tien-wen and Hou Hsiao-hsien. With Shu Qi, Chang Chen.

**THROUGH THE FOREST (À TRAVERS LA FORÊT)**

*France, 2005. Written and Directed by Jean-Paul Civeyrac.*
With Camille Berthomier, Aurélien Wiik, Morgane Hainaux, Alice Dubuisson. Shown with *Motion Report*, Serbia and Montenegro. Directed by Verica Patrnogic.

**TRISTRAM SHANDY: A COCK AND BULL STORY**

*UK, 2005. Directed by Michael Winterbottom.*
Written by Martin Hardy, based on Laurence Sterne's novel *The Life and Opinions of Tristram Shandy, Gentleman*. With Steve Coogan, Rob Brydon, Roger Allam, Gillian Anderson.

**WHO'S CAMUS ANYWAY? ▲**

*Japan, 2005. Written and Directed by Mitsuo Yanagimachi.*
With Shuji Kashiwabara, Hinano Yoshikawa, Ai Maeda, Hideo Nakaizumi.

## Special Events

**"The Beauty of the Everyday: Japan's Shochiku Company at 110"** – films shown: *The Army*, 1944, by Keisuke Kinoshita; *A Ball at the Anjo House*, 1947, by Kozaburo Yoshimura; *Black River*, 1957, by Masaki Kobayashi; *Carmen Comes Home*, 1951, by Kinoshita; *The Castle of Sand*, 1974, by Yoshitaro Nomura; *Every Night Dreams*, 1934, by Mikio Naruse; *Face*, 2000, by Junji Sakamoto; *The Hidden Blade*, 2005, by Yoji Yamada; *Japanese Girls at the Harbor*, 1933, by Hiroshi Shimizu; *Jirokichi*, 1952, by Daisuke Ito; *Late Spring*, 1949, by Yasujiro Ozu; *The Lights of Akakusa*, 1937, by Yasujiro Shimazu; *Love Affair at Akitsu Spa*, 1962, by Kiju Yoshida; *The Loyal 47 Ronin*, 1942/43, by Kenji Mizoguchi; *The Most Beautiful Day of My Life*, 1948, by Kozaburo Yoshimura; *Naked Youth* aka *Cruel Story of Youth*, 1960, by Nagisa Oshima; *The Neighbor's Wife and Mine*, 1931, by Heinosuke Gosho; *Night and Fog in Japan*, 1960, by Oshima; *No Advice Today* aka *Doctor's Day Off*, 1950, by Minoru Shibuya; *Ornamental Hairpin*, 1941, by Shimizu; *Our Neighbor Miss Yae*, 1934, by Shimazu; *Pale Flower*, 1963, by Masahiro Shinoda; *Scandal*, 1950, by Akira Kurosawa; *Souls on the Road*, 1921, by Minoru Murata – piano accompaniment by Donald Sosin; *Star Athlete*, 1937, by Shimizu; *The Story of the Last Chrysanthemums*, 1939, by Mizoguchi; *A Story of Floating Weeds*, 1934, by Ozu; *Three Outlaw Samurai*, 1964, by Hideo Gosha; *Woman of the Mist*, 1936, by Gosho; *Women of the Night*, 1948, by Mizoguchi; *The Young Women of Izu*, 1945, by Gosho.

**BEYOND THE ROCKS**

*USA, 1922. Directed by Sam Wood.*
Written by Jack Cunningham. With Gloria Swanson, Rudolph Valentino, Edythe Chapman.

**"Greeneland: Graham Greene and the Cinema"** – Adrian Wootton discussed the connections between the art of Graham Greene and the cinema, followed by a screening of *The Green Cockatoo*, UK, 1937. Directed by William Cameron Menzies. Written by Ted Berkman and Arthur Wimperis, based on Greene's story. With John Mills, René Ray, Charles Oliver, Bruce Seton.

**HAZE**

*Japan, 2005. Written and Directed by Shinya Tsukamoto.*
With Tsukamoto, Kaori Fujii.

**"HBO Films Directors Dialogues"** – in the Stanley Kaplan Penthouse: Jean-Pierre and Luc Dardenne in conversation with Kent Jones; Neil Jordan in conversation with Lisa Schwarzbaum; Michael Winterbottom in conversation with Stuart Klawans; Patrice Chéreau in conversation with Gregory Mosher; "The Squid, the Whale, the Filmmaker: A Conversation with Noah Baumbach," hosted by Phillip Lopate; Film Comment Focus: Steve Coogan in Conversation, with Gavin Smith.

**"Mary Ellen Mark: Moments in Film"** – a photography exhibit in the Frieda and Roy L. Furman Gallery.

**NEZUMI KOZO: NODA VERSION**

*Japan, 2005. Written and Directed by Noda Hideki.*
With Nakamura Kankuro, Nakamura Fukasuke.

**"Speaking Truth to Power: Media, Politics and Government"** – a panel discussion with WNYC Public Radio host Brian Lehrer, broadcast journalist Nick Clooney, NPR's Senior Foreign Editor Loren Jenkins, and legendary White House correspondent Helen Thomas.

**"Views from the Avant-Garde"** – curated by Mark McElhatten and Gavin Smith. Films from the USA unless otherwise noted.

**Program 1:** A *Trip to the Louvre (Une visite au Louvre x 2)*, by Jean-Marie Straub and Danièle Huillet, France.

**Program 2:** "The Daily Planet (Unearthed)" – *The Space Between*, UK, by Brad Butler and Karen Mirza; *Predictions*, by Katherin McInnis; *Total Power – Dead Dead Dead*, by Stephanie Barber; *Let Me Count the Ways: Minus 6*, by Leslie Thornton; *The Girl Who Lost Her Head (fragment)*, by Michele Smith; *Eclipse*, by Jeanne Liotta; *Detroit Park*, by Julie Murray; *Krypton Is Doomed*, by Ken Jacobs; *Blue Pole(s)*, by Fred Worden.

**Program 3:** David Gatten's *Secret History of the Dividing Line* – a true account in nine parts.

**Program 4:** "The Terrestrial Observatory" – *And I Make Short Films*, India, by S.N.S. Sastry; *Made in Chinatown*, by Jim Jennings; *Louis Aimé Augustin Le Prince – Leeds Bridge*, by Ken Jacobs; *Kosmos*, Germany, by Thorsten Fleisch; *Here*, by Fred Worden; *The Relentless Fury of the Pounding Waves*, Thailand, by Apichatpong Weerasethakul; *September Song*, by Luther Price; *Kolkata*, by Mark LaPore.

**Program 5:** *Blue Movie*, 1968, by Andy Warhol, with special guest star, Viva.

**Program 6:** Allen Ross's Grandfather Trilogy 1978-81 – *Papa*, *Thanksgiving 1979*, and *Burials*.

**Program 7:** Larry Gottheim – *Blues*, *Fog Line*, *Doorway*, and *Barn Rushes*, plus *The Opening* and *Your Television Traveler*.

**Program 8:** "Manual Override (Slip Inside This House)" – *Windows*, Thailand, by Apichatpong Weerasethakul; *Elsewhere*, by Luke Sieczek; *Sylvania*, by Bobby Abate, *Not Nine*, by Gail Vachon; *Catalog*, by Stephanie Barber; *Ruby Skin*, by Eve Heller; *Driven*, by Scott Stark; *Nice Biscotts #2* and *Same Day Nice Biscotts*, by Luther Price; *A Time to Die*, by Joe Gibbons; *Instructions for a Light and Sound Machine*, Austria, by Peter Tscherkassky.

**Program 9:** "Shadowhunger" – *Los Caudales*, by Timoleon Wilkins; *Pan of the Landscape*, by Christopher Becks; *Market Street*, by Tomonari Nishikawa; *C: Won Eyed Jail*, by Kelly Egan; *North Southernly*, by Vincent Grenier; *Hinterlands (Open Shadow)*, by Brian Short; *Shadows Choose Their Horrors*, by Jennifer Reeves.

**Program 10:** Heinz Emigholz – *The Basis of Make-Up III*, *Miscellanea III*, and *D'Annunzio's Cave*, Germany.

# 2006

SELECTION COMMITTEE: RICHARD PEÑA, CHAIRMAN, KENT JONES, PHILLIP LOPATE, JOHN POWERS, AND LISA SCHWARZBAUM.
SHORT FILMS SELECTION COMMITTEE: RICHARD PEÑA, GAVIN SMITH, AND GENEVIEVE VILLAFLOR.

THE 44TH NYFF POSTER ARTWORK WAS CREATED BY ©MARY ELLEN MARK.

### THE QUEEN ▲
*UK, 2006. Directed by Stephen Frears.*

Written by Peter Morgan. With Helen Mirren, Michael Sheen, James Cromwell, Alex Jennings. Shown with *South of Ten*, USA. Directed by Liza Johnson. (Opening Night.)

### VOLVER ▶
*Spain, 2006. Written and Directed by Pedro Almodóvar.*

With Penélope Cruz, Carmen Maura, Lola Dueñas, Blanca Portillo. (Centerpiece.)

### PAN'S LABYRINTH
*Spain/Mexico, 2006. Written and Directed by Guillermo del Toro.*

With Ivana Baquero, Doug Jones, Sergi López, Ariadna Gil, Maribel Verdú, Àlex Angulo. Shown with *Lump*, UK. Directed by Faye Jackson. (Closing Night.)

### AUGUST DAYS
*Spain, 2006. Written and Directed by Marc Recha.*

With David Recha, Marc Recha, Mariona Ordóñez, Pere Subirana, Fina Susín. Part fiction, part documentary, a re-creation of a trip through the back roads of Catalonia made by the director and his brother.

### BAMAKO
*Mali/France, 2006. Written and Directed by Abderrahmane Sissako.*

With Aïssa Maïga, Tiécoura Traoré, Hélène Diarra, Habib Dembélé. Shown with *Innocence*, France. Directed by Arnaud Gautier.

### BELLE TOUJOURS
*France/Portugal, 2006. Written and Directed by Manoel de Oliveira, inspired by Buñuel's* Belle du jour.

With Michel Piccoli, Bulle Ogier, Leonor Baldaque, Júlia Buisel. Shown with *The Caretakers*, USA. Directed by Elisabeth Subrin.

### CLIMATES
*Turkey/France, 2006. Written and Directed by Nuri Bilge Ceylan.*

With Ebru Ceylan, Nuri Bilge Ceylan, Nazan Kesal. Shown with *Salt Kiss*, Brazil/USA. Directed by Fellipe Gamarano Barbosa.

## FALLING
*Austria, 2006. Written and Directed by Barbara Albert.*

With Nina Proll, Birgit Minichmayr, Ursula Strauss, Kathrin Resetarits, Gabriela Hegedüs.

## 49 UP
*UK, 2006. Directed by Michael Apted.*

The latest chapter in Apted's project that documents a group of diverse men and women every seven years, from childhood through middle age.

## GARDENS IN AUTUMN
*France/Italy/Russia, 2006. Written and Directed by Otar Iosseliani.*

With Séverin Blanchet, Michel Piccoli, Muriel Motte, Pascal Vincent. Shown with *Alice Sees the Light*, USA. Directed by Ariana Gerstein.

## THE GO MASTER
*China, 2006. Directed by Tian Zhuangzhuang.*

Written by Ah Cheng. With Chang Chen, Sylvia Chang, Ito Ayumi, Emoto Akira, Mansaku Fuwa, Aki Fuji, Yi Huang. Shown with *The Day I Died*, Argentina/USA. Directed by Maryam Keshavarz.

## THE HOST
*South Korea, 2006. Written and Directed by Bong Joon-ho.*

With Song Kang-ho, Park Hae-il, Bae Doo-na, Ko A-sung, Byun Hee-bong.

## INLAND EMPIRE
*France, USA, 2006. Written and Directed by David Lynch.*

With Laura Dern, Jeremy Irons, Justin Theroux, Harry Dean Stanton.

## INSIANG
*The Philippines, 1976. Directed by Lino Brocka.*

Written by Lamberto E. Antonio and Mario O'Hara. With Hilda Koronel, Mona Lisa, Ruel Vernal, Rez Cortez, Marlon Ramirez, Nina Lorenzo, Mely Mallari. (Retrospective.) Shown with *In the Tradition of My Family*, USA. Directed by Todd Davis.

## THE JOURNALS OF KNUD RASMUSSEN
*Canada/Denmark, 2006. Written and Directed by Norman Cohn and Zacharias Kunuk.*

With Leah Angutimarik, Pakak Innuksuk, Neeve Irngaut Uttak, Natar Ungalaaq.

## LITTLE CHILDREN ▲
*USA, 2006. Directed by Todd Field.*

Written by Field and Tom Perrotta, based on Perrotta's novel. With Kate Winslet, Jennifer Connelly, Patrick Wilson, Jackie Earle Haley, Noah Emmerich, Jane Adams.

*Bamako* by Abderrahmane Sissako

## MAFIOSO
*Italy, 1962. Directed by Alberto Lattuada.*

Written by Rafael Azcona, Marco Ferreri, Agenore Incrocci, and Furio Scarpelli, based on a story by Bruno Caruso. With Alberto Sordi, Norma Bengell, Gabriella Conti, Ugo Attanasio. (Retrospective.) Shown with *Jimmy Blue*, USA. Directed by Joseph Infantolino.

## MARIE ANTOINETTE
*USA, 2006. Written and Directed by Sofia Coppola, based on a book by Antonia Fraser.*

With Kirsten Dunst, Jason Schwartzman, Rip Torn, Judy Davis, Asia Argento, Aurore Clément, Marianne Faithfull, Steve Coogan, Shirley Henderson.

## OFFSIDE
*Iran, 2006. Directed by Jafar Panahi.*

Written by Panahi and Shadmehr Rastin. With Sima Mobarak-Shahi, Safar Samandar, Shayesteh Irani, M. Kheyrabadi. Shown with *Fourteen*, USA. Directed by Nicole Barnette.

## OUR DAILY BREAD
*Austria, 2006. Directed by Nikolaus Geyrhalter.*

Written by Geyrhalter and Wolfgang Widerhofer. How the food we eat is harvested, slaughtered, and packaged is the subject of this documentary in which the central figures are the machines that make it all possible. Shown with *The Naked Race*, UK. Directed by Benoit Forgeard.

## PAPRIKA
*Japan, 2006. Directed by Satoshi Kon.*

Written by Kon and Seishi Minakami, based on Yasutaka Tsutsui's manga. With the voices of Megumi Hayashibara, Toru Emori, Katsunosuke Hori, Toru Furuya.

## POISON FRIENDS
*France, 2006. Written and Directed by Emmanuel Bourdieu.*

With Malik Zidi, Thibault Vinçon, Alexandre Steiger,

Thomas Blanchard. Shown with *Chronicles of a Jump*, Israel/USA. Directed by Zohar Lavi.

## PRIVATE FEARS IN PUBLIC PLACES (COEURS)
*France, 2006. Directed by Alain Resnais.*

Written by Jean-Michel Ribes, based on Alan Ayckbourn's play. With Sabine Azéma, Laura Morante, Lambert Wilson, Pierre Arditi, Isabelle Carré, André Dussollier.

## REDS
*USA, 1981. Directed by Warren Beatty.*

Written by Beatty and Trevor Griffiths. With Beatty, Diane Keaton, Jack Nicholson, Edward Herrmann, Jerzy Kosinski, Paul Sorvino, Maureen Stapleton. (Retrospective.)

## SYNDROMES AND A CENTURY
*Thailand/France/Austria, 2006. Written and Directed by Apichatpong Weerasethakul.*

With Nantarat Sawaddikul, Jaruchai Iamaram, Sophon Pukanok, Arkanae Cherkam.

## THESE GIRLS
*Egypt, 2006. Directed by Tahani Rached.*

A documentary following a band of rebellious teenage girls living on the streets of Cairo. Shown with *A Drop of Water*, France/Turkey. Directed by Deniz Gamze Erguven.

## TRIAD ELECTION
*Hong Kong. Directed by Johnnie To.*

Written by Yau Nai Hoi, Yip Tin Shing. With Louis Koo, Simon Yam, Nick Cheung, Cheung Siu Fai. Shown with *Cubs*, UK. Directed by Tom Harper.

## WOMAN ON THE BEACH
*South Korea, 2006. Written and Directed by Hong Sang-soo.*

With Kim Seung-woo, Go Hyun-jung, Kim Tae-woo, Song Seon-mi. Shown with *A Little Bit Under the Weather*, France. Directed by Annick Raoul.

# Special Events

PRESENTED AT THE WALTER READE THEATER UNLESS OTHERWISE NOTED

**"A Celebration of 50 Years of Janus Films"** – films shown: *L'avventura*, Italy, 1960, by Michelangelo Antonioni; *Ballad of a Soldier*, USSR, 1959, by Grigori Chukhrai; *Beauty and the Beast*, France, 1946, by Jean Cocteau; *Children of Paradise*, France, 1945, by Marcel Carné; *Cléo from 5 to 7*, France, 1962, by Agnès Varda; *The Cranes Are Flying*, Soviet Union, 1957, by Mikhail Kalatazov; *Cría cuervos*, Spain, 1976, by Carlos Saura; *Day of Wrath*, Denmark, 1943, by Carl Theodor Dreyer; *Death of a Cyclist*, Spain, 1955, by Juan Antonio Bardem; *The Earrings of Madame de…*, France/Italy, 1953, by Max Ophuls; *Fires on the Plain*, Japan, 1959, by Kon Ichikawa; *The 400 Blows* and *Antoine and Colette*, by François Truffaut; *High and Low*, Japan, 1963, by Akira Kurosawa; *Jules and Jim*, France, 1962, by Truffaut; *Knife in the Water*, Poland, 1962, by Roman Polanski; *Kwaidan*, Japan, 1965, by Masaki Kobayashi; *The Lady Vanishes*, UK, 1938, by Alfred Hitchcock; *The Makioka Sisters*, Japan, 1983, by Ichikawa; *The Organizer*, Italy, 1963, by Mario Monicelli; *The Phantom Carriage*, Sweden, 1921, by Victor Sjöström; *The Rules of the Game*, France, 1939, by Jean Renoir; *Sansho the Bailiff*, Japan, 1954, by Kenji Mizoguchi; *Seven Samurai*, Japan, 1954, by Kurosawa; *The Seventh Seal*, Sweden, 1957, by Bergman; *La Strada*, Italy, 1954, by Federico Fellini; *Summer with Monika*, Sweden, 1956, by Ingmar Bergman; *Viridiana*, Mexico/Spain, 1961, by Luis Buñuel; *Walkabout*, Australia, 1971, by Nicolas Roeg; *Wild Strawberries*, Sweden, 1957, by Bergman; *WR: Mysteries of the Organism*, Yugoslavia, 1971, by Dušan Makavejev; *Zero for Conduct*, France, 1933, by Jean Vigo.

**"HBO Films Directors Dialogues"** – in the Stanley Kaplan Penthouse: Stephen Frears in conversation with Lisa Schwarzbaum; Michael Apted in conversation with John Powers; Guillermo del Toro in conversation with Gavin Smith.

**"Looking at Jazz"** – in partnership with Jazz at Lincoln Center, a screening of jazz performances captured on film hosted by jazz pianist and scholar, Lewis Porter, who explores the relationship between jazz and film.

*Day of Wrath* by Carl Theodor Dreyer

**"The Return of Alejandro Jodorowsky"** – *The Holy Mountain*, Mexico/USA, 1973, and *El Topo*, Spain/Mexico, 1970.

**"Scenes from the City: 40 Years of Filmmaking in New York"** – a talk by James Sanders, filmmaker, writer, and editor of a book produced in conjunction with the Mayor's Office of Film, Theatre and Broadcasting.

**"Views from the Avant-Garde"** – curated by Mark McElhatten and Gavin Smith. Films from USA unless otherwise noted.

**Program 1:** "The Great Divide" – *Mirror World*, by Abigail Child; *More Than Meets the Eye: Remaking Jane Fonda*, by Scott Stark; *Dangerous Supplement*, South Korea/USA, by Soon-Mi Yoo; *The General Returns from One Place to Another*, by Michael Robinson; *site specific_ROMA 04*, Italy, by Olivo Barbieri; *Sahara Mohave*, by Leslie Thornton; *You Don't Bring Me Flowers*, by Michael Robinson; *Freedom and Homeland*, Switzerland, by Jean-Luc Godard and Anne-Marie Miéville.

**Program 2:** "Saul Levine: Notes from the Underground" – *Note to Patti*, *Note to Coleen*, *New Left Note*, *The Big Stick/An Old Reel*, and *Note to Poli*.

**Program 3:** "…Dissolves Into Air" – *The Riddle of Lumen*, by Stan Brakhage; *Between Two Deaths*, by Wago Kreider; *My Person in the Water*, by Leighton Pierce; *Cat's Cradle*, by Stan Brakhage; *This, and This*, by Vincent Grenier; *Clear Blue Sky*, by Tomonari Nishikawa; *0778 man.road.river*, Brazil, by Marcellvs L.; *Film for Invisible Ink case no. 71: Base-Plus-Fog*; by David Gatten; *Song and Solitude*, by Nathaniel Dorsky.

**Program 4:** Kenneth Anger – *Fireworks*, *Rabbit's Moon*, *Scorpio Rising*, and *Kustom Kar Kommandos*.

**Program 5:** "Above and Below" – *Silk Ties*, by Jim Jennings; *Crossings*, by Robert Fenz; *Views from Home*, UK, by Guy Sherwin; *Block*, UK, Emily Richardson; *site specific_LAS VEGAS 05*, Canada/Italy, by Olivo Barbieri; *THE PUSHCARTS LEAVE ETERNITY STREET*, by Ken Jacobs; *This Is My Heart*, Brazil/France, by Edson Barrus; *His Eye Is on the Sparrow*, by Bruce Conner; *Threshold of Transience aka The Dike of Transience*, Hungary, by Gulya Nemes; *Drive-Thru*, by Gretchen Skogerson.

**Program 6:** Paolo Gioli – *The Perforated Operator*, *Filmarilyn*, *Quando l'occhio trema*, *Traumatograph*, and *Images Disturbed by an Intense Parasite*.

**Program 7:** Ernie Gehr – *Serene Velocity*, *Table*, *The Morse Code Operator (or The Monkey Wrench)*, and *Before the Olympics*.

**Program 8:** "Mind and Matter" – *Reel 4 (Fountain with Black Sculptures, Heavenly Curtains, Airplanes II, Daffodils in the River, St. Jacob's Tower, Water, Swings, Bulrushes)*, Germany/France, by Helga Fanderl; *Nodes*, by Stan Brakhage; *Untitled #9*, by Greg Sharits; *Turbulent Blue*, by Luther Price; *Everyday Bad Dream*, by Fred Worden; *Black and White Trypps #2*, by Ben Russell; *Orbit*, by Kerry Laitala; *Light Work 1*, by Jennifer Reeves; *Transit*, by Greg Sharits; *Apparent Motion*, by Paul Sharits; *They Wakened Later, Simultaneously, Much Refreshed*, by Bruce McClure.

**Program 9:** *Brand Upon the Brain!*, Canada, by Guy Maddin, with Isabella Rossellini as the narrator. An earth-shaking live spectacle. Musical accompaniment by the Ensemble Sospeso.

*The Cranes Are Flying* by Mikhail Kalatazov

# 2007

NOTE: DUE TO CONSTRUCTION AT ALICE TULLY HALL, EXCEPT FOR OPENING AND CLOSING NIGHTS AT AVERY FISHER HALL, ALL PERFORMANCES WERE HELD IN THE FREDERICK P. ROSE HALL, THE HOME OF JAZZ AT LINCOLN CENTER.

SELECTION COMMITTEE: RICHARD PEÑA, CHAIRMAN, KENT JONES, SCOTT FOUNDAS, J. HOBERMAN, AND LISA SCHWARZBAUM. SHORT FILM SELECTION COMMITTEE: LAURA KERN, SUSAN MCCARTHY, RICHARD PEÑA, AND GAVIN SMITH. SILENT FILM COORDINATOR: SAYRE MAXFIELD.

THE 45TH NYFF POSTER ARTWORK WAS CREATED BY ©AGNÈS B.

*No Country for Old Men* by Joel and Ethan Coen

**THE DARJEELING LIMITED**
*USA, 2007. Directed by Wes Anderson.*

Written by Anderson, Roman Coppola, and Jason Schwartzman. With Owen Wilson, Adrien Brody, Schwartzman, Anjelica Huston. Shown with *Hotel Chevalier*, USA. Directed by Wes Anderson. (Opening Night.)

**NO COUNTRY FOR OLD MEN**
*USA, 2007. Written and Directed by Joel and Ethan Coen, based on Cormac McCarthy's novel.*

With Tommy Lee Jones, Javier Bardem, Josh Brolin, Woody Harrelson, Kelly Macdonald, Garret Dillahunt, Tess Harper. (Centerpiece.)

**PERSEPOLIS ▼**
*France, 2007. Written and Directed by Vincent Paronnaud and Marjane Satrapi.*

An animated adaptation of the original graphic novels by Satrapi. With the voices of Chiara Mastroianni, Catherine Deneuve, Danielle Darrieux, Simon Abkarian. Shown with *The Vulnerable Ones*, Democratic Republic of Congo. Directed by Bent-Jorgen Perlmutt. (Closing Night.)

**ACTRESSES**
*France, 2007. Directed by Valeria Bruni Tedeschi.*

Written by Bruni Tedeschi, Agnès de Sacy, and Noémie Lvovsky. With Bruni Tedeschi, Lvovsky, Mathieu Amalric, Louis Garrel.

**ALEXANDRA**
*Russia, 2007. Written and Directed by Aleksandr Sokurov.*

With Galina Vishnevskaya, Vasili Shevtsov, Raisa Gichaeva.

**THE AXE IN THE ATTIC**
*USA, 2007. Directed by Ed Pincus and Lucia Small.*

A documentary dealing with human survival following Hurricane Katrina that also offers a startling investigation into the ethics of documentary filmmaking.

**BEFORE THE DEVIL KNOWS YOU'RE DEAD**
*USA, 2007. Directed by Sidney Lumet.*

Written by Kelly Masterson. With Philip Seymour Hoffman, Ethan Hawke, Albert Finney, Marisa Tomei, Rosemary Harris.

**BLADE RUNNER: THE FINAL CUT**
*USA, 1982/2007. Directed by Ridley Scott.*

Written by Hampton Fancher and David Peoples, based on Philip K. Dick's novel *Do Androids Dream of Electric Sheep?*. With Harrison Ford, Rutger Hauer, Sean Young, Edward James Olmos, Daryl Hannah. On the occasion of its 25th anniversary, Scott fashioned a version of *Blade Runner* closest to what he originally intended.

**CALLE SANTA FE**
*Chile/France/Belgium, 2007. Directed by Carmen Castillo (Echeverría).*

The widow of Miguel Enríquez, the leader of the Movement of the Revolutionary Left, returns after three decades to the street in Santiago, Chile, where her husband was gunned down by secret police. Shown with *Orishas: Hay un Son*, France. Directed by Edouard Salier.

**THE DIVING BELL AND THE BUTTERFLY ▲**
*France/USA, 2007. Directed by Julian Schnabel.*

Written by Ronald Harwood, based on Jean-Dominique Bauby's book. With Mathieu Amalric, Emmanuelle Seigner, Marie-Josée Croze, Anne Consigny, Patrick Chesnais, Max von Sydow.

**FLIGHT OF THE RED BALLOON**
*France, 2007. Directed by Hou Hsiao-hsien.*

Written by Hou Hsiao-hsien and François Margolin. With Juliette Binoche, Simon Iteanu, Song Fang, Hippolyte Girardot, Louise Margolin.

**4 MONTHS, 3 WEEKS AND 2 DAYS**
*Romania, 2007. Written and Directed by Cristian Mungiu.*

With Anamaria Marinca, Laura Vasiliu, Vlad Ivanov, Alex Potocean.

**A GIRL CUT IN TWO**
*France, 2007. Directed by Claude Chabrol.*

Written by Chabrol and Cécile Maistre. With Ludivine Sagnier, Benoît Magimel, François Berléand, Mathilda May. Shown with *Saturday's Shadow*, UK. Directed by Nick Gordon.

**GO GO TALES**
*USA, 2007. Written and Directed by Abel Ferrara.*

With Willem Dafoe, Bob Hoskins, Matthew Modine, Asia Argento. Shown with *Death to the Tinman*, USA. Directed by Ray Tintori.

**I JUST DIDN'T DO IT ▼**
*Japan, 2007. Written and Directed by Masayuki Suo.*

With Ryo Kase, Asaka Seto, Koji Yamamoto, Masako Motai, Koji Yakusho.

*The Man from London* by Béla Tarr

### I'M NOT THERE
*USA, 2007. Directed by Todd Haynes.*

Written by Haynes and Oren Moverman. With Cate Blanchett, Ben Whishaw, Christian Bale, Richard Gere, Marcus Carl Franklin, Heath Ledger.

### IN THE CITY OF SYLVIA
*Spain/France, 2007. Written and Directed by José Luis Guerín.*

With Pilar López de Ayala, Xavier Lafitte, Laurence Cordier, Tanja Czichy.

### THE LAST MISTRESS
*France, 2007. Written and Directed by Catherine Breillat.*

Based Jules Barbey d'Aurevilly's novel. With Asia Argento, Fu'ad Aït Aattou, Roxane Mesquida, Claude Sarraute.

### THE MAN FROM LONDON
*Hungary/France/Germany, 2007. Directed by Béla Tarr.*

Written by László Krasznahorkai and Tarr. With Miroslav Krobot, Tilda Swinton, Erika Bók, János Derzsi.

### MARGOT AT THE WEDDING
*USA, 2007. Written and Directed by Noah Baumbach.*

With Nicole Kidman, Jennifer Jason Leigh, Jack Black, Zane Pais, Flora Cross, Ciarán Hinds, Matthew Arkin.

### MARRIED LIFE
*USA, 2007. Directed by Ira Sachs.*

Written by Oren Moverman and Sachs, based on John Bingham's book *Five Roundabouts to Heaven*. With Pierce Brosnan, Chris Cooper, Patricia Clarkson, Rachel McAdams

### MR. WARMTH: THE DON RICKLES PROJECT
*USA, 2007. Directed by John Landis.*

A portrait of a bygone era and of the comic Don Rickles. Shown with *The Boxing Lesson*, Romania, 2007. Directed by Alexandru Mavrodineanu.

### THE ORPHANAGE
*Spain, 2007. Directed by Juan Antonio Bayona.*

Written by Sergio G. Sánchez. With Belén Rueda, Fernando Cayo, Roger Príncep, Mabel Ribera, Geraldine Chaplin.

### PARANOID PARK
*USA, 2007. Written and Directed by Gus Van Sant, based on the novel by Blake Nelson.*

With Gabe Nevins, Dan Liu, Jake Miller, Taylor Momsen. Shown with *No Part of the Pig Is Wasted*, France, 2006. Directed by Emma Perret.

### REDACTED
*USA, 2007. Written and Directed by Brian De Palma.*

A fictionalized account of a 2006 atrocity committed against a teenage girl and her family by American troops in Mahmoudiya. Shown with *Cherries*, UK. Directed by Tom Harper.

### THE ROMANCE OF ASTREA AND CELADON
*France, 2007. Written and Directed by Eric Rohmer, based on Honoré d'Urfé's novel.*

With Andy Gillet, Stéphanie Crayencour, Cécile Cassel, Véronique Reymond. Shown with *Chinese Whispers*, Germany. Directed by Oliver Rauch.

### SECRET SUNSHINE
*South Korea, 2007. Written and Directed by Lee Chang-dong, based on an original story by Yi Chong-jun.*

With Jeon Do-yeon, Song Kang-ho.

### SILENT LIGHT
*Mexico/France/The Netherlands, 2007. Written and Directed by Carlos Reygadas.*

With Cornelio Wall, Elizabeth Fehr, Miriam Toews, Maria Pankratz, Peter Wall.

### USELESS
*Hong Kong, 2007. Directed by Jia Zhang-ke.*

A documentary about the production of clothing, from local tailors in Northern Chinese mining country to Parisian fashion installations. Shown with *Franz Kafka's A Country Doctor*, Japan. Directed by Koji Yamamura.

*Blade Runner* by Ridley Scott

# Special Events

PRESENTED AT THE WALTER READE THEATER UNLESS OTHERWISE NOTED

**"Chinese Modern – A Tribute to Cathay Studios"** – films shown: *The Battle of Love,* by Yue Feng, 1957; *June Bride,* by Tang Huang, 1960; *Mambo Girl,* by Yi Wen, 1957; *Our Dream Car,* by Yi Wen, 1959; *Sister Long Legs,* by Tang Huang, 1960; *Sun, Moon and Star (Parts 1 & 2),* by Yi Wen, 1961; *The Wild, Wild Rose,* by Wong Tin-lam, 1960.

**"The Future Is Now: Blade Runner at 25"** – film scholars Giuliana Bruno, Scott Bukatman, and Jane Gaines, along with members of *Blade Runner* creative team discuss the film on the occasion if its 25th anniversary.

### HAMLET
*Germany, 1920-21. Directed by Svend Gade and Heinz Schall.* Written by Erwin Gepard. With Asta Nielsen. A print restored to its original polychrome-tinted version by the German Film Institute. Presented with piano accompaniment by Donald Sosin.

**"HBO Films Directors Dialogues"** – in the Stanley Kaplan Penthouse: Wes Anderson in conversation with Kent Jones; Todd Haynes in conversation with J. Hoberman; Sidney Lumet in conversation with Gavin Smith; Julian Schnabel in conversation with Richard Peña.

**"In Glorious Technicolor: Martin Scorsese Presents":**
### DRUMS ALONG THE MOHAWK
*USA, 1939. Directed by John Ford.*
Written by Lamar Trotti and Sonya Levien, based on the novel by Walter Edmonds. With Claudette Colbert, Henry Fonda, Edna May Oliver.

### LEAVE HER TO HEAVEN
*USA, 1945. Directed by John M. Stahl.*
Written by Jo Swerling, based on Ben Ames Williams's novel. With Gene Tierney, Cornel Wilde, Jeanne Crain, Vincent Price.

**"Special Music Screenings"** – *Fados,* Portugal/Spain, 2007. Directed by Carlos Saura. A celebration of fado aka Portuguese blues; *The Other Side of the Mirror: Bob Dylan Live at the Newport Folk Festival 1963-1965,* USA, 2007. Directed by Murray Lerner. *Dylan in the '60s,* including duets with Joan Baez; *Runnin' Down a Dream: Tom Petty and the Heartbreakers,* USA, 2007. Directed by Peter Bogdanovich.

**"Tropical Analysis: The Films of Joaquim Pedro de Andrade"** – one of the father of Brazil's Cinema Novo movement of the late 1960s. Films shown: *The Brazilian Woodman,* 1982; *Conjugal Warfare,* 1975, shown with *Cat Skin,* 1962; *The Conspirators,* 1972; *Garrincha, Joy of the People,* 1963, shown with *Brasilia, Contradictions of a New City,* 1968; *Macunaíma,* 1969, shown with *The Master of Apipucos,* 1959; *The Priest and the Girl,* 1966, shown with *The Poet of the Castle,* 1959; short films by Andrade.

### UNDERWORLD
*USA, 1927. Directed by Josef von Sternberg.*
Written by Ben Hecht, Robert N. Lee, and von Sternberg. With George Bancroft, Evelyn Brent, Clive Brook. A new print with music accompaniment by the Alloy Orchestra.

**"Views from the Avant-Garde"** – curated by Mark McElhatten and Gavin Smith. Films from the USA unless otherwise noted.

**Program 1:** "From the Canyons to the Stars" – *All That Rises,* by Daicho Saito; *The Coming Race,* UK, by Ben Rivers; *Surging Sea of Humanity,* by Ken Jacobs; *Black and White Trypps Number Three,* by Ben Russell; *Energie!,* Germany, by Thorsten Fleisch; *North Shore,* by Fred Worden; *Armoire,* by Vincent Grenier; *Finestra davanti ad un albero (dedicato a Fox Talbot),* Italy, by Paolo Gioli; *Transit of Venus,* UK, by Nicky Hamlyn; *Observando el Cielo,* by Jeanne Liotta.

**Program 2:** *At Sea,* by Peter Hutton.

**Program 3:** "Unending" – *The Hyrcynium Wood,* UK, by Ben Rivers; *Nymph,* by Ken Jacobs; *Anonimatografo,* Italy, by Paolo Gioli; *What the Water Said 4-6* and *How to Conduct a Love Affair,* by David Gatten; *Tziporah,* Abraham Ravett; *Phantom,* Luke Sieczek; *In Memoriam,* by Mark LaPore; *Untitled (for David Gatten),* by Mark LaPore and Phil Solomon; *Rehearsals for Retirement* and *Last Days in a Lonely Place,* by Phil Solomon.

**Program 4:** Ken Jacobs and Rick Reed – *Dreams That Money Can't Buy,* a live Nervous Magic Lantern performance, and *Capitalism: Child Labor,* by Ken Jacobs.

**Program 5:** "Stranger Than a Strange Land" – *Warm Objects,* by Peggy Ahwesh; *Notes from a Bastard Child,* USA/Portugal, by Fern Silva; *The Mongrel Sister,* by Luther Price; *Victory Over the Sun,* by Michael Robinson; *Stranger Comes to Town,* by Jacqueline Goss; *Light Is Waiting,* by Michael Robinson; *SpaceDisco One,* by Damon Packard.

**Program 6:** "House Next Door" – *Old Dark House* and *We the People,* UK, by Ben Rivers; *Detroit Block,* Julie Murray; *Frontier Step,* by Gretchen Skogerson; *Dedication,* by Peggy Ahwesh; *House,* UK, by Ben Rivers; *Footnotes to a House of Love,* by Laida Lertxundi; *Office Suite,* by Robert Todd; *Prague Winter,* by Jim Jennings; *Electricity,* USA/Czech Republic, by Henry Hills; *Recorando el Ayer,* USA/Ecuador, by Alexander Cuestra; *Tahousse,* France, by Olivier Fouchard and Mahine Rouhi.

**Program 7:** Helga Fanderl – *Glaciers, Drawing Cobblestones, Gulf House, Leaden Waves, Shadows on a Red Wall, Tents on a Canal, Warrior's Market, Louie, Tombs, Broadway, Reflections, Courtyard, Gray Heron, Three Midtown Sketches, Pond in the Berry, Green Balloon, Carousel, Swinging Zora, Throwing the Net,* and *Under the Water Lilies.*

**Program 8:** Ernie Gehr – *Shadow, Cinematic Fertilizer 1 & 2,* and *10th Avenue.*

**Program 9:** "Bits and Pieces (Make Up to Break Up)" – *Antigenic Drift,* by Lewis Klahr; *Hide,* by Christophe Girardet and Matthias Müller; *The Counter Girl Trilogy,* by Courtney Hoskins; *Face Caught in the Dark,* Italy, by Paolo Gioli; *Beirut Outtakes,* by Peggy Ahwesh; *For Them Ending, For a Winter, Sunbeam Hunter, A Logic Sore, The Wedding Present,* and *40 Years,* by Jonathan Schwartz; *The Film of a Thousand and One Nights and a Night (Vol. 2),* by Scott Puccio; *Hanky Panky January 1902,* by Ken Jacobs; *Recreation,* by Robert Breer.

**Program 10:** *Pitcher of Colored Light,* USA/Switzerland, by Robert Beavers; *Reel from The Eniaos (Bliss),* by Gregory Markopoulos.

**Program 11:** "Memories" – The 6th annual Jeonju International Film Festival Digital Project: *Respite,* by Harun Farocki; *The Rabbit Hunters,* by Pedro Costa; *Correspondences,* by Eugène Green.

46th New York Film Festival
September 26th – October 12th 2008  Presented by The Film Society of Lincoln Center

# 2008

NOTE: DUE TO CONSTRUCTION AT ALICE TULLY HALL, ALL PERFORMANCES EXCEPT FOR OPENING AND CLOSING NIGHTS AT AVERY FISHER HALL, WERE PRESENTED AT THE ZIEGFELD THEATRE ON WEST 54TH STREET.

SELECTION COMMITTEE: RICHARD PEÑA, CHAIRMAN, SCOTT FOUNDAS, J. HOBERMAN, KENT JONES, AND LISA SCHWARZBAUM. SHORT FILM SELECTION COMMITTEE: ISA CUCINOTTA, LAURA KERN, RICHARD PEÑA, AND GAVIN SMITH. SILENT FILM COORDINATOR: SAYRE MAXFIELD.

THE 46TH NYFF POSTER ARTWORK WAS CREATED BY ROBERT COTTINGHAM. LIST ART POSTERS, ©LCPA.

### THE CLASS (ENTRE LES MURS)
*France, 2008. Directed by Laurent Cantet.*

Written by François Bégaudeau, Robin Campillo, and Cantet, based on Bégaudeau's book. With Bégaudeau, Nassim Amrabt, Laura Baquela, Cherif Bounaïdja Rachedi. (Opening Night.)

### CHANGELING
*USA, 2008. Directed by Clint Eastwood.*

Written by J. Michael Straczynski. With Angelina Jolie, John Malkovich, Jeffrey Donovan, Colm Feore. Shown with *Wait for Me*, USA. Directed by Ross Kauffman. (Centerpiece.)

### THE WRESTLER ▶
*USA, 2008. Directed by Darren Aronofsky.*

Written by Rob Siegel. With Mickey Rourke, Marisa Tomei, Evan Rachel Wood. Shown with *Security*, Germany. Directed by Lars Henning. (Closing Night.)

### AFTERSCHOOL
*USA, 2008. Written and Directed by Antonio Campos.*

With Ezra Miller, Jeremy White, Emory Cohen, Michael Stuhlbarg, Addison Timlin.

### ASHES OF TIME REDUX
*Hong Kong, 2008. Written and Directed by Wong Kar Wai, based on a story by Louis Cha.*

With Leslie Cheung, Brigitte Lin, Tony Leung Chiu Wai. A restoration and expansion of the director's legendary 1994 film. Shown with *Dust*, USA. Directed by Baker Smith.

### BULLET IN THE HEAD
*Spain/France, 2008. Written and Directed by Jaime Rosales.*

With Ion Arretxe, Iñigo Royo, Jaione Otxone, Ana Vila.

### CHE
*France/Spain, 2008. Directed by Steven Soderbergh.*

Written by Peter Buchman. With Benicio Del Toro, Demián Bichir, Santiago Cabrera, Elvira Mínguez.

### CHOUGA
*Kazakhstan/France, 2007. Written and Directed by Darezhan Omirbaev, based on Leo Tolstoy's* Anna Karenina.

With Ainur Turgambaeva, Aidos Sagatov. Shown with *Gauge*, USA. Directed by Alistair Banks Griffin.

### A CHRISTMAS TALE (UN CONTE DE NOËL)
*France, 2008. Directed by Arnaud Desplechin.*

Written by Emmanuel Bourdieu and Desplechin. With Catherine Deneuve, Jean-Paul Roussillon, Anne Consigny, Mathieu Amalric, Melvil Poupaud, Emmanuelle Devos, Chiara Mastroianni.

### FOUR NIGHTS WITH ANNA
*Poland/France, 2008. Directed by Jerzy Skolimowski.*

Written by Ewa Piaskowska and Skolimowski. With Kinga Preis, Artur Steranko, Jerzy Fedorowicz, Redbad Klijnstra, Jakub Snochowski. Shown with *PAL/SECAM*, Russia/USA. Directed by Dmitry Povolotsky.

### GOMORRAH ▲
*Italy, 2008. Directed by Matteo Garrone.*

Written by Maurizio Braucci, Ugo Chiti, Gianni Di Gregorio, Garrone, Massimo Gaudioso, and Roberto Saviano, based on Saviano's book. With Salvatore Cantalupo, Gianfelice Imparato, Maria Nazionale, Toni Servillo.

### HAPPY-GO-LUCKY
*UK, 2008. Written and Directed by Mike Leigh.*

With Sally Hawkins, Alexis Zegerman, Andrea Riseborough, Sinéad Matthews, Eddie Marsan.

### THE HEADLESS WOMAN
*Argentina/France/Italy/Spain, 2008. Written and Directed by Lucrecia Martel.*

With Guillermo Arengo, César Bordón, Claudia Cantero, Inés Efron. Shown with *I Hear Your Scream*, Argentina. Directed by Pablo Lamar.

### HUNGER
*UK, 2008. Directed by Steve McQueen.*

Written by McQueen and Enda Walsh. With Michael Fassbender, Liam Cunningham, Stuart Graham, Brian Milligan, Liam McMahon. Shown with *This Is Her*, New Zealand. Directed by Katie Wolfe.

### I'M GONNA EXPLODE (VOY A EXPLOTAR)
*Mexico, 2008. Written and Directed by Gerardo Naranjo.*

With Maria Deschamps, Juan Pablo de Santiago, Daniel Giménez Cacho, Martha Claudia Moreno.

### LET IT RAIN
*France, 2008. Directed by Agnès Jaoui.*

Written by Jean-Pierre Bacri and Jaoui. With Jaoui, Bacri, Jamel Debbouze, Pascale Arbillot. Shown with *Unpredictable Behaviour*, USA/Germany. Directed by Pasha Shapiro and Ernst Weber.

### LOLA MONTÈS
*France/West Germany, 1955. Directed by Max Ophuls.*

Written by Jacques Natanson, Ophuls, and Annette Wademant. With Martine Carol, Peter Ustinov, Anton Walbrook, Ivan Desny, Oskar Werner. (Retrospective.) Presented in honor of critic Andrew Sarris on the occasion of his 80th birthday. Sarris introduced the film, which he considers to be the greatest of all time.

### NIGHT AND DAY
*South Korea, 2008. Written and Directed by Hong Sang-soo.*

With Kim Yeong-ho, Park Eun-hye, Hwang Su-jeong, Kee Joo-bong.

### THE NORTHERN LAND
*Portugal, 2008. Written and Directed by João Botelho, based on Agustina Bessa-Luís's novel.*

With Ana Moreira, Rogério Samora, Ricardo Aibéo. Shown with *Surprise!*, France. Directed by Fabrice Maruca.

### SERBIS
*Philippines/France, 2008. Directed by Brillante Mendoza.*

Written by Armando Lao, based on a story by Lao and Boots Agbayani Pastor. With Gina Pareño, Jaclyn Jose. Shown with *Maybe Tomorrow*, France. Directed by Guilhem Amesland.

### SUMMER HOURS
*France, 2008. Directed by Olivier Assayas.*

Written by Assayas and Clémentine Schaeffer. With Juliette Binoche, Charles Berling, Jérémie Renier, Edith Scob. Shown with *Ralph*, UK. Directed by Alex Winckler.

### TOKYO SONATA
*Japan/The Netherlands, 2008. Directed by Kiyoshi Kurosawa.*

Written by Kurosawa and Sachiko Tanaka. With Haruka Igawa, Kai Inowaki, Teruyuki Kagawa, Kyoko Koizumi, Yu Koyanagi. Shown with *Love Is Dead*, France. Directed by Eric Capitaine.

### TONY MANERO
*Chile/Brazil, 2008. Directed by Pablo Larraín.*

Written by Alfredo Castro, Mateo Iribarren, and Larraín. With Castro, Amparo Noguera, Héctor Morales.

## TULPAN

*Kazakhstan/Germany/Poland/Russia/Switzerland, 2008. Directed by Sergey Dvortsevoy.*

Written by Dvortsevoy and Gennadij Ostrowskij. With Tulepbergen Baisakolov, Ondasyn Besikbasov, Zhappas Dzhailaubaev, Samal Eslyamova. Shown with *Deweneti*, France. Directed by Dyana Gaye.

## 24 CITY

*China/Hong Kong/Japan, 2008. Directed by Jia Zhang-ke.*

Written by Jia Zhang-ke and Zhai Yongming. With Joan Chen, Lu Liping, Zhao Tao, Chen Jianbin.

## WALTZ WITH BASHIR ▶

*Israel/Germany/France, 2008. Written and Directed by Ari Folman.*

An animated documentary featuring interviews with Boaz Rein Buskila, Ori Sivan, Roni Dayg, Carmi Cnaa'n. Shown with *I Don't Feel Like Dancing*, Germany. Directed by Joachim Dollhopf and Evi Goldbrunner.

## WENDY AND LUCY

*USA, 2008. Directed by Kelly Reichardt.*

Written by Jon Raymond and Reichardt. With Michelle Williams, Will Patton, John Robinson, Will Oldham. Shown with *Cry Me a River*, China. Directed by Jia Zhang-ke.

## THE WINDMILL MOVIE

*USA, 2008. Written and Directed by Alexander Olch.*

With Wallace Shawn, Bob Balaban. Straddling the line between documentary and fiction, a kind of critical autobiography of Richard P. "Dick" Rogers. Shown with *Quarry*, USA. Directed by Richard P. Rogers.

# Special Events

PRESENTED AT THE WALTER READE THEATER UNLESS OTHERWISE NOTED

## THE DAY SHALL DAWN

*Pakistan, 1959. Written and Directed by A.J. Kardar.*
With Tripti Mitra, Zurain Rakshi. Shown on the occasion of Pakistan's 50th anniversary.

**"Film Criticism in Crisis?"** – hosted by *Film Comment*. Panel participants included Emmanuel Burdeau, Pascual Espiritu, David Hudson, Jeong Seung-hoon, Kent Jones, Jonathan Rosenbaum, Gavin Smith, Pablo Suarez, and Jessica Winter.

**"HBO Films Directors Dialogues"** – in the Stanley Kaplan Penthouse: Darren Aronofsky in conversation with Richard Peña; Arnaud Desplechin in conversation with Kent Jones; Jia Zhang-ke in conversation with Scott Foundas; Wong Kar Wai in conversation with J. Hoberman.

**"In the Realm of Oshima"** – the films of Nagisa Oshima, a program co-organized by the Film Society and the Cinematheque Ontario. Curated by James Quandt. Films shown: *Band of Ninja*, 1967; *Boy*, 1969; *The Catch*, 1961; *The Ceremony*, 1971; *Cruel Story of Youth* aka *Naked Youth*, 1960; *Dear Summer Sister*, 1972; *Death by Hanging*, 1968; *Diary of a Shinjuku Thief*, 1968; *Double Suicide* aka *Night of the Killer*, 1967; *Empire of Passion*, 1978; *In the Realm of the Senses*, 1976; *Kyoto, My Mother's Place*, 1991; *The Man Who Left His Will on Film*, 1970; *Max Mon Amour*, 1986; *Merry Christmas, Mr. Lawrence*, 1983; *Night and Fog in Japan*, 1960; *100 Years of Japanese Cinema*, 1994; *Pleasures of the Flesh*, 1965; *Shiro of Amakusa, the Christian Rebel* aka *The Revolutionary*, 1962; *Sing a Song of Sex* aka *A Treatise on Japanese Bawdy Songs*, 1967; *The Sun's Burial* aka *Tomb of the Sun*, 1960; *Taboo*

*(Gohatto)*, 1999; *Three Resurrected Drunkards* aka *Sinner in Paradise*, 1968; *A Town of Love and Hope*, 1959, shown with *Diary of a Yunbogi Boy*, 1965; *Violence at Noon*, 1966.

**IT'S HARD BEING LOVED BY JERKS**
*France, 2008. Directed by Daniel Leconte.*
A chronicle of the legal battle that began with 12 cartoons satirizing Islamic fundamentalism.

**THE LAST COMMAND**
*USA, 1928. Directed by Josef von Sternberg.*
With Emil Jannings, Evelyn Brent, William Powell. Musical accompaniment by the Alloy Orchestra.

**"Martin Scorsese Presents In Glorious Technicolor": PANDORA AND THE FLYING DUTCHMAN**
*UK, 1951. Directed by Albert Lewin.*
With Ava Gardner, James Mason. A restored print.

**"The Place of Oshima"** – panel participants included David Dressoe, Aaron Gerow, Annette Michelson, and other scholars and critics.

**"Views from the Avant-Garde"** – curated by Mark McElhatten and Gavin Smith. Films from the USA unless otherwise noted.

**Program 1:** *In girum imus nocte et consumimur igni*, France, 1978, by Guy Debord.

**Program 2:** "The Warmth of the Sun" – *Dove Coup* UK, by Ben Rivers; *Whispers*, by Ernie Gehr; *Les Chaises*, USA/Canada, by Vincent Grenier; *Obar*, by Taylor Dunne; *After Writing*, by Mary Helena Clark; *Origins of the Species*, UK, by Ben Rivers; *Film for Invisible Ink, Case No. 142 Abbreviation for Dead Winter (Diminished By 1794)*, by

David Gatten; *Elements*, by Julie Murray; *False Friends*, Germany, by Sylvia Schedelbauer; *Hold Me Now*, by Michael Robinson; *And the Sun Flowers*, by Mary Helena Clark; *False Aging*, by Lewis Klahr.

**Program 3:** *Aberration of Starlight*, by Andrew Noren.

**Program 4:** *Winter* and *Sarabande*, by Nathaniel Dorsky.

**Program 5:** Bruce Conner tribute – *A MOVIE*, 1958, *THE WHITE ROSE*, 1966, *BREAKAWAY*, 1967, *VIVIAN*, 1964, *TEN SECOND FILM*, 1965, *REPORT*, 1967, *LOOKING FOR MUSHROOMS*, 1996, *TAKE THE 5:10 TO DREAMLAND*, 1977, *VALSE TRISTE*, 1979, and *EASTER MORNING*, 2008.

**Program 6:** "Time of the Signs" – *1859*, by Fred Worden; *Train of Thought*, by Jim Jennings; *New York Lantern*, by Ernie Gehr; *After Marks*, USA/India, by Fern Silva; *Nocturne [Avenue A, no lens]*, by Joel Schlemowitz; *Novel City*, by Leslie Thornton; *Trypps #5 (Dubai)*, USA/United Arab Emirates, by Ben Russell; *Today! (Excerpts #28, #19)*, by David Gatten and Jessie Stead; *Ah Liberty!*, UK, by Ben Rivers.

**Program 7:** *The Diptherians Episode Two: The Rhythm That Forgets Itself*, by Lewis Klahr; *Tattoo Step*, Canada, by Michael Maryniuk; *Mock Up on Mu*, by Craig Baldwin.

**Program 8:** "Still Wave" – *AMERICA IS WAITING*, 1982, by Bruce Conner; *Dig*, by Robert Todd; *Right*, by Scott Stark; *16-18-4*, Japan, by Tomonari Nishikawa; *The Acrobat*, by Chris Kennedy; *Nightparking*, by Gretchen Skogerson; *The Scenic Route*, by Ken Jacobs; *Phantogram*, by Kerry Laitala; *When Worlds Collide*, by Fred Worden; *Horizontal Boundaries*, by Pat O'Neill.

**Program 9:** *RR*, by James Benning.

# 2009

ALL MAIN EVENT SCREENINGS PRESENTED IN ALICE TULLY HALL.

SELECTION COMMITTEE: RICHARD PEÑA, CHAIRMAN, MELISSA ANDERSON, SCOTT FOUNDAS, J. HOBERMAN, AND DENNIS LIM.
SHORT FILM SELECTION COMMITTEE: ISA CUCINOTTA, LAURA KERN, RICHARD PEÑA, AND GAVIN SMITH.

THE 47TH NYFF POSTERS ARTWORK WAS CREATED BY ©GREGORY CREWDSON.

### WILD GRASS (LES HERBES FOLLES)
*France, 2009. Directed by Alain Resnais.*

Written by Laurent Herbiet and Alex Reval, based on Christian Gailly's novel *L'Incident*. With Sabine Azéma, André Dussollier, Anne Consigny, Emmanuelle Devos, Mathieu Amalric. (Opening Night.)

### PRECIOUS: BASED ON THE NOVEL "PUSH" BY SAPPHIRE ▼
*USA, 2009. Directed by Lee Daniels.*

Written by Geoffrey Fletcher. With Gabourey Sidibe, Mo'Nique, Paula Patton, Mariah Carey, Lenny Kravitz. (Centerpiece.)

### BROKEN EMBRACES
*Spain, 2009. Written and Directed by Pedro Almodóvar.*

With Penélope Cruz, Lluís Homar, Blanca Portillo, José Luis Gómez. (Closing Night.)

### ANTICHRIST
*Denmark, 2009. Written and Directed by Lars von Trier.*

With Willem Dafoe, Charlotte Gainsbourg, Storm Acheche Sahlstrøm.

### AROUND A SMALL MOUNTAIN (36 VUES DU PIC SAINT-LOUP)
*France, 2009. Directed by Jacques Rivette.*

Written by Shirel Amitay, Pascal Bonitzer, Christine Laurent, and Rivette. With Jane Birkin, Sergio Castellitto, André Marcon, Jacques Bonnaffé. Shown with *Plastic Bag*, USA. Directed by Ramin Bahrani. Narrated by Werner Herzog.

### THE ART OF THE STEAL
*USA, 2009. Directed by Don Argott.*

A documentary about the controversy surrounding the proposed move of the Barnes Foundation from Merion, PA, to Philadelphia, making it more accessible to the public.

### BLUEBEARD
*France, 2009. Written and Directed by Catherine Breillat.*

With Dominique Thomas, Lola Créton, Daphné Baïwir, Marilou Lopes-Benites. Shown with *Love Child*, Sweden. Directed by Daniel Wirtberg.

### ECCENTRICITIES OF A BLOND HAIR GIRL
*Portugal/France/Spain, 2009. Written and Directed by Manoel de Oliveira.*

With Ricardo Trepa, Catarina Wallenstein, Diogo Dória, Júlia Buisel. Shown with *Get Yer Ya-Yas Out!*, USA, 1969-2009, Directed by Bradley Kaplan, Ian Markiewicz, and Albert Maysles. Rare footage from the Rolling Stones's 1969 U.S. tour.

### EVERYONE ELSE
*Germany, 2009. Written and Directed by Maren Ade.*

With Birgit Minichmayr, Lars Eidinger, Hans-Jochen Wagner, Nicole Marischka.

### GHOST TOWN
*China, 2008. Directed by Zhao Dayong.*

A documentary portraying remarkable signs of life in a dilapidated, remote village in China's mountainous southwest.

### HADEWIJCH
*France, 2009. Written and Directed by Bruno Dumont.*

With Julie Sokolowski, David Dewaele, Yassine Salim, Karl Sarafidis. Shown with *Lili's Paradise*, Peru. Directed by Melina León.

*Sweet Rush* by Andrzej Wajda

### HENRI-GEORGES CLOUZOT'S INFERNO
*France, 2009. Directed by Serge Bromberg and Ruxandra Medrea, based on Clouzot's unfinished film.*

With Bérénice Bejo, Jacques Gamblin, Romy Schneider, Serge Reggiani. A reassemblage of 15 hours of rushes not seen since 1964, resurrecting Clouzot's aborted 1960s experimental film *L'Enfer*. Shown with *The Jung Files*, Spain. Directed by Gemma Ventura.

### INDEPENCIA
*Philippines/France/Germany/The Netherlands, 2009. Directed by Raya Martin.*

Written by Martin and Ramon Sarmiento. With Sid Lucero, Tetchie Agbayani, Alessandra de Rossi, Mika Aguilos. Shown with *A History of Independence*, France/Mali. Directed by Daouda Coulibaly.

### KANIKOSEN
*Japan, 2009. Written and Directed by Sabu, based on the book by Takiji Kobayashi.*

With Ryuhei Matsuda, Hidetoshi Nishijima, Hirofumi Arai, Mitsuki Tanimura.

### LEBANON ▶
*Israel, 2009. Written and Directed by Samuel Maoz.*

With Yoav Donat, Itay Tiran, Oshri Cohen, Michael Moshonov, Zohar Strauss. Shown with *The Slow Game*, Italy. Directed by Paolo Sorrentino.

### LIFE DURING WARTIME
*USA, 2009. Written and Directed by Todd Solondz.*

With Shirley Henderson, Ciarán Hinds, Allison Janney, Chris Marquette, Charlotte Rampling, Paul Reubens, Ally Sheedy. Shown with *Socarrat*, Spain. Directed by David Moreno.

### MIN YE... (TELL ME WHO YOU ARE)
*Mali/France, 2009. Written and Directed by Souleymane Cissé.*

With Sokona Gakou, Assane Kouyate, Alou Sissoko.

### MOTHER
*South Korea, 2009. Directed by Bong Joon-ho.*

Written by Bong and Park Eun-kyo. With Kim Hye-ja, Won Bin.

### NE CHANGE RIEN
*France/Portugal, 2009. Directed by Pedro Costa.*

A concert film featuring the French actress and chanteuse Jeanne Balibar. Shown with *Final Cut Template #2: Hollis Frampton*, USA. Directed by Doug Henry.

### POLICE, ADJECTIVE
*Romania, 2009. Written and Directed by Corneliu Porumboiu.*

With Dragoş Bucur, Vlad Ivanov, Ion Stoica, Irina Saulescu. Shown with *The Funk*, Australia. Directed by Cris Jones.

### A ROOM AND A HALF
*Russia, 2009. Directed by Andrey Khrzhanovsky.*

With Alisa Freyndlikh, Sergei Yursky, Grigoriy Dityatkovskiy, Artem Smola.

### SWEETGRASS
*USA, 2009. Directed by Ilisa Barbash and Lucien Castaing-Taylor.*

A breathtaking chronicle of a group of modern-day cowboys as they lead an enormous herd of sheep over the slopes of the Beartooth Mountains in Montana. Shown with *The History of Aviation*, France/Hungary, 2009. Directed by Bálint Kenyeres.

**SWEET RUSH**
*Poland, 2009. Written and Directed by Andrzej Wajda, based on the novella by Jarosław Iwaszkiewicz.*
With Krystyna Janda, Pawel Szajda, Jadwiga Jankowska-Cieślak, Julia Pietrucha.

**TO DIE LIKE A MAN**
*Portugal, 2009. Directed by João Pedro Rodrigues.*
Written by Rui Catalão, João Rui Guerra da Mata, and Rodrigues. With Fernando Santos, Alexander David, Gonçalo Ferreira de Almeida, Chandra Malatitch.

**TRASH HUMPERS**
*USA, 2009. Written and Directed by Harmony Korine.*
With Rachel Korine, Brian Kotzur, Travis Nicholson, Harmony Korine.

**VINCERE**
*Italy, 2009. Directed by Marco Bellocchio.*
Written by Bellocchio and Daniela Ceselli. With Giovanna Mezzogiorno, Filippo Timi, Fausto Russo Alesi, Michela Cescon, Pier Giorgio Bellocchio.

**WHITE MATERIAL**
*France, 2009. Directed by Claire Denis.*
Written by Denis, Maria N'Diaye. With Isabelle Huppert, Isaach De Bankolé, Christopher Lambert, Nicolas Duvauchelle, William Nadylam, Michel Subor. Shown with *Chicken Heads*, Palestine/USA. Directed by Bassam Ali Jarbawi.

**THE WHITE RIBBON**
*Germany/Austria/France/Italy, 2009. Directed by Michael Haneke.*

Written by Haneke, with Jean-Claude Carrière as a consultant. With Leonie Benesch, Josef Bierbichler, Rainer Bock, Christian Friedel, Burghart Klaussner.

**THE WIZARD OF OZ**
*USA, 1939. Directed by Victor Fleming, some sequences by King Vidor.*
Written by Noel Langley, Florence Ryerson, and Edgar Allan Woolf, based on the book by L. Frank Baum. With Judy Garland, Ray Bolger, Jack Haley, Bert Lahr, Billie Burke, Frank Morgan, Margaret Hamilton. Shown on the film's 70th anniversary. (Retrospective.)

# Special Events
PRESENTED AT THE WALTER READE THEATER UNLESS OTHERWISE NOTED

**"Approaching the Wizard: Flying Monkeys, Ruby Slippers and Yellow Brick Roads in American Cinema and Culture"** – in conjunction with the presentation of *The Wizard of Oz*, a discussion with John Fricke, Jane Lahr, Ned Price, and Robert Sklar.

**"Chandleresque: Raymond Chandler on Film and Television"** – commemorating the 50th anniversary of Chandler's death, a lecture by Adrian Wootton using film and audio clips.
**+ THE BLUE DAHLIA**
*USA, 1946. Directed by George Marshall.*
Written by Raymond Chandler. With Alan Ladd, Veronica Lake, William Bendix, Hugh Beamont.

**"Creating Film Culture: A Tribute to Dan and Toby Talbot and the 'New Yorker Years'"** – a conversation with the Talbots, Molly Haskell, and Jonathan Demme.
**+ MY DINNER WITH ANDRE**
*USA, 1981. Directed by Louis Malle.*
Written by Wallace Shawn. With Shawn and André Gregory.

**CROSSROADS OF YOUTH**
*South Korea, 1934. Directed by An Jong-hwa.*
A restored print accompanied by live narration, as well as singers and a small musical ensemble.

**"A Heart as Big as the World: The Films of Guru Dutt"** – (director and actor), India. Organized in collaboration with Uma da Cunha. Films shown (directed by Dutt unless otherwise noted): *Full Moon*, 1960, by M. Sadiq; *The Gamble* aka *A Game of Chance*, 1951; *The Hawk*, 1953; *In Search of Guru Dutt*, UK, 1989, by Nasreen Munni Kabir; *Master, Mistress and Servant*, 1962, by Abrar Alvi; *Mr. & Mrs. '55*, 1955; *Paper Flowers*, 1959; *Thirst* aka *The Thirsty One*, 1957.

**"HBO Films Directors Dialogues"** – in the Stanley Kaplan Penthouse: Marco Bellocchio in conversation with Phillip Lopate, Lee Daniels in conversation with Melissa Anderson, Claire Denis in conversation with Noah Baumbach, and Michael Haneke in conversation with Darren Aronofsky.

**THE NIGHT OF COUNTING THE YEARS** aka **THE MUMMY**
*Egypt, 1969. Directed by Shadi Abdel Salam.*
A restored print.

**"Pedro Almodóvar's History of Cinema: A Conversation"** – with Richard Peña.

**THE RED RIDING TRILOGY** – adapted from David Peace's series of novels about the Yorkshire Ripper. Premiered on Britain's Channel 4. *Red Riding 1974*, UK, 2009. Directed by Julien Jarrold; *Red Riding 1980*, UK, 2009. Directed by James Marsh; *Red Riding 1983*, UK, 2009. Directed by Anand Tucker.

**"(Re)Inventing China: A New Cinema for a New Society – 1949-1966"**: *Before the New Director Arrives*, 1956, by Lu Ban; *Big Li, Little Li and Old Li*, 1962, by Xie Jin; *Bridge*, 1949, by Wang Bin; *Family*, 1957, by Chen Xihe and Ye Ming; *Five Golden Flowers*, 1959, by Wang Jiayi; *Keep the Red Flag Flying* aka *Song of the Red Flag*, 1960, by Ling Zifeng; *Li Shang Shuang*, 1962, by Lu Ren; *Living Forever in Burning Flames*, 1965, by Shui Hua; *Mysterious Traveling Companion*, 1955, by Lin Nong and Zhu Wenshun; *New Year Sacrifice*, 1956, by Sang Hu; *Nie Er*, 1959, by Zheng Junli; *Platoon Commander Guan*, 1951, by Shi Hui; *The Red Detachment of Women*, 1961, by Xie Jin; *Sentries Under Neon Lights*, 1964, by Wang Ping and Ge Xing; *Seventy-Two Tenants*, 1963, by Wang Weiyi; *This Life of Mine* aka *The Life of a Beijing Policeman*, 1950, by Shi Hui; *Two Stage Sisters*, 1965, by Xie Jin; *Visitors on the Icy Mountains*, 1963, by Zhao Shinshui; *Woman Basketball Player No. 5*, 1957, by Xie Jin; *Woman Hairdresser*, 1962, by Ding Ran.

**"Views from the Avant-Garde"** – curated by Mark McElhatten and Gavin Smith. Films from the USA unless otherwise noted.

**Program 1:** *La rabbia di Pasolini*, Italy, by Pier Paolo Pasolini and Giuseppe Bertolucci.

**Program 2:** *Horizon Line*, by Katherin McInnis; *Scene 32*, USA/India, by Shambhavi Kaul; *What Part of the Earth Is Inhabited (After Pliny the Elder)*, by Erin Espelie; *night side*, by Rebecca Meyers; *dwarfs the sea*, by Stephanie Barber; *Journals and Remarks*, by David Gatten; *A Letter to Uncle Boonmee*, Thailand, by Apichatpong Weerasethakul; *(((((()))))*, by Leslie Thornton; *Trypps #6 (Malobi)*, USA/Suriname, by Ben Russell; *I Know Where I'm Going*, UK, by Ben Rivers.

**Program 3:** A Tribute to Chick Strand (1931-2009) – *Angel Blue Sweet Wings*, 1966, *Cartoon Le Mousse*, 1979, *Kristallnacht*, 1979, *Loose Ends*, 1979, and *Fake Fruit Factory*, 1986.

**Program 4:** *Sarah Ann*, The Netherlands/UK, by Pim Zwier; *Riff*, UK, by Lis Rhodes; *O'er the Land*, by Deborah Stratman.

**Program 5:** *In Comparison*, Germany, by Harun Farocki; *Scrap Vessel*, by Jason Byrne.

**Program 6:** *Puccini Conservato*, Canada/Italy, by Michael Snow; *Bethlehem*, by Peggy Ahwesh; *My Tears Are Dry*, Spain/USA, by Laida Lertxundi; *If There Be Thorns*, by Michael Robinson; *Wednesday Morning Two A.M.*, by Lewis Klahr; excerpt from *The Sky Socialist stratified*, by Ken Jacobs; *Still Raining, Still Dreaming*, by Phil Solomon.

**Program 7:** *The Three Ravens*, by Bobby Abate; *My Way 1*, by Amie Siegel; *I Miss*, by Annie Dorsen; *(If I Can Sing a Song About) Ligatures*, by Abigail Child; *the inversion transcription, evening track and attractor*, by Stephanie Barber; *non-Aryan*, by Abraham Ravett; *Faces by a Person Unknown*, Italy, by Paolo Gioli; *Vineland*, by Laura Kraning; *The Diamond (Descartes' Daughter)*, UK, by Emily Wardill; *Contre-jour*, Germany, by Christophe Girardet and Matthias Müller.

**Program 8:** *The Last Happy Day*, by Lynne Sachs; *Nothing Is Over Nothing*, by Jonathan Schwartz; *The Exception and the Rule*, UK/India/Pakistan, by Brad Butler and Karen Mirza.

**Program 9:** *untitled*, 1947, by Norman Mailer; *Holy Woods*, France, by Cécile Fontaine; *Sahara Mosaic*, by Fern Silva; *way fare*, Germany, by Sylvia Schedelbauer; *Lumphini 2552*, Thailand/Japan, by Tomonari Nishikawa; *Chromatic Frenzy*, by Kerry Laitala; *Vibration*, UK, 1975, by Jane Arden and Jack Bond.

**Program 10:** *Postcard #3: Niagara Rises*, by Carolyn Faber; *Sphinx on the Seine*, by Paul Clipson; *Piensa en Mi*, USA/Ecuador, by Alexandra Cuesta; *Quartet*, UK, by Nicky Hamlyn; *H(i)J*, Germany, by Guillaume Cailleau; *The Universe*, by Barry Gerson; *Straight Lines*, by Vincent Grenier; *Waterfront Follies*, by Ernie Gehr.

**Program 11:** *Trees of Syntax, Leaves of Axis*, Canada, by Daichi Saito; *Parallax*, Canada/France/Yemen/Bangladesh, by Christopher Becks; *Sound Over Water*, by Mary Helena Clark; *Physical Changes*, by David Dinnell; *Wound Footage*, Germany, by Thorsten Fleisch; *Cong in Our Gregational Pom-Poms*, by Bruce McClure.

# 2010

## THE SOCIAL NETWORK

*USA, 2010. Directed by David Fincher.*

Written by Aaron Sorkin, based on the book by Ben Mezrich. With Jesse Eisenberg, Andrew Garfield, Justin Timberlake, Armie Hammer, Max Minghella, Brenda Song, Rooney Mara. (Opening Night.)

## THE TEMPEST

*USA, 2010. Written and Directed by Julie Taymor, based on Shakespeare's play.*

With Helen Mirren, Alfred Molina, Russell Brand, Djimon Hounsou, Alan Cumming, Chris Cooper, David Strathairn, Ben Whishaw, Felicity Jones. (Centerpiece.)

## HEREAFTER

*USA, 2010. Directed by Clint Eastwood.*

Written by Peter Morgan. With Matt Damon, Cécile De France, Bryce Dallas Howard, Jay Mohr. (Closing Night.)

## ANOTHER YEAR

*UK, 2010. Written and Directed by Mike Leigh.*

With Jim Broadbent, Lesley Manville, Ruth Sheen, Peter Wight, Oliver Maltman, David Bradley.

## AURORA

*Romania/France/Switzerland/Germany, 2010.*

Written and Directed by Cristi Puiu. With Puiu, Clara Voda, Valeria Seciu, Luminita Gheorghiu, Gelu Colceag.

## BLACK VENUS

*France, 2010. Directed by Abdellatif Kechiche.*

Written by Kechiche and Ghalya Lacroix. With Yahima Torres, Andre Jacobs, Olivier Gourmet, Elina Löwensohn.

## CARLOS

*France/Germany, 2010. Directed by Olivier Assayas.*

Written by Assayas and Dan Franck, based on an original idea by Daniel Leconte. A revelatory 319-minute account of the career of the revolutionary terrorist known as Carlos the Jackal. With Édgar Ramírez, Alexander Scheer, Alejandro Arroyo.

*Mysteries of Lisbon* by Raúl Ruiz

### CERTIFIED COPY (COPIE CONFORME)
*France/Italy, 2010. Written and Directed by Abbas Kiarostami.*
With Juliette Binoche, William Shimell.

### FILM SOCIALISME
*Switzerland, 2010. Written and Directed by Jean-Luc Godard.*
With Catherine Tanvier, Christian Sinniger, Jean-Mark Stehlé, Agatha Couture.

### INSIDE JOB
*USA, 2010. Directed by Charles Ferguson.*
Written by Chad Beck, Adam Bolt, and Ferguson. A documentary about the current economic crisis that chronicles how financial growth and industry deregulation fostered an environment of recklessness and criminality.

### LENNONYC
*USA, 2010. Written and Directed by Michael Epstein.*
A portrait of John Lennon's New York years.

### MEEK'S CUTOFF
*USA, 2010. Directed by Kelly Reichardt.*
Written by Jonathan Raymond. With Michelle Williams, Bruce Greenwood, Zoe Kazan, Paul Dano, Shirley Henderson, Will Patton. Shown with *Day Trip*, New Zealand. Directed by Zoe McIntosh.

### MY JOY
*Ukraine/Germany/The Netherlands, 2010. Written and Directed by Sergei Loznitsa.*
With Vlad Ivanov, Viktor Nemets, Olga Shuvalova.

### MYSTERIES OF LISBON
*Portugal/France, 2010. Directed by Raúl Ruiz.*
Written by Carlos Saboga, based on Camilo Castelo Branco's novel. With Adriano Luz, Maria João Bastos, Ricardo Pereira, Clotilde Hesme. Melvil Poupaud, Léa Seydoux.

### OF GODS AND MEN
*France, 2010. Directed by Xavier Beauvois.*
Written by Beauvois and Etienne Comar. With Lambert Wilson, Michael Lonsdale, Olivier Rabourdin, Philippe Laudenbach, Jacques Herlin.

### OKI'S MOVIE
*South Korea, 2010. Written and Directed by Hong Sang-soo.*
With Jung Yu-mi, Moon Sung-keun, Lee Sun-kyun. Shown with *All Flowers in Time*, USA. Directed by Jonathan Caouette.

*Le quattro volte* by Michelangelo Frammartino

### OLD CATS
*Chile, 2010. Written and Directed by Pedro Peirano and Sebastián Silva.*
With Alejandro Sieveking, Catalina Saavedra, Bélgica Castro, Claudia Celedón. Shown with *Protect the Nation*, South Africa/Germany. Directed by Candice Reisser.

### POETRY
*South Korea, 2010. Written and Directed by Lee Chang-dong.*
With Yun Jung-hee, Lee David, Kim Hira, Ahn Nae-sang, Park Myeong-sin.

### POST MORTEM
*Chile/Mexico/Germany, 2010. Directed by Pablo Larraín.*
Written by Mateo Iribarren and Larraín. With Alfredo Castro, Antonia Zegers. Shown with *The Accordion*, Iran. Directed by Jafar Panahi.

### LE QUATTRO VOLTE
*Italy/Germany/France, 2010. Written and Directed by Michelangelo Frammartino.*
With Giuseppe Fuda, Bruno Timpano, Nazareno Timpano, and a herd of goats.

### REVOLUCIÓN
*Mexico, 2010. Directed by Mariana Chenillo, Fernando Eimbcke, Amat Escalante, Rodrigo García, Gael García Bernal, Diego Luna, Gerardo Naranjo, Rodrigo Plá, Carlos Reygadas, and Patricia Riggen.*
Ten short films commemorating the centenary of the Mexican Revolution. With Adriana Barraza, Ari Brickman, Carmen Corral, Jeannine Derbez, Robert Martinez.

### THE ROBBER
*Austria/Germany, 2010. Directed by Benjamin Heisenberg.*
Written by Heisenberg and Martin Prinz, based on Prinz's novel. With Andreas Lust, Franziska Weisz. Shown with *Mary Last Seen*, USA. Directed by Sean Durkin.

### ROBINSON IN RUINS
*UK, 2010. Written and Directed by Patrick Keiller.*
A personal essay purported to be constructed from footage recorded by the filmmaker's fictional alter ego (Robinson). Narrated by Vanessa Redgrave. Shown with *Translating Edwin Honig: A Poet's Alzheimer's*, USA. Directed by Alan Berliner.

### SILENT SOULS
*Russia, 2010. Directed by Aleksei Fedorchenko.*
Written by Denis Osokin. With Yuliya Aug, Igor Sergeyev, Viktor Sukhorukov, Yuriy Tsurilo. Shown with *Deu ci sia*, Italy. Directed by Gianluigi Tarditi.

### THE STRANGE CASE OF ANGELICA
*Portugal/Spain/France/Brazil, 2010. Written and Directed by Manoel de Oliveira.*
With Pilar López de Ayala, Ricardo Trêpa, Leonor Silveira, Ana Maria Magalhães. Shown with *Nulepsy*, UK, Directed by Jessica Sarah Rinland.

### TUESDAY, AFTER CHRISTMAS
*Romania, 2010. Directed by Radu Muntean.*
Written by Alexandru Baciu, Muntean, and Razvan Radulescu. With Mimi Branescu, Mirela Oprisor, Maria Polistasu. Shown with *Blokes*, Chile. Directed by Marialy Rivas.

### UNCLE BOONMEE WHO CAN RECALL HIS PAST LIVES
*UK/Thailand/France/Germany/Spain, 2010. Written and Directed by Apichatpong Weerasethakul.*
With Thanapat Saisaymar, Jenjira Pongpas, Sakda Kaewbuadee, Natthakarn Aphaiwonk.

### WE ARE WHAT WE ARE
*Mexico, 2010. Written and Directed by Jorge Michel Grau.*
With Francisco Barreiro, Alan Chávez, Paulina Gaitan, Carmen Beato.

*Meek's Cutoff* by Kelly Reichhardt

## Special Events

PRESENTED AT THE WALTER READE THEATER UNLESS OTHERWISE NOTED

### THE AUTOBIOGRAPHY OF NICOLAE CEAUSESCU
*Romania, 2010. Directed by Andrei Ujica.*
The life of the notorious Romanian dictator as he might have recalled it on the eve of his 1989 execution.

### "Biographical and Beyond: An Evening with David Thomson" – a discussion about Thomson's writing process, plus a screening of *Birth*, 2004, by Jonathan Glazer.

### BOXING GYM
*USA, 2010. Directed by Frederick Wiseman.*
His subject: Lord's Boxing Gym in Austin, Texas.

### CAMERAMAN: THE LIFE AND WORK OF JACK CARDIFF
*UK, 2010. Directed by Craig McCall.*
A documentary tracing the eight-decade career of the master cinematographer.
### + A MATTER OF LIFE AND DEATH
*UK, 1946. Directed by Michael Powell and Emeric Pressburger.*
With David Niven, Kim Hunter, Raymond Massey, Roger Livesey.

### "The Cinema Inside Me: Olivier Assayas" – the director discusses key moments in his own history of cinema with Richard Peña.

### DRACULA
*USA, 1931. Directed by George Melford.*
The Spanish-language version.

### "Elegant Elegies: The Films of Masahiro Shinoda" –
films shown (Japan): *The Assassin*, 1964; *Double Suicide*, 1969; *Dry Lake* aka *Youth in Fury*, 1960; *Killers on Parade*, 1961; *MacArthur's Children*, 1984; *Melody in Gray* aka *The Ballad of Orin*, 1977; *Moonlight Serenade*, 1997; *Pale Flower*, 1964; *Punishment Island*, 1966; *Samurai Spy*, 1965; *Silence*, 1971; *Tears on the Lion's Mane* aka *A Flame at the Pier*, 1962.

### "Fernando de Fuentes' Mexican Revolution Trilogy" –
*El compadre Mendoza*, 1934; *Let's Go with Pancho Villa*, 1936; *Prisoner Number 13*, 1933.

### FOREIGN PARTS
*USA, 2010. Directed by Verena Paravel and J.P. Sniadecki.*
A portrait of a shantytown neighborhood replete with auto-body repair shops.

### "HBO Films Directors Dialogues" – in the Stanley Kaplan Penthouse: David Fincher in conversation with Todd McCarthy; Kelly Reichardt in conversation with Melissa Anderson; Julie Taymor in conversation with James Shapiro; Apichatpong Weerasethakul in conversation with Dennis Lim.

### THE HOLE
*USA, 2009. Directed by Joe Dante.*
A 3-D frightmare that takes place in a placid Midwestern anytown, typically seen in sci-fi classics of the '50s.

### A LETTER TO ELIA
*USA, 2010. Directed by Kent Jones and Martin Scorsese.*
Scorsese speaks passionately of Elia Kazan as one of his formative filmmaking influences.
### + AMERICA, AMERICA
*USA, 1963. Directed by Elia Kazan.*
With Stathis Giallelis, Frank Wolff, Harry Davis.

### "The Marvelous World of Segundo de Chomon" – excerpts from the work of the "Spanish Méliès" presented with piano accompaniment by Makia Matsumura. Followed by a discussion with film scholar Tom Gunning.

### "Mike Leigh: Shooting London" – the director discusses the importance of London locations in his films. Moderated by Adrian Wootton – interspersed with film clips.

### NUREMBERG (THE SCHULBERG/WALETZKY RESTORATION)
*USA, 1948.*
A record of the Nuremberg trials originally made by Stuart Schulberg.

### "Views from the Avant-Garde" – curated by Mark McElhatten and Gavin Smith. Films from USA unless otherwise noted.

**Program 1:** "Pierre Clémenti: Unreleased Reels" – *Souvenir souvenir... (reel 27)*, France, 1967-78, *Positano (reel 30B01)*, France, 1968, and *La Deuxième femme (reel J)*.

**Program 2:** *O somma luce*, France, by Jean-Marie Straub; *Corneille-Brecht*, by Cornelia Geiser and Straub, France.

**Program 3:** Helga Fanderl – 29 films (France/Germany) in five movements. Super 8 to 16mm blow-ups.

**Program 4:** "History Is Homemade at Night: The Crazy, Beautiful World of Jeff Keen" – all films from the UK: *Marvo Movie*, 1967, *Cineblatz*, 1967, *Meatdaze*, 1968, *White Lite*, 1968, *Wail*, 1968, *Rayday Film*, 1968-70, and *White Dust*, 1970-72.

**Program 5:** Jennifer Montgomery – *The Agonal Phase* and *Transitional Objects*, 2000.

**Program 6:** Phil Solomon – *American Falls* and *What's Out Tonight Is Lost*, 1983.

**Program 7:** *Ruhr*, Germany/USA, by James Benning.

**Program 8:** "Mirror of Shadows and Cinders" – *Photofinish Figures*, Italy, by Paolo Gioli; *A Thousand Julys*, by Lewis Klahr; *Marie*, by Karen Yasinsky; *Dissonant*, The Netherlands/Belgium, by Manon de Boer; *Ape of Nature*, by Peggy Ahwesh; *The Soul of Things*, by Dominic Angerame; *Destination Finale*, Germany, by Philip Widmann; *Valleys of Fear*, by Erin Espelie; *SHU (Blue Hour Lullaby)*, Germany, by Philipp Lachenmann.

**Program 9:** "Station to Station" – *Crosswalk*, by Jeanne Liotta; *Servants of Mercy*, Portugal/USA, by Fern Silva; *Rite of Spring*, Portugal, 1963, by Manoel de Oliveira.

**Program 10:** "Visibility Unknown" – *The Flight of Tulugaq*, Brazil, by André Guerreiro Lopes; *New Year Sun*, by Jonathan Schwartz; *Trypps #7 (Badlands)*, by Ben Russell; *Burning Bush*, by Vincent Grenier; *Materia Obscura part*

one, Germany, by Jürgen Reble; *a loft*, by Ken Jacobs; *Mamori*, Canada, by Karl Lemieux; *Union*, by Paul Clipson; *Parties visible et invisible d'un ensemble sous tension*, France, by Emmanuel Lefrant; *Drifter*, by Timoleon Wilkins.

**Program 11:** "Since You Were Here…" – *Dust Studies*, by Michael Gitlin; *Washes*, by Norbert Shieh; *Get Out of the Car*, by Thom Andersen; *Recámara*, by Rosario Sotelo; *Cry When It Happens*, by Laida Lertxundi; *Night Shift*, by Gretchen Skogerson; *Future So Bright*, by Matt McCormick.

**Program 12:** "Turn on the High Beams 1" – *Untitled Galaxy*, by Jefre Cantu-Ledesma and Paul Clipson; *Fist 1 – Improper Frictions*, by Bruce McClure.

**Program 13:** "Sea Scrolls" – *Atlantis*, China/Belgium, by Pieter Geenen; *Dining Cars*, The Netherlands, by Arianne Olthaar; *Sea Series #7: Naufrage aux îles de Madeleine*, Canada, by John Price; *Antlantiques*, Senegal/France, by Mati Diop; *Distance*, by Julie Murray; *Travelogue*, by Vincent Grenier; *Shrimp Boat Log*, by David Gatten; *Blue Mantle*, by Rebecca Meyers.

**Program 14:** "Landing on the Edge" – *Place for Landing*, by Shambhavi Kaul; *Hearts Are Trump Again*, by Dani Leventhal; *Ray's Birds*, by Deborah Stratman; *In the Absence of Light, Darkness Prevails*, Brazil/USA, by Fern Silva; *Slave Ship*, by T. Marie; *Someone Should Be Happy Here*, by April Simmons; *THE HUNCH THAT CAUSED THE WINNING STREAK AND FOUGHT THE DOLDRUMS MIGHTILY*, by Stephanie Barber; *razor's edge*, by Stephanie Barber and Xav LePlae.

**Program 15:** "Séance" – *bust chance*, by Stephanie Barber; *Love Rose*, by Bobby Abate; *Kindless Villain*, by Janie Geiser; *So Sure of Nowhere Buying Times to Come*, by David Gatten; *Facts Told At Retail (after Henry James)*, by Erin Espelie; *Ghost Algebra*, by Janie Geiser; *Tokyo-Ebisu*, Japan, by Tomonari Nishikawa; *Possessed*, by Fred Worden; *These Hammers Don't Hurt Us*, by Michael Robinson.

**Program 16:** "Song Cycle"– *Pastourelle*, by Nathaniel Dorsky; *Ouverture*, France/Canada, by Christopher Becks; *The Suppliant*, USA/Switzerland, by Robert Beavers; *Hanging upside down in the Branches*, Germany, by Ute Aurand; *Film for Invisible Ink, case no. 323: ONCE UPON A TIME IN THE WEST*, by David Gatten; *In a Year with 13 Deaths*, by Jonathan Schwartz; *One*, USA/Austria, by Eve Heller; *Shibuya-Tokyo*, Japan, by Tomonari Nishikawa; *Beneath Your Skin of Deep Hollow*, Chile/Canada, by Malena Szlam; *Gesturings*, by Peter Herwitz; *Day Dream*, by Jim Jennings.

**Program 17:** "Fatal Attraction: An Introduction to Black and White Magic" – *…These Blazeing Starrs!*, by Deborah Stratman; *Tranquility*, Austria, by Siegfried A. Fruhauf; *To Another*, by J.B. Mabe; *Sugar Slim Says*, by Lewis Klahr; *Sorry*, by Luther Price; *Shutter*, Canada, by Alexi Manis; *The Floor of the World*, by Janie Geiser; *Toads*, by Milena Gierke; *Pigs*, by Pawel Wojtasik; *Shadow Cut*, Austria, by Martin Arnold; *Coming Attractions*, Austria, by Peter Tscherkassky.

**Program 18:** "Turn on the High Beams II" – *Crescent*, by Jefre Cantu-Ledesma and Paul Clipson; *Fist II – Into a Sotspot*, by Bruce McClure.

## THE 49TH NEW YORK **FILM FESTIVAL**
SEPTEMBER 30–OCTOBER 16, 2011

ALL PERFORMANCES IN ALICE TULLY HALL UNLESS OTHERWISE NOTED.

SELECTION COMMITTEE: RICHARD PEÑA, CHAIRMAN, MELISSA ANDERSON, SCOTT FOUNDAS, DENNIS LIM, AND TODD MCCARTHY. SHORT FILM SELECTION COMMITTEE: ISA CUCINOTTA, SCOTT FOUNDAS, LAURA KERN, RICHARD PEÑA, AND GAVIN SMITH.

THE 49TH NYFF POSTER ARTWORK WAS CREATED BY ©LORNA SIMPSON.

### CARNAGE
*France/Germany/Spain/Poland, 2011. Directed by Roman Polanski.*

Written by Polanski and Yasmina Reza, based on Reza's play *God of Carnage*. With Jodie Foster, Kate Winslet, Christoph Waltz, John C. Reilly. (Opening Night.)

### MY WEEK WITH MARILYN
*UK, 2011. Directed by Simon Curtis.*

Written by Adrian Hodges. With Michelle Williams, Eddie Redmayne, Kenneth Branagh, Dominic Cooper, Julia Ormond, Emma Watson, Judi Dench. (Centerpiece.)

### THE DESCENDANTS
*USA, 2011. Directed by Alexander Payne.*

Written by Nat Faxon, Alexander Payne, and Jim Rash, based on Kaui Hart Hemmings's novel. With George Clooney, Shailene Woodley, Beau Bridges, Robert Forster, Judy Greer. Matthew Lillard, Robert Forster. (Closing Night.)

### A DANGEROUS METHOD
*Germany/Canada, 2011. Directed by David Cronenberg.*

Written by Christopher Hampton, based his play *The Talking Cure* and John Kerr's book *A Most Dangerous Method*. With Keira Knightley, Viggo Mortensen, Michael Fassbender, Vincent Cassel, Sarah Gadon. (Special Gala.)

### THE SKIN I LIVE IN
*Spain, 2011. Directed by Pedro Almodóvar.*

Written by Pedro Almodóvar, with the collaboration of Agustín Almodóvar, based on Thierry Jonquet's novel *Mygale*. With Antonio Banderas, Elena Anaya, Marisa Paredes. (Special Gala.)

### THE ARTIST ▶
*France, 2011. Written and Directed by Michel Hazanavicius.*

With Jean Dujardin, Bérénice Bejo, James Cromwell, John Goodman, Penelope Ann Miller, Missi Pyle.

### CORPO CELESTE
*Italy/France, 2011. Written and Directed by Alice Rohrwacher.*

With Yle Vianello, Salvatore Cantalupo, Pasqualina Scuncia, Anita Caprioli, Renato Carpentieri.

*Melancholia* by Lars von Trier

### FOOTNOTE

*Israel, 2011. Written and Directed by Joseph Cedar.*

With Shlomo Bar-Aba, Lior Ashkenazi, Aliza Rosen, Alma Zack, Micah Lewensohn.

### 4:44 LAST DAY ON EARTH

*USA, 2011. Written and Directed by Abel Ferrara.*

With Willem Dafoe, Shanyn Leigh, Natasha Lyonne, Paul Hipp.

*Martha Marcy May Marlene* by Sean Durkin

### GEORGE HARRISON: LIVING IN THE MATERIAL WORLD

*USA, 2011. Directed by Martin Scorsese.*

An expansive documentary (208 minutes) about the Beatles's lead guitarist.

### GOODBYE FIRST LOVE

*France/Germany, 2011. Written and Directed by Mia Hansen-Løve.*

With Lola Créton, Sebastian Urzendowsky, Magne-Håvard Brekke, Valérie Bonneton.

### THE KID WITH A BIKE

*Belgium/France/Italy, 2011. Written and Directed by Jean-Pierre and Luc Dardenne.*

With Cécile De France, Thomas Doret, Jérémie Renier, Fabrizio Rongione, Egon Di Mateo, Olivier Gourmet.

### LE HAVRE

*Finland/France/Germany, 2011. Written and Directed by Aki Kaurismäki.*

With André Wilms, Kati Outinen, Jean-Pierre Darroussin, Blondin Miguel.

### THE LONELIEST PLANET

*USA/Germany, 2011. Written and Directed by Julia Loktev.*

With Gael García Bernal, Hani Furstenberg, Bidzina Gujabidze.

### MARTHA MARCY MAY MARLENE

*USA, 2011. Written and Directed by Sean Durkin.*

With Elizabeth Olsen, Sarah Paulson, Hugh Dancy, John Hawkes, Brady Corbet.

### MELANCHOLIA

*Denmark/Sweden/France/Germany/Italy, 2011. Written and Directed by Lars von Trier.*

With Kirsten Dunst, Charlotte Gainsbourg, Alexander Skarsgård, Charlotte Rampling, John Hurt, Stellan Skarsgård, Kiefer Sutherland, Brady Corbet.

### MISS BALA

*Mexico, 2011. Directed by Gerardo Naranjo.*

Written by Mauricio Katz and Naranjo. With Stephanie Sigman, Noe Hernández, James Russo, José Yenque.

### ONCE UPON A TIME IN ANATOLIA

*Turkey, 2011. Directed by Nuri Bilge Ceylan.*

Written by Ebru and Nuri Bilge Ceylan and Ercan Kesal. With Muhammet Uzuner, Yilmaz Erdoğan, Taner Birsel, Ahmet Mümtaz Taylan.

### PINA

*Germany/France, 2011. Written and Directed by Wim Wenders.*

A 3-D tribute to the choreographer Pina Bausch in which longtime members of the Tanztheater re-create many of their original roles.

*Shame* by Steve McQueen

### PLAY
*Sweden/France/Denmark, 2011. Written and Directed by Ruben Östlund.*

With Anas Abdirahman, Sebastian Blyckert, Yannick Diakité, Sebastian Hegmar.

### POLICEMAN
*Israel, 2011. Written and Directed by Nadav Lapid.*

With Yiftach Klein, Yaara Pelzig, Michael Aloni, Menashe Noy.

### A SEPARATION
*Iran, 2010. Written and Directed by Asghar Farhadi.*

With Leila Hatami, Peyman Moadi, Shahab Hosseini, Sareh Bayat, Sarina Farhadi.

### SHAME
*UK, 2011. Directed by Steve McQueen.*

Written by McQueen and Abi Morgan. With Michael Fassbender, Carey Mulligan, James Badge Dale.

### SLEEPING SICKNESS
*Germany/France/The Netherlands, 2011. Written and Directed by Ulrich Köhler.*

With Pierre Bokma, Jean-Christophe Folly, Jenny Schily, Hippolyte Girardot.

### THE STUDENT
*Argentina, 2011. Written and Directed by Santiago Mitre.*

With Esteban Lamothe, Romina Paula, Ricardo Felix, Valeria Correa.

### THIS IS NOT A FILM
*Iran, 2011. Directed by Jafar Panahi and Mojtaba Mirtahmasb.*

A day-in-the-life chronicle of the director Panahi, who is accused of collusion against the Iranian regime, but finds a middle ground between fiction and reality.

### THE TURIN HORSE ▼
*Hungary/France/Germany/Switzerland/USA, 2011. Directed by Béla Tarr.*

Written by Lázló Krasznahorkai and Tarr. With János Derzsi, Erika Bók, Mihály Kormos.

*Ben-Hur* by William Wyler

## Forums
FREE EVENTS PRESENTED AT THE EBM AMPHITHEATER OR THE APPLE STORE WHEN NOTED

Apple Store Talks (Upper West Side): Wes Anderson; Antonio Banderas; Willem Dafoe; Sean Durkin, Elizabeth Olsen, and John Hawkes; "Avant-Garde Influences Mainstream Movies!," presented by New York Women in Film in Television; Beyond the Screen: The Immersive Storytelling Forum: "The Age of Immersive Storytelling," "Documentaries and Transmedia Activism," "World Building in Games," "Audiences as Story Participants"; book signing with John Lithgow; discussion with Nuri Bilge Ceylan; Béla Tarr; indieWIRE Meets: Pedro Almodóvar; Xan Aranda; Antonio Campos, Sean Durkin, and Josh Mond; Jean-Pierre and Luc Dardenne; Gerardo Naranjo and Stephanie Sigman; the NYFF selection committee; and Jeffrey Schwartz; Plymptoons! Bill Plympton Talks About Drawing; "To Union or Not to Union: Casting & Working with Actors in Low Budget Indies," presented by SAGIndie; "Women Produce Well Developed Films," presented by the Producers Guild of America East; "Writing New York, Part I: Gotham, The Quintessential Urban Landscape – Does the Shoe Still Fit Without the Grit?,"; "Part II: Supporting Character, NYC," presented by the Writers Guild of America East.

## Masterworks
PRESENTED AT THE WALTER READE THEATER UNLESS OTHERWISE NOTED

**BEN-HUR**
*USA, 1959. Directed by William Wyler.*
Written by Karl Tunberg, based on Lew Wallace's novel. An 8K digital restoration of the original 70mm print. At Alice Tully Hall.

**THE GOLD RUSH**
*USA, 1925. Written and Directed by Charlie Chaplin.*
With Chaplin, Mack Swain, Tom Murray. Music accompaniment by members of the New York Philharmonic. At Alice Tully Hall.

**INVASION**
*Argentina, 1969. Directed by Hugo Santiago.*
Written by Jorge Luis Borges and Santiago, based on a story by Borges and Adolfo Bioy Casares. With Olga Zubarry, Lautaro Murúa, Juan Carlos Paz.

**"Velvet Bullets and Steel Kisses"** – a 37-film tribute to Japan's Nikkatsu Studio at the Walter Reade Theater. Films shown: *The Burmese Harp*, 1956, by Kon Ichikawa; *Capricious Young Man*, 1936, by Mansaku Itami; *Charisma*, 1999, by Kiyoshi Kurosawa; *Cold Fish*, 2010, by Sion Sono; *A Colt Is My Passport*, 1967, by Takashi Nomura; *Crazed Fruit*, 1956, by Ko Nakahira; *Dancer in Izu*, 1963, by Katsumi Nisikawa; *A Diary of Chuji's Travels*, 1927, by Daisuke Ito; *Earth*, 1939, by Tomu Uchida; *Gate of Flesh*, 1964, by Seijun Suzuki; *The Hell-Fated Courtesan*, 1975, by Noboru Tanaka; *Hometown*, 1930, by Kenji Mizoguchi; *I Look Up When I Walk*, 1962, by Toshio Masuda; *Intentions of Murder*, 1964, by Shohei Imamura; *Intimidation*, 1960, by Koreyoshi Kurahara; *Love Hotel*, 1985, by Shinji Somai; *Made to Order Cloth aka The Chivalrous Robber Jirokichi*, by Daisuke Ito, shown with *Jiraiya the Ninja*, 1921, by Shozo Makino; *Mud and Soldiers*, 1939, by Tomotaka Tasaka; *The Oldest Profession aka Confidential Report: Sex Market*, 1974, by Tanaka; *Pigs and Battleships*, 1981, by Imamura; *Retaliation*, 1968, by Yasuharu Hasebe; *Rusty Knife*, 1958, by Masuda; *Season of the Sun*, 1956, by Takumi Furukawa; *Singing Lovebirds aka Samurai Musical*, 1939, by Masahiro Makino; *Stray Cat Rock: Sex Hunter*, 1970, by Yasuharu Hasebe; *Sun in the Last Days of the Shogunate aka Shinagawa Path*, 1957, by Yuzo Kawashima; *Suzaki Paradise: Red Light*, 1956, by Kawashima; *Take Aim at the Police Van*, 1960, by Suzuki; *Tange Sazen and a Pot Worth a Million Ryo*, 1935, by Sadao Yamanaka; *Tattooed Core of Flowers*, 1976, by Masaru Konuma; *Ten Nights of Dreams*, 2007, by various directors; *Till We Meet Again*, 1955, by Yuzo Kawashima; *Tokyo Drifter*, 1966, by Suzuki; *The Warped Ones*, 1960, by Kurahara; *The Woman with Red Hair*, 1979, by Tatsumi Kumashiro; *The World of Geisha*, 1973, by Kumashiro.

**WE CAN'T GO HOME AGAIN**
*USA, 1972/2011. Directed by Nicholas Ray.*
Written by Tom Farrell and Nicholas and Susan Ray. With (as fictionalized versions of themselves) Richie Bock, Farrell, Danny Fisher. A digital restoration at Alice Tully Hall.

**YOU ARE NOT I**
*USA, 1981. Directed by Sara Driver.*
Written by Driver and Jim Jarmusch, based on a story by Paul Bowles. With Suzanne Fletcher, Evelyn Smith, Luc Sante.

## Short Films
PRESENTED AT THE ELINOR BUNIN MUNROE FILM CENTER

**Program 1:** *Blue*, New Zealand, by Stephen Kang; *The Five Stages of Grief*, USA, by Jessica Brickman; *The Bird Spider*, Spain, by Jaime Dezcallar; *Graffitiger*, Czech Republic, by Libor Pixa; *The Runner*, Serbia and Montenegro/USA, by Ana Lazarevic; *The Strange Thing About the Johnsons*, USA, by Ari Aster.

**Program 2:** *The Great Gatsby in Five Minutes*, USA, by Michael Almereyda; *Aaron Burr, Part 2*, USA, by Dana O'Keefe; *Memory by Design*, USA, by Nathan Punwar; *My Bow Breathing*, Italy, by E.M. Artale; *Grandmothers (Abuelas)*, UK, by Afarin Eghbal; *First Match*, USA, by Olivia Newman; *Traitors*, Morocco, by Sean Gullette.

## Special Events
PRESENTED AT THE WALTER READE THEATER OR THE ELINOR BUNIN MUNROE FILM CENTER UNLESS OTHERWISE NOTED

**ANDREW BIRD: FEVER YEAR**
*USA, 2011. Directed by Xan Aranda.*
A portrait of the rock musician.

**THE BALLAD OF MOTT THE HOOPLE**
*UK, 2010. Directed by Chris Hall and Mike Kerry.*
One of British rock's most popular live acts of the 1970s.

**CASTLE IN THE SKY**
*Japan, 1986. Written and Directed by Hayao Miyazaki.*
A 25th-anniversary screening, at Alice Tully Hall.

**CORMAN'S WORLD: EXPLOITS OF A HOLLYWOOD REBEL**
*USA, 2011. Written and Directed by Alex Stapleton.*
**+ THE INTRUDER**
*USA, 1962. Directed by Roger Corman.*
Written by Charles Beaumont, based on his novel. With William Shatner.

**CRAZY HORSE**
*USA/France, 2011. Directed by Frederick Wiseman.*
Behind the scenes at Paris's Crazy Horse cabaret.

**DON'T EXPECT TOO MUCH**
*USA, 2011. Written and Directed by Susan Ray.*
Nicholas Ray's widow examines his stormy romance with Hollywood.

**DREIBELEIN**
*Germany, 2011. A trilogy that tells a single story from three points of view:*
Part I: *Beats Being Dead*. Directed by Christian Petzold; Part II: *Don't Follow Me Around*. Directed by Dominik Graf; Part III: *One Minute of Darkness*. Directed by Christoph Hochhäusler.

**THE EXTERMINATING ANGEL**
*1962, Mexico. Directed by Luis Buñuel.*
The Opening Night film at the 1st New York Film Festival.

**FROM MORNING TO MIDNIGHT**
*Germany, 1922. Directed by Karl Heinz Martin.*
Written by Herbert Juttke, and Martin, based on Georg
Kaiser's play. With live accompaniment by the Alloy
Orchestra. Shown with *A Trip to the Moon*, France, 1902.
Directed by George Méliès.

**"HBO Films Directors Dialogues"** – Joe Berlinger and
Bruce Sinofsky in conversation with Eugene Hernandez;
Abel Ferrara in conversation with Dennis Lim; Julia Loktev
in conversation with Melissa Anderson; Wim Wenders in
conversation with Scott Foundas.

**HUGO**
*USA, 2011. Directed by Martin Scorsese.*
Written by John Logan, based on Brian Selznick's book. With
Asa Butterfield, Chloë Grace Moretz, Ben Kingsley. A surprise
preview, at Avery Fisher Hall.

**"Kevin Smith's Smoviola Presents":**
**THE ADVENTURES OF BUCKAROO BANZAI**
**ACROSS THE 8TH DIMENSION**
*USA, 1984. Directed by W.D. Richter.*
Written by Earl Mac Rauch. With Peter Weller, Ellen Barkin,
John Lithgow, Jeff Goldblum, Christopher Lloyd.

**MUSIC ACCORDING TO TOM JOBIM**
*Brazil, 2011. Directed by Nelson Pereira dos Santos.*
A musical tribute.

**THE 99: UNBOUND**
*UK/Kuwait/USA, 2011. Directed by Dave Osbourne.*
Written by Henry Gilroy.

**"On Cinema: Alexander Payne"** – a conversation conducted by Richard Peña.

**PARADISE LOST 3: PURGATORY**
*USA, 2011. Directed by Joe Berlinger and Bruce Sinofsky.*
The third part of an epic chronicle of the West Memphis Three.

**PATIENCE (AFTER SEBALD)**
*UK, 2011. Directed by Grant Gee.*
A documentary essay based on W.G. Sebald's book *The Rings
of Saturn*. Narrated by Jonathan Pryce.

**"Pauline Kael: A Life in the Dark, A Panel Discussion"**
**+ FINGERS**
*USA, 1978. Written and Directed by James Toback.*
With Harvey Keitel, Tisa Farrow, Jim Brown.

**THE ROYAL TENENBAUMS**
*USA, 2001. Directed by Wes Anderson.*
A 10th-anniversary screening.

**SALVADOR**
*USA, 1986. Directed by Oliver Stone.*
A 25th-anniversary screening.

**SODANKYLÄ FOREVER**
*Finland, 2010. Directed by Peter von Bagh.*
Twenty-five years of film history via Finland's Midnight Sun
Film Festival.

**SPIRITED AWAY**
*Japan, 2001. Directed by Hayao Miyazaki.*
A 10th Anniversary screening.

**"Susan Orlean: Rin Tin Tin, the Life and the Legend,**
**A Conversation"**
**+ CLASH OF THE WOLVES**

*USA, 1925. Directed by Noel M. Smith.*
Written by Charles Logue. With Rin Tin Tin.

**TAHRIR**
*France/Italy, 2011. Written and Directed by Stefano Savona.*
An account of the "Arab Spring" revolutions in Egypt.

**"20 Years of Art Cinema: A Tribute to Sony Pictures**
**Classics"** – film clips plus conversations with Michael
Barker, Tom Bernard, and Marcie Bloom.
**+ HOWARDS END**
*UK, 1992. Directed by James Ivory.*
Written by Ruth Prawer Jhabvala, based on E.M. Forster's novel.
With Anthony Hopkins, Emma Thompson, Vanessa Redgrave.

**VITO**
*USA, 2011. Directed by Jeffrey Schwarz.*
A portrait of New York film critic and gay-rights activist
Vito Russo.

**"Views from the Avant-Garde"** – curated by Mark
McElhatten and Gavin Smith. At the Walter Reade Theater
and Elinor Bunin Munroe Film Center. Films from the USA
unless otherwise noted.

**Program 1:** "The Soul and the Stem" – *Woman with Flowers*,
USA/Mexico, by Chick Strand; *Jan Villa*, India/USA, by
Natasha Mendonca; *The Sole of the Foot and Correspondence*,
USA/Germany, by Robert Fenz.

**Program 2:** Ben Rivers – *Sack Barrow* and *Slow Action*, UK.

**Program 3:** "Bitches Brew" – *Posthaste Perennial Pattern*, by
Jodie Mack; *Babobilicons*, 1982, by Daina Krumins; *You Are
Now Running on Reserve Battery Power*, by Jessie Stead; *Hull*,
by Tara Meranda Nelson; from *Jhana and the Rats of James
Olds: The Phone Call, Billy and the Magician, Little Kitten,
Level of Zero Buoyancy*, and *Romance Novels*, by Stephanie
Barber; *A Party Record Packed with Sex and Sadness*, by Bobby
Abate; *Praxis 8 – 12 Scenes*, Austria, by Dietmar Brehm; *Taste
Test*, by Andrew Lampert; *Bitch-Beauty*, by MM Serra.

**Program 4:** "Ladders and Tracks" – *Berlin Tracks 18h00-
20h00*, by Shiloh Cinquemani; *(k)now (t)here*, by Hey-Yeun
Jang; *Subway*, by Angela Ferraiolo; *Village, silenced*, by
Deborah Stratman; *Snakes and Ladders*, by Katherin
McInnis; *Longhorn Tremolo*, by Scott Stark; *Landfill 16*, by
Jennifer Reeves; *Barren*, by Katherin McInnis; *Back View*,
by Vincent Grenier; *The Toy Sun*, by Ken Kobland.

**Program 5:** *Upending*, 3-D, by the OpenEndedGroup.

**Program 6:** *Seeking the Monkey King*, by Ken Jacobs.

**Program 7:** Ernie Gehr – *Crystal Palace, Thank You for
Visiting, Mist*, and *ABRACADABRA*.

**Program 8:** George Kuchar – *Lingo of the Lost* and *Empire
of Evil*.

**Program 9:** "Cabinet of Curiosities" – *Between Gold*, by
Jonathan Schwartz; *Tin Pressed*, by Dani Leventhal; *Fifteen
an Hour*, by Kevin Jerome Everson; *Tableaux Vivants*, by
Vincent Grenier; *Curious Light*, by Charlotte Pryce; *Forms
Are Not Self-Subsistent Substances*, by Samantha Rebello;
*The Matter Propounded, of its Possibility or Impossibility,
treated in four Parts*, by David Gatten; from *Jhana and the
Rats of James Olds: Miniatures, Degas*, and *The Eclipse*, by
Stephanie Barber; *ransom notes*, Canada, by Kelly Egan;
*Conjuror's Box*, by Kerry Laitala.

**Program 10:** "Looking Through a Glass Onion" – *Passage
Upon the Plume*, by Fern Silva; *Shayne's Rectangle*, by

Dani Leventhal; *Line Describing Your Mom*, by Michael
Robinson; *Gossip*, by Bobby Abate; from *Jhana and the Rats
of James Olds: Tatum's Ghost*, by Stephanie Barber; *The
Death of the Gorilla*, 1966, by Peter Mays; *By foot-candle
light*, by Mary Helena Clark; *A Lax Riddle Unit*, Spain,
by Laida Lertxundi; *Sounding Glass*, Germany, by Sylvia
Schedelbauer; *The Evil Eyes*, by Bobby Abate.

**Program 11:** *Voluptuous Sleep*, by Betzy Bromberg.

**Program 12:** Nathaniel Dorsky & Jerome Hiler: *Words of
Mercury*, by Hiler; *The Return*, by Dorsky.

**Program 13:** "John Zorn: A Film in 15 Scenes" – *15 scenes, 254
shots*, by Gobolux; *Well Then There Now*, by Lewis Klahr; *Bare
Room*, by Joey Izzo; *arcana*, USA/Austria, by Henry Hills.

**Program 14:** Jean-Marie Straub – *Lothringen!*, France,
1994, by Straub-Huillet; *Un héritier*, France/South
Korea, *L'Inconsolable*, France, and *Schakale und Araber*,
Switzerland, by Straub.

**Program 15:** *Studies for the Decay of the West*, Germany,
by Klaus Wyborny.

**Program 16:** *The Unstable Object*, USA/Germany/Turkey,
by Daniel Eisenberg, with *Less and Less*, France, by Luc Moullet.

**Program 17:** Kevin Jerome Everson – *Quality Control* and
*The Prichard*.

**Program 18:** "The Red and the Black" – *River Rites*, USA/
Suriname, by Ben Russell; *Shadow, Seed, Spagyric*, by David
Baker; *Peril of the Antilles*, by Fern Silva; *A Preface to Red*,
USA/Turkey, by Jonathan Schwartz; *Protocol*, Canada/
Colombia, by Lina Rodriguez; *Imperceptihole*, by Lori Felker
and Robert Todd; *LIGHT LICKS: BY THE WATERS OF
BABYLON: I WANT TO PAINT IT BLACK*, by Saul
Levine; *Third Law: N Kedzie Blvd.*, by Mike Gibisser; *Slow
Burn*, by Jesse Cain.

**Program 19:** "Virgin Springs" – *Baptismal Sticks and
Stones*, by April Simmons; *Devil's Gate*, by Laura Kraning;
*Twice Removed*, by Leslie Thornton; *Ricky*, by Janie Geiser;
*Silent Springs*, by Erin Espelie; *Gazette*, Russia/Estonia, by
Eléonore de Montesquiou; *Kudzu Vine*, by Josh Gibson.

**Program 20:** *The Pettifogger*, by Lewis Klahr.

**Program 21:** *Twenty Cigarettes*, by James Benning.

**Program 22:** *Villatalla*, Switzerland/Chile/Italy, by
Jeannette Muñoz; *A Year*, Germany, by Renate Sami; *Young
Pines*, Germany/Japan, by Ute Aurand.

**Program 23:** *Chorus\*, Compound Eyes Nos. 1-5, Light
from the Mesa, Chorus*, and *Morphologies\**, by Paul Clipson.
*\*Featuring live musical performance by ARP.*

**Program 24:** *Two Years at Sea*, UK, by Ben Rivers.

**Installations:** in the EBM amphitheater – *Picture Taking*,
by Ernie Gehr; *Binocular Machine: Sheep Torso*, by Leslie
Thornton; *Armoire*, by Vincent Grenier; *By Pain and
Rhyme and Arabesques of Foraging*, by David Gatten;
*Tree Vortex Loop*, by Leighton Pierce; *Peeper Palace*, by
Dani Leventhal; *Soft Palate*, by Martin Arnold, Austria;
*Traders Leaving the Exchange, a Guard and the Street*,
by Les Leveque; *Night House Vortex*, by Leighton Pierce;
*John Krieg Exiting the Falk Corporation in 1971*, by
James Benning; *Self Control*, by Martin Arnold, Austria;
*Inferno Towering The*, by Anne McGuire.

THE 50TH NEW YORK FILM FESTIVAL SEPTEMBER 28–OCTOBER 14, 2012
FILM SOCIETY OF LINCOLN CENTER ALICE TULLY HALL | ELINOR BUNIN MONROE FILM CENTER | WALTER READE THEATER

# 2012

SELECTION COMMITTEE: RICHARD PEÑA, CHAIRMAN, MELISSA ANDERSON, SCOTT FOUNDAS, TODD MCCARTHY, AND AMY TAUBIN. SHORT FILM SELECTION COMMITTEE: ISA CUCINOTTA, LAURA KERN, RICHARD PEÑA, AND GAVIN SMITH.

THE 50TH NYFF POSTER ARTWORK WAS CREATED BY ©CINDY SHERMAN.

**LIFE OF PI ▲**
*USA, 2012. Directed by Ang Lee.*
Written by David Magee, from the novel by Yann Martel. With Suraj Sharma, Irrfan Khan, Rafe Spall, Gérard Depardieu. (Opening Night.)

**NOT FADE AWAY**
*USA, 2012. Written and Directed by David Chase.*
With John Magaro, Will Brill, Jack Huston, James Gandolfini, Christopher McDonald. (Centerpiece.)

**FLIGHT**
*USA, 2012. Directed by Robert Zemeckis.*
Written by John Gatins. With Denzel Washington, John Goodman, Don Cheadle, Melissa Leo, Bruce Greenwood, Kelly Reilly. (Closing Night.)

## AMOUR
*Austria/France/Germany, 2012. Written and Directed by Michael Haneke.*

With Jean-Louis Trintignant, Emmanuelle Riva, Isabelle Huppert, William Shimell.

## ARAF – SOMEWHERE IN BETWEEN
*Turkey/France/Germany, 2012. Written and Directed by Yeşim Ustaoğlu.*

With Özcan Deniz, Nihal Yalçin, Neslihan Atagül, Baris Hacihan, Ilgaz Kocatürk.

## BARBARA
*Germany, 2011. Directed by Christian Petzold.*

Written by Petzold, in collaboration with Harun Farocki. With Nina Hoss, Ronald Zehrfeld, Rainer Bock, Christina Hecke, Claudia Geisler.

## BEYOND THE HILLS
*Romania, 2012. Written and Directed by Cristian Mungiu, inspired by Tatiana Niculescu Bran's* Deadly Confession *and* Judges' Book.

With Cosmina Stratan, Chritina Flutur, Valeriu Andriuță, Cătălina Harabagiu, Gina Țandură.

## BWAKAW ▼
*Philippines, 2012. Written and Directed by Jun Robles Lana.*

With Eddie Garcia, Princess, Rez Cortez, Soliman Cruz.

## CAESAR MUST DIE
*Italy, 2012. Written and Directed by Paolo and Vittorio Taviani, based on an excerpt from Shakespeare's* Julius Caesar.

With Cosimo Rega, Salvatore Striano, Giovanni Arcuri, Antonio Frasca, Juan Dario Bonetti.

## CAMILLE REWINDS
*France, 2012. Directed by Noémie Lvovsky.*

Written by Maud Ameline, Lvovsky, Pierre-Olivier Mattei, and Florence Seyvos. With Lvovsky, Samir Guesmi, Judith Chemla, India Hair.

## THE DEAD MAN AND BEING HAPPY
*Spain/Argentina, 2012. Directed by Javier Rebollo.*

With José Sacristán, Roxana Blanco.

## FILL THE VOID
*Israel, 2012. Written and Directed by Rama Burshtein.*

With Hila Feldman, Rasia Israeli, Yiftach Klein, Renana Raz.

## FIRST COUSIN ONCE REMOVED
*USA, 2012. Directed by Alan Berliner.*

A chronicle of poet and translator Edwin Honig's loss of memory, language, and his past due to the onslaught of Alzheimer's.

## FRANCES HA
*USA, 2012. Directed by Noah Baumbach.*

Written by Baumbach and Greta Gerwig. With Gerwig, Adam Driver, Grace Gummer.

## THE GATEKEEPERS
*Israel, 2012. Directed by Dror Moreh.*

Six former heads of Israel's internal security agency, the Shin Bet, discuss their nation's past, present, and future.

## GINGER AND ROSA
*UK, 2012. Written and Directed by Sally Potter.*

With Elle Fanning, Alice Englert, Christina Hendricks, Annette Bening, Oliver Platt, Alessandro Nivola, Timothy Spall, Jodhi May.

## HERE AND THERE
*Spain/USA/Mexico, 2012. Written and Directed by Antonio Méndez Esparza.*

With Pedro De los Santos, Teresa Ramírez Aguirre, Lorena Guadalupe Pantaleón Vázquez.

## HOLY MOTORS
*France, 2012. Written and Directed by Leos Carax.*

With Denis Lavant, Edith Scob, Eva Mendes, Kylie Minogue.

## HYDE PARK ON HUDSON ▲
*UK, 2012. Directed by Roger Michell.*

Written by Richard Nelson. With Bill Murray, Laura Linney, Olivia Williams, Olivia Colman, Elizabeth Wilson.

## KINSHASA KIDS ▼
*Belgium/France, 2012. Written and Directed by Marc-Henri Wajnberg.*

With José Mawanda, Rachel Mwanza, Emmanuel Fakoko Bebson "de la rue" Elemba, Gabi Bolenge.

**THE LAST TIME I SAW MACAO**
*Portugal/France, 2012. Written and Directed by João Pedro Rodrigues and João Rui Guerra da Mata.*
With Rodrigues, Guerra da Mata, Cindy Scrash.

**LEVIATHAN ▼**
*USA, 2012. Written and Directed by Lucien Castaing-Taylor and Véréna Paravel.*
An anthropological excavation set inside one of the world's most dangerous professions: the commercial fishing industry.

◄ **LIKE SOMEONE IN LOVE**
*France/Japan, 2012. Written and Directed by Abbas Kiarostami.*
With Ryo Kase, Denden, Rin Takanashi.

**LINES OF WELLINGTON**
*Portugal, 2012. Directed by Valeria Sarmiento.*
Written by Carlos Saboga. With Nuno Lopes, Soraia Chaves, Marisa Paredes, John Malkovich.

**MEMORIES LOOK AT ME**
*China, 2012. Written and Directed by Song Fang.*
With Ye Yu-zhu, Song Di-jin, Song Yuan, Song Fang.

**NIGHT ACROSS THE STREET**
*France/Chile, 2012. Written and Directed by Raúl Ruiz, based on original stories by Hernán de Solar.*
With Christian Vadim, Sergio Hernández, Valentina Vargas.

**NO**
*Chile/USA/Mexico, 2012. Written and Directed by Pablo Larraín.*
Written by Pedro Peirano. With Gael García Bernal, Alfredo Castro, Antonia Zegers.

**OUR CHILDREN**
*Belgium, 2012. Directed by Joachim Lafosse.*
Written by Thomas Bidegain, Lafosse, and Matthieu Reynaert. With Niels Arestrup, Tahar Rahim, Émilie Dequenne.

**THE PAPERBOY**
*USA, 2012. Directed by Lee Daniels.*
Written by Daniels and Peter Dexter, based on Dexter's novel. With Nicole Kidman, Zac Efron, Matthew McConaughey, John Cusack, Scott Glenn.

**PASSION**
*USA, 2012. Written and Directed by Brian De Palma, based on an original screenplay by Alain Corneau and Natalie Carter.*
With Rachel McAdams, Noomi Rapace, Paul Anderson.

**SOMETHING IN THE AIR**
*France, 2012. Written and Directed by Olivier Assayas.*
With Dolores Chaplin, Victoria Lay, Lola Créton.

**TABU ▼**
*Portugal, 2012. Directed by Miguel Gomes.*
Written by Gomes and Mariana Ricardo. With Teresa Madruga, Laura Soveral, Ana Moreira.

**YOU AIN'T SEEN NOTHIN' YET**
*France, 2012. Directed by Alain Resnais.*
Written by Resnais and Laurent Herbiet, based on Jean Anouih's *Eurydice*. With Mathieu Amalric, Lambert Wilson, Michel Piccoli, Sabine Azéma, Anne Consigny.

## Gala Tributes

### "A Tribute to Nicole Kidman" ▼
Featuring an intimate onstage conversation followed by the U.S. premiere of her latest film, *The Paperboy* (part of the Main Slate).

### "Richard Peña: 25 Years"
The Program Director of the Film Society of Lincoln Center and Chairman of the New York Film Festival selection committee since 1988.

## Masterworks
PRESENTED AT THE WALTER READE THEATER UNLESS OTHERWISE NOTED

### COUSIN JULES
*France, 1972. Directed by Dominique Benicheti.*
Five years in the grim, silent life of an elderly French couple.

### DOWNPOUR (RAGBAR)
*Iran, 1972. Written Directed by Bahram Beyza'i.*
With Parviz Fanizadeh, Mohamad Ali Keshavarz, Jamshid Layegh. A restoration made possible by the World Cinema Foundation.

### FELLINI SATYRICON
*Italy, 1969. Directed by Federico Fellini.*
Written by Fellini and Bernardino Zapponi, based on Petronius's book. With Martin Potter, Hiram Keller, Max Born, Salvo Randone, Capucine.

### FIELD DIARY (YOMAN SADEH)
*Israel/France, 1982. Directed by Amos Gitai.*
A landmark documentary about the Israeli occupation of the West Bank.

### HEAVEN'S GATE
*USA, 1980. Written and Directed by Michael Cimino.*
With Kris Kristofferson, Christopher Walken, John Hurt, Sam Waterston, Brad Dourif, Isabelle Huppert, Joseph Cotten. A glorious new restoration of the original director's cut, personally supervised by Cimino himself.

### THE KING OF MARVIN GARDENS
*USA, 1972. Directed by Bob Rafelson.*
Written by Jacob Brockman, based on a story by Brockman and Rafelson. With Jack Nicholson, Bruce Dern, Ellen Burstyn, Julia Anne Robinson.

### LAWRENCE OF ARABIA
*UK/USA, 1962. Directed by David Lean.*
Written by Robert Bolt. With Peter O'Toole, Omar Sharif, Arthur Kennedy, Jack Hawkins.

### LITTLE SHOP OF HORRORS
*USA, 1986. Directed by Frank Oz.*
Written by Howard Ashman, based on his play and Roger Corman's film. With Rick Moranis, Ellen Greene, Steve Martin, Vincent Gardenia. Director's cut with 20 minutes of never-before-seen footage.

### THE MATTEI AFFAIR
*Italy, 1972. Directed by Francesco Rosi.*
Written by Tonino Guerra. With Gian Maria Volonté, Luigi Squarzina, Gianfranco Ombuen. Restoration by Cineteca di Bologna at the lab L'Immagine Ritrovata in collaboration with The Film Foundation, Paramount Pictures, and Museo Nazionale del Cinema of Turin.

### NATIVE SON
*USA/Argentina, 1981. Written and Directed by Pierre Chenal, based on Richard Wright's novel.*
With Wright, Gloria Madison, Willa Pearl Curtis, Nicholas Joy, Ruth Robert.

### NOTHING BUT A MAN
*USA, 1964. Directed by Michael Roemer.*
Written by Roemer and Robert M. Young. With Ivan Dixon, Abbey Lincoln, Gloria Foster, Julius Harris, Martin Priest. Shown with *Snow*, UK. Directed by Geoffrey Jones.

### OLD CZECH LEGENDS
*Czechoslovakia, 1953. Directed by Jiří Trnka.*
Six classic Czech folktales come to life in this brilliant puppet animation.

### THE OVERCOAT
*USA, 1926. Directed by Grigori Kozintsev and Leonid Trauberg.*
Written by Yuri Tynyanov, based on Nikolai Gogol's novel. With Emil Gan, Serfie Gerasimov, Andrei Kapler. With live musical accompaniment by the Alloy Orchestra. Shown with *Filmstudie*, Germany, 1926. Directed by Hans Richter.

### RE-INTRODUCING MARNIE: WILLIAM ROTHMAN ON HITCHCOCK'S LAST MASTERPIECE
*Marnie*, 1964, is presented and analyzed by leading Hitchcock scholar William Rothman.

### RICHARD III
*UK, 1955. Directed by Laurence Olivier.*
Text alterations of Shakespeare's play by Colley Cibber and David Garrick. With Olivier, Cedric Hardwicke, Ralph Richardson, John Gielgud.

### THE ROLLING STONES – CHARLIE IS MY DARLING - IRELAND '65
*UK, 1966. Directed by Peter Whitehead.*
A behind-the-scenes diary of the Rolling Stones on tour in Ireland in 1965.

### THE SATIN SLIPPER
*France/Portugal/West Germany/Switzerland, 1985. Written and Directed by Manoel de Oliveira, based on Paul Claudel's play.*
With Luis Miguel Cintra, Patricia Barzyk, Anne Consigny, Frank Oger.

### SNOW WHITE AND THE SEVEN DWARFS
*USA, 1937. Directed by William Cotrell and David Hand.*
Written by Ted Sears and Richard Creedon. A Walt Disney animated production based on the fairy tale by Wilhelm and Jacob Grimm. Shown with *Paperman*, USA. Directed by John Kahrs.

### "Cinéastes De Notre Temps/Cinéma, De Notre Temps"
– all French productions: *John Cassavetes*, 1969, by Herbert Knapp and André S. Labarthe; *Abel Ferrara: Not Guilty*, 2003, by Rafi Pitts; *Alain Cavalier: 7 Chapters, 5 Days, 2 Kitchens*, 1995, by Jean-Pierre Limosin, with *The "Home Cinema" of the Dardenne Brothers*, 2006, by Limosin; *Busby Berkeley*, 1971, by Knapp and Labarthe, with *A Conversation with George Cukor*, 1969, by Knapp and Labarthe; *Chantal Akerman By Chantal Akerman*, 1997, by Chantal Akerman, with *Philippe Garrel, Artist*, 1999, by Françoise Etchegaray; *Erich von Stroheim*, 1965, by Robert Valery; *Eric Rohmer: Evidence*, 1996, by Labarthe, in collaboration with Jean Douchet; *HHH, A Portrait of Hou Hsiao-hsien*, 1996, by Olivier Assayas; *Jacques Rivette: The Night Watchman*, 1990, by Claire Denis; *Jean-Pierre Melville: A Portrait in 9 Poses*, 1971-96, by Labarthe, with *Catherine Breillat: The First Time*, 2011, by Luc Moullet; *Jean Renoir, The Boss: The Rule and the Exception*, 1967, by Jacques Rivette; *Jean Vigo*, 1965, by Jacques Rozier; *Jerry Lewis (Part One)*, 1968, by Labarthe, with *David Lynch, Don't Look at Me*, 1989, by Guy Girard; *John Cassavetes*, 1969, by Knapp and Labarthe, with *Rome Is Burning (Portrait of Shirley Clarke)*, 1970, by Noël Burch and Labarthe; *Joseph Losey*, 1969, by Labarthe, with *Otto Preminger and the Dangerous Woman*, 1972-2012, by Labarthe; *Luis Buñuel: A Filmmaker of Our Time*, 1964, by Valery, with *Lang/Godard: The Dinosaur and the Baby*, 1967, by Labarthe; *Otar Iosseliani, The Whistling Blackbird*, 2006, by Julie Bertucelli; *The New Wave: Remedy or Poison?*, 1964, by Valery, with *Wild Man Pasolini*, 1966-91, by Jean-André Fieschi; *Raoul Walsh or the Good Old Days*, 1966, by Knapp and Labarthe, with *Josef von Sternberg: From Silence Comes the Other*, 1967, by Labarthe; *Samuel Fuller, Independent Filmmaker*, 1967, by Labarthe, with *Fuller at the Editing Table*, 1982, by Labarthe; *The Scorsese Machine*, 1990, by Labarthe, with *Scorsese at the Editing Table*, 1995, by Labarthe; *Shohei Imamura: The Free Thinker*, 1995, by Paulo Rocha, with *One Day in the Life of Andreï Arsenevitch*, 2000, by Chris Marker; *Where Does Your Hidden Smile Lie?*, 2001, by Pedro Costa, in collaboration with Thierry Lounas.

### "Men of Cinema: Pierre Rissient and the Cinema MacMahon" – a tribute to the influential critic-programmer-publicist Pierre Rissient and the legendary Paris cinema he helped to program in the 1950s: *Liebelei*, 1933, Germany, by Max Ophuls; *Night and the City*, 1950, USA, by Jules Dassin; *Objective Burma!*, 1945, USA, by Raoul Walsh; *The Prowler*,

1951, USA, by Joseph Losey; *Pursued*, 1947, USA, by Walsh; *The Tiger of Eschnapur*, 1959, West Germany/France/Italy, by Fritz Lang; *Whirlpool*, 1949, USA, by Otto Preminger.

## Short Films
PRESENTED AT THE ELINOR BUNIN MUNROE FILM CENTER

**Program 1:** *Crescendo*, Mexico, by Alonso Alvarez Barreda; *Up the Valley and Beyond*, USA, by Todd Rosken; *A Story for the Modlins*, Spain, by Sergio Oksman; *A Brief History of John Baldessari*, USA, by Henry Joost and Ariel Schulman; *Saint Pierre*, Canada, by Kevan Fun; *Frank Etienne Toward Beatitude*, France, by Constance Meyer.

**Program 2:** *Curfew*, USA, by Shawn Christensen; *Things I Heard on Wednesdays*, Egypt/USA, by Abu Bakr Shawky; *Night Shift*, New Zealand, by Zia Mandviwalla; *Zombie*, Spain, by David Moreno; *Nothing Can Touch Me*, Denmark, by Milad Alami; *Kavinsky*, Switzerland, by Daniel Schraner and Manuel Haefele.

## Special Events
PRESENTED AT THE WALTER READE THEATER OR THE ELINOR BUNIN MUNROE FILM CENTER UNLESS OTHERWISE NOTED

**"Cinema Reflected"** – illuminating documentaries and essay films about movies and the men and women who make them: *Casting By*, by Tom Donahue; *Celluloid Man*, by Shivendra Singh Dungarpur, India; *Final Cut - Ladies and Gentlemen*, by György Pálfi, Hungary; *Liv and Ingmar*, by Dheeraj Akolkar, Norway/UK/India; *Roman Polanski: Odd Man Out*, by Marina Zenovich; *Room 237*, by Rodney Ascher; *The War of the Volcanoes*, by Francesco Patierno, Italy, with *101*, by Luis Miñaro, Spain.

**"HBO Directors Dialogues/On Cinema"** – Noah Baumbach in conversation with Brian De Palma; David Chase in conversation with Scott Foundas; Abbas Kiarostami in conversation with Phillip Lopate; Ang Lee in conversation with Todd McCarthy; Robert Zemeckis in conversation with Richard Peña.

**"Midnight Movies"** – *The Bay*, by Barry Levinson, USA; *Berberian Sound Studio*, by Peter Strickland, UK; *Outrage Beyond*, by Takeshi Kitano, Japan.

**"On the Arts"** – films that reflect other performing arts through the prism of cinema: *Becoming Traviata*, by Philippe Béziat, France; *Deceptive Practice: The Mysteries and Mentors of Ricky Jay*, by Molly Bernstein and Alan Edelstein; *Ingrid Caven: Music and Voice*, by Bertrand Bonello, France; *Punk in Africa*, by Keith Jones and Deon Maas, South Africa/Czech Republic/Zimbabwe/ Mozambique; *The Savoy King: Chick Webb and the Music That Changed America*, by Jeff Kaufman.

**"Special Screenings"** – *The Met Live in HD: L'Elisir d'Amore*, by Bartlett Sher; *Oliver Stone's Untold History of the United States*, by Oliver Stone; *Once Every Day*, by Richard Foreman; *The Princess Bride*, by Rob Reiner, 1987.

**"Views from the Avant-Garde"** – curated by Mark McElhatten and Gavin Smith. At the Walter Reade Theater and Elinor Bunin Munroe Film Center. Films from the USA unless otherwise noted.

**Program 1:** *Sans soleil*, France, 1983, by Chris Marker.

**Program 2:** *The Blind Owl*, France, 1987, by Raúl Ruiz.

**Program 3:** "Invisible Attributes – By Sky and on Foot" – *The Creation As We Saw It*, UK, by Ben Rivers; *Morning of Saint Anthony's Day*, Portugal, 2011, by João Pedro Rodrigues; *Concrete Parlay*, by Fern Silva; *Walker*, Hong Kong/Taiwan, by Tsai Ming-liang.

**Program 4:** *anders, Molussien*, France, by Nicholas Rey.

**Program 5:** "Circles of Confusion" – *20Hz*, by Semiconductor; *Tension Building*, by Ericka Beckman; *Collections*, by Peggy Ahwesh; *Interstitial Project 1*, by Matt McCormick; *Birthstone*, by April Simmons; 2 Couplets from the Rain series: *Kiss the Rain* and *The Street of Everlasting Rain*, by Lewis Klahr; *Tokens and Penalties*, by Talena Sanders; *Interstitial Project 2*, by Matt McCormick; *Circle in the Sand*, by Michael Robinson.

**Program 6:** *The Parallel Road (Die Parallelstrasse)*, Germany, 1962, by Ferdinand Khittl.

**Program 7:** *The Extravagant Shadows*, by David Gatten.

**Program 8:** *The Poor Stockinger, the Luddite Cropper, and the Deluded Followers of Joanna Southcott*, UK, by Luke Fowler, with *A Day At Karl Marx's Grave*, Finland, 1983, by Peter von Bagh.

**Program 9:** "Phantom Residence" – *S P E C T R E*, 2011, by Sarah Grace Nesin; *Phantoms of a Libertine*, UK, by Ben Rivers; *The Room Called Heaven*, by Laida Lertxundi; *Mekong Hotel*, Thailand, by Apichatpong Weerasethakul.

**Program 10:** "Beyond the Borderline" – *Beyond Expression Bright*, by Erin Espelie; *The Name is not the Thing Named*, by Deborah Stratman; *Marshy Place Across*, by Lorenzo Gattorna; *Tectonics*, by Peter Bo Rappmund.

**Program 11:** Peggy Ahwesh & Joe Gibbons – *Martina's Playhouse*, 1989, and *From Romance to Ritual*, 1985, by Peggy Ahwesh; *Confidential Pt. 2*, 1980, and *Spying*, 1977-78, by Joe Gibbons.

**Program 12:** Jerome Hiler – *In the Stone House*, 1967-70/2012, and *New Shores*, 1970-90/2012.

**Program 13:** Nathaniel Dorsky – *August and After* and *April*.

**Program 14:** *STOP*, 1995-2012, by Jeff Preiss.

**Program 15:** "Touch and Go" – *When Faces Touch*, Italy, by Paolo Gioli; *Arbor*, by Janie Geiser; *Impressions*, by Marika Borgeson; *Point de Gaze*, by Jodie Mack; *Audition*, by Karen Yasinsky; *When Bodies Touch*, Italy, by Paolo Gioli; *Dragonflies with Birds and Snake*, Sweden/Germany, 2007-11, by Wolfgang Lehmann.

**Program 16:** *small roads*, 2011, by James Benning.

**Program 17:** "Doppleganger (The Eternal Return)" – *Strata of Natural History*, Switzerland/Chile, by Jeannette Munoz; *The Girl Chewing Gum*, UK, 1973, by John Smith; *The Man Phoning Mum*, UK, by John Smith; *Interstitial Project 3*, by Matt McCormick; *Waiting Room*, by Vincent Grenier; *Interstitial Project 4*, by Matt McCormick; *Transit of Venus I*, UK, 2005, and *Transit of Venus II*, UK, by Nicky Hamlyn; *WORK IN PROGRESS*, by Ernie Gehr.

**Program 18:** "Puzzling Evidence" – *Across and Down*, by Lori Felker; *Hotel Room*, Austria, 2011, by Bernd Oppl; *The Day of Two Noons*, by Mike Gibisser.

**Program 19:** "Atlas Minus…" – *The Strife of Love in a Dream*, France, 2011, by Camille Henrot; *21 Chitrakoot*, by Shambhavi Kaul; *A Few Extra Copies*, by Bobby Abate; *17 New Dam Rd.*, by Dani Leventhal; *The Voice of God*, India/Germany, 2011, by Bernd Lützeler; *The Tombigbee Chronicles Number Two* and *Chevelle*, by Kevin Jerome Everson; *Wadena*, by Peggy Ahwesh.

**Program 20:** "A Luther Price Bestiary" – a selection of 16mm films and 35mm slide work by Luther Price, 2007-12.

**Program 21:** "Chronocolor" – *Jake Seven*, by Mary Beth Reed; *Austerity Measures*, Greece, by Guillaume Cailleau and Ben Russell; *Another Void*, by Paul Clipson; *Which Ceaselessly Float Up*, double projection by Beige (Vanessa O'Neill and Kent Long); *Bloom*, by Scott Stark; *Never a Foot Too Far, Even*, Canada, 2011, double projection by Daichi Saito; *Deep Red*, The Netherlands, by Esther Urlus.

**Program 22:** *Fragments of Kubelka*, Austria, by Martina Kudláček.

**Program 23:** *Monument Film*, Austria, double projection by Peter Kubelka consisting of *Arnulf Rainer*, 1958-60, and *Antiphon*, as well as a three-panel installation in the Furman Gallery.

Supplementary Amphitheater Programs: *"EMPIRE,"* 2010, by Phil Solomon; *Vulgar Fractions*, by Peter Bo Rappmund; *Ponce de León*, by Ben Russell and Jim Drain; *Age Is…*, France/UK, by Stephen Dwoskin; *Foxfur*, by Damon Packard; *Deep State*, UK, by Brad Butler and Karen Mirza.

## Convergence
PRESENTED AT THE EBM AMPHITHEATER

Two days of panels, workshops, and "immersive experiences" designed for creators, designers, thinkers, and fans. It was focused on artists and filmmakers who are interested in the new tools and technologies that allow storytellers to involve audiences in new ways: Keynote Conversation: Tommy Pallotta; Panels: "Adult Swim and the Power of Musical Partnerships," with Laura Sterritt and Jason DeMarco; "Best of Breed Transmedia Content Innovators," with Daniel Laikind, Lindsay Ellis, Jeremy Redleaf, and Gary Delfiner, presented in collaboration with Digital Hollywood; "Bridging the Tech Divide," with Mark Harris, Barry Alexander Brown, and Michael Knowlton; "Location, Location, Location: The Future of Film in a Geotagged World," with Bill Plympton, Andrew Events, and Amy Neswald; "Multiple Producers, Multiple Platforms," with Blaine Graboyes, Peter Saraf, and James Pereclay, presented in Partnership with the Producers Guild of America, East; "Non Profit Design Summit," moderated by Lina Srivistava; "Novels in New Forms," with Nina Lassam, Amanda Harvard, Benjamin Samuel, and Rachel Fershleiser, presented in collaboration with Digital Hollywood; "Work in Progress: NY_HEARTS," with James Carter; "Writing Transmedia," with Nick Bernadone and George Strayton, presented in Partnership with Writers Guild of America, East. Presentations: *Renga*, immersive viewing, with Adam Russell, Jonathan Sear, and Jamin Warren in attendance; "TEDxUWS," an exploration of what story means in the 21st Century; "Transmedia Test Kitchen," presented by Brian Fountain and Matt Bolish; "Whispers in the Dark," presented by Jeff Wirth; Workshops: "McCarren Park Part I: Hipster Dinos, Transmedia, and Producing Something from Nothing," with Caitlin Burns, plus screening of *McCarren Park*; "McCarren Park Part II: Hipster Dinos, Transmedia, and How to Get Noticed Without Paying for It," with Caitlin Burns, plus clips from *McCarren Park*; "Transmedia on $8.00 a Day," presented by Brian Fountain; "XYEYE: Story Pitch Program," presented by Pamela Vitale; "You're Such a Character: New Roles for Audiences in Storytelling," presented by Andrea Phillips.

# CONTRIBUTOR BIOS

**DAVID ANSEN** was *Newsweek*'s movie critic from 1977-2008. He continues to write for the magazine as a freelancer. Since 2010 he has been the Artistic Director of the Los Angeles Film Festival. He has written documentaries for TNT, HBO, and PBS on Greta Garbo, Bette Davis, Groucho Marx, and Elizabeth Taylor.

**RICHARD CORLISS** has reviewed films and other aspects of popular culture for *Time* magazine since 1980. He was the editor of *Film Comment* from 1970-1985 and co-editor from 1985-1990. He is the author of the books *Talking Pictures* and *Greta Garbo* and, for the British Film Institute, a study of the Nabokov-Kubrick film *Lolita*. He wrote about movies and music for *The New York Times*, *The Village Voice*, *National Review*, *New Times* and *Soho Weekly News*. He lives in Manhattan with the great Mary Corliss.

**SCOTT FOUNDAS** is Associate Program Director for The Film Society of Lincoln Center, where he also serves as a member of the New York Film Festival selection committee and a contributing editor to *Film Comment*. From 2003–09, he was the lead film critic and film editor for the *L.A. Weekly*, and has written for *The New York Times*, Slate.com, and *Cahiers du cinéma*.

**ROGER GREENSPUN**'s articles on the movies have appeared in many journals and magazines. He has taught film history and criticism at Rutgers and in Columbia's School of the Arts. He has been a film critic for *Penthouse*, *The Soho News*, and *The New York Times*.

**MOLLY HASKELL** is a film critic and author who has written and lectured widely on film and the roles of women. Her books include *From Reverence to Rape: The Treatment of Women in the Movies*, *Love and Other Infectious Diseases: A Memoir*, and, most recently, *Frankly My Dear: Gone with the Wind Revisited*. She has taught at Columbia, Barnard, and Sarah Lawrence, served as film critic for *New York* magazine and *Vogue* and has written for many publications, including *The New York Times*, *New York Review of Books*, *Town & Country*, *The Guardian*, and *The Nation*. She is a member of the National Society of Film Critics, has served as a member of the selection committee of the New York Film Festival, and was Artistic Director of the Sarasota French Film Festival for seven years. Her work was featured in The Library of America's 2006 anthology, *American Movie Critics*, edited by Phillip Lopate, and she won a Guggenheim Fellowship in 2010.

**J. HOBERMAN** served two terms on the New York Film Festival selection committee (1982-84 and 2007-09), he is Gelb Professor of the Humanities at Cooper Union, the author, co-author, or editor of 12 books, and was for 33 years a film critic at *The Village Voice*.

**KENT JONES** is an internationally recognized writer and filmmaker. In 2007, Wesleyan University Press published *Physical Evidence*, a selection of his writings. He was Associate Director of Programming at The Film Society of Lincoln Center from1998-2009, and for seven of those years he served as a member of the selection committee for the New York Film Festival. In 2009, he was appointed Executive Director of the World Cinema Foundation. He has worked with Martin Scorsese throughout the years on numerous projects and several documentaries including *My Voyage to Italy*, the 2007 film *Val Lewton: The Man in the Shadows*, which he wrote and directed, and the Emmy-nominated and Peabody Award–winning 2010 film, *A Letter to Elia*, which he and Scorsese co-wrote and co-directed. He is a 2012 Guggenheim recipient, and he is preparing a feature film for the winter of 2013.

**LAURA KERN** is the managing editor of *Film Comment*. A former contributing film critic for *The New York Times*, she has also written for *Filmmaker*, indieWIRE, Variety.com, and *URB*. As a programmer, she collaborates on The Film Society of Lincoln Center's annual Film Comment Selects and Scary Movie series. She is also a member of the New York Film Festival's short-film selection committee.

**WENDY KEYS** held positions as both administrator and programmer at The Film Society of Lincoln Center from 1966–2008. She served as a member of the selection committees of the New York Film Festival and New Directors/New Films. From 1972-2008 she was the director/producer of the Film Society's annual Gala Tribute honoring major film artists. She curated many series and retrospectives at the Walter Reade Theater and Special Events at the Festival. In 2008 she directed and produced an award-winning documentary titled *Milton Glaser: To Inform and Delight*. She also produced a compilation of train scenes titled *All Aboard!* for the High Line. She serves on the Board of Human Rights Watch, is the founder of their Canada Committee, and co-programmed the first Human Rights Film Festival at the Public Theater. In addition, she is a member of the Board of The Film Society of Lincoln Center, the Friends of the High Line, and the Westhampton Beach Performing Arts Center.

**STUART KLAWANS** served on the selection committee for the New York Film Festival from 1992-95. He has been the film critic for *The Nation* since 1988 and is an occasional contributor to publications including *Film Comment*, *The New York Times*, and *Parnassus: Poetry in Review*. He is the author of *Film Follies: The Cinema Out of Order* and *Left in the Dark: Film Reviews and Essays*, and in 2007 received the National Magazine Award for reviews and criticism.

**JOANNE KOCH** began her career in film in 1950 at MoMA. In the late '60s she worked on film production and censorship issues at Grove Press, and in 1971 joined the staff of The Film Society of Lincoln Center, where she served as Executive Director until 2003. During those 32 years, in addition to her management role, she was the CFO, the publisher of *Film Comment*, a founder and member of the selection committee of New Directors/New Films, and co-producer of 17 of the Film Society's Gala Tributes. Most recently, until 2008, she acted as the Film Society's Project Director in connection with the construction and design of the Elinor Bunin Munroe Film Center. She serves on the Film Society's Board, lives in Greenwich Village, and is enjoying her nine grown grandchildren.

**PHILLIP LOPATE** is the author of a dozen works of nonfiction, fiction, and poetry, including *Waterfront, Being With Children, Portrait of My Body, The Rug Merchant, Notes on Sontag*, and *At the End of the Day*. He has edited the anthologies *Art of the Personal Essay* and *American Movie Critics*. He served twice on the New York Film Festival selection committee; his film criticism has appeared in *The New York Times, Vogue, Esquire, Film Comment, Cineaste*, and *Film Culture*, and is collected in the volume *Totally, Tenderly, Tragically*. He is Professor of Writing at Columbia University, where he directs the graduate nonfiction program, and lives in Brooklyn, NY, with his wife and daughter.

**RICHARD PEÑA** was the Program Director of the Film Society of Lincoln Center and the Director of the New York Film Festival from 1988-2012. He is also Professor of Film Studies at Columbia University, where he specializes in film theory and international cinema, and from 2006 to 2009 was a Visiting Professor in Spanish at Princeton University. He is also currently the co-host of Channel 13's weekly *Reel 13*.

**JOHN POWERS** is a longtime contributing editor at *Vogue*, where he writes about film, television, and politics. He is also the Critic at Large for NPR's *Fresh Air with Terry Gross* and a culture columnist for *The American Prospect*. The author of *Sore Winners (and the Rest of Us) in George Bush's America*, he lives in Pasadena, California, with his wife, Sandi Tan.

**LISA SCHWARZBAUM** is a critic at *Entertainment Weekly*. Previously, she was a feature writer and columnist at the *New York Daily News Sunday Magazine*. She has written for *The New York Times Magazine*, *Vogue*, and *More*, among many other publications. She is a member of the National Society of Film Critics and a former chair of the New York Film Critics Circle.

**GAVIN SMITH** is the editor of *Film Comment* and the co-programmer of the New York Film Festival's "Views from the Avant-Garde."

**DAVID THOMSON** has written for the *Independent on Sunday* and *The Guardian in London*, and he is an online movie critic at *The New Republic*. His publications include *The Biographical Dictionary of Film*, *Have You Seen?*, and, most recently, *The Big Screen*.

# OFFICERS AND BOARD OF DIRECTORS
## The Film Society of Lincoln Center – 2012

The New York Film Festival was presented from 1963 through 1968 by Lincoln Center for the Performing Arts in collaboration with The British Film Institute. In the first year, the Museum of Modern Art joined in the collaboration. Since 1969, the Festival has been presented by the Film Society of Lincoln Center, a separate constituent of Lincoln Center. Collaboration with the BFI continued through 1970.

# BOARD LEADERSHIP
## LINCOLN CENTER FOR THE PERFORMING ARTS 1963-68

JOHN D. ROCKEFELLER III, *Chairman*

WILLIAM SCHUMAN, *President*

## FILM SOCIETY OF LINCOLN CENTER – FROM 1969

WILLIAM F. MAY, *Founding Chairman, 1969-81*

MARTIN E. SEGAL, *Founding President, 1969-77*

ALFRED R. STERN, *President, 1978-87, Chairman, 1988-90*

BRENDAN GILL, *Chairman, 1982-83*

DOROTHY CULLMAN, *Chairman, 1984-87*

ROY FURMAN, *President 1988-93, Chairman, 1994-98*

JULIEN J. STUDLEY, *Chairman 1991-93, Chairman, Executive Committee, 1994-2005, Co-Chairman,*
    *Executive Committee, 2006-*

IRWIN W. YOUNG, *President, 1994-98*

IRA M. RESNICK, *Chairman, 1999-2004*

HENRY MCGEE, *President, 1999-2002, Co-President, 2003*

DANIEL H. STERN, *Co-President, 2003-04, President, 2005-*

ANN TENENBAUM, *Co-President, 2004, Chairman, 2005-, Co-Chairman, Executive Committee, 2006-*

# FESTIVAL STAFF LEADERSHIP
## LINCOLN CENTER FOR THE PERFORMING ARTS 1963-68

RICHARD P. LEACH, *Lincoln Center Executive Director, Programming, 1963*

AMOS VOGEL, *Festival Director 1963-68*

RICHARD ROUD, *Festival Program Director 1963-68*

SCHUYLER G. CHAPIN, *Lincoln Center Vice President, Programming, 1964-68*

SALLIE WILENSKY, *Festival Coordinator, 1964-68*

## FILM SOCIETY OF LINCOLN CENTER – FROM 1969

SCHUYLER G. CHAPIN, *Executive Director, 1969*

SALLIE WILENSKY, *Administrative Director, 1969-70*

RICHARD ROUD, *Festival Director, 1969-87*

GERALD FREUND, *Executive Vice President, 1970*

JOANNE KOCH, *Festival Administrator, 1971-76, Executive Director, 1977-98, Executive Vice President, 1999-2003*

WENDY KEYS, *Associate Director, 1977-86, Executive Producer, Special Projects, 1987-97*

RICHARD PEÑA, *Program Director and Chairman of the New York Film Festival Selection Committee, 1988-2012*

CLAUDIA BONN, *Director of Administration and Development, 1999-2002, Executive Director, 2003-07*

MARIAN MASONE, *Festival Manager, 2001-10, Associate Director of Programming/Special Programs, 1999-*

MARA MANUS, *Executive Director, 2008-09*

ROSE KUO, *Executive Director, 2010-*

# FESTIVAL PROGRAMMING HISTORY

The first three Festivals were programmed by Amos Vogel and Richard Roud. Beginning with the fourth, in 1966, a selection committee was established. The participants, in chronological order, were:

RICHARD ROUD, 1963-87, *European consultant,* 1988

AMOS VOGEL, 1963-68

ARTHUR KNIGHT, 1966-67, 1969-75, *West Coast consultant,* 1976-77

ANDREW SARRIS, 1966-75

SUSAN SONTAG, 1967-76, 1980-81

PENELOPE HUSTON, 1969

HENRI LANGLOIS, l969-76, *consultant on retrospective programs*

RICHARD CORLISS, 1971-87

ARTHUR MAYER, 1971-75

JOHN RUSSELL TAYLOR, 1972

ROGER GREENSPUN, 1975-78

CHARLES MICHENER, 1975-79

MARY MEERSON, 1978-89, *consultant on retrospective programs*

MOLLY HASKELL, 1978-80, 1984-86

TOM LUDDY, 1978-82, *West Coast consultant,* 1983

JACK KROLL, 1981-83

MARC WEISS, 1981-83, *American independent film consultant*

J. HOBERMAN, 1982-84, 2007-09

DAVID THOMSON, 1983-85

LAWRENCE SAPADIN, 1984-86, *American independent film consultant*

DAVE KEHR, 1985-87, 1998-2003

DAVID DENBY, 1986-87

LILLIAN JIMENEZ, 1987-89, *American independent film consultant*

CARRIE RICKEY, 1987-89

RICHARD PEÑA, 1988-2012

WENDY KEYS, 1988-98

PHILLIP LOPATE, 1988-90, 2004-06

DAVID STERRIT, 1988-92

DAVID ANSEN, 1990-96

STUART KLAWANS, 1992-95

JOAN JULIET BUCK, 1993

JONATHAN ROSENBAUM, 1994-96

ROBERT SKLAR, 1996-98

JOHN POWERS, 1998-99, 2004-06

KATHLEEN MURPHY, 2000-01

JOHN ANDERSON, 2000-03

MANOHLA DARGIS, 2000-02

KENT JONES, 2002-08

GEOFFREY O'BRIEN, 2003

LISA SCHWARZBAUM, 2004-07

SCOTT FOUNDAS, 2007-12

MELISSA ANDERSON, 2009-12

DENNIS LIM, 2009-11

TODD MCCARTHY, 2010-l2

AMY TAUBIN, 2012-

# NAME INDEX

# MOVIE INDEX

# PHOTO CREDITS

All film stills from THE KOBAL COLLECTION, unless otherwise noted.

The Kobal Collection, which owes its existence to the vision, courage, talent, and energy of the men and women who created the movie industry and whose legacies live on through the films they made, the studios they built, and the publicity photographs they took. Kobal collects, preserves, organizes, and makes these images available to enhance our understanding and enjoyment of this cinematic art.

The publisher wishes to thank all of the photographers (known and unknown) and the film distribution and production companies whose images appear in this book. We apologize in advance for any omissions or neglect and will be pleased to make any corrections in future editions.

*L'Age d'Or*: Vicomte Charles De Noailles; *Aileen Wuornos: The Selling of a Serial Killer*: Lafayette Films; *Alice in the Cities*: Filmverlag Der Autoren; *All About My Mother*: El Deseo/Renn/France 2; *Alphaville*: Chaumiane/Film Studio; *The American Friend*: Road Movies/Les Films du Losange/Filmverlag Der Autoren; *The Americanization of Emily*; MGM; *Amores Perros*: Alta Vista; *Andrei Rublev*: Mosfilm; *À nos amours*: The Criterion Collection; *The Artist*: La Classe Americane/uFilm/France 3 Cinéma; *Au hasard Balthazar*: Parc/Argos; *An Autumn Afternoon*: Shochiku; *Babette's Feast*: Betzer-Panorama Film/Danish Film Institute; *Bad Blood*: Photofest; *Bad Company*: Paramount; *Bad Education*: Canal +/TVE; *Badlands*: Warner Bros.; *Bamako*: Archipel 33; *Band of Outsiders*: Anouchka/Orsay; *Baran*: Fouad Nahas/Majid Majidi; *The Battle of Algiers*: Casbah/Igor; *Before Night Falls*: Elmar Pics/Daniel Daza; *La belle noiseuse*: Grise/Fr3/Canal +; *Ben-Hur*: MGM; *Beyond the Clouds*: Sunshine/Cube B/France 3 Cinéma; *Les Biches*: Films La Boetie/Alexandra; *Bird*: Warner Bros.; *The Bitter Tears of Petra von Kant*: Tango; *Black Cat, White Cat*: Pandora Film; *Black Narcissus*: ITV Global; *Black Rain*: Imamura Productions; *Blade Runner*: Ladd Company/Warner Bros.; *Blood and Sand*: 20th Century Fox; *Blood Simple*: River Road Prods.; *Blue*: Arts Council/BBC Radio/CH4 Film; *Blue (Trois Couleurs: Bleu)*: MK2/CED/CAB; *Bob le Flambeur*: OGC/Studios Jenner/Play Art/La Cyme; *Boogie Nights*: New Line/G. Lefkowitz; *Boys Don't Cry*: Fox Searchlight; *Breakfast on Pluto*: Sony Pictures Classics/Pathé/Pat Redmond; *Bullets Over Broadway*: Magnolia/Sweetland/Brian Hamill; *Bwakaw*: Fortissimo Films; *Caché*: Sony Pictures; *Camera Buff*: Zespoly/Film Polski; *Charulata*: R.D.Bansal; *Chariots of Fire*: 20th Century Fox/Allied Stars/Enigma; *Che*: Wild Bunch/Morena Films; *Chungking Express*: Jet Tone; *Colonel Redl*: Mafilm/Mokep/ZDF; *The Color of Paradise*: Varahonar Company/Hashem Attar; *The Conformist*: Mars/Marianne/Maran; *A Confucian Confusion*: Atomfilms; *Conversation Piece*: Rusconi/Gaumont; *The Covered Wagon*: Paramount; *The Crime of Monsieur Lange*: Oberon/Brandon; *Crumb*: Superior Pictures; *The Crying Game*: Palace Pictures; *Danton*: Les Films du Losange/Groupe X/Gaumont/Georges Pierre; *The Decameron*: Pea/Artistes Associes; *Day for Night*: Les Films du Carosse/PEFC/PIC; *The Death of Mr. Lazarescu*: Mandragora Movies; *Delicatessen*: Constellation/UGC/Hachette Premiere; *Diary for My Children*: Mafilm; *Distant*: NBC Films; *Distant Voices, Still Lives*: BFI/Channel 4/ZDF; *The Diving Bell and the Butterfly*: Pathé; *Dodsworth*: Goldwyn; *The Double Life of Véronique*: Sideral/Tor Studios/Canal +; *Down by Law*: Island; *The Draughtsman's Contract*: BFI/United Artists; *The Dreamlife of Angels*: Les Productions Bagheera; *Dream of Light*: Maria Moreno P.C.; *Dr. Mabuse the Gambler*: Nero; *Eating Raoul*: Bartel/Mercury; *Electra, My Love*: Mafilm/Hunnia Studio; *L'Enfant*: Canal +/Sony Pictures Classics/Christine Plenus; *Europa '51*: Ponti-De Laurentiis; *Exhibition*: Contrechamp; *Exotica*: Alliance/Ego Film; *The Exterminating Angel*: Uninci S.A Films 59/Altura; *Farewell My Concubine*: Tomson Films/China Film/Beijing; *Fata Morgana*: Werner Herzog Film GmbH; *Faust*: UFA; *F for Fake*: Films de L'astrophore; *Fireworks*: Bandai Visual; *Fitzcarraldo*: Herzog/Filmverlag Der Autoren/ZDF; *The Flower of My Secret*: CiBy 2000; *Flowers of Shanghai*: 3H Productions; *4 Months, 3 Weeks and 2 Days*: Saga Film; *The Front Page*: United Artists; *Gabbeh*: Mykanend/Sanaye; *Germany Year Zero*: Tevere/UGC; *Gertrud*: Palladium; *Get Out Your Handkerchiefs*: New Line Cinema; *Gomorrah*: Fandango; *Goodbye, Dragon Inn*: Homegreen Films; *The Great Dictator*: United Artists; *The Great McGinty*: Paramount; *The Green Room*: United Artists; *Grey Gardens*: The Criterion Collection; *Hail Mary*: New Yorker Films; *La Haine*: Lazennec/Canal +/La Sept/Guy Ferrandis; *Hallelujah the Hills*: Vermont; *Hamlet*: Lenfilm; *Happiness*: October Films; *Hard Times*: Artificial Eye/PFI; *Heart Like a Wheel*: 20th Century Fox/Dave Friedman/Photofest; *He Who Gets Slapped*: MGM;

*High School*: Frederick Wiseman; *Holy Smoke*: Miramax; *Hoop Dreams*: Fine Line/Kartemquin; *Hope and Glory*: Columbia; *Hotel Terminus: The Life and Times of Klaus Barbie*: Memory Pictures/Mark Ribeaux; *The House of Mirth*: Granada/Arts Council/Film 4/Jaap Buitendijk; *Hugo*: GK Films; *Hyde Park on Hudson*: Focus Features; *Ice*: AFI; *The Ice Storm*: Good Machine; *I'm Not There*: The Weinstein Company; *Infernal Affairs*: Basic Pictures/Media Asia Films Ltd.; *Inland Empire*: Studio Canal +; *In the Mood for Love*: Block 2 Pics/Jet Tone; *In the Realm of the Senses*: Argos/Oshima; *Intolerance*: Wark Producing Company; *Irma Vep*: Dacia Films; *J'accuse*: Pathé; *Jackie Chan's Police Story*: Paragon/Golden Harvest/The Ronald Grant Archive; *Jesse James*: 20th Century Fox; *Je t'aime, Je t'aime*: Fox Europa/Parc Film; *Joan of Arc at the Stake*: Sierra Pictures; *Le joli mai*: Sofracima; *Ju Dou*: Tokuma Enterprises; *Kaos*: Filmtre-Rai Channel 1/Cannon-Gala; *Kid Blue*: 20th Century Fox; *Kagemusha*: Toho/Kurosawa; *The King of Marvin Gardens*: Columbia; *King of New York*: Seven Arts/Photofest; *Kinshasa Kids*: MK2; *Knife in the Water*: Film Polski; *Koyaanisqatsi*: IRE; *The Lacemaker*: Action/FR3/Citel/Janus; *The Lady and the Duke*: Sony Pictures Classics; *Land and Freedom*: Parallax; *The Last Mistress*: Flach Film; *The Last of England*: Anglo Int/Brit Screen/Channel 4/Mike Laye; *The Last Picture Show*: Columbia; *Last Tango in Paris*: PEA; *Lebanon*: Ariel Films; *The Left-Handed Woman*: New Yorker Films/Everett Collection; *Leviathan*: Cinema Guild; *Life and Nothing But*: Hacette Premiere/AB Films/Little Bear; *The Life and Times of Rosie the Riveter*: First Run Features/Gordon Parks/Photofest; *Life Is a Bed of Roses*: Dussart/Soprofilms; *Life of Pi*: 20th Century Fox; *Like Someone in Love*: Eurospace/Sundance

Selects; *Lilies*: Pro-Fun Media; *Little Children*: New Line/Bona Fide Productions; *Lola Montès*: Gamma/Florida/Oska; *The Lost Honor of Katharina Blum*: Paramount-Orion/Everett Collection; *Love Affair, or the Case of the Missing Switchboard Operator*: Avala Film; *Loves of a Blonde*: CBK/Filmove Studio Barrandov; *La Luna*: 20th Century Fox; *The Manchurian Candidate*: United Artists; *The Man from London*: Ognon Pictures; *Man of Iron*: Film Polski; *The Man Who Laughs*: Universal; *The Man Without a Past*: Sputnik Oy; *The Marquise of O*: Les Films du Losange/Janus/Artemis; *The Marriage of Maria Braun*: Trio/Albatros/WDR; *Martha Marcy May Marlene*: Fox Searchlight Pictures; Martin Sheen and Terrence Malick on the set of *Badlands*: Warner Bros.; *Mean Streets*: Taplin-Perry-Scorsese; *Meek's Cutoff*: Evenstar Films; *Melancholia*: Zentropa; *Melvin and Howard*: Universal/Everett Collection; *Mephisto*: Mafilm/Studio Objectiv; *Mickey One*: Columbia; *Miller's Crossing*: 20th Century Fox; *Mon Oncle*: Spectra/Gray/Alterdel/Centaure; *The Mother and the Whore*: Les Films du Losange; *Mulholland Drive*: Studio Canal +/Les Films Alain Sarde/Universal/Melissa Moseley; *Muriel*: Lopert Pictures Corporation; *Murmur of the Heart*: Nouvelles Editions/Marianne/Vides; *My Brilliant Career*: NSW Film Corp; *My Darling Clementine*: 20th Century Fox; *My Dinner with Andre*: Andre/New Yorker/Criterion Collection; *My Left Foot*: ITV Global; *My Night at Maud's*: Pathé/Photofest; *My Own Private Idaho*: New Line; *Mysteries of Lisbon*: Clap Filmes; *The Mystery of Oberwald*: RAI; *Mystery of the Wax Museum*: Warner Bros.; *Mystic River*: Warner Bros./Merie W. Wallace; *My Week with Marilyn*: BBC Films; *Naked*: Film 4 International/British Screen/Thin Man Productions; *Napoleon*: SGF/

Gaumont; *The New Babylon*: Sovkino; *The Nightmare Before Christmas*: Touchstone/Burton/Di Novi; *The Night of the Hunter*: United Artists; *The Night of the Shooting Stars*: United Artists; *Nosferatu the Vampyre*: Werner Herzog/Gaumont; *Nostalghia*: Opera/RAI-2/Sovin; *Nothing Sacred*: Selznick/United Artists; *Notre Musique*: Avventura Films/France 3 Cinéma/Canal +; *Oh! What a Lovely War*: Paramount; *Olivier Olivier*: Oliane/Films A2/Canal +/Sofica; *Once Upon a Time in America*: Ladd Company/Warner Bros.; *Once Upon a Time in Anatolia*: NBC Film; *Our Daily Bread*: Nikolaus Geyrhalter Filmproduktion GmbH; *Palindromes*: Extra Large Pictures/Macall Polay; *Pan's Labyrinth*: Tequila Gang/WB; *Paradise Lost 3: Purgatory*: HBO; *Paris, Texas*: Road/Argos/Channel 4; *The Paperboy*: Millennium Entertainment; *Peggy Sue Got Married*: Rastar/Tri-Star; *Peeping Tom*: Anglo Amalgamated; *Pelle the Conquerer*: Svensk Filmindustri-Danish Film Institute; *Persepolis*: 2.4.7. Films; *The Piano*: Jan Chapman Prods./CiBy 2000; *Piccadilly*: B.I.P.; *Pierrot le fou*: Rome-Paris/De Laurentiis/Georges De Beauregard/ Georges Pierre; *The Plot Against Harry*: King Screen Productions; *Point Blank*: MGM; *Police, Adjective*: 42 KM Film; *The Pornographers*: East-West Classics; *Precious: Based on the Novel "Push" by Sapphire*: Lee Daniels Entertainment; *The President's Last Bang*: Kino International; *Princess Mononoke*: Dentsu/Nippon TV; *Prospero's Books*: Allarts/Camera 1/Cinea; *Pulp Fiction*: Miramax/Buena Vista; *Putney Swope*: Herald; *Le quattro volte*: Invisibile Film; *The Queen*: Pathé; *Ran*: Herald Ace-Nippon-Herald-Greenwich; *Rear Window*: Paramount; *The Red and the White*: Mafilm/Mosfilm; *Red Beard*: Toho; *Red Sorghum*: Xi'an Film Studio; *Rocco and His Brothers*: Titanus/Les

Films Marceau; *Roger & Me*: Warner Bros.; *La Ronde*: Sacha Gordine Productions; *Round Midnight*: Little Bear/PECF; *The Royal Tenenbaums*: Touchstone Pictures/James Hamilton; *Rushmore*: Touchstone Pictures/Van Redin; *Russian Ark*: Fora Film/Hermitage Bridge Studio; *A Safe Place*: B.B.S.; *Salaam Bombay!*: Miraai/Jane Balfour; *Salò*: Artistes Associes/PEA; *Sansho the Bailiff*: Daiei-Kyoto/Brandon; *The Scent of Green Papaya*: Les Productions Lazennec/LA SFP/LA SEPT/Canal +; *Secret Sunshine*: CJ Entertainment; *Secrets & Lies*: CiBy 2000; *The Servant*: Associated British; *Shame*: See-Saw Films; *Shanghai Triad*: Alpha Films; *The Shop on Main Street*: Barrandov Studios; *The Shout*: ITV Global; *Sid and Nancy*: Zenith-Initial/Goldwyn; *Sideways*: Fox Searchlight Pictures/Merie W. Wallace; *The Silences of the Palace*: Cinetele Films/Magfilms; *Simon of the Desert*: G. Alatriste; *Small Change*: Les Films du Carrosse; *Smile*: United Artists/The Ronald Grant Archive; *The Social Network*: Columbia Pictures; *The Sorrow and the Pity*: Norddeutscher Rundfunk; *The Squid and the Whale*: Samuel Goldwyn Films LLC; *The Stationmaster's Wife*: Photofest; *Steaming*: World Film Services; *The Story of Adele H.*: Les Films du Carrosse/Artistes Associes; *Strange Days*: Lightstorm Entertainment; *The Story of Adele H.*: Les Films du Carrosse/Artistes Associes; *The Story of Piera*: Everett Collection; *Strike*: Goskino; *The Suspended Step of the Stork*: Greek Film Centre/Arena/Vega/Erre; *The Sweet Hereafter*: Speaking Parts Limited/Alliance Communications; *Sweet Rush*: Akson Studio/Agencja Media; *Sympathy for Lady Vengeance*: Tartan Films; *Tabu*: The Match Factory; *Taste of Cherry*: Abbas Kiarostami; *A Taxing Woman*: Itami Films; *That Obscure Object of Desire*: Greenwich/Galaxie/In Cine; *Thelonious Monk: Straight, No Chaser*: Malpaso; *Temptress Moon*: Tomson Films/Shanghai Films; *Thérèse*: AFC/Films A2; *Thomas the Imposter*: Filmel; *Three Crowns of the Sailor*: Blaq Out; *Through the Olive Trees*: Farabi Cinema/Kiarostami; *Tih Minh*: Gaumont; *Time Regained*: Blufilm/Canal +/Gemini/Madragoa; *The Times of Harvey Milk*: Black Sands; *Titicut Follies*: Bridgewater Film Company; *Topsy-Turvy*: Thin Man/Greenlight; *The Torrent*: MGM; *A Touch of Zen*: Lian Bang; *The Trial of Joan of Arc*: Agnes Delahaye/Pathé; *The Trout*: Home Vision Entertainment/Photofest; *True Stories*: Warner Bros.; *The Turin Horse*: TT Film/Vega Film/Zero Friction Film; *Two Mules for Sister Sara*: Universal; *Underground*: CiBy 2000; *Unreconciled*: New Yorker Films/Photofest; *Les vampires*: Gaumont; *Vertigo*: Paramount; *Violette*: Filmel/FR3/Cinevideo; *Volver*: El Deseo S.A.; *Walkover*: Film Polski; *Waltz with Bashir*: Bridgit Folman Film Gang; *The War Game*: BBC; *Wendy and Lucy*: Field Guide Films/Film Science/Glass Eye; *Western Union*: 20th Century Fox; *Wild Grass*: Canal +; *Woman in the Dunes*: Teshigahara; *The Woman Next Door*: Les Films du Carrosse/T.F. 1; *A Woman of Affairs*: MGM; *A Woman Under the Influence*: Faces International/Sam Shaw; *Women on the Verge of a Nervous Breakdown*: El Desea-Laurenfilm; *The Wrestler*: Saturn Films; *WR: Mysteries of the Organism*: Neoplanta Film; *Xala*: Films Domireew; *Yaaba*: Les Films de l'Avenir/Thelma/Arcadia; *A Year of the Quiet Sun*: Film Polski; *Yol*: Güney Film/Cactus Film; *Y tu mamá también*: Anhelo Prod/IFC Films/Daniel Daza; *Zorns Lemma*: Anthology Film Archives

# ACKNOWLEDGEMENTS

We wish to thank the following photographers who have made their images available for this celebratory publication:

DAVID ALLOCCA/STARPIX

STEVE ASHTON

STEPHANIE BERGER

STAR BLACK

CORI WELLS BRAUN

MARK BUSSELL

JAMES DEE

TONY DE NONNO

ROBIN HOLLAND

ELLIOTT MOSS LANDY

JONATHAN LEVINE

HELAINE MESSER

SONIA MOSKOWITZ

TIMOTHY PARKS

CHUCK PULIN

JERRY SCHATZBERG

PAUL SCHUMACHER *and* METROPOLITAN PHOTOS

BOB SERATING

SUZANNE STEPHENS

*and a very special thank you to* DAVID GODLIS *for capturing the spirit of the NYFF for over 25 years*


## Additional thank yous:

SIMONA JANSONS *and* CRISTINA BLANCO *of Asia Pacific Offset*

NANCY E. WOLFF *of Cowan, DeBaets, Abrahams & Sheppard*

KAREN DAVIDSON *of the List Art Project*

JOAN DAVIDSON *and* ANN BIRCKMAYER *of the Furthermore Foundation*

AMY ARBUS

MATT BOLISH

JAMES BOURAS

CORD DUEPPE

ROY FURMAN

MARCELA GOGLIO

BENJAMIN GULLA

EUGENE HERNANDEZ

ANNA HUSTED

JUDITH JOHNSON

NICHOLAS KEMP

WENDY KEYS

MARIAN MASONE

JOHN MAZZOLA

TOM MICHEL

COURTNEY OTT

BÁRBARA PEIRÓ ASO

JOHN PELOSI

NICOLAS RAPOLD

STEVE TROHA

ROSE WEIL


## and, above all, thank you to:

LAURETTA DIVES *and* DARREN THOMAS *of The Kobal Collection*

VICKI ROBINSON, *for her endless patience and impeccable photo work*

CHRIS CHANG *and* GAVIN SMITH, *for their invaluable editorial assistance and input*